AA

KEYGUIDE

MEXICO

CONTENTS

186

71

206

122

UNDERSTANDING MEXICO

Understanding Mexico is an introduction to the country, its geography, economy, history and its people, giving a real insight into the nation. Living Mexico gets under the skin of Mexico today, while The Story of Mexico takes you through the country's past.

Mexico is difficult to encapsulate. The regional differences are huge. Manic Mexico City is a world away from the serenity of the country's quieter spots, and underlying everything is the heavy weight of history. The growth of regional powers such as the Olmecs was the precursor for the Maya in the southeast and the Aztecs in the Central Highlands. The Spanish Conquest exploited regional differences to impose its own beliefs and traditions on the population, while the more recent cultural invasion from north of the border, helped by the free trade agreement, has added another dimension to this already complicated country.

GEOGRAPHY

Mexico is the second-largest country in Latin America (after Brazil), covering an area of just under 2 million sq km (772,000sq miles), making it four times the size of France and roughly a quarter the size of continental USA, with which it has a frontier of 2,400km (1,490 miles).

The land mass consists of a plateau flanked by ranges of mountains roughly paralleling the coasts. The northern plateau is low, arid and thinly populated; it takes up 40 percent of the total area of Mexico, but holds only 19 percent of its people. Farther south, the level rises considerably; this southern central plateau is crossed by the volcanic cones of Orizaba (5,760m/18,898ft), Popocatépetl (5,452m/17,888ft), Iztaccíhuatl (5,286m/17,343ft), Nevado de Toluca (4,583m/15,036ft), Matlalcueyetl or La Malinche (4,461m/14,636ft), and Cofre de Perote (4,282m/14,049ft). This mountainous southern end of the plateau, the heart of Mexico, covers only 14 percent of the area of the country, but holds nearly half of its people, including the 20 or so million inhabitants of Mexico City.

Geographically, North America may be said to come to an end in the Isthmus of Tehuantepec. South of the Isthmus the land rises again into the thinly populated highlands of Chiapas.

CLIMATE

Climate and vegetation depend upon altitude. The *tierra caliente* (hot land) takes in the coastlands and plateau lands below 750m (2,460ft). The *tierra templada*, or temperate land, lies at 750m–2,000m (2,460ft–6,560ft). The *tierra fría*, or cold land, is from 2,000m (6,560ft) upwards. Above the tree line at 4,000m (13,125ft) are *páramos* (high moorlands).

The climate of the inland highlands is mostly mild, but with sharp changes of temperature between day and night, sunshine and shade. Generally, winter is the dry season and summer the wet season. There are only two areas where rain falls year round: south of Tampico along the lower slopes of the Sierra Madre Oriental and across the Isthmus of Tehuantepec into Tabasco state; and along the Pacific coast of the state of Chiapas. These wetter parts get most of their rain between June and September. Apart from these regions, the rest of the country suffers when the rainy season doesn't live up to its name and when the dry season does. Extremes of weather do happen, however. Between 2005 and 2007 both the Caribbean and Pacific coastlines were battered by severe storms and hurricanes.

PEOPLE

Out of a total population of around 106 million, about 9 percent are white, 30 percent *indígena* (indigenous) and 60 percent *mestizos*, a mixture in varying proportions of Spanish and *indígena*. A small percentage (mostly in the coastal zones of Veracruz, Guerrero and Chiapas) are a mixture of black and white or black and *indígena* or *mestizo*. Mexico also has infusions of other European peoples, Arabs and Chinese. There is a national cultural prejudice in favor of the indigenous rather than the Spanish element of the population, though this does not prevent *indígena* from being looked down on by the more Hispanic elements.

LANGUAGE AND DEMOGRAPHY

The official language of Mexico is Spanish, and though English is widely spoken, especially in the most tourist-oriented parts, your stay will be all the more rewarding if you try to communicate with people in their native tongue. As well as Spanish, the estimated 24 million *indígenas* are divided into 54 groups or subdivisions, each with its own language. The most common native language after Spanish is Nahuatl, the ancient language of the Aztecs.

Generally, indigenous people are far from evenly distributed; 36 percent live on the Central Plateau (mostly Hidalgo, and México); 35 percent are along the southern Pacific Coast (Oaxaca, Chiapas, Guerrero), and around 23 percent along the Gulf Coast (mostly Yucatán and Veracruz). In effect, 94 percent of them live in these three regions. There are also sizeable concentrations in the states of Nayarit and Durango, Michoacán, Chihuahua, Sinoloa and Sonora.

The main groups are: Pápago (Sonora); Yaqui (Sonora); Mayo (Sonora and Sinaloa); Tarahumara (Chihuahua); Huastec and Otomí (San Luis Potosí); Cora and Huichol (Nayarit); Purépecha/Tarasco (Michoacán); scattered groups of Nahua (Michoacán, Guerrero, Jalisco, Veracruz and other central states); Totonac (Veracruz); Tlapaneco (Guerrero); Mixtec, Mixe and Zapotec (Oaxaca state); Lacandón, Tzoltzil, Tzeltal, Chol and others (Chiapas); and Maya (Campeche, Yucatán and Quintano Roo).

POLITICS

Under the 1917 Constitution, Mexico is a federal republic of 31 states and a Federal District containing the capital, Mexico City. The president, who appoints the ministers, is elected for six years and can never be re-elected. The next elections are scheduled for 2012.

Congress consists of the 128-seat Senate, half elected every three years on a rotational basis, and the 500-seat Chamber of Deputies, elected every three years. The states enjoy local autonomy and levy their own taxes, and each has its own governor, legislature and court. The president has traditionally appointed the chief of the Federal District, but direct elections were held in 1997 for the first time.

ECONOMY

As an emerging global market, Mexico's economy ebbs and flows with the tide of world trade, yet in rural communities market stallholders barter produce as they have for millennia. City wealth contrasts with rural poverty, and globalization creeps in through fast-food outlets and shopping malls as centuries-old cultures cling to ancient traditions.

Mexico has been an oil producer since the 1880s and led the world in 1921. By 1971 the country had become a net importer, a position reversed in 1972 with the discovery of major new reserves. Today Mexico benefits greatly from the reserves and is the world's sixth-largest producer, with 65 percent of production coming from offshore wells in the Gulf of Campeche. Agriculture has been losing importance in the economy since the beginning of the 1970s and now contributes only an estimated 3.9 percent of GDP.

While the capital used to be a focal point for manufacturing, the government now offers incentives to companies relocating away from major industrial hubs. The boom came with the creation of 3,600 *maquiladoras* (assembly plants) along the US border, which employ some 1.3 million people, earning $1.5 billion annually for the economy. The country also benefits from more than $10 billion sent home from families living north of the border. Tourism is a large source of foreign exchange and the largest employer (about a third of the total workforce). Around 20 million visitors come to Mexico every year, 85 percent from the US. Since 1994, Mexico has been a member of the North American Free Trade Agreement (NAFTA; ▷ 15).

RELIGION

Though 90 percent of the population is ostensibly Roman Catholic (with another 7 percent Protestant and 3 percent atheist), the principal religion is a hybrid of Catholicism and pre-Conquest beliefs and traditions. Despite the apparent piety of many Mexicans, the country is determinedly secular. Because of its identification firstly with Spain, then with the Emperor Maximilian and finally with Porfirio Díaz, the Church has been severely persecuted in the past by reform-minded administrations, and priests are still not supposed to wear ecclesiastical dress.

Opposite *The Sierra de la Giganta mountain range in Baja California*

THE REGIONS OF MEXICO

Mexico City Mexico City is one of the world's great capitals—its architectural magnificence and vast public plaza survive side by side with the noise and pollution of traffic and 20 million people. At once bawdy, vibrant, gaudy, cultured, noisy, sometimes dangerous and always fascinating, the ancient Aztec capital is a celebration of chaotic humanity, good and bad.

The Yucatán Comprising the states of Campeche, Yucatán and Quintana Roo, the Yucatán Peninsula includes Mexico's Mayan Riviera, a tourist hotspot full of great Maya archaeological sites and superb Caribbean beach resorts.

Southern Mexico This vast area of the country spreads out from its narrow isthmus. On the southernmost edge, bordering Guatemala, is the fiercely traditional state of Chiapas, land of the Classic Maya, whose descendants still inhabit the highland villages today. To the north, Tabasco gave rise to the first great civilization of Mesoamerica, the Olmecs, while lively, cosmopolitan Oaxaca is one of the country's cultural highlights and the state of Guerrero is home to Acapulco, Mexico's most famous resort.

Central Mexico East Not far from the capital lie the colonial jewels of Puebla—the City of Angels—to the southeast, and the silver-mining town of Taxco to the south, while northeast the magnificent ruins of El Tajín host the spectacular *voladores* (flying men) ritual, an example of surviving pre-Hispanic traditions. The green,

fertile coastal plain backs the Gulf Coast, largely given over to the oil industry. The port of Veracruz, Spain's gateway to the New World, has a distinct culture and is home to the liveliest pre-Lenten carnival in all Mexico.

Central Mexico West Spanish-style architecture, built with the fortunes amassed from silver and gold, is at its most opulent and impressive in the magnificent towns and cities of the Colonial Highlands, while the Mexican stereotype is alive and well in the state of Jalisco, where you'll find tequila, the lasso-swinging *charros* and the romantic *mariachis*. The state capital, Guadalajara, is Mexico's second city—a huge, modern metropolis with an elegant Spanish core. West of Mexico City the state of Michoacán is home to the ancient Tarascan people, and is the best place to witness the spectacle of the *Día de los Muertos* (Day of the Dead), one of the most important dates in the Mexican calendar.

Northern Mexico and Baja California The miles of endless deserts and vast, barren landscapes of the north hold some of Mexico's most spectacular surprises. Baja California, the long, narrow peninsula that dangles southward from the US border between the Pacific Ocean and the Gulf of California for 1,300km (800 miles), is a stark and beautiful wilderness and one of the world's prime whale-watching sites, while in Chihuahua, Mexico's biggest state, is the Chihuahua al Pacífico, billed as "the world's most scenic railroad."

Above *Mexican traditions, such as this Aztec Conchero dance in Mexico City, are fiercely upheld throughout the country*

USA

BAJA CALIFORNIA NORTE

SONORA

CHIHUAHUA

COAHUILA

BAJA CALIFORNIA SUR

SINALOA

DURANGO

NUEVO LEÓN

ZACATECAS

TAMAULIPAS

NAYARIT

SAN LUIS POTOSÍ

JALISCO

COLIMA

MICHOACÁN

GUERRERO

VERACRUZ LLAVE

TABASCO

OAXACA

CHIAPAS

YUCATÁN

QUINTANA ROO

CAMPECHE

BZ

GT

HN

SV

Islas Revilla Gigedo

1 AGUASCALIENTES
2 GUANAJUATO
3 QUERÉTARO
4 HIDALGO
5 TLAXCALA
6 MÉXICO
7 DISTRITO FEDERAL
8 MORELOS
9 PUEBLA

Below *The twin towers of Santa Prisca dominate Taxco in Central Mexico East*

MEXICO CITY

History Wander the colonial Centro Histórico, Mexico City's heart; fascinating, chaotic and exotic in equal measure (▷ 86–87).

Museums The Museo Nacional de Antropología (▷ 72–75) is crammed with pre-Hispanic art and culture—a must before exploring the rest of the country.

Eating and shopping The district of Condesa (▷ 90–93) has become *the* place to eat, drink and be seen, while the more refined Polanco (▷ 80 and 91–92) is home to the city's finest shops and restaurants.

Café society Visit the beautiful, bohemian suburbs of San Angel (▷ 81) and Coyoacán (▷ 70), with their leafy, cobbled streets and chic sidewalk (pavement) cafés.

Art The Palacio de Bellas Artes houses many works by the great artist Diego Rivera, but don't miss the Museo Mural Diego Rivera on the opposite side of Alameda Central (▷ 67).

Music Visit Plaza Garibaldi (▷ 78) on a Friday or Saturday night and you're likely to be besieged by persistent *mariachi* bands.

THE YUCATÁN

Beaches Relax in the warm turquoise sea fringed with fine white-sand beaches and palm groves of the Riviera Maya (▷ 128–129).

Maya ruins Visit the sensational ruins at Uxmal (▷ 122–123), Tulúm (▷ 119) and Chichén Itzá (▷ 108–111).

Wildlife The Sian Ka'an Biosphere Reserve covers tropical forest, savanna and coastline and protects many bird species (▷ 118).

Diving Cozumel (▷ 133), the Island of the Swallows, is one of the most popular diving bases in the world, due to its extensive and rich variety of coral and underwater creatures.

Nightlife If you like to party, you'll love Cancún (▷ 107). It's also a good alternative entry point to Mexico City.

SOUTHERN MEXICO

Architecture Visit Oaxaca City for its colonial architecture (▷ 148–149) and the nearby ruins of Monte Albán (▷ 146–147).

Scenery Follow Route 190, from Oaxaca to Tehuantepec (▷ 158), as it serpentines unendingly through the beautiful Sierras.

Indigenous culture Soak up the atmosphere of the indigenous town of San Cristóbal de las Casas (▷ 96), from where you can explore the jungle waterfalls and multihued lakes.

Maya ruins The jungle setting of Palenque makes it the most atmospheric and beautiful of all the Maya sites (▷ 152–155).

CENTRAL MEXICO EAST

Shopping Take a trip to Puebla (▷ 182–183), the City of Angels, to buy beautiful Talavera tiles—after admiring them first on the colonial buildings (▷ 197).

Sightseeing The spectacular *volador* ritual, an example of surviving Totonac traditions, is performed regularly in Papantla and outside the magnificent ruins of El Tajín (▷ 185).

Ancient ruins Don't miss the awesome ruins of Teotihuacán, one of Mexico's most important pre-Hispanic sites and a short, easy trip from the capital (▷ 188–191).

Museums Xalapa (Jalapa) is home to the excellent Anthropology Museum, one of the best of its type in the country (▷ 193).

Carnaval Enjoy the legendary hospitality of the Veracruzanos and the eternally festive, tropical-port atmosphere that reaches its climax in spring during the liveliest carnival in Mexico (▷ 197).

CENTRAL MEXICO WEST

Culture To experience the Mexican stereotype go to Jalisco. Here you'll find the town of Tequila (▷ 219), the lasso-swinging Jaliscan *charros* (cowboys) and the country's most famous *mariachis*, those roving musicians dressed in their fine, tight-trousered suits.

Architecture A relatively short circuit north of Mexico City brings you to the Colonial Heartland, taking in the towns of Querétaro (▷ 216), Guanajuato (▷ 210–213), San Miguel de Allende (▷ 217) and Dolores Hidalgo (▷ 207), architectural gems built on the wealth from silver production.

Clockwise from right Bahía Concepción, ideal for snorkeling; a colorful café in Mexico City; Mayan ruins at Chichén Itzá

Festivals The *Día de los Muertos* (▷ 24), a key date in the Mexican calendar, is especially celebrated in Michoacán, particularly around Pátzcuaro (▷ 216), where on November 1 every village around the lake commemorates its dead.

Nature People flock to El Campanario Ecological Reserve each year in spring to see millions of monarch butterflies take to the wing as they migrate north, one of the most impressive sights in all of Mexico (▷ 18 and 216).

NORTHERN MEXICO AND BAJA CALIFORNIA

Wildlife Head down the Baja California Peninsula through spectacular desert scenery to bask on idyllic beaches and, if you time it right, to watch the migrating whales at Laguna Ojo de Liebre (Scammon's Lagoon; ▷ 248).

Train journey Board the Chihuahua al Pacífico (▷ 244 and 254), billed as "the world's most scenic railroad," which wends its way across bridges, through tunnels and over the Sierra Madre to Los Mochis.

Hiking Stop off at Creel or El Divisadero to absorb the views, discover the awe-inspiring landscapes, rock formations and wildlife, visit Mexico's tallest waterfall and penetrate the vertiginous depths of the Barranca del Cobre (▷ 243).

TOP EXPERIENCES

Gaze in awe at the 17th-century Franciscan Church of Santo Domingo, in Oaxaca, one of the best examples of baroque style in Mexico (▷ 150).

Soak up the sights, sounds and aromas of Oaxaca's Mercado de Abastos, the second-largest craft market in Mexico after Toluca. Beware of vendors trying to persuade you to taste *chapulines* (▷ 294)—grasshoppers fried in huge vats (▷ 149).

Be pampered at the Reserva Ecológica Nanciyaga on Lake Catemaco (▷ 178), where you can lie in a steaming patchouli-scented bath, followed by a vigorous massage and a vegetarian meal, all in a lush, tropical setting.

Witness the spectacle of Oaxaca's Guelaguetza, an impressive carnival celebration in July, when many different cultural groups gather in one place (▷ 166).

Get off your horse and drink in the authentic Wild West atmosphere of Durango (▷ 245), backdrop for many Hollywood Westerns and more recent classics such as *The Mask of Zorro*.

Wallow in the sumptuous surroundings of Bar La Opera, one of the capital's most sophisticated dining experiences (▷ 96).

Dive into the deep blue waters of one of Yucatán's many *cenotes* (sink holes). At Tres Ríos "eco" park, near Cancún (▷ 132 and 288), you can follow it up with horseback riding on the beach and snorkeling on the reef.

Drive through spectacular scenery to the 1,000m-deep (3,280ft) Cañon del Sumidero, where trails wind through lush vegetation with orchids, cascading waterfalls, crystalline rivers, frolicking monkeys and amazing birdlife (▷ 144).

Peer into the crater of Volcán Paricutín, near the town of Uruapan, following a 16km (10-mile) trek on horseback and a final 400m (440-yard) scramble on foot across the cold lava (▷ 221).

Above The Sumidero Canyon is home to monkeys and exotic birds
Below Treat yourself to dinner at Bar La Opera in Mexico City

Ponder the giant stepped pyramid of El Castillo at Chichén Itzá, one of the most visited and spectacular Maya sites (▷ 108–111). In 2007 the pyramid was voted one of "The New 7 Wonders of the World."

Attend a *charrería*, an authentic Mexican rodeo, where you can see wild-mare riding and team bull riding—accompanied by trumpets and local delicacies (▷ 290).

Down a shot of tequila, Mexico's national drink, in Cantina la Guadalupana (▷ 97), Mexico City, one of the best-known *cantinas* in the country.

LIVING MEXICO

Few countries in Latin America have such a large percentage of *mestizo* (mixed indigenous and European blood) and *indígena* (indigenous groups). Out of a total population of 106 million, almost 30 percent are indigenous while 60 percent are *mestizos*. Though the Spanish invaders set about converting the natives to Catholicism with a near hysterical zeal, pockets of resistance held out and today many indigenous groups have maintained their own cultural and religious identities. In Oaxaca, for example, some 20 percent of the population converse primarily in the Zapotec language, while the Lacandón and Huichol cultural groups, though small, have managed to avoid significant contact with the outside world thanks to their remoteness. That said, however, Mexico's indigenous people remain the most marginalized sector of society. The uprising by the Zapatista National Liberation Army (EZLN) in Chiapas in 1994, which deliberately coincided with the inauguration of the North American Free Trade Agreement (NAFTA), was a warning to the government that they cannot ignore the rights of indigenous people. The rest of the country, too, is showing signs of unrest as NAFTA fails to deliver prosperity to the masses and increased globalization leads to a creeping Americanization that is threatening the Mexican way of life.

Clockwise from left to right *Customers of a fast-food vendor share a joke in Guanajuato, Central Mexico; Mexicans are great consumers of fast food; a woman from Ocosingo wearing local traditional costume*

GIRL POWER

In this most macho of countries, one particular race stands out as a striking exception. The Zapotec women of the Isthmus of Tehuantepec are renowned for their strength, beauty and sound commercial acumen. Distinctive in their elaborately embroidered *huipiles* (blouses) and long, flowing *enaguas* (skirts), they can be seen running the daily markets held in the towns of Juchitán and Tehuantepec.

One local custom that illustrates who wears the pants in this matriarchal society is the *tirada de fruta* (fruit throwing), which takes place at various fiestas throughout the year. Sweets, toys and mangoes are distributed among the crowd, before women climb onto the rooftops and proceed to hurl fruit at the males they see gathered below them.

SUPER BARRIO

Is it a bird? Is it a plane? No, it's Super Barrio. Unlike his comic book contemporaries, however, Super Barrio is a real-life character who concentrates his efforts on campaigning for Mexico City's poor. He first emerged after the devastating earthquake of 1985, which killed many thousands of people, as one of three superheroes who took it in turns to don red and yellow tights, cape and wrestling mask, and assist the victims of the disaster. Since then he has been a constant source of energy and inspiration. Other people who have tried to follow in his footsteps include Super-Eco, an environmental crusader who wears bright green spandex, and El Chupacabras Crusader, defender of middle-class people experiencing financial difficulties.

DRUG TRADE

Mexico's "informal" sector accounts for up to a third of the country's economic output and employs a quarter of the working population. At the bottom of the heap are the armies of street children selling *chicles* (chewing gum), while at the top are Mexico's shadowy drug lords who earn vast sums from the narcotics trade.

Despite a series of joint US–Mexican anti-drug initiatives, the drug traffickers have continued to prosper. In 1999, General Jesus Gutiérrez Rebollo, ex-head of the country's anti-drug agency, was found guilty of being in the pay of the drug barons and sentenced to 40 years. His story has since been dramatized in Steven Soderbergh's Oscar-winning movie *Traffic* (2000), staring Michael Douglas.

FOOD ON THE RUN

Mexicans are famous for eating on the hoof, grabbing *tacos* or *quesadillas* at stands along roadsides. But sales of *tacos, tortas* and *tortillas* have been in decline because of competition from their fast-food equivalents north of the border, namely burgers, pizzas and hot dogs.

Between 1998 and 2004, *tortilla* consumption in Mexico fell by 25 percent, according to the National Corn Processors Chamber, who cite the sheer convenience of foreign imports and the social connotations attached to *tortillas*, which are viewed as the food of the poor, as reasons for the decline. Another reason is the mega marketing power of the big fast-food chains. It would be hard to imagine the many roadside *torta* stands offering a free toy with every sandwich!

HAPPY BIRTHDAY, NAFTA?

The 15th anniversary of NAFTA (North American Free Trade Agreement) between the US, Canada and Mexico fell in 2009, but although it was hailed as the panacea for the country's economic ills at its inception, few Mexicans now rejoice in its birth. True, Mexico's exports to the US grew threefold and its per capita income rose 24 percent, but most of the benefits of the agreement have been felt along the US border, where many US companies have relocated to take advantage of a cheap workforce, creating thousands of new jobs. Being tied so closely to the US economy means that Mexico has suffered directly from the economic slump in the US. Never the less, recent years have seen steady growth in the Mexican GDP.

Throughout Mexican history, art and architecture have been a fundamental part of the country's culture, from the massive Olmec heads of the mid-12th century BC to the eighth-century AD Mayan murals in the Temple of the Paintings at Bonampak, in southeast Chiapas. With the arrival of the Spanish in the 16th century came changes in style and content, but Mexico's indigenous painters and sculptors never completely abandoned their roots. This fusion of European and indigenous styles became a defining feature of the country's artists, architects and writers. Twentieth-century Mexican art was dominated by the great muralists Diego Rivera (1886–1957), José Clemente Orozco (1883–1949) and David Alfaro Siqueiros (1896–1974), who brought art to the people through a series of huge murals on public buildings depicting themes from Mexican history. Rivera and his fellow artists were devoted to the idea of *mexicanidad*, glorification of their native heritage and culture. In literature, too, this notion of "Mexicanness" dominated intellectual thought, most notably that of Octavio Paz in his 1952 novel *The Labyrinth of Solitude*, an analysis of Mexican society and how pre-Columbian cultures continue to influence the modern state. This synthesis of the ancient and modern has also been used to dazzling effect by the country's leading architects, Ricardo Legorreta (born 1931) and Luis Barragán (1902–88).

THE CULT OF KAHLO

The turbulent life of Frida Kahlo (1907–54) was brought to the world's attention by the big-budget 2002 movie *Frida*, starring Salma Hayek. Long before the film hit the screens, the cult of this great feminist icon had spread far beyond Mexico. Kahlo's often shocking art was driven by the physical pain she endured from horrific injuries sustained in a bus crash at the age of 18 and the mental anguish she suffered during her passionate and tortured relationship with revolutionary muralist Diego Rivera. The mystique surrounding her will only be fuelled by the book written by her niece, Isolda Pinedo Kahlo, claiming that Rivera helped her to die.

Above *Detail of Diego Rivera's mosaic mural on Teatro de los Insugentes, Mexico City*

NEW IDENTITY

Carlos Fuentes is Mexico's most celebrated novelist. Among his best-known works are *The Death of Artemio Cruz* (1962), which won international acclaim, and *The Old Gringo* (1985), which was made into a film starring Gregory Peck and Jane Fonda.

Fuentes' work has in the most part explored aspects of the history and cultural identity of Latin America, especially Mexico, but this search for national identity no longer permeates his writing, as witnessed in his novel, *Inez* (2002), a love story based around Berlioz's opera *The Damnation of Faust*. Fuentes says: "You have an absolute freedom in Mexican writing today in which you don't necessarily have to deal with the Mexican identity… because we have an identity… we know who we are. We know what it means to be a Mexican."

INSPIRATION FROM THE PAST

One of the great landmarks of Polanco is the Camino Real Hotel, with its unmistakable hot-pink and canary-yellow walls. Opened in 1968, it was the result of collaboration between two of Mexico's leading architects, Luis Barragán and Ricardo Legorreta. Barragán was, without doubt, the most influential Mexican architect of the 20th century, having been awarded architecture's Nobel Prize, the Pritzker Laureate, in 1980. His most famous disciple, Legorreta, has gone on to enjoy a career of unbridled success and international acclaim. The work of both men may be at the cutting edge of contemporary architecture, but their use of clean, simple lines and vivid color to reflect the natural elements in the environment is based on pre-Hispanic, indigenous building principles.

BREAKING THE SPELL

In 1967 Colombian writer Gabriel García Márquez wrote *One Hundred Years of Solitude* and lit the fuse of the so-called Latin American literature boom. Now a new boom is under way, led by thirtysomething Mexican writer Jorge Volpi, whose 1999 novel *Looking For Klingsor*, a spy thriller set in World War II Germany, has been translated into 16 languages. Together with Ignacio Padilla, Pedro Angel Palou, Eloy Urroz and Vicente Herrasti, Volpi forms the self-dubbed "crack generation," who have broken with literary conventions, particularly "magic realism," which has dominated the Mexican literary scene in recent decades. Controversially, the "crack generation" has criticized "boom" followers such as fellow Mexican Laura Esquivel and the Chilean writer Isabel Allende, who, they claim, reduce their literature to a mere formula.

Above *Passionate Mexican artist Frida Kahlo*
Below *Mural of Father Hidalgo by Orozco in Guadalajara*

LAST OF THE MURALISTS

Alfredo Zalce (1908–2003) was the last of Mexico's great revolutionary muralists, but unlike the "Big Three" (Rivera, Siqueiros and Orozco), he remains virtually unknown outside his native country. This is because Zalce spent his entire life avoiding fame and fortune and shunning all forms of publicity.

When the name of Michoacán's museum of contemporary art was changed to the Museo de Arte Contemporaneo Alfredo Zalce, the artist had to be tricked into attending the inauguration ceremony.

Many of his huge murals and statues are in Morelia, on display in public parks and government buildings such as the Palacio de Gobierno (State Capital building) and the Camara de Diputados (House of Representatives), but they can also be seen in Mexico City's excellent and extensive Museum of Anthropology (▷ 72–75).

When 16th-century conquistador Hernán Cortés was asked by the king of Spain to describe Mexico, he scrunched up a sheet of paper, dropped it on the table and said, "That is Mexico." From the scorched deserts of the north down to the steaming, tropical jungles of the south, this most geographically diverse of countries is dominated by mountains. Running down its flanks from the US border are the Sierra Madre Oriental (East) and Occidental (West), with a series of smaller ranges rising from the plateau in the middle of the country and in the northern deserts. These mountains were shaped by millions of years of geological activity and the process continues to this day: spectacular volcanic eruptions are a dramatic, and often tragic, feature of life for many Mexicans. The diverse landscapes are home to a rich mix of wildlife. Mexico is the world's third most biologically diverse country, after Brazil and Colombia. It has 700 species of reptile (more than any other country in the world) and 450 species of mammal. Unfortunately, the protection of Mexico's precious natural assets comes low on the list of priorities when compared with economic necessity, and many rare species, including the leatherback turtle, are under threat of extinction.

Clockwise from left to right *The monarch butterfly over-winters in the mountains of central Mexico; smoking Popocatépetl last erupted in 2001 and is constantly monitored for signs of activity; turtles are still hunted by poachers in spite of the penalties*

KING OF THE BUTTERFLIES
In the insect kingdom, one creature reigns supreme, the monarch butterfly (*Danaus plexippus*). In autumn tens of millions of these orange-winged marvels make the 3,000km (1,865-mile) migration south from the northern US and southern Canada to mountainous sites in central Mexico, most notably at the El Campanario Ecological Reserve in Michoacán (▷ 216). The following spring the butterflies begin the return trip north, breeding along the way, but they do not survive the journey; it is their offspring that arrive at their northern home in the summer, and the cycle starts again. The mystery is how each generation of monarchs finds suitable winter sites every year.

SEISMIC MATTERS

Less than 80km (50 miles) southeast of Mexico City and only 45km (28 miles) west of Puebla is the active volcano Popocatépetl (5,452m/17,888ft) and its dormant neighbor, Iztaccíhuatl (5,286m/17,343ft). Popocatépetl, or "smoking mountain" in the Aztec language, had lain dormant for 65 years until it began to spew out ash and red-hot rocks in a series of spectacular eruptions from 1994 to 2001. The authorities fear that this activity may have been a by-product of the massive earthquakes of 1985, which measured 8.1 and 7.5 on the Richter scale and left an estimated 6,000 people dead. Today, the volcano's snow-covered slopes remain out of bounds and "Popo" serves as a constant reminder of just how vulnerable this country is to seismic activity.

PLIGHT OF THE TURTLES

Though the sale of turtle meat and eggs has been banned in Mexico since 1990, the threat of up to nine years in prison has not been enough to deter the poachers.

The massacre of hundreds of Olive Ridley turtles at San Valentin in Guerrero state in January 2004 by armed poachers was only one in a long line of sickening incidents.

Prized for their supposed aphrodisiac qualities, turtle eggs are sold on the black market for up to $1.35 each. Though poverty is a major factor sustaining this illegal trade, lack of resources to enforce laws is another consideration.

Mexico's environmental watchdog, Profepa, has only 300 agents to protect the country's wildlife and therefore relies heavily on support from the Mexican army, navy and police force.

A ZONE OF CONTENTION

Scientists studying the fragile desert environment of the Mapimi Biosphere Reserve, near Durango in northern Mexico, face an unusual problem. The so-called Zona del Silencio (Zone of Silence) has developed from a half-baked local rumor into a full-blown conspiracy industry.

It all started when a US missile flew off course and landed in the reserve. The US military hastily removed the wayward craft, leaving the way open for a cult of so-called *zoneros* to develop. Among the many outrageous claims made for the area's mystical powers is a magnetic vortex attracting objects from outer space and acting as a conduit for extraterrestrial communication. The result is that the reserve has been overwhelmed by hordes of curious visitors and various itinerant oddballs who are putting genuine scientific research at risk.

ALIVE AND PECKING

The success of the campaign to save the thick-billed parrot *(Rhynchopsitta pachyrhyncha)* in the face of powerful logging interests made Mexico's hard-pressed environmentalists cheer. The endangered bird, which is endemic to the Sierra Madre Occidental, only nests above 2,300m (7,600ft), which is where the most valuable timber is found. Some 98.5 percent of the forests of the Sierra Madre have already been logged, and the Cebadillas de Yaguirachic, the parrot's most important nesting area, was targeted for logging in 2002. A cross-border agreement between Pronatura (Mexico's largest conservation organization) and the Wildlands Project based in Tucson, Arizona, has ensured a 15-year moratorium on any logging in the area, during which time local communities will hopefully replace lost revenues with income gained from ecotourism.

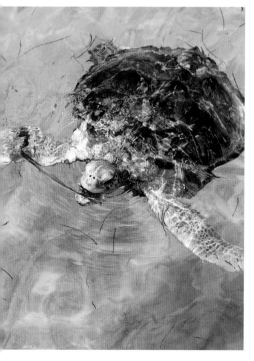

POPULAR CULTURE

When it comes to mass entertainment, US influence is ever present, yet Mexicans still prefer their own versions. Take TV, for instance—by far the most powerful medium. It is dominated by the huge number of *telenovelas* (soap operas), and every day millions of Mexicans tune in to watch their particular choice. The music scene, meanwhile, is a richly diverse one. Traditional genres such as cumbia, which originated in Colombia, salsa and merengue are as popular as ever in dance clubs, while Mexican rock, rap and hip-hop are getting more exposure through satellite channels such as MTV. In cinema, Mexico's image abroad has not always been a positive one, from the awful B-movies of the 1940s and 1950s to the evil villains of the Spaghetti Westerns. That screen image has been given an extreme makeover with the popularity of internationally acclaimed films such as *Amores Perros* and *Y Tu Mamá Tambien* that have proved homegrown talent can compete against the might of Hollywood.

MEXICAN NEW WAVE
Mexican cinema exploded onto the international stage in 2000 with the Oscar-nominated *Amores Perros (Love's a Bitch)*, directed by Alejandro González Iñárritu. He went on to make the critically acclaimed *21 Grams*, starring Benicio del Toro, but it was Gael García Bernal who grabbed the attention of the world's media with his role in the 2001 road movie *Y Tu Mamá Tambien (And Your Mother Too)*, which established him as the pin-up of Latin American cinema. Since then Bernal has shown his remarkable breadth of ability in two contrasting roles, first as a transsexual in Pedro Almodóvar's *Bad Education* (2004) and then as a young Che Guevara in *The Motorcycle Diaries* (2004). Could the next James Dean be Mexican?

Clockwise from left to right *A still from the 2004 film* The Motorcycle Diaries *starring Gael García Bernal; masked* luchadore Hurican *participates in a sport second only to soccer in popularity; Carlos Santana is Mexico's most famous rock export*

TELENOVELAS

In Mexico, *telenovelas* (soap operas) are not so much an entertaining diversion as an addiction. Prime-time TV (between about 4 and 10pm) features an endless stream of *telenovelas*, each one aimed at a specific target audience, from teenagers to housewives. So gushy and melodramatic are the *telenovelas* that they make the 1980s *Dynasty* saga look like a gritty and hard-hitting slice of social realism, but every day millions of mostly working-class Mexicans tune in to follow the twists and turns of each plot, no doubt treating the escapist fantasy as an antidote to the daily grind of their own lives. With viewing figures of up to 25 million regularly, *telenovelas* are big business for the two main TV channels, Televisa and Azteca, and the actors are huge stars, heavily featured in celebrity magazines.

MEXICAN ROCK

One of the most fertile musical genres to emerge from Latin America in recent years is Latin rock. The Mexican band Café Tacuba is a leading exponent of *rock en Español* and their 2003 album "Cuatro Caminos" won a Grammy for best Latin/alternative album. They formed in Mexico City 17 years ago, and their mix of rock, hip-hop, techno, merengue, ranchera and famously electric live performances have earned them a huge following far beyond their homeland.

It wasn't always so, however. Seen by the left as US cultural imperialism and by the right as a threat to traditional values, Mexican rock music was driven underground in the 1970s. Even the country's most famous rock export, Carlos Santana, was once barred from playing in public in Mexico City.

DEADLY DIVA

In such a macho culture as Mexico, it is ironic that one of the country's most effective political satirists is a woman. Astrid Hadad is the outrageous diva whose notorious stage show has earned her not only national headlines, but also a devoted international audience and the label "Mexico's Madonna." Hadad's distinctive style—dubbed "Heavy Nopal," after the cactus used in the making of tequila—mixes ranchera, bolero, rumba, rock and jazz with performing art, political barbs and a range of surreal and extravagant costumes (she can appear as the Virgin of Guadalupe, an Aztec pyramid covered in writhing snakes or even the bleeding heart of Jesus). Her razor-sharp wit is aimed at everyone and everything, from the Mexican government to macho culture.

BEHIND THE MASK

Since making its first appearance in the 1930s, professional wrestling, or *lucha libre*, has become one of the country's best-loved forms of entertainment, regularly watched by thousands of people.

Many of the top *luchadores* wear distinctively decorated masks to hide the wrestler's real identity. This mask-wearing serves as a metaphor for a country that has concealed its true face from the outside world since the time of the Conquest by Spain. Fights are sometimes billed as "mask vs. mask" and the most bitterly contested fight will result in the loser having to relinquish his mask to the victor.

The most famous of all Mexican wrestlers, *El Santo* (The Saint), went on to achieve more success by becoming a star of 1950s horror B-movies with titles such as *Santo versus The Mummy*.

As you fly into Mexico City you get the impression that the capital is lit with 20-watt light bulbs. In fact, the lights are as bright as those of any other big city, but they have to penetrate a haze of pollutants. With more than 24 million inhabitants, Mexico's capital is one of the largest conurbations in the world, with pollution levels and traffic congestion to match. And the problem gets worse as each year the capital, along with the country's other major cities, has to accommodate thousands of poor *campesinos* (peasant farmers), mostly from the south. From Mexico City to Ciudad Juárez in the north, city boundaries are shifting as shanty towns *(colonias)* appear, seemingly overnight, to house the new arrivals. Life for Mexico's rural population is tough. With only 13 percent of the land suitable for agriculture, farmers need all the help they can get, but the North American Free Trade Agreement (NAFTA) has not benefited them as they had hoped. The flow of migration from the countryside to the cities is likely to increase, and many more thousands will join the army of economic migrants heading for the US border and the hope of a better life in the First World.

THAT SINKING FEELING
Though not quite on the scale of the Leaning Tower of Pisa, Mexico City's cathedral suffers from serious subsidence. Inside, the two opposing side walls differ in height by about 1.5m (5ft) and there's a 6m (20ft) difference between the entrance and the high altar. In common with the rest of the city's central buildings, the cathedral's foundations are sinking. Pre-Hispanic Mexico City was a maze of canals, similar to those of Venice, and the Spanish built their new version directly on top, adding billions of tons of weight to a fragile foundation. The population explosion of the last century has added to the problem. At the beginning of the 1900s Mexico City stood more than 1m (3ft) above Lake Texoco; it now lies 3m (10ft) below.

Clockwise from left to right *The vast Plaza de la Constitución is the political and religious heart of Mexico City; the cathedral dominates Plaza de la Constitución in the capital; green VW Beetles comprise a large proportion of the taxi fleet in Mexico City*

BEETLEMANIA

On July 30 2003, the world's last original Volkswagen Beetle (number 21,529,464) rolled off the assembly line in Puebla. Though the "Vocho," as it is known, was superseded elsewhere by a new model, in Mexico demand was such that production in the country continued unabated for almost 40 years.

Nearly 2 million Beetles have been built at VW's Mexico plant in Puebla, many ending up as taxicabs, and one of the most distinctive features of the capital's traffic-choked streets is the sheer number of these cars, painted in their conspicuous yellow or green.

The last 3,000 to be made in Puebla, called the Ultima Edición (Last Edition), came with special features such as a CD player, and the very last one of those now stands in the VW museum in Wolfsburg, Germany, the car's spiritual home.

BREATHLESS IN THE CAPITAL

In 1958, Mexican novelist and elder statesman Carlos Fuentes wrote his remarkably prescient novel of life in the nation's congested capital, *Where the Air is Clear*. Within 40 years of publication, Mexico City was the air pollution capital of the world. By 1995, emissions of carbon monoxide, nitrogen dioxide, lead and sulfur dioxide all exceeded acceptable levels nine days out of ten, causing migrating birds to fall dead from the sky. In November 1996, 300 people died from respiratory illnesses. Since then, various government measures have helped to improve the city's air quality: the introduction of lead-free gasoline, fitting catalytic converters to all new vehicles and the relocation of industry. But there's a long way to go before *chilangos*, as the capital's residents are known, can breathe more easily.

TORTILLA CURTAIN

One of the most contentious issues in US—Mexican relations is the policing of the 3,168km (1,968-mile) border. Every night, under cover of darkness, tens of thousands of Mexicans desperate for a better life slip into the waters of the Río Grande and strike out for *el otro lado* (the other side). More than a million are apprehended each year by the US border patrol, but hundreds of thousands succeed, adding to the 3 million Mexican-born unauthorized residents in the US (Los Angeles has the largest population of Mexicans after Mexico City).

In 1994 the US government erected the "Tortilla Curtain," a steel fence with infrared cameras, lights and ground sensors, but the flow of illegal immigrants from Mexico continued. More recently, many US politicians have made moves to erect a new 3,220km (2,000-mile) fence.

RURAL POVERTY

Mexicans eulogize the countryside in countless *ranchero* ballads, but with only one in four of the population living outside towns and cities, such nostalgia may seem somewhat misplaced.

Though one in five Mexican workers are directly involved in agriculture, it accounts for only 3.9 percent of GDP. The majority are subsistence farmers working plots as small as 1ha (2.4 acres). NATFA (▷ 14, 15) has only made things worse for Mexico's millions of *campesinos*, who have had to compete with cheap agricultural imports from north of the border, as well as cope with a sharp fall in government subsidies. With the ending of all tariffs on food imported from the US and Canada in 2003, many rural Mexicans will be forced to abandon their tiny plots and head for the cities—or across the border.

Mexicans love a party, whether it's a child's birthday celebration where blindfolded guests try to smash open a *piñata* (papier-mâché donkey filled with sweets), or a tequila-fueled Carnaval with lavish parades and all-night dancing. In this predominately Catholic country, the festival calendar is full of religious events, *Semana Santa* (Holy Week) being the largest and most solemn affair, particularly in Taxco, San Luis Potosí and throughout Oaxaca. *Pascua* (Easter) is also celebrated throughout the country, but most spectacularly in the suburb of Iztapalapa, in the south of Mexico City, where more than a million visitors arrive annually to see its inhabitants stage a Passion play. Many festivals have their roots in pagan customs, such as Oaxaca's *Guelaguetza*, an exhausting two-week dance extravaganza, while others are a fusion of indigenous and Christian traditions, most notably the *Día de los Muertos* (Day of the Dead). Music, too, stirs the blood of the Mexican people. Most famous are the *rancheras*—passionate and soulful ballads that reach to the core of the national psyche. Aside from music and fiestas, Mexicans also express themselves through a huge diversity of folk art, crafting beautiful objects from anything they can get their hands on: wood, clay, silver—even root vegetables.

Clockwise from left to right *The guitar features in most forms of Mexican music and street musicians are a common sight; folk art is a popular means of self-expression in Mexico; the Voladores (flying men) of Papantla begin their twirling descent*

CACTUS VISIONS

Every year many Huichols, a native people who number only 15,000, make the pilgrimage from their homelands in Jalisco and Nayarit some 485km (300 miles) across the Sierra Madre to the *Wirikuta* (Field of Flowers) in the searing desert of San Luis Potosí, all for the sake of an innocuous-looking, potato-sized cactus. This cactus, the *peyote*, is at the heart of their sacred rituals and considered the fount of life. Through the chewing of the hallucinogenic *peyote* "button" in mystical ceremonies, the Huichol shamans believe they can communicate with the gods to predict the future and ensure the success of the maize crop. For the rest of the group, the visions resulting from eating *peyote* are interpreted through their art, in particular the creation of their vivid *nierika* (yarn paintings) and *chaquira* (beadwork).

FLYING TONIGHT

One dance craze unlikely to sweep Europe and North America is that performed by the daring Voladores de Papantla (the flying men of Papantla). This ancient Totonac ritual takes place every Sunday beside the cathedral in Papantla, and most days outside the ruins of nearby El Tajín (▷ 185). Five men dressed in elaborate costumes climb a 30m (100ft) pole crowned by a tiny platform. The leader then begins to play his flute and beat his drum while his four colleagues, each tied at the ankles to a rope that's fastened to a frame at the top of the pole, launch themselves backwards into midair. With arms outstretched to greet the sun, each *volador* (flyer) spins precisely 13 times before reaching terra firma. The total number of revolutions, 52, equals the number of years that comprise the pre-Colombian religious cycle.

MARIACHIS

The only thing more Mexican than tequila is *mariachi*, the musical ensemble born in the state of Jalisco during the 19th century.

Today, the most prestigious bands still hail from the town of Cocula. With their silver-studded *charro* (Mexican cowboy) suits and wide-brimmed hats, these wandering minstrels sing songs of love, death, honor, betrayal, machismo, politics and revolutionary heroes, all to the accompaniment of violin, guitars and trumpet, with often a Mexican harp doubling the bass line. Seen all over the country, the bands are part of a deep-seated and much-loved tradition, expressing an essential part of the Mexican soul.

RADISHING BEAUTIES

Every year, on December 23, one of Mexico's most unusual festivals takes place in Oaxaca. *La Noche de Rábanos* (The Night of the Radishes) is a bizarre mix of folk art and horticulture, when local artist-gardeners create ornate radish sculptures ranging from animals and famous people to nativity scenes. The radishes are harvested on December 18, giving the contestants five days in which to fashion these humble root crops into a sophisticated tableau. The winner receives 13,000 pesos. The strange event has its origins in colonial times, when a Spanish friar suggested that farmers carve their radishes into imaginative shapes in order to entice people to come to their market.

A DYING ART

Of all Mexico's religious festivals, one that stands out as the closest in spirit to indigenous traditions is the *Día de los Muertos* (Day of the Dead), celebrated on November 1 and 2. During these two days and nights, families communicate with their departed relatives by placing offerings of food and drink on elaborately prepared altars, and candlelit family picnics are held in cemeteries across the country. Markets sell all manner of decorative candles and wreaths of flowers, while bakers and confectioners create tiny candy coffins, bread rolls shaped like human bones and little sugar-coated *calaveras* (skulls). The most famous symbols of Day of the Dead, and one of the most potent expressions of Mexican folk art, are the grotesque papier-mâché skeletons, which were inspired by the macabre, late 19th-century political cartoons of José Guadalupe Posada (▷ 39).

COSTUME DRAMA

One of the most famous of all Mexican folk legends is that of the erroneously named China Poblana (Chinese-Pueblan). In the early 17th century, a Chinese princess (or Indian, depending on which version you read) was captured by Portuguese slave traders and taken to Manila, in the Philippines, where she was then sold to Captain Miguel de Sosa and his wife and shipped to her new home in Puebla.

Raised more as an adopted daughter than a slave, she went on to devote the rest of her life to helping the poor. Eschewing the elegant Spanish fashions of the day, she wore simple, full skirts and a loose, delicately embroidered *huipil* (blouse) covered with a shawl—a combination of the local indigenous dress and her own native costume—thus creating the distinctive peasant style which has since become the national costume of Mexico we see today.

TREE OF LIFE

The village of Metepec, south of Toluca, is known as the heart of production of the Árbol de la Vida or Tree of Life. These brightly painted and elaborate clay sculptures portraying Adam and Eve in the Garden of Eden and their imminent fall from grace are decorated with flowers and foliage, angels and saints, devils, a snake and the ubiquitous Mexican skeleton. Originating in the Middle East and arriving in Mexico via Spain, the trees have become the best-known expressions of Mexican folk art and are collected all over the world. Among the most avid collectors were Frida Kahlo and her husband Diego Rivera (▷ 16), who did much to promote public interest in the trees in the country's capital.

Top *Music plays a large part in local traditions and festivals and is performed widely throughout the country*
Above *A brightly decorated mask and sweetmeats, part of the Day of the Dead festivities*

THE STORY OF MEXICO

Though the earliest evidence of human life in Mexico dates from around 20,000BC, it wasn't until around 7000 to 6000BC that the numerous tribes of nomadic hunter-gatherers, collectively called the Chichimecas, began to settle in Mesoamerica, the area between south the present-day United States and northern Honduras and El Salvador. By 1500BC basic agricultural societies were forming and some constructed large public buildings. One of the earliest of these, dating from around 1350BC, at San Lorenzo, near Veracruz, was built by the Olmecs, the oldest known civilization of Mesoamerica. Their origins remains a mystery, but their artistic, social, numerical and astronomical achievements had a major influence on all of Mexico's subsequent cultures. The ascendancy of the Olmecs was relatively short-lived and by around 650BC they had been eclipsed by the Zapotecs, whose seat of power at Monte Albán, in Oaxaca, prospered from 500BC until AD700, when they lost out to the nearby Mixtecs. By this time, the metropolis of Teotihuacán, in the Valley of Mexico, had fallen into decline, while on the Gulf coast the Classic El Tajín civilization was still at its peak, and would remain so until around 1100.

Clockwise from left to right *The Pyramid of the Moon at the mysterious site of Teotihuacán; one of three colossal Olmec sculpted stone heads at Parque la Venta in Villahermosa; an Olmec figure with a child at Museo de Antropología in Xalapa*

FINDING THEIR BERINGS
It is traditionally accepted that man first came to America from Asia across a land bridge formed over the Bering Straits at the end of the Ice Age. However, recent discoveries, including that of a skull found in Baja California, suggest that the first Americans may not have come from Siberia or Mongolia. Scientists now think that initial settlement of the continent was driven by people from the South Pacific and Southeast Asia, and that they may have arrived by boat via a coastal route. They lived in small nomadic groups as hunter-gatherers but, from around 7000BC, they planted and harvested crops like beans, avocados, fruit and, most significantly, maize, which was to become their staple diet and spiritual source of life.

HEADS YOU WIN

The Olmecs' greatest achievement was their massive carved basalt heads, measuring up to 3.4m (11ft) tall and weighing more than 20 tons. They all feature thick-set, flattened faces and typically wear "helmets," which may have been used for protection in war or while playing the traditional Mesoamerican ball game (▷ 31).

The heads are thought to have been made as tributes to Olmec rulers, possibly recarved from the rulers' thrones, leading to the explanation that the stones which supported the rulers during their reign were thus refashioned to become "portrait-memorials" to them after their death.

It was the discovery of one of these heads in 1939, with the date of the completion of its carving marked on it, which led archaeologists to conclude that it was the Olmecs, and not the Maya, who were the "mother culture" of Mexico.

5,000 YEARS...AND COUNTING

Though the Maya were famed for their mathematical and astronomical genius, their calendars were based on earlier Olmec versions. The Olmecs had several, including a 260-day ritual calendar and a 365-day solar calendar. These worked using cogs, which were meshed to produce a 52-year cycle in which every day had a religious and prophetic significance. Another calendar was the "long count" that measured time in a linear fashion from the first day of creation. The beginning of the "long count," according to most scholars, was on or around August 13, 3114BC, leading to one unorthodox theory that this date equates to the beginning of the Olmec civilization. Evidence gleaned from Olmec—and later Maya—glyphs (ancient symbols representing numbers and letters) suggests that the present epoch will be completed in AD2012.

WHERE MEN BECOME GODS

Regarded as one of the most important archaeological sites in Mexico, Teotihuacán—"the place where men become gods"—was the largest city in the pre-Columbian New World. It covered more than 21sq km (8sq miles) and had a population of up to 200,000, which, by AD600, made it the sixth-largest city in the world. How Teotihuacán grew to be such a powerful city remains largely a mystery. Examples of Teotihuacán-style objects have been found as far afield as Tikal and Kaminaljuyú in Guatemala, suggesting that the city-state must have benefited from long-distance trade links. Nevertheless, after thriving for almost 1,000 years, the culture collapsed dramatically after the heart of the city was destroyed around AD700, possibly by Totonac invaders from Veracruz, or the Totomí from the north of Mexico.

ANIMAL MAGIC

The transmutation of man into wolf, or werewolf (half man, half wolf), has become a staple of the horror genre in film and literature, but the Olmecs were worshipping such notions many centuries ago, as shown by the recurring motif of the were-jaguar (half man, half jaguar) in their sculptures and pottery.

The principal deity of the Olmecs was the jaguar, the most powerful creature in the jungle, and it was believed that the were-jaguar possessed the intellect and spirit of man and the strength and ferocity of the jungle feline.

Only shamans could transform themselves into jaguars, which feat they achieved through the consumption of mind-altering plants. By taking on animal form the shaman could communicate with the spirit world and use his visions to guide his prophecies.

One of the great civilizations of human history was the Maya, who occupied the Yucatán Peninsula, Chiapas and Central America for more than 1,500 years, building great urban complexes at Calakmul (with some 60,000 inhabitants), Uxmal, Kabah, Mayapán, Cobá and Chichén Itzá. The Maya culture, which began to flourish just before the Christian era, made extraordinary developments in mathematics, astrology and hieroglyphics. But disaster struck around AD900, bringing about the abandonment of their ceremonial bases. The cause of this sudden collapse remains a mystery, though theories include famine brought on by drought, internal uprising and massacre by invading foreign tribes. Whatever the truth, the downfall of the Maya marked the end of the Classic period, and with it the end of the era of great imperial urban cultures in Mexico. Understanding the Maya has been a slow process because much was thought to have been destroyed by the Spanish in the years following the Conquest. What is known comes from deciphering hieroglyphics carved on monuments and ceramics. Their descendants still practice traditional customs and beliefs.

Clockwise from left to right *Temple of the Five Levels, the focal point of the ancient Maya site of Edzná; carved jaguar heads at Chichén Itzá; stone mosaic motifs of Sky Serpent masks decorate a facade at Uxmal Mayan site*

THE FLAT EARTH SOCIETY

The Maya belief held that the earth was flat, formed on the back of a basking crocodile that was bathing in a lake covered with water lilies. The earth had four corners, each with a cardinal point and an associated color. East was red and symbolized the sunrise, birth and fertility; west was black (the setting sun and death); north was white (upward and the heavens); south was yellow (downward and the underworld). The middle of the earth was represented by blue-green *(yax)*—the combined shades of water, jade and young maize.

These four corners were also represented by deities *(bacabs)* who ruled over the days at the end of the year. The sky, which was the overworld, was also held up at four corners by gods.

GIVING BLOOD

As the gods had given life to the Maya, along with life-sustaining maize, the Maya sought to praise their largesse by offering their own blood. Self-mutilation was carried out on the nose, tongue, ears and penis—often by using stingray spines or needles to pierce the skin. The blood would be spilt on tree bark, which was then burned as an offering to the gods. Another way of praising the gods was through human sacrifice. Ball-game losers (or possibly winners) and enemy captives would have their hearts ripped out or be decapitated and their blood offered to the gods. Such was the value of the enemy's blood that they would be kept imprisoned for years and their blood sapped on a regular basis, before finally being disposed of in suitably gruesome fashion.

IN THE EYE OF THE BEHOLDER

In Maya society great weight was placed on physical beauty, and body mutilation for aesthetic purposes was a common practice. A broad, elongated forehead was held in high regard and this led to the custom of children having their heads compressed between concave wooden boards to generate the desired effect. Being cross-eyed was also deemed to be attractive, so beads were dangled in front of children's eyes to achieve this. The Maya filed their teeth and encrusted them with obsidian and the much-prized jade. Quite what a bunch of cross-eyed, flat-faced kids with razor-sharp teeth must have looked like is anybody's guess, though many of the sculptures at Palenque (▷ 152–155) portray the results of such beautification treatments.

BITTER EXPERIENCE

Cocoa beans were revered by the Maya and used as cash currency. So valuable were they that fakes were made. Tricks of the trade included putting avocado seeds inside the cocoa pod to dye poor-quality beans and improve their appearance. This kind of dishonest behavior, however, landed many a Maya in metaphorical hot water.

The bean also had another use—one that prevails today. It was drunk by the Maya (and also the Aztecs) as a cold, bitter drink with spices such as vanilla, chili and honey added to the foaming broth. The beans would be roasted, ground down and mixed with water, then the extra ingredients added according to taste. It's said that the word chocolate derives from the Maya word *xocolatl*, which means "bitter water."

SUDDEN-DEATH PLAY-OFF

The ball game, invented 3,500 years ago by the Olmecs, was the first team sport in history and became a highly significant ritual for the Maya. The path of the heavy rubber ball represented the movement of the sun across the sky, and by playing the game the Maya were ensuring that this daily celestial journey continued. Each team had to move the ball around a stone court using only their hips, knees, elbows and heads, and the ball was not allowed to touch the ground. Points were scored for propelling the ball through a hoop attached to the walls of the rectangular court. For the participants, winning and losing was a matter of life or death. The losers (or winners—this remains uncertain) were decapitated in human sacrifice.

From humble beginnings on their island home of Aztlán, in northwest Mexico, the belligerent Aztecs—also known as the Mexica—migrated south to the Valley of Mexico in the late 13th century. Within 50 years, they prevailed over the rival city states who had been competing for power in the vacuum left by the demise of the great Toltec civilization, wiped out by drought in the mid-13th century. The Aztecs were first and foremost a supremely efficient military force. From their base at Tenochtitlán, on an island in the middle of Lake Texcoco, they set about expanding their territory, extracting tribute and victims for human sacrifice as they went, and by the late 1400s they were the most powerful state in the whole country. Their royal advisor, Tlacaecel, declared that the Aztecs were the chosen race who would keep the sun moving through the sky. Following this declaration of divine destiny, the Aztecs began a wave of military conquests across most of central Mexico and south as far as Guatemala, creating an empire to surpass that of the Toltecs, from whom they claimed to be descended. In 1502, Moctezuma II became the ninth Aztec emperor, his reign coinciding with the arrival of the Spanish conquistadors on Mexican soil.

UNLUCKY FOR SOME

The Aztec calendar comprised the *tonalpohualli*, used for religious purposes, and the *xiuhpohualli*, the agricultural and ceremonial calendar. The former counted days in a 260-day cycle, which was divided into 20 periods of 13 days. The latter was for counting years and worked on a 365-day solar cycle, divided into 18 periods of 20 days, with each "month" dedicated to a particular god and ritual. For example, the 11th month, *Ochpanitztli*, was for the mundane practice of road sweeping, while the 13th month, *Tepeihuitl* (feast of the hills), was marked by human sacrifices and cannibalism. There were also five "empty" or "nothing" days (*nemontemi*)—a bit like our public holidays—which signified the transition from the old to the new year.

Clockwise from left to right *Detail of a Diego Rivera mural illustrating five centuries of Mexican history, depicting the Aztecs; a brightly dressed* Conchero *dancer maintains Aztec tradition in the 21st century; during an Aztec ritual, a priest cuts the heart out of a living victim*

FOOD OF THE GODS

The Aztecs worshipped many hundreds of gods, but the one they revered most was Huitzilpochtli, god of the sun and god of war. Huitzilpochtli controlled their every decision and also inspired their notorious ferocity and blood lust.

It was Huitzilpochtli who ordered the Aztec people to head south and settle in the place where they would find an eagle with a serpent in its mouth, perched on a cactus sprouting from a rock—Tenochtitlán.

To sustain the god in his daily battle with the forces of darkness, and ensure that the sun would continue to rise every day, the Aztecs had to feed Huitzilpochtli with the blood and hearts of human victims. They did this by constantly waging war and taking prisoners who would then be used in sacrifice.

HEART OF THE EMPIRE

The heart of the Aztec empire was its capital, Tenochtitlán, founded on an island in the middle of Lake Texcoco in the mid-14th century. By the late 15th century Tenochtitlán had grown to become a vast city of magnificent temples and plazas, palaces, marketplaces and schools. These were all linked to the mainland by a series of causeways and surrounded by *chinampas*, floating gardens that produced enough crops to feed a population estimated at 200,000. At the heart of the city was the Great Temple, built in tribute to the god Huitzilpochtli, complete with skull rack on which to display the heads of sacrificial victims. At the dedication ceremony, in 1487, 20,000 prisoners of war were sacrificed in a non-stop, four-day bloodbath.

CRIME AND PUNISHMENT

The judicial system of the Aztecs was, in many ways, similar to that of modern western democracy, with accused criminals brought before a jury and a judge pronouncing guilt or innocence and meting out the appropriate punishment. That is where the similarity ends, however.

Any breach of the laws in Aztec society was punished harshly. Adultery and major theft carried the death penalty, as did the heinous crimes of commoners wearing cotton clothing or moving a field boundary, while kidnappers appeared to get off lightly by being sold into slavery. Drunkenness was not tolerated. The first occurrence resulted in offenders having their heads shaved and their property destroyed, and if they then proceeded to drown their sorrows, they'd face the death penalty.

RETURN OF THE KING

The Spanish invaders overthrew the mighty Aztec empire with ease, partly because of an ancient legend, which claimed that Quetzalcóatl would return from the east to restore the Toltec empire.

Quetzalcóatl, the plumed serpent, is said to have originated as a priest-king during the rule of the Toltecs in the 10th century. Banished for his pacifist views, he ended up on the Gulf Coast, where he then set sail for the Yucatán Peninsula, promising to return.

When the Spanish arrived, the Aztec ruler, Moctezuma II, mistook Hernán Cortés for Quetzalcóatl and welcomed him, granting him special protection and offering him treasure. The Spanish were quick to propagate this mythical interpretation of their presence among the indigenous population to help them win over their new subjects.

When Hernán Cortés set sail from Cuba, landing on the island of Cozumel in 1519, before founding present-day Veracruz, he had one thing on his mind. So strong was his lust for gold and silver that he ignored orders to return to Cuba and even scuttled his ships to prevent his soldiers having any thoughts of retreat. So began 300 years of colonial rule, characterized by unprecedented greed, cruelty and an obsession with wiping out all traces of indigenous religious beliefs and practices. For their efforts, Cortés' men were rewarded with massive land grants *(encomiendas)*, giving them complete ownership of everything and everyone and reducing the indigenous population to the role of virtual slaves. African slaves were even imported to boost a workforce decimated by European diseases such as smallpox, and by exhaustion resulting from forced hardship and drudgery. The Spanish also imposed a rigid social hierarchy, with the pure Spanish-born occupying the top government and church positions, educated *criollos* (Creoles or Mexican-born Spanish) becoming wealthy landowners, and the *mestizos* (mixed Spanish and indigenous blood) and *indígenas* (indigenous Mexicans) at the bottom of heap, with no place in the emerging colony.

LA MALINCHE

One of the most controversial and important figures in Mexican history is La Malinche, known to the Spanish as Doña Marina. Born an Aztec princess but captured in war, she was made a slave before being passed to Cortés as a gift by the *cacique* (military chief) of Tabasco. With her understanding of the Mayan dialects and Aztec tongue, Nahautl, La Malinche was employed by Cortés, first as interpreter, then, when she had learned Spanish, as his military adviser and finally his mistress, bearing him several offspring in the process. Having proved such an invaluable asset in the conquest of Mexico, she was branded a traitor by the indigenous people. To this day, to be called *un malinchista* in Mexico is to be called a person of questionable patriotism or even a traitor.

Clockwise from left to right *Hernán Cortes initiates Spanish colonial rule in Mexico, depicted in a mural by Diego Rivera; statue of the last Tarascan king in Colima; Puebla's Iglesia de Santo Domingo whose interior is decorated in gold*

EIGHTH WONDER OF THE WORLD

Perhaps the greatest legacies of the colonial period were the exuberant baroque churches of the mineral-rich cities of central Mexico. Imported from Spain in the mid-17th century, the baroque style came to dominate Mexican architecture, its outlandish decoration and expansive, curvaceous forms reflecting the growing social and economic confidence of the time. By the early 18th century it had evolved into the even more extravagant Churrigueresque, which was named after the Spanish architect José Benito Churriguera (1665–1725). One of the most astonishing precursors to the Churrigueresque style was the dazzling Capilla del Rosario (Rosary Chapel) in Puebla (▷ 183). Completed in 1690, the richly decorated interior was described by contemporaries as the eighth wonder of the world and now stands as testament to the ecclesiastical excess of the period.

VASCO DE QUIROGA AND THE UTOPIAN DREAM

One of the most remarkable of the first Spanish settlers was Vasco de Quiroga (c.1470–1565), sent by the Crown to arrest Nuno Beltrán de Guzmán, head of the first *audencia* (judicial body) in Mexico City and virtual dictator. Guzmán's reign of terror and corruption had almost wiped out the Purepechan (later known as Tarascan) kingdom, and Quiroga's duty was to repair some of the damage that had been done to the Crown's reputation.

Influenced by English statesman Sir Thomas More's ideas of Utopia, Quiroga's appointment as Bishop of Michoacán gave him the opportunity to put his dreams of an ideal community into practice. Quiroga built schools and hospitals, converted the Tarascans to Christianity, and gave them instruction in arts and crafts. These skills have been passed down and today the Tarascans are among the finest craftspeople in Mexico.

A VERY MEXICAN MIRACLE

Every Mexican knows the legend of the humble peasant, Juan Diego, who was stopped by a vision of the Virgin of Guadalupe at Tepeyac Hill in the northern outskirts of Mexico City on December 9, 1531. When the local bishop demanded proof of the miracle, the Virgin showered Diego in roses. Returning to show the doubting bishop the roses wrapped in his cloak, he found that they had disappeared, to be replaced by an image of the dark-skinned Virgin imprinted on the cloth. Now the Virgin is the country's patron saint and her feast day, December 12, is the largest nationwide religious holiday—proof that the Catholic Church was willing to turn a blind eye to the occasional Mexican adaptation of their precious tradition in order to ensure the success of their quest for wholesale conversion.

WHAT THE LORD GIVETH…

Every bit as ruthless as the Spaniards' search for gold and silver was their campaign of religious conversion. One of the most zealous practitioners was Father Diego de Landa (1524–79), first head of the Franciscans in the Yucatán. In 1562, on hearing that many Maya were still practicing their own faith in secret, he had the perpetrators tortured, then burned every Maya idol, object and manuscript he could find. Four years later, he wrote a painstakingly detailed account of Maya life before the Conquest, entitled *Relaciones de las Cosas de Yucatán* (Relation of the Affairs of Yucatán). Rediscovered in the 19th century, this book tells us much of what we know of the Maya today. How ironic that its author also did so much to destroy all evidence of this great civilization.

Mexico finally threw off the shackles of Spanish rule in 1821, under the Treaty of Córdoba, but it was a long and bloody struggle. An estimated 600,000 lives were lost over the 11 years from Father Hidalgo's *grito* (see right) to liberation. Several decades of reconstruction and political and economic chaos followed, characterized by weak government and foreign intervention. In the 30 years between 1821 and 1851, Mexico went through 40 governments, invasion by France and war with the United States, which resulted in the US gaining Texas, New Mexico, Arizona and Alta California—more than half of Mexican sovereign territory—for $25 million. The second half of the 19th century was wracked by war between the Liberals, who preferred secular federalism, and the Conservatives, who longed for the old days of a centralized and oligarchic system. Two men bestrode this period like political giants. The first, President Benito Juárez (1808–72), nationalized church property, with disastrous results for *campesinos* (peasants) who lost out to wealthy hacienda owners. While Juárez is seen as a hero of Mexican history.

CRY FREEDOM

On the morning of September 16 1810, in the village of Dolores (now Dolores Hidalgo; ▷ 207), the 60-year-old Creole priest, Father Miguel Hidalgo y Costilla, rang the church bells as usual to call the local people to Mass. What he had to say to them, however, would change the course of Mexican history. He urged his congregation to rise up against their Spanish oppressors and seize back the lands that had been stolen from their forefathers. With the now legendary cry *(grito)* of *Mexicanos, Viva Mexico!* (Mexicans, long live Mexico), he signalled the start of the long and bloody struggle for independence from Spain. Though he was tracked down and executed by Royalist forces, Hidalgo is revered as the father of Mexican independence.

Above *Detail of a mural in the elegant Palacio de Gobierno, in Saltillo*

A LOSING STREAK

Many tales surround Antonio López de Santa Anna, who occupied the presidency of Mexico no fewer than 11 times between 1833 and 1855. Santa Anna insisted on being referred to as "His Most Serene Highness" instead of the usual title "His Excellency."

The most bizarre incident relating to him, however, dates from 1842 when Santa Anna's left leg, amputated in 1838 after being hit by cannon fire in a battle with a French army at Veracruz, was disinterred, paraded through the capital and placed in an urn on a huge stone pillar at a ceremony attended by high government officials. Santa Anna not only lost his leg, but also ceded more than half of Mexican territory to the United States following the Mexican-American War (1846–48).

Above right *Statue of Father Hidalgo, in Guadalajara*
Below *Detail of a mural by Orozco, in Guadalajara, depicting the revolt by Father Hidalgo*

HERO OR VILLAIN?

One of the most famous participants in the Mexican-American War (1846–48) was John Riley, from County Galway in Ireland. Before the war began, the Legión Extranjera (Foreign Legion) was formed from European residents in Mexico, and expanded by the addition of deserters, mainly Irish, from the US army. Riley renamed them the St. Patrick's Brigade and gave them their distinctive green flag, with the shamrock on one side and St. Patrick on the other. The San Patricios, as they came to be known, were eventually captured by the US army and convicted of desertion. Most were hanged, but those who had deserted before the outbreak of hostilities were flogged, branded and set free, Riley among them. His story was dramatized in the 1999 film *One Man's Hero*.

MAXIMILIAN AND CARLOTA

One of the strangest events of Mexico's strife-ridden 19th century was the meeting, in October 1863, of Yucatán lawyer José Maria Gutiérrez with Maximilian, the Habsburg archduke of Austria, and his Belgian wife, Carlota.

Gutiérrez was there on behalf of a group of hardline Conservative émigrés to persuade the Emperor and Empress to come to Mexico and govern as puppets of Napoleon III of France in order to enforce their own political agenda. The gullible couple agreed, but their reign was a short one. Maximilian turned out to be more Liberal than Conservative and Napoleon, fearing trouble, pulled out his occupying army.

Carlota set off for Europe to drum up support for her isolated husband, leaving him to face capture and the firing squad alone. Maximilian was executed in 1867 in Querétaro, while Carlota ended her days, insane, in Belgium.

FLOUR POWER

It sounds like something out of a Marx Brothers movie, but the Pastry War, fought between Mexico and France in 1838, was a serious affair. It all began in Puebla, when a French baker's shop was ransacked by an angry mob of Mexican soldiers. The baker demanded compensation of 60,000 pesos, which the Mexican government refused to pay. News of the incident reached the French King, Louis-Philippe, who was already infuriated with Mexico for defaulting on its huge debt. The King demanded a 600,000-peso payment as compensation and when Mexico again refused to pay, he ordered the blockade of all Caribbean ports. The Mexican government remained defiant, leading in turn to the French invasion of Veracruz, during which Santa Anna lost his leg (see above left). The conflict ended when Mexico agreed to pay the compensation of 600,000 pesos in return for a French withdrawal.

The 19th century ended with Porfirio Díaz reigning supreme over a relatively peaceful and stable country, and a widening chasm between a wealthy elite and a poor, repressed majority. It was this stark contrast that led to growing demands for change, culminating in Francisco Madero issuing a call for revolution to begin at 6pm on November 20, 1910. Madero was supported initially by the five main regional leaders—Pascual Orozco, Pancho Villa, Venustiano Carranza and Álvaro Obregón in the north, and Emiliano Zapata in Morelos—forcing Díaz to flee to safety in France. Madero championed a schedule of political and social reform, but during his presidency (1911–13), he managed to alienate his revolutionary supporters. After a coup in February 1913, led by General Victoriano Huerta, Madero was brutally murdered, but the great new cry *Tierra y Libertad* (Land and Liberty) was not to be quieted until the election of Álvaro Obregón to the presidency in 1920. By that time, well over a million Mexicans had died or fled the country, and it wasn't until the regime of President Lázaro Cárdenas (1934–40) that the economic objectives of the revolution were fulfilled.

THE PORFIRIATO

One of Mexico's most notorious leaders was Porfirio Díaz. After promising not to seek reelection, once he took the reins of power he simply refused to let go. He won the presidency no fewer than eight times over a period of 34 years, which became known as the Porfiriato.

Under the slogan "order and progress" he suppressed all opposition using the dreaded *rurales*, a rural police force made up of the country's most notorious bandits. With peace restored, he sold off the country's oil fields, mines and railways to foreign interests, while rural workers had their lands seized by the hacienda owners. The Porfiriato may have been a prosperous time for wealthy investors, but for the vast majority it couldn't end soon enough.

Clockwise from left to right *A painting by Diego Rivera of Emiliano Zapata shows him in full revolutionary pose; a more formal portrait of General Zapata; statue of revolutionary leader Venustiano Carranza in Ensenada*

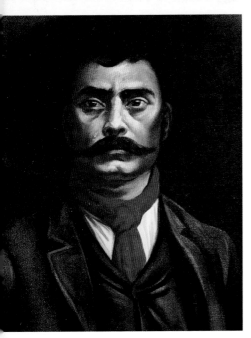

GUNNING FOR PANCHO

Mexico's other great mustachioed hero of the revolution was Doroteo Arango (1877–1923), or Francisco "Pancho" Villa, as he is better known. The cattle rustler turned bandit ruled over much of northern Mexico, and his resistance against the 1913–14 Huerta dictatorship made him a hero, not only in Mexico but also north of the border as Hollywood filmmakers and newspaper reporters came to witness and record his exploits. This acclaim soon turned to hatred, when Villa's men looted and burned US border towns in retaliation for the US government's support for the new president, Venustiano Carranza. Villa evaded capture by the US government's "punitive expedition" of 5,000 troops, but his luck ran out when he was gunned down by assassins in the city of Parral, on July 20, 1923.

REVOLUTIONARY HERO

The charismatic guerrilla leader Emiliano Zapata (1879–1919) has become the most famous symbol of the Mexican Revolution. Impatient for the implementation of land reforms promised by newly elected President Francisco Madero, Zapata's guerrillas took control of Morelos state in the south and began the process themselves under Zapata's "Plan of Ayala," which called for the expropriation and redistribution of hacienda lands to the rural poor.

Zapata was ambushed and murdered by rival revolutionary leader Venustiano Carranza, two years after his land reform plan was enshrined in the revolutionary constitution drawn up in 1917. Successive Mexican governments failed to realize Zapata's dream, but his name has lived on as a symbol of social justice.

CRISTERO WAR

In 2000, Pope John Paul II canonized 25 of the clergy killed in the Cristero War (1926–29). The war was a bloody civil conflict between government forces and Catholic rebels, which was provoked by violent Catholic resistance to the increasingly anti-clerical policies of the government of President Plutarco Elías Calles (1924–28).

It remains one of the most tragic episodes in Mexico's history and cost some 30,000 lives. In one particularly odious incident, on April 19, 1927, Father José Reyes Vega led a raid on a train allegedly carrying money. In the resulting shoot-out with the army escort, Father Vega's brother was killed and, in a vengeful rage, he ordered the wooden carriages to be set alight, killing 51 innocent civilian passengers. He was later killed in battle on April 19, 1929. Needless to say, Father Vega wasn't one of the Vatican's 25 new saints.

ART AND THE REVOLUTION

The Mexican Revolution inspired the country's great muralists José Clemente Orozco (1883–1949), David Alfaro Siqueiros (1896–1974) and Diego Rivera (1886–1957)—Los Tres Grandes—whose depictions of history and class struggle cover government buildings across the country. Their fame has overshadowed another of the country's artistic geniuses—José Guadalupe Posada (1851–1913), the greatest political and social satirist of his day. Using Mexico's Day of the Dead skeletons as a metaphor for the corrupt society of the Porfiriato, Posada's lampooning of tyrannical politicians earned him several spells in jail. He died penniless, his talent unrecognized. Now his art, and importance as a revolutionary catalyst, can be appreciated at the Bellas Artes National Institute and Biblioteca de Mexico (Library of Mexico) in Mexico City.

Twentieth-century Mexican politics was dominated by the Institutional Revolutionary Party (PRI), which had governed continuously since its creation in 1929 as the PNR, later PRM. Often compared to the former Soviet Communist Party, the PRI controlled political, social and economic life. Things began to change toward the end of the 20th century, however. The party's old-style corruption and cronyism cut little ice with Mexico's burgeoning urban middle class and its support waned. Growing internecine strife reached a violent crescendo in 1994 with the assassinations of the party's presidential candidate and secretary general. This proved the final nail in the electoral coffin. The victory of the Centre Action Party (PAN) candidate, Vicente Fox, in July 2000 marked the beginning of a new era in Mexico's history.

Above left *Women are playing important roles in today's Mexico*
Above right *President Felipe Calderón Hinojosa*

POLITICAL EARTHQUAKE

One of the main developments in Mexican political life in recent years has been the rise of "civil society" (non-partisan, single-issue, campaigning groups). From farmers and students to the gay and lesbian community, many thousands of Mexicans are finding their voice.

One of the largest groups is the feminist movement, which has been growing in strength ever since their key role in helping victims *(damnificados)* of the 1985 Mexico City earthquake. In the south of the country, women have been playing an active role in events for the past decade, not only comprising a third of the Zapatista rebel troops but also as leaders of the General Command, and inspiring local women to stand up against entrenched misogynist attitudes. But despite this, feminism has come late to Mexico, and women have had the vote only since 1954.

STYLE OVER SUBSTANCE?

Mexico's first 21st-century president, Vicente Fox, was the most US-style president the country has seen to date. An admirer of Bill Clinton, he has often been compared to the former US president. Fox promoted himself as a down-to-earth man of the people—he spent much of his election campaign touring the country on horseback—and preferred to appeal directly to Mexican voters, over the heads of Congress.

Critics dismissed him as being all style and no substance, and with the Mexican economy slipping into recession, a knock-on effect of the economic downturn in the US, the knives were being sharpened.

But in 2006 Felipe Calderón Hinojosa became the new president in a close and disputed election.

ON THE MOVE

On the Move gives you detailed advice and information about the various options for traveling to Mexico before explaining the best ways to get around the country once you are there. Handy tips help you with everything from buying tickets to renting a car.

ARRIVING BY AIR

Mexico is easily reached by air from the US, Canada, Europe, Australia, New Zealand and the rest of Latin America, with many international airlines flying direct to the country's two main airports—Mexico City (Ciudad de México) and Cancún in the Yucatán. In addition, airlines from the US and Canada fly to as many as 30 other Mexican destinations. For passport requirements, ▷ 269.

AIRLINES

Mexico's main national and international carriers are AeroMéxico and Mexicana. Most internationally recognized companies offer flights to at least Mexico's two main airports.

GETTING TO THE CITY FROM THE AIRPORT			
AIRPORT	**MEXICO CITY**	**CANCÚN**	**PUERTO VALLARTA**
DISTANCE TO CITY	13km (8 miles)	16km (10 miles)	6km (4 miles)
TAXI	Fixed-price taxis by zone. Tickets available from booths by exits of Terminal 1 salas A, E and F and the main exit of Terminal 2. Price: Approximately $18–$20 or more, depending on distance. Journey time: 1 hour minimum	*Colectivos* to the Hotel Zone or central Cancún from main terminal. Pay at kiosks outside airport. Price: $15–$25 Journey time: 30–45 minutes to central Cancún, 15–30 minutes to Hotel Zone	Taxis: Available directly outside terminal. All prepaid at kiosk. Price: $15–$25 Journey time: 30 minutes
BUS	Services from Boulevard Puerto Aéreo, 200m (220 yards) from Terminal 1 Sala A. Price: Very cheap Frequency: At least every 45 minutes Journey time: 1 hour minimum	Services from airport to center via Avenida Tulúm. Price: $5. Frequency: Half-hourly. Journey time: 30–45 minutes	Buses from opposite airport in main road (take walkway across). Price: $0.40 Frequency: 15–20 minutes Journey time: 30 minutes
METRO/TRAINS	Metro: From Terminal Aérea, outside Terminal 1 Sala A. Line 5, change at Pantitlán for Line 1 to city center. Advisable only if limited luggage, as often very crowded. Operates from 6am–1.30am on weekdays, 6am–1.30pm Sat and 7am–3am Sun Price: $0.20 Journey time: 45 minutes	N/A	N/A

AIRPORTS

Aeropuerto Internacional Benito Juárez (MEX) is 13km (8 miles) east of central Mexico City (tel (55) 24 82 24 24, for Terminal 1, and (55) 25 98 70 00 for Terminal 2). Terminal 1 is divided into six sections. **Sala A** receives national arrivals, while international arrivals are received at **Sala E**. All national and international departures leave from **Sala D,** but international check-in is at **Sala F**.

There is a tourist office (tel (55) 27 86 90 02) in Sala A. In addition to this there are airport information kiosks at salas A, D, E and F. Hotel reservations can be made at the hotel desk, prior to customs, and at the airport information kiosks. The tourist office has phones for making free calls to hotels. A travel agency at the east exit of the airport will reconfirm flights for $0.50.

There are *casas de cambios* and banks throughout the airport. Those in salas E and F are usually the least crowded. Opening hours of banks and *casas de cambios* ensure that there is a 24-hour service. Car rental offices are near the international arrivals in Sala E, along with 24-hour luggage lockers ($6 per day).

Terminal 2 handles international and national flights, including all AeroMéxico flights. Departure gates are on the upper level; arrivals and immigration are on the lower level. Terminal 2 is connected to Terminal 1 by a free monorail shuttle.

Cancún Aeropuerto Internacional

(CUN) is 16km (10 miles) south of the city. It has two terminals: the main Terminal 2 handles most domestic flights; the newer Terminal 3 handles most international arrivals and departures. There is free shuttle bus service between the terminals every 20 minutes.

Puerto Vallarta's Aeropuerto

Internacional Ordaz (PVR) is 6km (4 miles) north of central Puerto Vallarta and has very good domestic and international connections.

Acapulco's Aeropuerto Internacional General Juan N. Alvarez

(ACA) is 23km (14 miles) east of the city. It has direct connections with the US, including Atlanta, Miami, Chicago, Dallas, Houston, Los Angeles and Tucson. These destinations are served mainly by Mexican and US airlines.

Guadalajara's Aeropuerto Internacional Miguel Hidalgo y Costillo

(GDL) is 20km (12.5 miles) south of the city. It has good domestic and international connections, which makes it an excellent alternative to Mexico City.

Monterrey's Aeropuerto Internacional General Mariano Escobedo

(MTY) is 24km (15 miles) northeast of the city. With two terminals (connected by a subway), it has flights to and from many Mexican cities, as well as connections with the US (Dallas, Houston, Los Angeles and San Antonio), Canada and Cuba.

USEFUL TELEPHONE NUMBERS AND WEBSITES

	TELEPHONE	WEBSITES
AIRPORTS		
Mexico City	(55) 24 82 24 24	www.aicm.com.mx
Cancún	(998) 848 72 00	www.cancun-airport.com
Puerto Vallarta	(322) 221 13 25	www.puertovallarta.net
Acapulco	(744) 484 11 16	
Guadalajara	(33) 36 88 63 99	
Monterrey	(81) 83 69 07 53	
AIRLINES (MEXICO CITY)		
AeroMéxico	(55) 51 33 40 10	www.aeromexico.com
Air Canada	(55) 91 38 02 80	www.aircanada.com
American Airlines	01-800/904-6000	www.aa.com
British Airways	(866) 835 41 33	www.britishairways.com
Delta	01-800/123-4710	www.delta.com
Iberia	(55) 51 30 30 30	www.iberia.com
Lufthansa	(55) 52 30 00 00	www.lufthansa.com
Mexicana	(55) 54 48 09 90	www.mexicana.com
CRUISES/SHIPPING		
Strand Voyages (UK)	020 7010 7990	www.strandtravel.co.uk
The Cruise People (UK)	020 7723 2450	www.cruisepeople.co.uk
SGV Reisezentrum Weggis (Switzerland)	41 248 0048	www.frachtschiffreisen.ch
Carnival (US)	877/885-4856	www.carnival.com
BUSES		
ADO GL (Yucatán, Southeast, Gulf, Northeast)	01-800/702-8000	www.adogl.com.mx
ETN	01-800/800-0386	www.etn.com.mx
Grupo Estrella	01-800/507-5500	www.estrellablanca.com.mx
CAR RENTAL OFFICES		
Alamo		www.alamo.com
Avis		www.avis.com
Budget		www.budget.com
Hertz		www.hertz.com
TAXIS		
Mexico City Airport	(55) 24 82 24 24, ext. 2299 (for losses or complaints) or (55) 55 71 93 44 (for reservations)	

ON THE MOVE ARRIVING

ARRIVING BY LAND

Arriving in Mexico overland from the US is a popular option. The large number of border crossings ensures that entry into Mexico is relatively easy for foot passengers and those with their own vehicle. You must purchase Mexican automobile insurance before crossing the border as most US policies are invalid in Mexico. Almost every crossing now has a long-distance bus terminal, making travel from the border easy and relatively efficient. Below are the most widely used crossings between Mexico and the US, Guatemala and Belize.

All visitors traveling from the US to Mexico, including US citizens, will have to show a valid passport. You may be able to get into Mexico without one, but you will need it to get back to the US.

US
Tijuana
» Tijuana is the busiest border crossing into Mexico and is open 24 hours.

» The nearest American town is San Diego and it is recommended that you take time here to familiarize yourself with Tijuana (bus times, hotel prices, etc).

» If coming from San Diego airport, take the No. 992 bus from the terminal to the Greyhound station in the city. From here, the city trolleybus service will go right up to the San Ysidro border with Tijuana.

» The number of people and vehicles crossing the border each day makes it very easy to forget or miss the essential border formalities.

» There are no passport checks at the border, so it is possible to get through without completing US exit formalities. However, it is recommended that you seek out the correct place to do this as it will make the return trip much easier.

» If arriving on foot, it is important to get a Mexican tourist card from the office just over the pedestrian bridge. Having done this, it is another short walk to Tijuana itself.

» If arriving by vehicle, progress may not be so fast, as the massive freeway on the US side is cut to just three lanes on the Mexican side.

» It is important to carry out the correct exit and entry formalities—find the Migración office by heading through the right-hand lane called "Customs." Here, be sure to get a US exit stamp as well as a tourist card with a Mexico entry stamp on the card and your passport.

» It is also possible to get a vehicle permit here, but you will have to head 100m (110 yards) south to get the correct stamp at the vehicle registry office.

» Be sure to have all documentation regarding the vehicle available when crossing the border as the officials will require a copy of the documents (for example, vehicle permit, insurance, driver's license).

Otay Mesa
» This border crossing, 8km (5 miles) east of Tijuana, is far quieter. If arriving from the US you can find this on the SR-117 highway.

» The crossing is open 24 hours, but insurance and vehicle permit facilities do not exist.

Mexicali
» Mexicali borders the Californian city of Calexico (although it is heavily Mexicanized). The crossing is open 24 hours and progress is faster when leaving the US than when entering it.

» Be wary of the potential lack of interest from immigration officials on the Mexican side of the border—it is very important to go to them and get the correct entry formalities completed, as it will make later travel far easier.

Nogales
» If entering Mexico on foot, there is no checkpoint to go through. However, there is a customs area that may or may not be manned—you will be under official discretion as to whether you get searched or not when crossing. Open 24 hours.

» About 50m (55 yards) after the checkpoint is the immigration office where a tourist card and relevant stamps can be acquired. As with Tijuana and Mexicali, it is relatively easy to leave the border area without getting the official documentation. While doing this will not be an issue at the time, you run the risk of being returned to the border after a routine check later on in your journey.

» If entering Mexico with a vehicle, it is best to use the truck crossing 4km (2.5 miles) north of Nogales on the US side. The crossing is open 6am–8pm. US insurance can be found here.

» All the relevant vehicle documentation can be obtained at the Mexican Customs Post, 21km (13km) south of Nogales. However, be sure to have the necessary documents with you before you reach this point.

Ciudad Juárez
» The crossing from El Paso, Texas to Ciudad Juárez is simple, with minimal border formalities required.

» If arriving on foot, you can take a bus in El Paso from outside Gate 9 of the Greyhound terminal for $10. The driver should wait for you at the

Below *Sign indicating the Mexican border with Belize*

border as the relevant immigration process is carried out.

» You are automatically given 30 days to stay in Mexico, unless you request a longer stay at the immigration office.

Northeast Mexico

» There are five main crossings in this area and the major roads all converge at the Mexican city of Monterrey. The relevant documentation is required at every one.

» Nuevo Laredo is the most important Mexican town in the area and borders with Laredo on the US side.

» East of Nuevo Laredo is the crossing between McAllen in the US and Reynosa in Mexico.

» The crossing between Brownsville in the US and Matamoros in Mexico is quick and easy. It is possible to get a visa from the Mexican Consulate in Brownsville and permission is normally granted for six months at the immigration office at the border.

» Northwest of Nuevo Laredo, there is a crossing between Eagle Pass in the US and Piedras Negras in Mexico, and Del Rio in the US and Ciudad Acuna in Mexico.

GUATEMALA

Guatemala has three major border-crossing points with Mexico.

Ciudad Cuauhtémoc

» Open Monday to Friday, 8am–4pm and Saturday to Sunday, 9am–2pm. Remember that Mexico is one hour ahead of Guatemala.

» Tourist cards and visas can be obtained at the border, but you may only be granted 15 days. Extensions can be obtained in Oaxaca and Mexico City.

» The process is slightly longer for those entering Mexico with a vehicle. At the crossing, your vehicle will be fumigated ($8) and you should get a receipt for this. If you are re-entering Mexico, the documents from any prior entry will also be checked here.

» About 4km (2.5 miles) after the crossing, you must go to the Migración office where a tourist card and visa can be obtained or your existing visa checked.

» Finally, head to the Banjército to get the relevant vehicle papers you will need and a windshield sticker.

Talismán

» This is a 24-hour border crossing, 8km (5 miles) from Tapachula. The Mexican customs office is very close to its Guatemalan counterpart.

» You must pay an exit tax of $0.45 and there is a throng of children pushing to help you through the formalities—pay just one of them $2 to $3 to keep the others away.

» Be extremely careful at the toilet at the crossing—hold-ups and muggings have been reported here.

» If entering Mexico by vehicle, ensure that you have the necessary documents. These are issued at the Garuda de Aduana on Route 200 out of Tapachula. If you need to make photocopies, do so in Tapachula as there are no other facilities closer to the border.

» The procedures at this crossing are said to be difficult, so be patient.

Ciudad Hidalgo

» This crossing, south of Tapachula, is reputed to be the easiest and most efficient of the three from Guatemala. It is open 24 hours.

» Mexican immigration is close to the town plaza at the start of the bridge across the Río Suchiate.

Above *Cruise liners at Ensenada*

» There is a small charge to cross the bridge to Mexico.

BELIZE

» The only major crossing is between Santa Elena in Belize and Chetumal in Mexico, connected via a bridge over Río Hondo.

» It is open 24 hours and can often get incredibly busy with an influx of Belizeans heading into Mexico on shopping trips.

» An exit tax of $14 is charged, but the formalities are generally relaxed.

» Mexican tourist cards of 30 days can be obtained at the border. These can be extended by going to immigration in Cancún.

» If you need a visa, go to the Mexican Embassy in Belize City.

ARRIVING BY SEA
CRUISE SHIPS

Cruise ships from around the world regularly stop at many of Mexico's ports—both on the Pacific and the Gulf of Mexico. Popular destinations such as Acapulco, Cancún, Cabo San Lucas, Cozumel, Ensenada, Ixtapa-Zihuatantejo and Puerto Vallarta are well served by major cruise operators.

For specific schedules, itineraries and entry requirements it is best to contact travel agents or try out websites such as www.cruiseweb. com or www.mexicoexpo.com/ pages/h_cruise.html. For more contact details, ▷ 43.

TRAVEL INFORMATION

Mexico is a huge country but getting around can be relatively painless and straightforward, providing you are realistic, plan carefully and remain patient. Unless you have unlimited time, transport will be an issue at some point in your trip. While Mexico does have a good bus system and adequate highways, the country's vast distances mean you could find yourself on a bus for days just to get from one side of the country to the other. It is often better to spend a little more and take an internal flight. If you want to explore the hidden areas of Mexico you will need your own vehicle.

TIPS

» The main means of travel is via road, whether this be on a bus or in a private vehicle. Although the national bus system can be confusing, the fact remains that there will almost always be a bus from where you are to where you want to go. Most companies offer a varying degree of comfort and this is certainly something that should be considered, as the price will vary.

» If touring through difficult, mountainous terrain on a long bus journey do not necessarily expect to arrive according to the schedule.
» Many bus journeys can take more than several hours and so food and drink breaks are often part of the itinerary. While these come as a welcome relief to all, care must be taken when buying anything to eat or drink. Stick to whatever the locals choose and be ready to leave as soon as the driver has finished.
» Safety on buses is fine, providing you look after your belongings and are sensible with the route you take.
» Touring by car is a feasible means of getting around Mexico. It is often only with your own transport that some of the more inaccessible and untouched areas can be visited.
» Mexico has both toll and free highways—while the toll roads are expensive, they do cut journey times significantly.
» The free highways and other roads may be in a state of disrepair so be prepared; however, the routes they take are often interesting as they lead through small villages and towns.

» If driving into the major cities of Mexico, be prepared for the ultimate challenge as congestion can make progress very difficult.
» Car crime is a real threat all over Mexico and the relevant precautions should always be adhered to. Most hotels provide private parking facilities to ensure that your car will remain safe.
» Apart from a couple of train routes that are more geared up to sightseeing (▷ 49 and 243), Mexico does not offer any form of integrated rail network, so this method of travel is not really an option.
» Domestic air coverage is good throughout Mexico, with most medium-sized towns being accessible by internal flights. Although prices are high compared to bus travel, the amount of time saved with a flight may well make flying the best option.
» The two major domestic flight operators are Mexicana and AeroMéxico.

Above *A mixture of modern and traditional transportation in the city of Guadalajara*

GETTING AROUND IN MEXICO CITY

Mexico City is one of the largest capital cities in the world. Getting around it can be relatively simple or incredibly taxing, depending on the method of transportation you choose. The metro is cheap, clean, efficient and the most convenient form of public transportation as most of the city's sights are within walking distance of a station. The alternatives are bus and taxi, which are not only affected by the city's notorious congestion, but also add to the chronic pollution problems.

BUSES

» The buses have been consolidated into one system which is simple—all odd-numbered buses run from north to south, while all even-numbered buses run from east to west.

» Mexico City also has four long-distance terminals that broadly correspond with the points of the compass—Norte, Sur, Oriente, Poniente (North, South, East, West).

» It is often easier to identify the bus you want by the route and destination displayed in the windshield, rather than by the number of the bus itself.

» For all large buses, there is a standard charge of $0.25–$0.50, which must be paid in exact change.

» Coverage of the city by the bus routes is extensive, with 60 direct routes and 48 feeder (SARO) routes currently in operation.

» Be wary of thieves and pickpockets on some routes, particularly those in the tourist areas such as along Reforma and Juárez.

» One of the most useful buses for visitors is the No. 76, which leads from Uruguay along Reforma beside Chapultepec Park. Unfortunately the thieves know this too, so be extra vigilant when on this route.

» In addition to the standard buses, there are trolley buses in operation that charge just $0.35 per ticket.

THE METRO

» This is undoubtedly the best way of getting around the city. The French-built system is efficient and modern and is particularly useful at times when pollution is at its worst.

» The trains themselves are fast, regular, clean and quiet. However, they do get crowded at rush hour

(approximately 7.30am until 10am and 5pm until 7pm), and only two pieces of medium-sized luggage are normally allowed.

» As with the buses, watch out for pickpockets and thieves, especially at Pino Suárez, Hidalgo and Autobuses del Norte.

» In total, there are nine lines in service, leading all over the city. They are color-coded in the stations and on maps for ease of use. Maps are available throughout the city and among the best are the Atlas de Carreteras ($1.65) and the Guía Práctica del Metro ($9).

» At Insurgentes station (on the Pink Line 1) there is a metro information service and there are many other information kiosks in most of the interchange stations.

Below *A policeman in Mexico City*

» Use of the metro costs a standard $0.20 per ride and it is recommended that you buy a number of tickets in order to avoid queuing at a later date.

» Lines 1, 2, 3 and A run from 5am until 12.30am Monday to Friday, 6am until 1.30am on Saturday and from 7am until 12.30am on Sunday and national holidays.

» All the other lines open one hour later during the week, but operate the same times on weekends and also during holidays.

TAXIS

There are several different types of taxi operating within Mexico City and visitors should be aware of the dangers of using others than those listed below, as muggings and robberies often occur.

» *Turismo* taxis are by far the most expensive (sometimes as much as three times more than regular taxis) and can usually be found outside the most expensive hotels and major tourist sites. While these should generally be avoided, most drivers speak a little English and could be useful in the event of an emergency or a quick dash to the airport.

» *Sitio* taxis have fixed stands throughout the city and at the airport. They are cheaper than the Turismo taxis, but still cost a little more than ordinary cabs. However, they are safer—you pay at a booth before entering the taxi. Prices vary depending on the distance; generally about $5 for up to 4km (2.5 miles).

» Taxis on unfixed routes are the ones that can be hailed at any time. They are usually VW Beetles, or Nissans and other such Japanese cars, but can be clearly identified by their distinctive paintwork. They are green, while the newer cabs are red and white saloons. There are also yellow cars, but these are in the process of being phased out and so should not be used.

» The basic tariff is $0.70, with an additional $0.05 for each kilometer or 45 seconds traveled.

» The price increases by 20 percent between 10pm and 6am.

» Make sure that the meter is turned on and set at the basic tariff when you enter the taxi.

» You can bargain for a fixed price before setting off on your journey and you may have to do this, as some drivers may refuse to use their meter after 6pm.

» It is common to find that taxi drivers do not actually know of the street that you want—if this happens, try to give the name of the intersection of two streets to make it easier.

» Unless special help has been given (for example carrying heavy bags), no tip is necessary.

» Solo visitors, and especially women, should take great care when using taxis. If possible, take only the official Sitio taxis from your hotel. It has also been recommended by the tourist police in Mexico City that you make a note of registration and taxi numbers before getting in.

DRIVING

Driving your own vehicle in Mexico City is not to be recommended—the congestion is a huge issue, and getting anywhere in the city can take hours.

A far better option is to find a hotel with parking facilities and leave your vehicle there to explore the city on the public transportation system.

However, if you are intent on using your car then you must be aware of the pollution-related restrictions (*día sin auto hoy no circula*) that are in place throughout the week. These correspond to the last digit of your vehicle's numberplate and mean that your vehicle is not allowed on the street at all on the following days:
Monday (numbers 5 and 6)
Tuesday (numbers 7 and 8)
Wednesday (numbers 3 and 4)
Thursday (numbers 1 and 2)
Friday (numbers 9 and 0).

This system only runs on weekends if pollution levels are extremely bad. If this is the case then all even numbers and 0 are banned on Saturday, while all odd numbers are banned on Sunday.

This should not apply to foreign registered vehicles.

Above and below *Mexico City's distinctive taxi cabs: older taxis are green or yellow and white; newer cabs are red and white*

FERRIES AND TRAINS

Travel around Mexico is restricted largely to the air and road, though there are still some areas on the coast where ferry transport is a possibility, particularly Baja California and the Caribbean Coast. The rail network is virtually non-existent today, but a couple of journeys remain popular.

FERRY

There are three major ferry routes in the Baja California area—La Paz to Mazatlán, La Paz to Topolobampo and Santa Rosalía to Guaymas. All of these are car and passenger ferries and therefore convenient for anyone using their own vehicle. The operators offer various options for the long journey, from standard seating to a private cabin; prices vary accordingly.

Tickets for the long-haul services in Baja California can be bought at the terminal on the day of travel or at the company office in the middle of town if you want to reserve a place in advance. For these journeys, you are expected to be at the pier at least three hours before departure.

It is important to remember that you must have a valid tourist card and, if driving your own vehicle, you must make sure that it has a valid permit. Be prepared for delays, particularly from September on, as the chances of bad weather are increased. Essentially, keep your timescale flexible.

On the Caribbean Coast there are regular, quick services linking the area around Cancún with Isla Mujeres and Cozumel. They are good for both day trips and for longer stays.

For the shorter crossings on the Caribbean coast tickets can be bought at the terminal or pier from which the service departs. No advance reservations are needed as the operators run frequent services throughout the day.

TRAIN

There are very few passenger train services running in Mexico today. Although research has shown that most trains will still take passengers, the reality is that they seldom depart or arrive on time, making this an incredibly unreliable method of transportation. In fact, you are likely to reach your destination more through good luck than planning.

Although Mexico does not have an effective passenger rail network, two world-famous train rides continue to prosper.

Chihuahua al Pacífico

» The Chihuahua al Pacífico train journey goes from Chihuahua to Los Mochis. It is known for its spectacular descent through the Copper Canyon (▷ 243).
» For the best views, sit on the left side going to Los Mochis, and the right side on the way back.
» Such a famous railway line attracts a large volume of people—you will

have to book seats in advance at busy times. For more information and reservations, tel 01-800-122-4373, www.ferromex.com.mx or www.chepe.com.mx.
» There are two services—*Primera* and *Económica*. Be sure to take your own drinking water, food and toilet paper on both.
» The trains depart early (6am) and often end up at least 1 hour behind schedule.
» For the full trip expect to pay $145 for the *Primera* service and roughly half for the *Económica*.

Tequila Express

» This is an easy and convenient way of visiting Tequila from Guadalajara.
» For information, see www.tequilaexpress.com.mx or tel (33) 38 80 90 99. Book tickets through tour operators in Guadalajara.
» Departs 10am and returns 7pm; $85 for adults, $48 for children.

FERRY ROUTES		
ROUTE	**JOURNEY TIME**	**OPERATIONAL DETAILS**
La Paz to Mazatlán	*14–16 hours	Tuesday–Sunday at 2am. Prices: $84 and over. Baja Ferries (tel 612/125-6324; www.bajaferries.com)
La Paz to Topolobampo	*7 hours	Daily at 8am, Sunday–Friday at noon. Prices: $75 and over Baja Ferries (tel 612/125-6324; www.bajaferries.com)
Santa Rosalía to Guaymas	*9 hours	Tuesday, Wednesday, Friday, Sunday at 9am. Prices: $65 (foot passenger) to $248 (with own vehicle). Santa Rosalía Ferries (tel 01-615/152-1246; www.ferrysantarosalia.com)
Cancún to Isla Mujeres	30 minutes	9 times per day between 9am and 4.45pm. Prices: $15 (return)
Gran Puerto to Isla Mujeres	30–45 minutes	3 ferries operating every 30 minutes between 6am and 11.30pm. Prices: $4.50 (one way)
*Approximate journey times		

The domestic flight network in Mexico is extensive as many towns and cities have modern airports. However, while air travel within the country is efficient and safe, tickets are more expensive than in many other Latin American countries. This is because of the lack of competition within the market, created by the bankruptcy of Taesa in early 2000. Currently, the two main airlines are AeroMéxico and Mexicana. While there are other domestic airlines, their routes and schedules are limited. Mexico City is the hub for all domestic air travel and you may find that you have to go via here in order to get somewhere else—this not only adds to the cost, but also to the time taken up by travel.

BUYING TICKETS

» As competition slowly filters back into the Mexican air industry, ticket prices are gradually falling. The market is still dominated by the two big airlines who fly all over Mexico, but there are smaller airlines with schedules for some of the more popular routes. Where this is the case, prices will invariably be cheaper.

» As a general rule, it will be difficult to find out schedules and prices of the airlines unless they serve the particular town or city where you are based. Most travel agents should be able to help on this front, as can the internet.

» If you intend to fly frequently on your trip to Mexico, it may be worth considering the option of an air pass. Both Mexicana and AeroMéxico offer this service.

» Air passes can only be obtained by those arriving on transatlantic flights and have to be bought prior to visiting Mexico.

» Prices vary from between $50–$400 per coupon, but extra can be purchased and reservations are flexible. For more information, check the relevant websites.

MAIN DOMESTIC CARRIERS

AeroMéxico
(www.aeromexico.com), one of the two major national airlines. It has regular flights to most domestic destinations, as well as many services throughout the world.

Mexicana
(www.mexicana.com), the second major domestic airline. This offers very similar destinations as AeroMéxico, both domestically and internationally. Click Mexicana (www.clickmx.com) is a subsidiary airline of Mexicana. It offers low-cost flights to several domestic destinations.

Aerolitoral
(www.aerolitoral.com), a subsidiary airline of AeroMéxico. It offers mainly charter flights from its main hubs of Monterrey, Guadalajara and Chihuahua.

Aviacsa
(www.aviacsa.com), an independent operator with destinations in Mexico, the US, Central and South America.

LUGGAGE ALLOWANCE

This information is taken from the allowances issued by AeroMéxico. It may not be the same for the other domestic operators—double check before you fly.
25kg (55lb) in coach class.
30kg (66lb) in premier class.

Hand luggage allowance is one piece weighing no more than 10kg (22lb), in addition to a briefcase, handbag or laptop.

DOMESTIC FLIGHTS AND PRICES

Although Mexico has a large number of provincial airports, it is not always easy to fly direct between them. Mexico City is the hub of the entire system and you will often find that you will have to go via here in order to get to your next destination. Below is a list of the prices and times of flights from Mexico City to the major towns and cities elsewhere in Mexico; the prices quoted are for an adult return trip in high season with AeroMéxico.
Mexico City to Acapulco: 1 hour, $400, non-stop.
Mexico City to Cancún: 1 hour 55 minutes, $485, non-stop.
Mexico City to Guadalajara: 1 hour 10 minutes, $300, non-stop.

Mexico City to Monterrey: 1 hour 30 minutes, $285, non-stop.
Mexico City to Tijuana: 3 hours 30 minutes, $650, non-stop.
Mexico City to Oaxaca: 55 minutes, $275, non-stop.

» Apart from charter flights, the majority of flights between towns will go via Mexico City.

» Different airlines will offer various routes and you may be able to find direct flights from certain locations that no others have.

» For up-to-date information check operator websites and telephone numbers, as well as asking local travel agents, who should be able to provide information on any special offers being given by the airlines.

» If you want to fly from one town to another, rather than travel by road, it is worth checking to see whether you can do this direct, as the time difference between a bus journey and a flight with connections may not be all that much and the prices of the buses may be much lower.

ROUTES

» Monterrey to Cancún: There is no direct flight available and the journey will take a minimum of 5 hours.

» Guadalajara to Monterrey: There are direct flights available at certain times during the day with a travel time of around 1 hour 15 minutes. If there is a connection in Mexico City, the travel time will increase to 4 hours 30 minutes.

» Tijuana to Acapulco: Once again it is not possible to fly direct on both legs of the journey; at least one part will have a connection in Mexico City. If flying direct, the journey should take 3 hours 40 minutes, while the total time if connecting at Mexico City is 7 hours 40 minutes.

» Cancún to Oaxaca: The total journey time with a connection at Mexico City is 5 hours.

» Puerto Vallarta to Ciudad del Carmen: There is no direct flight for this route; the connection in Mexico City makes the journey around 8 hours 10 minutes.

Opposite *Taxis at Mexico City Airport*

NATIONAL AIRLINE CARRIER ROUTES

	AEROMEXICO	MEXICANA	AEROLITORAL	AVIACSA
Acapulco	✔	✔	✔	✔
Aguascalientes	✔	✔		
Campeche	✔	✔	✔	
Cancún	✔	✔		✔
Chihuahua	✔	✔	✔	
Ciudad del Carmen	✔	✔	✔	
Ciudad Juárez	✔		✔	✔
Ciudad Victoria	✔	✔		
Colima	✔	✔		
Cozumel		✔		
Culiacan	✔	✔	✔	
Durango	✔		✔	
Guadalajara	✔	✔	✔	✔
Hermosillo	✔	✔	✔	✔
Huatulco		✔		
Ixtapa	✔	✔		
Jalapa	✔	✔		
La Paz	✔	✔	✔	
Lazaro Cardenas	✔	✔		
León	✔	✔		
Los Cabos	✔	✔	✔	
Los Mochis	✔		✔	
Manzanillo	✔	✔		
Matamoros	✔		✔	
Mazatlán	✔	✔	✔	
Mérida	✔	✔	✔	✔
Mexicali	✔	✔	✔	
Mexico City	✔	✔	✔	
Minatitlan	✔	✔	✔	
Monclova				
Monterrey	✔	✔	✔	✔
Morelia	✔	✔		
Oaxaca	✔	✔	✔	✔
Piedras Negras	✔		✔	
Poza Rica	✔	✔	✔	
Puerto Vallarta	✔	✔		✔
Querétaro		✔		
Reynosa	✔	✔	✔	
Salina Cruz				
Saltillo		✔		
San Jose del Cabo	✔	✔	✔	
San Luis Potosí	✔	✔	✔	
Tampico	✔	✔	✔	✔
Tapachula	✔	✔	✔	✔
Tepic	✔	✔		
Tijuana	✔	✔	✔	✔
Torreon	✔	✔	✔	
Tuxtla Gutiérrez		✔		✔
Uruapan				
Veracruz	✔	✔	✔	✔
Villahermosa	✔	✔	✔	✔
Zacatecas	✔	✔		
Zihuatanejo	✔	✔	✔	

NATIONAL BUS NETWORK

Mexico's domestic bus network is efficient and much cheaper than air travel. While the journey can take a significant amount of time, travel by bus is a good option if you are not on a tight schedule. One of the main problems is trying to find exactly where the bus you want leaves from. In most towns and cities there is a central terminal, although in others there are two terminals according to first- and second-class travel, and there is sometimes even a division according to the different companies operating. As with most things in Mexico, the capital is the central hub for all bus travel—you can get anywhere from here—though most towns and cities operate services to other towns and cities in the region. Comfort and safety on buses can be an issue, but should not detract from using them as a reliable option.

BUS SERVICES

» Mexican buses are for the most part organized, clean and prompt.
» If you are planning to cover a long distance the full range of services is likely to be available, but this will probably not be the case if you are traveling between two small towns or villages.
» The distances involved in long-distance bus travel are huge, and so buses of all classes will make food and comfort stops.
» You can travel in absolute luxury or in second class, and the prices often reflect this. At the top end of the market are the luxury services, which compete with domestic airlines for comfort.

» Luxury buses offer an exceptional level of comfort and service, but this does add between 35 and 40 percent onto the price of regular first-class buses.
» First-class buses are probably the best means of road travel—they are a reliable and fairly economical means of covering large distances in relative comfort. All offer air-conditioning, toilets, videos etc.
» Second-class buses are really suitable only for shorter journeys. They are often in a state of disrepair and travel along poorly maintained routes, which makes for a bumpy and uncomfortable ride, particularly as they are often the most crowded buses.

BUYING TICKETS

» Some of the more organized bus companies now have computerized systems, so reservations can be made on certain journeys.
» There are many different bus companies, so prices do vary. The best means of comparing these is to go to the bus terminal itself and shop around—prices, classes and timetables should be posted at the company office in the terminal itself.
» Once you have paid for your ticket, be aware that most companies expect luggage to be checked in at least 30 minutes before scheduled departure time.
» Some companies offer as much as a 50 percent discount to those

SERVICES FROM MEXICO CITY

DESTINATION	COMPANIES	JOURNEY TIME	TERMINAL
Acapulco	Estrella de Oro, Turistar, Futura	5–6 hours	Sur
Aguascalientes	ETN, Fletcha Amarilla	6 hours	Norte
Cancún	ADO	24 hours	Sur
Chihuahua	Transportes Chihuahenses, Omnibus de México	20 hours	Norte
Cuernavaca	Pullman de Morelos	1 hour 30 minutes	Sur
Guanajuato	ETN, Primera Plus	5 hours	Norte
Guadalajara	ETN, Primera Plus, Futura, Fletcha Amarilla	7 hours	Norte, Poniente
Huatulco	Fletcha Roja	14 hours	Sur, Oriente
La Paz (via Mazatlán)	Futura, ABC (serves Baja California)	17 hours to Mazatlán, 19 hours ferry to La Paz	Norte
Manzanillo	ETN, UNO	12 hours	Norte
Mazatlán	Futura, Transportes del Pacífico	17 hours	Norte
Monterrey	Estrella Blanca, Futura	12 hours	Norte
Oaxaca	UNO, Cristobal Colon, ADO	7 hours	Oriente, Sur
Puerto Vallarta	ETN, Futura	12–14 hours	Norte
Querétaro	ETN, Primera Plus, Futura, Omnibus de México, Fletcha Amarilla	3 hours	Norte
San Luis Potosí	ETN, Primera Plus, Futura, Omnibus de México, Fletcha Amarilla	10–11 hours	Norte
Veracruz	ADO, UNO	5–6 hours	Oriente
Zacatecas	Omnibus de México	7–8 hours	Norte

BUS COMPANIES

BUS COMPANY	AREAS SERVED	CONTACT DETAILS
ADO	The Yucután, the southeast, the Gulf and northeast Mexico	01-800/702-8000 www.ado.com.mx
Estrella Roja	Mexico City, Puebla	01-800/712-2284 www.estrellaroja.com.mx
ETN	Northeast of Mexico City	01-800/800-0386 www.etn.com.mx
Estrella de Oro	Southwest of Mexico City	(55) 55 49 85 20 www.estrelladeoro.com.mx
Flecha Amarilla	Central Mexico	01-800/375-7587 www.flecha-amarilla.com
Grupo Estrella	Runs services through several companies all over Mexico	01-800/507-5500 www.estrellablanca.com.mx
Omnibus de México	North of Mexico City	01-800/765-6636 www.odm.com.mx
Primera Plus	Mid-central to southern Mexico	(55) 55 67 71 76 www.primeraplus.com.mx
UNO	North of Mexico City	01-800/702-8000 www.uno.com.mx

with international student cards, especially during holiday periods.

» Refunds are often given for cancellations as long as they are given at least three hours' notice before departure time.

» For up-to-the-minute information and the opportunity to purchase tickets for certain routes, the website www.magic-bus.com.mx is very useful.

LONG-DISTANCE TRAVEL FROM MEXICO CITY

Mexico City is the main departure and arrival point for all services. Due to the sheer scale of the operation there are four bus terminals, each serving a different region of the country.

Terminal del Norte: This serves northern Mexico, as well as the US border. There are good facilities here, including a *casa de cambio* and cafés.

Terminal del Sur: This serves the Cuernavaca, Acapulco, Oaxaca and Zihuatanejo areas. This terminal can get extremely busy and it is best to reserve tickets in advance.

Terminal Poniente: This serves all locations in the west of Mexico.

Terminal Oriente: This serves southeast Mexico (including Yucatán and Oaxaca) and has a tourist

information office among several other facilities.

Mexico City Airport: Although not a designated terminal, it has very convenient services to Puebla, Toluca, Cuernavaca and Querétaro.

SAFETY ON BUSES

Bus travel in Mexico is basically a safe means of travel. However, there are some points to bear in mind before you leave.

» If possible, avoid using buses at night, especially in the states of Guerrero, Oaxaca, Veracruz and Chiapas. Highway robbery is an issue, but journeying by day and trying to keep to the toll roads helps to avoid this problem.

» If you have luggage that needs to be stowed on board, be sure to watch it onto the bus and always keep the receipt.

» Try to avoid buses where your luggage is stowed on the roof (this

usually occurs in outlying areas) as this leaves you open to theft, especially at night.

» Always clip or lock your smaller bags to the luggage rack when inside the bus.

USEFUL TIPS

» Try to sit at the front of a bus on long journeys—by the time of arrival they can get smelly.

» Bring warm clothing if the bus has air-conditioning—it can get very cold.

» If visiting the Yucatán Peninsula, always try to book in advance, especially during holiday times.

» Be aware of the busiest times of the year, when seats are hard to come by—these tend to be school holidays, August and the 15 days leading up to New Year.

Below *Coaches that run on the main Mexico City to Acapulco route operate from and to Terminal del Sur in Mexico City*

DRIVING

Driving in Mexico is a suitable option for travel, providing the correct planning and precautions are taken. In recent years great efforts have been made to upgrade the road network—a number of well-maintained interstate highways now link the main towns and cities. While these charge fees, the contrast with the lower quality, older roads is noticeable and journey times can be significantly shorter. Driving can be an excellent way to see the country's more inaccessible areas, but it is important to be aware of Mexico's distinct driving culture. It is vital to have the correct documents and to be conscious of some of the potential dangers involved. Driving is on the right.

DOCUMENTATION

It is illegal to drive without the correct documents. The police may not be as liberal as you are used to, but there should be no problem as long as you remember always to have copies of the following:

» Valid vehicle permit; this is required whether it's a rental car or your own
» Driver's license
» Passport
» Rental car agreement (if applicable)
» Current car registration card (original) and a copy of the proof of ownership (title papers)
» Valid tourist card
» Proof of insurance

SPEED LIMITS

Interstate highways: 110kph (68mph)
Open country: 70kph (43mph)
Built-up areas: 40kph (25mph)

TOLL ROADS

» Toll roads are called cuota; they generally work out at about 1 peso ($0.10) per kilometer. The network of these roads is now quite extensive, but they are expensive—between $5 and $18 or more for routes that bypass the middle of cities.
» The high cost makes these roads too expensive for many Mexicans, so they are often empty and fast.
» To avoid toll roads either ask for local advice or follow trucks, though this may involve unpaved roads.

» The free roads are often fine, and have much more interesting scenery.

OVERTAKING AND JUNCTIONS

» Mexican drivers have very different procedures when overtaking or meeting oncoming traffic. Be careful in these situations as you may be taken by surprise.
» Road procedures vary from town to town and state to state, so make sure you acquaint yourself with the local rules to avoid problems.
» When two vehicles converge or when a vehicle is stuck behind a

Above *Typical canyon road in the state of Chihuahua*

slower one, the driver who flashes his lights first has the right of way.

» If a bus or truck wants to turn across the road you are on, you must give way if that vehicle flashes its lights—in doing this it is effectively claiming right of way.

» At crossroads where there are no traffic lights, the vehicle that comes to a complete stop first has the right of way over everyone else.

BREAKDOWNS

» If your vehicle breaks down on a highway, give warning to other drivers, either with a warning triangle or red cloth attached to your car. If you don't have these, lay branches some distance in front of and behind your car.

» The Mexican Tourist Department offers a free assistance service called the *Angeles Verdes* (Green Angels). They patrol the main roads, often speak English, carry fuel, offer first aid, towing and tourist information, and can make minor repairs if required. The service is free; free hotline number (tel 01-800-903-9200).

ACCIDENTS

» It is important not to leave your vehicle if you are involved in an accident.

» Inform your insurance company immediately. Always carry your insurance policy identification card.

» If the parties cannot agree on whose fault the accident was, or if minor bodily injury occurs, the vehicles may be impounded until the case is resolved.

» If there is a more serious injury, you may be confined to a hotel or hospital until the claim has been settled.

» Call the operator (02) and ask to be connected to Mexico City to call a helpline for road accidents; tel (55) 56 84 97 15 or (55) 56 84 97 61.

FUEL

» All fuel is unleaded and all stations are owned by Petróleos Mexicanos (PEMEX).

» Prices are uniform throughout the country—currently about $2.50 per gallon ($0.69 per liter).

» There are two types of petrol— *Magna* is the cheaper (in the green

pumps), while *Premium* is more expensive (in the red pumps).

» Fuel stations are not self-service— specify how much you want (in fuel or price) and make sure the meter is set at zero. A small tip is expected.

WARNINGS

» If you have any work done to your vehicle in Mexico, try to supervise and keep records of everything, and where it was carried out.

» Do not interact with police, but be sure to watch any proceedings closely.

» If you are stopped for something you know you didn't do, do not pay an on-the-spot fine. Instead, demand to see the chief at the tourist police headquarters.

» All cars must display a number plate on both the front and the back.

» If your car breaks down and is irreparable, it must be donated to the Mexican people through the Secretaría de Hacienda.

» Be wary of drug searches, especially on the west coast. If this happens, bear the following precautions in mind:

» Keep copies of medicinal prescriptions and medicine in the original containers.

» Keep evidence of all conditions requiring medication with a hypodermic syringe or emergency treatment.

» Never take any packages from other people or take hitchhikers across the borders.

SHAKEDOWNS

Unfortunately, bribe-seeking policemen that pull over tourists for minor traffic infractions are all too common in Mexico. If you feel the traffic stop was without merit, insist the officer take you to the local police station. They will usually relent. If you prefer to get back on the road quickly, $20 to $60 cash will usually buy your freedom. Of course, serious traffic violations or accidents are non-negotiable.

Left *Make sure you have sufficient fuel for your journey, especially in rural areas*

MEXICAN ROAD SIGNS

Parking Okay	No Parking	No Parking Section Ends Here	Speed Limit	Inspection Area	Stay Right
Stop	Yield (Give Way)	Railroad Crossing	Detour		Speed Bumps

This chart gives the distance in kilometers of a car journey between key towns in Mexico. Journey times can vary considerably depending on the state of the roads.

	Acapulco de Juárez	Cancún	Chihuahua	Ciudad de México	Ciudad Juárez	Guadalajara	Guaymas	La Paz	Matamoros	Mazatlán	Mérida	Monterrey	Oaxaca	Querétaro	San Luis Potosí	Tampico	Tapachula	Tijuana	Veracruz	Villahermosa
Cancún	2061																			
Chihuahua	1857	3260																		
Ciudad de México	329	1732	1419																	
Ciudad Juárez	2125	3528	377	1796																
Guadalajara	850	2253	1120	521	1497															
Guaymas	2147	3550	747	1818	681	1297														
La Paz	4623	6026	2951	4294	2571	3773	2476													
Matamoros	1328	2445	1223	999	1600	1029	1970	4129												
Mazatlán	1367	2770	1008	1038	1385	517	780	3256	1311											
Mérida	1739	322	2829	1410	3206	1931	3228	5704	2123	2448										
Monterrey	1334	2451	903	1005	1280	759	1650	3809	320	991	2129									
Oaxaca	671	1550	1914	495	2291	1016	2313	4789	1387	1533	1228	1393								
Querétaro	542	1945	1206	213	1583	416	1713	4157	884	933	1623	736	708							
San Luis Potosí	744	2147	1004	415	1381	347	1578	3955	682	798	1825	534	910	202						
Tampico	840	1921	1405	475	1782	748	1979	4356	524	1199	1599	530	637	556	401					
Tapachula	1101	1614	2535	1116	2912	1637	2934	5410	1829	2154	1292	1835	677	1329	1531	1305				
Tijuana	2822	4554	1479	2822	1099	2301	1004	1472	2657	1784	4232	2337	3317	2685	2483	2884	3938			
Veracruz	778	1425	1868	449	2245	970	2267	4743	1020	1487	1103	1026	367	662	864	496	809	3271		
Villahermosa	1123	938	2213	794	2590	1315	2612	5088	1507	1832	616	1513	612	1007	1209	983	676	3616	487	
Zacatecas	939	2342	809	610	1186	311	1383	3760	768	603	2020	448	1105	397	195	596	1726	2288	1059	1404

CITY TRANSPORTATION

Public transportation in Mexico's towns and cities is varied but effective. In Mexico City, Monterrey and Guadalajara, the metro is one of the easiest and cheapest ways of getting around. Elsewhere, various types of buses offer a sometimes complex, but extensive coverage at very reasonable prices. Every town and city has numerous taxis and in a large city these can often be the most effective means of getting from A to B. Public transportation is normally safe, but take precautions to ensure that this remains the case.

BUSES
» Most tourist offices will be able to give you information on the best routes and buses to take to your destination; if this is not the case then ask the bus driver.

» As in Mexico City, the destination of a particular bus should be marked on the front of the windshield—double check before getting on.

» Prices vary from town to town, but most bus travel will be a fixed fare, regardless of how far you are going on a particular route. Ask a local or a bus driver to find out current prices—in Guadalajara, for example, the regular price is $0.45; in Oaxaca it is $0.50.

» In some of the bigger towns and cities, be prepared for an uncomfortable journey as the buses are often packed, especially at peak times. As on long-distance buses, make sure you are extra vigilant with your belongings.

COLECTIVOS, COMBIS AND PESEROS
» These are essentially minibuses that have a capacity of about 14 people and operate along set lines in much the same way that buses do.

» They are less expensive than taxis and usually less crowded than buses.

» It is possible to flag down a *colectivo* if you are not at the start of the route; tell the driver where you are intending to go before getting on, just to be sure you have the correct one.

» Prices vary normally, depending on how far you travel. While they are more expensive than the buses, the journey is significantly faster and generally more comfortable.

TAXIS
» There are numerous taxis in every town and city throughout Mexico.

» Outside Mexico City, taxi colors vary, so check what the official

marks are. It is generally safe to hail an official taxi from anywhere other than Mexico City.

» Although all taxis should have a meter, it is sometimes a good idea to fix a price before setting off.

» *Sitio* taxis around airports and bus terminals are a safe form of transportation; you pay at a booth or kiosk before getting in.

» If you are not familiar with the town or city that you are in, arrange a taxi through your hotel—it may be more expensive than regular taxis, but is safer.

» No tipping is required unless the driver has given an extra service such as carrying heavy luggage to a hotel or airport terminal.

CYCLING
» Cycling can be a good way of getting around towns and cities, although in bigger places the busy and polluted roads are not always particularly safe or convenient.

» In the busiest places a rear-view mirror is a recommended safety precaution.

» Cycling is particularly popular in Baja California and there are bicycle repair and rental shops in towns such as La Paz.

» The main cities have bicycle repair shops, but in the smaller places you are unlikely to find much more than the basics, such as spokes, tires and inner tubes.

» If repairs need to be made to your bicycle, be wary of mechanics who get quickly to work rather than admit that they do not really know what they are doing.

Left The motocarro *motorcycle attached to a trailer is the typical mode of transportation in Tehuantepec*

Mexico is constantly improving its accessibility for visitors with disabilities. The major cities and resorts such as Cancún and Acapulco have many hotels which should be able to cater to most needs. However, outside of these areas, the facilities are generally not adequate for independent disabled travel. One of the best ways to visit the country is with a specially organized tour group, of which there are many—through these you do not have to stay confined within a resort.

BY TRAIN

Train travel is virtually impossible for anyone with a disability. This is the case everywhere, including Mexico City metro, where only a few of the stations have ramps and elevators, or special assistance for the visually impaired. The Chihuahua–Los Mochis railway journey does have limited disabled access. People are generally willing to offer assistance on and off the trains. For details, check the operator's website.

BY AIR

Most, if not all, airports in Mexico are accessible for wheelchair users. If you do not see the necessary facilities (such as an elevator), do not be afraid to ask for assistance. To be sure that your destination will be accessible for you, check with the relevant airline before starting your journey.

BY BUS

Very few, if any, town buses have wheelchair access. A better

option is to use the official taxis. Long-distance buses are much more amenable to disabled travel. Although they may not have specific access for wheelchairs, there is a lot of space inside and members of staff should be more than willing to help if you ask.

BY FERRY

The relatively new ships operated by Baja Ferries between La Paz, Mazatlán and Topolobampo have access for wheelchair users. Ramps, elevators and escalators on the vessel ensure that the journey is comfortable. It is still worth enquiring at a travel agent shop or on the pier itself before you travel.

AROUND TOWN

Much of Mexico remains particularly difficult for visitors with disabilities. Away from the major resorts, such as Cancún, sidewalks (pavements) are rarely ramped and are often uneven or broken. In some places it is unlikely that there will be handrails on the stairwells. However, this should not necessarily prevent you from visiting the sights around town. Many people hire taxi drivers who are willing to help those with mobility problems to visit the sights for an extended period of time.

USEFUL INFORMATION SOURCES FOR VISITORS WITH DISABILITIES

The tourist board is not overly helpful in finding out how accessible particular destinations and sites are in Mexico, so the best thing is to contact either a disability organization or travel agent for further information.

www.makoa.org has a vast number of resource links for people with disabilities, including information on travel; look under Travel and Recreation Resources. www.globalaccessnews.com is very useful for visitors with disabilities. There is information on Mexico, although it focuses largely on Cancún and Puerto Vallarta.

UK: RADAR, 12 City Forum, 250 City Road, London, EC1V 8AF (tel +44 (0)20 7250 3222; www.radar.org.uk).

US: SATH, 347 5th Avenue, Suite 605, New York City, NY 10016 (tel +1 212/447-7284; www.sath.org).

Canada: The Easter Seals Society, One Concord Gate, Suite 700, Toronto, ON M3C 3N6 (tel +1 800/668-6252; www.easterseals.org).

SPECIALIST TOUR OPERATORS

Specialist tour operators are often the best means of visiting Mexico with a disability. Among the best are:
» Directions Unlimited, 123 Green Lane, Bedford Hills, NY 10507, tel 800/533-5343. U.S. travel agent can customize tours for individuals with disabilities.
» Disability Action Group, 189 Airport Road West, Belfast BT3 9ED, Northern Ireland, tel 02890-297880; www.disabilityaction.org. Information about access for disabled British visitors.
» Disabled Persons' Assembly, PO Box 27-524, Wellington 6035, New Zealand, tel 04-801-9100, gen@dpa.org.nz; www.dpa.org.nz. Has lists of tour operators and travel agencies catering to visitors with disabilities.

REGIONS

This chapter is divided into six regions of Mexico (▷ 8–9). Places of interest are listed alphabetically in each region.

SIGHTS 66
WALKS 86
WHAT TO DO 90
EATING 96
STAYING 100

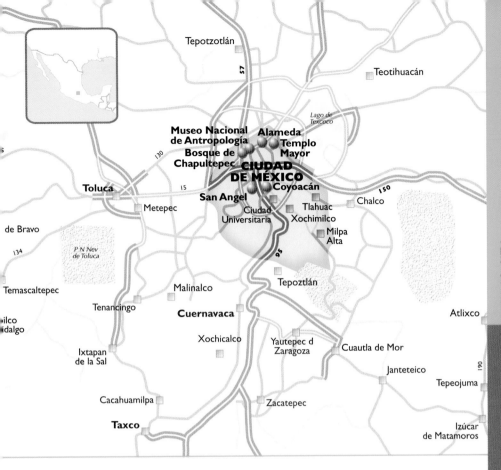

MEXICO CITY

Virtually pulsating with a richness of life and culture, this vibrant city has an exciting blend of history and modernity. With its sprawling parks, stunning colonial palaces, ornate churches and fascinating museums, Mexico City is a magnet for visitors. Its urban energy is electric and Mexico's capital truly does have it all, from its laid-back sidewalk cafés and cantinas to its impressive monuments and glorious pyramids.

Filled with historic and cultural treasures, Mexico City was founded more than 675 years ago as the ancient city of Tenochtitlan and capital of the Aztec Empire. Today, more than 22 million people call this dynamic city home. With its abundance of ancient ruins and colonial masterpieces, some have referred to it as "The City of Palaces." Indeed, the central downtown area resembles a European city, with its broad boulevards and ornate buildings, dotted with parks, public art, and colorful gardens. In the center of it all are the partially excavated ruins of the main Aztec temple. Just beyond the city, one can see pyramids rise.

As steeped as the city is in history, it's also quite modern and chaotic, almost buzzing with energy. Some not-to-be-missed treasures here include Templo Mayor, Teotihuacan, Museo Nacional de Arte, and the Catedral Metropolitana. While walking around this great city, watch your step; Mexico City was built on an old lake bed, and some buildings have sunk below street level, which means streets and sidewalks are uneven in many places.

Mexico City is a jewel and has much to offer. But just like when visiting any major city, be aware of your surroundings and when possible, don't travel alone. If you plan to take a taxi from the airport, make sure you only use authorized or *sitio* taxis. Avoid wearing expensive jewelry and don't carry a lot of cash. Additionally, stick to the main tourist streets when walking, and avoid walking at night.

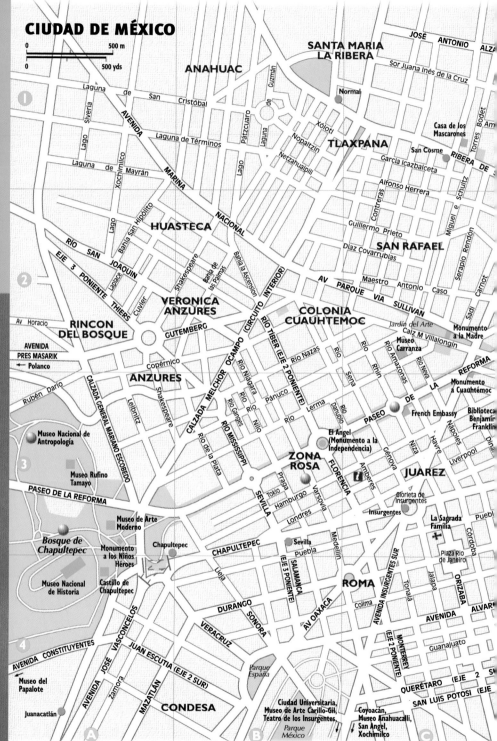

CIUDAD DE MÉXICO

0 ————— 500 m
0 ————— 500 yds

ANAHUAC

SANTA MARIA LA RIBERA

JOSÉ ANTONIO ALZA

Sor Juana Inés de la Cruz

Laguna de San Cristóbal

Normal

Casa de los Mascarones

Torres Bodet

AVENIDA

Laguna de Términos

Pátzcuaro

Laguna de

Guzmán

Xólotl

Nopaltzin

TLAXPANA

San Cosme

RIBERA DE

García Icazbalceta

Garcia Rendón

MARINA

Lago Xochimilco Mayrán

Lago

Netzahualpill

Alfonso Herrera

Contreras

Miguel e Schultz

Laguna de

Lago San Hipólito

Bahía San Hipólito

HUASTECA

NACIONAL

Guillermo Prieto

SAN RAFAEL

Serapio Rendón

Carnot

RIO SAN JOAQUIN

Laplace

Shakespeare

Bahía de las Palmas

Bahía de Ascensión

Díaz Covarrubias

EJE 3 PONIENTE THIERS

Cuvier

VERONICA ANZURES

AV PARQUE VIA SULLIVAN

Maestro Antonio Caso

Sadi

Av Horacio

RINCON DEL BOSQUE

GUTEMBERG

(CIRCUITO INTERIOR)

COLONIA CUAUHTEMOC

Jardín del Arte

Calz M Villalongín

Monumento a la Madre

AVENIDA PRES MASARIK
← Polanco

Copérnico

RIO TIBER (EJE 2 PONIENTE)

Río Nazas

Río Rhin

Museo Carranza

REFORMA

CALZADA GENERAL MARIANO ESCOBEDO

Leibnitz

ANZURES

Río Niágara

Río

Río

Pánuco

Lerma

Sena

Río Amazonas

Río Neva

Monumento a Cuauhtémoc

Rubén Darío

Shakespeare

CALZADA MELCHOR OCAMPO

RIO GANGES

RIO NILO

Río Danubio

PASEO DE LA

French Embassy

Biblioteca Benjamín Franklin

Museo Nacional de Antropología

RIO MISSISSIPPI

Río de la Plata

El Ángel (Monumento a la Independencia)

Córdova

Napoles

Niza

Havre

Liverpool

Dina

JUAREZ

Museo Rufino Tamayo

ZONA ROSA

FLORENCIA

Amberes

Glorieta de Insurgentes

PASEO DE LA REFORMA

SEVILLA

Tokio

Praga

Hamburgo

Varsovia

Insurgentes

La Sagrada Familia

Puebl

Museo de Arte Moderno

Londres

Sevilla

Medellín

Córdoba

Bosque de Chapultepec

Monumento a los Niños Héroes

Chapultepec

CHAPULTEPEC

Puebla

SALAMANCA (EJE 3 PONIENTE)

Plaza Río de Janeiro

ORIZABA

Museo Nacional de Historia

Castillo de Chapultepec

Lieja

DURANGO

Colima

ROMA

AVENIDA INSURGENTES SUR

Tonalá

Jalapa

ALVAR

SONORA

AV OAXACA

AVENIDA

MONTERREY (EJE 2 PONIENTE)

Guanajuato

AVENIDA CONSTITUYENTES

JUAN ESCUTIA (EJE 2 SUR)

VERACRUZ

Museo del Papalote

JOSÉ VASCONCELOS

Zamora

MAZATLÁN

Parque España

QUERÉTARO (EJE 2

SAN LUIS POTOSI (EJE

Juanacatlán

CONDESA

Ciudad Universitaria, Museo de Arte Carillo-Gil, Teatro de los Insurgentes, Parque México

Coyoacán, Museo Anahuacalli, San Angel, Xochimilco

A   **B**   **C**

asílica de Guadalupe ↑

↑ Plaza de las Tres Culturas

ESTACIÓN DE FERROCARRILES BUENAVISTA

MARTÍNEZ DE LA TORRE (EJE 1 NORTE)

CENTRO

Buenavista

Guerrero

MOSQUETA

Lerdo

Glorieta General José de San Martín

MORELOS

GUERRERO

J Meneses

Magnolia

Zarco

Soto

REFORMA

Garibaldi

LÓPEZ

RAYÓN

Rep de Ecuador

Dr Enrique González Martínez

Nervo

Buenavista

Ignacio Zaragoza

Aldama

Guerrero (Eje Poniente)

Violeta

Obispo

Plaza Garibaldi

ALLENDE

Rep de Nicaragua

REP de ARGENTINA

Museo del Chopo

AVENIDA INSURGENTES CENTRO

Mina

PASEO

DE

LA

Mina

Pensador Mexicano

Belisario Domínguez

Rep de Perú

Santo Domingo

Museo de la Medicina Mexicana

OSME

PUENTE DE ALVARADO

Revolución

Frontón México

Edison

Museo de San Carlos

Hidalgo

San Juan de Dios

San Juan de Dios

Rep de Cuba

CHILE

Plaza Santo Domingo

J Ma Iglesias

Museo de la Alameda

Museo Franz Mayer

Museo Nacional de Arte

Monte de Piedad

Monumento a la Revolución

Plaza de la República

Nueva Lotería

Museo Mural Diego Rivera

Colón

Dr Mora

AVENIDA HIDALGO

Donceles

TACUBA

CENTRO

Alameda Central

Palacio de Bellas Artes

Bellas Artes

Casa de los Azulejos

Allende

Catedral Metropólitana

TABACALERA

Ramírez

Donato Guerra

AVENIDA JUÁREZ

Plaza de las Esculturas

Juárez

Independencia

Torre Latinoamericana

AV FRANCISCO I MADERO

5 de Mayo

Zócalo

Zócalo (Plaza de la Constitución)

Av Morelos

Secretaría de Gobernación

Enrico Martínez

BALDERAS

Artículo 123

Victoria

Templo de San Francisco

16

DE SEPTIEMBRE

Palacio de Iturbide

Venustiano

Carranza

Gral Prim

ucerna

BUCARELI (EJE 1 PONIENTE)

González

Ernesto Pugibet

Luis Moya

San Juan de Letrán

REP

DE

URUGUAY

ma

Museo de Cera

Abraham

La Cuidadela

Vizcaínas

BOLÍVAR

ISABEL LA CATÓLICA

S Jerónimo

Isabel la Católica

5 de Febrero

20 DE NOVIEMBRE

Iglesia y Hospital de Jesús Nazareno

Museo de la Ciudad

Plaza de la Ciudadela

ARCOS DE BELÉN

Balderas

Salto del Agua

JOSÉ MARÍA IZAZAGA

Nezahualcóyotl

Museo de la Charrería

Pino Suárez

Mercado de la Merced

Cuauhtémoc

DR RÍO DE LA LOZA

Arena México

FRAY SERVANDO TERESA DE MIER

PINO SUÁREZ

Plaza Morelia

Dr Lavista

Durango

Morelia

BREGÓN

AVENIDA CUAUHTÉMOC

Glorieta Simón Bolívar

Obispo

Rep de Perú

Rodríguez

Rep de

Bolivia

R Puebla

Leona Vicario

Margil

N

Mina

Tujano

Belisario

Domínguez

Santo Domingo

Museo de la Medicina Mexicana

Rep de Argentina

Cármen

Rep de Venezuela

Pensador

Mex

Rep de Cuba

ALLENDE

Plaza Santo Domingo

Secretaría de Educación Pública

San Pedro y San Pablo

Loreto

Museo Franz Mayer

Museo de la Estampa

Teatro de la Ciudad

CHILE

Palma

Monte de Piedad

G Obregón

San Ildefonso

Anfiteatro Simón Bolívar /Colegio de San Ildefonso

San Juan de Dios

AVENIDA HIDALGO

Santa Veracruz

Sta Veracruz

EJE CENTRAL LÁZARO CÁRDENAS

Museo Nacional de Arte

El Caballito

Donceles

Museo de la Caricatura

Seminario

Justo Sierra

Bellas Artes

Palacio de Minería

Allende

TACUBA

Templo Mayor

Rep de Guatemala

Santísima Trinidad

Alameda Central

Palacio de Bellas Artes

Casa de los Azulejos

5 de Mayo

La Profesa

Catedral Metropólitana

Palacio Arzobispal

Museo José Luis Cuevas

Moneda

Escuela Nacional de Artes Plásticas

AVENIDA JUÁREZ

FRANCISCO I MADERO

Sagrario Metropolitano

Soledad

Torre Latinoamericana

Dolores

Templo de San Francisco

Palacio de Iturbide

Carrie

Palma

MONTE DE PIEDAD

Zócalo

Zócalo (Plaza de la Constitución)

Museo de las Culturas

Academia

Independencia

16

de

Septiembre

Palacio Nacional

200 m

Hospital General

Artículo

123

San Juan de Letrán

Venustiano

Carranza

20 DE NOVIEMBRE

PINO SUÁREZ

Suprema Corte de Justicia

Corregidora

Manzanares

Amón diga

200 yds

Hospital General

Victoria

Rep

de

Uruguay

Mexico City Metro

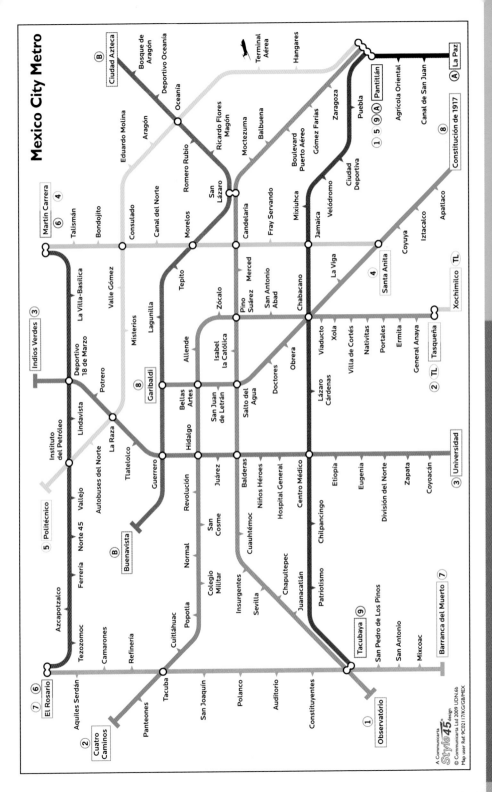

A Communicarta
Style45 design
© Communicarta Ltd 2009 UDN.6b
Map user Ref: 9C021177KG/GB/MEX

ALAMEDA

An attractive park with fountains and heroic statues under the shade of eucalypti, cypresses and ragged palms, Alameda is overlooked by the Palacio de Bellas Artes—an art deco gem and home to the Ballet Folclórico de México. The Alameda park has served several functions in its long history—from Aztec market, to execution ground for the Spanish Inquisition, to temporary camp for US soldiers in the late 1840s. Its heyday was in the 19th century when all social classes mingled here for their Sunday stroll. Badly affected by the 1985 earthquake, the surrounding area is being transformed by new building work.

INFORMATION
✚ 63 E2 (inset E2) 🚇 Bellas Artes

LANDMARKS

Flanking the eastern side of the park is the Palacio de Bellas Artes (Tue–Sun 10–6), the work of Italian architect Adamo Boari. A large, flamboyant art deco building, it houses a museum, theater, cafeteria, excellent bookshop on the arts (▷ 93) and a museum with old and contemporary paintings, prints, sculptures and handicrafts. The building also contains frescoes by Rivera, Orozco, Tamayo and Siqueiros. On the top floor a museum of architecture details the building's history. Perhaps the most remarkable thing about the theater is its glass curtain designed by Tiffany, but this can only be seen during performances, either by the Ballet Folclórico de México or the many operas and orchestral concerts that are staged here (▷ 92).

At the southeast corner of the park is the Torre Latinoamericana (daily 9am–10pm), which has a viewing platform with telescopes on the 44th floor. On the south side is the Juárez Hemiciclo, a white marble monument inaugurated in 1910 to honor president Benito Juárez. Opposite, the colonial Iglesia de Corpus Christi is used to display and sell folk arts and crafts. Farther west a sunken section of the sidewalk (pavement) shelters the Plaza de las Esculturas (1998), with its 19th-century sculptures. Across Avenida Hidalgo is the Museum Franz Mayer, which houses decorative arts from the 16th through 19th century. This former hospital building has frescos, archways, and carved wood doors.

Diego Rivera's huge mural, *Sueño de una Tarde Dominical en la Alameda Central (Dream of a Sunday Afternoon in Alameda)*, was removed from the earthquake-damaged Hotel del Prado on Avenida Juárez in 1985. It now occupies its own purpose-built museum, the Museo Mural Diego Rivera (Tue–Sun 10–6) at the west end of the Alameda. One of Rivera's finest works, it presents a pageant of Mexican history from the Conquest up to the 1940s.

Opposite *Mexico City is the soul of the country with a vibrant atmosphere*
Below *The Palacio de Bellas Artes, designed by Adamo Boari in 1904*

INFORMATION

✚ 62 A3 · 🎟 Free · 🚇 Chapultepec
🍴 The park is dotted with food stands selling hamburgers, quesadillas and cotton candy (candyfloss), and there is an open-air café in the Museo de Arte Moderno

TIP

» The Auditorio Nacional, one of the city's most important concert halls, is in Chapultepec Park at Paseo de la Reforma 50 (tel (55) 52 80 92 50). Free classical music concerts are given on Sunday at noon by the Bellas Artes Chamber Orchestra; arrive early for a seat.

BOSQUE DE CHAPULTEPEC

Bosque de Chapultepec is the lungs of the city, a vast green park with boating lakes, botanical gardens and shady picnic spots, and is home to some of the city's finest museums. This beautiful green space, with its thousands of *ahuehuete* trees (sacred to the Aztecs), covers 646ha (1,600 acres) and has enough to keep you occupied for a couple of days. Sunday is the liveliest time to go, when families and daytrippers throng to the zoo (▷ 95) and museums (which are free for nationals on Sundays). However, it can get very crowded, so expect a wait at some sights.

EAST TO WEST

Paseo de la Reforma runs east to west along the top of the park, connecting it to the middle of the city. On entering the park from the eastern gate, you will pass the large, six-columned Monumento a los Niños Héroes, commemorating the young soldiers who defended the castle (Castillo) of Chapultepec (then a military academy) against the 1847 American occupation. Behind the monument is Chapultepec Hill, visible from afar, with the imposing Castillo perched on top giving a view over the Valley of Mexico from its balconies. It now houses the Museo Nacional de Historia (Tue–Sun 9–5), but its opulent rooms were once used by Emperor Maximilian and Empress Carlota during their brief reign in the 1860s. There is an impressive mural by David Siqueiros (1896–1974), *From the Dictatorship of Porfirio Díaz to the Revolution*, in Sala XIII, near the entrance, and a notable one by Juan O'Gorman (1905–82) on the theme of Independence.

NORTH AND SOUTH

Just south of Paseo de la Reforma is the Museo de Arte Moderno (Tue–Sun 10–6), where José-Clemente Orozco (1883–1949), Siqueiros and Diego Rivera (1886–1957) are well represented in the excellent permanent collection of modern Mexican art. World-class temporary exhibitions are also regularly staged. There is a good bookshop, gift shop and an open-air cafeteria behind the first building.

North of here is the Museo Rufino Tamayo (Tue–Sun 10–6), with a fine collection of works by this Modernist painter (1899–1991), as well as his private collection of European and American 20th-century art, including works by Henry Moore, Francis Bacon and Picasso. Next door is the world-famous Museo Nacional de Antropología (▷ 72–75).

Above *Monumento a los Niños Héroes, in front of the Castillo*

BASÍLICA DE GUADALUPE

Buses marked "La Villa" travel north along Paseo de la Reforma through the suburbs of Mexico City to the Basilica of Guadalupe, the most venerated shrine in Mexico. It was here, in December 1531, that the Virgin appeared to Juan Diego and imprinted her portrait on his cloak (▷ 35). A basilica was built on the site in 1533, growing to become the huge baroque structure you see today. At the back, a museum (Tue–Sun 10–6) is stacked with religious art and some curious 19th-century votive offerings. A new basilica was built in 1976 and it is here that Juan Diego's cloak, set in gold, is now housed. To see it, step onto the moving walkway behind the altar. (Note: shorts are not permitted in the basilica.) From the plaza you can walk up Cerro de Tepeyac past numerous chapels to the Capilla de las Rosas, with fine views on a clear day. On December 12 thousands of people assemble here to celebrate the anniversary of the Virgin's appearance (▷ 293).

✚ Off map 63 D1 ✉ Plaza de las Américas ☎ (55) 55 77 60 22 🕐 Daily 8–8 🚇 La Villa Basílica

Right *The 16th-century Catedral Metropolitana stands on the zócalo*
Below *Facade of the House of Tiles*

CASA DE LOS AZULEJOS

Blue-and-white 18th-century Puebla tiles cover the front of the 16th-century Casa de los Azulejos (House of Tiles). They were made in 1653 in a factory managed by Dominican friars. Occupied by the Zapatista army during the Revolution, the house is now one of the Sanborn chain of restaurants. The central courtyard (the main dining room) has Moorish arches, stone pillars and an ornamental fountain. On the far side of the courtyard a stone staircase leads to the wooden balconies above. José Clemente Orozco's evocative fresco, *Omniscienda (Omniscience)*, on the inside stairwell, dates from 1925.

✚ 63 E2 (inset E2) ✉ Avenida Madero 4 ☎ (55) 55 12 13 31 🕐 Daily 7am–1am 🖐 Free 🚇 Bellas Artes

CATEDRAL METROPOLITANA

This immense cathedral, which dominates the *zócalo*, is the largest and oldest in Latin America. It was first built soon after the Conquest, and completed in 1525, four years later, using stones taken from the Aztec Temple of Huitzilópochtli (Templo Mayor) nearby. The structure you see today dates from 1573. Guided visits take you up to the bell tower to see the largest of the bells, Santa Maria de Guadalupe, weighing 13 tons. Like many of the city's heavy colonial buildings, the cathedral is sinking into the soft lake bed below and a lengthy schedule of work is under way to build new foundations. The tilt is quite obvious. However, for the first time in years, the interior is free of scaffolding and the immensity of the building can be fully appreciated. The most attractive feature is the enormous gilt Retablo de los Reyes behind the main altar, built between 1718 and 1737, depicting European monarchs.

Next door is the beautiful 18th-century church of El Sagrario, which has a fine Churrigueresque facade decorated with sculpted saints and a gilt interior.

✚ 63 F2 (inset F2) ✉ Plaza de la Constitución ☎ (55) 55 10 04 40 🕐 Daily 7.30am–8pm 🖐 Free 🚇 Zócalo

INFORMATION

✚ Off map 62 C4 ⊕ Viveros, Miguel
Angel Quevedo, General Anaya

COYOACÁN

Coyoacán is one of the most culturally dynamic areas of Mexico City, packed with cultural centers that come alive at weekends. This charming district south of the historic heart is where Hernán Cortés had his headquarters during the battle for Tenochtitlán in 1521. It is also one of the most beautiful and best-preserved parts of the city, with scores of fine old buildings (▷ 88). If coming from metro Viveros or Miguel Angel de Quevedo, it is worth approaching via the elegant, tree-lined Avenida Francisco Sosa, said to be the first urban street laid in Spanish America. Halfway between Avenida Universidad and the Jardín Centenario is pretty Plaza Santa Catarina, where on Sundays, after 1pm, people gather to tell stories (all welcome).

A 10-minute walk from here will take you to the Jardín Centenario, formerly the atrium of a Franciscan monastery, and now home to the lively Sunday crafts market. Overlooking the garden is the bulky 16th-century Iglesia de San Juan Bautista (Mon–Sat 8–1, 5–8.30, Sun 8am–8.30pm), with a magnificent interior. Directly to the northeast lies the pretty Plaza Hidalgo, with the Palacio de Cortés, built on the site of Cortés's original house. Just off Plaza Hidalgo, half a block up Avenida Hidalgo, is the Museo Nacional de Culturas Populares (Tue–Thu 10–6, Fri–Sun 10–8), which hosts excellent folkloric exhibitions and a schedule of films, dance and concerts. The Foro Cultural Coyoacán (▷ 93) on Calle Allende is half a block north of Plaza Hidalgo.

CELEBRATED FORMER RESIDENTS

Indeed, Coyoacan is a tranquil oasis that offers glimpses of traditional Mexican life with its cobblestone streets, gorgeous flower gardens, park-like plazas, and lovely colonial mansions steeped in history. Visitors flock here to shop for paintings and crafts, enjoy the museums and sidewalk cafés, and savor the towns' artistic environment. Many of them also spend time visiting the former homes and studios of Diego Rivera, Frida Kahlo, and Leon Trotsky.

Admirers of Frida Kahlo should visit the Museo Frida Kahlo (▷ 89), northeast of Plaza Hidalgo. Two rooms are preserved as they were when Kahlo and her husband Diego Rivera lived there, while the rest contain Kahlo's wonderful collection of traditional costumes and folk art, as well as her wheelchair and several paintings. In the same direction, at Calle Río Churubusco 410, is the Casa de León Trotsky (▷ 89).

Below *Coyoacán is a beautiful district that comes alive at weekends with displays of color and traditional culture*

CIUDAD UNIVERSITARIA
www.unam.mx

The city university, 18km (11 miles) south from central Mexico City, via Avenida Insurgentes Sur on the road toward Cuernavaca, was founded in 1551 and has occupied a number of sites. The present-day campus was built between 1950 and 1955 and is one of the largest universities in the world, with 300,000 students. The most notable building is the 10-floor Biblioteca Central (Central Library), its outside walls iridescent with a mosaic mural by Juan O'Gorman telling the story of scientific knowledge, from Aztec astronomy to molecular theory. The nearby Rectoría building is covered with vast, semi-sculptured murals by David Alfaro Siqueiros.

Also in this area of the campus is the Museo Universitario de Ciencias y Arte (MUCA), with a wide-ranging collection including traditional masks from all over Mexico, as well as exhibitions on contemporary art and culture. Beyond this, the grassy Plaza Mayor marks the beginning of the enormous grounds of the main campus. Across the highway is the massive Estadio Olímpico (Olympic Stadium), used in the 1968 Olympic Games and 1986 World Cup. It is now home to the university's

fútbol team. Close by is the Jardín Botánico, with a cactus collection, jungle plants and arboretum.

Farther south on Avenida Insurgentes is a cultural complex including the Sala Nezahualcóyotl (where concerts are held), the Teatro Juan Ruiz de Alarcón and a bookshop.

➕ Off map 62 B4 ✋ Free 🚇 Copilco (then 20-min walk) or Universidad (then 30-min walk) 🚌 Bus marked CU along Eje Lázaro Cárdenas or bus 17, marked Tlalpan

COLEGIO DE SAN ILDEFONSO
www.sanildefonso.org.mx

The former Colegio de San Ildefonso is home to some interesting murals by José Clemente Orozco and Diego Rivera, among others. Built in 1749 in splendid baroque style as the Jesuit School of San Ildefonso, it then became the Escuela Nacional Preparatoria, before being converted into one of the city's most important temporary exhibition spaces. Don't miss the Orozco murals—*The Trench* (ground floor) and the *The Aristocrats* (first floor). In the Anfiteatro Bolívar look out for Rivera's *Creation* (1922), and by the stairs between the first and second floors, Fernando Leal's evocative *The Fiesta of Lord of Chalma*, both in excellent condition. A pleasant first-

floor cafeteria under the colonnades of the principal courtyard serves snacks and good cappuccino.

➕ Inset 63 F2 ✉ Calle Justo Sierra 16 ☎ (55) 57 02 63 78 🕐 Tue–Sun 10–6 (box office closes 5.30) 💵 $4.50 (free on Tue) 🚇 Zócalo

INSURGENTES

Heading out of the city along Avenida Insurgentes toward the suburbs of San Angel and Coyoacán there are several sites worth looking for. The Polyforum Cultural Siqueiros (daily 10–6), nowadays used as a convention hall, is covered on the outside by striking murals. Inside the ovoid dome is a wonderful gigantic mural by Siqueiros.

A little farther south and along Avenida San Antonio is the Plaza México, the largest bullring in the world (▷ 95). Continuing south at the corner with Calle Mercaderes is the Teatro de los Insurgentes (www.teatroinsurgentes.com.mx), with its curved facade, designed by Diego Rivera, sporting a gigantic pair of hands holding a mask.

➕ Off map 62 B4 🚌 Buses from Plaza de la República marked Insurgentes Sur

Above *Detail of Diego Rivera's striking mural that covers the curved facade of Teatro de los Insurgentes*

INTRODUCTION

This huge museum in the northern part of Bosque de Chapultepec (▷ 68) is a work of art in itself and contains an awesome collection of pre-Hispanic finds. Ranged around a central courtyard, it is shaded by a gigantic concrete mushroom, with an area of 4,200sq m (45,200sq ft)—the world's largest concrete and steel expanse supported by a single pillar, sculpted by José Chávez Morado. Water, symbolizing eternal life, cascades down around this pillar, on which scenes from Mexico's history are carved. The two-floor building has a facade 350m (1,148ft) long. All of the ground-level exhibition rooms can be reached from the central patio.

On the right as you enter the courtyard are the first rooms, an excellent introduction to anthropology and to Mesoamerican prehistory. Some rooms have outdoor areas with sculptures, reconstructions of houses and other exhibits. A walk counterclockwise will lead you in and out of the various rooms and allow you to take restful breaks.

The upper floor is devoted to indigenous cultures today, with fabulous collections of clothing, masks, pottery, musical instruments, items from domestic life and much more. Because of the enormous number of exhibits to see and information to digest, allow at least two days to do justice to the museum. Floor plans are available at the ticket booth. (Labeling is in Spanish and English.)

The crowning glory of Chapultepec Park, the National Museum of Anthropology is not only famed for its vast collection of pre-Hispanic objects, but also for the building's design. The brainchild of architect Pedro Ramírez Vásquez, built in just 19 months between 1963 and 1964, the museum derives its inspiration from Mexico's ancient archaeological sites. Covering around 44,000sq m (473,600sq ft), over a third of which is outdoors, this is a vast archaeological treasure trove. The collection itself began to be amassed in the late 19th century, with many further additions over the years.

INFORMATION

www.mna.inah.gob.mx

✚ 62 A3 ✉ Paseo de la Reforma and Calzada Gandhi, Chapultepec Park ☎ (55) 55 53 63 81/55 53 63 86 🕐 Tue–Sun 9–7 💰 $4.80 except Sun (Sun free to Mexican nationals and therefore very crowded; arrive early) 🚇 Chapultepec, Auditorio or any colectivo along Reforma marked Auditorio ◀ Guided tours in English or Spanish Tue–Sat 9.30–5.30, free, with minimum of 5 people. Audioguide available in English, $6 📖 English and Spanish books, plus some in French and German, and guides to Mexican ruins including maps. Guide books of the museum ($6) 🍽 On-site cafeteria good but pricey ❓ Permission required to photograph (no tripod or flash allowed) $3; $5 for video camera

Above *Main entrance to the museum*
Opposite *This massive statue, outside the main entrance, was thought to be an Aztec rain god or water goddess*

TLALOC?

The large exhibit (almost 9m/30ft tall and weighing 167 tons, ▷ 72) just outside the main entrance was found near San Miguel, close to the town of Texcoco, and thought to be the image of Tlaloc, the Aztec rain god. Latest theories indicate it might possibly be his sister, Chalchiuhtlicue, the water goddess.

WHAT TO SEE

GROUND FLOOR

PRECLÁSICO

The first cultures (Preclassic) of the Valley of México are covered in this room, spanning the years 2300BC to AD100. The miniature female figurines are of particular note, dating from 1700BC to 1300BC. The Tlatilco burial site, reconstructed exactly as it would have been found when excavated, contains the lovely acrobat figure that was found in the grave of a shaman, hinting at the existence of mysterious religious rites.

TEOTIHUACÁN

Displayed here are some of the most important objects found at this site (▷ 188–191), the first great city of the Valley of México. It is immediately obvious that the craftsmanship has become more sophisticated. The stunning turquoise, obsidian and shell-covered stone burial mask as well as the complex incense pot representing Xochipilli (the god of flowers) stand out among other exquisite pieces. Of particular note is the massive full-scale reconstruction of part of the Temple of Quetzalcóatl.

TOLTEC

With pieces from several Toltec cities, most notably Xochitécatl and Tula, this room covers the years between AD750 and 1200. From Tula come the Atlantes of Tula—stone sculptures of warriors with their arms pointing down—and the Chac Mool from Chichén Itzá, a reclining figure with a receptacle on its stomach for sacrificial offerings. From Xochicalco (▷ 187), near Cuernavaca, come the weighty stone columns; note the intricately carved column depicting Tlaloc, god of water, with his characteristically long tongue.

MÉXICA

The Aztec room, displaying stunning objects from perhaps the most bewitching of pre-Hispanic cultures, is the highlight of the museum. Greeting you at the entrance is the Ocelotl-Cuauhxicalli, a jaguar baring its teeth with a hollow in its back for the placing of sacrificial human hearts. The huge statue of Coatlicue, goddess of the earth, shows her wearing a necklace of hands and hearts and a skirt of serpents under which her eagle claw feet protrude.

The undisputed focal point is the 24-ton Piedra del Sol (Sun Stone), also known popularly though not accurately as the Aztec Calendar, the epitome of the cosmological and mathematical knowledge of the people of pre-Hispanic America. This vision of the Aztec universe was found by early colonists, reburied, then rediscovered in 1790. In the middle is the sun god, Tonatiuh, with his tongue shaped like a sacrificial knife.

OAXACA

This room is dedicated to the Zapotec and Mixtec cultures from the Oaxaca Valley, with most pieces coming from Monte Albán (▷ 146–147), a site first developed by the Zapotecs but taken over by the Mixtecs. Be sure to look for the Zapotec jade bat god and the jaguar motif pottery, as well as the rare Mixtec musical instruments, including an intriguing flute made from a human femur.

GOLFO DE MÉXICO

Covering the modern-day regions of Tuxtla, Veracruz and Tabasco, the Gulf Coast room is dedicated to Olmec civilization, a sophisticated culture that preceded Teotihuacán. The colossal heads are the highlights in this room, noted for their mysteriously African features. But look, too, for the handsome sculpture of the distinctive *hombre barbado*, or the wrestler, a wonderfully evocative piece.

Below *Mayan bas-relief from Yaxchilán*

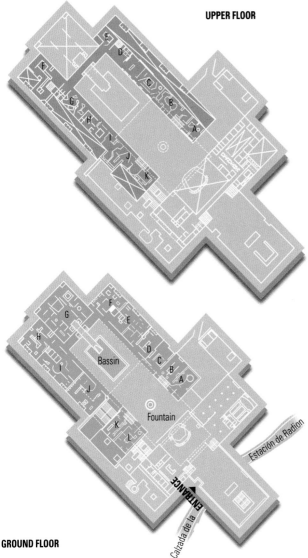

UPPER FLOOR

GALLERY GUIDE
Upper floor: ethnography section,
counterclockwise from right to left:
A: Indigenous peoples of Mexico
B: Gran Nayar
C: Purépecha
D: Los Otomainos
E: Puebla
F: Oaxaca
G: The Gulf of Mexico
H: Lowland Mayans
I: Highland Mayans
J: The Northeast
K: Nahuas

Ground floor: counterclockwise from
the first room on the right:
A: Introduction to Anthropology
B: Cultures of Mesoamerica
C: Origins
D: Preclassic
E: Teotihuacán
F: Toltec
G: México
H: Oaxaca
I: Gulf of Mexico
J: Maya
K: Western cultures
L: Northern cultures

GROUND FLOOR

MAYA

Next comes the room dedicated to Maya culture, whose influence at its apogee between AD300 and 900 spread as far as modern-day Costa Rica. The undisputed highlight of this, one of the better rooms on this side of the museum, is the sunken reproduction of the tomb of Pakal from the Temple of the Inscriptions at Palenque (▷ 152–155), which also includes the spectacular jade death mask of the king.

NORTE (NORTH) AND OCCIDENTE (WEST)

The primarily agricultural cultures of the north and west of Mexico have generally bequeathed a less impressive historical legacy. However, these rooms have an interesting reconstruction of adobe houses from Paquimé (Casas Grandes; ▷ 243) in Chihuahua state, as well as some pottery from Chicomoztoc—the desert site which some historians believe is where the Aztecs originated.

MERCADO DE LA MERCED

This giant indoor market, considered the largest market in the Americas, spills out over several blocks in a riot of commercial activity. It sells everything from fresh market produce to shoes and cheap nylon clothes. Wander south of the *zócalo* and east along Calle República de El Salvador past tiny alleyways crammed with stands and bustling with street vendors.

✚ Off map 63 F3 ✉ Calle Rosario Puerta 4, between calles Santa Escuela and General Anaya ⏰ Daily 7–7

MUSEO ANAHUACALLI

Museo Anahuacalli, also known as the Diego Rivera Museum, was built by the painter to house his large collection of pre-Hispanic sculptures and pottery. The extraordinary pseudo-Mayan tomb, in the shape of a pyramid, was begun in 1933 and finished in 1963, after Rivera's death. It contains a web of small, gloomy passageways opening into rooms through angled, flat-topped Mayan arches. The first floor is a huge art studio displaying some of Rivera's sketches. There are splendid views from the rooftop.

✚ Off map 62 B4 ✉ Calle Museo 150 ☎ (55) 56 17 43 10/56 17 37 97 ⏰ Tue–Sun 10.30–5 🖐 $4.50, with student card $2, free with ticket to Frida Kahlo Museum in Coyoacán (and vice versa) 🚐 *Combi* 29 from the Taxqueña metro to Estadio Azteca 🚌 Bus marked División del Norte from outside Salto del Agua metro

MUSEO DE ARTE CARRILLO-GIL

www.macg.inba.gob.mx

This excellent modern museum houses the private art collection of Álvaro Carrillo-Gil (1899–1974). The renovated building lies north of San Angel's Plaza Jacinto, 10 minutes' walk up Avenida Revolución. The collection, amassed from the 1930s to 1960s, is dominated by paintings by José Clemente Orozco (174), David Alfaro Siqueiros (47) and Diego Rivera (27, mainly of his Cubist period), as well as Carrillo-Gil's own paintings. There are also works by Rodin, Picasso and Klee, along with changing exhibitions of Mexican contemporary art. A central ramp links the building's three floors. There is also a fine selection of 17th- and 18th-century Japanese Ukiyo-e (woodblock prints).

✚ Off map 62 B4 (San Angel) ✉ Avenida Revolución 1608, San Angel ☎ (55) 55 50 62 60 ⏰ Tue–Sun 10–6 🖐 $3 (free Sun)

MUSEO DE LA CIUDAD DE MÉXICO

www.arts-history.mx

Occupying a splendid 18th-century colonial residence, the Museo de la Ciudad, founded in 1964, showcases the city's cultural past and present through temporary exhibitions, educational courses and permanent exhibits such as photographs detailing the construction of the metro system and minor pre-Hispanic and colonial objects. The building consists of two magnificent courtyards built of grey stone and embellished with elaborate cornices. Note also the fine wooden doors. Upstairs there is a chapel built in 1778 and a music room. In the attic is the studio of Joaquín Clausell (1866–1935), a journalist, painter and caricaturist who was exiled in Paris during the Porfirio Díaz dictatorship. His political sketches line the staircase leading up to the attic, and there are copies of the controversial *El Demócrata* newspaper, which he edited. He often hosted meetings of the leading intellectuals and artists of the day in this studio. There is an excellent bookshop at the museum's entrance and on the other side of the road a memorial marks the spot where Hernán Cortés is supposed to have first met the Aztec ruler Moctezuma II.

✚ Off map 63 F3 ✉ Avenida Pino Suárez 30 ☎ (55) 55 42 06 71/55 42 00 83 ⏰ Tue–Sun 10–6 🖐 $2 🚇 Pino Suárez

Left *Museo Anahuacalli was built by painter Diego Rivera in a dramatic setting on the edge of Coyoacán*

MUSEO FRANZ MAYER

www.franzmayer.org.mx

On the northern side of the Alameda two churches flank the Jardín Morelos: Santa Veracruz, built in 1730 and heavily tilting to one side, and San Juan de Dios, with its richly carved baroque exterior and unusual red hexagonal stone slabs. A former hospital is attached to the latter, and it is here that the fabulous collection of applied art belonging to the Franz Mayer Museum is housed. Mayer, a financier who arrived in Mexico from Germany in 1905, was also an avid collector of Mexican crafts and decorative arts. As well as Mexican glass, silver, clocks, furniture, textiles and a fine collection of Talavera ceramics from Puebla, there are European paintings from the 14th to 20th centuries and a library with rare first editions. Note the Mexican 17th-century paintings inlaid with mother-of-pearl and the fine painted screen from the same period, depicting a view over Mexico City. The cloister behind San Juan de Dios, attached to the museum, is now a pleasant café.

✚ 63 E2 ✉ Avenida Hidalgo 45, Plaza de la Santa Veracruz ☎ (55) 55 18 22 66 ◉ Tue–Sun 10–5, Wed 10–7 ✋ $4.50, $2.50 with student card ($0.50 if only visiting the cloister), free Tue ◎ Bellas Artes, Hidalgo

MUSEO NACIONAL DE ANTROPOLOGÍA

▷ 72–75.

MUSEO NACIONAL DE ARTE

www.munal.com.mx

An equestrian statue of Charles IV of Spain, once in the *zócalo*, marks the main entrance to the National Art Museum, built in 1904 and designed by Italian architect Silvio Contri. Inside are magnificent staircases made by the Florentine firm Pignone. Magnificently refurbished in 2003, the museum houses a large collection of Mexican paintings, drawings, sculptures and ceramics from the 16th century to 1950. It's best to start on the second floor in order to keep to chronological order.

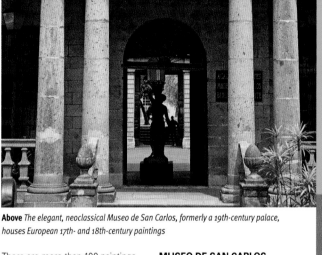

Above *The elegant, neoclassical Museo de San Carlos, formerly a 19th-century palace, houses European 17th- and 18th-century paintings*

There are more than 100 paintings by José Maria Velasco (1840–1912), Diego Rivera's teacher—look for his landscapes in Room 22. Other highlights include the 19th-century photography on the second floor, and the miniature portraits by Hermenegildo Bustos (1832–1907) in Room 23. There are also works by Rivera, Orozco, Siqueiros, Rufino Tamayo, and Tina Modotti.

✚ 63 E2 (inset E2) ✉ Calle Tacuba 8 ☎ (55) 51 30 34 95 ◉ Tue–Sun 10.30–5.30 ✋ $3; free on Sun ◎ Bellas Artes

MUSEO DEL PAPALOTE

This delightful museum, specially designed for children, is an excellent place for them to have fun while learning about the human body, communications and the world we live in. It is full of hands-on, interactive exhibits, including a stomach-churning flight simulation 565km (350 miles) above earth.

✚ Off map 62 A4 ✉ Avenida Constituyentes 268, Bosque de Chapultepec ☎ (55) 52 37 17 73 ◉ Sun–Wed 10–8, Thu 10am–11pm, Fri–Sat 10–10 ✋ $9, IMAX extra ◎ Constituyentes

MUSEO DE SAN CARLOS

www.bellasartes.gob.mx

The Museo de San Carlos has a wide-ranging collection of 17th- and 18th-century European paintings and stages temporary exhibitions. Housed in a fine neoclassical 19th-century palace, its permanent collection is displayed in first-floor galleries around an oval courtyard and contains works by Ingres and Rubens. Look for *Mujeres Bretones a la Orilla del Mar (Women from Brittany on the Sea Shore)* by Manuel Benedito Y Vives (1875–1963), in the first gallery.

During its lifetime the building has served as a residence to Mexican dictator Santa Anna, a school and a cigarette factory. The pretty garden directly behind the museum is dedicated to Latin America's revolutionary Left, with busts of Che Guevara and Cuban student leader Julio Antonio Mella, who was assassinated in Mexico City in 1929.

✚ 63 D2 ✉ Puente de Alvarado 50 ☎ (55) 55 66 80 85 ◉ Wed–Mon 10–6 ✋ $2.50 (free Sun) ◎ Revolución, Hidalgo

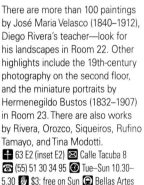

PALACIO DE ITURBIDE

www.arts-history.mx
Next to the Convento San Francisco is the beautifully restored Iturbide Palace, now owned by Mexico's national bank, Banamex. It was built between 1779 and 1784 for the Conde de Valparaíso, and ranks among the city's most elegant baroque buildings. At the time of construction the interior courtyard would have been the most sumptuous in the area, with graceful arches and columns adorned with elaborate masonry. From 1821 to 1823 the palace was the home of the Emperor Agustín de Iturbide, a royalist general who, during the struggle for Independence, changed sides, throwing in his lot with the rebels led by Vicente Guerrero. In 1821 he signed a treaty with the last Spanish viceroy acknowledging Mexican independence and in 1822 declared himself emperor, only to be forced to abdicate a year later, and executed the year after that. It now hosts temporary art exhibitions.

➕ 63 E2 (inset E2) ✉ Avenida Madero 17 ☎ (55) 12 26 01 20 🕐 Daily 10–7 🖐 Free 🚇 Bellas Artes

PALACIO NACIONAL

The National Palace takes up the whole of the eastern side of the zócalo. Built on the site of the Palace of Moctezuma at the time of the Conquest, it has been rebuilt and added to many times; President Calles added the third tier of arches around the central patio in the 1920s. Over the central door hangs the Liberty Bell, rung every year at 11pm on September 15 by the President to commemorate Mexican Independence. Inside, a series of Diego Rivera murals, begun in 1929, are among the artist's finest. The enormous work covering the staircase is a sweeping panorama of Mexican history, *México a Través de los Siglos (Mexico Through the Centuries)*. The right-hand panel depicts pre-Hispanic Mexico with a highly idealized vision of life in Tenochtitlán. The large central panel, finished in 1935, relates Mexican history from the Conquest in 1521 through war and oppression, invasion, Independence and revolution. Almost every figure of consequence through the ages appears here: note Padre Hidalgo waving the banner of Independence and Benito Juárez with his Constitution. The left-hand panel is known as *El Mundo de Hoy y de Mañana (The World Today and Tomorrow)*. Along the first floor frescoes depicts daily life in Aztec Tenochtitlán.

➕ Inset 63 F2 ✉ Plaza de la Constitución ☎ (55) 91 58 12 59 🕐 Mon–Sat 9–6, Sun 9–2 🖐 Free. Some form of ID is essential to enter the building 🚇 Zócalo

PASEO DE LA REFORMA

Cutting across the city diagonally from the Bucareli roundabout to the Bosque de Chapultepec is the wide, tree-lined Paseo de la Reforma, laid out by Emperor Maximilian during the 1860s to emulate the fashionable French 19th-century boulevards. It is lined with fine mansions, banks and offices, luxury hotels and chic boutiques. During the Porfirio Díaz dictatorship a series of monuments relating to key moments in the country's history was added: first (from north to south) is a statue of Christopher Columbus at Glorieta Colón; next, at the crossing with Avenida Insurgentes, is Cuauhtémoc, the last Aztec emperor; and finally, at the intersection with calles Tiber and Florencia, a marble column—45m (148ft) high and supporting a golden winged Victory—representing Independence, inaugurated in 1910 and known as "El Angel." One block north of Paseo de la Reforma, on Calle Rio Lerma 35, is the Museo Carranza (daily 9–6), a 1908 mansion once home to Presidente Venustiano Carranza, author of the 1917 Constitution. It is now a museum about his life and the 1910 Revolution.

➕ 62 C3 🚌 Any bus from Chapultepec or from the western end of the Alameda marked Paseo de la Reforma

PLAZA GARIBALDI

Go to Plaza Garibaldi on a Friday or Saturday night, when up to 200 *mariachis* in their traditional costume of sombrero, tight silver-embroidered trousers, pistol and *sarape* blanket will serenade you (for a fee). The whole square throbs with life, although it would be wise to keep a close eye on your belongings in the crowds. Should you find yourself here during the day wander east down Calle Honduras and browse the overwhelming range of bridal shops and stands selling bouquets, garlands and all possible other wedding accessories.

➕ 63 E1–F1 🚇 Garibaldi

Left *Statue of a* mariachi *in Plaza Garibaldi*
Opposite *Diego River's stunning panoramic mural depicts Mexican history*

HUELGA

Above *Plaza de las Tres Culturas is the site of the Aztec's main market and ceremonial area; the ruins are open to the public*

PLAZA SANTO DOMINGO

Two blocks north of the cathedral is a small plaza surrounded by fine colonial buildings. There is the Antigua Aduana (former customs house) on the east side; the Portales de Santo Domingo on the west side, where public scribes and owners of hand-operated printing presses still carry on their business; the Convento de Santo Domingo (1737), in Mexican baroque, on the north side; and the old Edificio de la Inquisición, where the tribunals of the Inquisition were held, at the northeast corner. The latter is now the Museo de la Medicina Mexicana (daily 10–6; closed during university holidays), housing, among other exhibits, an entire room dedicated to skin diseases—strictly for those with a strong stomach.

➕ 63 F2 🚇 Allende

PLAZA DE LAS TRES CULTURAS

Lázaro Cárdenas leads to Santa María la Redonda, at the end of which is Plaza Santiago de Tlatelolco, the city's oldest plaza after the *zócalo* and one that holds great symbolism for Mexicans. The square is now known as the Plaza de las Tres Culturas since it shows elements of Aztec, colonial and modern architecture. It was here that the Aztecs held their main market, and on it, in 1524, the Franciscans built a huge church and convent using the stones of the Aztec temples. What's left of the original market and ceremonial area has been restored and is open to the public.

Mexico's modern era is represented by the massive, multifloor Nonoalco-Tlatelolco public housing scheme (heavily damaged in the 1985 earthquake) and the Mexican Foreign Ministry looming over the ruins. A plaque sums up Tlatelolco's significance in the Mexican psyche: "On 13 August 1521, Tlatelolco, heroically defended by Cuauhtémoc, fell to Hernán Cortés. It was neither a triumph nor a defeat, but the painful birth of the *mestizo* race that is Mexico today." The poignancy is reinforced by a memorial to the massacre of October 1968, in which students were killed in clashes with police.

➕ Off map 63 F1 ✉ Eje Central Lázaro Cárdenas, Esq. Flores Magón ☎ Zona Arqueológica Tlatelolco (55) 55 83 02 95 🕐 Daily 8–6 🎫 Free; donations encouraged 🚇 Tlatelolco

POLANCO

North of the Bosque de Chapultepec lies the trendy area known as Polanco, laid out in a grid pattern. The area is one of the most chic districts in the city, and includes the striking Camino Real Hotel (▷ 100), worth a walk-in visit. Also here are exclusive private residences, commercial art galleries, fashion stores and expensive restaurants—collectively a monument to the consumer society. One glaring example of this is the huge Palacio de Hierro department store at the corner of calles Molière and Homero. There is little of cultural value with the exception of the Sala de Arte Siqueiros, on Tres Picos 29 (Tue–Sun 10–6) and a couple of unremarkable modern churches.

➕ Off map 62 A2 ❓ *Colectivos* marked Horacio from metro Chapultepec or Polanco

SECRETARÍA DE EDUCACIÓN PÚBLICA

The Ministry of Education, three blocks north of the *zócalo*, was built in 1922. Among frescoes by different artists are some by Diego Rivera; they illustrate the lives and sufferings of the common people as well as satirizing the rich. Look for *Día de los Muertos (Day of the Dead)* on the first floor (far left in the second courtyard) and, on the second floor, *El Pan Nuestro (Our Daily Bread)*, showing the poor at supper, in contrast to *El Banquete de Wall Street (The Wall Street Banquet)* and *La Cena del Capitalista (The Capitalist's Supper)*. A passageway connects the Secretaría with the courtyards of the older Ex-Aduana de Santo Domingo (Mon–Fri 9–6), where there is a Siqueiros mural, *Patriots and Parricides*.

➕ Inset 63 F2 ✉ Entrance on Avenida Argentina 28 ☎ (55) 53 28 10 97 🕐 Mon–Fri 9–6 🎫 Free 🚇 Zócalo

TEMPLO MAYOR

▷ 82–83.

TEMPLO DE SAN FRANCISCO

Opposite the Casa de los Azulejos is the Templo de San Francisco, founded in 1525 by the "Apostles of Mexico," the first 12 Franciscans to reach the country. By far the most important church in colonial days, Mass here was attended by the viceroys themselves, including Hernán Cortés. For 200 years the monastery was plagued by earthquakes, modifications and demolitions and the church we see now dates from the rebuilding that took place in 1716.

➕ 63 E2 (inset E2) ✉ Avenida Madero ☎ (55) 55 18 46 90 🕐 Daily 7am–8pm 🎫 Free 🚇 Bellas Artes

SAN ANGEL

This suburb of plazas, narrow streets and attractive colonial mansions is home to the Bazar Sábado, a splendid Saturday folk art and curiosity market. Villa Obregón, popularly known as San Angel, lies 13km (8 miles) southwest of central Mexico City, with its narrow, cobbled streets and the charm of an era now largely past. Most of the distinguished architecture in the area is from the 19th century.

Many visitors come for the Saturday Bazar Sábado, but the area has plenty to offer on other days. Look for the triple domes of the Iglesia del Carmen, covered with painted tiles, and the domes of the former Convento del Carmen, now the Museo Colonial del Carmen (Tue–Sun 10–5), which houses 17th- and 18th-century furniture and paintings. Opposite, on Calle Revolución, is the Centro Cultural San Angel, which stages exhibitions, concerts and lectures (for information tel (55) 56 16 12 54). See also the beautifully furnished and preserved old Casa del Risco (Tue–Sun 10–5), near the Bazar Sábado, on Callejón de la Amargura, former home of Mexican intellectual and politician Don Isidro Fabela (1882–1964). Look for the peculiar fountain made from mother-of-pearl, old plates and broken vases in the patio.

THE ARTISTIC QUARTER

Also worth a visit is the Iglesia de San Jacinto (access in the southeast corner of Plaza San Jacinto), first built in 1596 when this area was an outlying village known as Tenanitla. Don't miss the immaculate walled garden behind the church, a popular spot for wedding photos.

The Museo Estudio Diego Rivera (Tue–Sun 10–6) at Avenida Altavista y Calle Diego Rivera, opposite the San Angel Inn (▷ 99), is where Rivera and Frida Kahlo lived and worked. Actually two houses joined by an overhead walkway, the innovative design is the work of Juan O'Gorman. It's worth remembering just how daring his use of concrete and stark angular lines would have been in this traditional district in the early 1930s. The museum contains several works by Rivera, as well as belongings and memorabilia, although as you ascend the narrow spiral staircase and pass through the diminutive rooms it's slightly difficult to imagine the larger-than-life Rivera fitting in here. Until, that is, you reach his wonderfully well-appointed studio, any artist's dream.

INFORMATION
✚ Off map 62 C4 🚌 Bus from Chapultepec Park Ⓜ Miguel Angel de Quevedo

Above *San Angel has attracted many artists over the years, including Diego Rivera and Frida Kahlo who lived here*

INFORMATION

✛ Inset 63 F2 ✉ Calle Seminario 4 and Calle Moneda, entrance in northeast corner of the *zócalo* ☎ (55) 55 42 02 56 🕐 Tue–Sun 9–6 👣 Museum and temple $4.80, students free with ISIC (free Sun). $3.50 to use video camera 🚇 Zócalo 🖐 Guided group tours in English and Spanish available. Reservations necessary. Minimum 10 people. $18 per person 📖 Bookshop in museum 🍴 Drinks and snacks

TIPS

» Pass by in the evening when the pyramid is flood-lit.
» Leave plenty of time for the museum: it is just as interesting as the ruins.

Above *Thousands of captives from rival tribes were sacrificed at Templo Mayor, represented by stone skulls in the wall*

INTRODUCTION

The Templo Mayor was the spiritual and ceremonial heart of Tenochtitlán, former capital of the Aztec Empire. Its fascinating and informative museum has reconstructions of how Tenochtitlán would have looked at its height. To the eastern side of the cathedral lie the partially excavated foundations of the greatest temple of Tenochtitlán, capital of the Aztecs. The entrance to the site is on Calle Seminario. Once inside, the fixed route takes you along raised metal platforms and walkways from which you can view the ruins. Leave enough time for the museum at the end of the circuit (entered on the same ticket), as it helps put in context what you have seen. As well as reconstructions of life in Tenochtitlán, the museum contains many beautiful sculptures found during various excavations.

The layout of the museum's eight rooms aims to reproduce symbolically the Templo Mayor's two-part structure: start by ascending the right-hand side of the building through Rooms 1 to 4, dedicated to Huitzilpochtli (god of war), then descend the left-hand side through Rooms 5 to 8, dedicated to Tlaloc (god of rain). The rooms cover all aspects of life in Tenochtitlán, from the Aztec religion, war and sacrifice to trade and agriculture.

Although it was known that Tenochtitlán's ceremonial fulcrum lay under central Mexico City, it was believed that the Templo Mayor, or Teocalli, lay directly beneath the cathedral. However, in 1978 workmen discovered an enormous stone disc depicting the goddess of the moon, Coyolxauhqui, in the northeastern corner of the *zócalo*. Further exploration revealed the hidden foundations of Teocalli. The existing buildings were cleared and excavations begun. In 1987, the adjoining museum was opened to house the sculptures and reliefs found in the main pyramid of Tenochtitlán. The building, in the middle of the city's colonial heart, was designed by the architect Pedro Ramírez Vazquez to be as discreet as possible.

According to the Spanish chroniclers who arrived in the city with Hernán Cortés, the grandeur of the entire sacred complex, with its gleaming white stucco pyramids and frescoes depicting great battles, was overwhelming. What you see here are the bare foundations, so it can only be imagined how great this temple would have looked at the height of the empire.

WHAT TO SEE

ETAPA IV (ARCHAEOLOGICAL SITE)

The different stages of construction have been categorized into *etapas* (stages) to identify from which era each building belongs. Due to the Aztec practice of building a new temple every 52 years at the completion of their calendar cycle, seven have been identified piled on top of each other. Note here the small platform with four serpent heads, dating from 1486 to 1502, that would have marked the foot of one of the two wide staircases that led to the sanctuaries on top. The enormous undulating serpents at the north and south corners of this platform still retain traces of their original red, blue and yellow, and date from the temple's second expansion between 1469 and 1481.

Room 1: The archaeological excavations of the temple: an explanation of the process used to excavate the Templo Mayor.

Room 2: War and Sacrifice: an insight into the importance of war during the growth of the Aztec Empire, and the role of sacrifice.

Room 3: Trade and tax systems: information on the peoples conquered by the Aztecs and how trading relationships developed after war.

Room 4: Huitzilopochtli, god of war. Of note are the huge stone eagle warriors.

Room 5: Tlaloc, god of rain.

Room 6: Flora and fauna of Tenochtitlán: animals the Aztecs would have been familiar with.

Room 7: Agricultural methods: includes a model of how the Aztec market would have looked.

Room 8: Arrival of the Spanish: this room focuses on the fall of Tenochtitlán and displays exhibits found on the site from the colonial era as well as later Aztec pieces.

Left *One of the huge stone eagle warriors*
Below *Part of the museum's large collection of Aztec pottery*

THE COYOLXAUHQUI DISC (MUSEUM VESTIBULE)
The museum's central feature is the find that sparked off excavations—the vast, circular disc, weighing about 8 tons and depicting the dismembered body of Coyolxauhqui, who was killed by her brother Huitzilopochtli. According to Aztec myth, Coyolxauhqui's mother became miraculously pregnant. Desperately ashamed, Coyolxauhqui vowed to kill her mother to restore honor. But before she could, her brother Huitzilopochtli jumped out of his mother's womb fully grown and armed and cut his sister to pieces in revenge, before throwing her down a mountain. Thus Coyolxauhqui is always portrayed dismembered and lying at the foot of the Temple of Huitzilopochtli.

THE TZOMPANTLI (THE VESTIBULE)
The spectacular replica of a *tzompantli* (wall of skulls) is on your right as you enter the vestibule. Although the structure has been rebuilt to demonstrate the structure of an Aztec *tzompantli* and is not the temple's original, the skulls themselves were found on the site during the excavations, which have been in place since 1978. All Aztec temples included a *tzompantli*, where the skulls of sacrificed victims were traditionally placed.

THE TEOTIHUACÁN MASK (ROOM 3)
This striking dark green stone mask with its beady black eyes and one earring is one of many such masks originating from Teotihuacán. These pieces impressed the Aztecs with their expressive features and superb craftsmanship. The mask is beautifully inlaid with obisidian and shells.

THE OLMEC MASK (ROOM 3)
Below *The* tzompantli *(wall of skulls) is a replica, but the skulls themselves were found on the excavation site*

Similarly, this unique mask, 3,000 years old and originating from the Olmec area of coastal Veracruz, was found in one of the most sacred inner rooms of the temple. The Aztecs recognized its artistic significance and certainly would have venerated such a precious and ancient object.

XOCHIMILCO

Xochimilco—"the place where flowers grow" in Nahuatl—lies 28km (17 miles) southeast of central Mexico City. It is an extraordinary network of canals and islands, and an important supplier of market produce and flowers to the capital. This is the one place where it is still possible to envisage the ancient city as it was: built on islands in the lake interconnected by causeways, with a floating commercial life against a vibrant backdrop. In order to make the lake fertile, the Aztecs developed a form of agriculture using *chinampas*, "floating gardens," formed by mud and reeds. Nowadays Xochimilco is famed for its carnival-like atmosphere on Sundays, when brightly painted punt-like boats laden with hundreds of daytrippers from the capital jostle along the waterways amid a riot of color and music. As you glide down canals past luxuriant gardens, smaller boats carrying anything from fruit and jewelry to entire *mariachi* bands will sell their wares, or music, for a fee. In Xochimilco town, the Saturday market still sells plump, succulent fruit and a profusion of flowers, as it has done for centuries.

On the main square is the town's indisputable architectural jewel, the Iglesia de San Bernardino de Siena.

Begun in 1535 and completed in 1595, it contains a magnificent Renaissance altarpiece, one of the oldest and best preserved in the Americas. Its convent, built by the Franciscans in 1585, has finely detailed masonry.

➕ Off map 62 C4 🕐 Official tariffs operate, although prices actually depend on your ability to negotiate. A small punt seats 12 and generally costs $20 an hour 🚌 Take a bus or *colectivo* (any heading south down Avenida Insurgentes), or the metro to Tasqueña, and from there get the *tren ligero* to Xochimilco at the end of the line 🚤 There are seven *embarcaderos* (landing stages) in the town, the largest of which are Fernando Celada and Nuevo Nativitas

ZÓCALO

The vast main square, whose official name is Plaza de la Constitución, is the city's political and religious heart. Its name comes from the monument to Independence that was supposed to stand in the middle of the square. However, as General Santa Anna only got as far as erecting the statue's base, the square became known popularly as "the plinth"—the *zócalo*. On the north side sits the cathedral (▷ 69) and to the east is the Palacio Nacional (▷ 78). Opposite are the Portales de los Mercaderes (Arcades of the Merchants), where small shops and businesses have traded since 1524. Opposite the cathedral is the Monte de Piedad, a government-run pawn shop (Mon–Fri 8.30–6, Sat 8.30–1) in a 16th-century building supposedly used by Moctezuma II.

There is a continuous stream of entertainment: groups performing pre-Hispanic spectacles in costume dance to the pounding of drums while street entertainers and vendors vie for attention. It is the place to hold official ceremonies and celebrations, demonstrations and marches. Activists use the central space as a campsite, displaying banners facing the Palacio Nacional.

The ceremonial lowering of the flag in the middle of the square takes place daily at 6pm, accompanied by much pomp and circumstance. It is raised again at 6am.

➕ 63 F2 (inset F2) 🚇 Zócalo

ZONA ROSA

In the politically charged late 1960s an area of the Juárez district came to be known as the Pink Zone, a part of town that was bohemian and hedonistic and saw itself as non-political and non-partisan—neither red nor white. The area, between Chapultepec and the historic heart, continues to support an impressive range of restaurants, nightclubs, hotels, and bars. Although it lost ground to Polanco after the 1985 earthquake, it has since seen something of a revival, with new shops, internet cafés and European-style streetside restaurants opening up. While the area has no obvious visitor attractions, it's ideal for eating out and bar-hopping—and its size means you can easily negotiate it on foot. Multilingual tourist police patrol the streets but at night it's advisable to travel by taxi.

➕ 62 B3 ✉ Between Paseo de la Reforma and Avenida Chapultepec 🚇 Sevilla, Insurgentes, Cuauhtémoc

Above *Brightly decorated boats glide along Xochimilco's canals laden with people and musicians*

EXPLORING MEXICO CITY'S CENTRO HISTÓRICO

The heart of Mexico City, with its Aztec, colonial and modern architecture, is a lively mix of ancient and modern—layered and packed together in a fascinating profusion of urban life.

THE WALK

Distance: 1.6km (1 mile)
Time: 3–4 hours
Start/end at: Plaza de la Constitición (Zócalo), Mexico City

HOW TO GET THERE

Take Line 2 of the metro to Zócalo.

★ If you're an early riser, start with breakfast at the rooftop terrace restaurant of the Majestic Hotel (▷ 101) and look out across the spectacular view of the huge *zócalo*. The main square of the city has much to delay the curious, with the cathedral on the north side and the Palacio Nacional to the east.

Leave the square at the northeast corner. Head east on Calle Moneda.

❶ Cobbled Calle Moneda is criss-crossed with old streets packed with the noise and trade of a street market and fringed by the Palacio Arzobispal, Palacio Nacional (▷ 78) and Museo de las Culturas.

After three blocks, just past Iglesia de Santa Ines, a left turn up Calle Academia leads to the Museo José Luis Cuevas.

❷ Housed in the cloister of a former convent, the Museo José Luis Cuevas displays exhibits of the erotic works of the artist. A huge bronze, *La Giganta*, dominates the central patio.

After two blocks you reach the richly carved facade and fine towers of the 17th-century Iglesia de La Santísima Trinidad. On leaving the church turn right for two blocks, then left down Calle de Mixcalco to arrive at the southern side of the Plaza de Loreto after one block.

❸ The Plaza de Loreto is an attractive square with a fountain in the middle. The Iglesia de Santa Teresa la Nueva looks on from the east, while from the north, the Iglesia de Loreto is a fine example of primitive neoclassicism.

Continuing west on Calle de Mixcalco, now called 2a Calle del Maestro Justo Sierra, your stroll takes in the Sociedad Mexicana de Geografía y Estadística (Mexican Society for Geography and Statistics) on the left, the Antigua Colegio de San Ildefonso (No. 16) on the right, and back on the left a superb view—albeit somewhat obscured by railings—of architecture spanning the centuries, with the Templo Mayor in the foreground and the cathedral in the distance. With your back to the monumental architecture, turn right up República de Argentina—you're in the home of the pirate CD now and the competing sounds of salsa, merengue, house and hip hop are bewildering. After two blocks turn left along República de Venezuela to reach Plaza Santo Domingo (▷ 80).

❹ On entering the plaza, immediately to your left is the Secretaría de Educación Pública (▷ 80), home to a bonanza of Rivera murals. To your right is the Edificio de la Inquisición, now housing the Museo de la Medicina Mexicana (▷ 80), which describes the history of Mexican medicine. On the west side of the plaza, printers hand-print invitations to weddings and family occasions. The Mexican baroque Convento de Santo Domingo overlooks the busy plaza of artists and workers.

After exploring the square, continue down Belisario Dominguez. If you're in need of refreshment, drop in at the Hosteria Santo Domingo (No. 72), Mexico City's oldest restaurant. Turn left at República de Chile, heading south for three blocks, then turn right onto Calle Tacuba.

❺ Now in a more traditional retail part of the city, you pass Metro Allende and, shortly on the right, Café Tacuba, the popular haunt of Mexico's lunch crowd. Farther on, to the right, is the Museo Nacional de Arte (▷ 77), which faces the late 18th-century Palacio de Minería.

One block west is the magnificent Post Office, its gilding sparkling in the midday sun, and then you reach the Alameda (▷ 67).

❻ This large city park with overgrown trees is the best place for a quiet moment in the sprawling, magnificent metropolis. Once the site of an Aztec market, the name

Alameda comes from the *álamaos* or poplar trees planted in the square in the 16th century by Viceroy Luis de Velasco. On the eastern side is the art nouveau facade of the Palacio de Bellas Artes, and to the southeast is the 44-floor Torre Latinoamericana, a survivor of countless earthquakes since its completion in 1956.

Leave the Alameda at the southeast corner and head east along Calle Francisco Madero. Turn left at the first small street, Condesa Marconi, pausing to pop into the ornate Casa de los Azulejos (▷ 69), decorated with Talavera tiles. Continue north and turn right on Calle 5 de Mayo, looking in on Bar La Opera, at the first intersection with Calle Filomeno Mata, where Pancho Villa blasted a hole through the ceiling before being assassinated in 1923. A couple of blocks farther east along Calle 5 de Mayo are the divine handmade sweet creations of Dulcería de Celaya (▷ 90–91), which you can nibble at on your return to the *zócalo*.

TOURIST INFORMATION
Northwest corner of the *zócalo*.

WHERE TO EAT
CAFÉ TACUBA
▷ 96.

CASA DE LOS AZULEJOS
▷ 69.

HOSTERIA SANTO DOMINGO
Fine traditional dining; or just pop in for a snack.
✉ Belisario Dominguez 72 ☎ (55) 55 26 52 76 🕐 Daily 9am–10pm

MAJESTIC HOTEL
▷ 101.

SUSHI ROLL
▷ 99.

PLACES TO VISIT
If you plan to visit any of the places of interest on the walk you will need proof of ID with a photograph—a photocopy will often be sufficient.

MUSEO NACIONAL DE LAS CULTURAS
✉ Calle Moneda 13 🕐 Tue–Sun 10–6 ✋ Free

MUSEO JOSÉ LUIS CUEVAS
✉ Calle Academia 13 🕐 Tue–Sun 10–5 ✋ $2, free Sun

MUSEO DE LA MEDICINA MEXICANA
✉ Republica de Brasil 33 ☎ (55) 29 75 42 🕐 Daily 10–6, closed during university holidays ✋ Free

TORRE LATINOAMERICANA
✉ Corner of Calle Madero 🕐 Daily 9am–10pm ✋ $5

Opposite *Market stands set up in front of the cathedral in the zócalo*

SAN ANGEL AND COYOACÁN

The figures of Frida Kahlo, Diego Rivera and Hernán Cortés stand tall in Mexican history. They each called the southern suburb of Coyoacán home, and a walk through the area takes in the city's past.

THE WALK

Distance: 7km (4.5 miles)
Time: 3–4 hours
Start at: Museo Estudio Diego Rivera
End at: Plaza Hidalgo or Plaza de la Conchita

HOW TO GET THERE

Take a taxi from Miguel Angel de Quevedo (Line 3) or Barranca del Muerto to reach Museo Estudio Diego Rivera.

★ From this Modernist museum (▷ 81), built by the Mexican functionalist architect Juan O'Gorman, walk up to the San Angel Inn and, looking straight ahead, take Lazcano, spurring off the main road diagonally. Continue ahead and turn right at the end of the road down Calle de Reina, a cobbled street with balconies festooned with flowers. Turn left along Calle del General Aureliano Rivera, then take the second right to Plaza San Jacinto.

❶ Plaza San Jacinto is a whirlwind of activity, especially at the Bazar del Sábado, a great place to pick up souvenirs and handicrafts, or have a bite to eat or a drink. Just off the plaza is the 16th-century Iglesia de San Jacinto.

Continue round the plaza and leave from the southeastern corner, heading down Calle del Dr. Gálvez, a short road of just 50m (55 yards) that meets the busy Avenida Revolución. Cross over here and turn left. Continue for about 200m (220 yards), then look for a gap in the stone wall through an arched doorway that leads to the church and the Museo Colonial del Carmen.

❷ This 17th-century former Carmelite monastery is now a museum housing colonial furniture and art.

Turn right out of the courtyard, cross the first road and take the right fork, cutting the corner to turn right onto Avenida La Paz. At Avenida Insurgentes Sur, cross over and cut through the Parque de la Bombilla, taking the left fork after passing the Monumento a General Alvaro Obregón.

❸ This memorial commemorates the assassination of the Mexican president in 1928 during the Cristero Revolt.

Head out of the park behind the monument and turn right at the cobbled street (away from the main road) and in 20m (22 yards) turn left, before the guarded checkpoint, toward Plaza Federico Gamboa, across Calle Chimalistac.

❹ The small, shaded Plaza Federico Gamboa hides the 17th-century chapel of San Sebastián Mártir, which has a fine baroque altarpiece. The square is home to artists and writers, including Gabriel Garcia Marquez (born 1928).

Continue through the plaza, turn left at the intersection with Callejon San Angelo, then cross over Miguel Angel de Quevedo to join Calle Allende before turning right onto Avenida Arenal which, on crossing Avenida Universidad, becomes Avenida Francisco Sosa.

Opposite *The Museo Frida Kahlo*

right and continue straight ahead, taking the third left down Calle Allende and passing the Museo Frida Kahlo again to return to the Plaza Hidalgo. A short extension down Calle Higuera leads to the Plaza de la Conchita.

❾ Overlooking Plaza de la Conchita is the exquisite facade of the Iglesia de la Conchita, and to the southwest the Casa de La Malinche, the home of the mistress of Spanish conquistador Hernán Cortés (▷ 34).

TOURIST INFORMATION
✉ Avenida Revolución at Madero
☎ (55) 56 16 20 97

WHERE TO EAT
SAN ANGEL INN
Top-class dining in the former Carmelite monastery (▷ 99).
✉ Calle Diego Rivera 50 ☎ (55) 56 16 05 37
🕐 Mon–Sat 12.30–3am, Sun 1–9.30

PLACES TO VISIT
MUSEO COLONIAL DEL CARMEN
✉ Avenida Revolución 4 and 6 ☎ (55) 56 16 28 16 🕐 Tue–Sun 10–5 ✋ $4

CASA DE LEÓN TROTSKY
✉ Calle Río Churubusco 410 ☎ (55) 55 54 06 87 🕐 Tue–Sun 10–4.45 ✋ $4

MUSEO FRIDA KAHLO
✉ Londres 247 ☎ (55) 55 54 59 99
🕐 Tue–Sun 10–6 ✋ $4.50

❺ To the side of a small bridge crossing Avenida Río Magdalena is the 17th-century Capilla de San Antonio Panzacola, at the end of Avenida Francisco Sosa, one of the oldest streets in Latin America, lined with balconies hung with flowers, and ornate doorways and arches.

Continue east and at Calle Salvador Novo turn right for a quick visit to the Museo Nacional de la Acuarela. Back on Avenida Francisco Sosa, the road heads west, passing the shady Plaza Santa Catarina before arriving at Jardín Centenario—the heart of Coyoacán.

❻ The garden and nearby Plaza Hidalgo to the east form one of the city's great meeting places. Architecturally the tone is set by the 18th-century Palacio de Cortés to the north, and to the southwest by the bold exterior of the 16th-century Templo de San Juan Bautista, ornately decorated with frescoes and gilded altars. On any day of the week the plaza hums and stirs, stepping up a notch on weekends when all of Mexico appears to stroll through the street fairs, enjoying live music and street performers. From here, head to the eastern side of Plaza Hidalgo and turn left down Calle Allende. Passing between Parque Allende and the market.

❼ In six blocks you will reach the Museo Frida Kahlo, the long-time home of Mexico's best-known artist.

If you're tiring, head back down the street to Jardín Centenario. But a short trip left out of the museum, taking the third left up Calle Morelos for three blocks, leads to Casa de León Trotsky.

❽ The exiled Russian revolutionary made his home here in 1937, where he was eventually murdered in 1940. You can see the bullet holes of a previous attempt on his life and in the high-walled garden is the tomb where his ashes are laid.

Leave the Trotsky Museum, turn

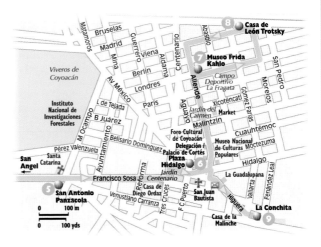

REGIONS   MEXICO CITY • WALK

Above *Mexican folk art and crafts from all over the country are popular souvenirs*

SHOPPING

THE AMERICAN BOOKSTORE
This is Mexico City's oldest English-language bookshop and by far the best place to pick up some vacation reading.
✉ Boulevard 23, between Calle Madero and Calle 16 de Septiembre ☎ (55) 55 12 03 06 ⦿ Mon–Sat 10–7 Ⓜ Allende, Zócalo

ARTESANÍAS DEL CENTRO
You can always find an interesting buy in this curious little establishment crammed with paintings, scented candles, silver crosses, images of the Virgin Mary, clocks and even the odd José Guadalupe Posada-style skeleton.
✉ Calle Palma Norte 506-F ☎ (55) 55 12 04 47 ⦿ Mon–Sat 10–8 Ⓜ Allende

BRIQUETTE AU CHOCOLAT
This Parisian-style chocolatier in the Condesa district stocks a divine range of exquisitely presented sweets and chocolates, both European and Mexican. Superbly made gift boxes are available. Try the almond Olives de Provence.
✉ Calle Fernando Montes de Oca 81C, corner with Calle Yautepec ☎ (55) 52 11 02 76 ⦿ Mon–Sat 10–8.30 Ⓜ Juanacatlan

CENTRO SANTA FE
The largest shopping mall in all Mexico makes its home in the city's ritzy Santa Fe district. The center's 300 tenants include department stores, shops, clothing boutiques, restaurants and a movie theater.
✉ Avenida Vasco de Quiroga 3800, Santa Fe ⦿ Sun–Fri 11–8, Sat 11–9 🚌 From the Tacubaya metro station take any bus marked "Santa Fe"

LA CIUDADELA
If you missed out on a purchase somewhere else on your trip, you will most likely find it again here. Selling crafts from all regions of the country, La Ciudadela comprises row upon row of pottery, jewelry and indigenous clothes stands. Prices are not much higher than in the provinces, but bargaining won't get you far.
✉ Calle Balderas 95 ⦿ Mon–Sat 11–7, Sun 11–5 Ⓜ Balderas

COLECCIÓN BELLAS ARTES MÚSICA
This is one of the best places in the country to buy Mexican classical and traditional music, including an excellent collection of Manuel Ponce piano music, as well as a comprehensive selection of western classical music and jazz. The staff are well informed and can recommend the best CDs of Mexican music.
✉ Lobby of the Palacio de Bellas Artes, Avenida Hidalgo ☎ (55) 55 10 15 98/55 12 25 93 ⦿ Tue–Sun 11–7 (later on performance nights) Ⓜ Bellas Artes

COYOACÁN CRAFTS MARKET
Sundays are packed in Coyoacán when the suburb comes to life and the hippie crafts market takes over the Plaza Hidalgo. Mexican embroidered clothing, rainsticks, jewelry, sandals, incense and candles can be found here, to the accompaniment of music. Food stands line the sides of the Jardin Centenario and the cafés and restaurants spill out onto the sidewalk (pavement). Finding a table can be tricky so it is a good idea to reserve in advance.
✉ Plaza Hidalgo ⦿ Sat–Sun 10–7 Ⓜ Viveros

DANIEL ESPINOSA JEWELRY
Top-quality jewelry from one of Mexico's most highly acclaimed young designers is showcased here. Espinosa has exhibited his work in

the US and Europe. Expect to pay high prices for the original designs and fine workmanship.
✉ Calle Tamaulipas 72, Condesa ☎ (55) 52 11 39 94 🕓 Mon–Sat 11–8 Ⓜ Juanacatlan

DULCERÍA DE CELAYA
Founded in 1874, this little pastry shop displays its traditional Mexican sweets in glass cabinets in an elaborate belle époque interior. The specialty is *Rompope*, a sweet concoction made of milk, sugar, egg yolk and cinnamon that you add to rum. Among the other mouthwatering delicacies are limes stuffed with coconut, *turrones* and *suspiros meringues*—fluffy meringue puffs.
✉ Avenida 5 de Mayo, 39 ☎ (55) 55 21 17 87 🕓 Mon–Sun 10.30–7.30 Ⓜ Allende, Zócalo

ESSENCIAS Y PERFUMES EUROPEOS
A popular perfume factory whose walls are lined with plastic bottles, this shop creates exact replicas of the famous designer brands at a fraction of the price. Find Coco Chanel, Calvin Klein, Nina Ricci and Lancôme, among many others.
✉ Calle Tacuba 54 and 72 ☎ (55) 55 10 13 66/55 12 18 72 🕓 Mon–Sat 10–7 Ⓜ Allende

FONART (FONDO NACIONAL PARA EL FOMENTO DE LAS ARTESANÍAS)
www.fonart.gob.mx
The best quality textiles, pottery and silver from all over Mexico are sold in this wonderful crafts shop on the west side of the Alameda. Founded in 1974, FONART aims to rescue, promote and diffuse the traditional crafts of all the Mexican states and peoples. The products are fairly traded and the organization is well worth supporting. Prices are relatively high, but the excellent quality merits them.
✉ Avenida Júarez 89 ☎ (55) 55 21 01 71 🕓 Mon–Fri 10–7, Sat 10–6, Sun 10–4 Ⓜ Hidalgo

GANDHI BELLAS ARTES
A very popular and well-stocked bookshop with branches around the city. The Bellas Artes branch has the widest range of English-language books. Also very good for CDs, videos, guides and maps.
✉ Avenida Juárez 4 ☎ (55) 26 25 06 06 🕓 Mon–Sat 10–9, Sun 11–8 Ⓜ Bellas Artes

LAGUNILLA
This open area of *tianguis* (stands) laden with antiques, books and bric-à-brac rivals La Merced in size and diversity. It is a great place to wander on a Sunday when the atmosphere is festive and bargains are snapped up with panache and much shouting.
✉ Calle Rayon, two blocks north of Plaza Garibaldi 🕓 Mon–Sat 9–8, Sun 10–7 Ⓜ Plaza Garibaldi

LIBROS Y ARTE
This excellent chain of literary and art bookshops has its largest branch in the Palacio de Bellas Artes, with a large selection of books on Mexican art and anthropology, travel guides, children's books, posters and videos.
✉ Palacio de Bellas Artes, Avenida Hidalgo ☎ (55) 55 21 97 60 🕓 Daily 10–7 (later on performance nights) Ⓜ Bellas Artes

MERCADO DE LA MERCED
You're sure to find something to your liking at this mecca for serious shoppers. It's the city's biggest market and there's something for all. Load up on exotic spices, colorful shawls, gorgeous pottery, embroidered dresses, and authentic arts and crafts. Housed in several modern buildings, shops also line the streets all the way to the *zocálo*.
✉ Circunvalacion between General Anaya and Adolfo Gurrion 🕓 Daily 7–6

PALACIO DEL HIERRO
This huge chrome-and-glass structure at the intersection of Molière with Homero houses a selection of global designer brands, including the expensive but ever fragrant Crabtree & Evelyn toiletries. There's also a very good food hall.

✉ Calle Molière 222, Polanco ☎ (55) 52 83 72 00 🕓 Sun–Fri 11–8.30, Sat 11–9 Ⓜ Polanco

PARQUE ALAMEDA
Next door to the Sheraton Hotel, this glittering shopping mall houses coffee shops and expensive perfumeries and sports shops.
✉ Avenida Juárez 🕓 Daily 8am–9pm (shop times vary) Ⓜ Hidalgo, Juárez

PERFUMERÍA EDELWEISS
A tiny old-fashioned perfumery with a profusion of bottles displayed from floor to ceiling in mahogany and glass cabinets, Edelweiss stocks all the famous brands at excellent discount prices.
✉ Boulevard 14, between Avenida 5 de Mayo and Calle Tacuba ☎ (55) 55 12 08 48 🕓 Mon–Sat 10–7 Ⓜ Allende

PLAZA DEL ÁNGEL
A delightful Victorian-style gallery between Florencia and Amberes, Plaza del Ángel offers around 20 antiques shops filled with furniture, bric-à-brac, art and Mexican crafts all under one roof—perfect for easy browsing. On Saturdays it turns into a lively street fair.
✉ Entrances on Calle Hamburgo 150 and Calle Londres 161 🕓 Individual shops tend to keep their own hours, but most are open Mon–Fri 11–7 and Sat–Sun noon–4, with some closing on Mon Ⓜ Insurgentes

SAN ANGEL BAZAR
This is a very popular open-air crafts market, relaxed and friendly despite the crowds and traffic chaos. In addition to the usual items from across the country you can find some original jewelry, textiles and Talavera pottery at good prices, and the beautiful location in the heart of San Angel makes this a great way to spend your Saturday. Trendy and popular bars and cafés line the sides of the plaza. Parking is difficult.
✉ Plaza San Jacinto, San Angel 🕓 Sat 10–6 Ⓜ Miguel Angel de Quevedo

SANBORNS
www.sanborns.com.mx
This chain has more than 70 mini

department stores throughout Mexico City. They tend to be good for quality crafts and ceramics—usually at a fair price—as well as music, books (including an English-language section) and a pharmacy. Locations include a few along Paseo de la Reforma and in the Hotel Calinda Geneve in the Zona Rosa.

SEARS

A good starting point for virtually anything you might need, Sears is a western-style department store selling everything from perfume and lingerie to designer clothes, electronic equipment and household goods. Prices tend to be on a par with those of Europe and the US.
✉ Avenida Juárez 4 ☎ (55) 55 30 72 12 ⊙ Mon–Thu 11–10.30, Fri–Sun 11–9 Ⓜ Bellas Artes

TALLERES DE LOS BALLESTEROS

www.ballesteros.net
Come here for excellent quality, top-end jewelry and tableware, in both modern and traditional designs. There's another branch of the shop in Zona Rosa at Amberes 24.
✉ Calle Presidente Masarik 126 ☎ (55) 55 45 41 09/55 45 16 66 ⊙ Mon–Sat 10–7 Ⓜ Polanco

TANE

www.tane.com.mx
Located inside the Hotel Presidente Intercontinental, Tane carries some of the most exquisite silver and gold jewelry in the entire country. You'll also find high quality flatware, candle sticks and other unique objets d'art. Tane has six other stores around the city.
✉ Campos Eliseos 218 ☎ (55) 52 81 08 20 ⊙ Mon–Fri 11–7 Ⓜ Auditorio

ENTERTAINMENT AND NIGHTLIFE

BALLET FOLCLÓRICO DE MÉXICO

www.balletamalia.com
A performance by the Ballet Folclórico in its home theater (an attraction in itself with its dazzling interior and glittering jeweled stage curtain) is a must. This long-standing, world-famous company puts on spectacular shows of elaborately choreographed Mexican dances interspersed with traditional music and song. Peasant dances may be a trifle glamorized and costumes more at home in the West End than in Mexican villages, but the overall spectacle is dazzling.
✉ Palacio de Bellas Artes, Avenida Hidalgo ☎ (55) 55 29 93 20 ⊙ Performances usually Sun at 9.30am and 8.30pm, Wed at 8.30pm, Fri at 8pm 🎟 Tickets from $40 Ⓜ Bellas Artes

BARRACUDA

You could be forgiven for thinking you are in London or New York in this swanky post-modern bar, attracting the city's rich, beautiful and wealthy. The mojitos are superb and the service impeccable.
✉ Calle Nueva León 4-A, Condesa ☎ (55) 52 11 94 80 ⊙ Wed–Sun 7pm–2am Ⓜ Chilpancingo

CAFEÍNA

Monday evenings are especially spirited in this trendy bar, when lovers of Brazilian music can drink excellent caipirinhas to the sweet tones of MPB and samba. There is a dance floor, which gets packed, and live music every evening.
✉ Calle Nueva León 73, Condesa ☎ (55) 52 12 00 90 ⊙ Mon–Sat 6pm–2am 🎟 Cover $10 for women, $15 men Ⓜ Chilpancingo

CANTINA EL CENTENARIO

Here is a Mexican cantina at its best—pass through the saloon doors into a noisy den of happy revelers knocking back tequilas and munching on nachos. Service is strictly no frills, and the michelada (beer with ice, lime juice and salt) is likely to put hair on your chest.
✉ Calle Vicente Suárez 42, Condesa ☎ (55) 55 11 02 76 ⊙ Mon–Wed 12–11.30, Thu–Sat noon–12.30am Ⓜ Juanacatlan, Chilpancingo

CENTRO NACIONAL DE LAS ARTES

www.cenart.gob.mx
This is one of the most important cultural centers in the city, comprising theaters, concert exhibition halls and 10 cinemas. The city's Orquesta Sinfónica Carlos Chávez often plays at this venue, as do visiting string quartets and solo recitalists.
✉ Calle Río Churrubusco with Calle Canal de Miramontes ☎ (55) 41 55 00 00 ⊙ Daily 11–10 Ⓜ General Anaya

CINEARTE

www.contempocinema.com
This small art cinema is hidden away on the first floor of the gallery Plaza del Ángel. It has two modern

Below Detail of Diego Rivera's mural on the facade of Teatro de los Insurgentes

cinemas, digital sound, a café and bar. Wednesdays are half price.
✉ Plaza del Ángel, Londres 161, Zona Rosa ☎ (55) 52 08 40 44 Ⓜ Insurgentes

CINEMEX CASA DE ARTE
www.cinemex.com
This is an exclusive cinema showing foreign-language and art films, with a café, bar and valet parking.
✉ Plaza Masaryk, Calle Anatole France 120, Polanco ☎ (55) 52 57 69 69 Ⓜ Polanco

CINETECA NACIONAL
Home to cinema festivals and regular screenings of art-house movies, the Cineteca often shows English-language films.
✉ Avenida Mexico Coyoacán 389 ☎ (55) 41 55 12 00 Ⓜ Coyoacán

EL COLMILLO
Firmly established as a landmark on the international DJ map, Bar Colmillo keeps the dance floor heaving with a mix of Asian dub, hip hop and psychedelic trance, while the groovy Upstairs Lounge, with armchairs and ambient tunes, offers respite for the weary.
✉ Calle Versalles 52 ☎ (55) 55 92 61 14 🕐 Wed–Sat 10.30am–4am ✋ Cover from $9 Ⓜ Cuauhtemoc

FORO CULTURAL COYOACÁN
Tucked behind Coyoacán's Casa de Cortés, this lively cultural center, full name Foro Cultural Coyoacanese Hugo Argüelles, has a dynamic schedule of events that includes theater, dance and concerts—from Beatles cover groups to string quartets. There are discounts for students, and there's a good café on site.
✉ Calle Allende 36 ☎ (55) 55 54 07 38 🕐 Daily 11–10

HOOKAH LOUNGE
This super-chilled-out bar in the city's hippest district is reminiscent of scenes from *A Thousand and One Nights*. You can relax here, sprawl out on sumptuous cushions, smoke a bubble pipe with honey tobacco and snack on Arabic *mezze*.

✉ Calle Campeche 284, Condesa ☎ (55) 52 64 62 75 🕐 Mon–Sat 1pm–2am, Sun 1pm–11pm Ⓜ Chilpancingo

HOSTERÍA DEL BOHEMIO
Guests here, in the interior patio of the ex-San Hipolito convent, are treated to live jazz and *nueva trova* from the shadows of the candlelit tables around the patio. Coffee, cakes, savory snacks and beer are on the menu.
✉ Avenida Hidalgo 107 ☎ (55) 55 12 83 28 🕐 Daily 5pm–1am Ⓜ Hidalgo

JORONGO BAR
Locals swear by this popular joint, which is packed nearly every night of the week. Enjoy lively mariachi music or romantic boleros in the plush surroundings of the bar inside the Hotel Maria Isabel Sheraton, which faces the Angel Monument. Relax and mingle with friendly locals while enjoying the ambiance and soaking up the wonderful traditional music that has been part of the scene here for decades.
✉ Hotel Maria Isabel Sheraton, Reforma 325, Zona Rosa ☎ (55) 52 42 55 55 🕐 Daily 7:30pm–2am ✋ Cover: $7

MAMA RUMBA
Decked out in patriotic red, blue and white Cuban flag tablecloths and vibrating to the rhythms of merengue and salsa, this is one of the best-known and best-loved Cuban bars in town. Quality live music every night, a spacious dance floor and a restaurant serving spiced-up Cuban cuisine are all on the menu.
✉ Plaza San Jacinto 23, San Ángel ☎ (55) 55 50 80 99 🕐 Bar Thu–Sat 9pm–4am, restaurant Thu–Sun 1–11 ✋ $5 entrance fee after 10pm 🚌 Any bus heading south down Avenida Insugentes, or walk/taxi from metro Miguel Ángel de Quevedo

MAMBO CAFÉ
Excellent groups from Puerto Rico, Cuba and the Dominican Republic play in this café that oozes Caribbean spirit. Dancers are flashy and confident and competitions

are sometimes held. Don't let this put you off; the atmosphere is welcoming and every race, social class and age enjoys dancing here.
✉ Avenida Insurgentes Sur 644 ☎ (55) 55 23 94 52 🕐 Wed–Sun 9pm–2am 🚌 Any bus heading south down Avenida Insurgentes

MARIACHIS
The songs that *mariachis* play might sound familiar and range from traditional boleros to classical music, and even the Beatles—but their style and presentation are completely unique to Mexico. Known for their strolling presentation, distinctive style of dress, and their sound of brass and guitars, they symbolize the romance and tradition of Mexico. You'll find a large concentration of *mariachis* around the Plaza de Garibaldi, five blocks north of the Palacio de Bellas Artes. If you stick around for a song or two, make sure to put something in the tip jar—the going rate is $2 per song.
✉ Plaza de Garibaldi 🕐 Daily

PALACIO DE BELLAS ARTES
The finest offering of folkloric ballet in the city can be found at the Palacio de Bellas Artes, where the famed Ballet Folklorico de Mexico performs on Wednesday and Sunday. A typical program features a diverse evening of Aztec ritual dances, a fiesta in Veracruz, a wedding celebration, and agricultural dances from Jalisco, all of which showcase marimba players, singers, and dancers.
✉ Eje Central and Avenida Juarez, Centro Historico-Alameda ☎ (55) 55 12 25 93 ✋ Tickets $36–$60

PUNTO Y APARTE
www.cabaretito.com
Hidden away on an upper floor, up a cramped and crooked staircase, this lively and intimate gay bar has a cabaret every evening from 9pm, a good selection of wines and good-value snacks and pasta.
✉ Calle Amberes, 62 ☎ (55) 55 33 54 42 🕐 Daily 2pm–1am Ⓜ Insurgentes

SALA MANUEL PONCE

The pick of the city's jazz is here, in this smaller concert hall in the Palacio de Bellas Artes, along with Cuban music and world-music groups. Check the monthly schedule with the box office (open from noon) and reserve tickets in advance.

✉ Palacio de Bellas Artes, Avenida Hidalgo ☎ (55) 55 12 25 96 🚇 Bellas Artes

SALA NEZAHUALCOYOTL

Some of the world's leading musicians, as well as local and student performers, appear at this excellent recital hall within the UNAM campus.

✉ Ciudad Universitaria ☎ 56 65 07 09/56 22 71 25 🎫 Tickets usually from $8 🚇 Copilco

TEATRO DE LA CUIDAD

The Opera de México and Orquesta Sinfónica often give performances in this beautiful theater just next door to the Museo Nacional de Arte.

✉ Calle Donceles 36 ☎ (55) 55 18 49 26 🚇 Bellas Artes, Allende

TEATRO DE LOS INSURGENTES

This modern, rather run-down theater (n hosts musicals and popular shows, mostly in Spanish. Occasionally a visiting theater group from Europe or the US will perform.

✉ Avenida Insurgentes ☎ (55) 55 98 68 94 (box office) 🕐 Box office open Tue–Sun 10–6 🚌 Any bus heading south down Avenida Insurgentes

T-GALLERY

Groovy acid jazz is played live every evening in this bar packed with an eclectic mix of antiques and odds and ends—all for sale, incidentally. Arrive early to get a private room with velvet sofas or you may find yourself perching on the stairs with the crowds.

✉ Calle Saltillo 39 ☎ (55) 52 11 12 22 🕐 Daily 5pm–2am 🚇 Chilpancingo

WHISKEY BAR

This first international location of Rande Gerber's hot chain of bars is quite the sensation and has become one of the most happening

Above The bright yellow Museo del Papalote is specially designed for teaching children about the world and science

clubs in the city. A beautiful setting combined with great music is the backdrop for a crowd that is typically just as beautiful. The Whisky Bar is actually four bars in one, and also includes an outdoor terrace lounge. This is the place to see and be seen.

✉ At the W Mexico City hotel, Campos Eliseos 252, at Andres Bello ☎ (55) 91 38 18 00 🕐 Sun–Wed until 2am, Thu–Sat until 3am

YUPPIES SPORTS BAR

Television screens showing 24-hour sporting events dominate this enormous pub-style bar. The menu includes Tex-Mex *tacos*, chicken wings, pizza and *nachos*. Yuppies Sports Bar is, perhaps not surprisingly, popular with international visitors.

✉ Calle Genova 34, with Calle Hamburgo ☎ (55) 55 33 09 19 🕐 Daily 1pm–1.30am 🚇 Insurgentes

SPORTS AND ACTIVITIES

CHAPULTEPEC GOLF CLUB

www.golfchapultepec.com

Day passes for golf clubs in Mexico City can be difficult to come by, as rules require that you attend with an existing member. This is a challenging 18-hole course (par 72).

☎ (55) 55 89 14 08 🚇 Chapultepec

ESTADIO AZTECA

www.ticketmaster.com.mx (tickets)

Home to the capital's biggest soccer club, América, Estadio Azteca is the vast stadium where the World Cup finals of 1970 and 1986 were held. Guided tours on the hour every hour from 10 until 3.

✉ Calzada de Tlalpan 3465 ☎ (55) 56 17 80 80 🚇 Tasqueña, then bus 26 toward Xochimilco

HIPÓDROMO DE LAS AMÉRICAS

The full gamut of Mexican society gathers under one roof for Mexico City's weekly races. For the most exclusive experience, the Turf Club is the place to base yourself, but wherever you are there are always plenty of bookies on hand, eager for you to part with your cash.

✉ Avenida Industria Militar, Colonia Lomas de Sotelo ☎ (55) 53 87 06 00 🕐 Fri–Sun 3pm 💵 Entry from $3 🚌 Buses marked Hipodromo heading west on Avenida Reforma

PLAZA MÉXICO

www.lamexico.com

Mexico's bullfighting season runs from October to April (▷ 288). Bullfights usually start at 4pm on Sundays at this 47,000-capacity bullring, the world's largest. Seats are usually available the day of the fight, and on sunny days it's worth paying more to sit in the shade.

✉ Calle Augusto Rodin No. 241 ☎ (55) 56 11 44 13 💵 $3–$55 🚌 Buses heading south down Avenida Insurgentes

RANCHO DEL CHARRO

www.nacionaldecharros.com

This is the place to see exciting rodeo action, including remarkable feats of horsemanship and showy

FESTIVALS AND EVENTS

JANUARY

FEAST OF SAN ANTONIO ABAD

The Blessing of the Animals takes place at the church of Santiago Tlatelolco on Plaza de las Tres Culturas, San Juan Bautista Church in Coyoacán and the Church of San Fernando, north of Juárez and Reforma. Pets and livestock are decorated with flowers and ribbons and blessed in the church.

🕐 January 17

SEPTEMBER

EL GRITO DE INDEPENDENCIA (THE CRY OF INDEPENDENCE)

This fiesta commemorates Mexican Independence from Spain, or more specifically, the day Father Hidalgo

pageantry. *Mariachi* bands add to the atmosphere.

✉ Avenida de los Constituyentes 500, Bosque de Chapultepec ☎ (55) 52 77 87 06 🕐 Shows usually held at noon on Sun 🚇 Chapultepec

ROCK CLIMBING

Popular with nature lovers, Parque Nacional los Dinamos has some of the best rock climbing near the city with many bolted and bolt-free climbing routes along the narrow gorge of the Magdalena river. Walls of varying difficulty reach as high as 30m (100ft) and there are several different rock formations requiring a variety of climbing techniques. Mochilazo offers guided day trips and rock climbing courses as well.

✉ Mochilazo: Avenida de la Glorieta 15, Fraccionamiento las Arboledas ☎ (55) 52 39 54 85; www.mochilazo.com.mx

HEALTH AND BEAUTY

ENRIQUE BRICKER

This beauty salon offers reliable quality cuts without an appointment, as well as tanning and facials.

✉ Calle Londres 136-A ☎ (55) 52 08 17 63 🕐 Mon–Sat 10.30–10.30 🚇 Insurgentes

rang the bell of his small church in Dolores Hidalgo calling on his parishioners to fight for liberty. Every year at 11pm on September 15, the President stands on the balcony of the National Palace and shouts "Viva México" several times while the crowd below replies "Viva," and the great bell hanging over the entrance is rung. On the last shout, fireworks shatter the sky and the party continues all night.

✉ Palacio Nacional, Zócalo 🕐 September 15–16

DECEMBER

FIESTA DE NUESTRA SEÑORA DE GUADALUPE

▷ 293.

FOR CHILDREN

MUSEO DEL PAPALOTE

▷ 77.

PARQUE ZOOLÓGICO CHAPULTEPEC

The city's zoo at the western end of the lake occupies a large section of Chapultepec Park and is home to more than 2,000 animals from five continents. The landscape is desert, tropical and temperate forests, and the animals seem well cared for. The ocelots and spider monkeys are highlights, as are the pandas. The zoo is popular with families and can be overcrowded at weekends.

✉ Bosque de Chapultepec 🕐 Tue–Sun 9–4.30 💵 Free 🚇 Chapultepec

PISTA DE HIELO SAN JERÓNIMO

This well-kept and spacious indoor ice-skating arena toward the south of the city has two cafés on site.

✉ Avenida Contreras 300 ☎ (55) 56 83 19 29 🕐 Tue–Thu 11–3, 5–7.30, Fri 11–9, Sat 11.30–9, Sun 11–8 💵 $8 unlimited time 🚇 Metro to Universidad then taxi

PRICES AND SYMBOLS

The restaurants are listed alphabetically within Mexico City. The prices given are the average for a two-course lunch (L) and a three-course dinner (D) for one person, without drinks. The wine price is for the least expensive bottle. All the restaurants listed accept credit cards unless otherwise stated.

For a key to the symbols, ▷ 2.

BAR LA OPERA

Founded in 1876, this elegant restaurant one block from Bellas Artes oozes lavish belle époque charm and sophistication with its sumptuous red velvet upholstery, large gilt mirrors and mahogany furniture. Bar La Opera's famous clientele include Pancho Villa, who left his mark with a bullet hole you can still see in the ceiling. The eclectic and original dishes include grilled fish in a Veracruzana sauce and *paella* Valenciana.

✉ Avenida 5 de Mayo ☎ (55) 55 12 89 59 🕐 Mon–Sat 1pm–midnight, Sun 1–6 🍴 L $20, D $32, Wine $12 🚇 Bellas Artes

LA BODEGUITA DEL MEDIO

The Mexico City branch of Ernest Hemingway's favorite Cuban bar, the Bodeguita del Medio, is housed in an attractive early 19th-century house, its walls covered in the signatures of previous diners. This is an atmospheric bar and restaurant—and the ideal place to sip a refreshing *mojito* (a Cuban cocktail made with rum, soda water, sugar and lime) to the sound of Cuban son. Try the *tostones* stuffed with seafood, and for real Cuban authenticity ask for the cigars.

✉ Calle Cozumel 37, Condesa ☎ (55) 55 53 02 46 🕐 Sun and Sat 1.30pm–2am, Mon 1.30–11 🍴 L $10, D $20, Wine $16 🚇 Sevilla

CAFÉ LA BLANCA

You'll come across this no-nonsense eatery halfway along Avenida 5 de Mayo. Open early for excellent-value breakfasts and during the week for two-course set lunches, its menu also lists several Mexican dishes. The large canteen-style, open-plan dining room has a circular soda bar, which, together with the retro orange plastic chairs, gives a classic 1950s feel. Good espresso coffee is served here.

✉ Avenida 5 de Mayo 40 ☎ (55) 55 10 92 60 🕐 Daily 7am–11pm 🍴 L $8, D $10, Wine $9 🚇 Zócalo, Allende

Above *The 16th-century Casa de los Azulejos houses the flagship restaurant of the Sanborn's chain*

CAFÉ TACUBA

One block east of the Museo Nacional de Arte, this immensely popular restaurant occupies a 17th-century mansion. *Quartetos* and *mariachis* play here every evening from 8pm against the backdrop of blue-and-white Spanish tiles. Founded in 1912, the restaurant specializes in Mexican dishes, including excellent *enchiladas*, *tamales* and fruit desserts. Mexican politician Danilo Fabio Altamirano was assassinated here in 1936. One of the country's most famous rock bands takes its name from the restaurant.

✉ Calle Tacuba 28 ☎ (55) 55 18 49 50/55 21 20 48 🕐 Daily 8am–11.30pm 🍴 L $15, D $20, Wine $15 🚇 Allende

CAMBALACHE

www.grupocambalache.com

Don't be put off by this Argentine steak house being a chain restaurant: For sizzling steaks in an intimate atmosphere there's none better. Diners tuck into the filling portions under oak beamed ceilings, served by friendly and professional staff. And vegetarians and fish lovers aren't excluded either—there's a decent selection of non-meat dishes, including a succulent salmon fillet layered with crunchy black pepper.

✉ Calle Arquímedes 85, Polanco ☎ (55) 52 80 20 80 🕐 Daily 1pm–1am 🖐 L $30, D $45, Wine $20 🚇 Polanco

EL CAMPIRANO

Just off Avenida 5 de Mayo, this smart restaurant-bar is open every day for excellent buffet breakfasts (until 12.30) and buffet lunches (until 6.30). The mouthwatering and temptingly displayed dishes include *mole poblano*, seafood *paella, lomo al higo* (beef in a fig sauce), *chiles rellenos* (stuffed chilies) and an enticing selection of 28 different and interesting salads!

✉ Calle Bolivar 20 ☎ (55) 55 21 08 15/55 10 09 20 🕐 Daily 8.30–12.30, 1.30–6.30 🖐 L $15, Wine $12 🚇 Allende

CANTINA LA GUADALUPANA

A stone's throw from Plaza Hidalgo in the southern neighborhood of Coyoacán, this is one of the best-known *cantinas* (locals bars serving simple food) in Mexico. With its saloon doors, heavy wooden furniture and bulls' heads on the paneled walls, you'd be forgiven for thinking you're in a small town in deepest Mexico with your horse tethered up outside rather than a bustling suburb of Mexico City. Bean soup and squid cooked in its own ink are good options if you're struggling to choose from the extensive menu. Or just come for a drink. Credit cards are not accepted.

✉ Avenida Higuera 14, Coyoacán ☎ (55) 55 54 62 53 🕐 Mon–Sat noon–11 🖐 L $9, D $14, Wine $9 🚇 General Anaya, Viveros

CASA DE LOS AZULEJOS

This 16th-century palace (the House of Tiles, ▷ 69), directly across from the Templo de San Francisco, is now home to Sanborn's Restaurant, the flagship establishment of a chain of 36 across the city. As well as the restaurant, in the high-ceilinged central courtyard, overlooked by wooden balconies, there is a drugstore, chocolate shop and bookshop with foreign-language magazines. Serving toned-down but delicious dishes, Sanborn's is an excellent option for those unused to the fire of Mexican cuisine. Many people come to this restaurant just to enjoy the building.

✉ Calle Madero 4 ☎ (55) 55 12 13 31 🕐 Daily 7am–1am 🖐 L $12, D $15, Wine $9 🚇 Bellas Artes

LA CASA DE LAS SIRENAS

www.lacasadelassirenas.com.mx
This elegant, sun-drenched terrace restaurant occupies a 1750s colonial house just behind the cathedral. The traditional mahogany wood bar serving 250 types of tequila is linked to the terrace by a series of sloping corridors and staircases filled with period furniture. From the restaurant, where the atmosphere is relaxed and the service always impeccable, there is a splendid view over the *zócalo*. The menu includes many Mexican specialties, meat and fish dishes, and breakfast is served on weekends.

✉ Calle República de Guatemala 32 ☎ (55) 57 04 33 45 🕐 Mon–Thu 8am–11pm, Fri–Sat 8am–2am, Sun 8–7 🖐 L $18, D $20, Wine $14 🚇 Zócalo

CENTRO CASTELLANO

The best Spanish restaurant in town, Centro Castellano was founded in 1959 by Don Ricardo Vega Velasco and for four decades has excelled in serving the very best Spanish dishes in a warm and welcoming stone-flanked taverna. Cuts of ham and wooden tankards hang from low beams. From among the exquisitely presented dishes, try the superb *gazpacho Andaluz* and the specialties *lechón al estilo Segovia* (suckling pig), *lomo de huachinango a las brasas* (red snapper cooked over charcoal) or the *paellas*.

✉ Calle República de Uruguay 16–18 ☎ (55) 55 18 60 80/55 21 35 16 🕐 Mon–Sat 1–11, Sun 1–8 🖐 L $12, D $22, Wine $12 🚇 San Juan de Letrán

CHEZ WOK

Renowned chef Kwong Poon Li is at the helm of this gourmet Chinese restaurant just off Avenida Presidente Masaryk. Describing its cuisine as "Imperial China," a good few of Chez Wok's highly original creations also come fused with Mexican ingredients—try the Mexican spring roll with quail. There are good options for vegetarians too. The immaculate dining room is elegant and discreet.

✉ Calle Tennyson 117, Polanco ☎ (55) 52 81 34 10 🕐 Mon–Sat 1–11, Sun 1–5 🖐 L $25, D $45, Wine $16 🚇 Polanco

CHUCHO EL ROTO

You'll get tasty breakfasts and good-value lunches in this bright, cheerful café, half a block from the Plaza San Jacinto in San Angel. A pretty pattern of lilies decorates the orange and blue walls, and a flower-covered balustrade separates the pine tables from the sidewalk outside. Highlights on the simple menu include *enchiladas de mole Oaxaqueña* and *enchiladas suizas*. Mexican breakfasts are just $5.

✉ Calle Madero 8, San Angel ☎ (55) 56 16 20 41 🕐 Daily 8am–10pm 🖐 L $8, D $8 🚇 Miguel Ángel de Quevedo

CÍRCULO VASCO ESPAÑOL

Founded by exiled Basques in the late 19th century, this classy eatery includes signature dishes from that region in Spain such as *rueda de robalo a la clonostiarra* (sea bass cooked with parsley and white wine). The hearty breakfast with a chili-and-cheese omelet is a favorite choice of diners.

✉ Avenida 16 de Septiembre 51 ☎ (55) 55 18 29 08 🕐 Daily 9–8 🖐 Breakfast $8, L $15 🚇 Zócalo

FOCOLARE

This unashamedly touristy restaurant caters to large groups with its evening folk dance show "Noches Mexicanas" (Monday–Saturday 8.45; reservations essential), a spectacle of color and music. The attractive dining room is adorned with local baskets and terra-cotta tiles, and tables are grouped around a central catwalk stage. Try the original *camarones al tequila* (shrimps with tequila) and the delicious *pato en salsa de Jamaica*. Focolare specializes in Yucatecan cuisine. There is a $9 cover charge for the show.

✉ Calle Hamburgo 87, Zona Rosa ☎ (55) 52 07 85 03 ◷ Daily 1pm–midnight ✍ L $12, D $20, Wine $16 Ⓜ Insurgentes, Sevilla

FONDA EL REFUGIO

More than 50 years of quality have made this modest restaurant a landmark on the local dining scene. It features dishes from each major region of Mexico. The *mole* made with pumpkin seeds, and chilis stuffed with beef are two standards. Try a coconut candy for dessert.

✉ Liverpool 166 ☎ (55) 52 07 27 32 ◷ Mon–Sat 1–11, Sun 1–10 ✍ L $10, D $16, Wine $10 Ⓜ Insurgentes

LOS GIRASOLES

www.restaurantelosgirasoles.com
Slick waiters in patriotic red, green and white neckties and leather aprons buzz around this lively Mexican restaurant on the Plaza Manuel Tolsa, next to the Museo de Arte Nacional. Oaxacan pottery, flagstones dotted with handsome *azulejo* tiles and roughly hewn walls add to the atmosphere. The extensive menu, also available in English, includes Aztec-inspired dishes such as maguey worms fried in butter and chili, as well as turkey breasts in a tamarind mole sauce and the Yucatán-inspired *cochinita pibil*—spicy shredded pork.

✉ Calle Tacuba 8–10 ☎ (55) 55 10 06 30/55 10 32 81 ◷ Sun–Mon 1–9, Tue–Sat 1pm–midnight ✍ L $15, D $25, Wine $18 Ⓜ Bellas Artes, Allende

HACIENDA DE CORTÉS

The interior patios and flowering gardens of this colonial-style hacienda tucked behind Plaza la Conchita make this restaurant an exceptionally pleasant place to dine. The large, shaded outdoor patio area lends itself to leisurely breakfasts

and the dining room inside is softly lit with brass lamps. Try the delicious fish fillet with butter, almonds and parsley or the plentiful set breakfasts (9–1), which are excellent value at $6.

✉ Fernández Leal 70, Coyoacán ☎ (55) 56 59 37 41 ◷ Mon–Sat 9am–10.30pm, Sun 9–7 ✍ L $12, D $15, Wine $10 Ⓜ General Anaya, Viveros

HOSTERÍA DE SANTO DOMINGO

Mexico City's oldest restaurant can be found in the former Santo Domingo convent, just half a block from the square of the same name in the historic downtown area. Tables are spread through a labyrinth of rooms on different levels connected by archways and steps under beamed ceilings, in contrast to the cavernously large—and somehow rather soulless—upper-level back area. House specials include chorizo sausage accompanied by a salad of tender *nopal* cactus, chili stuffed with beef, raisins (sultanas), pine nuts and *acitrón* (candied cactus) and *chiles en nogada* (peppers stuffed with minced meat). There is piano music every evening from 8.

✉ Belisario Domínguez 72 ☎ (55) 55 10 14 34/55 26 52 76 ◷ Daily 9am–9.30pm ✍ L $15, D $22, Wine $12 Ⓜ Allende, Zócalo

EL HUEQUITO

www.elhuequito.com.mx
Three blocks south of Avenida 5 de Mayo, between República de Uruguay and República de El Salvador, this brightly painted and lively American-style diner is casual, cheap and friendly. In addition to the delicious breakfasts served here, the restaurant serves an extensive choice of tasty, toned down Mexican specials such as *enchiladas al suizo*, *tacos* and *quesadillas* as well as hamburgers, T-bone steak and ice cream. There is a good children's menu, and live music on Thursdays and Fridays from 8pm.

✉ Calle República de Bolivia 58 ☎ (55) 55 10 4199/55 21 02 07 ◷ Mon–Sat 7.30am–11pm, Sun 8am–9pm ✍ L $7, D $12, Wine $12 Ⓜ San Juan de Letrán

EL JOLGORIO

Tucked away down Avenida Higuera, the attractive and fashionable El Jolgorio restaurant specializes in Arabic-Indian-Mexican fusion cuisine. The reasonably priced and inventive dishes are divided on the menu into earth, water, fire and air, and include couscous salads, curried meats and vegetarian dishes. The restaurant has a superb-value set lunch from Monday to Thursday ($7).

✉ Avenida Higuera 22 E, Coyoacán ☎ (55) 56 58 83 39 ◷ Mon 2–7, Tue 1–7, Wed–Fri 1–11, Sat 2–11, Sun 11–11 ✍ L $12, D $16, Wine $12 Ⓜ General Anaya, Viveros

JUGOS CANADÁ

A perfect place for a quick snack and vitamin-C boost, this juice bar is casual and inexpensive. The walls are covered with tropical fruits, which are plucked, chopped and squeezed in front of you and served in plentiful quantities. *Tortas*, hamburgers and hotdogs are under $5 and the salad of fresh fruits, yogurt, granola and honey is a must. Credit cards are not accepted.

✉ Avenida 5 de Mayo 49, corner with República de Chile ☎ (55) 55 18 37 17 ◷ Tue–Sat 8am–10pm, Sun 9–9 ✍ L and D $5 Ⓜ Zócalo

MESÓN ANTIGUA SANTA CATARINA

Situated on the square of the same name in Coyoacán, this pink-and-blue café-restaurant has a rickety wooden staircase that emerges onto a splendid open dining room overlooking the square: A perfect place for enjoying a leisurely afternoon sangria. The good Mexican food served on ceramic dishes is very reasonably priced and the breakfasts are delicious.

✉ Plaza Santa Catarina 6, Coyoacán ☎ (55) 56 58 48 31 ◷ Daily 8am–11pm ✍ L $8, D $15, Wine $30 Ⓜ General Anaya, Viveros

MEXICO VIEJO

One block north of the *zócalo* on the corner with República de Brasil, this inviting restaurant offers impeccable

service in a sunflower-yellow ranch-style dining room. Popular with local business people, it is particularly recommended for its delicious breakfasts of *huevos rancheros* or hotcakes, and for its four-course set lunches on weekdays ($7).

✉ Calle Tacuba 87 ☎ (55) 55 10 37 48/ 55 12 97 43 ⏰ Mon–Sat 8am–9pm, Sun 8–6 (breakfast until 12.30, lunch until 6) 🍴 L $12, D $16, Wine $14 🚇 Zócalo

LES MOUSTACHES

www.lesmoustaches.com.mx
Dine in style in this elegant French restaurant, one of the top eating experiences in town. A gastronomic feast in a Porfiriato-era mansion near the US embassy, Les Moustaches is by reservation only. Choose from such culinary delights as salmon in a saffron sauce with wild rice, and *lenguado Veronique* (sole in a white wine sauce with glazed grapes). The wine list is superb and a sommelier is at hand to offer expert advice should you need it.

✉ Río Sena 88 between La Reforma and Río Lerma, Zona Rosa ☎ (55) 55 33

33 90/55 25 12 65 ⏰ Tue–Sat 1–11.30, Sun–Mon 1–6 🍴 L $28, D $35, Wine $25 🚇 Insurgentes

LOS MURALES

www.century.com.mx
Attached to Hotel Century just off Avenida Insurgentes, the strength of this understated business restaurant is its delicious vegetarian lunch buffet. Between numerous trips to the buffet—spread with salads, pastas, Mexican dishes and desserts—the attentive waiters refill your glass with *agua de fruta* and then green tea, all included. There is also an excellent weekend breakfast buffet until 11am.

✉ Avenida Liverpool 152, Zona Rosa ☎ (55) 57 26 99 11 ⏰ Daily 7am–10.45pm 🍴 L $12, D $20, Wine $15 🚇 Insurgentes

SAN ANGEL INN

www.sanangelinn.com
For a taste of how the city's elite dine, this exquisitely converted monastery decorated in colonial style with original tiled stone

fountains and beautiful interior patios is the place to see and be seen. Throughout its 300-year history, this hacienda, in the delightful colonial district of San Angel, has played host to generals, revolutionaries and ambassadors, and the likes of Bridget Bardot, Henry Kissinger and Muhammad Ali. Start with a margarita or a martini, then choose from the European cuisine and sumptuous desserts which are served in a delightful, softly lit dining room, hung with iron chandeliers.

✉ Calle Diego Rivera 50 at Calle Altavista, San Angel ☎ (55) 56 16 22 22/56 16 05 37 ⏰ Mon–Sat 1–1, Sun 1–9.30 🍴 L $20, D $30, Wine $20 🚇 Miguel Angel de Quevedo, then take a taxi

SUSHI ROLL

There are few surprises in this impressively authentic sushi bar, a popular lunch spot with local office workers. The place has a clean look, with whitewashed walls and spotlighting. The menu includes everything you might expect, with prices depending on whether the fish is imported or caught locally. This being Mexico, you'll find a bowl of chilies next to the soy sauce on the table.

✉ Avenida 5 de Mayo 15B, corner with Filomeno Mata ☎ (55) 55 12 13 87/55 21 12 17 ⏰ Mon–Sat 1–8, Sun 1–6 🍴 L $10 🚇 Bellas Artes

LA TERRAZA, HOTEL MAJESTIC

www.majestic.com.mx
For a spectacular vista over the *zócalo*, head to the Hotel Majestic's seventh-floor rooftop restaurant. This is an expensive option but it is a perfect observation point for watching the frenetic action below. Stylish breakfasts until noon; thereafter fairly standard Mexican and international food.

✉ Avenida Francisco Madero 73 ☎ (55) 55 12 86 00 ⏰ Daily 7am–midnight 🍴 L $12, D $15, Wine $9 🚇 Zócalo

PRICES AND SYMBOLS

The prices are the average for a double room for one night including breakfast, unless otherwise stated. All the hotels listed accept credit cards unless otherwise stated. Note that rates can vary widely throughout the year.

For a key to the symbols, ▷ 2.

CAMINO REAL

www.caminoreal.com/mexico/
Designed by Mexican architect Ricardo Legorretta, the Camino Real, minutes from the Museo Nacional de Antropología, is a luxury hotel with daring style. Influenced by pre-Hispanic pyramids and colonial haciendas, the hotel also has a futuristic feel to it. Add bubbling fountains and bold colors and you have a wonderfully original hotel. Style aside, there's also a tennis club, spa and massage parlor, as well as a 24-hour café, three restaurants and a trendy bar. All rooms have a view of the attractive gardens, the pool or interior patios.
✉ Avenida Mariano Escobedo 700, Polanco ☎ (55) 52 63 88 88 ✋ $150 weekdays; $125 weekends, excluding breakfast ($8)
ⓘ 712 ⊙ ⊛ ⛊ ⊚ Chapultepec, Polanco

LA CASONA

www.hotellacasona.com.mx
An exquisite pink mansion listed by the National Institute of Fine Arts as a protected building is home to this small and utterly delightful hotel three blocks from metro Sevilla and within 10 minutes' walk of the Bosque de Chapultepec. The lobby is furnished with antique English dressers, while watercolors and Mexican masks adorn the walls. The dining room leads out to a pretty patio with a tiled fountain. Rooms are all individually decorated, and are without exception light and pleasant. American breakfast is included.
✉ Avenida Durango 280, corner with Cozumel, Polanco ☎ (55) 52 86 30 01
✋ $145 ⓘ 29 (12 nonsmoking)
⊙ ⊚ Sevilla

GILLOW

Next door to the imposing (and sinking) Iglesia de la Profesa, just two blocks from the *zócalo*, this hotel offers an unpretentious atmosphere in a pleasant setting. The airy rooms—all with large beds, writing desks and enormous closets—are built around a tall central well, and those with the best views are on the sixth floor. The

Above *Baroque-style Hotel de Cortés is a former guesthouse for pilgrims*

restaurant, the Capilla, offers three-course set meals for $10.
✉ Calle Isabel la Católica 17 ☎ (55) 55 10 07 91 ✋ $65, excluding breakfast ⓘ 103 ⊛ Allende

HOLIDAY INN

www.hotelescortes.com
Breakfast on the sunny sixth-floor terrace with fantastic views over the *zócalo* is the highlight of this gleaming, swanky hotel. Once the residence of Hernán Cortés, it occupies one of the original colonial buildings on the square. Although a little small, bedrooms have all the expected conveniences and are painted in pastel hues. The super location, slick service and elegant furnishings make this an excellent central choice. Parking is available.
✉ Avenida 5 de Mayo 61 ☎ (55) 51 30 51 30 ✋ $130 ⓘ 105 ⊙ ⛊ ⊚ Zócalo

HOSTAL MONEDA

www.hostalmoneda.com.mx
The friendly Hostal Moneda is located in the heart of downtown, just one block east of the cathedral, with easy access to Chapultepec

Park and Coyoacán. Breakfast is served on the sunny rooftop terrace, which has splendid views of the cathedral. Each room is equipped with lockers and hot water, and internet access is available in the reception area. Other facilities include a laundry.

✉ Calle Moneda 8 ☎ (55) 55 22 58 03 ✋ Private rooms $40, dorms (3, 4, 5 or 6 beds) starting at $15 per person ⓘ 37 Ⓜ Zócalo

HOTEL DE CORTÉS

www.hoteldecortes.com.mx

This hotel at the northwestern end of the Alameda is a baroque-style, 17th-century, former pilgrims' guesthouse. The rooms overlook the brightly painted central courtyard, where breakfast is served, so they can be a little dark. Children under 12 stay free.

✉ Avenida Hidalgo 85 ☎ (55) 55 18 21 81/85 ✋ $137 ⓘ 29, including 10 suites (12 non-smoking) Ⓜ Hidalgo

HOTEL SUITES AMBERES

www.suitesamberes.com.mx

Just five minutes' walk from the Insurgentes metro stop is this pleasant complex of studio apartments for long stays. The airy apartments come with a fully equipped kitchenette, lounge, terrace, television and internet access. Some can sleep up to six people. There is a rooftop gym and sauna with views over the city.

✉ Calle Amberes 64, Zona Rosa ☎ (55) 55 33 13 06 ✋ $133 (prices are negotiable for stays longer than 7 days) ⓘ 28 apartments 🄲 🄿 Ⓜ Insurgentes

HOTEL TOLEDO

This budget hotel's location—between Bellas Artes and San Juan de Letrán metro stations—is its greatest asset. The convenience of being a one-minute walk from budget cafés, an ATM and a Sanborn's makes up for the fact that the Toledo is past its heyday. Carpets are frayed but rooms are clean and all have television. Prices are good for people on their own too. There is no breakfast room.

✉ Avenida López 22 ☎ (55) 55 21 50 79/55 21 32 49 ✋ $24, excluding breakfast ⓘ 58 Ⓜ Belles Artes, San Juan de Letrán

JUÁREZ

This small and friendly hotel tucked into a quiet alleyway just off Avenida 5 de Mayo is one of the best budget options in the city, thanks in large part to its excellent location just a minute away from the *zócalo*. The rooms, though small, are clean and pleasant and all have television—ask for one with a window. It's popular with budget visitors, so it's definitely worth reserving in advance.

✉ Avenida 5 de Mayo 17 ☎ (55) 55 12 69 29/55 18 47 18 ✋ $25, excluding breakfast ⓘ 39 Ⓜ Zócalo

MAJESTIC

www.majestic.com.mx

At the heart of the *zócalo*, this Best Western occupies an imposing 16th-century building. The attractive lobby is a haven of Moroccan arches, palms and Spanish tiles. The quiet rooms overlooking the central courtyard are all decorated in 1930s style with enormous beds, soft lighting and bathtubs. The breakfast buffet, served in the La Terraza restaurant (▷ 99) overlooking the *zócalo*, is magnificent. Next door, the El Campanario bar is open until 2am, with live music from 7.30pm.

✉ Avenida Francisco Madero 73 ☎ (55) 55 21 86 00; from US 1-800 528 12 34 ✋ $120, excluding breakfast ($6) ⓘ 85, including 5 suites Ⓜ Zócalo

MANAGUA

Rooms in this popular budget option are basic but the hotel is 200m (220 yards) from metro Hidalgo, putting you within minutes of the Alameda, not to mention good-value eateries and internet cafés. Reservations are recommended.

✉ Plaza de San Fernando 11 ☎ (55) 55 12 13 12/55 21 49 61 ✋ $20, excluding breakfast ⓘ 75 Ⓜ Hidalgo

MARCO POLO

www.marcopolo.com.mx

Small but stylish, the Marco Polo offers everything you need

for a comfortable and luxurious stay. Bedrooms are sumptuously furnished—all include a lounge—while bathrooms are glitteringly pristine. Also featured in each room are internet access and a bar with complimentary fruit and coffee.

✉ Calle Amberes 27, Zona Rosa ☎ (55) 55 11 18 39 ✋ $90–$160 ⓘ 59, 4 penthouse suites with Jacuzzi, 13 suites for longer stays 🄿 Ⓜ Insurgentes

MARLOWE

México City's airport tourist office refers many visitors to this modern mid-range hotel just one block from Bellas Artes and the Alameda, and it's easy to see why. This makes a pleasant, simple base offering good value in an excellent location. Rooms are kept scrupulously clean, staff are professional and there is a gym, sauna and restaurant.

✉ Avenida Independencia 17 ☎ (55) 55 21 95 40 ✋ $60, excluding breakfast ($7) ⓘ 120 🄿 Ⓜ Bellas Artes

EL ROBLE

www.hotelroble.com.mx

El Roble is the best value mid-range hotel in the vicinity. The polished marbled reception is appealing, as are the rooms, which although a little dark, are well appointed, clean and carpeted—all with television. Parking is available ($3 per day).

✉ Calle Uruguay 109 ☎ (55) 55 22 78 30/55 22 80 83 ✋ $39, excluding breakfast ($5) ⓘ 61 Ⓜ Zócalo

SHERATON CENTRO HISTÓRICO

www.sheratonmexico.com

The 26-floor Sheraton has fabulous views across the park and east toward Reforma. Opened in 2003, this luxurious hotel, a study in understated elegance, has spacious rooms decorated in cool pastel shades and furnished in stylish dark mahogany. Sliding doors, marble bathrooms and intelligent sensor lighting all add to the Zen-like calm. Facilities include satellite television, internet access and a sauna.

✉ Avenida Juárez 70 ☎ (55) 51 30 53 00 ✋ $160–$300, excluding breakfast ($10) ⓘ 457 🄲 🄴 🄿 Ⓜ Hidalgo

THE YUCATÁN

The Yucatán Peninsula—the land of Maya pyramids and Caribbean beach resorts—includes the states of Campeche, Quintana Roo and Yucatán. Love it or hate it, the super resort of Cancún, on the northeast tip of the peninsula, is Mexico's tourism calling card to the world. Meanwhile, the ancient Maya ruins of Chichén Itzá, rising from the scrub jungle of Yucatán, were named one of the "New 7 Wonders of the World" in 2007. Throw in the Maya ruins of Uxmal and Tulum, among many others, and the scuba diving paradise of Cozumel, and it's no wonder the peninsula is the most heavily visited region in all Mexico.

Of course, it's not all sun, sugar-white sand and electric-turquoise blue water. The colonial city of Merida has all the classic architecture and charm of the Mexican interior's better known vestiges of Spanish colonialism. On the peninsula's west coast, the fascinating city of Campeche makes an ideal base for exploring mysterious archaeological sites such as Uxmal. Farther south, in the jungle near the Guatemala border, the ancient ruined cities along the Río Bec route include beautiful Becán and Calakmul, home to the highest Maya pyramid in Mexico.

Finally, there's the Caribbean coast. From the paradisiacal Riviera Maya (Cancún south to Tulum) to the pristine Sian Ka'an Biosphere Reserve to the undiscovered Costa Maya (Sian Ka'an to the Belize border), these are the Mexican beaches of your daydreams. Palms sway in the breeze, the margaritas are icy cold and the ocean is as warm as bathwater. Whether you long to dance 'til dawn at a Cancún nightclub, go for a night-time scuba dive off Cozumel or fall asleep early in a thatch-roofed beachfront *cabaña*, the Yucatán is ready, willing and able to oblige.

AKUMAL

www.mayayucatan.com

Akumal sits on a gorgeous stretch of coastline, with pristine beaches, azure sea and magical *cenotes* (natural sinkholes). Aside from its laid-back ambience, which makes a pleasing contrast to Cancún and Playa del Carmen, the resort's main attraction is its excellent swimming and snorkeling, with exquisite coral and a series of caves. Divers swarm to the underwater world, marveling at the many species of coral and series of caves separated by canyons beyond the coral wall.

Akumal, meaning "the place of the turtles," is so named because of the turtles that used to come ashore here to lay their eggs. These days numbers are declining as building development increases.

Head north of Akumal, passing through Half Moon Bay, to reach the stunning Ya Kul lagoon (daily 8–5), a popular snorkeling destination.

✚ 317 S8 🚌 Buses from Cancún, Playa del Carmen and Tulúm

BECÁN

Becán, meaning "path of the serpent," is an important Maya site in the Río Bec style, characterized by heavy masonry towers simulating pyramids and temples, usually found in pairs. Built in the Late Classic period (AD600–900), it was the political, religious and administrative capital of the Río Bec zone.

The site is surrounded by a moat, now dry, which is believed to be one of the oldest defense systems in Mesoamerica. Seven entrance gates cross the moat to the city. The buildings are a strange combination of decorative towers and fake temples, as well as structures used as shrines and palaces. The twin towers are set on a pyramid-shaped base supporting a cluster of buildings that seem to have been used for a variety of functions: religious, administrative, and residential.

Above *Clear waters teem with marine life*
Opposite *The sandy beach at Akumal*

✚ 317 R9 ✉ 15km (9.5 miles) west of Xpujil 🕐 Daily 8–5 👋 $4

CALAKMUL

www.calakmul.org

Calakmul, within the Reserva de la Biósfera Calakmul, is one of the largest archaeological sites in Mesoamerica; it is also the biggest of the Maya cities, with about 10,000 buildings—many of them unexcavated. The city was discovered in 1931 by American explorer Cyrus Longworth Lundell (1907–93), who named it "the city of two adjacent mounds."

In the middle of the site is the Gran Plaza, overlooked by a pyramid whose base covers 2ha (5 acres). One of the buildings grouped around the Gran Plaza is believed—due to its curious shape and location—to have been designed for astronomical observation. The Gran Acrópolis, the largest of all the structures, is divided into two sections: Plaza Norte, with its ball court, was used for ceremonies; Plaza Sur was used for public activities.

Within the reserve there are more than 800 plant species, and a variety of wildlife including pumas, deer, and howler monkeys.

✚ 317 R9 ✉ 213km (132 miles) southeast of Campeche, 60km (37 miles) off the main Escárcega–Chetumal road 🕐 Daily 8–5 👋 $4 🚌 Buses from Campeche and Xpujil 📷 Agencies in Chetumal offer tour packages (two people minimum)

CAMPECHE
▷ 106.

CANCÚN
▷ 107.

CELESTÚN

www.mexonline.com/celestun

The Reserva de la Biósfera Celestún, on the spit of land separating the Río Esperanza estuary from the Bahía de Campeche, on the west coast of Yucatán, was created to protect thousands of migratory waterfowl. The area's major attraction is North America's sole colony of pink flamingos. Pelicans, fish, crabs, and shrimps also inhabit the lagoons, and manatees, toucans and crocodiles can sometimes be glimpsed in the quieter waterways. There are more than 234 species of mammal, including spider monkeys, ocelots, jaguars, and sea turtles. The reserve's springs and freshwater pools are good for swimming.

Celestún town is a small, dusty fishing resort, although the long beach, with little shade, is relatively clean with clear water ideal for swimming. Along the beach fishing boats bristle with *jimbas*—cane poles used for catching octopuses. Boat trips to view the wildlife can be arranged at the river bridge 1km (half a mile) back along the Mérida road.

✚ 317 Q8 ✉ 90km (56 miles) west of Mérida 🚌 Buses from Mérida

INFORMATION

www.campechetravel.com
✚ 317 Q8 🛈 Avenida Ruíz Cortines
s/n, Plaza Moch-Couoh ☎ (981) 811 92
29 🚌 Buses from Mérida

TIPS

» Campeche's streets in the Old Town are numbered rather than named. Even numbers run north/south, beginning at Calle 8 near the *malecón*, east to Calle 18 inside the walls; odd numbers run east (inland) from Calle 51 in the north to Calle 65 in the south.

» Take the 45-minute Centro Histórico tour. A regular tram runs from the main plaza daily 9–1 and 5–9, and you can just hop on and off.

» Buses marked "Circuito Baluartes" provide a regular service around the perimeter of town.

CAMPECHE

Campeche, an ideal base from which to explore the archaeological sites of Campeche state, is one of Mexico's most engaging cities, renowned for its colonial architecture. It was here in 1517 that the Spanish, under Francisco Hernández de Córdoba, first disembarked on Mexican soil. Infamous bands of buccaneers constantly raided the port and in 1663 they slaughtered the city's inhabitants. Over the next five years, the Spanish settlement was fortified with a series of formidable bulwarks and *baluartes* (bastions), some of which now house museums. If the heart of the city is the shady *zócalo* (main square), with its small central pagoda, the soul is the *malecón* (seafront promenade), which was destroyed by a hurricane in 1996, but has since rebuilt and is now a handsome promenade.

WALKING THE CIRCUITO BALUARTES

Begin at the *zócalo*, where the Franciscan Catedral de la Concepción (1540–1705) stands. Inside is the *Santo Entierro* (Holy Burial), a sculpture of Christ on a mahogany sarcophagus with silver trim. Right in front of the *zócalo* is the Baluarte de la Soledad, the central bulwark of the city walls, now housing the Museo de la Cultura Maya (Tue–Sat 9–2, 4–8, Sun 9–1), which displays Maya stelae (carved upright stones) and sculpture. Walking westward, you will pass the Palacio de Gobierno and the Congreso.

Next on the *circuito* is the Templo de San José, on Calle 10, a baroque church with a tiled facade, followed by the Baluarte de Santa Rosa, now the visitor information office. Then comes Baluarte de San Juan, from which a large chunk of the old city wall still extends and connects with Puerta de la Tierra, where a *Luz y Sonido* (Light and Sound) show takes place (Wed, Fri and Sat 8pm). A short detour north takes you to the Casa de Teniente del Rey (King's Lieutenant's House), which houses the Museo Regional de Campeche (Calle 59, Tue–Sat 8–2, 5–8, Sun 9–1). This museum charts the history of Campeche state since Maya times. The *circuito* then leads past the Baluarte de San Francisco and the market, just outside the line of the city walls, then down to the northwest tip of the old city. Here the Baluarte de Santiago has been turned into a walled garden, the Jardín Botánico Xmuch'Haltun.

The Fuerte de San Miguel, on the *malecón*, southwest of the city, houses the archaeological museum (Tue–Sat 9–8, Sun 9–1), which has a well-documented display of pre-Columbian exhibits.

Below *Baroque Templo de San José has a beautiful tiled facade*

CANCÚN

Cancún is Mexico's party capital, delivering round-the-clock entertainment. It lies close to the ancient wonders of the Maya world and the natural beauty of the Riviera Maya. Cancún, a beachside metropolis with little authentic Mexican flavor and yet the number-one visitor destination in Mexico, is loved and loathed in equal measure. The 25km (16-mile) Hotel Zone, set on a narrow strip of land in the shape of a number seven alongside the coast, is an ultra-modern boulevard, with five-star hotels, high-tech nightclubs, high-class shopping malls and branches of McDonald's, Burger King and Planet Hollywood. The main avenue is Tulúm, formerly the highway running through the city; now it is the location of the handicraft market, the main shops, banks and the municipal tourist office. There are restaurants here, too, but the better ones are along Avenida Yaxchilán, which is also the main focus for nightlife. Cancún City—a modern sprawl that evolved from temporary shacks housing the thousands of workers in the Hotel Zone—has little to attract visitors.

THE BEACH AND BEYOND

With pale white sand stretching for 19km (12 miles), a turquoise sea, coral gardens, lagoons and mystical *cenotes* (natural sinkholes), watersports enthusiasts flock to Cancún. The diving is world class, reefs have visibility of 24m (80ft) and there are many dive schools offering PADI courses. The panoply of watersports operators and all-inclusive resorts means there are facilities for windsurfing, jetskis and waterskiing. With waters teeming with dorado, grouper and billfish, game fishing is big, and Cancún plays host to several international fishing tournaments; March to July is the high season.

Late-afternoon shopping is another major recreational activity, and along the strip numerous malls overflow with designer labels, perfume emporiums, jewelry stores and Mexican handicrafts. Prices here are higher than anywhere else in Mexico. Cancún's diversity extends to gastronomy and nightlife, with top-class international restaurants, tassel-shaking cabarets and all manner of live musical performances, ranging from Cuban jazz quartets to rapper artists such as 50 Cent.

The sights and natural wonders beyond Cancún offer much greater reward. You can rent a jeep and cruise the Riviera Maya as far as Tulúm (▷ 119), taking in the archaeological site of Cobá and the tranquil beach of Akumal (▷ 105).

INFORMATION
www.cancunmx.com
✚ 317 S7 ℹ Avenida Cobá s/n
☎ (998) 884 65 31 🕐 Mon–Fri 9–2, 4–7 🚌 Buses ply the Hotel Zone strip heading into the middle of town
✈ Cancún airport, 16km (10 miles) south

TIP
❯❯ Taxis are inexpensive and abundant. The flat rate within central Cancún is $1–$1.50; to the Hotel Zone $5–$8.

Above Cancún likes to party and its nightlife scene is vibrant

INFORMATION

✚ 317 R8 ✉ Highway 180 ☎ (985)
851 01 37 🕐 Daily 8–6 💵 $9.50, child
(under 13) free. You are given a yellow
band to wear so that you may leave and
re-enter as often as you like on day of
entry 🖐 Guides charge around $40 for
1.5-hour tours 🍴 Drinks and snacks at
entrance (expensive), at the *cenote* and
on the path to Old Chichén ❓ Visitor
center at entrance has a restaurant, free
cinema (short film in English at noon and
4pm), museum, shops, exchange facilities
and luggage deposit (free)

Above *The Group of the Thousand
Columns next to the pyramidal Temple
of the Warriors*

INTRODUCTION

Iconic, majestic and harmonious, Chichén Itzá is one of the most spectacular
Maya sites, adorned with exquisite sculptures and tributes to its mighty gods,
a fascinating insight into the astrological and mathematical genius of the Maya.
Chichén Itzá is Mexico's most-visited Maya sight. The giant stepped pyramid
of Kukulkán, or El Castillo, dominates the site, watched over by Chac Mool
(or Chaac Mool), a reclining statue once used to receive sacrificial offerings.
Frequent buses and tours connect the coastal resorts and the nearby city of
Valladolid to the east. It requires at least one day to do the site justice.

　Chichén Itzá was built in the Late Classic period and once covered 25sq
km (10sq miles); the administrative, cultural and religious focus—occupied by
priests and ruling elite—was concentrated in an area of 6sq km (2sq miles). The
Itzáes, who settled here in the ninth century, were descended from the Putun
or Chontal Maya. By the end of the 10th century the city was more or less
abandoned, and although it was re-established in the 11th to 12th centuries
it is not known by whom. Whoever the people were, a comparison of some
of the architecture with that of Tula, north of Mexico City, indicates they were
heavily influenced by the Toltecs of central Mexico. Despite the site's decline,
its potent majesty continued down the years to such an extent that Spanish
conqueror Francisco Montejo (1479–1549) considered making it his capital.

WHAT TO SEE

EL CASTILLO (PIRÁMIDE DE KUKULKÁN)

The Castle is one of the Maya world's most impressive structures. Also known as the Pyramid of Kukulkán—the "feathered serpent", the greatest of the Maya gods—it rises majestically to a height of 30m (98ft) and dominates the buildings in the northern half of the site. Four flights of stairs, each with 91 steps, lead up to the final platform—making a total of 365 steps, corresponding to the number of days in the solar calendar. The head of a plumed, open-mouthed serpent decorates the base of the pyramid. There is also an interior ascent of 61 steep, very narrow steps leading to a chamber lit by electricity. The red-painted jaguar that probably served as the throne of the high priest burns bright, with its jade eyes and flint fangs. The northwest side of the pyramid is oriented toward the sacred *cenote* (▷ 110), where Kukulkán would come to receive tributes. The castle, together with the Platform of Venus and the *sacbé* (white road), represented the religious and political power of the Itzá people. *Sacbeob*, known as white roads because they were built of limestone and surfaced with cement, were sacred Maya paths, thought to have been used for ceremonial purposes or as transportation routes.

One of the best times, and also the busiest, to view El Castillo is on the morning and afternoon of the spring (March 21) and autumn (September 21) equinoxes, when the alignment of the sun's shadow casts a snake-shaped shadow on the steps of the Castle. To the ancient Maya, this image represented Kukulkán. The phenomenon was also an expression of the divine spirit of Maya cosmology, an allegory of the earth's renewal with the changing of the seasons; the spring and autumn equinoxes heralded the arrival of the crop planting and harvesting seasons.

HEADS YOU WIN, OR LOSE

In the ball court, at eye-level, a relief shows the decapitation of the winning captain, one of the most significant and powerful examples of Maya art. At one time historians thought it was the losing team that was sacrificed, yet the latest theories suggest it was the captain of the winning side, as his success made him a fitting tribute to the gods.

Left *Detail of a carved serpent's head on the Temple of the Warriors*
Below *Mayan ball players had to throw the ball through one of these rings*

SITE PLAN

1 Castillo
2 Ball Court
3 Temple of the Jaguar
4 Platform of the Skulls (Tzompantli)
5 Platform of Eagles
6 Platform of Venus
7 Well of Sacrifice
8 Temple of the Warriors
  and Chac Mool Temple
9 Group of the Thousand Columns
10 Market
11 Tomb of the High King
12 House of the Deer
13 Red House
14 El Caracol (Observatory)
15 Nunnery
16 "Church"
17 Akabdzib

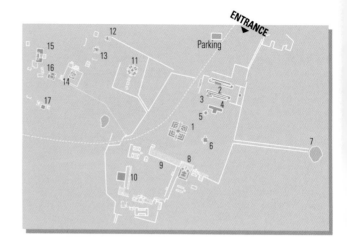

CENOTE SAGRADO

Running north of El Castillo is the *sacbé* (white road) leading to the Cenote Sagrado (Sacred Well), dedicated to the rain god Chac. Women and children, animals and valuable propitiatory objects of all kinds were thrown into its deep blue cavern as sacrifices. It was first dredged between 1904 and 1907, when a vast quantity of pottery, jade, copper and gold objects was found. In 1962 it was explored again, and some 4,000 further pieces were recovered, including beads, polished jade, lumps of copal resin, small bells, a statuette of rubber latex, another of wood, and a quantity of animal and human bones. Another well, the Cenote de Xtoloc, to the south of El Castillo, was probably used as a water supply.

TEMPLO DE LOS GUERREROS

To the east of El Castillo is the Temple of the Warriors, with its famous reclining Chac Mool statue at the entrance to the two enclosures. Chac Mool was a messenger to the gods and the ancient Maya would place offerings on his stomach. The temple is richly decorated with motifs representing the military elite to whom the temple was dedicated. The pyramidal platform has now been closed off to avoid erosion. Inside are vivid carvings of plumed serpents, warriors, and priests. Next to it is the Mil Columnas (Thousand Columns Group), so called for its procession of pillars with intricate relief carvings.

CHICHÉN VIEJO

About 500m (550 yards) from the main clearing are the buildings of the earlier city, Old Chichén. El Caracol (Snail), or the Observatory, is included in this group, so named because of its interior spiral stairway, which resembles a snail's shell, and its astrological associations. Above the doors of the observation tower carvings represent the rain god Chac. The structure's windows are aligned with the cardinal points in order to make astrological calculations. So incredibly sophisticated were the Maya systems that they are believed to have predicted solar eclipses occurring between the seventh and 24th centuries.

Next to El Caracol is the Casa de las Monjas, or Nunnery, which has two patios in the Puuc architectural style. The upper facade is stunning—a latticework of glyphs and sculpted masks of the gods. A 30-minute walk to the right of Las Monjas leads to the Templo de los Tres Dinteles (Temple of the Three Lintels).

Right *Images of Chac, the rain god, adorn the temples*

INFORMATION

www.islacozumel.com.mx/

✚ 317 S8 ℹ Altos Plaza de Sol, Colonia Centro ☎ (987) 869 02 11 ⊙ Mon–Fri 9–2.30 ⛴ Ferries from Playa del Carmen

INTRODUCTION

Mexico's largest Caribbean island and one of the world's most popular diving destinations also teems with wildlife and birdlife, as well as some small archaeological sites of interest. Cozumel, encircled by more than 25 reef formations, is a fabulous diving site. At the northern end, the archaeological site of San Gervasio, with a temple dedicated to Ixchel, goddess of fertility, is unmissable. San Miguel de Cozumel, the only town, has little character—due mainly to the construction of a US air base during World War II. The best public beaches are from San Miguel town. (Note that some roads are suitable only for 4WDs.)

A circuit of the island on paved roads is easily done in a day. Head due east out of San Miguel (take the continuation of Avenida Juárez). Make the detour to San Gervasio then carry on to the Caribbean coast at Mescalito's restaurant. Here, turn left for the northern tip (road unsuitable for ordinary vehicles), or right for the south, passing Punta Morena, Chen Río, Punta Chiqueros, El Mirador (a low viewpoint), and Paradise Cove. Here, the paved road heads west, while an unpaved road continues south to Punta Celarain and an interesting old lighthouse.

Cozumel was settled by the Maya as early as AD300 and went on to become a major seaport for Mayan trade between Veracruz and Honduras. The Maya successfully resisted Spanish attempts to colonize the Yucatán Peninsula until 1519, when Hernán Cortés arrived with his men and destroyed many of the island's temples, marking the start of the bitter struggle to control the peninsula. Following Cortés' departure, the island was struck by a smallpox epidemic and the population rapidly decreased to under 300 by 1570. Thirty years later it was abandoned.

Pirates used Cozumel as a base during the 17th century, and in 1848 settlers from the mainland fled here to escape the bloodthirsty reprisals of the Maya,

Above *A scuba diver approaches an overhang at Tormentos Reef*

who were wreaking revenge for the many atrocities perpetrated against them by the Spanish. In 1961, French explorer Jacques Cousteau arrived, and when he discovered that the surrounding waters possessed some of the best scuba diving sites in the world, this quiet little fishing community developed into the major diving destination it is today.

WHAT TO SEE

ARCHAEOLOGICAL SITES

There are some 32 archaeological sites on Cozumel; those on the east coast are mostly single structures (thought to have been lookouts or navigational aids). The easiest to see are the restored ruins of the Maya-Toltec period at San Gervasio (daily 7–5) in the north—7km (4 miles) from Cozumel town, then 10km (6 miles) to the left up a paved road. Guides are on hand, or you can buy a self-guiding booklet at the *librería* (bookstore) on the square in San Miguel, or at the flea market. It is an interesting site, quite spread out, with *sacbeob* (sacred white roads) between the groups of buildings. There are no large structures, but it has a pleasant plaza and an arch, and pigment can be seen in places. It is also a great place to listen to birdsong and watch for butterflies, lizards, land crabs, and insects.

BEACHES

In the north of the island the beaches are sandy and wide. South of San Miguel, they tend to be narrow and rocky. The east (Caribbean) coast is rockier, but very picturesque; swimming and diving on the unprotected side is dangerous due to strong undercurrents. The only safe place to swim is the sheltered bay at Chen Río. Punta Morena is a good surf beach with reasonable accommodations and seafood.

MUSEO DE LA ISLA COZUMEL

The Museo de la Isla Cozumel on the waterfront provides a well-laid-out history of the island from pre-Columbian times to the arrival of Juan de Grijalva and Hernán Cortés in the 16th century, with engaging anecdotes revealing the seminal moments in Cozumel's history. Displays also present the island's flora and fauna. There is a good bookshop, an art gallery, a library, an auditorium, and a rooftop restaurant with excellent food and views.

✉ Avenida Rafael Melger, between Calle 4 and Calle 5 Norte ☎ (987) 872 14 34 ⊙ Daily 9–5 🖐 $3.50

PUNTA CELARAIN

The ecological park of Parque Punta Sur covers a variety of natural landscapes including lagoons and mangrove jungles. A snorkel center has opened here too, and there is a viewing platform. On the road north, opposite the turn-off to El Cedral, is a sign to El Cedral beach club, an excellent fish restaurant on a lovely beach; it is popular with dive groups for lunch. Next is Playa San Francisco, and a few kilometers beyond that the Wyndham Resort, the last big hotel south of San Miguel. Just beyond this is Parque Chankanaab (daily 7–5), a lagoon behind the beach (9km/6 miles from San Miguel). Now a national park, it has a botanical garden with local and imported plants, a rather artificial "Maya Area," swimming (ideal for families with young children), snorkeling, swimming with dolphins, dive shops, lockers, souvenirs, and good—but expensive—restaurants.

✉ Parque Punta Sur ☎ (987) 872 09 14

BILLFISH

Cozumel hosts an annual international billfish tournament at the end of April/ beginning of May which attracts anglers from all over the world; the sea fishing is excellent, with abundant swordfish, marlin and tuna.

TIP

» There are no local buses, but Cozumel town is small enough to explore on foot. To get around the island, take an organized tour or a taxi; otherwise, rent a jeep, moped or bicycle.

Below *A deep-sea fishing boat off Cozumel where swordfish, marlin, tuna and billfish are abundant*

CHETUMAL

www.corozal.com

Visitors en route to Belize and Guatemala often use Chetumal, the state capital of Quintana Roo, as a stopover. It is also a good base to explore the ruins of the Río Bec group in Campeche state—Xpujil, Becán and Chicanná. Though attractions are thin on the ground, this small Mexican city has a more authentic feel than most of the other towns on the Riviera Maya. The avenues are broad and busy, and those at its heart are lined with huge stores selling inexpensive imported goods.

The Museo de la Cultura Maya on Avenida Héroes de Chapultepec (Tue–Thu and Sun 9–7, Fri–Sat 9–8) has good models of sites and touch-screen computers explaining the Maya calendar and glyphs. Although there are few original Maya pieces, it gives an excellent overview of Maya culture. Chetumal Bay has been designated a Natural Protected Area for manatees.

✛ 317 S9 ✉ Avenida 5 de Mayo ☎ (983) 835 05 00 ⏱ Mon–Fri 9–5 🚌 Buses from Valladolid

CHICANNÁ

Chicanná, meaning "house of the serpent's mouth," is named for its most outstanding feature—the dramatic entrance to one of the temples in the shape of a monster's mouth with fangs jutting over the lintel and lining the access stairway. Many of the structures have intricate baroque carvings in Chenes style.

Chicanná is considered to have been used as a small residential base for the rulers of the ancient regional capital of Becán. It was occupied during the Late Preclassic period; the final stages of activity at the site have been dated to the Post Classic era. Consistent with the Río Bec style, there are numerous representations of Itzamná, the Maya god of creation.

✛ 317 R9 ✉ 12km (7.5 miles) west of Xpujil ⏱ Daily 8–5 🎟 $3.50 🚐 Agencies in Chetumal offer day tours to Chicanná, Xpujil and Becán

CHICHÉN ITZÁ

▷ 108–111.

COBÁ

The great appeal of the little-excavated archaeological site of Cobá is its jungle setting and lakes. An important Maya city in the eighth and ninth centuries AD, with a population estimated to have been between 40,000 and 50,000, Cobá was abandoned for unknown reasons. The urban extension of Cobá is put at some 70sq km (27sq miles).

An unusual feature is the network of *sacbeob* (white roads). More than 40 of these sacred roads pass through the site, some local, some of great length—such as the 100km (62-mile) road to leading to Yaxuná in Yucatán state.

Lago Macanxoc, within the site, is a habitat of many turtles and fish, and is a good bird-watching area. Toucans may be seen very early in the day, and greenish-blue and brown mot-mots in the early morning. Both Lago Macanxoc and Lago Cobá, as well as their surrounding forest, can be seen from the summit of the Iglesia, at 24m (79ft) the second-tallest structure at Cobá.

There are three other groups of buildings to visit: the Macanxoc Group, about 1.5km (1 mile) from the Cobá Group; Las Pinturas, 1km (half a mile) northeast of Macanxoc, which has a temple and the remains of other buildings that employed columns in their construction; and the Nohoch Mul Group, at least another 1km (half a mile) from Las Pinturas. Nohoch Mul has the tallest pyramid to be found in the northern Yucatán (42m/138ft), a magnificent structure providing superb views of the dense jungle on all sides. An excellent way to explore the ruins and jungle is to rent a bicycle, or tricycle and driver, at the entrance to the Cobá Group.

✛ 317 S8 ✉ 40km (25 miles) inland from Tulúm ☎ (998) 883 36 71 ⏱ Daily 7–6 🎟 $4.80 🚌 Buses from Valladolid 🚐 Bilingual tours

COZUMEL

▷ 112–113.

DZIBILCHALTÚN

The Maya city of Dzibilchaltún includes more than 8,000 structures. The site (in two halves, connected by a *sacbé*) was founded as early as 1000BC; it was occupied for thousands of years but reached its peak between AD600 and 1000. The most important building is the Templo de las Siete Muñecas (Temple of Seven Dolls), named for the seven clay dolls buried within it. These can now be seen in the site museum. The structure is aligned with the four cardinal points and there is a show here each year for the spring and autumn equinoxes on March 21 and September 21. At the west end is the ceremonial hub with temples, houses, and a large plaza with an austere, open chapel.

Nearby is Cenote Xlacah, 44m (144ft) deep. You can swim in the clear water (take a mask and snorkel as it is full of fascinating fish). A nature trail, lined with indigenous trees, all labeled, starts halfway between the temple and the *cenote*, rejoining the *sacbé* halfway along.

✛ 317 R8 ✉ 14km (8.5 miles) north of Mérida ⏱ Daily 8–5 🎟 $6 ℹ VW *combis* leave from Calle 69, between 62 and 64 in Parque San Juan, every 1 or 2 hours between 5am and 7pm, stopping at the ruins en route to Chablekal 📖 Site map available from museum by ticket office

Below *A pelican, a common sight around Chetumal, where the bay is a Natural Protected Area*

EDZNÁ

Edzná, meaning "house of grimaces" or "house of the Itzáes" and built in a tranquil valley, was a huge Maya ceremonial base. Occupied from about 600BC to around AD800 or 900, it was constructed in the simple Chenes style like Chicanná, but mixed with Puuc, Classical and other influences. The focal point is the magnificent Templo de los Cinco Pisos (Temple of the Five Levels), a stepped pyramid with four levels of living quarters for the priests and a shrine and altar at the top; 65 steep steps lead up from the Central Plaza. Opposite is the Paal U'na (Temple of the Moon). Excavations are being carried out on the scores of lesser temples, but most of Edzná's original sprawl remains hidden under thick vegetation.

Imagination is needed to picture the network of irrigation canals and holding basins built by the Maya along the valley below sea level. Some of the site's stelae remain in position (two large stone faces with squinting eyes are covered by a thatched shelter); other fine examples can be seen in various Campeche museums.

There is also a good example of a *sacbé* (white road). In July (the exact date varies), a Maya ceremony to Chac is held here to encourage or to celebrate the arrival of the rains, as appropriate.

🚻 317 R9 ✉ 61km (38 miles) southeast of Campeche 🕐 Tue–Sun 8–5 💲 $3.90 🚍 Tourist bus from Campeche town wall 🚌 Daily tours from Viajes Programados, Calle 59, Edificio Belmar, in Campeche

EK-BALAM

Ek-Balam ("Black Jaguar") is surrounded by traditional Maya villages. A series of temples, sacrificial altars and residential buildings is grouped around a central plaza, elaborately finished with carved sculptures or polychrome stucco; the most impressive of these is a gruesome mask with protruding fangs on the main facade of the acropolis, which appears to be a monster, and winged idols believed to be angels, imagery unique to Ek-Balam.

Occupied from 300BC, this site formed the hub of the Tah kingdom that dominated the eastern Yucatán state. It flourished during the Late Classic period, reaching its zenith around AD600 to 1200. The acropolis is the second-largest standing pyramid in the state of Yucatán after the Kinich Kakmó pyramid in Izamal (▷ 116), with richly carved stucco and a series of interconnecting passageways. The site's most important discovery was the tomb of the ruler Ukit Kan Lel Tok, containing valuable objects such as jewelry and weapons.

🚻 317 S8 ℹ️ 25km (16 miles) north of Valladolid 🕐 Daily 8–5 💲 $3 ❓ *Colectivos* to Temozón, from where you can bicycle the remaining 12km (7.5 miles) to the ruins

GRUTAS DE BALANKANCHÉ

The Balankanché Caves lay hidden until Humberto Gómez, a tour guide from Chichén Itzá, discovered them in 1959. In addition to being extraordinarily beautiful, with a tangible sense of mysticism, the caves are of significant archaeological importance. Close to the entrance, dripping stalactite formations cluster around a gigantic stalagmite, 7m (23ft) tall, that resembles a ceiba tree, the sacred tree of the Maya. Inside, a variety of ceremonial objects, believed to be offerings to the rain god Tlaloc (the Aztec equivalent of Chac), were discovered. Within the same echoing chamber is the Balam Throne, a sacred altar. The museum houses a collection of ceremonial objects including pots and *metates* (grinding stones). It is very damp and hot within the caves, but there are lovely gardens outside. There is a son et lumière show, but it is rather poor.

🚻 317 S8 ✉ 6km (4 miles) east of Chichén Itzá 🕐 Daily 9–5 (allow about 45 minutes for the 300m/985ft descent) 💲 $4.70 🚍 Buses from Chichén Itzá and Pisté-Balankanché 🚌 Guided tours in English at 11, 1 and 3

ISLA HOLBOX

Isla Holbox lies just off the northern tip of the Yucatán Peninsula, a world apart from the resorts of Cancún and Playa del Carmen, with long stretches of dazzling pink-tinged sand glistening with mother-of-pearl shells shelving to an emerald ocean.

In the small fishing village founded in 1847, dusty streets dotted with painted wooden houses and *palapa* (palm-thatched) restaurants are home to an eclectic population. The best way to explore the island is by golf cart or moped. Local fishermen run eco-tours where you can swim and snorkel alongside whale sharks (Jul–Sep only) and barracuda; though very few nasty occurrences have been reported, extreme caution is advised.

There are five uninhabited islands beyond Holbox, including the bird-watching paradise of Isla de Pajaros (Bird Island).

🚻 317 S7 🚍 Buses to Chiquilá for boats three times daily, and direct from Tizimín

Above Ferries from the mainland and boats dock at Isla Mujeres' laid-back, low-rise main village

ISLA MUJERES

www.isla-mujeres.com.mx

Just a 20-minute ferry trip from Cancún, Isla Mujeres (Island of Women) is a refreshing antidote to the urban sprawl of the big resorts and the hurly-burly of package tourism. The town is strictly low-rise, with brightly painted buildings giving it the feel of a Caribbean island. The island's laws prohibit any building higher than three floors, and US franchises are not allowed to open branches here. There are several good beaches on the northwest coast, 5 minutes' walk from the town. Laid-back restaurants and nightspots with live music are plentiful. Away from the town, at the south of the island, is El Garrafón, a national park established to protect the coral reef (▷ 133).

A 15-minute walk from El Garrafón will take you to the only known Maya shrine to a female deity: Ixchel, goddess of the moon and fertility. At the heart of the island are the curious remains of a pirate's domain, Casa de Mundaca (▷ 127).

➕ 317 S7 ℹ️ Avenida Rueda Medina 130 ☎ (998) 877 03 07 🕐 Mon–Fri 9–4 🚢 Ferry from Cancún

IZAMAL

Izamal is known as the "golden city" for its colonial heart, entirely painted in rich yellow. Once a major Classic religious site said to be founded by Itzamná, the god of creation who sometimes appeared as a priest, 20 Maya structures have been identified—several of them on Calle 27. Izamal became one of the hubs from which the Spanish attempted to Christianize the Maya. Fray Diego de Landa, the historian of the Spanish Conquest of Mérida, founded the huge Franciscan convent and church—Convento de San Antonio de Padua. Constructed on top of a Maya pyramid, it was begun in 1549 and has the second-largest atrium in the world. The surrounding stone walls are embellished with carvings of Maya origin. In 1993 the throne was built for the Pope's visit. The image of the Inmaculada Virgen de la Concepción in the church was made the Reina de Yucatán (Queen of Yucatán) in 1949, and the patron saint of the state in 1970.

Just a couple of blocks away are the ruins of a great mausoleum known as the Pirámide Kinich Kakmó. At 195m (640ft) long, 173m (567ft) wide and 36m (118ft) high it is the fifth-highest pyramid in Mexico.

From the top of the Kinich Kakmó pyramid there is an excellent view of the town and surrounding *henequén* (sisal) and citrus plantations.

➕ 317 R8 🕐 Daily 8–5 🚌 Buses from Mérida

KOHUNLICH

A local Mayan discovered the ruins of Kohunlich in 1967. Kohunlich means "cahoon ridge:" A *cahoon* is the Belizian name for a type of palm, and these soaring trees line the pathways around the site. The ruins' most outstanding feature is the Pirámide de los Mascarones (Pyramid of the Masks), flanked by striking masks carved in stucco. Tinged with red, each mask is more than 2m (6.5ft) tall. Iconic and enigmatic, they are believed to be a representation of gods, or Kohunlich's ruling elite, yet their true identification eludes archaeologists and historians. This peaceful, isolated site, built during the Early Classic period, doesn't receive the same number of visitors as the sites farther north.

➕ 317 R9 ✉ 61km (38 miles) west of Chetumal 🕐 Daily 8–5 💲 $4 🚌 Buses and *colectivos* from Chetumal 🚢 Many agencies in Chetumal (▷ 114) offer tours

LAGUNA BACALAR

Close to the border with Belize is the Laguna Bacalar, a crystal-clear freshwater lagoon, 42km (26 miles) long and 2km (1.2 miles) wide. It is one of Mexico's largest and most mesmerizing lakes, also known as the Laguna de Siete Colores for its different shades of greens and blues. The lake teems with fish and waterbirds, and on the lakeshore the birdlife is resplendent. If you are lucky, you may see rare giant tropical otters, as well as monkeys and toucans. Activities include kayaking, swimming and skin-diving.

Overlooking the lake is the stone Spanish fort of San Felipe, believed to have been built around 1729 by the Spanish to defend the area from English pirates and smugglers (there is a plaque praying for protection from the British). British ships roamed the islands and reefs, looting Spanish galleons laden with gold on their way from Peru to Cuba. There are many old shipwrecks on the reef and around the Banco Chinchorro, 50km (31 miles) out in the Caribbean.

The village of Bacalar is a subdued town, which goes about its business seemingly oblivious to the trickle of largely Mexican visitors. There is a dock for swimming north of the plaza, with a restaurant and disco next to it. About 3km (2 miles) south of the village is the startlingly clear, stunningly blue Cenote Azul, 90m (295ft) deep, which teems with fish and invites swimming and snorkeling.

➕ 317 S9 ✉ 37km (23 miles) north of Chetumal 🚌 Buses from Chetumal

MÉRIDA

Mérida is a convenient base for exploring the archaeological sites on the Puuc and Convent routes. Its backstreets are dotted with colonial buildings, and there's plenty of lively bustle. The capital of Yucatán state and its colonial heart is Mérida, a frenetic, tightly packed city full of buildings in varying states of repair, from the grandiose to the dilapidated. Originally a large Maya city called Tihó, it was conquered by Francisco de Montejo on January 6 1542. He dismantled the Maya pyramids and used the stone as the foundations for the Catedral San Ildefonso (1556–98).

ZÓCALO

The city revolves around the large, shady *zócalo* (Plaza Mayor), site of the Catedral San Ildefonso. Completed in 1598, it is the oldest cathedral in Latin America and has a fine baroque facade. Inside is the Cristo de las Ampollas (Christ of the Blisters), a statue carved from a tree that burned for a whole night after being hit by lightning without showing any damage at all. To the left of the cathedral is the 19th-century neoclassical Palacio de Gobierno (Government Palace), with its collection of enormous murals by Campeche artist Fernando Castro Pacheco (1918–66), which can be viewed daily until 8pm. Casa de Montejo, on the south side of the plaza, now a branch of the Banamex bank, is a 16th-century palace built by the city's founder. Away from the main plaza along Calle 60 is Parque Hidalgo, a tree-filled square bordering the 17th-century Iglesia de Jesús. A little farther along Calle 60 is the early 20th-century Teatro Peón Contreras, with a neoclassical facade, marble staircase and Italian frescoes.

MUSEUMS

The Museo de Antropología e Historia in Palacio Cantón has an excellent collection of original Maya objects from various sites in Yucatán, including jade jewelry dredged from *cenotes* and deformed skulls with sharpened teeth. Museo Macay, on the main plaza, has a permanent exhibition of Yucatecan artists. The Museo de la Canción Yucateca has an exhibition of objects and instruments relating to the history of music in the region. The Pinacoteca Juan Gamboa Guzmán is a gallery showing classic and contemporary painting and sculpture.

INFORMATION

➕ 317 R8 ℹ Teatro Peón Contreras, Calle 60 and 57 (just off Parque Hidalgo) ☎ (999) 924 92 90 🕐 Daily 8am–9pm ✈ Mérida airport, 8km (5 miles) south

Museo de Antropología e Historia

✉ Paseo de Montejo 485 ☎ (999) 928 32 58 🕐 Tue–Sat 8–8, Sun 8–2

Museo Macay

✉ Calle 60 ☎ (999) 924 52 33 🕐 Wed–Mon 10–6

Museo de la Canción Yucateca

✉ Calle 57 ☎ (999) 923 72 24 🕐 Tue–Fri 9–5, Sat–Sun 9–3

Pinacoteca Juan Gamboa Guzmán

✉ Calle 59 ☎ (999) 924 52 33 🕐 Tue–Sat 8–8, Sun 8–2

TIPS

» During July and August Mérida is subject to heavy rains during the afternoon—as well as being very hot.
» Mérida is renowned for the quality of its hammocks (▷ 285) and Panama hats.

Below *The baroque facade of the Catedral San Ildefonso, Latin America's oldest cathedral*

REGIONS THE YUCATÁN • SIGHTS

117

PLAYA DEL CARMEN

A 50-minute drive south of Cancún, the former fishing village of Playa, as it is locally known, has developed rapidly to become a major visitor resort. The beach is dazzling white, with clear shallow water, and the vast number of diving and watersports schools create a youthful, energetic beach culture. Activities include yoga, massage, salsa classes, and Spanish lessons. Because of its good transportation links, many visitors choose Playa as a base for trips to the archaeological sites of Tulúm and Cobá, Cozumel and the less developed beaches of the Riviera Maya.

While Playa has not had the high-rise treatment of Cancún, the beach area is still very commercialized and international. The focal point is the pedestrianized Avenida 5, one block from and parallel with the beach, which funnels south to a classy mall. This busy strip is punctuated with Hemingway-themed *palapa* (thatched) restaurants, sports bars, international restaurants, cafés, designer-label outlets, and souvenir shops with a hard sell.

➕ 317 S8 ℹ️ Avenida Juárez and Avenida 15 ☎ (984) 873 28 04 🕐 Mon–Sat 9–8, Sun 9–5 🚌 Buses from Cancún

PUERTO MORELOS

The quiet, unspoiled fishing village of Puerto Morelos, with pristine, uncrowded beaches and good diving and snorkeling opportunities, is a low-key place to relax for a few days, or stop over en route to larger towns farther south, such as Playa del Carmen.

The village is little more than a large plaza right on the waterfront with a couple of streets running off it, but there is a good supply of hotels and restaurants.

If on arrival at Cancún airport you don't wish to spend the night in the city, you could get a taxi directly to Puerto Morelos. This is also the place to catch the car ferry to the island of Cozumel.

A local cooperative of tour operators has an office on the plaza

Above *Playa del Carmen is famous for its white sand and watersports*

and offers snorkeling, kayaking, bird-watching, and fishing trips.

➕ 317 S8 🚌 Buses from Playa del Carmen to Cancún stop on the main highway turn-off close to Puerto Morelos, where taxis are available ✈ Cancún airport 18km (11 miles) north

RESERVA DE LA BIÓSFERA SIAN KA'AN

Declared a UNESCO World Heritage Site, Sian Ka'an, meaning "place where the sky is born" lies south of Tulum and covers 4,500sq km (1,740sq miles) of the Quintana Roo coast down to the Punta Allen peninsula. While independent travel is difficult, the rewards are great. The opportunities for spotting wildlife and birdlife in the reserve are excellent, and the vast area is also studded with more than 20 unrestored Maya ruins, all the more mystical and powerful for their primordial setting. About one-third of the reserve is tropical forest, one-third savannah and mangrove and one-third coastal and marine habitat—including 110km (68 miles) of barrier reef, the second-largest reef in the world. Mammals include jaguars, pumas, ocelots and other big cats, monkeys, tapirs, peccaries, manatees, and deer. Turtles nest on the beaches; and there are crocodiles, plus a wide variety of land and aquatic birds.

The small community of Punta Allen at the tip of the peninsula makes its living mostly by lobster

fishing, using traditional Maya methods. There are one or two small hotels and restaurants here, but you'll need provisions for the drive down.

➕ 317 S8–S9 ✉ 3km (2 miles) south of Tulúm ℹ️ Centro Ecológico Sían Ka'an (CESiak) offers guided tours of the reserve ☎ (984) 104 05 22; www.cesiak.org ❓ Don't try to get there independently without a car. It is possible to drive into the reserve from Tulúm village as far as Punta Allen; beyond that you need a launch 🤚 $2

RÍO LAGARTOS

This attractive little fishing village on the north coast of Yucatán state is the focal point for boat rides through the biosphere reserve, which contains thousands of pink flamingos as well as many other species of bird. Boat trips to the flamingo reserve can be arranged by walking down to the harbor, where you'll receive many offers from boatmen.

The largest colony of flamingos is near Las Coloradas (15km/ 9 miles away), recognizable by a large salt mound on the horizon—make sure your boatman takes you there rather than to the smaller groups of birds along the river (▷ 135). Fifteen minutes' walk east from the Río Lagartos harbor is an *ojo de agua*, a pool of sulfurous water for bathing, supplied by an underground *cenote*.

➕ 317 S7 ✉ 100km (62 miles) north of Valladolid

TULÚM

The 12th-century Maya-Toltec ruins of Tulúm, with its city walls of gleaming white stone, overlooking the dazzling turquoise waters of the Caribbean, are one of the Yucatán's most visited sites. Perched on craggy coastal cliffs, Tulúm was once an important trading port whose fortress was still occupied when the Spanish arrived in 1518. Although this relatively small site does not rank among the greats, today the walled ruins have become a magnet for sun-worshippers and archaeological enthusiasts alike. To gain an illuminating new perspective on the ruins, consider one of Tulum's "Visitas Nocturnas," a 45-minute night-time tour on which you'll see the city's structures bathed in deep shades of red, blue and amber light.

TEMPLO DEL DIOS DESCENDENTE

The Templo del Dios Descendente (Temple of the Descending God) is named after the upside-down stucco figure carved over its entrance. The significance of this god is unclear, although he may have symbolized rain or the setting sun (Cozumel was the home of the rising sun), or have been the Bee God, Ah Mucen Cab, an important deity in the region. Similar images can be seen on the other buildings.

EL CASTILLO

El Castillo is the main structure on the site, fronted by serpent columns, which were built in several stages. It commands a view of both the sea and the forested Quintana Roo lowlands stretching westward. All its main openings face west, as do most, but not all, of the doorways at Tulúm. The majority of the main structures are roped off so that you cannot climb the Castillo, nor get close to the surviving frescoes, especially on the Templo de los Frescos (Temple of the Frescoes). The facade of the palace is decorated with carved reliefs of the Descending God (▷ above).

Right in the middle of the site is a small beach cove—most visitors come prepared with bathing suits. There are also quieter beaches nearby, which require a relatively easy clamber down the cliffs. In the Tulúm area there are more than 50 *cenotes*, with opportunities for cave diving (▷ 288 and 289).

INFORMATION

✚ 317 S8 ✉ 130km (80 miles) south of Cancún toward Chetumal ⏰ Daily 7–6 ✋ $4.50 🚌 Buses from Valladolid. Frequent buses ply the coast from Cancún to Chetumal, stopping at Tulúm en route ❓ There is a visitor complex at the entrance to the ruins

TIP

» Prior to the "Visitas Nocturnas" an interesting audiovisual introduction to the site is shown. You're then given headphones that feature an audio walking tour available in several languages, including English. Tours cost $22 per person and depart every 10 to 15 minutes between 8 and 10pm.

Below and overleaf *The Maya-Toltec ruined El Castillo at Tulúm has a fabulous clifftop location above blue Caribbean waters and forested lowlands*

INFORMATION

➕ 317 R8 🕐 Daily 8–5 💲 $9.50
🚌 $40 per 1.5-hour tour 🅴 Expensive
café in the visitor center ❓ *Son et
lumière* shows in Spanish 8pm in summer,
7pm in winter

INTRODUCTION

One of the most important Maya sites in Mexico, with outstandingly intricate stone carvings and mosaics, Uxmal encapsulates the purity and beauty of the Puuc style. Uxmal means "that which was thrice built" or "place of abundant harvest." The site dates back to the Preclassic era, although the majority of its 150 or so structures were built during the Late Classic period and final stages of the Classic period. Maya cities in this region are characterized by the quadrangular layout of the buildings—set on raised platforms, with a plain lower section and a richly embellished upper section—and a man-made underground water-storage system. Representations of the rain god Chac, who was believed to have been supremely important due to the area's low rainfall, are omnipresent.

At its peak, Uxmal was one of the largest of the Maya cities, with a population of around 25,000. Its rulers probably also governed nearby Kabah, Labná and Sayil (▷ 130–131). Much of the city's prosperity came from the fertility of the soil, and sophisticated engineering techniques meant that rainwater could be collected in *chultunes*, or cisterns. Unlike at Chichén Itzá, there were no *cenotes* to provide a water supply. With the growth of Chichén Itzá under Toltec rule, Uxmal declined in power and prosperity and was finally allied with nearby Mayapán in the Late Post Classic period. The buildings were abandoned for reasons unknown in the 10th century, and may have come under the Toltec influence.

WHAT TO SEE

CASA DEL ADIVINO (PYRAMID OF THE MAGICIAN)

This oval-shaped pyramid is set on a large rectangular base; rather than "thrice built," there is evidence that five stages of building were used in its construction. This is one of the most enigmatic Maya structures, and many myths surround its creation. According to one legend, the god Itzamná is supposed to have built the pyramid in one night, without any assistance. It is 38m (125ft) tall, with steep staircases leading to two temples at the top. The Fangs of Chac and fine stone latticework mark the doorways. The ancient city

Above *The Pyramid of the Magician was built in five stages*

of Uxmal was constructed in strict accordance to the position of the planets, and the western stairway of the Pyramid of the Magician aligns with the setting sun at the summer solstice (June 21). Sacrificial rituals at Uxmal were carried out from this pyramid—the priest would rip out the beating heart of the living victim before tossing the body down the staircase.

CASA DE LAS MONJAS

The Nunnery has four low buildings set around a large courtyard. It was named by the Spanish, who thought the 74 rooms resembled convent cells. Chac, the rain god, is represented with fine masks arranged vertically on the corners of the buildings. The northern building, the oldest and most ambitious, is the purest representation of the Puuc style, while the east building is decorated with double-headed serpents and intricate latticework on its cornices. Plumed serpents adorn the facade of the west building.

PALACIO DEL GOBERNADOR

The House of the Governor is considered to be one of the most outstanding buildings in Mesoamerica. Its facade was constructed with more than 20,000 stones. Above the central entrance is an elaborate trapezoidal motif, with a string of Chac masks interwoven into a flowing, undulating, serpent-like shape extending to the facade's two corners. The stately two-headed jaguar throne in front of the structure suggests the building may have had a royal or administrative function.

CASA DE LAS TORTUGAS

Compared with many buildings at Uxmal, the House of the Turtles is rather sober. It is named for the carved turtles on the upper cornice; below, a short row of tightly packed columns resemble the Maya *palapas*—houses made of sticks with thatched roofs, still used today.

EL PALOMAR

The Dovecote is the oldest (AD700–800) and most damaged of the buildings at Uxmal, and in many ways sits rather incongruously with the Puuc style. What remains is still impressive: A long, low platform of wide columns is topped with clusters of roof combs, whose serrated appearance bears a similarity to dovecotes.

TIPS

» A visit to Uxmal makes a grand end to the Puuc route tour (▷ 130–131), and sunset is the perfect time to view the site in its full glory.

» Views of the whole site can be had from the top of the fifth temple, reached via the eastern staircase.

Below *The tears of this carved stone turtle on the House of Turtles were believed by the Maya to bring rain*

VALLADOLID

Roughly halfway between Mérida and Cancún is Valladolid, a relaxed, vibrant little town with some fine colonial architecture; it has experienced a steady increase in visitors due to its proximity to Chichén Itzá. The heart of town is the leafy central plaza, with a fountain that is illuminated in the evening. Here, elderly *Vallisoletanos* take siestas beneath the trees, young couples share ice cream and in the evening dance to the brass bands which often play from 8pm. The Franciscan cathedral dominates the plaza, honey-gold in the late-afternoon light. There is a slightly medieval feel to the city, with some of the streets tapering off into mud tracks. Valladolid's location makes it an ideal place to settle for a few days while exploring the ruins of Chichén Itzá, Cobá, Tulúm, the fishing village

Below A stand selling colorful traditional clothing in the local market at the little town of Valladolid

of Río Lagartos, and the three beautiful *cenotes* in the area. With its excellent-value hotels and a welcoming, low-key atmosphere, it is a much more appealing base than Mérida.

Iglesia de Santa Ana, one block east of the plaza on Calle 41, has a small town museum (daily 9–9) with a lovely courtyard garden. It shows the history of rural Yucatán and has exhibits from the ruins of Ek-Balam (▷ 115). A 10-minute walk east from the plaza, on calles 36 and 39, is Cenote Zací (daily 8–6), where you can swim (except when there is algae in the water). There is a restaurant on site and lighted promenades. For other *cenotes* in the area, ▷ 289.

✚ 317 S8 ℹ East side of *zócalo* ☎ (985) 856 18 65 🕐 Daily 9–9

XCALAK

Xcalak, at the tip of Quintana Roo, across the bay from Chetumal, is a curious blend of Mexican and Belizean culture that appeals to those in search of a remote, rugged, Caribbean landscape with good facilities for outdoor activities. The area is famous for its excellent fishing and the scuba diving is highly rated. The village itself has very little in the way of visitor infrastructure, with just a few shops selling beer and basic supplies, and one small restaurant serving Mexican food.

A few kilometers north of Xcalak, Hotel Villa Caracol rents comfortable (though expensive) *cabañas* (huts) and provides sportfishing and diving facilities. Trips can be arranged from Villa Caracol to the fabulous Banco Chinchorro, an unspoiled island which has a large coral reef 26km (16 miles) offshore and a graveyard of shipwrecks spanning centuries, or to San Pedro in Belize. In the village you may be able to rent a boat to explore Chetumal Bay and Banco Chinchorro. Do not try to walk from Xcalak along the coast to San Pedro; the route is virtually impassable.

✚ 317 S9 🚤 Private launch from Chetumal ❓ *Colectivos* from Chetumal

XCARET

www.xcaret.com
Xcaret, south along Route 307 from Cancún, is promoted as an eco-archaeological Maya theme park. Geared toward daytrippers from the Riviera resorts, it is either a glossy, multimedia sprint though the nature, culture and traditions of the Maya, or an overpriced, tasteless, tacky theme park—depending on your point of view. Originally a port called Polé, the ancient Maya site of Xcaret was the departure point for voyages to Cozumel. Attractions include an underground river winding through *cenotes*, caves and tunnels lit by natural light shafts, a dolphin enclosure with interactive dolphin programs, a butterfly pavilion, a bird sanctuary, horseback-riding and bicycling. Many visitors come here for the glitzy evening show "Xcaret Spectacular," a gala performance that includes a re-enactment of a pre-Hispanic ball game, and traditional music and dance performances.

➕ 317 S8 ✉ 72km (45 miles) south of Cancún ☎ 01 (800) 292 27 38 🕐 Daily 8.30am–10pm ✋ Adult $62, child (under 1.4 meters tall) $31. Additional charges for activities ❓ 1km (half-mile) walk from entrance to Xcaret. Alternatively take a taxi, or a tour from Playa del Carmen or Cancún. You can also walk along the beach from Playa del Carmen; it takes 3 hours

XEL-HÁ

www.xelha.com.mx

Meaning "where the water flows," the national park of Xel-Há, on the Riviera Maya, surrounds a small bay with a beautiful clear lagoon. Here you can snorkel (arrive as early as possible to see the fish, as the lagoon is full of visitors throughout most of the day), swim in *cenotes*, snuba dive (without tanks) or visit the dolphin enclosure, spa or "hammock island." Of the land-based activities, the highlight is the marvelous "path of conscience"

through the jungle, which leads to one of the lagoon bays. The path is lined with sculptures and anecdotes relating to nature. Across the road from the park are the Xel-Há ruins, also known as Los Basadres.

➕ 317 S8 ✉ 10km (6 miles) north of Tulúm ☎ (984) 884 71 65 🕐 Daily 8.30–6 (closing times vary) ✋ Adult $75, child (under 1.4 meters tall) $50. Additional charges for activities 🚌 Buses from Cancún, Playa del Carmen, and Tulúm

XPUJIL

The tiny village of Xpujil, on the Chetumal–Escárcega highway, is convenient for the three sets of ruins in this area—Xpujil, Becán (▷ 105) and Chicanná (▷ 114). It has two hotels and a couple of shops. Xpujil is a small site constructed in the Río Bec style, which is characterized by heavy masonry towers simulating pyramids and temples, usually found rising in pairs

at the ends of elongated buildings. The main building has an unusual set of three towers with rounded corners and steps that are too steep to climb, suggesting they may have been purely decorative. On the facade, on either side of the main entrance, are the open jaws of an enormous reptile in profile, possibly representing Itzamná, the Maya god of creation.

Xpujil's main period of activity was AD500 to 750; it began to go into decline around 1100. It can be very peaceful and quiet here in the early morning, compared with the throng of visitor activity at the more accessible sites such as Chichén Itzá and Uxmal.

➕ 317 R9 ✉ 100km (62 miles) west of Chetumal 🕐 Daily 8–5 ✋ $3.50

Above *The clear, semi-freshwater lagoon of the ecological reserve at Xel-Hó, full of tropical fish, is a snorkeler's delight*

ISLA MUJERES

Pristine white coral sands and azure sea provide the perfect antidote to the brash urban sprawl of Cancún.

THE DRIVE

Distance: 22km (14 miles)
Time: 1 day
Start/end at: El Muelle Pier

HOW TO GET THERE

Ferries leave from Puerto Juárez in Cancún every 30 minutes between 9am and 4.45pm, $12.50 return.

★ On leaving the ferry terminal, on El Muelle Pier, turn right and after two blocks you will come to Rentador Gomar where you can rent a golf cart/moped, the best way to get around. From Gomar, take the first left along Calle Nicolas Bravo, heading inland. After two blocks you reach the main square.

❶ Plaza Municipal, with its central pagoda, is overlooked by Iglesia de La Concepción and flanked with a baseball court, ice-cream parlors, the main supermarket and a children's merry-go-round. The square is at its most vibrant on Sunday evenings, when families from across the island set up stands selling *tacos*, regional delicacies and handicrafts.

Head one block toward the waterfront, turn left onto Calle Guerrero, then right after one more block onto Calle Madero, which brings you to the sea. Park your golf cart or moped and walk out on to the main promenade of the shore.

❷ This windward stretch of coast is wild and rugged and off-limits to swimmers. You can take a 15-minute detour south along the coastal promenade where there are hotels, bars and streets lined with painted clapboard houses.

Continue north along the coast (about a 10-minute walk) to the most beautiful beach on the island.

❸ Playa del Norte is the archetypal Caribbean beach: glimmering turquoise sea, a wide stretch of fine white sand, palms and an infectiously mellow vibe. The sea is shallow for more than 90m (300ft) and there is good snorkeling. The blazing scarlet sunsets here are spectacular.

Walk along the beach toward the lighthouse. Just before reaching it, leave the beach and turn left onto Calle López Mateos. Some 100m (110 yards) along the street, on the left-hand side, is the cemetery.

❹ Here, amid tombs decorated with funerary sculptures, angels and flowers, is the grave of slave trader/pirate Fermín Mundaca, whose tale of unrequited love is legendary on La Isla. Ask a local to point it out to you. Mundaca built Vista Alegre (see right) for the young girl he loved, but she rejected him and he died, broken-hearted, in Mérida.

Leave the cemetery and turn right immediately onto Hidalgo, the town's main avenue. Continue to Calle Madero and turn left here to collect your golf cart or moped, then return to Avenida Rueda de Medina and head south. The road continues to the Punta Sur, passing the naval base, airport and Miraflores and Cañatol districts, before arriving at Playa Paraíso and Playa Lancheros, just south of Laguna Makax.

5 Playa Paraíso is an expensive mini-resort for Cancún daytrippers. Playa Lancheros is a lovely stretch of beach and recreation center.

From Playa Lancheros, the main highway (known as the Corredor Panorámico) hugs the coast as it heads south. In between chic apartment buildings, luxury hotels and spas there are fleeting glimpses of the sea, with the high-rise beach metropolis of Cancún on the horizon. The road ends at El Garrafón.

6 This snorkeling center, 8km (5 miles) from the town, has been developed into a recreational resort in the style of Xcaret (▷ 124) on the mainland.

A 15-minute walk from here takes you to the tip of the island and the ruins of a Maya shrine, Santuario Maya a la Diosa Ixchel—unique in being dedicated to a female deity.

7 There is a cultural center near the shrine, with large sculptures by several international artists. The views from the lighthouse are particularly stunning.

Return to the highway and head north. In the middle of the island, southeast of the lagoon, a dirt road leads off the main highway to Casa de Mundaca, home of the pirate Fermín Mundaca.

8 A big arch gate marks its entrance. Paths have been laid out among the trees, but all that remains of the estate (Vista Alegre) are one small building and a circular garden with raised beds, a well and a gateway. Look for the poignant carving on the garden side of the gate, *La entrada de La Trigueña* (La Trigueña was the girl's nickname).

From Casa de Mundaca, head north to Avenida Rueda Medina—Laguna Makax is on your left. It's a 10-minute ride back to El Muelle Pier from here.

TOURIST INFORMATION
www.islamujeres.com
www.isla-mujeres.com.mx
✉ Avenida Rueda Medina 130, Cancún
☎ (998) 877 03 07

PLACE TO VISIT
CASA DE MUNDACA
🕐 Daily 9–5

WHERE TO EAT
BISTRO FRANCÉS
▷ 137.

EL BALCÓN DE ARRIBA
▷ 137.

Opposite *Detail of a plaque on the pointed arch of Casa de Mundaca*
Below *Snorkeling in the clear waters*

THE RIVIERA MAYA

A warm turquoise sea, white sands and palm groves stretch from Cancún south to Tulúm. Threaded between exclusive palaces, commercial recreational parks and the archaeological sites of the Ruta Maya, a less trodden path of traditional fishing villages, virgin beaches and exotic wildlife awaits discovery.

THE DRIVE

Distance: 285km (177 miles)
Time: 1 day
Start at: Cancún airport
End at: Cancún

★ The Riviera Maya officially begins at Cancún and continues south along the four-lane Highway 307 to Tulúm. Each turn-off is well marked. The first stop, 20km (12.5 miles) from the airport, is Puerto Morelos.

❶ Puerto Morelos (▷ 118) is the oldest fishing village on the Riviera, charming and unspoiled. You can park close to the village and walk along deserted stretches of beach or

go snorkeling. A 1km (half-mile) path south from Puerto Morelos leads to Jardín Botánico Dr. Alfredo Barrera Marin, with exotic species of flora and fauna in tropical rain forest.

From Puerto Morelos, return to Highway 307, passing Playa Paraiso and Punta Maroma, two of the best beaches along the coast. Continue south for 37km (22.5 miles) to Playa del Carmen.

❷ Playa del Carmen (▷ 118) has metamorphosed from a subdued fishing village into a beach party hotspot. Along the main thoroughfare, Avenida 5,

US franchises nudge up against souvenir shops, designer-label stores, tequila bars, spas, and all-you-can-eat buffets; it's a hard sell, essentially catering to a sun-and-fun tourist market. For a more genuine Mexican atmosphere, take a stroll along Avenida Juárez, or to find a less crowded stretch of beach, walk along Avenida 5 north as far as Calle 12, then turn onto the beach and continue north for 40 minutes along Playa de Cocos, where several beach bars provide wonderful vantage points.

A 3-hour walk south from Playa del Carmen, or a 20-minute drive south

a luxury resort. There is a wonderful *cenote*; turn right onto the beach, head south to a jungle trail and in five minutes you'll reach it. During the turtles' nesting season, the beach is strictly off limits from 6pm. About 4km (3.5 miles) south from Xcacel is the well-signed Hidden Worlds Cenotes Park.

7 Hidden Worlds is widely regarded as the most impressive submerged cave system on the Riviera Maya. *Cenote* snorkel tours of varying lengths enter a labyrinth of stalactite and stalagmite laden caverns. In tight, narrow passages with low ceilings, your snorkel tube will actually bump against hanging stalactites. Claustrophobics need not apply.

About 17km (10.5 miles) south from Hidden Worlds is Tulum (▷ 119).

8 The ruins lie 4km (2.5 miles) north of Tulúm village, and are well signposted from Highway 307. Parking is just off Highway 307, in an area known as El Crucero.

From Tulúm, it is 136km (84 miles) back to Cancún. An optional detour, if time permits, or if you plan to stay overnight in Tulúm, is to head inland for 47km (29 miles) to Cobá (▷ 114).

WHEN TO GO
If you are staying in Cancún or Tulúm make reservations in advance as it's crowded at Christmas, *Semana Santa* and national holidays.

TOURIST INFORMATION
✉ Avenida Cobá and Avenida Bonampak, Cancún ☎ (998) 884 65 31

WHERE TO EAT
MEDIA LUNA, PLAYA DEL CARMEN
▷ 137.

WHERE TO STAY
CABAÑAS COPAL, TULÚM
▷ 139.

along Highway 307, brings you to the ancient Maya site of Xcaret.

3 Xcaret (▷ 124), the former port of Polé, has been transformed into a Maya Disneyland aimed at Cancún daytrippers. However, the surroundings are glorious, with turquoise waters, fine powdered-sand beaches and mysterious jungle trails.

Continue south along Highway 307 for 29km (18 miles) towards Akumal. Look for the turn-off to the resort on the left-hand side of the road, signposted to the Akumal Caribe Hotel.

4 Akumal (▷ 105) is an exclusive resort that has seen much development, but despite the proliferation of complexes it has a relaxed ambience. You can walk north from Akumal for 3km (2 miles) to the Yal Ku lagoon (daily 8–5), another excellent snorkeling spot.

Return to Highway 307 and in 1km (half a mile), on the right-hand side of the road, is a green sign for Aktun Chen, another of the Maya Riviera's

eco-parks. Turn onto this unpaved road to the park, in 3km (2 miles).

5 Aktun Chen, meaning "cave with an underground river inside," lies in more than 400ha (988 acres) of rain forest. There are three caves with a *cenote* 12m (40ft) deep. The stalactites and stalagmites formed more than 5 million years ago are spectacularly illuminated. Guided tours last 1.5 hours.

Continue south on Highway 307 for another 5km (3 miles) to Xcacel, reached by a dirt road from the main highway (watch out for the steep drop from the highway) that eventually leads to a guard shack—pay the security guard 20 pesos.

6 Xcacel is a superb beach and one of Mexico's most important sites for nesting sea turtles, with deep sands and minimal reef. Behind the beach are more than 362ha (894 acres) of jungle, mangrove swamps, dunes, and beaches. The area was a federal reserve until 1992, when the property was bought by a hotel chain for $2.5 million. Controversy has since raged over the construction of

THE CONVENT AND PUUC ROUTES HIGHLIGHTS

The Puuc and Convent routes, in the central west of Yucatán state, are dotted with Maya villages, ancient ruins, convents and *cenotes* (sinkholes).

THE DRIVE

Distance: 264km (164 miles)
Time: 1 day
Start/end at: Mérida

★ Get an early start from Mérida, aiming to be on the Periférico to Route 18 (signs say Kanasín, not Ruta 18) by 7.30am. Follow the signs to Acancéh, where on the main plaza you will find a Grand Pyramid, a colonial church and a modern church. Continue south on Route 18 for 8km (5 miles) to Tecoh.

❶ Tecoh has an ornate church and convent dedicated to the Virgin of the Assumption. There are carved stones around the altar. Both church and convent stand at the base of a large Maya pyramid.

From Tecoh, continue on Route 18 and pass through the small village

of Telchaquillo, which has a *cenote* in the plaza. In 4km (2.5 miles), a turn-off to the right brings you to the Maya ruins of Mayapán.

❷ Considered the last great Maya capital, Mayapán is a walled city with 4,000 mounds, six of which are in varying stages of restoration. There are murals depicting death and war, painted in the style of the codices of the Post Classic period, and sculpture in stucco. Mayapán once formed a triple alliance along with Uxmal (▷ 122–123) and Chichén Itzá (▷ 108–109).

Return to Route 18 and continue for another 22km (14 miles) to Tekit, a large village containing the Iglesia de San Antonio de Padua. The next village, Mama, 8km (5 miles) farther, has the oldest church on the route and is famous for its ornate altar and

bell-domed roof. In 9km (5.5 miles) is Chumayel, where the legendary Maya document *Chilam Balam* was found. Another 12km (7.5 miles) on is Maní, the most important stop on this route.

❸ At Maní you will find a large church, convent and museum with good multi-lingual explanations. It was here that Fray Diego de Landa (1524–79), the Bishop of Yucatán, ordered important Maya documents and objects to be burned during an intense period of Franciscan conversion of the Maya people to Christianity.

From Maní head west to the town of Ticul, which is on both the Convent and Puuc routes.

Above *The ruined three-tiered palace at the Mayan site of Sayil*

❹ Ticul is known for its *huipiles*, the embroidered white dresses worn by older Maya women (prices and quality here are much better than in Mérida) and for producing the area's ubiquitous red-clay planter pots and leather shoes.

About 16km (10 miles) southeast of Ticul, on Route 184, is the town of Oxkutzcab, with a large market on one side of the plaza and a 15th-century church on the other. The area around Ticul and Oxkutzcab is intensively farmed with citrus fruits, papayas and mangoes. Around 6km (4 miles) southwest of Oxkutzcab are the caves at Loltún.

❺ The Grutas de Loltún extend for 8km (5 miles) along illuminated pathways. Excavations in the Huechil cave revealed mammoth and bison remains, and there are relief carvings, petroglyphs and murals.

From Loltún, continue 30km (19 miles) southwest to Labná.

❻ Once a city of 1,500 to 2,500 inhabitants, Labná has an unusual monumental arch. Most Maya arches are purely structural, but this one was constructed for aesthetic purposes, clearly meant to be seen from afar. The two facades on either side of the arch differ greatly in their decoration; the western one is decorated with delicate latticework and stone carving imitating the wood or palm-frond roofs of Maya huts. Across the eastern facade, a line of zigzag carvings is believed to represent the feathered serpent, a potent symbol in Maya mythology. The palace also has some 70 *chultunes* (water cisterns).

Continue for another 9km (5.5 miles) to Xlapak, whose ruins have not been as extensively restored as the others in this region. After 13km (8 miles) from this turning is Sayil, or the Place of the Ants.

❼ Sayil, dating from AD800 to 1000, has many areas still under

reconstruction, including the ball court and *mirador* (lookout point). Stelae (inscribed stone slabs) are displayed near the entrance. In its day, the three-tier palace included 90 bathrooms for some 350 people. A broad mask with huge fangs forms the central motif on the facade.

From Sayil, turn right after approximately 5km (3 miles)—the route is well marked—to the Classic Puuc site of Kabah.

❽ Kabah is renowned for its Palacio de los Mascarones (Palace of the Masks). Its structures, most notably the Temple of the Sun, were built on platforms, making them distinct from other buildings. The facade has the image of Chac (God of Rain) repeated 260 times, the number of days in the Almanac Year. The central chamber is entered via a Chac mask.

Some 37km (23 miles) north, along Route 261, is Uxmal) (▷ 122–123). From here it is 74km (46 miles) along Route 261 back to Mérida.

TOURIST INFORMATION
✉ Teatro Peón Contreras, Calle 60 and Calle 57, Mérida ☎ (999) 924 92 90
🕓 Daily 8am–9pm

PLACES TO VISIT
GRUTAS DE LOLTÚN
🕓 Tours Tue–Sun 9.30, 11, 12.30, 2, 3 and 4 ✋ $5

LABNÁ, XLAPAK, SAYIL, KABAH
🕓 Daily 8–5 ✋ Labna free; others $3.50

WHERE TO EAT
HACIENDA TEPICH
Yucateca dishes include rabbit.
✉ Km 12.5 Mérida-Mayapán
☎ (999) 950 13 72

HACIENDA UXMAL
You'll find excellent regional and international cooking here.
✉ Km 78 Carreterra-Campeche ☎ (997) 976 20 12 🕓 Daily 7.15am–10pm

PRINCIPE TUTUL-XIU
Mexican dishes are on the menu.
✉ Calle 26, Mani ☎ (999) 798 40 86
🕓 Daily 11–7

BECAL
PANAMA HATS
Becal is known for its Panama hats, called *jipis* (pronounced "hippies") and ubiquitous throughout the Yucatán. Many of the town's families have workshops in cool, damp, backyard underground caves— necessary for keeping the shredded leaves of the *jipijapa* palm, from which the hats are made, moist and pliable. Most vendors will give visitors a tour of their workshop, but they are quite zealous in their sales pitches. Prices are better for *jipis* and other locally woven items (cigarette cases, shoes, belts) in the market than in the shops near the plaza.

CAMPECHE
ALAMEDA PARK
There are plenty of bargains at the main market in Alameda Park. You can find excellent, inexpensive Panama hats (*jipis*), finely and tightly woven so that they retain their shape even when crushed into your luggage (within reason). Note, though, that they are cheaper at source if you buy them in Becal (▷ above).
✉ Calle 57 (south end), Campeche
🕐 Daily

CASA DE ARTESANÍA TULSULNA
In general, handicrafts in Campeche are less expensive than in Mérida. Occupying a colonial house, this shop sells intricately embroidered regional dresses and blouses, hats, jewelry, baskets, and weavings.
✉ Calle 10 No. 333, Campeche ☎ (981) 816 90 88 🕐 Mon–Fri 9–8, Sat 10–2

CANCÚN
AQUAWORLD
www.aquaworld.com.mx
A variety of water sports can be organized on the beaches along the Hotel Zone. Aquaworld, Cancún's "water kingdom," offers "jungle" tours, parasailing, introductory scuba-diving courses and advanced certification, waterskiing and windsurfing. You can also rent waverunners, jetskis and kayaks. Take a dinner cruise to round off the day.
✉ Boulevard Kukulcán Km 15.2, Cancún ☎ (998) 848 83 27 🕐 Daily 6.30am–10pm

CARLOS N' CHARLIES
A bit of Cancún legend, this is the type of joint where you might have to wait a while for a drink because the staff have decided to sing with the live band on stage. The

Above *Getting ready to jetski from the beach at Cancún*

occasional press-ganged conga line is always good fun.
✉ Boulevard Kukulcán Km 8.5, Cancún ☎ (998) 883 44 68 🕐 Daily 12pm–5am

COCO BONGO
Coco Bongo is a nightlife mega-complex, a three-level club with myriad bars and improvised dance floor spaces populated largely by energetic young Americans.
✉ Boulevard Kukulcán Km 9.5, Cancún ☎ (998) 883 50 61 🕐 Disco from 10pm

ECO-PARK KANTÚN CHÍ
www.kantunchi.com
Within easy reach of Cancún, and a popular day trip, this lush ecological park in the heart of the Riviera Maya has a network of underground caves packed with stalactites and stalagmites which you can explore, and a series of *cenotes* (natural sinkholes) where you can swim. Tours include guides and snorkeling equipment. There is also a small zoo.
✉ Carretera Cancún–Tulúm Km 266.5 ☎ (984) 873 00 21 🕐 Daily 9–5 ✋ Park: $23 adult, $13 child. Cave: $38 adult and child over 12 years

HANDICRAFT MARKET

Avenida Tulúm, near the market in the middle of town, is a huge network of stands, all selling the same merchandise: silver jewelry from Taxco, ceramic Maya figurines, hammocks, jade chess sets. Prices are hiked up to the limit, so bargain hard—most vendors expect to get half what they first ask for.

✉ Avenida Tulúm, Cancún ⏰ Daily 8am–10pm

LA ISLA

www.laislacancun.com.mx

Opposite the Sheraton Hotel, this partly outdoor mall is a pleasurable shopping experience in the Hotel Zone. You'll find Zara, Nautica, Mexican handicrafts stores, familiar US brands, coffee shops, and a food court. On the upper level there is a multiplex cinema.

✉ Boulevard Kukulcán Km 12.5, Cancún ☎ (998) 883 50 25 ⏰ Daily 10–10

COZUMEL

DEEP BLUE

www.deepbluecozumel.com

This is the best of the smaller diving schools in Cozumel, offering personalized support with a maximum of eight people per small boat. Matt and Deborah, an English/Colombian couple, run the school, which is PADI and NAUI certified.

✉ A R Salas 200, Avenida 10 Sur, Cozumel ☎ (987) 872 56 53 ✋ Open Water Diver $400; 3- to 5-day dive packages $192–$300; cavern and cenote-diving, including two dives, transport and lunch $140

PUNTA SUR ECOLOGICAL RESERVE

This eco-tourism development occupies the southern tip of the island, with natural landscapes including lagoons and mangrove jungles. A snorkel base has opened here as well as a viewing platform, and there is a Mayan ruin in the shape of a shell, El Caracol, which is believed to have been used as a lighthouse. There are four boat rides a day on the Columbia lagoon. You can arrange a round-trip taxi service from San Miguel.

✉ 27km (17 miles) from downtown San Miguel on the Costera Sur (coastal highway), Cozumel ☎ (987) 872 09 14 ⏰ Daily 9–4.30 ✋ $10

ISLA MUJERES

AVENIDA HIDALGO

This main avenue is lined with souvenir shops, most of them selling similar things: Maya figurines and masks, hammocks, blankets and silver jewelry from Taxco. Bargaining is obligatory—try to get the item for half the original asking price, which is what vendors expect to receive.

✉ Isla Mujeres

BAHÍA

Snorkeling trips depart from the ferry dock daily between 10 and 11am. They include two hours snorkeling and lunch, returning at around 2.30pm.

✉ Avenida Rueda Medina 166, Isla Mujeres ☎ (998) 877 03 40 ✋ $30 per person

BUHOS

This almost legendary beach bar-restaurant, in an idyllic Caribbean setting, is fun and lively, with great music, tasty food ranging from fajitas to lobster, and a wide repertoire of cocktails and beer. A sunset cocktail here is a must.

✉ Cabañas Maria del Mar: Avenida Carlos Larzo, 1, Isla Mujeres ☎ (998) 877 01 79 ⏰ Daily 7.30am–11pm

COSMIC COSAS

This is a very friendly, US-run bookstore with new and used books bought, sold and exchanged, mostly beach-read novels and a few out-of-date guidebooks. There are also CDs for sale, an internet café and a dog-adoption notice board. This is a good place to meet fellow visitors.

✉ Calle Matamoros 82, Isla Mujeres ☎ (998) 877 05 55 ⏰ Mon–Sat 9am–10pm

CORAL SCUBA DIVE CENTER

www.coralscubadivecenter.com

This is the only dive school on the island affiliated with PADI; it has over 20 years' experience, bilingual

staff and more than 50 local dive sites, including reef, adventure, coral gardens or the Ultra Freeze shipwreck options.

✉ Avenida Matamoros 13-A, Isla Mujeres ☎ (998) 877 07 63 ⏰ Daily 9–9 ✋ Introductory course $59; two-tank dive $60; two-tank reef dive $39; eight-dive package $154; snorkel trips $22. Equipment rental, an additional $15

EL GARRAFÓN

www.garrafon.com

This ecological recreational park (▷ 116) offers day passes, which include snorkeling in the shallow reef next to the shore, a visit to the Maya ruin and Caribbean village, and the use of the pool and hammocks. In addition, all-inclusive packages comprise lockers, towels, snorkel equipment, and unlimited food and drink at the restaurants and open bar. Additional activities, such as zip lines (bungee jumping) and snuba-diving (scuba-diving without a tank), are available at extra cost. The reef is 320m (1,050ft) long, extending some 12m (40ft) from shore, with a maximum depth of 3m (10ft).

✉ Punta Sur, Isla Mujeres ☎ (998) 193 33 60 ⏰ Daily 10–5 ✋ Adult $69, child $50, admission includes meals

ISLA CONTOY EXPRESS TOUR

Boat trips on board the Caribbean Express leave Isla Mujeres at 8.30am, arriving at Isla Contoy at 10am, following snorkeling on the reef. A lunch of Yucatán fish is served before returning at 2.30pm.

✉ Avenida Rueda Medina, Abasolo and Matamoros, Isla Mujeres ☎ (998) 877 13 67 ⏰ Daily ✋ Adult $60, child (6–11) $50

LA PEÑA

Close to the main square, the breezy roof terrace here is a perfect place to relax to laid-back music until 10pm with an industrial-strength cocktail. There is a good mix of people and the staff are welcoming. Plans are afoot to open a courtyard restaurant and movie lounge.

✉ Avenida Guerrero, Centro, Isla Mujeres ☎ (998) 845 73 84 ⏰ Daily 7.30pm–around 3am

PLAYA PARAÍSO

This lovely stretch of beach, just a 30-minute walk from El Garrafón (▷ 116), close to the tip of Punta Sur, has been transformed into a mini-resort for Cancún daytrippers.
✉ Isla Mujeres

RICARDO GAITÁN

Ricardo Gaitán is the specialist guide for bird-watching tours to Isla Contoy, 30km (19 miles) north of Isla Mujeres. Knowledgeable and professionally run trips include snorkeling on Ixlache reef, fishing and a barbecued fish lunch. Tours of the island are provided.
✉ Contoy Pier, Avenida Rueda Medina, Isla Mujeres ☎ (998) 877 13 63 ◷ Daily, leaving 9am, returning 4.30pm 🖐 $60

MÉRIDA

CASA DE LAS ARTESANÍAS

One of the most expensive, places to buy handicrafts in Mérida is in this former monastery. The quality is high in finely embroidered *huipiles*, textiles, hammocks, pottery, and jewelry. Local art exhibitions are often held in the courtyard gallery.
✉ Calle 63 No. 503A, Mérida ☎ (999) 928 66 76 ◷ Mon–Sat 8–8, Sun 9–7

MAIN MARKET

Here you'll find good leather *huaraches* (sandals) and excellent cowboy boots for men and women.
✉ Corner of Calle 56 and Calle 57, Mérida
◷ Daily from 5am

MERCADO DE ARTESANÍAS

Many well-made handicrafts are on sale here, as well as good postcards, but prices are high and the salespeople are pushy.
✉ Calle 67, between 56 and 58, Mérida
◷ Daily 9–5

PANCHOS

Although this bar-restaurant is very touristy, it has live music every night, and the patio, with candles, fairylights and infectious merriment makes it a popular evening stop-off.
✉ Calle 59, between Calle 60 and Calle 62, Mérida ☎ (999) 923 09 42 ◷ Daily 6pm–2am

TEATRO PEÓN CONTRERAS

This theater first opened its doors in 1908 and is considered one of the best in Mexico, acclaimed for its classical ballet performances. The stage is grandiose and there is a wonderful marble staircase. Visiting politicians and celebrities have included former US president Bill Clinton. There is a bookshop and exhibitions are held regularly.
✉ Calle 60 with 57, Mérida ◷ Shows at 9pm 🖐 Tickets vary

ZÓCALO

Many of the souvenir shops dotted in the streets around the plaza specialize in hammocks. They also sell silver jewelry from Taxco, Panama hats, *guayabera* shirts, *huaraches*, baskets, and Maya figurines. Always bargain hard; the salesmen are pushy.
✉ Mérida

PLAYA DEL CARMEN

BLUE PARROT BEACH CLUB

www.blueparrot.com
This is the best nightspot in Playa, with an excellent bar with swing seats, a dance floor, and tables right on the beach. Monday through Thursday are "Ladies Night." Guest DJ's appear Friday through Sunday. The famous "Blue Parrot Fire Show" is nightly at 10.30pm. Cocktails cost about $6–$8, but there's a happy hour from 5 to 8pm.
✉ Calle 12 at the beach, Playa del Carmen ☎ (984) 206 33 50 ◷ Daily noon–4am

BOURBON STREET

A mellow, Deep South vibe, live Louisiana blues, and jazz and rock (nightly from 9pm) are on offer at this streetside bar. It's a good place to prop up the bar and meet people. In addition to draft beer and good cocktails, Cajun food is served.
✉ Avenida 5, between Calle 6 and Calle 8, Playa del Carmen ☎ (984) 803 30 22 ◷ Daily noon–2am

IKARUS

www.ikaruskiteboarding.com
This was the first kitesurfing company in Mexico to follow

Professional Air Sport Association standards. Classes are held at Puerto Morelos—halfway between Cancún and Playa del Carmen—or Tulúm. Students can obtain Level 1 pilot certification.
✉ Avenida 5, Calle 16, Playa del Carmen ☎ (984) 803 20 68 🖐 $75 per hour

SEÑOR FROG'S

Right on the beach with its own marina, volleyball court and beach club, the brash and loud Señor Frog's is one of the most popular drinking holes in the area. Entertainment ranges from monthly music festivals to nightly DJs.
✉ Centro Commercial Plaza Marina, Playa del Carmen ☎ (984) 873 09 30 ◷ Daily 10am–3am

SKYDIVE PLAYA

www.skydive.com.mx
For an extreme adrenalin rush, try the skydiving courses or tandem dives here, with soft beach landings and lots of freefall time. An introductory course is given before each dive. Skydive is a member of the Parachute Association, with licensed instructors.
✉ Playa Marina Loc 32, Playa del Carmen ☎ (984) 873 01 92 ◷ Daily 9–dusk 🖐 $229 for tandem dive with certified instructor

TANK-HA DIVE CENTER

www.tankha.com
You will find experienced, qualified, multilingual instructors at this very professional, long-established company. It offers snorkeling and diving for all levels, along with PADI and courses up to Divemaster.
✉ Calle 10, between Avenidas 5 and 10, Playa Del Carmen ☎ (984) 873 03 02/879 34 27 ◷ Office open daily 8am–10pm 🖐 PADI open-water course $350 (includes DAN medical insurance); one-tank dive $40; two-tank dive Cozumel $135 (including transport from Playa); two-tank *cenote* dives $110

PROGRESO

MUNDO MARINO

Luis Cámara, the friendly owner of this souvenir shop, once caught a great white shark, and many shark-related souvenirs are on sale.

✉ Calle 80, Progreso ☎ (969) 915 13 80

🕐 Mon–Fri 9–8, Sat 10–2

PUERTO MORELOS
LA PALAPA DE FÉLIX

The marina in Puerto Morelos offers activities within the national park such as excursions and boat trips. The snorkeling here is excellent, and there are fishing trips and visits to nearby *cenotes* (sinkholes).

✉ SM1 MZ 14, Lote 8, Puerto Morelos

☎ (998) 884 23 16 🕐 Daily 8–2

✋ Snorkel tour $25

RÍO LAGARTOS
BIRD-WATCHING

Early-morning boat trips (2.5–4 hours) can be arranged in this fishing village to see the flamingos; they usually nest during May and June and stay through July till August (although salt mining is disturbing their habitat).

✋ $40 in an 8- to 9-seater boat (fix the price before embarking)

TICUL
HUIPILES

Ticul, 80km (50 miles) south of Mérida, is a pleasant little village known for its *huipiles*—embroidered white dresses worn by older Maya women. You can buy them in Mérida, but the prices and quality of those in Ticul are much better. Look out for them on Calle 23.

TULÚM
AQUATECH DIVE CENTRE

Open-water and cavern diving, sport fishing, snorkeling and underwater photography are available at this dive school. The resort is 105km (65 miles) south of Cancún.

✉ Villas de Rosa, Akumal, Tulúm ☎ (984) 875 90 20 ✋ Packages can be arranged which include accommodations in beachfront condos ($120 per night). A one-tank dive costs $40–$60

HIDDEN WORLD'S CENOTES

www.hiddenworlds.com

Located at Dos Ojos, this is the second-largest underground cave

FEBRUARY
MÉRIDA CARNIVAL

During this week Mérida erupts with floats, dancers in regional costume, music, dancing around the plaza, and children dressed in animal suits. There are parades starting from the Monument to the Flag on Paseo Montejo heading south to Parque San Juan in downtown, the route lined with stands selling regional snacks. Local and international musicians perform at concerts.

✉ Mérida 🕐 Week before Ash Wednesday

MARCH AND SEPTEMBER
FIESTAS DEL EQUINOXIO

Twice a year, on the morning and afternoon of the spring and fall

system in the world. Trips can be organized for first-time snorkelers as well as under-water veterans.

✉ Dos Ojos Caverns, just off Route 307, south of Puerto Aventuras, Tulúm ☎ (984) 115 45 14 ✋ Snorkeling from $40; diving trips from $50

VALLADOLID
ANTONIO "NEGRO" AGUILAR

Antonio Aguilar was a baseball champion in the 1950s and '60s, playing for the Leones de Yucatán and the Washington Senators. Now semi-retired, he runs a shop selling sports equipment and renting out bicycles. Antonio will draw you a map of the best routes and advise you on what to take.

✉ Calle 44 No. 195, Valladolid 🕐 Daily 9–7 ✋ $5 for 3 hours

CENOTE X-KEKÉN

More commonly known as Dzitnup, this beautiful, underground *cenote*, just 7km (4 miles) from Valladolid, is stunningly lit. The cavernous ceiling drips with stalactites. Swimming is excellent, the water is cool (it may be a little dirty at times) and

equinoxes, the alignment of the sun casts a serpentine-shaped shadow on the steps of El Castillo at Chichén Itzá which gradually moves down to meet a serpent's head carved at the base. Expect large crowds on these days, and make hotel reservations well in advance if you are considering staying.

✉ Chichén Itzá 🕐 March 21 and September 21

MAY
CANCÚN JAZZ FESTIVAL

Jazz lovers descend on Cancún to savor a host of top jazz musicians from around the world who come to take part in free nightly concerts which are held throughout the city toward the end of May.

✉ Cancún 🕐 Memorial Day weekend

bats flit around. Exploratory walks can be made through the tunnels leading off the *cenote*; you will need a flashlight. Be careful as the steps can be slippery. Also be prepared for children offering to take you round the *cenote*. Almost directly opposite is the less-crowded Cenote Samula.

✉ 7km (4 miles) southwest of Valladolid 🕐 Daily 8–6 ✋ $2.50 ❓ *Colectivos* leave hourly from the front of Hotel María Guadalupe on Calle 44, between Calle 39 and Calle 41; they return until 6pm, after which you will have to get a taxi back to Valladolid. You can also take any bus heading west to the turn-off (it's then a further 2km/1.2-mile walk) or rent a taxi or bicycle

CENOTE ZACÍ

In the middle of town, several blocks from the main plaza, this artificially lit, open-air *cenote* has good swimming; it is sometimes closed due to algae in the water. There is a popular restaurant with an excellent view over the *cenote* and good food, lighted promenades, and a mini-zoo.

✉ Calle 36, between Calle 37 and Calle 39, Valladolid ☎ (985) 62 107 🕐 Daily 8–5 ✋ Adult $1.50, child $0.75

PRICES AND SYMBOLS

The restaurants are listed alphabetically within each town. The prices given are the average for a two-course lunch (L) and a three-course dinner (D) for one person, without drinks. The wine price is for the least expensive bottle. All the restaurants listed accept credit cards unless otherwise stated.

For a key to the symbols, ▷ 2.

CAMPECHE

LA PIGUA

Campeche is renowned for its fish and seafood, in particular *camarones* (shrimps) and *pan de cazón* (bread with dogfish), and La Pigua is one of the best places to sample it. This seafood restaurant has played host to many famous visitors, including the late Celia Cruz, Queen of Salsa. The emphasis is on freshness and quality rather than presentation.

✉ Avenida Migual Alemán 179, Campeche ☎ (981) 811 35 65 ⏰ Daily 1–5.30, 7.30–11 🖐 L $12, D$16, Wine $14

CANCÚN

LA HABICHUELA

www.lahabichuela.com
La Habichuela is one of the oldest and most popular restaurants in Cancún. Maya sculptures, elegant candlelit tables and live jazz music complement the delicious Caribbean cuisine here. The house special is *cocobichuela*—lobster and shrimp in a piquant curry sauce served in a coconut shell ($32). To finish off, try the divine chocolate pyramid of Chichén Itzá.

✉ Avenida Margaritas 25, Downtown, Cancún ☎ (998) 884 31 58 ⏰ Daily noon–midnight 🖐 L $27, D $32, Wine $20

PERICOS

www.pericos.com.mx
This is an archetypal Cancún eating house—a tacky, *cantina*-style restaurant (local bar serving food) with staff in bandit costume. Still, it is hugely popular, serving generous portions of food, including jumbo shrimp platters and filet mignon alongside pitchers of frozen margaritas. The atmosphere is ebullient, with live *mariachi* music.

✉ Avenida Yaxchilán 61, Cancún ☎ (998) 884 31 52 ⏰ Daily noon–midnight 🖐 L $16, D $25, Wine $20

CHETUMAL

SERGIO'S PIZZA

This is the best-value place in town: relaxing, dimly lit and informal.

The food is well presented, the pizzas are delicious and the "Sergio salad," with pulses, vegetables, mushrooms, and greens in a *tortilla* shell and topped with grilled chicken breast, is perfect. Good for late-night suppers, with tasty sweet breads and creamy broccoli soup.

✉ Avenida Alvaro Obregon 182, Chetumal ☎ (983) 832 04 91 ⏰ Daily 9am–midnight 🖐 L $12, D $17, Wine $15

COZUMEL

PRIMA TRATTORIA

This busy Italian restaurant uses organic ingredients from the owner's garden in its pastas, northern Italian seafood and wood-oven pizzas. The portions are generous, though many dishes are coated liberally with cream or cheese. The presentation and service are good, and there is breezy outdoor seating. Try the fettuccini with prawns and steak prima, followed by a slice of key lime pie. There is a non-smoking area.

✉ Avenida Adolfo Rosala Salas 109, San Miguel de Cozumel ☎ (987) 872 42 42 ⏰ Daily 4pm–midnight 🖐 D $24, Wine $18

ISLA MUJERES

EL BALCÓN DE ARRIBA

On the main high street that leads to the Playa Norte, this charming little restaurant runs the gamut of tasty fresh fish and seafood dishes—try the excellent grilled red snapper with *achiote* sauce—and is especially noted for its tempura. The broad menu also includes a couple of vegetarian options. The portions are large, the staff are friendly. Credit cards are not accepted.

✉ Avenida Hidalgo 12, Isla Mujeres ☎ (998) 877 05 13 ◷ Daily 8am–11pm ✋ L $12, D $17, Wine $17

BISTRO FRANCÉS

By 8.30am this French bistro is packed for the best-value and most varied breakfast combinations ($8) on the island, including crêpes, French toast, and *huevos rancheros*. By night there is candlelit dining and French-inspired cuisine, including French onion soup and fresh fish fillet with lime and capers. Credit cards are not accepted.

✉ Avenida Matamoros 29, Avenida Juárez and Avenida Hidalgo, Isla Mujeres ◷ Daily 8–noon, 6–10 (closed one day per week, usually Sat) ✋ D $18, Wine $15

MÉRIDA

AMARO

www.restauranteamaro.com
Amaro is one of the most popular restaurants in Mérida. While the food is rather overpriced, the setting is romantic, with candlelit tables in the courtyard and live music from 9pm. The vegetarian cuisine has many regional twists. There are pasta dishes, salads and pizzas, including an avocado pizza that has gained quasi-legendary status.

✉ Calle 59 No. 507, between Calle 60 and Calle 62, Mérida ☎ (999) 928 24 51 ◷ Daily 11am–2am ✋ L $12, D $16, Wine $16

DULCERÍA Y SORBETERÍA COLÓN

An essential ritual in Mérida is to take a 20-minute stroll from the *zócalo* along Paseo Montejo and stop and cool off with an ice cream from this legendary parlor,

established in 1907. The light and refreshing sorbets and ice creams are made from pure fruit, mixed with water or milk. The breezy, open-air tables overlook the Plaza Grande. Credit cards are not accepted.

✉ Calle 61 and 62, Mérida ☎ (999) 928 14 97 ◷ Daily 8am–11pm ✋ $2.50

PLAYA DEL CARMEN

CASA TUCAN

www.casatucan.de
This expertly managed, German-run hotel/restaurant/bar serves wonderful dishes, with a vegetarian slant. Shells encrusted into the tiled floor, snug alcoves, a tree protruding through the roof, and eggyolk-yellow handpainted walls create a tempting breakfast spot. There is a variety of evening specials.

✉ Calle 4 between avenidas 10 and 15, Playa del Carmen ☎ (984) 873 02 83 ◷ Daily 8am–11pm ✋ L $12, D $18, Wine $12

MEDIA LUNA

Tables here overlook Avenida 5, and background music adds to the hip lounge-bar vibe. The Mediterranean cuisine includes baked squash, Roquefort and caramelized onion salads, and chicken with goat's cheese and sun-dried tomatoes. The cocktails are great, and the breakfast specials are also worth checking out. Credit cards are not accepted.

✉ Avenida 5, between Calle 12 and Calle 14, Playa del Carmen ☎ (984) 873 05 26 ◷ Daily 4–10.30 ✋ L $11, D $19, Wine $19

TODO NATURAL

Large portions of salads, pasta and rice dishes (as well as Mexican fare), using tasty wholesome ingredients, are served at this health-food restaurant. Most items on the menu are vegetarian, but there are also inventive fish and chicken dishes. Todo Natural is worth a visit for the goldfish-bowl-sized *jugo* (fruit juice) alone. There is usually live music at the weekend.

✉ Avenida 5, Playa del Carmen ☎ (984) 873 22 42 ◷ Daily 7am–11pm ✋ L $12, D $20, Wine $18

XLAPAK

Unassuming from the outside, this small café-juice-bar-restaurant-gallery-internet- café-language-school along the northern stretch of Avenida 5 is a great late-afternoon hangout. The smoothies are the main draw at just $2, and are a meal in themselves. The Mexican fare includes stuffed chicken breast coated with tamarind sauce, a tasty rendition of *mole Oaxaqueña* with chicken, and fish stuffed with shrimps. Xlapak's daily *comida corridas* (set lunches) are arguably the best in town. Credit cards are not accepted.

✉ Avenida 5, Playa del Carmen ◷ Daily 8am–11.30pm ✋ L $7, D $18, Wine $16

TULÚM

CABAÑAS COPAL

www.cabanascopal.com
Candles and classical music set the scene at this beachside *palapa*, an ecotourism restaurant serving dishes with a health-conscious, vegetarian slant. Light lunches include *nopal* (cactus leaf) and *chaya* (a large-leafed vegetable) salads, and *tostadas de nopal*. For dinner, there is spaghetti or *fajitas* with shrimp, and one of the house specials, traditional Maya *tikin xik*—broiled fish cooked with spices and sour orange juice, seasoned with herbs and tomato, baked in banana leaves.

✉ Carretera Tulum Ruinas Km 5, Tulúm ☎ (800) 123 32 78 ◷ Daily 7am–11pm ✋ L $12, D $15, Wine $12

VALLADOLID

HOTEL EL MESÓN DEL MARQUÉS

www.mesondelmarques.com
El Mesón, on the north side of Plaza Principal, is one of the best restaurants in town. The serene patio with an ornate water fountain and gently strummed folk music makes this an idyllic place to relax. The broad menu includes an excellent chicken *pibil*. There is even a low-calorie menu. This is a place not to be missed.

✉ Calle 30 No. 203, Valladolid ☎ (985) 856 20 73 ◷ Daily 8am–10.30pm ✋ L $15, D $20, Wine $17

PRICES AND SYMBOLS

The prices are the average for a double room for one night including breakfast, unless otherwise stated. All the hotels listed accept credit cards unless otherwise stated. Note that rates can vary widely throughout the year.

For a key to the symbols, ▷ 2.

CAMPECHE
HOTEL BALUARTE

www.baluartes.com

Hotels in Campeche may not offer the best value, compared to other parts of Mexico, but the Baluarte is one of the city's best mid-range options. Close to the *malecón*, the modern four-story complex has bright, functional rooms with television, and well-stocked bathrooms. There is a small pool area, restaurant and rooftop bar.
✉ Avenida 16 de Septiembre 128, Campeche ☎ (981) 816 39 11 🛏 $65 🛈 100 💲 🏊

CHETUMAL
HOTEL LOS COCOS

www.hotelloscocos.com.mx

Los Cocos, a five-minute walk from the Museo de la Cultura Maya (▷ 114), is one of the plusher options in the city, and much better value than the Holiday Inn across the road. Functional rooms are equipped with all the basics, but the major draw in hot, humid Chetumal is the swimming pool, surrounded by shady palms and peaceful gardens. The café/bar, while quite expensive, serves what is considered to be the best breakfast in town.
✉ Avenida Héroes 134, Chetumal ☎ (983) 835 04 30 🛏 $85 🛈 85 💲 🏊

CHICANNÁ
CHICANNÁ ECO VILLAGE RESORT

Ideally placed for exploring the Río Bec archaeological sites, this welcoming eco-lodge surrounded by lush jungle hosts an eclectic mix of travelers. Each cabin is basic but very comfortable with crisp white paintwork, private bath and a table. Also on site is a pool deck with Jacuzzi, a sociable bar area, a satellite television room, a library and hammocks strewn through the extensive gardens. The restaurant, La Biósfera, serves delicious wholesome cooking, including an intriguing banana cream soup.
✉ Carretera Escarcega Km 150, Chicanná ☎ (981) 811 91 91 🛏 $100–$115 🛈 42 rooms in bungalows 🏊

Above *María del Mar, on Isla Mujeres, has a real Caribbean atmosphere*

COBÁ
ARCHAEOLOGICAL VILLA

Overlooking the Cobá lakeshore and just 10 minutes' walk from the ruins, these peaceful villas in landscaped gardens provide a great base to explore the archaeological sites of the Maya Riviera (particularly early in the morning before tour groups arrive). Family-oriented facilities include a large swimming pool, a library, a television room, a pool table, a boutique, and a restaurant.
✉ Domicilio Conocido, Zona Arqueologica, Cobá ☎ (984) 206 70 01 🛏 $90 🛈 43 💲 🏊

ISLA MUJERES
HOTEL PERLA DEL CARIBE

http://perla-del-caribe.myislamuheres.com

This hotel is enviably positioned on the northeastern side of the island, a stone's throw from a sliver of beach. The simple, neutral-toned rooms are airy, flooded with light, very clean and have decent mattresses; most have ocean views. The staff are very friendly and will usually offer discounts for longer stays. Credit cards are not accepted.

Avenida Francisco Madero 2, Isla Mujeres ☎ (998) 877 04 44 ✋ $50 🛈 90 💲 🏊

MARÍA DEL MAR
www.cabanasdelmar.com
María del Mar has a variety of accommodations, from top-of-the-range *cabañas* to swanky rooms in the Castle complex, which are decorated in neutral shades and have a sitting area. It is also close to the nicest stretch of beach on the island. Throughout the complex, a relaxed and sociable Caribbean vibe prevails with hammocks, rocking chairs, a swimming pool, and a bar serving excellent cocktails.
✉ Avenida Carlos Larzo 1, Isla Mujeres ☎ (998) 877 01 79 ✋ Castle $160, Tower $150, *cabañas* $140 🛈 Castle complex 18, Tower complex 24, *cabañas* 31 💲 🏊

NA BALAM
www.nabalam.com
On one of the finest stretches of beach on the island, Na Balam combines a relaxed Caribbean vibe with eastern spirituality. Tropical thatched bungalows with hammocks slung from each patio, some with private pools, are scattered around labyrinthine pathways dotted with palms. White and wicker predominate in the reception areas and bar/restaurant, which is one of the best on the island. There is yoga on Monday, Wednesday and Friday at 9am.
✉ Calle Zazil-Há 118, Playa Norte, Isla Mujeres ☎ (998) 877 02 79 ✋ $150 standard 🛈 42 💲 🏊

MÉRIDA
CASA MEXILIO
This colonial guesthouse is the best place to stay in the heart of Mérida. There is a *mudéjar*-style courtyard, antiques, a swimming pool with deck, and a garden ablaze with flowers and wild vegetation. Each of the rooms is comfortable, with Maya, Spanish and eastern themes. Reserve well in advance.
✉ Calle 68 No. 495, Mérida ☎ (999) 928 25 05/0-800 210 43 41 (US toll-free) ✋ $60–$120 🛈 13 🏊

HACIENDA XCANATUN
www.xcanatun.com
A palpable sense of history and grandeur pervades each room of this 18th-century hacienda, carefully restored by Jorge Ruz Buenfil, whose father was Alberto Luz-Lullier, the esteemed archaeologist who discovered Pakal's tomb in Palenque. It is equipped with all modern conveniences, in addition to a superlative restaurant, a holistic spa, two swimming pools, and a garden retreat. Although some 8km (5 miles) north of Mérida, this is the most lavish option in the area.
✉ Carretera Mérida-Progreso Km 12, Mérida ☎ (999) 930 21 40 ✋ $270–$340 🛈 18 suites 💲 🏊

PLAYA DEL CARMEN
BLUE PARROT
www.blueparrot.com
Sociable and upbeat, the Blue Parrot attracts an eclectic mix of people with its varied accommodations options and fantastic, if pricey, bar on one of the liveliest stretches of the beach. Waterfront *palapas* with hammocks slung outside are basic, while studios and deluxe rooms come with all creature comforts. There are daily yoga classes, massages are available and there is a dive school on site. Music and revelry continue until 4am.
✉ Calle 12 and 14, Playa del Carmen ☎ (984) 206 33 50/(800) 435 06 68 (US toll-free) ✋ $165/$155 (deluxe/double room), beachfront *palapa* ($79) 🛈 72

HUL-KÚ
www.hotelhulku.com
At the beachside hotels in Playa you'll pay a premium for dingy, basic rooms, but just a couple of streets back from the water there are some excellent-value hotels. This is one. Spotless rooms with cable television and fans are decorated with bamboo furniture and Mexican ceramics. There is a calming, leafy pool area, with hammocks, lounge chairs and plenty of reading material on hand. Credit cards are not accepted.
✉ Avenida 20, Playa del Carmen ☎ (984) 873 00 21 ✋ $65–$110 🛈 29 💲 🏊

TULÚM
CABAÑAS COPAL
www.cabanascopal.com
This exotic ecotourism complex and holistic spa is perched above the spectacular beach. It has a mystical atmosphere with daily yoga classes, a restaurant/bar (▷ 137) and an internet café. This is rustic chic at its finest: each serene *caseta* and *cabaña* has mosquito nets, mosaic tiled bathrooms, and the more expensive cabins have stunning panoramic views. With no electricity or phone, this is a blissful escape.
✉ Tulúm Beach, Tulúm ☎ (800) 123 32 78 ✋ $95–$130 (*cabaña* for 4), $205–$285 (*casita*) 🛈 45 *palapas*, 15 rooms

VALLADOLID
GENESIS EK-BALAM
www.genesisretreat.com
Close to the archaeological site of Ek-Balam, 25 minutes' drive north of Valladolid, Genesis Ek-Balam is an ecological retreat. Each screened *cabaña* is basic but comfortable and site facilities include "eco showers," a garden bathtub, coffee shop and chemical-free bio-filtered swimming pool. There are lovely gardens in which to observe wildlife, and activities include Maya language classes. You can also rent mountain bikes to explore the nearby ruins and *cenotes*. The restaurant serves regional dishes and snacks.
✉ Off Highway 295, Valladolid ☎ (985) 852 79 80 ✋ $45; solo travelers receive 10 percent discount 🛈 6 *cabañas*, 3 tents 🏊

HOTEL SAN CLEMENTE
www.hotelsanclemente.com.mx
This inviting hotel next to the cathedral is excellent value. The peaceful colonial building has plenty of character, with an arcaded patio with a central fountain and benches among palms and flowers humming with birdlife. The swimming pool area is equipped with lounge chairs and umbrellas. Each room is spacious and clean with cable television. Staff are helpful.
✉ Calle 42 No. 206, Valladolid ☎ (985) 856 22 08 ✋ $40 🛈 63 💲 🏊

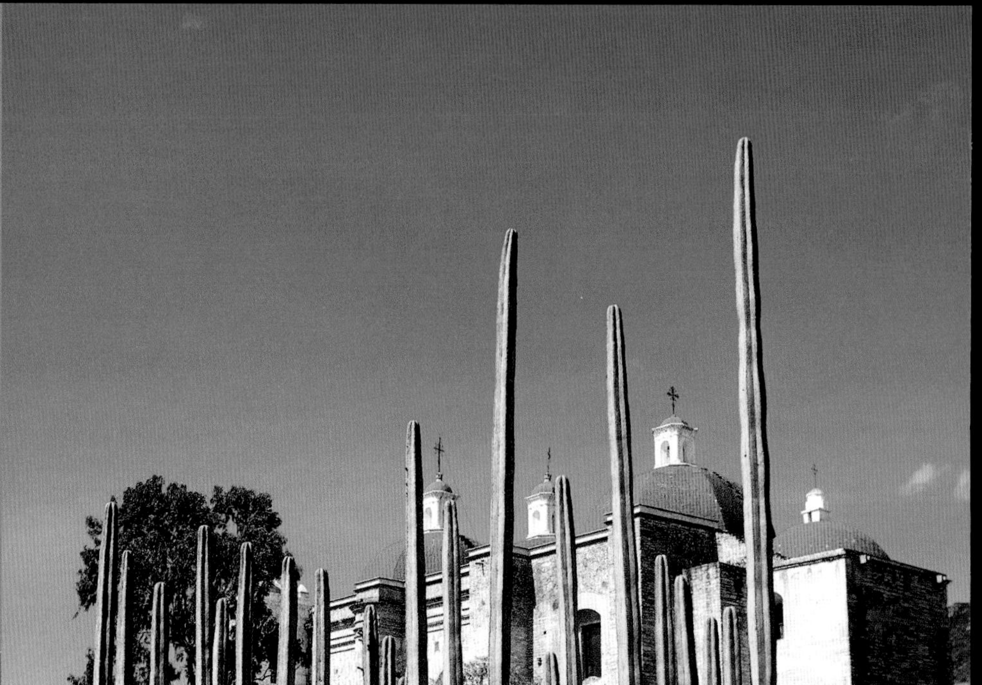

SOUTHERN MEXICO

Acapulco's world famous cliff divers are as much a symbol of Mexico as the *taco*. And it's here in the country's southern region that mass international tourism to Mexico began when the beach resort of Acapulco took off in the 1950s. Years later, backpackers and bohemian types discovered the magnificent colonial city of Oaxaca, a fascinating place surrounded by authentic craft villages and the archaeological sites of Monte Albán and Mitla. Adventurous travelers are drawn farther east, where deep in the rain forest of Chiapas lie the mysterious Maya ruins of Palenque and the indigenous culture of San Cristóbal de las Casas.

Recent decades have seen the rise of Ixtapa-Zihuatanejo as a first-class beach resort destination. Luxury seekers are drawn to the modern hotels of Ixtapa, while those looking for a quieter vacation opt for the intimate inns and sleepy fishing village charms of Zihuatanejo. Foodies flock to the region for what is arguably the best cuisine in the country. The fresh fish and seafood found on the coast has few equals. The culinary traditions of Chiapas have deep roots. And when it comes to sheer diversity of cuisines, no state can compete with Oaxaca, best known for its *mole* sauces.

Whether you spend your days visiting the massive stone Olmec heads in La Venta, taking a cooking class in Oaxaca or parasailing over Acapulco, you'll need somewhere to lay your weary head. The region's accommodations run the gamut from all-inclusive mega resorts in Acapulco to funky beach hotels in Puerto Escondido to converted monasteries and old colonial homes in Oaxaca. No matter where you stay, rest easy knowing that in Southern Mexico, as in the rest of the country, it's the kind and hospitable Mexican people that make traveling here a joy.

ACAPULCO

Mexico's premier beach playground has a spectacular setting, backed by the high mountains of the Sierra Madre del Sur. Acapulco, wrapped around the 11km (7-mile) curve of Acapulco Bay, is the archetypal package holiday resort—unashamedly loud and brash, with high-rise hotels, trendy restaurants and swanky shops rubbing shoulders with heaving nightclubs, golf courses, tour touts and street vendors. Some 380km (245 miles) from Mexico City, it thrived during colonial times as the nearest Pacific port to the capital. From the moment the first Spanish galleon set sail for Manila in 1565, its fate was sealed as the terminal for the prosperous new trade route with the East, but its fortunes changed after Independence. The arrival of the international airport in the 1950s halted the decline and Acapulco quickly became the "in" place for Hollywood stars, who flocked here during the 1960s to party in their exclusive homes, before the happening scene moved to the other side of the country.

THE BEACHES

Acapulco's main attractions are its golden beaches, particularly playas Hornos, Hornitos, Condesa and, on the eastern side of the bay, Playa Icacos. Beside the latter is the CICI Acapulco Magico water park (daily 10–6) with a pool with a wave machine, a water slide and arena with performing dolphins and sea lions. On the southern shore of the Peninsula de la Playas, at the western end of the bay, are playas Caleta and Caletilla, whose calm (but murky) waters make them popular with families with small children. Playa Angosta, in a tiny, sheltered cove on the western side of the peninsula, is a 20-minute walk from the *zócalo*. Some 10km (6 miles) northwest of Acapulco is Pie de la Cuesta, a long narrow spit separating the booming ocean surf from the mangroves and palms of Laguna Coyuca.

The cliff divers at La Quebrada plunge 40m (130ft) into the water below, timing their dives to coincide with the incoming waves (daily at 1pm, 7.15pm, 8.15pm, 9.15pm and 10.15pm).

FUERTE DE SAN DIEGO

Away from the beach life is the Fuerte de San Diego (Tue–Sun 9.30–6.30), where the last battle for Mexican Independence was fought. It has been transformed into an attractive museum recalling the history of Mexico, and of Acapulco in particular.

INFORMATION

www.sectur.guerrero.gob.mx
➕ 315 K10 ℹ Costera Miguel Alemán 4455 ☎ (744) 484 44 16 ⏱ Daily 8am–11pm ✈ Aeropuerto Internacional Alvarez (ACA), 23km (14 miles) east

TIPS

» The most useful bus route runs the full length of Costera Miguel Alemán, linking the older part of town to the beaches and hotels. Bus stops on the main thoroughfare are numbered, so find out which number you need to get off at.
» Though a beach resort, you'll need to lose the shorts and sandals and dress to impress if you want to sample the city's legendary nightlife.

Above *Acapulco is justly famous for its beaches, cliff divers and nightlife*
Opposite *The Sierra Madre del Sur plunge into the ocean at Acapulco*

AGUA AZUL

This series of stunning jungle waterfalls and rapids runs through the lush valleys of the Sierra Madre. You can follow a path on the left of the rapids for 7km (4 miles), with superb views and secluded areas for picnics. Swimming is good—the water is clear and blue during fine weather, muddy brown in bad—but stick to the roped areas; the various graves on the steep path alongside the rapids testify to the dangers. Watch out for the Liquidizer, a particularly dangerous area of white foaming water. Even in the designated areas the currents are ferocious, and you must beware of hidden tree trunks. The main swimming area at Agua Azul—its name means "blue water"—is surrounded with restaurants and local children selling fruit.

Misol-Há, north of Agua Azul, is a waterfall 40m (130ft) high. A narrow path winds behind the falls, allowing you to stand behind the immense curtain of water. You can swim here also, and there are simple facilities and restaurants.

Warning: Military checks occasionally take place between Palenque and San Cristóbal de las Casas. If you are stopped at night, turn off the car engine and lights and switch on the inside light. Always have your passport handy.

✚ 316 Q10 ✉ 35km (22 miles) south of Palenque, Carretera 199 to Ocosingo ☎ 01 55 53 29 09 95 ext. 7002, Misol-Há ext. 7006 ◉ Daily 8–6 🖐 $1.50 x 2 per person (caseta at entrance to town and at the falls means you pay twice) ⬛ Travel agencies in Palenque and many of the hotels offer tours to Agua Azul, including a visit to the waterfall at Misol-Há, 22km (14 miles) from Palenque ❓ Colectivos from Avenida Hidalgo and Calle Allende in Palenque for Agua Azul and Misol-Há

BONAMPAK

Bonampak was built in the Late Classic period on the Río Lacanjá, a tributary of the Río Usumacinta. It is famous for its realistic murals in the Templo de las Pinturas (Temple of Paintings), dated AD800, which tell the story of a battle and the bloody aftermath involving sacrificial torture and execution of prisoners. Painted on the walls, vaulted ceilings and benches of the temple's three rooms, the murals also describe the rituals surrounding the presentation at court of the future ruler. The people participating were mainly the ruling elite, and a strict hierarchy was observed whereby minor nobility attended eminent lords.

In Room 1, the celebration opens with the young prince, clothed in white robes, being presented to an assembly of lords. The king, dressed simply, watches from his throne, while lords in sumptuous clothing and jewelry, and musicians line up for a procession.

The right of the heir to accede to the throne and the need to take captives to be sacrificed in his honor is depicted in the paintings of Room 2. Here, a ferocious battle is in progress in which the ruler, Chaan Muan, shining heroically, proves his right to the throne. Then, on a stepped structure, Chaan Muan oversees the torture and mutilation of the captives; one victim has clearly been decapitated, his head resting on a bed of leaves.

The paintings that cover the walls of Room 3 appear to celebrate these sacrifices in an exuberant display of music and dance.

✚ 317 Q10 ✉ 176km (109 miles) southeast of Palenque ◉ Daily 8–5 🖐 $7 🚌 Buses from Palenque ✈ Flights from Palenque to Bonampak and Yaxchilán ⬛ Tour operators from Palenque offer a 13-hour day trip to Bonampak and Yaxchilán (▷ 159)

CAÑON DEL SUMIDERO

www.sumidero.com

From Tuxtla Gutiérrez, a drive through spectacular scenery leads to the rim of the 1,000m-deep (3,280ft) Sumidero Canyon, now a national park. During the Spanish Conquest indigenous warriors, unable to endure the subjugation, hurled themselves off the edge. Myriad trails wind through lush vegetation with orchids, cascading waterfalls and crystalline rivers. Frolicking monkeys and cavorting birdlife are more or less guaranteed, while the promise of jaguars and pumas is usually unfulfilled. In addition to hiking, swimming and lazing in hammocks, the park offers many and various adventure activities, including kayaking and cycle rides. The animal hospital is particularly popular with children.

About 15km (9 miles) beyond the national park, the colonial town of Chiapa del Corzo is the embarkation point for boat trips to the canyon (▷ 166), but it's worth allowing a couple of hours to explore the town, which was a Preclassic and Proto-Classic Maya site and shares features with early Maya sites in Guatemala. The ruins are behind the Nestlé plant.

Other sights of interest include the fine 16th-century Moorish-influenced fountain and the 16th-century Iglesia de Santo Domingo, which has an engraved altar made of solid silver.

✚ 316 P10 ✉ Parque Ecoturístico Cañon del Sumidero, 10km (6 miles) north of Tuxtla Gutiérrez ☎ (961) 104 80 54 ◉ Daily 10–4.30 🖐 Adult $28.50, child (5–12) $20.50 ⬛ Tours from San Cristóbal, including a boat trip ❓ Colectivos from San Cristóbal

Below The jungle waterfalls at Agua Azul create a spectacular display as they tumble over limestone rocks

COMALCALCO
www.comalcalco.gob.mx

In pre-Hispanic times the ancient city of Comalcalco wore the mantle of the most important political capital in Tabasco. Comalcalco in Nahuatl means "place of the earthenware pans" and, unlike other Maya sites, its palaces and pyramids were built of fired bricks rather than stone. The city was populated by the Chontal or Putun people, who were noted for their trading. The archaeological zone includes a ceremonial area built during the Preclassic period, the North Plaza complex and the Great Acropolis. The axis of Temple I, which forms part of the North Plaza, is aligned with the setting sun. At the entrance to the site, a museum houses many of the treasures unearthed during excavations, including fragments of intricate stucco decoration that would once have covered the entire base of the temple, and clay figurines symbolizing Maya society.
➕ 316 P9 ✉ 52km (32 miles) northwest of Villahermosa ⏰ Daily 8–5 ✋ $3.90
🚌 Buses from Villahermosa

HUATULCO
www.baysofhuatulco.com.mx

East along the coastal road from Pochutla is Huatulco, a meticulously engineered and environmentally aware international vacation resort. The complex is surrounded by a forest reserve and nine splendid bays. Golf, swimming pools, nightlife, international and Mexican cuisine, beaches, watersports, excursions into the forest, and tours of some of the archaeological sites are all available.

The complex encompasses several interconnected towns and development areas. Tangolunda is set aside for large luxury hotels and resorts, with a golf course, the most expensive restaurants, souvenir shops, and nightlife. Chahué, on the next bay west, has a town park with

Right Brightly painted fishing and tour boats moored in Santa Cruz marina, part of the Huatulco international resort

a spa and a beach club, a marina and a few hotels.

Some 6km (4 miles) west of Tangolunda is Santa Cruz Huatulco, once an ancient Zapotec settlement and Mexico's most important Pacific port during the 16th century (later abandoned). Tour boats leave from its marina, which has facilities for visiting yachts, hotels, restaurants, shops, and a few luxury homes. There is an attractive open-air chapel by the beach, the Capilla de la Santa Cruz, and a well-groomed park. La Crucecita, 2km (1 mile) inland, is the hub of the Huatulco complex, with the more economical hotels, restaurants and shops.
➕ 316 M11 ℹ Sedetur, Boulevard Benito Juárez, near the golf course, Tangolunda ☎ (958) 581 01 77

IXTAPA-ZIHUATANEJO
www.ixtapa-zihuatanejo.com

The two resorts of Ixtapa and Zihuatanejo are promoted as a package even though they are 7km (4 miles) apart and totally different in character.

Ixtapa is a popular modern resort, with its fashionable hotels, restaurants, bars, discos, shopping complex, golf courses, yacht marina and beaches.

The beautiful, laid-back fishing port of Zihuatanejo, on the other hand, makes a welcome change

from high-rise Ixtapa, and still retains much of its Mexican village charm. There is a handicraft market by the church, some beachside cafés and a small Museo Arqueológico on Avenida 5 de Mayo. The Plaza de Toros, at the entrance to town, hosts seasonal *corridas* (bullfights).
➕ 314 J10 ℹ Palacio Municipal, Zihuatanejo ☎ (755) 554 20 01
⏰ Mon–Fri 8–6, Sat 10–2

LAGUNAS DE MONTEBELLO

From Comitán de Dominguez you can reach this exhilarating region of more than 50 lakes, lagoons and caves, which became a national park in 1959. One group of lakes is known as the Lagunas de Siete Colores—due to oxides in the water and refracted light, they take on wonderful hues ranging from deep emerald, turquoise and violet to steely gray. The national park has more than 7,000 pine groves, forests of oak, and a jungle with orchids. Five of the lakes are accessible by paved road; you must hike to the others (not recommended in the rainy season). The most attractive are Agua Tinta and Bosque Azul. Buses go as far as Laguna Bosque Azul, a one-hour journey. It is also possible to camp in the park.
➕ 316 Q11 ⏰ Daily 8–5 ✋ $3 (charge for vehicle) 🚌 *Combis* or buses from Comitán

MONTE ALBÁN

INFORMATION

www.oaxaca.gob.mx

✚ 315 M10 ☎ (951) 516 12 15
🕐 Daily 8–5 ✋ $4.80 🚌 Several
buses depart from Hotel Trébol, one block
south of the *zócalo* in Oaxaca. *Autobuses
Turísticos* (tourist buses) depart from
Hotel Rivera del Angel, Calle Mina 518
🚌 $20 per hour for an official guide.
Non-official guides hang around the site.
Beware of overcharging and check their
credentials 📖 Informative literature and
videos in several languages ☕ Café in
museum complex serves pricey snacks
and better-value lunches

INTRODUCTION

Enigmatic and compelling, the ancient capital of the Zapotecs has
a legacy of sophisticated architecture and fascinating iconography,
with temples, tombs, plazas, and ball courts revealing Zapotec culture
at its zenith. Monte Albán lies 10km (6 miles) west of Oaxaca, on a hilltop
dominating the valley, and is easily reached by car or public transportation.
Restoration was carried out between 1992 and 1994, when a museum and
visitor center were built. Walls, terraces, pyramids, tombs, staircases and
sculptures reveal the Zapotecs' cultural achievements and monumental
architecture. The Gran Plaza, 400m (1,310ft) up a steep mountain, without
immediate access to water or arable land, is the focal point.

Monte Albán was one of the first cities in Mesoamerica and one of the most
populous. It was founded around 500BC and flourished until AD750, exerting
considerable political and economic control over the other communities in
the central valley of Oaxaca and surrounding mountains. Although it had been
developing a policy of offense and capture as early as 200BC, the expansion of
the city really gained impetus with the growth of Teotihuacán (▷ 188–191).

WHAT TO SEE

GRAN PLAZA

The main plaza may have been the site of the marketplace, but this theory is
undermined by the back-breaking hill and the restricted access. It would also
seem ideal for religious ceremonies and rituals, but the absence of religious
iconography contradicts this interpretation. The imagery at Monte Albán is
almost exclusively militaristic, with allusions to tortured prisoners and captured
settlements. The Gran Plaza is delineated north and south by the two largest
structures in the city, which have been interpreted as palace and/or public

Above *Ruins of the ancient Zapotec
capital at Monte Albán*

building (Plataforma Norte/North Platform) and temple (Plataforma Sur/South platform). Apart from these, the ball court and arrow-shaped building in front of the South Platform, there are 14 other structures—six along the west side, three in the middle and five along the east side.

EDIFICIO DE LOS DANZANTES

One structure, known as the Edificio de los Danzantes (Building of the Dancers), to the west of the Gran Plaza, has bas-reliefs, glyphs and calendar signs (probably fifth century BC). The intriguing, strangely shaped figures that give the building its name are possibly dancing, but their symbolism is unclear.

BALL COURT

The ball court is east of the Gran Plaza, marked by two structures at the sides of the rectangular base, with slanting walls. The western side is covered with a sculpture representing a grasshopper.

BEYOND THE GRAN PLAZA

From AD450 to AD600, Monte Albán had 14 districts beyond the confines of the Gran Plaza: theories suggest that each of the 14 structures within the Main Plaza corresponded with one of the districts outside. Each pertained to a distinct ethnic group or polity, brought together to create a pan-regional confederacy. The arrow-shaped structure functioned as a military showcase; it also has astronomical connotations.

THE CONFEDERACY

The presence of structures on or bordering the Main Plaza that housed representatives of various ethnic groups supports the theory that Monte Albán came into being as the site of a confederacy or league, and its neutral position, unrelated to any single polity, lends credence to this suggestion. The absence of religious iconography, which might have favored one group over the others, emphasizes the secular role of the area, while the presence of the Danzantes sculptures suggests a trophy-gathering group. In all, about 310 stone slabs depicting woeful captives have been found. Some of them are identified by name glyphs, which imply hostilities against a settlement and the capture of its warriors. The fact that most of them are nude denotes the contempt with which they were treated by their captors: nudity was considered shameful by the peoples of Mesoamerica.

THE COLLAPSE

Monte Albán reached its maximum size around AD600, with a population of between 15,000 and 30,000. Shortly after that date, the city changed dramatically. The population shrank by nearly 82 percent, the Gran Plaza was abandoned, and most people moved nearer the valley floor, but behind protective walls. The abandonment of the Gran Plaza was a direct result of the collapse of the political institution focused there. This has been seen as a consequence of the fact that, early in the seventh century, Teotihuacán was already showing signs of decadence. Gaining momentum, the decadence led to the abandonment of that great centre. It is unlikely to have been coincidental that the Gran Plaza at Monte Albán was abandoned around this time.

MUSEUM

At the site entrance is an impressive little museum that traces the history of Monte Alban and displays several original stelae, figurines and pottery pieces. Though some of the more intriguing artifacts have been moved to the Museo Nacional de Antropología in Mexico City, the museum does display an eerie collection of human skulls, including some child skulls purposefully deformed for beautification. Visitors will also find a bookstore, café and craft shop.

TIPS

» To allow more time at the ruins (3 hour minimum is recommended), take the tourist bus to Monte Albán, then walk the 4km (2.5 miles) downhill to Colonia Monte Albán and get a city bus back from there.

» The Centro Cultural Santo Domingo in Oaxaca (▷ 150) houses the contents of Tomb 7 and presents the rise and fall of Monte Albán.

• The place is radiant at sunset, but permission is needed to stay that late (take a torch/flashlight).

Below *Detail of an intriguing bas-relief on the Edificio de los Danzantes (Building of the Dancers)*

INFORMATION

www.aoaxaca.com

✚ 315 M10 (also walk, ▷ 162–163)

ℹ Juarez 703 ☎ (951) 502 12 00

🕐 Daily 8–8 ✕ Aeropuerto Xoxocotlán
(OAX), 9km (5.5 miles) south

Above *The unmissable Iglesia de Santo Domingo, one of the best examples of baroque in the western world*

INTRODUCTION

Oaxaca is a graceful blend of pre-Columbian and colonial influences, with the finest baroque church in Mexico, a crop of engaging museums and galleries, ebullient feast days, kaleidoscopic markets and the curious complexities of Oaxaqueña cuisine.

Oaxaca is the cosmopolitan capital of the state of Oaxaca. Declared a UNESCO World Heritage Site in 1987, this relatively compact city, blessed with an average temperature of 22°C (72°F), is best explored on foot. It is one of Mexico's most handsome cities, and at every turn breezy patios and majestic stone buildings reveal its importance during the colonial period, while the vibrant markets displaying local crafts and regional delicacies, traditional *Guelaguetza* folk dances (▷ 166), and feast days point to its indigenous roots. The highlights for those with little time include the animated *zócalo* (main square), the sublime Iglesia de Santo Domingo and monastery, the hypnotic Mercado Abasto, and the mystical Monte Albán archaeological site (▷ 146–147) overlooking the town. The major sights are concentrated around the zócalo or along Calle Macedonio Alcalá, a cobbled pedestrian mall that joins the square with the Iglesia de Santo Domingo. Avenida Independencia is the main street running east–west; the most photogenic part of the old city lies to the north, and the commercial area, housing the cheaper hotels, to the south. Avenida Independencia is also a dividing line for the north–south streets, which change names here.

Nomadic tribes, related to the Olmecs, are believed to have first inhabited Oaxaca's central valleys more than 10,000 years ago. The period 700BC to 300BC witnessed the construction of the spectacular Monte Albán (▷ 146–147), which reached its zenith between AD500 and AD750 to become the leading Zapotec base. By AD800 the city had been abandoned, for reasons unknown. As Zapotec culture declined, Mixtec culture began to flourish and conquest by the Aztecs in 1486 added to the complex mosaic of cultures encountered by the Spaniards. In 1529 the Spaniards erected a city—the Villa de Antequera—that rapidly developed a more Spanish character.

It was only in 1872 that it was named Oaxaca, a word from the Nahuatl Huaxyacac language meaning "in the nose of the gourds." Alonso García Bravo, architect of Mexico City and Veracruz, and one of Spain's most esteemed town planners, was commissioned to design the city. He began by creating the Plaza Central or *zócalo*, then built the cathedral over a former Aztec burial site.

On the other side of the square, municipal buildings provided the basis for civil power, establishing a harmonious balance between the sacred and the secular. The city flourished during the Viceroyalty as Oaxaca's sheep farms, sugar cane, and gold and silver mines produced more wealth. Today, Oaxaca has the largest indigenous population (around 1.2 million) in Mexico, speaking more than 150 dialects.

WHAT TO SEE
ZÓCALO

The *zócalo* is the heart of town. Oaxacan life ebbs and flows through its leafy central park, along its arcades and beneath shady porticos lined with open-air cafés and restaurants. Around the ornate central bandstand men have their shoes shined while munching on *chapulines* (deep-fried grasshoppers) and, in the shade of giant laurel trees, vendors offer charms to prevent the loss of the soul. The square has a perpetual carnival air, with gaudy helium balloons bobbing over romantic fountains, pearly-pink cotton candy (candyfloss) stands and live music. Political demonstrations are often held opposite the graceful arcades of the Palácio de Gobierno (Government Palace), which occupies the south side of the square and contains two fine murals painted by Arturo García Bustos in 1980. The 17th-century cathedral (daily 7am–8pm) has a fine baroque facade and an antique pipe organ. In front, scattered among the laurels and shocking-pink bougainvillea, stands sell everything from cloth dyed with purple snails to fruit sherbets. In the evening music and dance events provide great free entertainment.

TIPS

» To get an insight into Oaxaca's history and culture before you begin exploring the city and archaeological sites in the area, visit the Museo de las Culturas de Oaxaca in the Centro Cultural Santo Domingo (▷ 150).

» Women should be aware of *gavacheros*, local young men who hang around the *zócalo* picking up foreign women and seeking favors.

Below *Sun filters through the high-level windows of Iglesia de Santo Domingo, highlighting the opulent decoration*

IGLESIA DE SANTO DOMINGO

Four blocks from the *zócalo* is Oaxaca's unmissable sight—the Franciscan church of Santo Domingo with its adjoining monastery, now the Centro Cultural de Santo Domingo (see below). The church is considered one of the best examples of baroque style in Mexico, possibly the western world. When English novelist Aldous Huxley visited in 1933, he enthused that it was "one of the most extravagantly beautiful churches in the world." Elaborately carved by the Dominicans in 1608, it underwent extensive refurbishment in the 1950s that revealed wonderful ceilings and walls 9m (30ft) thick and ablaze with gold leaf. The church is dominated by a three-level gilded altar, and a spectacular polychrome bas-relief on the ceiling above the entrance reveals the family tree of Santo Domingo de Guzmán, founder of the order.

✉ Calle Macedonia Alcalá and Avenida Gurrión ⛅ Daily 7–1, 4–7.30 ❓ Flash photography not allowed

CENTRO CULTURAL SANTO DOMINGO

Housed in the former convent of Santo Domingo, the cultural complex includes the Museo de las Culturas de Oaxaca, Biblioteca Francisco Burgoa, Jardín Etnobotánico and a bookstore. Construction of the convent started in 1575 and Dominican friars occupied the convent from 1608 to 1812. Subsequently the Mexican army occupied it until 1972, when it became the regional museum.

Exhibits in the museum's 14 galleries are well displayed, with detailed explanations in Spanish (audiovisual tours are available in English). The history of Oaxaca from pre-Hispanic times to the contemporary period is presented through an archaeological collection and includes spectacular riches found in Tomb 7 of Monte Albán (▷ 146–147). There are also displays of different aspects of Oaxacan culture such as crafts, cooking and traditional medicine, and temporary exhibits, including the work of contemporary Mexican artists.

The Biblioteca Francisco Burgoa (admission included) houses a collection of 24,000 volumes dating from 1484. There are temporary exhibits and the library is open to scholars for research.

The Jardín Etnobotánico preserves southern Mexico's native plants. Species include the agaves used to make *mezcal, pulque* and tequila and plants used in folk medicine.

✉ Calle Macedonia Alcalá and Avenida Gurrión ☎ (951) 516 29 91 🕐 Tue–Sun 10–6 ⛅ $4.80 ❓ Flash photography not allowed. Jardín Etnobotánico ☎ (951) 516 76 15

Below *The facade of Basílica de la Soledad has many fine sculptures*
Right *Edible grasshoppers are among the delicacies to be found at Benito Juárez market*

BASÍLICA DE LA SOLEDAD

The massive 17th-century Basílica de la Soledad has fine colonial ironwork and sculpture. Construction began on the site of the hermitage to San Sebastián in 1582, but was halted until 1682 because of earthquakes. The building was consecrated in 1690 and the convent was finished in 1697. Sculptures include an exquisite Virgen de la Soledad, which at one time was endowed with a crown of pure gold and embellished with some 600 glittering diamonds. The interior of the basilica is lavishly gilded, and the plaques on the walls are painted like cross-sections of polished stone. The Museo Religioso de la Soledad at the back of the church has a display of religious objects.

✉ Avenida Independencia 107 🕐 Basílica de la Soledad: daily 7–10. Museo Religioso de la Soledad: Mon–Sun 8–2, 4–7

MARKETS

The markets and varied crafts of Oaxaca are among the foremost attractions of the region. There are four main markets, all of which are worth a visit; polite bargaining is the rule everywhere. The Mercado de Abastos, also known as the Central de Abastos, at the corner of Periférico and Las Casas, is the largest in Oaxaca and the second-largest craft market in Mexico after Toluca; it's a cacophony of sights, sounds and aromas, busiest on Saturdays and not to be missed. Prices here tend to be lower than in the smaller markets. In the middle of town is the Mercado 20 de Noviembre (Calle Aldama, on the corner of 20 de Noviembre), with clean stands selling prepared foods, including barbecued tasajo (dried beef), cheese and sweet breads. To the rear of the market on Mina and 20 de Noviembre, a deep chocolatey aroma fills the air from the numerous chocolate mills, including Mayordomo (▷ 166). Next door to the Mercado 20 de Noviembre, the larger Mercado Benito Juárez sells household goods, fruits, vegetables, crafts, and regional products such as quesillo (string cheese), bread and chocolate. Mercado Artesanal (Zaragoza and J. P. García) has a good selection of crafts.

🕐 Daily 7am–8pm

Above Vibrantly colored, hand-woven traditional blankets on display at Benito Juárez market

INFORMATION

www.palenquemx.com

☩ 316 Q10 ✚ Avenida Juárez,
esq Abásalo ☎ (916) 345 03 56
🕓 Mon–Sat 9–9, Sun 9–1

Archaeological Site

☎ (916) 348 34 06 🕓 Daily 8–5
✋ $4.80 🚌 Minibuses from Palenque
town 🗣 Multilingual guides, $40 for
1.5 to 2 hours; ask at the ticket office
🍴 Expensive restaurant at museum on
way back to town. Vendors outside gates

Above *The Palace stands at the center of
the Mayan ruins of Palenque, considered
the most beautiful in Mexico*

INTRODUCTION

Suffused in mystery, Palenque is a fine example of a Maya sanctuary of the
Classic period, eerily atmospheric amid wild jungle, and hailed as the most
beautiful of all the Maya ruins in Mexico. Palenque has a mystical charm that
enchants archaeologists, historians and visitors alike. From Palenque town,
minivans run every 10 minutes along the 7km (4-mile) road to the ruins. Here
there are handicraft stands and an information booth where guided tours can
be organized.

Two rulers, Pakal the Great and his son Chan Bahlum, immortalized their
divine ancestry and military accomplishments here in a mesmerizing series
of palaces, temples, glyphs, and stucco. At the heart of the site is El Palacio,
a group of buildings arranged around four patios to which a tower was later
added, the Templo de las Inscripciones (Temple of the Inscriptions), rising
above the tomb of Pakal.

Palenque grew from a small agricultural village at the height of the
Classic period to one of the most important cities in the pre-Hispanic world.
Usumacinta, the alluvial plain to the north, provided Palenque's inhabitants
with the resources to construct this majestic city. During the reign of Pakal
the Great, the city rapidly rose to the first rank of Maya states. The duration of
Pakal's reign is still a bone of contention among Maya scholars because the
remains found in his sarcophagus do not appear to be those of an 81-year-old
man—the age implied by the texts in the Temple of the Inscriptions.

WHAT TO SEE

EL PALACIO

The Palace stands in the middle of the site on an artificial platform over 100m (328ft) long and 9m (30ft) high. When Chan Bahlum's younger brother, Kan Xul, became king he devoted himself to enlarging the palace and built the four-floor tower in memory of their dead father. The top of the tower is almost on a level with Pakal's mortuary temple, and on the winter solstice (December 21) the sun, viewed from here, sets directly above his crypt. Large windows where Maya astronomers could observe and chart movement of the planets pierce the walls of the tower. Kan Xul reigned for 18 years before being captured and probably sacrificed by the rulers of Toniná, to the south.

TEMPLO DE LAS INSCRIPCIONES

The Temple of the Inscriptions, along with Temples XII and XIII, lies to the southwest of the Palacio group and is one of the few Maya pyramids to have a burial chamber incorporated at the time of its construction. It was erected to cover the crypt in which Pakal the Great, the founder of the first ruling dynasty of Palenque, was buried. Discovered in 1952 by Alberto Ruz Lhuillier, the burial chamber measured 7m (23ft) long, 7m (23ft) high and 3.75m (12ft) across, an incredible achievement considering the weight of the huge pyramid pressing down upon it. According to the inscriptions, Lord Pakal was born in AD603 and died in 684. Inside, Ruz Lhuillier discovered the king's bones adorned with jade ornamentation. Around the burial chamber various stucco figures depict the Bolontikú—the Nine Lords of the Night—from Maya mythology. A narrow tube was built alongside the stairs, presumably to give Pakal spiritual access to the outside world. Pakal also left a record of his forebears in the inscriptions. These three great tablets contain one of the longest texts of any Maya monument. There are 620 glyph blocks; they tell of Pakal's ancestors, astronomical events, and an astonishing projection into the distant future (AD4772). One of the last inscriptions reveals that, 132 days after Pakal's death, his son, Chan Bahlum, ascended to power as the new ruler of Palenque.

TIP

» There have been reports of criminals hiding in the jungle and occasional muggings in out-of-the-way places. Leave valuables at your hotel to minimize any loss.

Below *The Temple of the Foliated Cross*

THE SARCOPHAGUS LID

Pakal's sarcophagus is fashioned out of a solid piece of rock, with a carved limestone slab covering it. Every element in the imagery of the lid is consistent with Maya iconography. The central image is that of Pakal falling back into the fleshless jaws of the earth monster who will transport him to Xibalba, the realm of the dead. A cruciform world-tree rises above the mouth to the underworld. The long inscription around the edge of the lid includes a number of dates and personal names that record a dynastic sequence covering almost the whole of the seventh and eighth centuries. Although the imagery of the sarcophagus lid refers to Pakal's fall into Xibalba, the location of the tower of the palace ensures that he will not remain there. The sun, setting over the crypt on the winter solstice, will have to do battle with the Nine Lords of the Night before re-emerging triumphantly in the east. Pakal, who awaits the sun at the point where the final battle has been fought, will accompany the sun as he re-emerges from Xibalba in the east.

Above *Detail of a Mayan stone carving in one of the courtyards of the Palace*

TEMPLE XIII

In 1994 a secret passageway was unearthed alongside the Temple of the Inscriptions, which led to an underground temple with three rooms. In the middle room were the remains of a woman within a stone coffin. While the coffin bore no inscriptions, archaeologists have concluded that the woman was of royal lineage, and she was christened the "Red Queen" because her remains were covered in cinnabar (mercury sulfide).

GRUPO DE LA CRUZ

To the extreme southeast of the middle of the site lie the temples of the Group of the Cross, which include the Templo del Sol (Temple of the Sun), with detailed relief carvings. The three temples in this group all have dramatic roof combs, originally believed to have a religious significance, although traces of roof combs have been found on buildings now known to have been purely residential. Human and mythological time come together in the inscriptions of these temples. In each tableau carved on the tablets at the back of the temples, Chan Bahlum, the new ruler, receives the regalia of office from his father, Pakal, now in the underworld and shown much smaller than his living son. The shrines in the three temples are dedicated to the Palenque Triad, a sacred trinity linked to the ruling dynasty of the city, whose genealogy is explained in the inscriptions. They were certainly long-lived: the parents of the triad were born in 3122BC or 3121BC and the children were born on October 19, October 23 and November 6, 2360BC. It has been shown that these were dates of extraordinary astronomical phenomena: the gods were intimately related to heavenly bodies and events. On each set of balustrades, Chan Bahlum began his text with the birth of the patron god of each temple. On the left side of the stairs he recorded the time between the birth of the god and the dedication of the temple. Thus, mythological time and contemporary time were fused.

NORTH GROUP

North of El Palacio, past the remains of a small ball court, lies the often overlooked North Group (Grupo Norte). There are several temples here, but the main attraction is the Temple of the Count (Templo del Conde), named for Jean-Frédérick Waldeck, an eccentric French explorer and self-styled count who lived at Palenque in the early 19th century. His namesake structure is a classic, moderately sized temple that sits atop a five-tiered base and contains an inner sanctuary.

QUEEN BATHS

Near the North Group, a steep hiking path through the jungle leads to the Queen Baths, a pretty cascade named for the royalty that once bathed in the falls. Swimming is no longer allowed in the pool below the waterfall, but the banks are a cool shady place to relax after a day of exploring. Throughout Palenque there are short paths leading to other small cascades. Mosquito repellent is highly advised.

MUSEUM

Many of the stucco carvings retrieved from the site are displayed in the site museum on the way back to town, as well as pieces of jade jewelry, funerary urns and ceramics.

🕐 Tue–Sun 9–4.30

PALENQUE TOWN

Palenque town's sole purpose is to cater to visitors heading for the archaeological site nearby. There is plenty of accommodations for every budget, with dozens of inexpensive *posadas* (inns) around the middle of town, and a visitor *barrio* (district), La Cañada, with more expensive hotels, restaurants and bars. Palenque is also a convenient place to stop en route to the southern Chiapan towns of San Cristóbal and Tuxtla Gutiérrez. Visitors coming to Palenque from Mérida, Campeche and other cities in the Yucatán Peninsula will find it much hotter here, particularly in June, July and August.

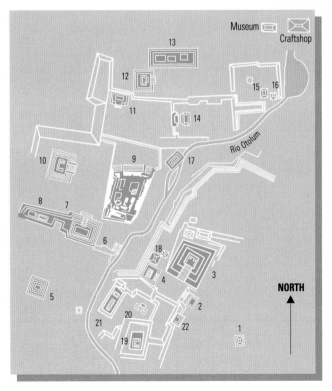

SITE PLAN

1 Mirador
2 Temple of the Foliated Cross
3 Temple of the Cross
4 Temple of the Sun
5 Temple of the Lion
6 Temple of the Inscriptions
7 Temple XIII
8 Temple of the Skull
9 Palace
10 Temple XI
11 Temple X
12 Temple of the Count
13 North Group
14 Ball Court
15 Encampment
16 Queen Baths
17 Otolum Aqueduct
18 Temple XIV
19 Temple XX
20 Temple XXI
21 Temple XXII
22 Temple XVII

Left *A small fishing boat makes its way between the moored pleasure craft in Puerto Escondido*

end; surfing is best near the middle. About 1km (half a mile) west again is Mazunte, the least-developed major beach. Nude bathing is prohibited; the safest swimming is at either end of the bay. At the east end of Mazunte is the Centro Mexicano de la Tortuga (▷ 167).

🕂 315 M11 ✈ Huatulco airport, 32km (20 miles) east, Puerto Escondido airport, 90km (56 miles) west

PUERTO ESCONDIDO

Reached via a corkscrew mountain drive on the pacific coast of Oaxaca state, Puerto Escondido has been transformed from a sleepy fishing village into one of the most popular destinations in southern Mexico. With stunning beaches, world-class surfing and a relaxed alternative lifestyle, its appeal is obvious. Hotels, restaurants and cultural complexes cater to surfers, yoga gurus and independent visitors. Daily rituals revolve around the beach, contemplating glorious sunsets. At night, restaurants serve up feasts of fresh shrimp and seared tuna to the sound of chilled-out music or the lapping of the waves. Experienced surfers make the pilgrimage to Playa Zicatela, the premier Mexico surfing scene. Playa Principal, abutting El Adoquín pedestrian mall, has the calmest waters, but is not very clean. A few fishermen still bring in the catch of the day here. Playa Manzanillo and Puerto Angelito share the Bahía Puerto Angelito and are an easy 15-minute walk away; they are pretty, with reasonably safe swimming, but rather commercial. The state tourist police patrol both the main beach and tourist areas.

Safety is an important issue in and around Puerto Escondido. Never walk on any beach at night, even if you are in a group.

🕂 315 M11 🛈 Sedetur, Avenida Juárez, at the entrance to Playa Bacocho ☎ (954) 582 01 75 🕔 Mon–Fri 9–5, Sat 10–1
🚌 Buses from Oaxaca

MITLA

Mitla is one of the foremost sites in the state of Oaxaca and remarkable for its ornate stonework, considered by many archaeologists to be without peer. Inhabited in the Classic period, Mitla reached its zenith in the Post Classic period and was still inhabited when the Spanish arrived. There are five groups of buildings, of which the most notable is the Grupo de las Columnas (Group of Columns), in the eastern part of the site. Here, the principal elements are the Salón de las Columnas (Hall of Columns) and the Patio de las Grecas (Hall of Mosaics), notable for its geometric stone mosaics. In the north and east of the complex are tombs where Zapotec priests and kings were buried.

In the village of Mitla, near the main square, you will find a lively tourist market.

🕂 316 M10 ✉ 42km (26 miles) southeast of Oaxaca ☎ (951) 568 03 16 🕔 Daily 8–5 🎫 $3.50 🚌 Buses from Oaxaca 🚍 Half-day tours to Tule, Tlacolula and Mitla from Oaxaca

MONTE ALBÁN
▷ 146–147.

OAXACA
▷ 148–151.

PALENQUE
▷ 152–155.

PUERTO ANGEL

From Pochutla, a pretty road winds south through hilly forest country before dropping to the sea at Puerto Angel. This low-key fishing port lies above a flask-shaped bay, and the central beach is an ideal spot from which to watch the activity of the small dock. Unfortunately the turquoise water is polluted. Nearby is Playa del Panteón, a small beach in a lovely setting, but crowded in season. There are cleaner and more tranquil beaches east of town, including Estacahuite (beware of strong currents and sharp coral).

Some 4km (2.5 miles) west of Puerto Angel is Zipolite, one of Mexico's few nudist beaches. It has gained a reputation for drugs and violence, but things are improving. The steeply shelved beach has dangerous undercurrents, especially near the rocks at the east end.

Another 3km (2 miles) west is San Agustinillo, a long, pretty beach with safe swimming at the west

SAN CRISTÓBAL DE LAS CASAS

San Cristóbal's fascinating blend of colonial architecture and indigenous culture, eclectic restaurants, and lively bars and cafés make this an ideal base to explore Chiapas. In the town's main square, Plaza 31 de Marzo, is the neoclassical Palacio Municipal, dating from 1885, and a gazebo built during the era of Porfirio Díaz (▷ 38). Nearby stands the 16th-century Catedral de San Cristóbal, painted in earthy yellow, brown and white, with a baroque pulpit added in the 17th century. It is flanked by the Iglesia de San Nicolás, which dates from 1613. The 16th-century Casa de la Sirena (Avenida Insurgentes 1), now the Hotel Santa Clara, is a rare example of colonial residential architecture. North, along Avenida 20 de Noviembre, is the Iglesia y Ex-Convento de Santo Domingo, by far the most dramatic building in the city, with an elaborate baroque facade in molded mortar, striking when viewed in the late afternoon sun. For a drive around indigenous villages around San Cristóbal, (▷ 160–161).

INDIGENOUS CULTURE

Twenty-one indigenous groups live in San Cristóbal and they form an important part of the town's atmosphere—each district is distinguished by it own dress and handicrafts. The main market is in front of the Iglesia de Santo Domingo, with dozens of stands selling traditional textiles, handmade dolls, wooden toys and jewelry. The cultural center Na Bolom (daily 10–6), at Avenida Vicente Guerrero 33, is an excellent resource on all aspects of indigenous culture. It was founded in 1951 by the Danish archaeologist Frans Blom and his wife, Swiss photographer Gertrudis Duby. After the death of Frans in 1963 Gertrudis continued campaigning for the conservation of the Lacandón area. Since her death in 1993, at the age of 92, the center has continued to function as a non-profit organization dedicated to conserving the Chiapan environment and helping the Lacandón people. Knowledgeable volunteers conduct tours and provide fascinating anecdotes about the life of the Bloms and their friends.

The Museo de Los Altos, in the Ex-Convento de Santo Domingo (Tue–Sun 9–6), charts the history of San Cristóbal, with an emphasis on the plight of the indigenous people. The Centro de Desarrollo de la Medicina Maya (Mon–Fri 9–2, 4–6), at Avenida Salomón González Blanco 10, has a herb garden with detailed displays on the use of some of the medicinal plants.

INFORMATION

www.turismochiapas.gob.mx

✚ 316 P10 ℹ Delegacíon Regional de Turismo, Hidalgo 1-B ☎ (967) 678 65 70 ◉ Mon–Sat 8–8, Sun 9–2 ✈ San Cristóbal airport, 15km (9 miles) north

TIPS

» San Cristóbal has a mild climate compared to Palenque and Tuxtla Gutiérrez. During June, July and August it is warm and sunny in the morning, while in the afternoon it tends to rain heavily, with a sharp drop in temperature, rising again in the evening.

» If you are coming from San Cristóbal to Palenque by car you can use the 210km (130-mile) paved road; avoid night-time journeys because of the risk of armed robberies.

» If you don't take an organized tour to the nearby villages it is advisable to travel with a guide; contact Na Bolom (tel (967) 678 14 18; ▷ left).

» Don't take cameras to the villages as photography is seen as invasive and profiteering.

Above *Colorful bunting adorns the entrance to the church of Santa Guadaloupe in Santo Domingo*

RESERVA DE LA BIÓSFERA EL TRIUNFO

In the Sierra Madre, the Triunfo Biosphere Reserve is one of the most pristine and diverse wildlife regions in the country. Most importantly, it protects Mexico's only cloud forest, over 2,750m (9,000ft) above the Pacific coast. The main hiking route into the forest runs from Jaltenango (reached by bus from Tuxtla) to Mapastepec on the coastal highway. It's about 29km (18 miles) from Jaltenango to Finca Prusia; then follow a good mule track for 3 hours to the El Triunfo camp (1,650m/5,410ft).

Endemic species of wildlife include the rare azure-rumped tanager and the horned guan, birds found only here and across the border in the nearby mountains of Guatemala. Other birds and mammals include the quetzal, harpy eagle, jaguar, tapir and the white-lipped peccary.

Turn left in the clearing for the route down to Tres de Mayo, 25km (15.5 miles) away; this is an easy descent of 5 hours to a pedestrian suspension bridge on the dirt road to Loma Bonita. From here, take a pick-up to Mapastepec.

Below *The impressive facade of Tuxtla Gutiérrez' San Marcos Cathedral*

➕ 316 P11 ✉ Park entrance about 184km (114 miles) south of Tuxtla Gutiérrez via Angel Albino Corzo ☎ (961) 612 36 63 (Institute of Natural History, Tuxtla) 🕐 Daily 8–5

TEHUANTEPEC

Santo Domingo Tehuantepec, to give its full name, is a vibrant town that conserves the region's indigenous roots. Robust Zapotec matrons in bright dresses stand in the back of motorized tricycles known as *motocarros*. Life moves slowly here, focused on the plaza, which has arcades on one side and a market next to it. Many churches with attractive white buildings were built here during the early colonial period. Houses are low, in white or pastel shades. The Río Tehuantepec runs two blocks from the plaza.

The Casa de la Cultura (Mon–Fri 10–4) is housed in the 16th-century Dominican former convent Rey Cosijopi. Although it's quite run down, original frescoes can be seen on some of the walls. There is a library and simple exhibits of regional history, archaeology and costume. Ask the caretaker to open it up.

The Museo Casa de la Señora Juana C. Romero (Mon–Fri 10–4) is a chalet built entirely with materials brought from France; Romero's great-granddaughter lives there today, and you can ask for permission to visit the house.

➕ 316 N11 ℹ Sedetur, Carretera Transístmica 7, 2nd floor ☎ (971) 715 12 36

TUXTEPEC

The large commercial city of Juan Bautista Tuxtepec, on the border of Veracruz and Oaxaca states, is the natural place to overnight if you are journeying between the two. It's tranquil and unpretentious, and prices here are lower than in other parts of Oaxaca.

Avenida Independencia, the main commercial avenue, runs along the riverfront. Here you will find a bustling market selling ripe tropical fruits, vegetables and cilantro (coriander) placed incongruously between bleeping alarm clocks, plastic hair adornments, cheap T-shirts, and sacks of chilies. Shops selling electronic goods blare out *Veracruzana* rhythms and Caribbean salsa, while local women wearing colorful traditional Oaxacan dress confidently negotiate the traffic-clogged streets.

Sleepy Parque Benito Juárez, the main plaza, with its ample Palacio Municipal to the south and a modern cathedral to the east, comes alive in the evenings when families and cotton candy (candyfloss) vendors jostle for space.

Farther west is Parque Hidalgo, with a statue of the father of Mexico's Independence.

➕ 316 M10 ℹ Cámara Nacional de Comercio Serytour, Libertad esq Allende, opposite Parque Juárez 🕐 Mon–Fri 9–2, 5–8, Sat 9–1 🚌 Buses from Córdoba, Mexico City, Veracruz and Oaxaca

TUXTLA GUTIÉRREZ

www.turismochiapas.gob.mx
The capital of Chiapas state is a busy, shabby city with several points of interest for the visitor. The main sights are a long way from the middle of town and are generally too far to walk.

In the Parque Madero at the east end of Tuxtla is the Museo Regional de Chiapas on Calzada de los Hombres Ilustres 885 (Tue–Sun 9–4), displaying a fine collection of Maya objects, and with an auditorium and a library.

Some 3km (2 miles) south of town up a long hill is the superb Zoológico Miguel Álvarez del Toro (Tue–Sun 8.30–4.30), founded by Dr. Miguel Alvarez del Toro, who died in 1996. His aim was to provide a free zoo for the children and indigenous people of the area. Many of the animals are kept in open areas rather than cages. Take mosquito repellent with you.

➕ 316 P10 ℹ Boulevard Belisario Domínguez 950, Secretaria de Fomento Economico ☎ (961) 602 52 98 🕐 Mon–Sat 9–2 ❓ *Colectivos* to the zoo from Mercado, Calle 1a Ote Sur and Calle 7 Sur Ote

Above *One of the four colossal carved stone heads from the ancient Olmec city of La Venta*

LA VENTA

The almost impenetrable forest of La Venta was once the hub of the ancient Olmec culture. An expedition of archaeologists in 1925 found huge sculptured human and animal figures, urns and altars. When the discovery of oil in the 1950s threatened the destruction of the monuments, poet Carlos Pellicer established the Parque Nacional de La Venta, also called the Museo Nacional de la Venta, on Boulevard Adolfo Ruiz Cortines, around 3km (2 miles) from central Villahermosa (daily 8–5). Thirty-three exhibits lie scattered in small clearings. The huge heads, one of them weighing 20 tons, were created by the Olmecs, a culture that flourished between about 1150BC and 150BC. Exposure to the elements has damaged certain figures but to see them in natural surroundings is an experience you should not miss.

🚹 316 P10 ✉ 120km (74 miles) west of Villahermosa

VILLAHERMOSA

www.tabasco.gob.mx
Villahermosa, the capital of Tabasco state, stands on the Río Grijalva.

It is a busy, prosperous city, with a warren of modern, colonial-style pedestrian malls throughout the central area. Visitors from Chiapas will find it more expensive, hotter and more humid. A few minutes' walk from the middle of town, southwest along the river bank, is the Centro de Investigaciones de las Culturas Olmecas (CICOM), a new modern complex with a large public library, an expensive restaurant, airline offices, and souvenir shops.

The Museo Regional de Antropología Carlos Pellicer (Tue–Sun 9–7), covering three floors, has well laid-out displays of Maya and Olmec objects. Two other museums worth visiting are the Museo de Cultura Popular, at Calle Zaragoza 810 (Tue–Sun 9–8), and the Museo de Historia de Tabasco, at Avenida 27 de Febrero esq Juárez (Tue–Sun 9–8, Sun 10–5). On the corner of Avenida Pino Suárez and Bastar Zozaya is the Mercado Pino Suárez, where every nook and cranny is taken up with goods of all sorts (▷ 167).

Day trips from Villahermosa can be made to Yumká, 16km (10 miles) east, a 108ha (267-acre) safari park with three major habitats—jungle, savannah and lagoon. Visitors can walk through rain forest or take boat tours through each zone (▷ 167).

Within reach of Villahermosa is the ancient site of La Venta (▷ 159), one of Tabasco's notable attractions.
🚹 316 P10 ℹ Esq Calle 13, Avenida de los Ríos ☎ (993) 316 36 33
🕐 Mon–Fri 8–8

YAGUL

Yagul is an outstandingly picturesque archaeological site. Serene, ghostly and absorbing, it is often described as the most moving of Oaxaca's ruins, with its acropolis majestically overlooking the Oaxaca Valley. It was a large Zapotec and later Mixtec religious base that flourished following the decline of Monte Albán (▷ 146–147). The city enjoyed a renaissance just prior to the arrival of the Spanish.

Yagul's labyrinthine structures

bear striking similarities to those of Monte Albán, and the Palacio de los Seis Patios (Palace of the Six Patios) also resembles the Salón de las Columnas (Hall of Columns) at Mitla (▷ 156).

The ball court, set in a landscape punctuated by candelabra cactus and agave, is said to be the second-largest found in Mesoamerica; it is also one of the most perfect discovered to date.

If you take the path behind the ruins (the last part is steep) there are fine tombs and a superb view from the hill.
🚹 316 M10 ✉ 36km (22 miles) southeast of Oaxaca, just off Route 190 to Mitla ☎ (951) 516 01 23 🕐 Daily 8–5 💷 $3.50 🚌 Buses to Mitla from Oaxaca; ask to get off at the paved turn-off to Yagul, 1km (half a mile) uphill to the site 🔲 Guided tours in English on Tue are arranged by Oaxaca travel agencies

YAXCHILÁN

Southeast of Palenque is Yaxchilán, one of the least accessible but most rewarding of the Maya sites. Built along a terrace and hills above the Río Usumacinta, it is reached by a combination of car and boat.

The site is spectacular, as much for its position amid luxuriant vegetation, saturated with the sounds of birds, insects and howler monkeys, as for the exquisite inscriptions on its buildings.

Yaxchilán developed from a small agricultural village to become one of the most outstanding Maya bases in the region. With the rise of Cráneo-Mahkina II to the throne in AD526, it became the regional capital. The temples are ornately decorated with stucco and stone and the lintels are carved with scenes of ceremonies and conquests.
🚹 317 Q10 ✉ Carretera 307, direction of Escudo Jaguar, 1-hour *(lancha)* boat trip to Yaxchilán 🕐 Daily 8–5 💷 $4.60 per person 🚢 1-hour boat journey from Echeverría. Be there before 9am to meet other visitors wanting to share a boat ✈ Flights from Palenque to Bonampak and Yaxchilán, in a light plane for 5 people

INDIGENOUS VILLAGES NEAR SAN CRISTÓBAL

San Cristóbal de las Casas provides the ideal base for half-day or full-day excursions to the area's indigenous villages. Steeped in ancestral traditions, potent mysticism and bloody revolution, they provide powerful insights into the lost world of Chiapas.

THE DRIVE

Distance: 280km (174 miles) total distance to visit all towns
Time: One half-day per excursion
Start/end at: San Cristóbal de las Casas

EXCURSION 1
To Zinacantán and San Juan Chamula

★ Leave San Cristóbal (▷ 157) on the San Juan Chamula road and head west for 5km (3 miles) until the road forks. Take the left fork and continue for a further 5km (3 miles) to Zinacantán.

❶ Zinacantán in the Tzotzil language means "place of the bats," referring to the abundance of bats in the area and the discovery of a stone in the form of a bat, which later became a titular god. Before the arrival of the Aztecs, Zinacantán was an important

commercial hub and considered the capital of the Tzotziles. The main gathering place is around the church; the roof was destroyed by fire ($0.50 charged for entering church, official ticket from tourist office next door; photography inside is strictly prohibited). Annual festival days here are January 6, January 19–22 and August 7–11; visitors are welcome.

The Tzotzil village of San Juan Chamula lies 12km (7.5 miles) northwest of San Cristóbal de las Casas. From Zinacantán take the left fork north, instead of turning onto the San Cristóbal road.

❷ The painted church in San Juan Chamula is particularly beautiful. To visit it you will need to obtain a permit ($1) from the village tourist office on the square, and remember

photographing inside the church is strictly forbidden. Some Indians believe cameras steal their souls, and photographing their church is stealing the soul of God. There are no pews or formal services: family groups sit or kneel on the floor, chanting, with candles burning in memory of their loved ones. A food market is held on Sundays, and there are many permanent handicraft stands on the way up the small hill southwest of the village. Take heed of signs saying that it is dangerous to walk in the area. Return to San Cristóbal the way you came.

EXCURSION 2
To Tenejapa

★ Head northeast from San Cristóbal de las Casas for 28km (17 miles), a journey of approximately one hour and 15 minutes, to reach the little-visited village of Tenejapa.

3 Tenejapa has a traditional fruit and vegetable market on a Thursday with a clutch of other stands. You can buy excellent woven items from the weavers' cooperative near the church. There is a fine collection of old textiles in the regional ethnographic museum adjoining the handicraft shop. The cooperative can also arrange weaving classes.

EXCURSION 3
To Amatenango del Valle
★ From San Cristóbal de las Casas, head south on the Pan-American Highway through roads lined with cornfields to Amatenango del Valle in the Teocicca Valley.

4 Amatenango del Valle is a Tzeltal village with around 7,400 inhabitants. The women make and fire pottery in their yards in strict accordance to traditional ways by building a fire around the pieces, rather than using a kiln.

EXCURSION 4
To Ocosingo and Toniná
★ Ocosingo (often written as Ococingo) lies 58km (36 miles) northeast of San Cristóbal de las Casas. Follow the route to Palenque, a scenic two-hour drive along a paved serpentine road.

5 Ocosingo, nestling in one of Mexico's most beautiful valleys, is a largely Tzeltal village with a local airport, a lively market and several hotels. It was one of the cells of fighting in the uprising in January 1994. The town makes a good base for visiting the Maya ruins of Toniná, about 12km (7.5 miles) southeast.

The road is unpaved but marked with signs once you leave Ocosingo. Beside the road is a marsh, frequented by thousands of swallows in January.

6 Toniná is the perfect place to enjoy the countryside and Maya architecture in peace and quiet. The huge pyramid complex, with seven stone platforms creating a man-made hill, is 10m (33ft) higher than the Temple of the Sun at Teotihuacán

and is the tallest pyramidal structure in the Maya world. The stelae (engraved slabs) take diverse forms, as do the wall panels; some are in styles and of subjects unknown at any other Maya site. In December 1990 the well-preserved Mural of the Four Swans was discovered on the sixth level.

From Toniná it is around 86km (53 miles) back to San Cristóbal de las Casas.

TOURIST INFORMATION
MUNICIPAL OFFICE
✉ Palacio Municipal, San Cristóbal de las Casas ☎ (967) 678 06 65 ⊘ Mon–Fri 9–8

SAN CRISTÓBAL DE LAS CASAS DELEGACÍON REGIONAL DE TURISMO
✉ Hidalgo 1-B, San Cristóbal de las Casas ☎ (967) 678 65 70 ⊘ Mon–Sat 8am–10pm, Sun 9–2

WHERE TO EAT
There are few eating options in the villages. Tours arranged by Na Bolom include lunch in Zinacantán. San Cristóbal de las Casas has good restaurants and cafés (▷ 167).

CASA DEL PAN
▷ 170.

PALOMA
▷ 171.

WHERE TO STAY
NA BOLOM
▷ 173.

POSADA EL PARAÍSO
▷ 173.

TIPS
» It is best not to take cameras to villages as photographing is seen as invasive and profiteering. There are good postcards and photographs on sale.
» During the rainy season (May to October), heavy flooding can result in the roads being impassable.

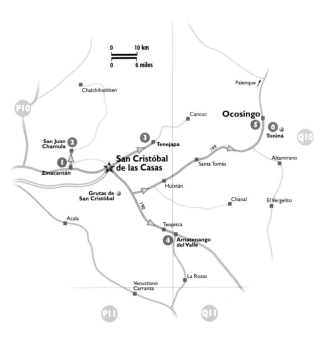

OAXACA CITY

From the serenity of colonial churches and romantic patios to the exuberance of lively street markets and festivals, a walk through Oaxaca reveals a cultural maelstrom.

THE WALK
Distance: 5km (3 miles)
Time: 3 hours
Start/end at: *Zócalo*

★ Begin at the *zócalo*, the heart of Oaxaca (▷ 148–151), with the Palacio de Gobierno behind you, and head north to the Alameda de León, where you will find the 17th-century cathedral on the right.

❶ The cathedral has a fine baroque facade. Construction began in 1535, but the building was not consecrated until 1733, after being damaged by earthquakes. The 14 side chapels contain many examples of 18th-century sacred art.

From the cathedral, head north across the Alameda, passing through craft stands and food carts, to Calle Macedonio Alcalá, a cobbled pedestrian walkway.

❷ Along Macedonio Alcalá are many colonial buildings with swirling wrought-iron balconies. Archways and ornate doorways lead to leafy patios, craft shops, museums, art galleries, gourmet restaurants, and cafés. At No. 202 is one of the finest museums in Oaxaca.

❸ Housed in a late 17th-century mansion with a stone facade, the Museo de Arte Contemporáneo de Oaxaca presents contemporary art works from renowned Oaxacan artists, including Rufino Tamayo (1899–1991). The building is a perfect example of Spanish colonial architecture, with rooms fanning out from three interior courtyards. On the next block you can make a short detour by turning right onto Calle Murguia. This brings you to one of Mexico's most renowned hotels, the Camino Real (▷ 172), housed in the former Convento de Santo

Catalina. Two blocks south at Calle 5 de Mayo and Avenida Independencia is the Teatro Macedonio Alcalá.

❹ The elegant belle époque Macedonio Alcalá theater dates back to the mid-19th century, with a reproduction Louis XV entrance and white marble staircase. Regular performances are held here, (currently closed for restoration).

Return along Avenida Independencia to Calle Macedonio Alcalá and walk four blocks north, past oil canvases displayed on Avenida Abasolo, to reach the Iglesia de Santo Domingo.

❺ With the construction of the Iglesia de Santo Domingo, Mexican baroque reaches its apogee. The adjoining monastery houses the Centro Cultural Santo Domingo (▷ 150), which includes the unmissable Museo de las Culturas

Opparite *The high vaulted ceiling in the Iglesia de Santo Domingo*

de Oaxaca, Jardín Etnobotánico, the Biblioteca Francisco Burgoa and Hemeroteca (newspaper library).

Continue north, passing the Instituto de Artes Gráficas de Oaxaca (IAGO) on your left after one block, to reach Calle Cosijopi, where there is a small, peaceful garden. Take a left turn in one block to Calle García Vigil, where you will see the remains of an aqueduct and an area referred to as the Arcos de Xochimilco.

⑥ The Arcos de Xochimilco is a picturesque district of cobbled alleys draped in jacaranda, with closet-sized *taco* cafés, fountains, gigantic cacti and ornate street lanterns. The aqueduct once brought water from San Felipe del Agua to the city.

Take Calle García Vigil south, past Museo Casa de Juárez, then south for four blocks to Avenida Morelos. Turn right and walk a block and a half to the Museo Rufino Tamayo.

⑦ This museum has outstanding pre-Columbian objects dating from 1250BC to AD1100, donated by Oaxacan painter Rufino Tamayo.

At the next left, turn onto Calle Tinoco y Palacios, and in one block is the Iglesia de San Felipe Neri, with its elaborate altars, which brings you to Avenida Independencia, the commercial part of the city. Turn right and walk two-and-a-half blocks. Steps lead up to the Jardín de la Soledad (▷ 151).

⑧ This massive 17th-century building houses a much-revered statue of the Virgin. Don't miss the small museum at the back.

Walk back on Avenida Independencia toward the cathedral for three-and-a-half blocks, then turn right onto Calle 20 de Noviembre and head south for four blocks. Between the markets, Mercado Benito Juárez and Mercado

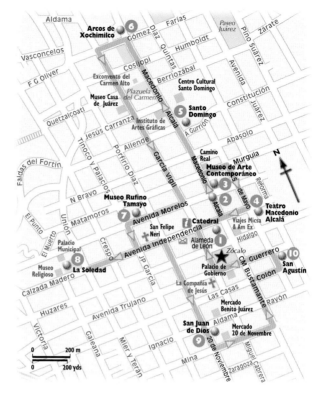

20 de Noviembre, is the Iglesia de San Juan de Dios.

⑨ Inside are Indian paintings of the Conquistadors arriving in Oaxaca in 1629 and an anti-Catholic uprising in 1700. This was the first church to be built in Oaxaca, and was originally dedicated to Santa Catalina Mártir.

Turn left one block after the church onto Calle Mina and continue for two blocks, left into Calle Bustamante for two blocks, right into Calle Colón and first left into Calle Armenta y Lopez. (Along Calle Mina a deep chocolate aroma emanates from the many chocolate mills in the area.) Turn left onto Armenta y Lopez and head in the direction of the *zócalo* and the Iglesia de San Agustín.

⑩ The church of San Agustín has an intricate facade, with a Guerrero bas-relief of St. Augustine holding the City of God above adoring monks.

From the church, turn left and it's just one block west to the *zócalo*.

TOURIST INFORMATION
✉ Municipal Tourism Office, Juarez 703
☎ (951) 502 12 00 ◉ Daily 8–8

PLACES TO VISIT
MUSEO DE ARTE CONTEMPORÁNEO DE OAXACA
✉ Calle Macedonio Alcalá 202 ☎ (951) 514 22 28 ◉ Wed–Mon 10.30–8

IGLESIA DE SANTO DOMINGO, MUSEO DE LAS CULTURAS DE OAXACA, JARDÍN ETNOBOTÁNICO, BIBLIOTECA FRANCISCO BURGOA AND HEMEROTECA
▷ 150.

MUSEO RUFINO TAMAYO
✉ Avenida Morelos 503 ◉ Mon, Wed–Sat 10–2, 4–7, Sun 10–3

WHERE TO EAT
MARÍA BONITA
▷ 169.

CRAFT VILLAGES AROUND OAXACA

Beyond the city of Oaxaca you'll find ghostly ancient ruins, Zapotec villages steeped in mysticism, hypnotic craft markets and a dramatic landscape with cascading waterfalls and abundant wildlife.

THE DRIVE

Distance: 126km (78 miles)
Time: 1 day
Start/end at: Oaxaca

★ Leave Oaxaca (▷ 148–151) on the main highway, Route 190, heading east. The road is poorly paved in parts with potholes and risk of occasional flooding. Continue for 12km (7.5 miles) until you reach a sign on the right to El Tule.

❶ El Tule has what is thought to be the world's largest tree, a *savino (Taxodium mucronatum)*, estimated at 2,000 years old. On the left, near the basilica as you drive into town, it stands about 40m (130ft) high, 42m (138ft) around the base, weighs an estimated 550 tons, and is watered by an elaborate pipe system. El Tule also has a market with good food on sale at Guerrero 4-A.

Continue east along Route 190 for 5km (3 miles) to San Jerónimo

Tlacochahuaya, which has a 16th-century church with plateresque rococo altarpieces and vivid Indian murals. Upstairs, in the cloisters to the rear, there is an ornate organ. Continue along the highway for another 3km (2 miles) to Dainzú. Take the turn-off on the right, shortly after the Km 20 sign, then follow the unpaved road for approximately 1.5km (1 mile).

❷ Secluded and peaceful, the labyrinthine archaeological site of Dainzú flourished alongside Monte Albán (▷ 146–147), reaching its apogee around AD350. The site is significant for its depictions of ball players wearing feline masks and gloves, and for the superlative jaguar carvings on Structure G.

Return to Route 190 and after around 7km (4 miles) turn left at Km 27, where a paved road leads to Teotitlán del Valle after 4km (2.5 miles).

❸ The name Teotitlán comes from a Nahuatl word meaning "place of the gods," and the village's 4,500 inhabitants call themselves beeni *xiguiee*, "charmed/magic people," who believe that they are descended from the clouds. Bright wall-hangings and *tapetes* (rugs) are woven with subjects ranging from pre-Columbian scenes to reproductions of paintings by famous artists such as Diego Rivera and Rufino Tamayo. There is a daily artisans' market held near the 16th-century church, and the Museo Comunitario.

From Teotitlán you can make an optional detour involving a one-hour hike north through stunning scenery to the town of Benito Juárez, one of the highest points of the valley.

❹ At Benito Juárez in the Sierra Norte, soaring aromatic pine forests and cascading waterfalls teem with flora and fauna. Hike, or rent a mountain bike from Tourist Yú ù (▷ 166), near the turn-off from Route 190 and head to El Mirador (3,050m/10,005ft) for spectacular views of the Tlacolula Valley.

Return to Route 190 and continue for approximately 8km (5 miles) to the village of Tlacolula.

⑤ Tlacolula has one of the oldest Sunday markets in Mesoamerica; a scintillating array of traditional crafts lines the main street and surrounds the church, which is similar in style to the Iglesia de Santo Domingo in Oaxaca, with intricate white and gold stucco, lots of mirrors, silver altar rails and sculptures of martyrs in gruesome detail. Two beheaded saints guard the door to the main nave. The town is renowned for its *mezcal* liquor preparation, with more than 24 varieties.

About 3km (2 miles) north of Tlacolula is the peaceful Zapotec village of Santa Ana del Valle.

⑥ Santa Ana del Valle is one of the best places to buy quality weavings, and has an important rug market. There is an 18th-century baroque

temple and a small but engaging community museum with displays revealing the seminal events of the Mexican Revolution and ancient textile techniques; ask any villager to point you toward the keyholder.

Return to Route 190 and continue east for 7km (4 miles) to the turn-off north for Yagul.

⑦ Yagul (▷ 159) is one of the most intimate and ethereal ancient sites in the region, with an acropolis gloriously poised overlooking the Oaxaca Valley.

From Yagul, return to Route 190 and in 5km (3 miles) you'll reach a paved road, which branches left and leads to Mitla (4km/2.5 miles).

⑧ Mitla (▷ 156) flourished during the Post Classic period (AD750–1521) and is renowned for its majestic stonework mosaics.

From Mitla, drive for 12km (7.5 miles) to San Pedro Ayutla. Take the diversion for San Lorenzo Albarrades and in 8km (5 miles) is San Isidro Roaguía, where you will find the stunning Hierve el Agua waterfalls.

⑨ Hierve el Agua is a series of petrified waterfalls created by the water's high mineral concentration. The most spectacular fall plummets 30m (98ft). Once a sacred site for the Zapotecs, the falls were used 2,400 years ago by early inhabitants who constructed wells for terraced crops. A 2km (1.2-mile) pathway leads to El Anfiteatro, a lookout point with dizzying views of the valley.

Return to Route 190 and retrace your route to Oaxaca.

TOURIST INFORMATION
✉ Municipal Tourism Office, Juarez 703, Oaxaca ☎ (951) 502 12 00 ⊙ Daily 8–8

PLACES TO VISIT
MUSEO COMUNITARIO
✉ Teotitlán del Valle ☎ (951) 524 44 63 ⊙ Tue–Sun 10–6

PENSAMIENTO MEZCAL
One of the *mezcal* factories on Route 190, this establishment offers tours of the production process.
✉ Route 190, km 32, Tlacolula ☎ (956) 562 00 17

WHERE TO EAT
EL DESCANSO
This pleasant modern restaurant serves good local cuisine.
✉ Avenida Juárez 51, Teotitlán del Valle ☎ (951) 524 41 52 ⊙ Daily 9–6

EL CENTEOTL
Rather expensive, this place is one of the finest restaurants for traditional *cocina oaxaqueña*.
✉ Domicio Conocido, Yagul ☎ (951) 516 61 86 ⊙ Daily 11–7

Opposite *Textiles and rugs are a specialty of Oaxaca's craft villages*

WHAT TO DO

ACAPULCO

BABY'O

This small, intimate dance venue is a welcome antidote to the crop of superclubs that make up the city's late-night scene. Everything from techno to hip-hop is played to a largely 20-something crowd.
✉ Costera Miguel Alemán, Acapulco ☎ (744) 484 74 74 ⏰ Daily 10pm–5am ✋ Cover charge $10–$20 for women, $40–$60 for men

BENITO JUÁREZ

TOURIST YÚ Ù

In this government-run ecotourism project you can stay in rustic cabins in the mountains and experience traditional Oaxacan village life. Activities include trout fishing, hiking, cycling, and horseback-riding. The scenery is idyllic, with cascading waterfalls and brooks crisscrossing lushly carpeted valleys.
✉ Comité de Ecoturismo de Benito Juárez, Benito Juárez ☎ (951) 514 21 55 (Sedetur) ✋ $10 per person camping; $30 cabaña

CHIAPA DEL CORZO

PARQUE ECOTURÍSTICO CAÑON DEL SUMIDERO, SA DE CV

www.sumidero.com
The boat trip from Chiapa del Corzo to Cañon del Sumidero has magnificent views of the canyon,

the Cueva de Silencio, the Cueva de los Colores, and cliffs 600m (1,968ft) high, including the Arból de Navidad with its waterfall. The tour ends as the canyon opens out into the valley with a series of waterfalls (▷ 144).
✉ Chiapa del Corzo ☎ (961)104 80 54 ⏰ Daily 10–5 ✋ Adult $28.50, child $20.50; boat transfers to the park are included in admission and depart regularly from the Chiapa del Corzo embarcadero beginning at 9am. Two hour boat trips into Sumidero Canyon, without a visit to the park, depart from the embarcadero and cost $12 per person

HUATULCO

HIKING

In the Huatulco area, the mountains of the Sierra Madre del Sur drop from the highest point in the state of Oaxaca (3,750m/12,300ft) to the sea. There are ample opportunities for day hiking. In the hills north of Huatulco coffee plantations can be visited, including a meal with traditional dishes and bathing in freshwater springs or waterfalls.
✋ $50 per person

OAXACA

AMATE BOOKS

This has the best selection of English-language books in Oaxaca, with a good choice of Latin-

Above *The villages around Oaxaca and San Cristóbal de las Casa are best for handicrafts*

American literature and archaeology books, glossy art volumes featuring Mexican artists Rufino Tamayo and Frida Kahlo, and guides to Oaxaca.
✉ Calle Macedonio Alcalá 307, Oaxaca ☎ (951) 516 69 60 ⏰ Mon–Sat 10–9, Sun 2–7

CAMINO REAL

www.caminoreal.com
The Hotel Camino Real is the setting for the Gualaguateza spectacles—exuberant folk traditions of the various cultural groups in the region.
✉ Calle 5 de Mayo 300, Oaxaca ☎ (951) 516 61 00 ⏰ Show Fri 8pm, dinner at 7pm ✋ $36 (includes buffet dinner)

CHOCOLATE MAYORDOMO

Mayordomo mill grinds cacao beans, almond, sugar and cinnamon into a paste for making hot chocolate. Outlets sell Oaxacan mole (▷ 297), grasshopper salt and mezcal.
✉ Calle Mina and 20 de Noviembre, Oaxaca ☎ (951) 516 33 09 ⏰ Daily 7am–9pm

LA MANO MÁGICA

Contemporary art and high-quality artesanía draw many collectors to La Mano Mágica. The wool and silk tapestries feature the creations of one of Oaxaca's most renowned weavers, Arnulfo Mendoza. You can watch tapestries being woven. Mano Mágica also organizes cultural tours and cooking classes in Teotitlán del Valle on the first and third Friday of the month (8.30–3; $85 including transport, and lunch).

✉ Calle Macedonia Alcalá 203, Oaxaca ☎ (951) 516 42 75 🕐 Mon–Sat 10.30–3, 4–8

MUJERES ARTESANAS DE LAS REGIONES DE OAXACA

MARO was founded by a group of women to preserve the traditional methods of regional handicrafts. There is a good selection of textiles, ceramics, *alejibres* (animals carved in copal wood then brightly painted), and embroidered dresses.

✉ Calle 5 de Mayo 204, Oaxaca ☎ (951) 516 06 70 🕐 Daily 9–8

SEDETUR

For the highest-quality rug collection, visit this shop selling crafts. The profits go to the artisans.

✉ Calle Murguia 206, Oaxaca ☎ (951) 516 01 23 🕐 Daily 9–8

SOL Y LUNA

This is one of the top spots in Oaxaca for Latin music. The music kicks off after 9.30pm with excellent salsa and merengue, tango and flamenco. Food is also served.

✉ Calle Reforma 502, Oaxaca ☎ (951) 514 80 69 🕐 Daily 6.30pm–1.30am, closed Sun 💶 Cover $6

TIERRAVENTURA

www.tierraventura.com
This ecotourism organization runs adventure and cultural trips to the indigenous villages, Sierra Mixteca, the mountains and the Oaxaca coast. Personalized tours range from one day to several weeks; themes include horseback-riding, shamanism, hikes and traditional Indian medicine.

✉ Abasolo 217, Oaxaca ☎ (951) 501 13 63 🕐 Mon–Sat 10–2, 5–7 💶 1-day tour $60–$85; 2-day tour $120–$180; 4-day tour $430

PUERTO ANGEL
CENTRO MEXICANO DE LA TORTUGA

Endangered sea turtles are studied and conserved here. You can see many species in viewing tanks. A trail leads from the beach to Punta Cometa, a spit of land with lovely views and spectacular sunsets.

✉ East end of Mazunte beach, Puerto Angel 🕐 Wed–Sat 10–4.30, Sun 10–2.30 💶 Adult $2, child (under 12) $1 🎫 Guided tours in Spanish and English

SAN CRISTÓBAL DE LAS CASAS
LA CASA DEL JADE

The museum has a collection of replicas and jade jewelry from the Toltec, Zapotec and Olmec cultures, including re-creations of King Pakal's tomb (▷ 152–155). You can visit the workshop and watch the craftsmen.

✉ Museo Mesoamericano de Jade, Avenida 16 de Septiembre 16, San Cristóbal de las Casas ☎ (967) 678 25 57 🕐 Mon–Sat 9–9, Sun 9–5

LAS GRUTAS DE SAN CRISTÓBAL

Horses can be rented at Las Grutas, 10km (6 miles) southeast of San Cristóbal, for a five-hour ride (guide extra) through the forest.

✉ Km 94, San Cristóbal de las Casas 🕐 Daily 9–6 💶 Horseback-riding $15

LAS VELAS

Just one block from the *zócalo* is one of the town's most popular hangouts, with live music every night. Happy hour is from 8pm–midnight. Live music ranging from reggae to blues, Latin jazz and salsa continues until the early hours.

✉ Francisco Madero 14, San Cristóbal de las Casas ☎ (967) 678 04 17 🕐 Daily 8pm–4am

SAN MARTÍN TILCAJETE
WOODCARVINGS

San Martín Tilcajete, 1km (half a mile) west of the main road, is the center for the production of *alejibres*—animal carvings. They often have a look of the supernatural about them.

✉ 21km (13 miles) from Oaxaca

SAN TOMÁS JALIEZA
TEXTILES

Santo Tomás Jalieza is the center for cotton and wool textiles produced with backstrap looms and natural dyes. Friday is market day.

✉ 24km (15 miles) south of Oaxaca

TEOTITLÁN DEL VALLE
WEAVING

The best prices for weavings are at the stores along the road as you come into the town of Teotitlán del Valle. Make sure you know whether you are getting all wool or a mixture, and check the quality. A well-made rug will not ripple when unfolded on the floor.

✉ 32km (20 miles) east of Oaxaca

VENTANILLA
TOURS

From the visitor center in the village local residents run tours, combining a rowboat ride through mangroves for up to 10 people, a visit to a crocodile farm and a walk on the beach. Horseback-riding tours along the beach are also available. Simple meals are available in the village. Guides speak Spanish only.

💶 Tour $5 per person

VILLAHERMOSA
MERCADO PINO SUÁREZ

Mercado Pino Suárez is crammed with goods, from barbecued *pejelagarto* (pike-like fish) to cowboy hats, fabrics and spices. The local drink, *pozol*, an acquired taste, is believed to cure a hangover. You can watch it being made as the *pozoleros* grind the hominy into a thick dough then mix it with cacao.

✉ Corner of Avenida Pino Suárez and Calle Bastar Zozaya, Villahermosa 🕐 Daily 9–7

YUMKÁ

Parque Yumká is an easy day trip from Villahermosa. This safari park containing jungle, savannah and lagoon is a "zoo without cages," offering walking, trolley and boat tours of each habitat.

✉ Camino Yumka, Ejido dos Montes, Villahermosa ☎ (993) 356 01 07 🕐 Daily 9–4 💶 $5. Round trips for about $10

PRICES AND SYMBOLS

The restaurants are listed alphabetically within each town. The prices given are the average for a two-course lunch (L) and a three-course dinner (D) for one person, without drinks. The wine price is for the least expensive bottle. All the restaurants listed accept credit cards unless otherwise stated.

For a key to the symbols, ▷ 2.

ACAPULCO
PIPO'S

One of Acapulco's oldest and best-loved restaurants has been luring the locals for years with its fresh fish, friendly service and reasonable prices. The airy dining room is decorated with the obligatory fishing paraphernalia and the English menu features a good selection of seafood, including clams, crayfish, lobster, shrimp, crab and octopus. Try the *huachinango Veracruzano* (red snapper baked with tomatoes, peppers, onion, and olives). There's another branch of Pipo's at Costera Miguel Aleman and Canadá (tel 748 401 65).

✉ Almirante Breton 3, Acapulco ☎ (744) 484 01 65 ⏰ Daily 1–9.30 🍴 L$10, D$25, Wine $12

HUATULCO
LAS CÚPULAS

www.quintareal.com

Stunning panoramic views of Tangolunda Bay make this elegant hotel restaurant one of the best placed in Huatulco. The furnishings are sumptuous, the service impeccable and the cuisine mouthwatering, with an eclectic menu of regional and international dishes presented with panache: definitely worth splashing out on. For a civilized start to the evening, have a cocktail at the bar next door and soak up the dazzling views. Las Cúpulas is also a popular breakfast venue.

✉ Quinta Real Hotel, Paseo Benito Juárez 2, Zona Hotelera, Bahía Tangolunda Huatulco ☎ (958) 581 04 28 ⏰ Daily 7–midnight 🍴 D $28, Wine $20

OAXACA
EL BICHO POBRE II

Both local Oaxaqueños and visitors flock to this hugely popular restaurant, with its large, airy, open plan—if rather Spartan—dining room. The specialty is the *botano surtido*, a massive platter of regional delicacies including *chalupas*, *tamales* and *quesadillas*. The *mole*

Above *Pipo's is one of Acapulco's longest established and best-loved restaurants, and is popular with locals*

negro con pollo and *sopa azteca* are also highly rated. If you need any guidance the friendly staff and chefs will describe each dish.

✉ Calzada de la República 600, Colonia Jalatlaca, Oaxaca ☎ (951) 513 46 36 ⏰ Daily 8am–9pm 🍴 L $8, D $11, Wine $14

LA BIZNAGA

Close to the Iglesia de Santo Domingo, La Biznaga is run by chef and owner Fernando Lopez, whose philosophy is "slow food." The cuisine, fusing traditional Oaxacan ingredients and recipes with intriguing international twists, is served on the patio. Salmon with pesto and cilantro (coriander), garlic prawns with tamarind sauce, beef with goat's cheese, and a sublime chocolate torte with fruit cassis are just a selection of the gastronomic delights to be found on the changing menu. Credit cards are not accepted.

✉ Calle García Vígia 512, Oaxaca ☎ (951) 516 18 00 ⏰ Mon–Thu 1–10, Fri–Sat 1–11 🍴 L $15, D $24, Wine $19

CAFÉ ALEX

Three blocks west of the *zócalo* in the buzzing commercial area, Café Alex serves good breakfasts ranging from a traditional Oaxacan feast of *chilaquiles* with eggs, sour cream and *quesillo*, refried beans and tortilla to wholesome fresh-fruit platters topped with granola and yogurt and drenched in honey. The quirkily decorated dining rooms, with rust-red walls combined with 1970s wood paneling, are usually jam-packed with locals and visitors keeping the service brisk and the atmosphere lively. Credit cards are not accepted.

✉ Avenida Díaz Ordáz 218 and Avenida Trujano, Oaxaca ☎ (951) 514 07 15 🕐 Mon–Sat 7am–10pm, Sun 7am–1pm ✋ $5 (breakfast)

LA CASA DE ALCALÁ

You enter this colonial home on the main pedestrian mall through a wrought-iron arched gateway. Adobe walls decorated with black-and-white photographs of early 19th-century Oaxaca encircle the peaceful patio, with its ornate fountain and cobbled floor. The staff are extremely friendly and efficient, serving traditional Oaxacan dishes and international fare. Try the *pechuga campestre* (chicken filled with pumpkin) and *mole Oaxaqueña*. Breakfast set menus are also very good value. High chairs are available for children.

✉ Macedonia Alcalá 303, Oaxaca ☎ (951) 514 08 20 🕐 Mon–Sat 8am–11pm, Sun 8am–10pm ✋ L $12, D $25, Wine $15

CASA OAXACA

www.casa-oaxaca.com

Chef and manager Alejandro has developed a cult following among Oaxacan artists and it's not hard to understand why. The stylish and serene patio, with live music in the evenings, is the perfect backdrop to Alejandro's philosophy that food is art. The choice changes weekly but dishes always contain the freshest organic ingredients. Perfectly executed combinations such as sea bass with lime and squash blossoms served with tomato marmalade, or jumbo shrimp with ginger sauce served over *jícama* (raw root vegetable) complement Oaxaqueña specialties such as *chiles en nogada* or black *mole*. The service is impeccable, the wine list monumental and, by international standards, excellent value.

✉ Calle García Vigil 407, Oaxaca ☎ (951) 514 41 73 🕐 Breakfast 9am–11.30am, dinner 6.30–8.30 ✋ D $30, lunch not available. Five-course tasting menu $30, Wine $20

CATEDRAL

www.restaurantecatedral.com.mx

Housed in a grand old colonial building just blocks from the *zócalo*, Catedral dishes up traditional Oaxacan cuisine such as suckling pig, pumpkin-blossom soup and an outstanding black *mole* with chicken. The kitchen also turns out imaginative international dishes, as well as delicious breakfasts—from standard waffles and pancakes to Tiotitlan style eggs with tomato sauce, *epazote* (a local herb) and cheese. Romantics should request a table in the stone courtyard next to the burbling fountain. After dinner, the adjacent bar hosts live music on weekends beginning at 10pm.

✉ Calle García Vigil 105, Oaxaca ☎ (951) 516 32 85 🕐 Wed–Mon 8am–1am ✋ L $12, D $22, Wine $12

COMO AGUA PARA CHOCOLATE

Laura Esquivel's eponymous novel inspired the fresh and expertly run Like Water for Chocolate restaurant just off the *zócalo*. Chicken with *tamarindo* (tamarind) sauce, duck with ginger and orange sauce, and a variety of vegetarian options, including stuffed pumpkin squash and pasta with pesto, line up alongside stylishly presented and well executed Oaxacan specialties. There is a relaxing candlelit bar, but while main course prices are very reasonable, drinks here are generally overpriced.

✉ Calle Hidalgo 612, Oaxaca ☎ (951) 516 29 17 🕐 Daily noon–11pm ✋ L $11, D $14, Wine $24

LA CRÊPE

With views across Oaxaca from its first-floor balcony, one block from the Iglesia de Santo Domingo, La Crêpe is fresh and modern with an inventive menu of snacks and light meals—perfect for lunch. Owner Vicente began his career with a little pancake cart in Mexico City and has now established a loyal following among locals, expatriates and visitors. Dishes are always well presented, and include Mediterranean-inspired salads with lashings of olives, pine nuts and heavenly goat's cheese, wholesome seeded baguettes and, of course, sweet and savory crêpes. Credit cards are not accepted.

✉ Macedonio Alcalá 307, Oaxaca ☎ (951) 516 22 00 🕐 Mon–Sat 7.30am–11pm, Sun 7.30am–10pm ✋ L $10, D $15, Wine $12

MARÍA BONITA

Just north of the Iglesia de Santo Domingo, this snug, family-run restaurant with cobbled floors, yellow walls and rustic tables has an extensive menu of delicious Oaxacan cooking served in clay pots or on terra-cotta earthenware plates. The enthusiastic staff will lovingly list the ingredients and describe the preparation of each recipe. This is a great place to try one of the *moles*, *quesadilla*-style *tlayudas* with *quesilla* and pumpkin flowers, or chilies stuffed with *chapulines*, and the set menus are great value.

✉ Macedonio Alcalá 706B, Oaxaca ☎ (951) 516 72 33 🕐 Tue–Sat 8.30am–9pm, Sun 9–5.30 ✋ L $9, D $13, Wine $14

EL NARANJO

www.elnaranjo.com.mx

Inspired regional dishes using the finest organic ingredients are served with aplomb in the fragrant courtyard of this 17th-century house, one block from the *zócalo*, south of Avenida Independencia. The seven signature *mole* dishes on the menu provide a great initiation into one of Oaxaca's most memorable tastes and textures. The rolled *tortillas* with *picadillo Oaxaqueño* topped with *mole*, and the *sopa de nuez y chipotle* (pecan and chili soup) are first class.

✉ Avenida Trujano 203, Oaxaca ☎ (951) 514 18 78 🕐 Mon–Sat noon–11 🖐 L $15, D $25, Wine $15

PALENQUE

DON MUCHO
www.palenquemx.com/elpanchan
Part of the Palenque experience has to involve stopping for lunch or dinner, or chilling out at least, at the heady jungle retreat of El Panchan. The total antithesis of the functional frenzy of Palenque, the atmosphere is laid back, the vibe offbeat and the music chilled. The Italian-Mexican menu varies from pasta with pesto to *fajitas,* club sandwiches and wood-oven pizzas drizzled with olive oil (after 6pm only). The breakfast deals are the best in town, with a chocolate and banana shake making a suitable initiation. In the evening there are plenty of amateur performances to accompany the gastronomic delights, from fire dancers to circus performers. Credit cards are not accepted.

✉ El Panchan Camping Carretera Zona Arqueológica Km 4.5, Apartado Postal 55, Palenque 🕐 Daily 9am–11pm 🖐 L $8, D $13, Wine $12 🖐 Take a *colectivo* from the high street in Palenque, marked *"ruinas,"* and ask the driver to drop you at El Panchan (2km/1 mile before the ruins). To return after 6.30pm, catch a ride or share a taxi

PIZZERIA PALENQUE
It is difficult to miss this small streetside pizzeria in the heart of Palenque town. The pro-active waiters usually take it in turns to announce "pizza" to every passerby. Still, for all its lack of subtlety, stark lighting and a fair coating of traffic fumes, the thin-crust pizzas laden with an inventive medley of toppings, served swiftly and with a smile, are the best you'll find in Palenque, with good prices. Credit cards are not accepted.

✉ Avenida Juárez 168, Palenque ☎ (916) 345 03 32 🕐 Daily 1pm–11pm 🖐 L $8, D $12, Wine $17

RESTAURANTE LAS TINAJAS
Backpackers flocked to the original Las Tinajas, famed for its massive portions, in the heart of Palenque. The smaller, original restaurant has now spread its wings to larger premises a couple of doors down, with outdoor seating and a breezy open-plan design. A broad menu includes the house special, *pollo pibil*, huge steaks, *enchiladas*, *quesadillas*, salads, pasta and club sandwiches. Left-over take-out boxes are the norm. With every dish cooked to order, grumbling tour groups can often wait up to an hour. The breakfast deals are excellent value, although the five-egg omelets are rather overwhelming.

✉ Avenida 20 de Noviembre, esq Absalo Carlos Caraveo Gómez, Palenque ☎ (916) 100 11 47 🕐 Daily 7.30am–10pm (or until the last customer leaves) 🖐 L $11, D $14

PUERTO ESCONDIDO

CABO BLANCO
Diners come to this Puerto institution for its excellent grilled fish and seafood, served with inspired sauces. Tasty Asian dishes, including piquant Thai curries, make a refreshing change and inventive vegetarian food usually appears on the menu. After dinner the restaurant turns into a lively beach bar with a true Zicatela vibe, and in the high season there is music on Thursday and Saturdays.

✉ Calle del Moro, Zicatela, Puerto Escondido ☎ (954) 582 03 37 🕐 Daily 8am–11pm 🖐 L $11, D $17, Wine $17

EL CAFECITO
Under the same ownership as the hugely popular Carmen's patisserie on a path to the beach from the main road, this coffee shop and bistro serves superlative breakfasts—the chocolate bread is particularly good, accompanied by a deliciously robust coffee. The more cosmopolitan restaurant has blissful sea-view dining, and a tropical tone prevails with wicker chairs and relaxed music. Fresh fish draws a loyal clientele who enthuse over the seared tuna steaks and

the excellent-value shrimp platters. Credit cards are not accepted.

✉ Calle del Moro, Zicatela Beach, Puerto Escondido ☎ (954) 582 05 16 🕐 Wed–Mon 6.30am–10pm 🖐 L $8, D $15, Wine $16

SAN CRISTÓBAL DE LAS CASAS

CASA DEL PAN
www.casadelpan.com
This fantastic bakery, with a sunny, calm café-restaurant, is one of the best places to start the day in San Cristóbal. Wonderful wholemeal breads and huge fruit platters heaped with granola and honey, hotcakes, omelets and *huevos rancheros* are all served abundantly and with ceremonial panache by the welcoming staff. There is often live music in the evenings and other cultural activities. The set lunches are good value, and there are sandwiches and refreshing salads for vegetarians. Credit cards are not accepted.

✉ Calle Dr. Navarro 10, San Cristóbal de las Casas ☎ (967) 678 58 95 🕐 Tue–Sun 8am–10pm 🖐 Breakfast $6, L $8, D $12, Wine $14

EL EDEN
Two blocks from the main plaza and tucked away inside the Hotel Posada Paraiso, a couple of Swiss ex-pats helm the wonderful El Eden restaurant. The two dining rooms are small, simple and quiet, but the chef makes a bold statement that he's serious about food. This is the place for steak cooked to tender perfection. The house salad (prepared tableside) and fondues are other popular choices.

✉ Avenida 5 de Febrero 19, San Cristóbal de las Casas ☎ (967) 678 00 85 🕐 Daily 8–10 🖐 L $8, D $18; Wine $12

EL FOGÓN DE JOVEL
El Fogón is well established on the tour group itinerary for its rather manufactured brand of typical Chiapaneca food. The colonial house, one block from the cathedral, decorated with a bizarre combination of regional handicrafts

and international flags, is warmed by open fires and enlivened with *marimba*. Overpriced main dishes vary in quality, with the house special being a rather greasy pork *pibil*. The appetizers, however, are simple and satisfying, with delicious *tortillas, guacamole, salsa verde,* and double-cream cheese. Round off the meal with the local firewater—*posh*.

✉ Avenida 16 de Septiembre, San Cristóbal de las Casas ☎ (967) 678 11 53 🕐 Daily 1–10 🍴 L $12, D $18, Wine $18

MADRE TIERRA

This Anglo-Mexican restaurant and bakery, opposite the Iglesia de San Francisco, is worth a visit for its wholemeal breads and chocolate cheesecake alone. By day you can eat in the arcaded courtyard, while inside, candles, intimate alcoves, bookcases, and an arty vibe make a snug setting for the cool nights. Lighter snacks, including pizzas, spinach *empanadas* and quiche, are the better choices, as the main dishes, which include curry and spinach cannelloni, can be rather bland and often not very hot. The bakery also sells bagels, cinnamon rolls and chocolate croissants. Credit cards are not accepted.

✉ Avenida Insurgentes 19, San Cristóbal de las Casas ☎ (967) 678 42 97 🕐 Daily 8am–10pm 🍴 L $8, D $12, Wine $14

NATURALISSIMO

Just one block from the cathedral, deliciously wholesome food is served in a lovely courtyard. Great breakfasts include a help-yourself fruit bar with creamy yogurt, crunchy granola and honey, and other nutty tropical tastes. The main reason to visit, however, is for the *comida corrida* (set lunch) served from noon–6 daily; three courses including soup, salad bar, *jugo* and a *plato fuerte* (main dish). There is also a bakery where you can buy cakes as well as yogurt. Credit cards are not accepted.

✉ Calle 20 de Noviembre 4, San Cristóbal de las Casas ☎ (967) 678 99 97 🕐 Daily 7am–11pm 🍴 Breakfast $5, L $5, D $9, Wine $12

PALOMA

Paloma, one of San Cristóbal's more sophisticated restaurants, is geared to a slightly older crowd. An eclectic menu includes delicious salmon with Dijon sauce, chicken in peanut sauce and, for vegetarians, *quesadillas* and ravioli with *acelgas* (a root vegetable) and cheese. There is also a laid-back bar with comfy wicker chairs, a civilized spot to round off an evening listening to jazz (every night from 9pm), maybe with a cappuccino and a slice of chocolate cake.

✉ Avenida Miguel Hidalgo 3, San Cristóbal de las Casas ☎ (967) 678 15 47 🕐 Daily 9am–midnight 🍴 L $12, D $20, Wine $17

EL PUENTE

This lively cultural center is three blocks from the *zócalo*. The leafy bar-restaurant with laid-back music, Zapatista posters on the walls and internet access is one of the best spots in San Cristóbal to relax, read and meet other visitors. The broad menu includes leafy spinach salads, pasta dishes, *enchiladas*, soups, sandwiches and juices. There is also a cinema showing Mexican and international films every night; the schedule is posted on the door. Credit cards are not accepted.

✉ Calle Real de Guadalupe 55, San Cristóbal de las Casas 🕐 Daily 8am–midnight 🍴 L $6, D $10, Wine $14

LA SELVA CAFÉ

This sleekly run, continental-style coffee shop is just two blocks south of the *zócalo*. Owned by a coffee growers' collective, there are more than 30 types of organic coffee. The light, airy art gallery is lively in the evenings with a youthful, bohemian crowd. There are excellent liqueur cappuccinos, thick hot chocolate and sinful cakes, while healthier options include refreshing Mediterranean salads and wholemeal baguettes. Credit cards are not accepted.

✉ Avenida Crescencio Rosas and Cuauhtémoc, San Cristóbal de las Casas ☎ (967) 678 72 43 🕐 Daily 8.30am–11pm 🍴 Breakfast $5, L $9, D $12

TUXTLA GUTIÉRREZ
LAS PICHANCHAS

www.laspichanchas.com.mx
A lovely *casona* with a pretty courtyard houses the ebullient Pichanchas, established in 1976 and one of the best restaurants in Tuxtla, despite being on the tourist trail. Accompanying the highly rated regional cooking are traditional dance performances and *marimba* music at 2–5 and 8–11. The restaurant is famous for its *tamales,* and other house specials include *juacané* chicken breast (stuffed with beans and smothered in Hierba Santa sauce).

✉ Avenida Central Oriente 837, Tuxtla Gutiérrez ☎ (961) 612 53 51 🕐 Daily noon–midnight 🍴 L $11, D $15, Wine $17

Left *Restaurante Las Tinajas serves generous portions and great breakfasts*

PRICES AND SYMBOLS

The prices are the average for a double room for one night including breakfast, unless otherwise stated. All the hotels listed accept credit cards unless otherwise stated. Note that rates can vary widely throughout the year.

For a key to the symbols, ▷ 2.

ACAPULCO
LOS FLAMINGOS

Los Flamingos was the favored hangout of many Hollywood greats, who bought it as a private club. The views from the balconies are without peer. Rooms are a little bare, with shower-only bathrooms and most without air-conditioning, but the sea breezes are cooling. Impeccably tended gardens, polite service and a superb restaurant add to the charm and appeal. Free transport is provided.

✉ Avenida López Mateos, Acapulco ☎ (744) 482 06 90 ✋ $65–$125 ① 46 rooms, 2 suites 🏊

HUATULCO
MISIÓN DE LOS ARCOS

www.misiondelosarcos.com
This homey, characterful hotel in the La Crucita area makes a refreshing change from the rather impersonal, all-inclusive mega-complexes that predominate in Huatulco. Each room is elegantly finished. There is also a coffee shop-cum-ice cream parlor, internet access and a fully equipped gymnasium. This is probably the best value for money in Huatulco.

✉ Gardenia 902 y Tamarindo, Huatulco ☎ (958) 587 01 65 ✋ $50–$85 ① 13 🔄 🍽

OAXACA
CAMINO REAL

www.caminoreal.com
A former convent, in the heart of the old town, has been converted into the internationally renowned Camino Real. There are hushed, leafy patios with ornate fountains, while the carved stone arcades are decorated with tapestries and frescoes. Rich fabrics lend a luxurious quality to each tranquil room with views onto the street or the gardens and swimming pool. Impeccable service extends to the excellent El Refectorio restaurant.

✉ Calle 5 de Mayo 300, Centro Histórico, Oaxaca ☎ (951) 516 61 00 ✋ $225, $320 Camino Real Club (includes buffet breakfast), $360 junior suite ① 91 (all nonsmoking) 🔄 🏊

Above *Los Flamingos hotel in Acapulco, a favourite with Hollywood stars*

CASA OAXACA

www.casa-oaxaca.com
Just four blocks from the *zócalo*, this distinctive hotel blends clean minimalist furnishings and artful design with elegance. The restored colonial house is popular with the Oaxacan artistic community, and international figures such as Gabriel García Marquez have dined in the restaurant (▷ 172). Guests may find that the the lack of some facilities that you would expect at this price, including air-conditioning and TV, may not be to their taste. However, there is a sauna.

✉ Calle García Vigil 407, Oaxaca ☎ (951) 514 41 73 ✋ $170–$270 ① 7 🏊

HOSTAL DON MARIO

www.hostaldonmario.8m.com
Rufino Tamayo was born in this sunny colonial house, close to the Arcos de Xochimilco. With a welcoming family feel and patios flushed with jacaranda, this is a great budget choice. Spiral staircases lead to the bedrooms, spread over three floors. While basic, each room is spotless and

airy with a fan, and those on the third floor have private bathrooms and access to a patio with views across the city. There is also internet access, information on tours in the area and a small handicraft shop.
✉ Cosijopi 219, Oaxaca ☎ (915) 514 20 12 ✋ $20 ⓘ 9

HOSTAL SANTA ROSA
You'll be at the heart of the action, one block from the *zócalo*, at this pristine hostal. Spacious, airy rooms have cable TV, phone and ceiling fans. The large bathrooms, regularly topped up with scented goodies, are surgically scrubbed each day. There is also a tour agency in the lobby and a restaurant offering good-value *comida corrida*.
✉ Trujano 201, Oaxaca ☎ (951) 514 67 14 ✋ $45 ⓘ 17

PALENQUE
MARGARITA AND ED
www.elpanchan.com
El Panchan—Maya for "heaven on earth"—is host to a mix of philosophies, foods and intellectual interests. Don Moisés, founder of Panchan, originally came to Palenque as an archaeologist. This is by far the plushest of the accommodations options on the site, comprising comfortable thatched-roof cabins with private bath, sundeck and hot water. A mix of people, evening entertainment, interesting conversation, and more than a whiff of spirituality makes this a perfect place for immersing yourself in the mystique of Palenque.
✉ El Panchan Camping, Carretera Zona Arqueológica Km 4.5, Apartado Postal 55, Palenque ✋ $16

MAYA TULIPANES
www.mayatulipanes.com
This modern hotel has one of the best positions in Palenque. The spacious, functional rooms, with cable television and noisy air-conditioning, vary greatly, with many being rather musty and rough around the edges and all generally lacking character. However, the lovely pool area, tropical jungle and

pleasant staff make up for these shortcomings. The bar/restaurant also serves very good regional food with candlelit, outdoor seating—and there is internet access.
✉ Cañada 6, Palenque ☎ (916) 345 02 01 ✋ $80 ⓘ 72 😊 🏊

PUERTO ANGEL
CAÑÓN DEVATA
Here, bungalows and a guesthouse are surrounded by forest in a landscaped canyon—the result of an ecological project conceived by painter Mateo López. Labyrinthine pathways lead to bright, comfortable bungalows decorated with paintings and sculptures, many the work of Mateo himself. Hammocks, wonderful views, fascinating hosts, and an excellent organic restaurant add to the appeal of the *posada*, which is often booked months in advance. Reservations are advised. Credit cards are not accepted.
✉ Playa del Panteón, Puerto Angel ☎ (958) 584 31 37 ✋ $35–$50 (bungalows), $25 (guesthouse) ⓘ 22
🚫 Closed May and Jun

PUERTO ESCONDIDO
ALDEA DEL BAZAR
A veritable sultan's palace, the Aldea del Bazar extends its Moorish theme to the staff, kitted out in Middle Eastern garb. Rooms are spacious, many with twin and double beds and a sitting room, and there is a lush garden with palms, a pool, a *temazcal* (pre-Hispanic sauna). The restaurant serves excellent and highly rated cuisine.
✉ Benito Juárez 7, Fracc. Bacocho, Puerto Escondido ☎ (954) 582 05 08 ✋ $95 ⓘ 47 😊 🏊

SAN CRISTÓBAL DE LAS CASAS
NA BOLOM
www.nabolom.org
The house where archaeologist Franz Blum and his wife, Gertrude, a Swiss photographer and fervent campaigner for the preservation of the Lacandón Indians, lived is now a cultural complex and guesthouse (▷ 157). Each room has a private

bathroom and fireplace and guests enjoy free access to the museum and library. A buffet-style meal is served at 7pm and guests, staff and volunteers from the center sit together at the long dining table where Frida Kahlo, Diego Rivera and François Mitterrand—to name a few—were once entertained. Credit cards are not accepted.
✉ Vicente Guerrero 33, San Cristóbal de las Casas ☎ (967) 678 14 18 ✋ $70–$80 ⓘ 15

POSADA EL PARAÍSO
www.hotelposadaparaiso.com
Everything in this Mexican-Swiss-owned hotel, from the reception area to the bright patio bedrooms, is impeccably finished. Decorated throughout in tones of siena and aqua-marine, each pristine room has high ceilings with exposed beams, brick bathrooms, a desk, and a telephone. The restaurant serves pricey but faultless food.
✉ Avenida 5 de Febrero 19, San Cristóbal de las Casas ☎ (967) 678 00 85 ✋ $55 ⓘ 14

TUXTLA GUTIÉRREZ
CAMINO REAL
This modern, five-floor hotel is one of the best in Tuxtla, combining fabulous service with intoxicating jungle surroundings. The rooms are first class, with cable TV and lavish bathrooms. The *cenote*-style swimming pool, sauna, gym, massage rooms, and excellent restaurant make this a great place to be pampered for a few days.
✉ Belisario Dominguez 1195, Tuxtla Gutiérrez ☎ (961) 617 77 77 ✋ $110 ⓘ 184 😊 🏊 📺

VILLAHERMOSA
QUALITY INN CENCALI
www.qualityinnvillahermosa.com
This hotel offers excellent value for money. Plush carpeted rooms include balconies, cable TV and bathrooms with tubs. The restaurant serves an abundant breakfast.
✉ Juárez y Paseo Tabasco, Villahermosa ☎ (993) 316 66 11 ✋ $85 ⓘ 160 😊 🏊

CENTRAL MEXICO EAST

Parts of this region are a mecca for adventure travelers, considering they can scuba dive along Veracruz's coastal reefs; hike Mexico's highest mountain, a dormant volcano called the Pico de Orizaba; and enjoy superb white-water rafting. For the non-adventurous, there is exploring of a different kind—great museums, historical sites, fascinating ruins, and wonderful cuisine—tasty fare such as *picadas*, a Veracruz tradition (a thick *masa* pancake with cheese and sauce); and puffy *gordita negra* (*masa* cooked with black-bean paste and flavored with the toasted leaf of the *aguacatillo*.)

About 104km (65 miles) northwest of Veracruz is the town of Xalapa (pronounced hah-lah-pa), the capital of the state of Veracruz and the middle of Mexico's prime coffee-growing area. Xalapa's anthropology museum has excellent examples of the monumental sculptures made by the Olmec. Also, very near Xalapa are three popular rivers for rafting and several rafting companies that supply all of the gear you'll need for an excursion.

From Xalapa, many visitors next make tracks to El Tajin and the city of Papantla. El Tajin is one of the most important archaeological sites in Mexico. The major stopover for seeing the ruins is Papantla, a hilly city north of Veracruz. One of the products of Papantla, since the time of the Aztecs, is vanilla beans. Native to Mexico, vanilla was used primarily to flavor chocolate, also indigenous to Mexico.

The city of Puebla, west of Veracruz, is worth visiting as well. It's famous for being home to beautiful colonial buildings decorated with hand-painted Talavera tiles. Check out the cathedral, which was completed in 1649—it has the tallest bell towers in Mexico. Puebla is also considered the place that gave birth to some of Mexico's classic and most delicious dishes: *mole poblano* and *chiles en nogada*, as well as *tinga* (pork or chicken stewed with chilies) and *mixiotes* (spiced rabbit, lamb, or chicken wrapped and steamed in a sauce.)

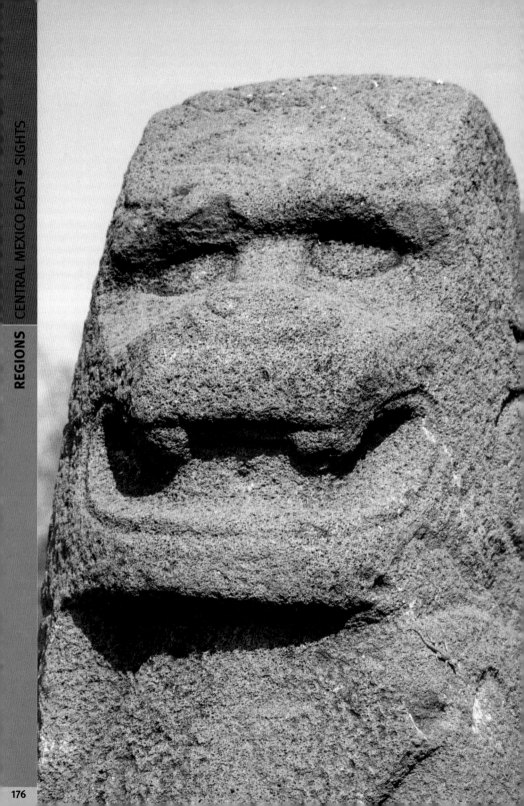

ACTOPAN

www.actopan.com

The 16th-century town of Actopan is set in the verdant Valle del Mezquital. Its Otomí name means "fertile lands." For visitors, however, Actopan's wealth lies in its beautifully preserved old core: Narrow, cobbled streets cluster around the *zócalo* and come alive on Wednesdays when the traditional *tianguis* (market stands) sell regional products—textiles, hats, fruit—as they have done for 400 years. Founded in 1548, the fine Augustinian ex-Convento de San Nicolás Tolentino (Tue–Sun 9–5) houses a religious art museum within its cloisters; there is an unusual open chapel beside the main church.

From Actopan, a 56km (35-mile) branch road runs to one of Mexico's great archaeological sites: Tula de Allende (▷ 221), which was capital of the Toltecs.

✚ 315 L8 🚌 Buses from Pachuca and Tula

BARRANCA DE METLAC

The road east from Puebla to Veracuz is one of the loveliest drives in Mexico. As the *altiplano* (high plateau) gradually recedes behind you, the road descends into a lush and fertile coffee-producing area. The exuberant vegetation is best appreciated from the bridge, 130m (425ft) above the river, which crosses the dramatic Barranca de Metlac, 8km (5 miles) from Orizaba on the road to Fortín de las Flores. The steep banks plunge down to the torrent below in a cascade of luxuriant vegetation, flame trees and hummingbirds.

✚ 315 M9 🚌 Take Highway 150 out of Orizaba toward Córdoba

CACAHUAMILPA

The road to Ixtapan de la Sal from Cacahuamilpa passes by the Grutas de Cacahuamilpa, known locally as "Las Grutas." These are some of the largest caves in North America and a major visitor attraction. From the vast cave entrance a slippery path (walking sticks available at the entrance for $1) winds its way down through eerie cathedral-like halls punctuated by 75-million-year-old columns and elaborate stalactite and stalagmite formations. At its highest point the ceiling is 70m (230ft) above the cave floor, while at its deepest there are 180m (590ft) of solid rock above you. Guides take you on a 2km (1.2-mile) circuit, lighting the chambers to reveal their full majesty and pointing out fanciful shapes in the spectacular rock formations. It is more fun to visualize your own figures and objects, which you can do as you make your own way back to the entrance.

✚ 315 L9 🕐 Daily 10–5 🖐 $6 including a 2-hour tour 🚌 Minibuses from Taxco 🚍 Take Highway 166 out of Taxco and turn right at the Cacahuamilpa sign

CACAXTLA

A remarkable series of pre-Columbian frescoes depicting battle scenes with giant eagles and elaborately costumed jaguar warriors can be seen at the ruins of Cacaxtla on a hilltop near San Miguel del Milagro, between Texmelucan and Tlaxcala. The colors are still sharp and some of the figures are larger than life size. Occupied by the Olmec-Xicalanca civilization between AD400 and 1200, Cacaxtla was a thriving market town (its name means "place of the woven market baskets") that maintained strong trade links with the Gulf civilizations. Many obsidian knives, ceramic pots from El Tajín and shells from the Gulf were found during excavations and are displayed in the site museum. A huge roof covering the entire pyramid base protects the paintings from the elements.

From Cacaxtla, the pyramid at Xochitécatl 3km (2 miles) away is clearly visible, perched impressively on a hill and accessible only on foot. An exclusively ceremonial site, Xochitécatl is considerably older than Cacaxtla; the Pirámide de la Serpiente was built in 700BC. Following an eruption by Popocatépetl in AD100 the site was abandoned, then reoccupied from AD500 to 950. Don't miss the unusual spiral pyramid dedicated to the cult of Ehécatl, god of wind.

✚ 315 L9 🕐 Daily 9–6 🖐 $4.50 (includes access to Xochitécatl) 🚌 Buses from Puebla to just beyond Nativitas, where a sign on the right points to San Miguel del Milagro and Cacaxtla 🚍 From Puebla take Highway 119 toward Tlaxcala. At Zacatelco, turn off onto the minor road marked Nativitas and Cacaxtla

Right *Illuminated caves in Cacahuamilpa National Park*

Opposite *Detail of an Olmec jaguar head*

CATEMACO

www.catemaco.info

Picturesque Catemaco is set on the western shore of the enchanting mountain-ringed Lake Catemaco and is a famous focal point for traditional witchcraft and spiritual purification rites. Although something of a tourist attraction nowadays, the cult is still taken seriously and all manner of *brujos* (witches), warlocks, wizards and sorcerers live in the area. Calm pervades the town, whose dusty streets only stretch about six blocks inland from the lakeshore. One of the highlights is a boat trip on the lake (boat owners along the lakeside charge $30–$35 per boat and stop at all the major sites). You will visit the shrine to the Virgin del Carmen, set in a tiny grotto where the Virgin appeared, and stop at the Isla de los Monos, home to a colony of macaque monkeys introduced from Thailand for the University of Veracruz.

About 7km (4 miles) round the northern shore of the lake, on the road to Coyamé, is the Reserva Ecológica Nanciyaga, which offers walks in the surrounding rain forest, and *temazcal* treatments consisting of steaming patchouli-scented baths, vigorous massages and a vegetarian meal. Nanciyaga's lush, tropical setting was used to film the movie *Medicine Man* (1992), starring Sean Connery.

🕂 316 N9 🚌 Buses from Veracruz and San Andrés Tuxtla

CEMPOALA

The ruins of Cempoala (Zempoala) are an inspiring archaeological site set in lush vegetation and sugar cane plantations. Watered by the Río Chachelacas and only 8km (5 miles) from the Gulf coast, the city was founded by the Totonacs in approximately AD1200. In April 1519, at the invitation of Cempoala's chief, Xicomecoatl, the newly disembarked Hernán Cortés visited then promptly conquered the city and forced its inhabitants to become the Spaniards' allies against the fierce Aztecs. Arriving in Cempoala, Cortés' troops reported brilliant temples covered in shells, stucco work that shone like silver and an ordered city of 30,000 inhabitants, comparable to Seville in Spain at the time.

There is a small museum with findings from the site, including a female stone figure surrounded by obsidian knives found in the Templo de la Muerte. Don't miss the Templo de las Caritas, once decorated with rows of little carved heads and now partially hidden by tall sugar cane, to the right of the main site.

🕂 315 M9 🕙 Daily 10–6 💲 $3.50
🚌 Buses from Veracruz to Cardel, then a local bus to Cempoala

CHOLULA

www.poblanerias.com

Now effectively a suburb of Puebla, when Cortés arrived in 1519 Cholula was a thriving ceremonial settlement with 100,000 inhabitants and 400 temples grouped round the Gran Pirámide de Tepanapa (daily 9–5.30). When razing the shrines, Cortés vowed to build a chapel for each one destroyed, hence the rather surprising number of churches, around 70. Entering town you can't miss the 16th-century Iglesia de Nuestra Señora de los Remedios (▷ 194–195) atop its great pyramid, with a fine view of Cholula's many spires and domes, and the snow-capped, majestic Popocatépetl (▷ 181). The pyramid, now overgrown and ruined, has 8km (5 miles) of excavated tunnels.

About 1km (half a mile) of tunnel is open to the public, giving an idea of the layers that were superimposed over 10 centuries to create the structure. The museum near the tunnel entrance has a copy of the 60m (197ft) *Mural de los Bebedores (The Drinkers)*, depicting a *pulque*-drinking ritual, found inside the tunnels. The Franciscan fortress church of San Gabriel is on the *zócalo*; next to it is the Capilla Real, modeled on the great mosque of Córdoba in Spain.

🕂 315 L9 🚌 Buses from Puebla

COATEPEC

Coatepec, an enchanting place to spend an afternoon, is reached along a lush and winding highway. It is famous for its fruit liqueurs and orchids, and is also an important base for the surrounding coffee haciendas; the whole town is infused with the sweet scents of roasting coffee beans, vanilla and freshly baked bread—still delivered by bicycle to the town's residents. The pretty *zócalo* bristles with cotton candy (candyfloss) sellers picking their way through the palms, flowers and old men snoozing, while the surrounding streets appear to end at the foot of the captivating, snow-capped Pico de Orizaba (▷ 181), in whose shadow the town sits.

Around 19km (12 miles) southwest of Coatepec is the 40m (130ft) Cascado de Texolo, a lovely place for a cold swim, bird-watching and walking. Many of the scenes in the movie *Romancing the Stone* (1984) were filmed here.

🕂 315 M9 🚌 Buses from Xalapa (Jalapa). For the Cascada de Texolo take the bus from Los Sauces marked Xico and get off at the entrance to the village. You will then have to walk 3km (2 miles) down a paved road through coffee plantations

Left *Tourist boats tied up along the shores of Lake Catemaco*

CUERNAVACA

Colonial Cuernavaca, with its year-long warm and sunny climate, is a weekend resort for the capital's elite, who fuel the city's buzzing cultural and intellectual life. Cuernavaca's proximity to Mexico City, its warm climate and attractive provinciality have made it a prime spot for escaping the metropolis. Already popular as a resort with the Aztec elite long before it was conquered by Cortés, the tradition continues today with the ultra-modern, high-walled homes of wealthy *capitalinos*. Its Nahuatl name of Cuauhnáhuac, meaning "adjacent to the tree," was soon corrupted by the Spanish to Cuernavaca (cow horn). The remarkably plain Catedral de la Asunción (daily 8–2, 4–6), on Calle Hidalgo, three blocks west of the Plaza de Armas, was founded in 1529. Note the fine 17th-century murals depicting the martyrdom of the Mexican saint San Felipe de Jesús on his journey to Asia. By the cathedral entrance stands the small Iglesia de Tercera Orden, built in 1529, whose facade carved by Indian craftsmen contains a small figure said to be one of the only two known statues of Cortés in Mexico.

MUSEUMS

The Palacio de Cortés at the eastern end of the tree-shaded *zócalo* is now the Museo Regional Cuauhnáhuac (Tue–Sun 10–5), exhibiting local archaeological finds such as the remains of a mammoth and articles from Xochicalco (▷ 187); note the lovely seated stone sculpture of the goddess Diosa Xochiquetzal and colonial art and weaponry. Cortés built the palace in 1531 for his second wife, Doña Juana de Zuniga.

Next to the cathedral on Calle Nezahualcoyotl 4 is the Museo Robert Brady (Tue–Sun 10–6), housing a fabulous collection of paintings by, among others, Diego Rivera, Frida Kahlo and Paul Klee, as well as colonial furniture, textiles, pre-Hispanic objects, and African art belonging to Brady, an American artist, who lived here until his death in 1986. The house, a former 16th-century convent, is grouped around a delightful pool and garden.

The 18th-century Jardín Borda (Tue–Sun 10–5.30) on Calle Morelos 103 was much loved by Emperor Maximilian and his wife, Carlota. Inspired by Granada's Generalife in Spain, these enchanting formal gardens are guarded by two fine watchtowers called *chocolateros*. According to legend, it was customary to sip a cup of afternoon chocolate in the tower while admiring the scenery.

INFORMATION

www.cuernavaca.gob.mx
www.morelostravel.com
✚ 315 L9 ⓘ Avenida Morelos Sur 187
☎ (777) 314 38 72 ⊕ Mon–Fri 8–7
🚌 Buses from Mexico City 📖 Good
bookshop 🚗 From central Mexico City,
follow Avenida Insurgentes Sur south,
past Ciudad Universitaria, and then take
Highway 95D

TIPS

» Sunday morning Mass in the cathedral at 11am is accompanied by a *mariachi* band.
» The café in the Jardin Borda is an ideal place to take a break, with tables by an immaculate lawn and trickling fountain.
» The Diego Rivera murals in the Palacio de Cortés depict Mexican history from Conquest to Revolution and focus on the revolutionary Emiliano Zapata.

Above *Painting of a battle scene in the Palacio de Cortés*

Opposite *Bells outside Córdoba cathedral*
Right *Permanently snow-capped Pico de Orizaba is Mexico's highest peak*

CÓRDOBA
www.cordoba.com.mx

Highway 150 from Puebla to Veracruz passes through this pleasant colonial city in the rich coffee-producing valley of the Río Seco. Founded in 1618 by 30 families, its leafy and elegant Plaza de Armas is arcaded on three sides and lined with cafés where you can taste the delicious local brew. The Portal de Zevallo on the north side is where the last Spanish viceroy, Don Juan O'Donojú, signed the Treaty of Córdoba with General Iturbide in 1821, acknowledging Mexican independence from Spanish colonial rule. On the east side is the Catedral de la Immaculada Concepción. The Museo de la Ciudad at Calle 3 No. 303 (daily 9–2, 4–8) has interesting Totonac and Olmec pieces.

➕ 315 M9 ℹ️ Avenida 3 and Calle 1 ☎ (271) 717 17 00 🕐 Mon–Fri 10–2, 4.30–7 🚌 Buses from Mexico City, Puebla, Veracruz and Orizaba

ORIZABA
www.todossomosorizaba.com.mx

Orizaba was once the much-loved resort of Emperor Maximilian, but lost most of its charm in the 1973 earthquake when the bullring and many 19th-century buildings were lost. Although the town is now heavily industrialized—Cervecería Moctezuma has brewed its beer here since 1896—its setting at the foot of the majestic volcano Pico de Orizaba (or Citlaltépec), at 5,760m (18,898ft), is unrivalled. Sites of interest in town are clustered around the *zócalo*.

On the north side is the many-domed Iglesia San Miguel, finished in 1729; at the daily market nearby, women in traditional dress sell local produce. On the staircase of the Palacio Municipal (daily 8am–10pm), on the other side of the river, is a mural by José Clemente Orozco (1926). The ex-Palacio Municipal (now a café) on the *zócalo* is a

rather odd cast-iron pavilion brought piece by piece from France after the famous 19th-century Paris Centennial Exposition.

➕ 315 M9 ℹ️ Basement of Palacio Municipal, Avenida Colón Poniente 230 ☎ (272) 726 22 22 🕐 Mon–Fri 8–2 🚌 Buses from Puebla and Veracruz

PACHUCA
www.hidalgo.gob.mx

Pachuca de Soto, capital of Hidalgo state, is one of the oldest silver-mining towns in Mexico. The Aztecs, the Spaniards and more recently the English all mined here, leaving the hills honeycombed with old workings and terraced with tailings. Although Pachuca is largely modern there are a number of colonial mansions dotted along its narrow, steep and crooked streets. The Plaza de la Independencia is dominated by the huge Reloj Monumental, a neoclassical clock tower built just before the Revolution in 1910, with four marble figures representing Liberty, the Constitution, Reform, and Independence. The Museo de la Fotografía (Tue–Sun 10–6), in the cloister of the former Convento de San Francisco on Arista y Hidalgo, is the principal museum of note. It has a fascinating section on the history of photographic techniques and a superlative archive of early Mexican photography, including pictures by

Agustín Casasola (1874–1938), who documented the Revolution. The Museo de la Minería (Wed–Sun 10–2, 3–6) at Calle Mina 110 has an interesting display on the history of mining in Pachuca.

➕ 315 L8 ℹ️ Avenida Revolución 1300 ☎ (771) 718 44 89 🕐 Mon–Fri 8.30–4.30 🚌 Buses from Mexico City

POPOCATÉPETL AND IZTACCÍHUATL
www.cenapred.unam.mx/mvolcan.html

The snow-capped, volcanic peaks of Popocatépetl (Popo), 5,452m (17,888ft) and Iztaccíhuatl, 5,286m (17,343ft), rise majestically to the east of the capital en route to Puebla. Their names recall the tragic legend of the beautiful princess Ixtaccíhuatl (White Lady) who, believing her lover Popocatépetl (Smoking Mountain) had been killed in battle, poisoned herself in grief. When the warrior returned alive he laid her body on the mountain and jumped into its crater. The three summits of Iztaccíhuatl represent the head, breasts and knees of the princess.

In 2000, Popocatépetl had its largest eruption for 500 years. Smoke and ash rose up more than 10km (6 miles). For the foreseeable future it will not be possible to climb, or get close to, Popo.

➕ 315 L9

INFORMATION

www.poblanerias.com

⊕ 315 L9 🏠 Calle 5 Oriente 3, Avenida Juárez ☎ (222) 246 20 44 ⊙ Mon–Sat 10–7, Sun 10–1 ✈ Aeropuerto Hermanos Serdán; mostly domestic flights

INTRODUCTION

Puebla is one of Mexico's oldest and most historically important cities, home to a multitude of magnificent baroque churches, Churrigueresque facades and sparkling tiled domes. Nowadays Puebla de los Angeles, "the city of the angels," is largely industrial and in parts very modern, but the colonial heart is small enough to walk around quite easily. Most of the city's sights of interest are concentrated in the middle around the *zócalo*. The gridded streets are numbered in a complex system and called Poniente (west), Oriente (east), Norte (north) or Sur (south), depending on their location in relation to the *zócalo*; it's worth getting hold of a map. The city is well served by a comprehensive bus and *colectivo* system for transportation to sights farther out of the old heart.

Founded in 1531, Puebla was constructed on an entirely new site, unusual in this part of the country, where the Spanish used pre-Hispanic sites on which to build their towns. According to some sources, friar Julián Garcés saw angels in a dream indicating where the city should be built. More likely, the Spanish were keen to make a break from the powerful ancient sites of Cholula and Tlaxcala. The city prospered due to its location en route from the rich mines of the highlands to the port of Veracruz. Further wealth was generated from the manufacture of Talavera tiles and ceramics, a skill brought to Puebla by artisans from Talavera de la Reina in Spain. The tiles, an outstanding element of Puebla's architecture, are used extensively on the colonial buildings and inside the cloisters and closed interior patios across the city.

WHAT TO SEE

ZÓCALO

Dominating the lively, arcaded *zócalo* is the city's bulky gray Catedral de la Inmaculada Concepción, the second-largest cathedral in the country and rather more impressive inside than out. Notable for its marble floors, onyx and marble statuary and stunning gold-leaf altarpiece, it was begun in 1575 and completed in the middle of the following century when Bishop Juan de Palafox y Mendoza injected a large portion of his inheritance into the project. He also partly funded the 74m (243ft) towers.

Above *Decorated ceramic pots and plates for sale in Puebla*

To the right of the cathedral on Calle 5 Oriente 5 is the Biblioteca Palafoxiana (Tue–Sun 10–4.30), the library founded by Bishop Palafox, who donated his 6,000-volume collection in 1646. It now contains 46,000 antique volumes, as well as the city's Casa de la Cultura, which hosts regular art exhibitions and concert recitals. Two blocks south of the cathedral is the Patio de los Azulejos (Mon–Fri 9–5), at Calle 3 Sur 110, with a tiny entrance on Avenida 16 de Septiembre. The former almshouses for retired priests have fabulous tiled facades, a fine example of these *mestizo* craftsmen's skill.

CHURCHES

Many of Puebla's numerous churches—about 60 in all—have domes that sparkle with the glazed Talavera tiles for which the city is famous, and exuberant baroque interiors. The magnificent Capilla del Rosario (Rosary Chapel), inside the Iglesia de Santo Domingo at Calle 5 de Mayo 407, displays a beauty of style and lavishness of form that served as a model and inspiration for all later baroque in Mexico. Both the chapel and the altar of the main church are covered in very detailed gold leaf. Note the strong indigenous Indian influence in Puebla's baroque architecture, which can also be seen in the churches of Tonantzintla and Acatepec (▷ 195). Two lovely churches excelling in baroque plasterwork and Talavera tiles are those of San Cristóbal, Calle 4 Norte and Calle 6 Oriente, built in 1687 with modern Churrigueresque towers and Tonantzintla-like plasterwork inside; and the 18th-century San José, Calle 2 Norte and Calle 18 Oriente, with a tiled facade and beautiful altarpieces inside. One of the oldest local churches is San Francisco at Avenida 14 Oriente 1009, with a glorious tiled facade and a mummified saint in its side chapel.

MUSEO AMPARO

This is Puebla's most outstanding museum, modern and well laid out, with exhibits spread over two colonial buildings with tranquil patios. Although far smaller than the anthropology museums of Mexico City and Xalapa (Jalapa), the museum owns one of the most comprehensive and well-presented pre-Hispanic collections in Mexico. The glass reproduction of a *tzompantli* (wall of skulls) with alternating Totonac and Olmec heads is an impressive introduction. Olmec art is well documented here, with an enormous and mysterious huge stone head for which this culture is famed. Some colonial painting and furniture is also on display. There are excellent audiovisual explanations in several languages, although you will need to rent the headsets.
✉ Calle 2 Sur 708 🕐 Wed–Mon 10–6 💲 $3.50

TIPS
» Churches close at varying and constantly changing times, but most shut for lunch between 1 and 4pm.
» *Chiles en nogada* is a must. One of Mexico's most delicious and patriotic dishes (its colors are those of the national flag), it is only made between July and September when the *nuez de castilla* (walnuts), a crucial ingredient, are harvested.
» Pick up the fortnightly *Andanzas* magazine, which lists cultural events in the city.

Below left *The Iglesia de Santo Domingo houses the Capilla del Rosario*
Below *Multicolored blankets in the Parián market*

SAN ANDRÉS TUXTLA

www.sanandrestuxtla.gob.mx

The larger of the two Tuxtlas on the road to Catemaco, San Andrés Tuxtla is a warren of narrow, winding streets. The bustling daily market is well stocked with Oaxacan foods such at *totopos* (fried tortilla chips with cheese) and *tamales de elote* (crispy tortillas, spicy meat and cakes of maize flour steamed in leaves), tropical fruits and medicinal herbs.

The town is surrounded by tobacco plantations, and is famed for its cigar trade; a visit to a cigar factory is a must. The most central factory, founded in 1830, is Santa Clara (Mon–Fri 9–1, 3–7, Sun 9–11) on Calle 5 de Febrero 10. The 30 or so factory workers welcome visitors and allow you to observe the production process, from the selection of dried leaves to the hand-rolling of the *puros* (cigars). You can even have a go at it yourself and there's a small shop on site with excellent prices.

✚ 316 N9 ℹ️ Secretaría de Relaciones Exteriores, Palacio Municipal, on the *zócalo* 🕐 Mon–Fri 10–2, 4–7 🚌 Buses from Catemaco, Tuxtepec, Veracruz

SANTIAGO TUXTLA

www.santiagotuxtla.gob.mx

This small, pleasant, colonial town set along the river enjoys a cool climate 1,700m (5,580ft) above the Gulf coast in the attractive volcanic area of Los Tuxtlas, known as the Switzerland of Mexico for its mountains and perennially green vegetation. The area was the heartland of the Olmec civilization that flourished between 1500BC and 600BC. In the middle of the *zócalo* is the town's chief attraction—the largest of the 16 known Olmec heads, carved in solid stone, measuring 3.4m (11ft) high and 1.5m (5ft) wide. Thought to represent a dead person due to its closed eyes, drooping mouth and stylized headpiece, it has the characteristics flattened nose and thick lips common to all the Olmec heads, which, some

theorists believe, raise questions of the possible presence of, or contact with, Negroid peoples in the Americas at that time.

Also on the *zócalo* is the Museo Tuxteco (Mon–Sat 9–6, Sun 9–5), displaying among other things local Olmec and Totonac objects used in traditional witchcraft *(brujería)*, the first sugar-cane press to be used in Mexico and another fine Olmec stone head.

✚ 316 N9 🚌 Buses from Veracruz, San Andrés Tuxtla and Catemaco

TAMPICO

www.tamaulipas.gob.mx

The busy port town of Tampico, on the tropical Gulf of Mexico, was founded in 1522 by Gonzalo de Sandoval, sacked by pirates in the 17th century and refounded in 1823. Oil was discovered here in 1901, marking the beginning of a new era of wealth and prosperity based on the huge refinery at Río Pánuco.

Despite new construction, Tampico retains an air of faded grandeur with its ramshackle, peeling colonial buildings laced with wrought-iron verandas and wooden-slatted windows. Caribbean in atmosphere, the animated Plaza de la Libertad springs to life in the sweltering evenings when local *jarocho* musicians and dancers perform in the elegant Victorian bandstand. A more sedate area is the Plaza de Armas, with Catedral Santa Iglesia, whose clock comes from England and altar from Carrara in Italy, and the art nouveau former Palacio Municipal, now a bank.

✚ 311 L7 ℹ️ Calle 20 de Noviembre 218 ☎ 212 26 68 🕐 Mon–Sat 9–7 🚌 The bus station is 10km (6 miles) out of town. Buses from San Luis Potosí and Veracruz

TAXCO

▷ 186.

TEOTIHUACÁN

▷ 188–191.

TEPOZTLÁN

Scenic Tepoztlán lies at the foot of the spectacular Parque Nacional El

Tepozteco, ringed by volcanoes and perched between rocky crags. Until recently an isolated rural village, its picturesque, steep cobbled streets with plodding, heavily laden donkeys are now lined with fashionable crafts boutiques and pretty cafés, attracting daytrippers from Cuernavaca at weekends. On the western side of the *zócalo* a crowded outdoor market sells fresh produce and crafts. Opposite, a gated entrance and overgrown churchyard lead to the remarkable 16th-century church and ex-convent of María de la Natividad (Tue–Sun 10–5). It was built by the Dominican order in 1580, occupied by French soldiers under Emperor Maximilian between 1864 and 1867 and again by revolutionaries in 1910. The interior patios are decorated with restored frescoes.

The small Tepozteco pyramid (daily 9–5.30) high up in the mountains above the town was built around 1130 and is dedicated to the god of *pulque* (a drink made of fermented maguey cactus). It is a strenuous 2km (1.2-mile) climb uphill from the end of Avenida Tepozteco, but spectacular views make the effort worthwhile.

✚ 315 L9 🚌 Buses from Cuernavaca and Mexico City

Below *The busy main plaza in San Andrés Tuxtla is overlooked by the twin towers of the cathedral of San Jose*

EL TAJÍN

The most impressive archaeological site on the Gulf coast, El Tajín has a rich body of iconography telling of the interplay between humans and the gods, and the dignified sacrifice of warriors and ball players. The great city of El Tajín ("thunderbolt" in Totonac) is one of the most enigmatic archaeological sites in Mexico. At its zenith in about AD600 it would have covered 1,050ha (2,595 acres), but by the time of the Conquest it had been completely forgotten, only to be rediscovered in 1785. Little is understood about El Tajín; no one even knows who built it. Some suggest the Huastecs, others the Totonacs. Its date of construction is less contested. The important structures were built between AD300 and AD900, with a surge of energy around AD600 when Teotihuacán and Monte Albán were being abandoned.

MAIN BUILDINGS

In the most important of the 17 ball courts, the Juega de Pelota Sur (South Ball Court), the bas-relief tableaux along the walls provide a fascinating glimpse into the philosophy that underpinned the ball game (▷ 31), including a portrait of a decapitated player—his head by his feet with the death god, Mictlantecuhtli, at his side—demonstrating an important association with human sacrifice. The obsession with the ball game suggests that the city was an immense academy where young men were trained in its skills and rules.

The Pirámide de los Nichos, one of the most famous structures at El Tajín, is punctuated by 365 niches, which would have originally been painted deep red on a black background. Their purpose is unknown; perhaps they held offerings, one for each day of the year. The pyramid is crowned with a sanctuary lined with engraved panels, one of which shows a cacao plant bearing fruit. Cacao was of great commercial value to the people of the area and there is some evidence that the rulers of El Tajín controlled its cultivation in the zones surrounding the site.

TAJÍN CHICO

The structures on this artificially tiered natural hill above the main site are thought to have been elite residences and administrative buildings. The Edificio de las Columnas was the special domain of the ruler, 13 Rabbit, who governed at the city's zenith.

INFORMATION

✚ 315 M8 ⏰ Daily 8–5 💲 $4.80, free with student card, $3.50 for use of video camera 🚌 Buses from Papantla and Poza Rica ℹ️ Guides at the entrance charge $20 for a 75-min tour. Limited written information on site 📖 Small pamphlets in Spanish for $1. Buy a guidebook in the Anthropology Museum, Mexico City, $6 🍽️ Open at 10am

TIPS

» Arrive when the site opens at 8am; the air is cool, the grass dewy and parrots squawk in the palms.
» Papantla and Tuxpán are much more pleasant places to overnight than nearby Poza Rica.
» The Voladores de Papantla (flying dancers) perform at El Tajín daily during high season, weekends in low season (▷ 25).

Above *The Pyramid of the Niches rises in six tiers of 3m (10ft) each, crowned by a temple*

INFORMATION

www.taxco.guerrero.gob.mx

✚ 315 K9 ℹ Avenida de los Plateros 1 ☎ (762) 622 22 74 🕐 Mon–Fri 8–3, Sat 9–11am 🚌 Buses from Mexico City

TIPS

» Taxco is a small town and, although hilly and cobbled, it is best experienced on foot.

» If you are buying silver, make sure it is genuine: check for the hallmark sterling or .925.

» To reach Ixcateopan de Cuauhtémoc, take the road north out of Taxco toward Teloloapan. *Combis* leave from the Estrella de Oro bus station in Taxco every 30 minutes.

TAXCO

The colonial town of Taxco, clinging to its steep hill, is distinguished for its remarkable silver jewelry. Mexico's most famous silver town is a warren of whitewashed, terra-cotta-tiled houses lining the steep and twisting cobbled streets that climb up the hillside to the Plaza Borda. French immigrant José de la Borda became fabulously rich after discovering the San Ignacio vein in the 18th century and he founded the town as you see it today, spending a fortune on building the Iglesia de Santa Prisca. Although no longer mined in large quantities, silver—in the shape of jewelry—remains the town's main livelihood and literally hundreds of silver shops *(platerías)* cater to visitors.

AROUND TOWN

The plaza is dominated by the magnificent, baroque, rose-hued Iglesia de Santa Prisca, whose twin towers soar above everything except the mountains. Built between 1751 and 1759, its interior is a dazzling display of Churrigueresque altarpieces with paintings by Miguel Cabrera (1695–1768), with scenes from the life of the Virgin behind the altar. The Museo de Arte Virreinal (Tue–Sat 10–5.45, Sun 10–4) on Calle J Ruiz de Alarcón 12 is housed in the Casa Humboldt, named after the renowned German explorer Baron von Humboldt (1769–1859), who stayed here once in 1801. Exhibits include superb religious art and ecclesiastical objects from Santa Prisca as well as some interesting background on Taxco's importance on the trade route from Acapulco.

The Museo Guillermo Spratling (Tue–Sun 9–5), behind Santa Prisca at Calle Porfirio Delgado 1, contains the personal collection of pre-Hispanic memorabilia belonging to this American architect and writer. Spratling arrived in Taxco in 1929 to set up a jewelry workshop, and his designs in silver helped bring the city to world recognition.

There are superb views from the Teleférico (cable car; daily 8–7) to Monte Taxco, reached by walking 2km (1.2 miles) up Calle Benito Juárez to the northern end of town.

IXCATEOPAN DE CUAUHTÉMOC

Some 45km (28 miles) from Taxco is the pretty village of Ixcateopan de Cuauhtémoc. Most of the buildings, and even the cobblestones, are made of marble. A statue commemorating Cuauhtémoc, the last Aztec emperor, stands at the entrance to the village, his birthplace. His skeleton is said to rest in the glass-covered tomb in the 16th-century Iglesia de Santa María de la Asunción, now a museum.

Below *Panoramic view across the rooftops of Taxco*

TEOTIHUACÁN

▷ 188–191.

TLACOTALPAN

Small, quiet Tlacotalpan lies on the Río Papaloapan, about 15km (9 miles) from Alvarado on the spectacular road inland to Tuxtepec and Oaxaca. Picturesque, secluded and very laid-back, the town has a distinctly Caribbean feel, its low houses fronted by stuccoed columns and arches painted in pastel shades. Large French windows with wrought-iron grilles reveal cool, dark interiors, heavy 19th-century furniture, rocking chairs and white linen curtains that float in the welcome breeze from whirring fans. There are two churches on the zócalo, the Parroquía de San Cristóbal (daily 8–7) on the west side and the Capilla de la Candelaria (daily 7am–8pm) on the north side. Opposite, on Calle Manuel Allegre, the Museo Salvador Ferrando (Tue–Sun 10–6) contains local 19th-century paintings and furniture.

🚩 316 N9 (southwest of Cuernavaca) 🛈 Zócalo ☎ (288) 884 21 51 ⏰ Daily 9–3, 5–7 🚌 Buses from Veracruz via Alvarado, or direct from Santiago Tuxtla, San Andrés Tuxtla, Tuxtepec

TLAXCALA

The quaint town of Tlaxcala, with its simple buildings washed in pinks and yellows, is the capital of the state of the same name, where wealthy ranchers breed fighting bulls but the landless peasantry is still poor. The Palacio de Gobierno (daily 9–6), which takes up one side of the main square, has some vivid murals inside painted by Desiderio Hernández Xochitiotzin (born 1922) depicting the indigenous history of Tlaxcala. On the intersection of Calle Mariano Sanchez with Calle 1 de Mayo is the Museo de Artes y Tradiciones Populares (Tue–Sun 10–6), where Otomí people demonstrate traditional arts such as embroidery, weaving, cooking, and pulque-making (a cactus-based liquor). You can't miss the twin white towers of the Basílica de

Above The bell tower and ornate decoration on the upper facade of the church of San José in Tlaxcala

Ocotlán (daily 9–6), perched on a hill overlooking Tlaxcala—walk up Avenida Guridi y Alcocer for 1km (half a mile). Its facade of lozenge-shaped vermilion bricks frames the white stucco portal, while the Churrigueresque interior is covered with gold leaf.

The ruined pyramid of Xicoténcatl, at San Estaban de Tizatlán, 5km (3 miles) outside Tlaxcala, has two sacrifical altars with original color frescoes preserved under glass.

🚩 315 L9 🛈 Avenida Juárez y Landizábal ☎ (246) 465 09 60 ⏰ Mon–Fri 9–7, Sat–Sun 10–6 🚌 Buses from Puebla, Mexico City

VERACRUZ

▷ 192.

XALAPA

▷ 193.

XOCHICALCO

The name of this pre-Hispanic hilltop site means "place of the flower house," although the surrounding hills are now dry and barren, but the views are spectacular. This city and ceremonial hub, discovered in 1770, was one of the principal settlements of Mexico's central plain, occupying a strategic site on the north–south trade route. Its heyday occurred from AD650 to AD900, after which it was abandoned mysteriously. The city's elaborate defensive features suggest, however, that it had enemies: archaeologists have discovered a complex system of doors and tunnels within the city walls. At its highest point is the Pirámidé de Quetzalcóatl (Pyramid of the Plumed Serpent), faced with andesite slabs which fit together invisibly without mortar. The friezes depict skeletal jaguars and figures of a serpent. The site also has two impressive ball courts, as well as numerous minor temples and living quarters. About 500m (550 yards) from the ruins down the hill an innovative new museum is housed in hexagonal rooms. Look for the remnants of the original piping system that ensured dampness would not deteriorate the friezes on the buildings. There are also some interesting photographs depicting the temples in a severe state of disrepair, taken by Hungarian Pál Rosti, who visited the site in 1856.

The site is large and requires at least two to three hours to see it.

🚩 315 L9 (southwest of Cuernavaca) ⏰ Daily 9–5 💲 $4.80; extra $3.50 for video cameras 🚌 Buses from Cuernavaca

TEOTIHUACÁN

INTRODUCTION

The site has some of the most remarkable relics of an ancient civilization in the world, including the massive Pyramid of the Sun, and was home to a mysterious people who existed at the same time as the Roman Empire. Allow at least two to three hours to see the site properly—longer if you're really interested. Arrive early before the vast numbers of wandering vendors and tour groups, who descend around 11am.

The site can be roughly divided into three distinct areas of interest connected by the 4km-long (2.5-mile) Avenida de los Muertos (Avenue of the Dead). At the southern end is La Ciudadela, in the middle section is the Pirámide del Sol and the museum, and at the northern end is the Pirámide de la Luna, surrounded by some smaller temples. To the west lie the mostly unexcavated sites of Tetitla, Atetelco, Zacuala, and Yayahuala. Teotihuacán is thought to date from around 300BC to AD750, with its heyday between AD450 and 650. Much of the city and the identity of its creators remains a mystery. Some archaeologists have suggested an ecological disaster—soil exhaustion or desertification of the surrounding area after years of deforestation—to explain the city's collapse. Even the name Teotihuacán is something of a misnomer; it was the Aztecs who gave the city the name by which we now know it: "the place where men become gods." Equally, the Avenue of the Dead was named mistakenly by the Aztecs, who thought it was lined with the burial chambers of Teotihuacán's rulers. It does appear, however, that the city housed some 200,000 people at its apogee, spread over an area of around 20sq km (8sq miles), making it the sixth-largest city in the world at the time. Excavations show that the ceremonial hub you see today was surrounded by areas occupied by artisans, workmen, merchants, and representatives of those crafts and professions that contribute to a functioning

INFORMATION

http://archaeology.la.asu.edu/teo/
✚ 315 L9 ⏰ Daily 7–5; if entrance near bus stop is not open at 7am, try entrance near Pyramid of the Moon. Museum daily 9–6; entrance included on ticket ✋ $4.80; extra $3.50 for video cameras; $4.50 parking fee. *Son et lumière* display $4 per person 🚌 Buses from Mexico City, Terminal del Norte, usually Gate 8. Note that the site is more generally known as Pirámides rather than Teotihuacán 📖 Official guidebook ($2) gives a useful route to follow. Students give free guided tours on weekends

Above *Detail of painted wall plaster on display in the museum*
Opposite *The Pyramid of Quetzalcóatl is decorated with serpents' heads and Tlaloc masks*

» Take water and food—most shops (overpriced) are limited to the west side of the site.

» If you're short of time, the best place to start is the Pyramid of the Moon (Gate 3), the area of most interest.

» The simplest way to visit Teotihuacán is on an organized tour, though an early departure from Mexico City doesn't mean you'll arrive at the site early, since tours tend to stop off at the Basílica de Guadalupe and a souvenir shop en route. Hostel Moneda offers day trips, which include pick-up and return from central hotels, a stop at the Basílica, English-speaking guide and lunch for $29; leaving 9am, returning 5.30pm (tel (55) 55 22 48 20).

» You can park in any of the five lots. Lot 1 is the closest to the Visitor Center.

» Keep in mind that you'll likely be doing quite a bit of walking, and perhaps some climbing, so be sure and wear comfortable shoes.

» There is a restaurant in the new Museo Teotihuacan, which is a convenient place to grab a snack or lunch unless you opt to pack a picnic lunch or buy something from a vendor.

Below *Mural in the Jaguars' Palace, Palacio de Quetzalpapálotl*

city. There is certainly no doubting the city's influence—research indicates that an individual from Teotihuacán arrived at Copán in Honduras and usurped the power of the rightful ruler, extending the influence of Teotihuacán throughout the Maya region.

WHAT TO SEE
LA CIUDADELA
This enormous square, dominated by the impressive Templo de Quetzalcóatl on its east side, was mistakenly thought to be the site of a fortress *(ciudadela)* by the Spanish. At Teotihuacán it was common practice to build on top of existing temples, creating overlapping structures akin to an onion—each layer represented a different era. Underneath the newest of the temples archaeologists have found an earlier pyramid with decoration that is unique to the site. Lining the staircase are huge carved heads of the much-revered feathered serpent, as well as Tlaloc, the beady-eyed rain god. You can still make out traces of pigment—remember that the rather dour pyramids you see today would once have been brightly painted.

PIRÁMIDE DEL SOL AND AROUND
Following the Avenue of the Dead north, you will reach the Pyramid of the Sun, the tallest pyramid on the site and the third largest in the world, measuring 65m (213ft) high and 213sq m (2,292sq ft) at its base. The sides are terraced, and wide stairs lead to the summit. The pyramid was heavily restored between 1905 and 1910 in time for Mexico's centennial Independence celebrations: controversial archaeologist Leopoldo Batres (1852–1926) has been blamed for taking the top off the pyramid and removing the original 4m (13ft) covering of stone and stucco. What you see now are the jutting stones on the sloping sides that would have held in place decorative panels, known as the *talud-tablero* technique. Underneath the pyramid, and not open to the public, is a system of natural caves discovered in 1971; some historians believe this may have been the most important point of the whole city—a sacred womb or site of an ancient underground spring. Nowadays, the pyramid's spiritual cast is most obvious on the spring equinox on March 21, when sun-worshippers flock

Above and left *Carvings of a plumed butterfly or quetzalpapálotl*

here to see the sun's alignment with the west face of the pyramid. Making a sojourn to the top of the pyramid is worth the 248-step climb. The ascent to the peak can be exhilirating and the view is breathtaking.

Just south of the Pyramid of the Sun is the site museum, surrounded by a sculpture garden. As well as an excellent model of old Teotihuacán, the museum has many fascinating objects including masks, ceramics and larger sculptures of deities—all well displayed.

PIRÁMIDE DE LA LUNA

Smaller than the Pyramid of the Sun, but built on higher ground, the Pyramid of the Moon is at the northernmost end of the Avenue of the Dead. You approach it through the Plaza de la Luna. The climb to the summit is hard, though it's worth getting at least as far as the first platform—48 steep steps—for wonderful views down the Avenue of the Dead. Excavations carried out in 2001 have uncovered numerous remains of sacrificial victims toward the middle of the pyramid, throwing into doubt earlier theories that human sacrifice wasn't a feature of life at Teotihuacán.

PALACIO DE QUETZALPAPÁLOTL

To the west of the Pyramid of the Moon is the Palace of the Precious Butterfly, where the priests serving the sanctuaries of the moon lived. The area has been restored, together with its columned patio—note especially the obsidian inlet in the highly decorated carved pillars. Following the path left of the palace and through a warren of chambers thought to have been the living quarters of priests, you will find the Palacio de los Jaguares (Jaguars' Palace). Impressive murals of cat-like creatures are displayed under protective shelters. Continue through a narrow tunnel to the right and you will emerge in the Temple of the Feathered Shells, with shells, flowers and green parrots decorating the base of an earlier temple.

MUSEO DE LA PINTURA MURAL TEOTIHUACANA

Exiting from Gate 3 behind the Jaguars' Palace, cross the parking area and the road to reach the excellent Museum of Teotihuacán's murals (opening hours same as site; price included in site admission). From the road a 350m (1,150ft) path leads past unexcavated temples covered in cacti to the museum, which houses around 40 murals from the site. Jaguars, shells and maguey, as well as figures of Tlaloc and Quetzalcóatl, appear again and again in the multihued paintings. Outside the museum, a shady botanical garden is an excellent place to relax.

INFORMATION

www.veracruz-puerto.gob.mx/turismo/
✚ 316 M9 🚹 Palacio Municipal,
Plaza de Armas ☎ (229) 989 88 17
🕐 Mon–Sat 8–8, Sun 10–6 🚌 Buses
from Mexico City, Xalapa, Puebla. The
bus terminals are 4km (2.5 miles) from the
middle of town, on Avenida Díaz Mirón

TIPS

» Veracruz' beaches leave much to be
desired. The beach at Mocambo is the
best, but the sand can be dirty.
» It is generally hot and humid in
Veracruz, however, between July and
September the region can be plagued by
heavy rains and from October to January
the beaches and *malecón* tend to be
empty, and many resorts close.

Above *Replica of the* Marigalante, *at rest
in the harbor*

VERACRUZ

The tropical town of Veracruz exudes Caribbean style and rhythm. Languid
evenings in the *zócalo* are enlivened by marimba players and couples dancing
the romantic *danzón*. On Good Friday, in 1519, Hernán Cortés and his troops
disembarked at Isla de los Sacrificios on the Gulf Coast of Mexico and founded
the town of Villa Rica de la Veracruz. In fact, this first settlement was a few
kilometers to the north; the present site was established in 1598.

For 400 years Veracruz was the setting for all manner of military defeats,
foreign occupations and heroic deeds. Basically, it is a Caribbean city; its
culture (called *jarocho*) is a fusion of Andalucian and African elements, reflected
in its Afro-Mexican ethnicity, music—featuring marimbas, flutes and harps—
and dance. This is one of the country's most enjoyable places to sit back, relax
and be entertained.

COLONIAL VERACRUZ

The heart of the city is the Plaza de Armas. White-paved, palm-fringed and
studded with attractive cast-iron lampstands and benches, it is watched over
by the Palacio Municipal, cathedral and several hotels in colonial buildings. The
floodlit plaza comes alive during the sultry evenings with a crush of dancers
and marimba players. You could enjoy the local *julep* drink—made with dark
rum, vermouth, sugar and mint—in the *portales* of the plaza, while you listen
to the sound of marimbas. Two blocks east of the plaza, the *malecón* (seafront)
also bristles with activity at night-time, and you can often catch street
performers and fire-eaters entertaining the crowds.

The city's main historic attraction is the fortress of San Juan de Ulúa
(Tue–Sun 10–5), joined by a causeway to the mainland. For 300 years the
fortifications failed to deter buccaneers and a series of foreign invasions, and
in 1825 the Spanish made their final stand here. Later, the fortress became a
political prison where Mexico's "Robin Hood," Chucho el Roto, was imprisoned,
and Benito Juárez established his constitutional government in exile between
1858 and 1861.

The Baluarte de Santiago (Tue–Sun 10–7), at Avenida 16 de Septiembre, is
one of nine forts that once formed part of the city walls. Built in 1635, it now
contains a small pre-Hispanic gold collection recovered from a shipwreck.
The Museo de la Ciudad (Tue–Sun 10–6), at Calle Zaragoza 397, traces the
history of Veracruz from the Conquest to 1910 and displays some lovely Olmec
sculptures, as well as interesting information on the trans-Atlantic slave trade.
Boca del Río, once a small fishing village a short drive east along the coast, is
now a developed area of beach hotels, bars and restaurants.

XALAPA

Xalapa (Jalapa), capital of Veracruz state since 1885 and home to the university—a hub of great creativity, energy and cultural flair—is surrounded by rich vegetation in the shadow of the 4,282m (14,049ft) peak of Cofre de Perote. Set in the lush, coffee-producing area of Mexico, the inland capital of Veracruz state enjoys a warm and damp climate. Walled gardens, stone houses and steep, cobbled streets overflow with flowers, and early mornings in the Parque Juárez ring to the sound of birdsong. Interspersed between colonial buildings are flamboyant, Gothic-style, 19th-century mansions, while surrounding the old heart is the modern town with its wide, congested avenues. Around Parque Juárez note the 18th-century cathedral with its sloping floor and the Palacio de Gobierno with murals by the Chilean artist José Chavez Morado (1909–2002).

MUSEUMS

In the northern suburbs of Xalapa, on the road out to Mexico City, is the outstanding Museo de Antropología (Tue–Sun 9–5), displaying a remarkable collection of treasures from the Olmec, Totonac and Huastec coastal cultures. Inaugurated in 1986 and considered the best anthropology museum in the country after Mexico City's for its scale and quality, it provides a superb, comprehensive introduction to the Gulf Coast civilizations, the highlight being its splendid Olmec stone sculptures. The 1.5m-wide (5ft) carved basalt heads from San Lorenzo are up to 1,000 years old, and each one has a different expression as well as the characteristically flat nose. Note the exquisite jade masks from 900BC and the lovely *El Señor de las Limas*, a stone sculpture of a priest sitting cross-legged holding a limp child in his arms. Look for the Xipetotec standing stone figure with flayed skin representing the victim of a sacrificial rite and, less gruesome, the adorable little toys from central Veracruz—dogs on wheels and smiling clay figurines on swings.

An exceedingly pleasant retreat from the bustle of the city is the Museo Hacienda El Lencero (Tue–Sun 10–5), 10km (6 miles) outside Xalapa on the road to Veracruz. This colonial hacienda was built by Juan Lencero, a soldier who arrived in Mexico with Hernán Cortés. It later became the residence of general and president Antonio López de Santa Anna, and today is a well-preserved example of a 19th-century house with original furniture and lovely grounds.

INFORMATION

www.xalapa.gob.mx/turismo/
diversos.htm

➕ 315 M9 ℹ Palacio Municipal, Enriquez 214 ☎ (228) 842 12 14 🕐 Mon–Fri 9–3, 4–8.30 🚌 Buses from Mexico City, Puebla, Veracruz

TIPS

» Watch out for the daily downpour that usually occurs at the end of the afternoon.
» Pick up the monthly cultural magazine *La Agorera* from the arts center, Agora de la Ciudad, Parque Juárez.
» Put the ruins of El Tajín into greater context by visiting the Anthropology Museum first.

Below *Two colossal Olmec carved heads on display in the Museo de Antropología*

THE CHURCHES OF PUEBLA

From the stunning Capilla del Rosario in the heart of Puebla, to exquisite marvels in tiny, dusty villages scattered around the city, this drive takes in some of the most spectacular examples of baroque architecture in Mexico.

THE DRIVE
Distance: 60km (37 miles)
Time: 5 hours
Start/end at: Puebla

★ Start in the *zócalo*, heart of the city of Puebla (▷ 182–183).

❶ The great Catedral de la Inmaculada Concepción (▷ 182–183) sits at the southwest corner, facing Calle 16 de Septiembre. Although the gray exterior walls are unremarkable, the interior has wonderful marble and onyx statuary. Mestizo artist Manuel Tolsa designed the gold-leaf altarpiece in 1797.

Turn right out of the cathedral and walk up Calle 16 de Septiembre. Beyond the *zócalo*, the street becomes pedestrianized. After three-and-a-half blocks you will cross Calle 4 Oriente. On the northeast corner stands the Iglesia de Santo Domingo.

❷ Inside the church, the Capilla del Rosario, on the left-hand side, is an extraordinarily lavish display of gold leaf and baroque flounces. Completed in 1659, the decorative stucco work here provided the inspiration for all later baroque art and architecture in Mexico.

From central Puebla, follow Avenida Reforma west. After 2km (1 mile) it becomes Prolongación Reforma. On leaving the city it becomes Carretera Federal Mexico-Puebla, passing through Cholula. The views of Popocatépetl and Ixtaccíhuatl are stunning on the left-hand side. After 16km (10 miles), you will come to the town of Huejotzingo.

❸ In Huejotzingo, Avenida Carlos Zetina borders the eastern side of the *zócalo*. Halfway along is the Convento Franciscano, set back on the right-hand side. The second oldest church and monastery in

Mexico, it was begun by the first Franciscans to arrive in the country in 1529 and finished in 1570. Note the Moorish *mudejar* influences in the fortress-like exterior and stonework around the door frame. Inside the church is one of the only remaining original 16th-century altarpieces in the country. The monastery has a lovely walled garden and cloisters.

Return to Cholula on the same road—Carretera Federal Mexico-Puebla—which becomes Calle 12 Poniente in town. At the *zócalo*, turn right, following the sign *"Zona archaeológico."*

❹ Sitting atop the ancient pyramid of Cholula (▷ 178) is the small, beautiful Iglesia de Nuestra Señora de los Remedios, a riot of white, cream and gold stucco decoration that glitters in the light from the clear glass windows in the dome.

Originally built by the Spanish in 1594, the church was destroyed by an earthquake in the mid-19th century and rebuilt between 1864 and 1874 in neoclassical style.

From the *zócalo*, follow Boulevard Miguel Alemán south, which becomes Carretera Cholula-Tonanzintla. After 3km (2 miles) is the tiny village of Tonantzintla.

❺ In Tonantzintla, turn right off Avenida Hidalgo, where the road curves to the left, onto Avenida Hombres Ilustres. Park and walk two blocks west to the pedestrianized main square. Here the ornate tower of the church, built in the first half of the 18th century, features figurines clothed in blue and green, while the tiled dome glitters in blue and yellow. The Moorish-style arched doorway is surrounded by terra-cotta and blue-and-white star-shaped tiles. Inside, look for the gold-leaf angels' dark, indigenous faces, the tropical fruit, maize and children wearing feathers that are surrounded by white swirls edged with gold. The Virgin above the altar sits in the middle of this splendor in her own pavilion, surrounded by flowers and angels emerging from white swirls.

Return to the Carretera Cholula-Tonanzintla and continue in the same direction—toward Puebla—for 1km (half a mile), passing the Panteón la Puríssima, a large cemetery, on your left, until you reach San Francisco Acatepec.

❻ On entering San Francisco Acatepec, directly ahead of you is the village's 17th-century baroque church of San Francisco. The wonderfully tiled mosaic and polychrome facade, a feast of detail, is constructed from local Talavera glazed ceramics. The density and brilliance of the interior shimmers with gold leaf, and the

Right *Statue of a saint on the facade of the church of Santa Maria, Tonantzintla*
Opposite *Cholula's Nuestra Señora church*

ornate altarpiece appears to flow seamlessly into the decorations of the dome and side chapels. Within the four arches of the dome there are figures of the four Apostles: St. Mark with a lion; St. Matthew with an angel; St. Luke with a bull; and St. John with an eagle.

Continue on the same road toward Puebla. After crossing the Anillo Periférico, the road becomes the Carretera a Atlixco. Continue through the suburbs of Puebla, where the road becomes Boulevard Atlixco, until you reach Avenida Juárez. Turn right onto Juárez and follow this road for 1km (half a mile) to the *zócalo*.

TOURIST INFORMATION
✉ Calle 5 Oriente No. 3, Puebla ☎ (222) 246 20 44 ◷ Mon–Sat 10–7, Sun 10–1

PLACE TO VISIT
CONVENTO FRANCISCANO DE SAN MIGUEL DE HUEJOTZINGO
✉ Plazuela Fr. Juan de Alameda ☎ (222) 276 02 28 ◷ Daily 10–5 💵 $3.50

WHERE TO EAT
EL CONVENTO
Located inside the former El Convento de la Concepción, this elegant restaurant offers international and Mexican dishes.
✉ Calle 7 Poniente 105, Puebla ☎ (222) 229 09 09 ◷ Mon–Sat 2pm–midnight

CHOLULA
Cholula's *zócalo* is full of cafés and restaurants. Try Los Jarrones (Portal Guerrero 4, tel (224) 247 10 98; daily 8am–11pm), and take advantage of its sunny terrace, which fronts the square.

COATEPEC

LA EUROPEA

One block from the *zócalo*, La Europea is stuffed with first-rate tents, rucksacks, bicycling and fishing gear, binoculars, camping, hiking and kayaking equipment.
✉ Calle 5 de Mayo 5, Coatepec ☎ (228) 816 71 87 ⊙ Mon–Sat 10.30–3, 5–9

CUERNAVACA

LOS AMATES DE AXOCHIAPAN

This spa, off Highway 160 between Cuernavaca and Puebla, consists of two thermal sulfuric pools rich in calcium and iron and naturally heated to 30°C (86°F), changing rooms, a restaurant, children's games and gardens.
✉ Axochiapan, Carretera Ahuaxtl–Teotlalco, Cuernavaca ☎ (735) 351 03 55 ⊙ Daily 9–6 🚌 Take the Cuatla—Izucar de Matamoros highway. At the Amayuca intersection, turn right toward Tepalcingo

AQUA SPLASH

www.aquasplash.com.mx
With 13 pools, 8 water slides, children's pools and games, wave machines, restaurants, gardens for picnics and parking, this excellent, modern and well-run water theme park is well worth inserting into your itinerary. Easily reached by car from Cuernvaca, it gets very crowded on weekends.
✉ Carretera Tequesquitengo-Jojutla, Km 4.5, Cuernavaca ☎ (734) 343 34 24 ⊙ Daily 8–6 🚌 From Cuernavaca take Highway 95 toward Acapulco, pass the tollbooth at Alpuyeca, then leave the highway and take minor road toward Tequesquitengo. Turn right onto the road to Jojutla and park entrance is 4km (2.5 miles) from the turn-off

CENTRO COMERCIAL LAS CAMPANAS

This fantastic bric-à-brac and craft shop is a dream, full of Guatemalan *huipil* shawls, local pottery, furniture, old records and secondhand clothing. Cash only is accepted.
✉ Calle Comonfort 2, Cuernavaca ☎ (777) 314 34 45 ⊙ Daily 10–2, 4–8

PUEBLA

BARRIO DEL ARTISTA

The cobbled Plazuela del Torno, now surrounded by artists' studios open to the public, owes its name to the spinning wheels that traditionally occupied the square. Most evenings there is live music.
✉ Calle 6 Oriente with Calle 6 Norte, Puebla ⊙ Daily 10–6

CAFÉ RENTOY

This well-liked groovy café and wine bar on the northeast corner of the Barrio del Artista square serves a wide range of cocktails. On the cobbled *plazuela*, live musicians perform jazz, Cuban *son* and *trova* every evening from 6 to 8pm and midnight to 2am. There's jazz on Sundays from 2pm.
✉ Calle 8 Norte 602, Puebla ☎ (222) 246 44 59 ⊙ Sun–Thu 8am–11pm, Fri–Sat 8am–3am

IMAGINA MUSEO INTERACTIVO

Animal skeletons and life-size model dinosaurs are highlights of this interactive museum. The Planetarium next door has IMAX screens showing films daily.
✉ Centro Cívico 5 de Mayo, Cerro de Guadalupe, Puebla ☎ (222) 235 34 19 ⊙ Mon–Fri 9–6, Sat–Sun 10–7 ✋ $5 🚌 Ruta 72 marked *"centro cívico"* from Boulevard de los Héroes del 5 de Mayo, three blocks east of the *zócalo*

MERCADO DE ARTESANÍAS "EL PARIÁN"

Occupying the ancient Plaza San Roque, the market's mass of

craft stands specialize in Talavera ceramics at excellent prices, embroidered blouses, glass, local sweets, onyx and much more.
✉ Calle 2 Oriente with Calle 6 Norte, Puebla 🕐 Daily 10–7.30

TALAVERA URIARTE
www.uriartetalavera.com.mx
Founded in 1824, this is one of the most prestigious Talavera factories in Puebla, allowing visitors to observe every stage in the pottery-making process. The interior patio is beautifully tiled and displays the factory shop's wares: superb ceramics and pottery at high prices.
✉ Calle 4 Poniente 911, Puebla ☎ (222) 232 15 98 🕐 Mon–Fri 9–6.30, Sat 10–6.30, Sun 11–6

TEATRO PRINCIPAL
Inaugurated in 1760, this is the oldest still-operating theater in the Americas, hosting ballets, musicals, plays and symphony concerts. You can visit the plush interior outside performance times.
✉ Calle 6 Norte with Calle 8 Oriente, Puebla ☎ (222) 232 60 85 🕐 Open for visits daily 10–4.30 ✋ Tickets from $7

TAXCO
LUNA COLECTION
The interior of Luna Colection resembles an Aladdin's cave with sparkling precious stones on display. You'll find lovely handmade silver pieces at good prices.
✉ Plaza Borda 1, Taxco ☎ (762) 622 64 47 🕐 Daily 9–8

TEPOZTLÁN
SANTA FE
This boutique sells embroidered dresses, silver jewelry and unusual pots made from dried orange peel, all handmade in town.
✉ Avendia Revolución 24, Tepoztlán 🕐 Sat–Sun 11–7, Mon–Fri times vary

VERACRUZ
ACUARIO DE VERACRUZ
www.acuariodeveracruz.com
This modern aquarium has 25 spacious pools. Its star attractions are the sharks, barracudas and rays.

FEBRUARY
DÍA DE LA MEXICANIDAD
Ixcateopan de Cuauhtémoc
The anniversary of the death of Cuauhtémoc, the last Aztec ruler, is celebrated in his birthplace, the village of Ixcateopan 20km (12 miles) from Taxco. Runners come from Mexico City via Taxco carrying a torch representing the identity of the Mexican people. Aztec dancers in traditional costume and plumed headdresses come from all over Mexico to dance all night and most of the following day.
🕐 February 22–23

FEBRUARY/MARCH
CARNAVAL
This is the largest Carnaval in Latin America outside Brazil. The night parades are spectacular shows of water, light and music. For seven

✉ Boulevard M. Avila Camacho, Veracruz ☎ (229) 931 10 20 🕐 Mon–Thu 9–7, Fri–Sun 9–7.30 ✋ Adult $7, child $3.50

MEXICO VERDE
www.mexicoverde.com
This eco-adventure holiday company offers hikes to waterfalls and crystalline natural pools, rappelling (abseiling) down rock faces and rafting down the River Pescado through 17 Class III and IV rapids, as well as child-friendly adventures.
✉ Veracruz ☎ (800) 362 88 00 🕐 Mon–Fri 10–1, 4–7.30, Sat 10–1 ✋ 1 day to 4 days from $85 to $480

EL PALACIO
El Palacio is a great place to watch couples dancing danzón, listen to the marimba players and soak up the atmosphere of a Veracruzana night. Try the local tipple—julep—made from dark rum, mint and sugar, or the el torito with peanut liqueur. Amex cards are not accepted.
✉ Calle Miguel Lerdo 127, Veracruz ☎ (229) 932 24 10 🕐 Daily noon–4am

days, the fantastically decorated carros alegóricos (floats), carrying scantily clad women shaking to Latin American rhythms, present a feast of color and sparkle and attract millions of visitors. The opening ceremony on the zócalo is the "Quema del mal humor," the burning of bad moods, then everyone can proceed to dance and sing to the music.
✉ Veracruz 🕐 Starting second Tuesday before Ash Wednesday

JULY/AUGUST
FERIA DE SANTIAGO APOSTOL
These festivities celebrate Santiago (St. James the Apostle), the town's patron saint. Processions, rodeos, horse-racing, street theater and dancing take place over five consecutive days.
✉ Santiago Tuxtla 🕐 Last week of July

PLAZA DE ARTESANÍAS
This large market is the best place for Cuban guayaberas, huarache ponchos, hammocks and sweets. Credit cards are not accepted.
✉ Calle Serdan with Calle Landero and Cos, Veracruz 🕐 Daily 9am–10pm

XALAPA
EL GIRASOL
Crafts from all over Mexico are sold in these artesanía shops. Amex cards are not accepted.
✉ Callejón del Diamante 6-6, Xalapa ☎ (228) 818 01 45 ✉ Xalapeōs Ilustres 22, Xalapa ☎ (228) 841 41 98 🕐 Mon–Sat 10–2, 4–8, Sun 12–2

RIO AVENTURA EXPEDICIONES
www.rioaventura.com.mx
Try this adventure tourism company for horseback-riding, rafting, hiking and rappelling (abseiling) around Jalcomulco. Food and equipment are included in the price and the guides speak English.
✉ Jalcomulco ☎ (229) 121 69 41 🕐 Daily 9–7 ✋ Day trips from $45

PRICES AND SYMBOLS

The restaurants are listed alphabetically within each town. The prices given are the average for a two-course lunch (L) and a three-course dinner (D) for one person, without drinks. The wine price is for the least expensive bottle. All the restaurants listed accept credit cards unless otherwise stated.

For a key to the symbols, ▷ 2.

CATEMACO
LOS SAUCES

Cool breezes from Lake Catemaco waft over the terrace of this fish restaurant, the best choice along the lakeside *malecón*. The specialty is the *mojarro*, small perch from the lake, best sampled with *tachogobi*, a traditional spicy, fresh tomato sauce. Breakfasts are served until midday. Credit cards are not accepted.
✉ Paseo del Malecón, Catemaco ☎ (294) 943 05 48 ⏰ Daily 8am–10pm 🖐 L $10, D $22, Wine $12

COATEPEC
CASA BONILLAS

Two blocks from the *zócalo*, this very popular restaurant was established in 1934 and specializes in exquisite seafood dishes. It is justly proud of

its prawns in a home-made *salsa verde* made from chili, orange juice and butter. There is a bar attached with less expensive lunch snacks. Amex cards are not accepted.
✉ Calle Juárez 20 with Calle Cuauhtémoc, Coatepec ☎ (228) 816 00 09 ⏰ Daily 8–8; bar closes 11pm Thu–Sat 🖐 L $12, D $20, Wine $14

CÓRDOBA
EL BALCÓN

Situated on the balcony of the historic Portales de Zevallos, this restaurant affords lovely views of the plaza below, animated by dancers and musicians in the evenings. Sample the local Córdoban coffee or the Veracruzana *julep* drink made from dark rum and mint.
✉ Avenida 1 No. 101, Córdoba ☎ (217) 712 19 89 ⏰ Mon–Sat 5.30–10, Sun 2–4.30 🖐 L $8, D $20, Wine $16

CUERNAVACA
LA INDIA BONITA

High walls protect La India Bonita's lush central patio and its fountains, making it easy to forget you're in the heart of Cuernavaca. Specials include a tender lamb fillet in *pulque* salsa. From 7pm on Saturdays there is a Mexican dance show.

Above *Fonda de Santa Clara in Puebla is picturesque and popular*

✉ Calle Morrow 15, Cuernavaca ☎ (777) 318 69 67 ⏰ Tue–Fri 9–5, 8–10, Sat 9–5, 9–11, Sun 9–5 🖐 L $15, D $30, Wine $15

LAS MAÑANITAS

www.lasmananitas.com.mx
Las Mañanitas, set in a restored hacienda with immaculate grounds, has a reputation as one of the finest restaurants in Mexico. Innovative regional cuisine is the order of the day, featuring *sopa de tortilla* and chicken in *mole verde*.
✉ Calle Ricardo Linares 107, Cuernavaca ☎ (777) 362 00 00 ext.240 ⏰ Daily 8–noon, 1–11 🖐 L $30, D $40, Wine $15

PACHUCA
MI ANTIGUA CAFE

On the south side of the *zócalo*, this modern café is the place to come for good espressos and breakfasts. Also on the menu are light lunches of imaginatively filled baguettes and crêpes, and cheesecakes with pots of Darjeeling tea in the afternoon. Credit cards are not accepted.
✉ Calle Matamoros 115, Pachuca ☎ (771) 107 18 37 ⏰ Mon–Sat 8am–11pm, Sun 9am–10pm 🖐 L and D $12

PUEBLA

CAFE Y LIBRERÍA TEOREMA

Delicious coffees are served in a studious atmosphere, the walls lined with books and paintings, and tables scattered with newspapers. Choose from specialty coffees with amaretto, brandy or whisky, lunch snacks, or a coffee-and-cake deal from 5 to 7pm. There's live jazz, trova and rock every evening from 9.30, plus a huge cocktail menu.
✉ Avenida Reforma 540, Puebla
☎ (222) 298 00 28 🕐 Mon–Fri 10am–12.30am, Sat and Sun 10am–2am
✋ L and D $5

FONDA DE SANTA CLARA

This picturesque, taverna-style restaurant one block west of the zócalo is popular with locals and visitors alike, and has a relaxed atmosphere in which to sample some of the most original cuisine in Mexico. The mole poblano and chiles en nogada are house specials.
✉ Calle 3 Poniente No. 307, Puebla
☎ (222) 242 26 59 🕐 Daily 10–10
✋ L $12, D $16, Wine $14

SAN ANDRÉS TUXTLA

MARISCOS CHAZARO

Jorge Chávez Flores, owner of this family-run fish restaurant, prepares exquisite prawn cocktails. The restaurant is cooled by whirring fans and decorated with the fantastic marine life he has caught. The specialty is the prawns in extra hot chile chipotle sauce—only for the brave. Credit cards are not accepted.
✉ Avenida Madero 12, San Andrés Tuxtla
☎ (294) 942 13 79 🕐 Mon–Sat 8.30–7, Sun 8.30–5 ✋ L $10, D $15, Wine $12

TAMPICO

LA TROYA

An excellent view over the animated and rowdy Plaza de la Libertad makes this the most entertaining restaurant in town. It occupies the balcony of a 19th-century art nouveau building, now the Hotel Posada del Rey, one of the oldest in Tampico. A wide choice of Mexican and international cuisine, including a good paella, is on the menu.

✉ Inside Hotel Posada del Rey, Calle Madero 218, Tampico ☎ (833) 214 11 55
🕐 Daily 7am–11pm ✋ L $10, D $17, Wine $13

TAXCO

CAFÉ EL ADOBE

Terra-cotta adobe walls, a mosaic-tiled floor, low arches and attractive balcony lend this restaurant a hacienda-style feel. Breakfasts are excellent and good value, and the menu includes many variations on the principal Mexican antojitos (appetizers), including the original tacos taxqueños, as well as seafood, steaks and desserts.
✉ Plazuela San Juan 13, Taxco ☎ (762) 622 14 16 🕐 Daily 8am–11.30pm ✋ L $8, D $18, Wine $12

CAFÉ SASHA

www.cafesasha.com
On the first floor of a colonial building, some of the tables in this intimate vegetarian restaurant are squeezed onto tiny balconies overlooking the cobbled street below. The food is moderately priced and consistently good. Choose from vegetarian pasta dishes, crêpes, Chinese noodles and delicious carrot cake. Breakfast is excellent. Credit cards are not accepted.
✉ Calle Juan Ruiz de Alarcón 1, Taxco
🕐 Daily 8am–midnight ✋ L $7, D $11, Wine $12

TEPOZTLÁN

LA TAPATÍA

On the south side of the zócalo, this informal restaurant is decorated with local textiles, and prepares its delicious tropical juices, vegetarian set lunches and Mexican quesadillas and tacos with organic ingredients. Amex cards are not accepted.
✉ Avenida Revolución 18, Tepoztlán
☎ (739) 395 10 21 🕐 Daily 8–8 ✋ L $6, D $12, Wine $11

VERACRUZ

GRAN CAFÉ DEL PORTAL

A cafe lechero (white coffee) and pastry in this famous establishment opposite the cathedral is a must. The Cuban Caldevilla family opened the premises as a candy store in 1824 and Spaniard Don Pepe, whose grandson still owns the café, later created the social gathering point it is today. Old photos of Veracruz line the walls and waiters are dressed in white coats. The menu includes meat, fish and Mexican dishes.
✉ Calle Independencia 1187, Veracruz
☎ (229) 931 27 59 🕐 Daily 8am–11pm
✋ L $8, D $18, Wine $12

MARISCOS TANO

Just off the malecón, this excellent restaurant has dried eels, turtles and small sharks hanging menacingly from the ceilings. Start with the delicious Campechano fresh crab and prawn cocktail with lime and coriander before moving on to the house special, arroz a la tumbada, a local paella-style dish. Credit cards are not accepted.
✉ Calle Mario Molina 20, Veracruz
☎ (229) 931 50 50 🕐 Daily 9am–9.30pm
✋ L $9, D $13, Wine $10

NEVERÍA TRIGUEROS

There is nowhere better than this popular, relaxed juice and ice-cream bar to sample the traditional Veracruzana mondonga de fruta. Consisting of a mountain of chopped tropical fruit topped with a generous dollop of ice cream or yogurt, it is usually a considered a breakfast but also makes a refreshing snack.
✉ Calle Zaragoza, 147 between Calle Mario Molina and Calle Serdan, Veracruz
☎ (229) 932 39 50 🕐 Daily 8am–1am
✋ L and D $6

XALAPA

LA FONDA

Tucked away up a side street off Calle Enriquez, this popular place serves three-course set lunches, which include agua de frutas (fruit-flavored water) and coffee. In the long, open kitchen cooks in white dresses and head scarves stir steaming cauldrons of hot soups and bake tortillas on an open fire. Credit cards are not accepted.
✉ Callejón del Diamante with Enriquez, Xalapa ☎ (228) 818 72 82 🕐 Mon–Sat 8–6 ✋ L $5

PRICES AND SYMBOLS

The prices are the average for a double room for one night including breakfast, unless otherwise stated. All the hotels listed accept credit cards unless otherwise stated. Note that rates can vary widely throughout the year.

For a key to the symbols, ▷ 2.

CATEMACO

PARQUE ECOLÓGICO NANCIYAGA

www.nanciyaga.com

Situated in the most northerly stretch of tropical rain forest on the planet, 7km (4 miles) from Catemaco on the northern side of Lake Catemaco, this eco-lodge is one of the most original places to stay in southern Veracruz. Comfortable wooden cabins with verandas and hammocks are scattered among the trees. There are canoes for rent, and swimming in the healing spring waters, aromatherapy massages, guided walks in the jungle and a *temazcal* spiritual treatment for an extra fee.
✉ Catemaco-Coyame Road Km 7, Catemaco ☎ (294) 943 01 99 🖐 $90
🛈 10 cabins with fans

COATEPEC

POSADA COATEPEC

This magnificent hacienda in the middle of Coatepec has an interior patio painted with detailed frescoes, 19th-century furniture and a Victorian carriage. Rooms are individually decorated with enormous beds, soft lighting and attractively tiled bathrooms. An walled garden, a swimming pool, a fountain, and a sauna add to the appeal.
✉ Calle Hidalgo 9, Coatepec ☎ (228) 816 05 44 🖐 $115, excluding breakfast; suites $150–$190 🛈 23, 10 with air-conditioning
🔄 Some 🏊 Outdoor

CUERNAVACA

CASA COLONIAL

This understated, luxurious hotel stands opposite the cathedral, in the

Above *Camino Real Puebla is set in a beautifully restored building, converted from a 16th-century convent*

heart of Cuernavaca, known as the City of Eternal Spring. It occupies an 18th-century house and garden, and features lofty, beamed ceilings, open fires, heavy dark-wood furniture and antique chests. The rooms are all individually decorated and have gleaming, traditionally tiled bathrooms, perfect white linen, terra-cotta-tiled floors and softly glowing lanterns.
✉ Calle Netzahualcoyotl 37, Cuernavaca ☎ (777) 312 70 33 🖐 $98 (at weekends $125); Continental breakfast in hotel restaurant $6.50 🛈 19 🏊

PACHUCA

HOTEL DE LOS BAÑOS

The corridor leading to the reception of this excellent-value hotel, just one block from the *zócalo*, is lined with gilt mirrors and tiles. More blue-and-white tiles cover the central, enclosed patio of this 19th-century building. Rooms are carpeted and comfortable, with elaborately carved wooden furniture.

✉ Calle Matamoros 205, Pachuca ☎ (771) 713 07 00 👷 $29 🛏 56

PUEBLA

CAMINO REAL PUEBLA
www.caminoreal.com/puebla/
One block from the *zócalo*, this sumptuous hotel occupies the reconverted and beautifully restored El Convento de la Concepción. Founded in 1593, it was a functioning convent until 1861, when it was used as a military barracks. Rooms surround the two interior stone patios, whose deep-yellow walls are covered with their original flowery frescoes, and are exquisitely furnished with huge oak beds, antique wardrobes and colonial-era art. The elegant El Convento restaurant offers exquisite international and Mexican dishes. Parking is available.

✉ Calle 7 Poniente 105, Puebla ☎ (222) 229 09 09 👷 $220 ($105 on weekends), excluding breakfast 🛏 84 rooms and suites

MESÓN SACRISTÍA DE LA COMPAÑÍA
www.mexicoboutiquehotels.com/mesonsacristia
This boutique hotel in a 200-year-old building near the Plazuela de los Sapos has individually and elegantly decorated rooms with four-poster beds, antique dressers, Talavera pottery, and exquisite gold-leaf details around the door frames. The public areas are crammed with beautiful objects and paintings, but luckily everything you see in the hotel is for sale, should you fall in love with something. There is also an antiques shop on site. Parking is available.

✉ 6 Sur 304, Callejón de los Sapos, Puebla ☎ (222) 242 35 54 👷 $160–$210 🛏 9

TAXCO

AGUA ESCONDIDA
Hotel Agua Escondida puts you right at the heart of things, in the *zócalo* district of the town. This great value

hotel has the amenities of its larger competitors, such as a swimming pool, restaurant and café/bar, with the added benefits of friendly service and a vibrant, typically Mexican atmosphere. Just sit back on the terrace and enjoy the views of the parish church of Santa Prisca (▷ 186).

✉ Plaza de la Borda 4, Taxco ☎ (762) 622 11 66 👷 $68–$75 🛏 58 🏊

LOS ARCOS
Just one block down the hill from the Plaza Borda, this colonial mansion is set around a delightful courtyard shaded by a handsome jacaranda tree. The lobby is in the former carriageway, opening out onto the stone arches of the courtyard. Rooms are pleasantly decorated and furnished and bathrooms sparklingly clean. There is a fantastic roof terrace with views of Santa Prisca and the town spreading into the valley below.

✉ Juan Ruiz de Alarcón 4, Taxco ☎ (762) 622 18 36 👷 $43, excluding breakfast (plenty of cafés serving breakfast in nearby Plaza Borda) 🛏 21

TEPOZTLÁN

POSADA DEL TEPOZTECO
http://posada.planetbyte.com.mx
Surely the loveliest place to stay in Morelos state, this beautifully renovated colonial hacienda affords spectacular views over the Tepozteco National Park from its gardens and terraces. The rooms are large, many with a private terrace and Jacuzzi, and the restaurant extends into the flower garden, where there is an ivy-covered fountain and a pleasantly shaded pergola for relaxed al fresco dining.

✉ Calle Paraíso 3, Tepoztlán ☎ (739) 395 00 10 👷 $170–$200 🛏 20 (including 6 suites) 🏊

TLACOTALPÁN

POSADA DOÑA LALA
Situated on the *zócalo*, with a breezy restaurant terrace at the rear looking over the river promenade, this family-run and very friendly hotel offers simple but attractive rooms

with high ceilings, large beds made from dark wood, and crisp white sheets. There is also an attractive garden with a swimming pool and a family restaurant. Parking is available for guests.

✉ Calle Carranza 11, Tlacotalpán ☎ (288) 884 25 80 👷 $55–$65, excluding breakfast ($5) 🛏 35 🛎 Some rooms 🅿 Outdoor

VERACRUZ

GRAN HOTEL DILIGENCIAS
www.granhoteldiligencias.com
This modern 5-star hotel takes pride of place on the *zócalo*. The grand, marble-covered reception with cool white decor employs extremely efficient, English-speaking staff. Rooms are immaculate if a little soulless. The terrace overlooking the square has an inviting pool and sun-lounge area. Valet parking is available.

✉ Calle Independencia 1115, Veracruz ☎ (229) 923 02 80 👷 $120 🛏 121 🛎 🏊 🍽

MOCAMBO
www.hotelmocambo.com.mx
This fabulous hotel, 8km (5 miles) south of Veracruz, was built in the 1930s and still retains its air of grandeur, albeit somewhat faded. Its palatial art deco interior is bright and airy. The rooms have air-conditioning, TV and balcony with a view of the gardens or the ocean.

✉ Boulevard Ruiz Cortinez 4000, Mocambo Beach, Veracruz ☎ (229) 922 02 02 👷 $110–$130 🛏 123 🛎 🏊

XALAPA

MESÓN DEL ALFÉREZ
This is the pleasantest place to stay in the middle of town. Rooms in the converted colonial house are brightly painted, furnished in rustic farmhouse style and open onto the central patio. Rooms looking onto the congested street side can be noisy, so opt for an interior one. Children under 10 stay free.

✉ Calle Sebastián Camacho 2–6, corner with Calle Zararzoga, Xalapa ☎ (228) 818 01 13 👷 $65 🛏 20, including 2-floor suites

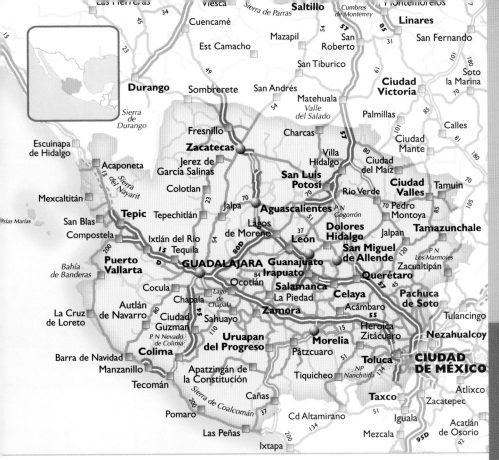

CENTRAL MEXICO WEST

The colonial silver mining cities of Mexico—San Miguel de Allende, Queretaro, San Luis Potosi, Guanajuato, and Zacatecas—are situated in the rugged mountains of the Sierra Madre Occidental. The smallest of the cities is San Miguel de Allende, with its charming cobblestone streets. Many artists and writers call San Miguel home. The center of the city is the public library, which is located in the former convent of Santa Ana. It may be small but that doesn't mean that San Miguel doesn't know how to party in big ways—the city is known for celebrating festivals and it has up to 40 of these a year.

Guanajuato, founded in 1559, soon became a very rich town, with world-famous mines that earned their owners titles of nobility. Along with Zacatecas and San Luis Potasi, Guanajuato was one of Mexico's most important mining cities. Quite picturesque, Guanajuato is also one of Mexico's great colonial settlements.

Recognized as the most historic city in the region, Santiago de Queretaro was founded by the Spanish in 1531 during their first large-scale expedition into the vast northern stretches of their new territory. Queretaro is also one of the two principal places in the world where opals are mined commercially (southern Australia is the other.) Shoppers can find locally mined opals and other semiprecious stones in several stores here.

Zacatecas, like Guanajuato, is known for the wealth of silver extracted from its mines. Stroll about the city, with its hilly terrain, and take in its wonderful museums, beautiful architecture, and restaurants offering up tasty cuisine.

San Luis Potosi is the largest and most industrial of the silver cities, with almost a million inhabitants. Known for its great plazas, it also has rich colonial architecture. The center of town is the Plaza de Armas, which dates from the mid-1700s and is shaded by beautiful magnolia trees. East of the plaza is one of the city's most famous squares, Plazuela del Carmen, named for the Templo del Carmen church.

AGUASCALIENTES

Aguascalientes hosts the annual San Marcos National Fair, one of Mexico's biggest cultural festivals, and is home to the excellent José Guadalupe Posada Museum. Founded in 1575, Aguascalientes is capital of the state of the same name. It owes its name, "hot waters," to the mineral springs once abundant here. Nowadays Spanish heritage jostles for space with modern shopping malls, but there are some pretty parks.

AROUND THE PLAZA

Most of the city's visitor attractions lie on or near Plaza de la Patria, dominated by a soaring, fluted column on top of which rests an eagle poised to kill a snake. On the south side is the Palacio de Gobierno (Mon–Fri 8–6, Sat 8–2), begun in 1665, with a splendid interior courtyard decorated with vivid murals by Chilean artist Osvaldo Barra Cunningham (1922–99).

On the west side of the plaza is the cathedral (Mon–Sat 9–5, Sun 8–7), built on the site of a hermitage used by workers heading for the silver mines to the north, and finished in 1738. To the south of the cathedral is the Teatro Morelos, where in 1914 the revolutionary factions led by Pancho Villa, Emiliano Zapata and Venustiano Carranza met to find common ground. The meeting ended in failure. About 10 blocks south is the Museo José Guadalupe Posada (Tue–Sun 11–6), hosting a small display of his prints and original engravings. Born in Aguascalientes, Posada (1852–1913) has near legendary status in Mexican art (▷ 39).

East of Plaza de la Patria on Zaragoza 505 is the neoclassical Museo de Aguascalientes (Tue–Sun 11–6), home to a collection of contemporary art, including paintings by Saturnino Herrán (1887–1919) and José Clemente Orozco (1883–1949). Next door is the Iglesia de San Antonio, inaugurated in 1908, with a baroque facade in faded yellow.

INFORMATION

www.aguascalientes.gob.mx

✚ 314 J7 ☷ Palacio de Gobierno, south side of Plaza de la Patria

☎ (449) 915 95 04 🕐 Tue–Sun 9–8

✖ Aguascalientes airport, 21km (13 miles) south

TIP

» With more than 1.5 million visitors, the *Feria de San Marcos* is Mexico's biggest fair (▷ 233). Booking a hotel room in advance is essential, and if rodeo and ranchero country music isn't your thing then the city is best avoided altogether from mid-April to early May.

Opposite *Detail of a mural by Osvaldo Barra Cunningham in the courtyard of the Palacio de Gobierno*
Below *Tiered arches surround the courtyard of the Palacio de Gobierno*

BARRA DE NAVIDAD AND SAN PATRICIO MELAQUE

www.barradenavidad.com

Toward the southern end of the 450km (280-mile) stretch of coastline between Puerto Vallarta and Manzanillo known as La Costa Alegre, the villages of Barra de Navidad and Melaque are small, laid-back resorts at either end of Bahía de Navidad (Christmas Bay), famous for its calm waters.

Although there is creeping commercialization, both villages feel much more down to earth than many of the purpose-built resorts along La Costa. Melaque is better for shopping, while Barra de Navidad has more hotels and restaurants, as well as a footnote in history proudly marked by a monument in the main square—it was from here that Spanish ships set out in 1564 to conquer the Philippines. Local buses shuttle back and forth between the two villages, or you can walk along the beach.

✚ 314 H9 ℹ Jalisco 67 ☎ (315) 355 51 00 ⏰ Mon–Fri 9–5 🚌 Buses from Manzanillo, Guadalajara, Puerto Vallarta

Above A boat moves through the calm waters of Barra de Navidad

CELAYA

Celaya is famous for its confectionery—especially *cajeta*, a sweet caramel spread, available on practically every street corner, which according to purists is better when made with goat's milk *(leche de cabra)*—and its churches, most of them built by Francisco Eduardo Tresguerras (1759–1833), a native of the town. His masterpiece is considered to be the neoclassical Templo del Carmen (daily 10–1, 3–6) with its fine yellow-tiled dome. Just outside the main door on Calle Madero is his mausoleum. Tresguerras also rebuilt much of the huge Convento de San Francisco (daily 9–4), with an imperious courtyard surrounded by handsome confessional boxes.

Outside the monastery stands the Torre Hidráulica, or *bola de agua* (ball of water), as it's popularly known. It marks the centenary of Mexico's independence from Spain and has become the symbol of the city. Nowadays Celaya is an industrial city based on food processing and chemicals.

✚ 315 K8 ℹ Casa del Diezmo, Juárez 204 ☎ (461) 612 74 76 ⏰ Mon–Fri 9–5, Sat 10–1 🚌 Buses from Mexico City, Aguascalientes, Querétaro and intermittent services to Morelia, Guadalajara, San Luís Potosí

CHAPALA

www.amigosdelago.org

Chapala, on the northern shore of Laguna de Chapala, Mexico's largest lake, is a resort town with gorgeous lake views and a reliably agreeable climate. It is for this reason that "Lakeside," as it's often called, is home to one of the world's largest communities of expatriate Americans and Canadians. As a result, the town and its surroundings have good sporting facilities, plenty of hotels and restaurants, and handsome private residences—the village of Chula Vista on the way toward Ajijic is known by locals as the "Beverly Hills" of Lakeside.

In Chapala, boat trips around the lake or to the Isla de los Alacranes are available from the pier at the end of Calle Madero ($25–$30 per person). Here you can pick up fried *charales*, a local delicacy similar to whitebait.

✚ 314 J8 ℹ Madero 407 above the Sol de Chapala liquor store ☎ (376) 765 31 41 ⏰ Mon–Fri 9–7, Sat 9–1 🚌 Buses from Guadalajara

CHICOMOSTOC

Chicomostoc (also known as La Quemada) is an archaeological site on Highway 70. Mystery surrounds the identity of the people who inhabited this citadel, but the most popular theory suggests that this was the site of Las Siete Cuevas (The Seven Caves). According to legend it was a stopping point in the wanderings of the México tribes before they went on to found Tenochtitlán. The Palacio de las Once Columnas (Palace of the Eleven Columns) is Chicomostoc's outstanding structure, and the museum contains a good scale model of the site. But it is its location on a rocky outcrop that makes the trip worthwhile—the views are breathtaking.

✠ 314 J7 ✉ 48km (30 miles) southwest of Zacatecas ⊙ Site and museum: daily 10–5 ✋ $3.90 🚌 Buses from Zacatecas

COLIMA

www.visitacolima.com.mx

This clean and attractive state capital, dubbed the "city of palms," has recovered remarkably quickly from a large earthquake that killed at least 25 people and damaged many buildings in January 2003.

The town's focal point is the verdant Jardín de Libertad, dominated by the late 19th-century cathedral (daily 6–2, 4–8.30). Next door is the neoclassical Palacio de Gobierno (Mon–Fri 9–5, Sat 10–1), home to a mural painted in 1953 by local artist Chávez Carrillo that pays homage to Father Miguel Hidalgo (see right).

On the southern side of the square lies the Museo Regional de Historia (Tue–Sat 9–6, Sun 5–10pm), with an impressive collection of pre-Hispanic ceramics from La Campana and El Chanal.

North of Jardín de Libertad is the Andador Constitución, a pedestrian street lined with stands selling crafts. There is also a DIF state-run artisan's shop (▷ 230). Walking east along Colima's main drag, Avenida Madero, you will pass two more tranquil plazas, the Jardín Torres Quintero and the Parque Núñez.

Farther afield, at Calzada Pedro Galván in the Casa de Cultura complex, is the interesting Museo de las Culturas de Occidente María Ahumada (Tue–Sun 9–6.30), which contains a huge display of pre-Hispanic figurines.

✠ 314 H9 ℹ Palacio de Gobierno, Avenida Hidalgo 96 ☎ (312) 312 43 60 ⊙ Mon–Fri 8.30–8, Sat 10–2

DOLORES HIDALGO

It was in Dolores Hidalgo that local priest Don Miguel Hidalgo y Costilla tolled the church bells to mark the beginning of the uprising against Spanish rule in 1810 (▷ 36). Nowadays the town is a tranquil place with a lovely main square, dominated by a statue of Hidalgo. The town attracts a steady stream of mainly Mexican visitors who come to visit the shrine-like Museo Casa Hidalgo (Mon–Sat 9–5.45, Sun 9–4.45) on Calle Morelos and Avenida Hidalgo, two blocks south of the main square, as well as the famous Iglesia de Nuestra Señora de los Dolores, built between 1712 and 1778 (daily 5.30am–9pm). Confusion surrounds the fate of the bell rung by Hidalgo—it either hangs in the Palacio Nacional in Mexico City or was melted down for arms. Whatever the case, the bells you see are not the originals. What Dolores Hidalgo can claim as its own, however, is its extraordinary tradition of home-made ice cream, available at stands around the Jardín.

✠ 315 K8 ℹ Main square ☎ (418) 182 11 64 ⊙ Mon–Sat 10–7 🚌 Buses from San Miguel de Allende, Guanajuato, Mexico City

Left *Facade of the church of Our Lady of Sorrows, Dolores Hidalgo*

INFORMATION

www.guadalajara.gob.mx

314 H8 Booth in Plaza de la Liberacion, Paseo de Gollado 105 (33) 36 68 16 00 Mon–Fri 9–8 Bus terminal 10km (6 miles) from central Guadalajara Aeropuerto Internacional Miguel Hidalgo, 20km (12 miles) south of city

TIPS

» Tonalá, 15km (9 miles) southwest of Guadalajara on the road to Mexico City, is noted for its Sunday and Thursday markets (▷ 230).

» El Público newspaper has a good entertainment supplement, Ocio, every Friday, with music, film and art listings for the week ahead. There is also an English-language monthly listings paper, Guadalajara Weekly, from tourist offices.

» The old bus station, south of the central area, serves towns within 100km (60 miles) of the city, mainly with second-class buses. To get to Zapopán take a blue TUR bus from Calle Alcade ($0.50).

Below The cathedral is a mixture of styles: Churrigueresque, baroque, and neoclassical

GUADALAJARA

Mexico's second city, home to masterpieces by muralist José Clemente Orozco, is full of graceful colonial arcades, or portales, which flank the old plazas and shaded parks. It also has some of the region's best craft shopping.

AROUND THE CATHEDRAL

The heart of the city is Plaza de Armas. On its north side is the cathedral, built in a medley of styles—its two spires were replaced after an 1818 earthquake destroyed the originals, and the dome dates from 1875. On the east side of the plaza in elegantly severe baroque style is the Palacio de Gobierno, which houses a striking Orozco mural depicting the looming figure of Independence hero Miguel Hidalgo.

East of the cathedral is the Plaza de la Liberación, overlooked by the Teatro Degollado, where Guadalajara's famous Ballet Folclórico dance company perform (▷ 230). On the square's north side is the Museo Regional de Guadalajara (Tue–Sat 9–5.45, Sun 9–4.45), with a superb prehistoric section and one of the finest displays of 17th- to 18th-century colonial art in Mexico.

PLAZA TAPATÍA AND SOUTH

Heading east behind the theater brings you to the modern Plaza Tapatía, lined with huge department stores. At its eastern end is the Instituto Cultural Cabañas (Tue–Sat 10.15–6, Sun 10.15–2.45), an elegant neoclassical cultural center with excellent temporary exhibitions. It displays 53 Orozco murals depicting key events in Mexican history. South of here is the vast, covered Mercado Libertad (market), known locally as San Juan de Dios (▷ 230).

GUADALAJARA'S SUBURBS

In the northwestern part of the city is the Basilica of Zapopán, which houses a much-venerated image of the Virgin of Zapopán above the main altar. Next door is an excellent museum of Huichol indigenous art (Mon–Sat 9–1.15, 3.30–6, Sun 10–2).

About 7km (4 miles) southeast of the city is the attractive suburb of Tlaquepaque, worth a visit for its numerous arts and crafts shops (▷ 230). And for attractive outside bars and a Sunday afternoon mariachi serenade, there's no better place than the Parián, next to Jardín Hidalgo, the main square.

GUADALUPE

Now really a suburb of Zacatecas, Guadalupe is a dusty little place whose chief attraction is the Convento de Guadalupe (daily 10–4.30). From here the colonization and evangelization of Mexico's northern tribes took place. The convent was also an orphanage and children's hospice. Nowadays it has an excellent Museo de Arte Religioso (daily 10–4.30) with some fascinating colonial-era paintings by local *mestizo* artists depicting traditional biblical scenes in a way that makes quite clear their antipathy toward Spanish rule.

🚪 314 J7 🚌 Buses from Zacatecas

GUANAJUATO

▷ 210–213.

GUAYABITOS

www.guayabitos.com

Just off Highway 200 is Guayabitos, a languid little resort popular with Mexican families who want to avoid the bustle of the nearby resort of Puerto Vallarta. Guayabitos is much cheaper than Puerto Vallarta and built on a different scale entirely—in fact there's really very little to the place except a street lined with hotels, restaurants, and shops selling inflatable plastic toys.

The beach is pleasant and the sea calm, although in high season it can get very crowded. Many of the hotels have swimming pools overlooking the beach and there is a good selection of bungalows in the more peaceful, southern end of town. Whale-watching tours run from December to March.

🚪 314 G8 ℹ️ At the entrance to town just off Highway 200 🕐 Official opening hours daily 10–1, 2–5, but often shut in the afternoons ✈️ Puerto Vallarta airport 42km (26 miles) to south, Tepic airport to the north

IXTAPAN DE LA SAL

Ixtapan de la Sal is a pleasant leisure resort with medicinal hot springs, surrounded by attractive pine forests on Route 55. In the middle of this quiet, whitewashed town is the municipal spa (daily 7–6), refurbished in 2004 and equipped with thermal and mud baths, hydro-massage facilities, individual changing rooms and masseurs. It's very pleasant, particularly in the mornings before midday, but can get crowded during school holidays.

For those after a more exclusive experience, the Ixtupan Parque Acuatico is set in private grounds at the edge of town, with its own Olympic-size wave pool, river, water slides, thermal baths, restaurants, and picnic spots. Basic admission is $16. Spa treatments and private baths are extra.

Alternatively, try the Hotel Ixtapan Spa on Boulevard San Román, which offers total pampering—including aromatherapy, Thai and Swedish massages, facials and "detox" packages, as well as three tennis courts and an 18-hole golf course.

🚪 315 K9 🚌 Buses from Mexico City, Toluca, Taxco, Coatepec, Cuernavaca

IXTLÁN DEL RÍO

Ixtlán del Rio is an unremarkable small town with an agricultural economy. The chief reason for stopping here is to visit the ruins of Los Toriles, a Toltec ceremonial base on a warm, windswept plain 2km (1.2 miles) out of town on Highway 15. The archaeological remains open to the public cover around 8ha (20 acres) and include 15 structures, representing the key ceremonial hub of the original 50ha (123-acre) settlement.

The city enjoyed its heyday from around AD750 to 900. Its most significant structure is the Temple to Quetzalcóatl, noted for its unusual circular shape and cruciform windows. It is topped by two small pyramids thought to commemorate the sun and moon, though archaeologists believe the site was dedicated to the god of wind. There is a small museum on site.

🚪 314 H8 🕐 Los Toriles: daily 9–6 ✋ $3.50 🚌 Buses from Tequila, Guadalajara and Tepic 🚗 To reach Los Toriles by car from Ixtlán del Río, pass the Cristo Rey bullring on your right before turning left at the sign and over the railway tracks into the site

Above *The tiled roof of Capilla de Napoles in the Convento de Guadalupe*

INFORMATION

www.guanajuato-travel.com

➕ 315 K8 ℹ️ Plaza de la Paz 14
☎ (473) 732 19 82 🕐 Mon–Fri 9–7.30,
Sat 10–5, Sun 10–2 🚌 Buses from
Mexico City, León ✈ Aeropuerto del
Bajío 40km (25 miles) west

INTRODUCTION

For centuries Guanajuato, seemingly hewn out of the rock, was the wealthiest city in Mexico. Today it is full of twisting, narrow alleyways, magnificent colonial mansions, baroque and neoclassical churches and hidden squares. Nestled in a narrow gorge amid wild, striking scenery, Guanajuato emerges from the hills as a patchwork of colonial buildings that tumble down the steep hillside, the roofs appearing to be suspended from the floor of the building above. It was declared a UNESCO World Heritage Site in 1988, and has been spared industrial development—there are no traffic lights or neon signs. The Guanajuato River, which cuts through the city, has now been covered and underground streets opened up to relieve the stress of traffic in the narrow streets above—an unusual, often confusing system.

The polluted subterranean Avenida Miguel Hidalgo passes directly underneath the Avenida Juárez, which runs straight through the heart of the city. Almost everything of interest is either along here or just off it, down one of the steep, winding *callejones* (alleyways). The only way to see the city is on foot; wander around and lose yourself in the warren of cobbled streets where you will inevitably stumble upon a charming *plazuela*, ornate fountain or one of the many baroque churches.

The city's name derives from the Tarascan word Quanax-Huato, "place of frogs," and they are much in evidence—in stone sculpture, on T-shirts and as souvenir gifts. The nomadic Chichimec people inhabited this region before the Conquest and continued to invade the town long after it was founded in 1570. Decreed a city in 1741 by King Philip V of Spain, for centuries Guanajuato was the wealthiest city in Mexico, its mines producing silver and gold in staggering quantities, enriching both the city and the Spanish Crown. Today, Guanajuato is above all a cultural and university city. The *Festival Cervantino* (▷ 233) is the largest cultural event in the country and an important showcase for alternative and contemporary dramatic arts. Guanajuato's most famous son at present is Mexico's former first non-PRI president, Vicente Fox.

Above *Looking down over the city of Guanajuato, with its church spires and colorful houses*

WHAT TO SEE

JARDÍN DE LA UNIÓN

The city's triangular *zócalo*, the Jardín de la Unión, is dominated by the neoclassical Teatro Juárez (Tue–Sun 9–1.45, 5–7.45 except on performance days), inaugurated in 1903 by Porfírio Díaz, with Doric columns and a sumptuous art nouveau interior—all red velvet, gilt fittings and crystal chandeliers. Next door is the 17th-century Iglesia de San Diego, with a stunning rococo facade. After a huge flood in 1780 the level of the streets was raised and in the gap between the church and the theater you can look down onto the original level of the street, where much of the original church foundations lie. The Iglesia de la Compañía, built in 1734 by the Jesuits, with a stunning, pinkish-gray baroque facade, is behind the *zócalo*. Clear glass in the dome lights up the interior and reveals one of the finest Churrigueresque gilt retablos in the country. Note the unusual red-brick ceiling at the entrance to the church.

On Plaza de la Paz, directly to the east of the Jardín de la Unión, is the yellow and ocher Basílica de Nuestra Señora de Guanajuato, with a dazzling gold interior draped with glass chandeliers and an ornately painted vaulted ceiling and dome. The wooden Virgin, seated among silver and jewels, was given to the city in 1557 by King Philip II of Spain in gratitude for the enormous wealth that was pouring into his country from the city's mines. According to legend, on arrival in Mexico the Virgin was already 800 years old, having survived centuries of Moorish occupation hidden in a cave in Andalucía.

ALHÓNDIGA DE GRANADITAS

The massive Alhóndiga de Granaditas was built originally as a granary, then later turned into a fortress, and is now the most important of Guanajuato's museums, with items from the pre-Columbian and colonial periods. It was the scene of one of the Independence movement's earliest and bloodiest battles. After the Cry of Independence *(El grito)* went up in Dolores Hidalgo, Father Miguel Hidalgo marched on the city, forcing the outnumbered Spanish to retreat into the Alhóndiga. A young miner, Juan José de los Reyes Martínez, known as "El Pípila," volunteered to crawl to the doors, protected from Spanish bullets by a stone slab on his back, and set fire to the entrances. He died in the attempt, and thus began the wanton slaughter of Spanish soldiers and royalist prisoners. Later when Hidalgo was himself caught and executed, along with

TIPS

» Although there is a lot to see in Guanajuato, many of the interesting places are along and around Avenida Juárez and can be visited on foot in a day or two.

» *Las callejóneadas* is a tradition whereby students don black capes and wander down *callejones* (alleyways) singing and drinking flasks of wine. The groups gather daily at 4pm on Jardín de la Unión, and the public can join in.

Below left *Jardín de la Unión is the city's zócalo, a popular meeting place*
Below *Views over the city are wonderful from the monument to El Pípila*

Below *The bearded face of Don Quixote stands out amid the complex carvings on the unusual Cervantes Monument*

three other leaders in Chihuahua, their severed heads were fixed, in revenge, at the four corners of the Alhóndiga, where they remained for 10 years. The hooks are still there on the outside walls.

✉ Avenida Juárez ⏰ Mon–Sat 10–2, 4–8, Sun 10–noon

MUSEO ICONOGRÁFICO DEL QUIJOTE
This small museum consists of a collection of paintings and artworks—including a Picasso drawing and a couple of Salvador Dalí paintings, as well as sculptures, busts, miniatures, medals, pipes and trinkets devoted entirely to Don Quixote (▷ 233).

✉ Calle Manuel Doblado 1 ⏰ Tue–Sat 10–6.30

MUSEO DIEGO RIVERA
Diego Rivera (1886–1957) was born at Calle Pocitos 47, now the Museo Diego Rivera, housing a permanent collection of 90 of his paintings. The Rivera family lived on the ground floor, where the artist's bed and other household objects are displayed. Upstairs, browse a good collection of Rivera's early works. The house also contains some sketches of earlier murals that basically made his reputation as well as paintings from 1902–56. The fourth floor houses a small auditorium for lectures and conferences. It's also where you'll find a large

representation of one of Rivera's most famous murals, *Un Sueno Dominical en la Alameda*.

☒ Calle Pocitos 47 ⊕ Tue–Sat 10–7, Sun 10–3

MUSEO DEL PUEBLO

Opposite the university is the home of the Marqués de San Juan de Rayas, one of the city's notoriously wealthy silver barons. Now displaying an assorted collection of local art, the museum's highlight is the room covered in murals by José Chávez Morado (1909–2002), one of the most important Mexican muralists of the 20th century. Chavez Morado had an obvious eye for the macabre, collecting death portraits, eerie portraits of the living, and religious paintings on the topic of mortality. Also in the museum collection are paintings by Hermenegildo Bustos, a portrait artist of the 19th century. Additionally, there is a small collection of pre-Hispanic artifacts and several folk-art testimonials that are dedicated to the miraculous powers of various saints.

☒ Calle Pocitos 7 ⊕ Tue–Sat, 10–3, Sun 10–3

IGLESIA DE LA VALENCIANA

The splendid Iglesia de La Valenciana (daily 7–7) is 5km (3 miles) out of town on the road to Dolores Hidalgo. Built between 1765 and 1788 for the workers of the Valenciana silver mine, it opened in 1548 and was for hundreds of years the richest church in the world. Behind the elaborate facade carved in pink *cantera* stone, the church is a profusion of Churrigueresque gilt, with three huge gold-painted wooden altarpieces and a wooden pulpit of sinuous design.

About 400m (440 yards) down a dusty path to the left of the church is the mine (daily 9–8), still functioning though on a much reduced scale. Guides are on hand to show you around the workings, nowadays little more than some rusting machinery and decayed buildings. To the left of the church is the Casa del Conde de la Valenciana (▷ 231), a stunning colonial hacienda. Formerly the mining company's headquarters, it is now an attractive craft shop with a pleasant café in the courtyard.

MUSEO EXHACIENDA SAN GABRIEL DE BARRERA

Years ago, more than 150 haciendas of wealthy colonial mine owners surrounded Guanajuato. Today, most are either in ruins or restored and privately owned. But one has been made into the Museo Exhacienda San Gabriel de Barrera. A lovely place known for its elaborate gardens in many styles—Spanish, Moorish, and others—the hacienda gives a good picture of 18th-century life in grand style. The hacienda also has its own chapel. A shop on site showcases all of the many wonderful crafts produced in this area.

☒ About 3km (2 miles) from town on the road to Marfil ✋ $3 ⊕ Wed–Sun 10–5

TEMPLO DE CATA

High above the city, perched on the mountain to the north, is this small "miners' church." Cata is the name of the mine nearby as well and the neighborhood that surrounds the church. A baroque facade, with only one tower standing, decorates the outside. The church's Senor de Villaseca or "El Triguenito" has traditionally been a popular figure in Guanajuato, especially with miners, truckers, and taxi drivers.

☒ Carretera Panoramica ⊕ Daily 9–5 ✋ Free

EL PIPILA

One of the best vantage points in the area for photographs is here, with the city unfolding before you, and terrific views in every direction. The statue is the city's monument to Jose de los Reyes Martinez, better known as El Pipila, legendary hero of the War of Independence.

☒ Above the hill behind the church of San Diego ⊕ Daily 24 hours ✋ Free

Above *Decorative street lamps and palm trees are a feature of this World Heritage Site*

Above *León, with its fountains and statues, is a delightful place to spend a relaxing day*

LEÓN

www.leon-mexico.com

Set in the fertile plain of the Gómez river, León is one of Mexico's fastest-growing cities. Much of the outskirts are taken up by light manufacturing industries and agrobusiness. The good news is that León is the place to pick up top-quality leather goods and shoes at rock-bottom prices; you'll find the best bargains near the bus station.

In the middle of town, the pedestrianized Plaza Fundadores is dominated by the Jesuit-built cathedral, completed in 1837, and the Palacio Municipal, with a fine clock tower said to have been built as a result of a winning lottery ticket bought by a local doctor. Also on the main square is the Casa de Cultura, which hosts contemporary art exhibitions (check notice boards in doorways for current events). Just three blocks away at Madero 721 is the unusual Templo Expiatorio (daily 7am–9pm), a soaring Gothic church begun in 1921 and only finished in 2000. In addition to striking modern stained-glass windows, there is an interesting crypt (Fri–Sun 10–1) at the left-hand side of the main entrance. Farther afield at Boulevard Francisco Villa 202 you will find the Explora Science Museum (▷ 231), with its giant IMAX screen and old steam engines.

✚ 314 J8 ℹ️ Adolfo López Mateos 1511 ☎ (477) 763 44 01 🕐 Mon–Fri 9–7

🚌 Buses from Mexico City, Guanajuato, Querétaro, Aguascalientes ✈️ Del Bajío International airport (also serving Guanajuato), 20km (12 miles)

MALINALCO

Perched above the attractive town of Malinalco are the remarkable partly excavated ruins of the same name. The site (reached by more than 400 steps) is on the Cerro de los Ídolos and, although small, offers spectacular views. The undisputed highlight is the temple carved from a single monolithic rock, thought to have served as a ritual base for the jaguar and eagle orders of the Aztec warrior class. Particularly impressive is the entrance to the temple, which takes the form of a menacing snake. According to legend, Malinalxochtle, sister of the supreme god of the Aztecs, Huitzilopochtli, argued with her brother and left to settle in the area around what is today Malinalco. The Aztecs built the site in 1501, having subdued the Malinalcans in 1476.

Also worth visiting is the Augustinian Templo y Ex-Convento del Divino Salvador (1540), in the middle of town. Behind an attractive plateresque facade and nave with a patterned ceiling, the convent has interesting two-floor cloisters painted with elaborate frescoes. The streets surrounding the church are particularly busy on Wednesday, market day—a good time to pick up locally made breads and fruit liqueurs at the stands in the main square.

✚ 315 L9 🕐 Daily 10–5 💲 $3.90
🚌 Buses from Mexico City

MANZANILLO

www.manzanillo.gob.mx

Spread along the twin bays of Santiago and Manzanillo, the city and working port of Manzanillo enjoys an undeniably picturesque setting. It's a sprawling place, difficult to get around without a car, though the middle has a certain shabby charm, the beaches are attractive and the tropical climate is pleasant all year round. But it is for anglers, above all, that Manzanillo is paradise. This is the swordfish capital of the world, as well as a good place to catch marlin and tuna. Keen golfers will also find first-class facilities (▷ 231).

✚ 313 H9 ℹ️ Boulevard Miguel de la Madrid 1294 ☎ (314) 333 13 80 🕐 Mon–Fri 9–7, Sat 9–2 🚌 Buses from Colima, Guadalajara, Mexico City ✈️ Playa de Oro airport 13km (8 miles) from central Manzanillo

MEXCALTITÁN

According to local folklore, the island of Mexcaltitán ("in the house of the moon" in Nahuatl) is where, in 1091, the Aztecs began their journey south, eventually founding Tenochtitlán in 1325. It is a wonderfully picturesque place, an oval-shaped island sitting in a lagoon measuring 6km (4 miles) by 3km (2 miles). Just 350m (1,150ft) in diameter, the island doesn't take long to wander around; the main building of note is the 19th-century Templo Parroquial del Señor de la Ascensión on the pretty main square. In the rainy season (June to August) many of the streets are flooded and locals paddle around in canoes—hence the epithet "the Venice of Mexico."

✚ 314 G7 ✉️ Santiago Ixcuintla is 65km (40 miles) north of Tepic on Highway 15. From here take a bus or shared taxi to the Batanga quay 45km (28 miles) away 🚤 Boats from Batanga (15 mins)

MORELIA

The attractive city of Morelia, birthplace of Independence hero José María Morelos y Pavón, has a historic heart built of rose-tinted stone. Morelia, capital of Michoacán state, is a city with grand colonial buildings, courtyards and shady plazas. Founded in 1541 and formerly called Vallodolid, it changed its name to Morelia in 1828.

The cathedral, completed in 1744 in sober baroque with a fine facade and two towers said to be the tallest of all Mexico's church towers, is set between the city's two main plazas, the Plaza de Armas and the Plaza Melchor Ocampo. Opposite the cathedral is the Palacio de Gobierno (Mon–Fri 8–5), adorned with murals depicting key episodes in Mexican history. To the east is the most ornate church in the city, Guadalupe (also known as San Diego).

AROUND PALACIO CLAVIJERO

Two blocks west of the cathedral is the Palacio Clavijero, with the Mercado de Dulces y Artesanías (▷ 231) alongside. On the corner of calles Madero and Nigromante is the Colegio de San Nicolás de Hidalgo, the second-oldest institute of higher education in the Americas.

Two blocks north is the tree-lined Jardín de las Rosas, overlooked by the Museo del Estado (Mon–Sat 9–2, 4–8, Sun 9–2), whose eclectic collection includes traditional Tarascan looms, textiles and pottery, a typical Day of the Dead altar (▷ 26), and a reconstructed 19th-century apothecary.

SOUTH OF THE CATHEDRAL

One block from the Plaza de Armas down Calle Abasolo is the Mercado Hidalgo, with scores of local eateries under the arcades. On Calle Corregidora, next to the 16th-century Templo de los Agustinos, is the Casa Natal de Morelos (daily 9–7), where the local Independence hero was born in 1765, the exact spot marked by a plain monument and flag. The house Morelos bought for his sister in 1801 on the corner of calles Morelos Sur and Saldaña is now the Museo Casa de Morelos (daily 9–7). As well as exhibits on the guerilla priest's life, the background to the War of Independence is put in context.

INFORMATION

www.visitmorelia.com
➕ 315 K9 ℹ️ Tato Vasco 80 ☎ (443) 317 80 52 🕐 Mon–Sat 9–6, Sun 10–2 🚌 Buses from Salamanca, Uruapan, Zamora, Mexico City ✈ Airport 27km (17 miles) north

Above *Sunlight shines through windows in the ornately decorated dome of the church of Guadalupe*

PÁTZCUARO

Above Lake Pátzcuaro (▷ 228), the town of Pátzcuaro is one of the most picturesque in Mexico, with narrow cobbled streets and houses with deep overhanging eaves. As well as the attractive main square, highlights include fine murals of local history by Juan O'Gorman in the Biblioteca (daily 8–5) on the Plaza Gertrudis Bocanegra. East from here along Calle La Paz is the Basílica de Nuestra Señora de la Salud (daily 8–4, Sun until 7), containing a much-revered figure of Our Lady of Health. Also worth visiting is the Museo de Artes Populares (Tue–Sat 9–7, Sun 9–3), a regional handicrafts museum on Calle Enseñanza. The island of Janitzio, with its giant statue of Morelos, rises sharply from the middle of Lake Pátzcuaro.

🚩 314 J9 ℹ️ West side of the Plaza Quiroga under Portales Hidalgo ☎ (434) 342 12 14 🕐 Mon–Fri 10–3, variable in afternoon, usually 5–7, Sat–Sun 10–2 🚌 Buses from Mexico City, Morelia, Uruapan

PUERTO VALLARTA

www.visitpuertovallarta.com
Puerto Vallarta is a highly commercialized resort, with all the trappings of any US or European city, including Burger Kings, glitzy nightclubs and chain hotels. On the plus side, the town stretches along the beautiful Banderas Bay, where you can often see dolphins cavorting in the waters. Playa Los Muertos is probably the best beach in town,

but beware the undertow. There is an attractive old core with steep cobbled lanes that rise above the city: here, at Calle Zaragoza 445, film stars Richard Burton and Elizabeth Taylor had their love nest (closed for renovation). There is plenty to do in the surrounding area, from hiking and mountain-biking to watersports.

🚩 314 G8 ℹ️ Presidencia Municipal, corner of Juárez and Independencia ☎ (322) 223 25 00 🕐 Daily 8–9 ✈️ Aeropuerto Internacional Ordaz, 6km (4 miles) north

QUERÉTARO

www.queretaro.travel
The elegant and wealthy city of Querétaro has superb colonial mansions and some of the country's finest ecclesiastical architecture.

This modern industrial city retains a well-preserved historic core with fine plazas linked by narrow, cobbled streets and elegant mansions. Founded in 1531, it served as the site where Father Hidalgo and his fellow conspirators plotted their 1810 rising. On discovering that the Corregidor (Mayor) had learned of their intentions, his wife, Doña Josefa Ortiz de Dominguez, now known as La Corregidora, got word to Hidalgo, despite being locked up in a room by her husband. Hidalgo immediately gave the cry "El grito" (for Independence). It was here, too, that Emperor Maximilian surrendered after defeat, was tried and then shot on June 19 1867, on the Cerro de las Campanas (the Hill of Bells), west of the city.

Queretero's main square is the Jardín Zénea, dominated by the Iglesia de San Francisco. The adjoining monastery houses the Museo Regional (Tue–Sun 10–6), with exhibits on the Independence movement and objects relating to the imprisonment and death of Emperor Maximilian. To the southeast is the smaller Jardín Corregidora, surrounded by cafés. The 16th-century Convento de la Santa Cruz (Tue–Sun 10–2, 4–6), on

Left Sunset at Puerto Vallarta

Calle Independencia, was founded by the Franciscans in 1683. In 1867, during the final weeks of his reign, Emperor Maximilian was imprisoned here. Guided tours take you to the árbol de la cruz, a tree whose thorns grow in the shape of a cross. There are lovely views of the 18th-century aqueduct from behind the convent. The Teatro de la República, on Calle Hidalgo, is where Maximilian and his generals were tried, and where the Constitution of 1917 was drafted.

🚩 315 K8 ℹ️ Plaza de Armas ☎ (442) 238 5073 🕐 Mon–Fri 9–4 🚌 Main bus station 6km (4 miles) southeast of central Querétaro. Buses from Mexico City

QUIROGA

The inhabitants of Quiroga voted in 1852 to rename their town (then called Cocupao) after Bishop Vasco de Quiroga, who was responsible for most of the Spanish building in the area and for teaching the Purépecha people the various crafts they still practice: work in wool, leather, copper, ceramics, and cane. The chief reason to visit is the craft market, at its best on Sunday when locals from the surrounding villages sell their wares.

🚩 314 J9 🚌 Buses from Pátzcuaro, Guadalajara, Morelia

RESERVA ECOLOGICA EL CAMPANARIO

This ecological reserve above the village of El Rosario is the gateway to one of the natural wonders of the world: the wintering ground of the monarch butterfly (▷ 18). The best time to visit is January and February, when huge clusters of them hang from branches. When warm air blows through the reserve they rise en masse in swirling red clouds. The reserve is at a high altitude and you will need to walk a few kilometers to see the butterflies. Warm clothes and sensible shoes are essential.

🚩 315 K9 🕐 Daily 9–6 💵 $4, plus tip for compulsory guide 🚌 Buses from Zitácuaro to Ocampo, then local bus to reserve (15-min walk) ℹ️ Angangueo and Zitácuaro cater to butterfly-watchers. Alternatively, arrange transport from Mexico City (4 hours away)

SAN MIGUEL DE ALLENDE

This colonial gem on a steep hillside facing the broad sweep of the Río Laja has numerous boutiques, restaurants and an active cultural scene—thanks to its expatriate community. Known simply as San Miguel until 1826, when the town was renamed in memory of the Independence hero born here, San Miguel de Allende is a wonderfully picturesque town of colonial mansions, pretty patios and cobbled lanes. It also has a large non-Mexican community, due partly to the art school established here in the 1930s by US artist Stirling Dickinson. In summer, the town buzzes with students studying at the many Spanish-language schools.

JARDÍN PRINCIPAL

Social life revolves around the Jardín Principal. Around it are the colonial Palacio Municipal (1736) and on the south side the striking Parroquía (daily 6am–9pm), whose neo-Gothic facade was added in the late 19th century. On the corner of Calle Allende and Calle Umaran is the Casa de Don Ignacio de Allende (Tue–Sun 9–5), a small museum focusing on Allende's role in the Independence movement.

AROUND TOWN

Five minutes' walk to the north through cobbled streets is the Plaza Cívica, in the middle of which stands a fine monument to General Ignacio Allende. A couple of blocks farther is the good crafts market (daily 11–6). West of the main square lies the Centro Cultural "El Nigromante," also known as the Escuela de Bellas Artes (Tue–Sat 10–5.30, Sun 10–2). It houses excellent temporary exhibitions along with murals by David Alfaro Siqueiros.

Heading south down Calle San Antonio is the Instituto Allende, once a Carmelite convent and private residence of the impressively named Don Tomás de la Canal y Bueno de Baeza, and now a cultural center offering language classes, tours and summer courses, from jewelry-making to art therapy. It is also a good source of information on homestays and apartments or rooms for rent. One steep block up from the shady Parque Juárez at the southern end of town is El Chorro, the site of the original spring upon which the town was founded, and where you can see pretty outdoor washing tubs still used today.

INFORMATION

www.turismosanmiguel.com

➕ 315 K8 ℹ️ Plaza Principal, next to the church ☎ (415) 152 09 00
🕐 Mon–Fri 8.30–8, Sat 10–8, Sun 10–5.30 🚌 Buses from Guanajuato, Querétaro ✈ Aeropuerto del Bajío at Silao near León, 56km (35 miles) southwest

Above *The neo-Gothic Parroquía*
Below *Locally made basketware for sale in the town*

Above *The ceiling of San Luis Potosí's Capilla de Aranzazú*

SAN BLAS

This old colonial port is a holiday resort, popular with surfers attracted by the legend of the world's longest surfable wave (1.7km/1 mile) which hits this coast between May and October. The town's past is reflected in the old customs house, now a cultural center (Tue–Sun 11–6), toward the waterfront.

On the hill overlooking San Blas are the ruins of the Contaduría (daily 10–4), together with the Iglesia de la Marinera. Both are worth visiting for the good views—but beware the mosquitoes.

Since Hurricane Kena hit in 2002 authorities have done much to improve facilities, especially at El Borrego beach. The best beaches, however, are outside town: Playa Los Cocos, 16km (10 miles) to the south, is the most beautiful, and is deserted during the week.

Local agencies organize ecotourism trips and also rent out surfboards (▷ 232).

➕ 314 G8 ℹ️ Casa del Gobierno, Zócalo ☎ (323) 285 02 21 🕐 Mon–Fri 9–3 🚌 Buses from Guadalajara, Tepic, Puerto Vallarta

SAN LUIS POTOSÍ

www.slp.gob.mx

Originally founded in 1592 as a Franciscan mission, San Luis developed into a rich mining town after the Spanish discovered deposits of gold and silver in the surrounding hills. Despite the city's largely industrial sprawl, the historic heart retains its colonial charm: pedestrianized cobbled streets interspersed with church domes and tiled mansions are set around the stately Jardín Hidalgo, dominated by the cathedral, whose exterior is crafted from pink *cantera* stone and flanked by ornately carved bell towers. Opposite is the Palacio de Gobierno, which Benito Juárez occupied in 1863 when San Luis became his temporary capital. The most beautiful of the city's churches is the Templo del Carmen on the square of the same name, with its vivid tiled dome, fine pulpit and striking gold-leaf retablos. Behind the palms and fountain of the lovely Plaza San Francisco is the Museo Regional Potosino (Tue–Sat 10–7, Sun 10–5), with an excellent collection of pre-Hispanic items, mainly from the Huastec culture. On the upper floor is the magnificent baroque Capilla de Aranzazú, executed in a flourish of Churrigueresque.

The recently renovated Museo de la Máscara, at Calle Villerías 2 has reputedly the most diverse collection of masks in Mexico, some dating from pre-Hispanic times (Tue–Fri 10–2, 5–7).

➕ 315 K7 ℹ️ Palacio Municipal, Jidalgo 5, half a block west of Plaza de los Fundadores ☎ (444) 812 27 70 🕐 Mon–Fri 8–8, Sat 10–8 🚌 Buses from Tampico, Mexico City, León, Zacatecas

TAPALPA

Tapalpa, a pretty village popular as a weekend retreat, is on a winding road that offers spectacular views. At over 2,000m (6,560ft) above sea level and set amid attractive pine forests, it has something of an alpine feel to it and is frequented by extreme-sports enthusiasts, in particular hang-gliders. Cobbled lanes, fountains and ornamental lamps in the colonnades make Tapalpa an appealing place to wander around. Look for the Templo de la Merced (Tue–Sun 10–4) and its restored gold-leaf retablo.

On Sundays there is a lively local market held around the Jardín Principal. The local brew, called *Ponche*, is made out of seasonal fruits including guava, pomegranate or tamarind with cinnamon sticks and a shot of alcoholic spirit, usually *mezcal*, and can be a boon on chilly evenings.

➕ 314 H8 🚌 Buses from Guadalajara

TEPIC

Capital of Nayarit state, Tepic was founded in 1531 at the foot of the extinct volcano of Sangagüey. The Plaza Principal is dominated by the cathedral (daily 8–1, 3–7), with two fine Gothic towers and a wedding-cake interior decorated in creamy primrose and gold. Outside during the day numerous stands sell Huichol crafts, including bags (carried only by men) and bright beadwork. Five blocks north along Avenida México is the Plaza Constituyentes, overlooked by the handsome pink Palacio de Gobierno adorned with two unusual corner towers. The Museo Regional (Mon–Fri 9–6, Sat 9–3) on Avenida Mexico is worth a look for its collection of Toltec objects and Huichol crafts. The Casa de Amado Nervo at Calle Zacatecas Norte 281 (Mon–Fri 10–2, Sat 10–2) has an exhibition dedicated to Nervo (1870–1919), the local-born Modernist poet.

➕ 313 H8 ℹ️ Avenida México ☎ (311) 214 80 71 🕐 Daily 8–8 🚌 Buses from San Blas, Guadalajara

TEPOTZOTLÁN

In the town of Tepotzotlán (not to be confused with Tepoztlán near Cuernavaca), just off the road to Querétaro, is the splendid former Jesuit church and convent of San Francisco Javier, which houses the Museo Nacional del Virreinato (Tue–Sun 9–6). As well as a striking Churrigueresque facade, the church interior, with its five gold-leaf retablos, is breathtaking. The Camarín de la Virgen is a veritable feast for the eyes—an octagonal chamber bedecked with highly elaborate floor-to-ceiling baroque carvings. The convent, built around attractive patios and backing onto a lovely walled garden, is something of an anticlimax by comparison, but comes to life just before Christmas, when Nativity plays are performed.

➕ 315 L9 🚍 Buses from Mexico City

TEQUILA

www.tequilaexpress.com.mx

Approaching Tequila you will see field upon field of blue agave, the raw material used to make the famous Mexican drink. In pre-Conquest times, the Indians used the agave sap to brew a mildly alcoholic drink, *pulque*, still drunk today. The Spaniards, wanting something more refined and stronger, developed *mezcal* and set up distilleries to produce what later became tequila. The first of these was established in 1795 by royal decree and is still in existence today: La Rojena, the distillery of José Cuervo, at the end of Sixto Gorjón. A tour includes a video on the history of the drink and the firm, a look at the tequila-making process, a tasting and an opportunity to visit the shop (hour-long tours Sun–Fri every hour 10–4, Sat 10–6). Tequila Sauza, dating from 1873 and found on the main square, runs hour-long tours (Sun–Fri 11, 12.30 and 4, Sat 11 and 12.30). Also worth a visit is the Museo Nacional de Tequila (Tue–Sun 10–5),

illustrating the history and evolution of both town and drink.

➕ 314 H8 ℹ️ Booth in front of Iglesia de Purísima Concepción 🕐 Daily 11–7 🚍 Buses from Guadalajara 🚉 Tequila Express

TEQUISQUIAPAN

This picturesque town, in the southwest of Querétaro state, is at the geographical midpoint of the country. Its other claim to fame is as a center for thermal baths, making it a popular vacation destination with Mexican families. Bathing can be arranged by your hotel or by local tour agencies (▷ 232). The central Plaza Cívica is surrounded by colonnades and dominated by the neoclassical Parroquía de Santa María. Local crafts including basketware and pottery are for sale at the market at Calle Ezequiel Montes and Calle Carrizal.

➕ 315 K8 ℹ️ Plaza Principal ☎ (414) 273 02 95 🕐 Mon–Fri 9–3, 5–7, Sat–Sun 10–8 🚍 Bus station 4km (2.5 miles) from middle of town. Buses from San Juan del Río, Querétaro

TOLUCA

At 2,680m (8,793ft), Toluca is the highest city in Mexico and capital of the state of the same name. Named after the god Toltzin, meaning "he

who leans his head" in Nahuatl, Toluca is nowadays an industrial powerhouse whose outskirts dwarf its colonial heart. The spacious Plaza de los Mártires is at the city's heart, overlooked by the somewhat gloomy Palacio Nacional and the enormous cathedral, begun in 1870 but not finished until 1978. Next door is the Iglesia de Veracruz (Tue–Sat 9–2, 4–7, Sun 8–5), which houses a black Christ. Northeast of the main square lies the Plaza Garibay, whose highlight is the splendid Jardín Botánico Cosmovitral (Tue–Sun 9–5), a former market that in 1980 was reopened as a botanical garden. If possible, visit on a sunny day when the light is streaming through the stained-glass windows. Toluca's real claim to fame, however, is its Friday market, said to be the biggest in the country. Unfortunately, it's increasingly being taken over by cheap junk, but it still attracts crowds from Mexico City. The market takes place around the bus station.

➕ 315 K9 ℹ️ Calle Urawa 100, Puerta 110, Col. Izcalli ☎ (722) 219 19 51 🚍 Buses from Mexico City, Guadalajara

Below left and right *Pottery frog for sale at Tequisquiapan's market, near the Parroquía de Santa María*

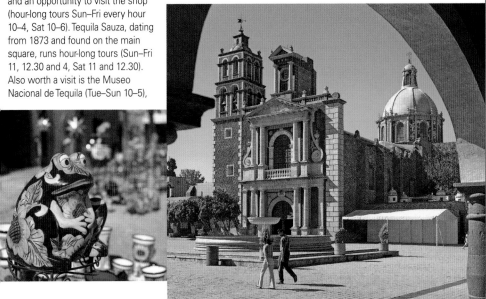

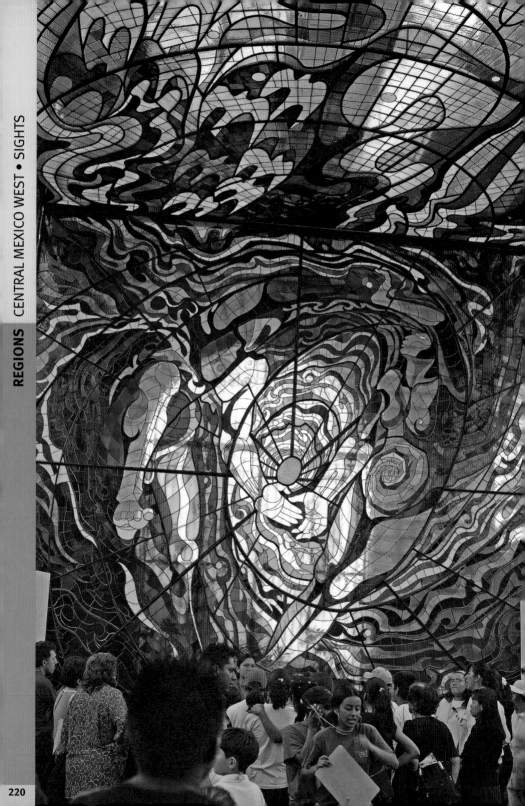

TULA DE ALLENDE

A half-day excursion from Mexico City can be made easily to Tula de Allende, thought to be the most important Toltec site in Mexico, whose apogee was between AD900 and 1200. The site covers 17sq km (6.5sq miles), but the most interesting parts are in a compact area. There are two ball courts, several pyramids in varying states of disrepair and some interesting friezes. What has made Tula famous, however, are the four huge *Atlantes*—5m-high (16ft) warrior-pillars in black basalt—on top of the main pyramid. Note the butterfly emblem on the warriors' chests—Toltec warriors venerated Izpapalotl, the obsidian butterfly, as their protector in battle. These figures would have originally supported a roof above the pyramid. Around the bottom of this pyramid, under a corrugated plastic shelter, are impressive friezes of skulls being devoured by a rattlesnake. There are good views from the site, and the *Atlantes* look their best in the late afternoon sunshine.

🚻 315 L8 ✉ 84km (52 miles) northwest of Mexico City 🕐 Daily 9–5 💵 $3.90, half-price for ISIC holders; $3.50 extra for video cameras 🚌 Buses from Mexico City, Querétaro, Guanajuato, León

URUAPAN

Uruapan means "place where flowers are beautiful" in Purepecha. Nowadays the thriving agricultural economy around town is avocados, and Uruapan is known as the "world capital of the avocado." Its reputation for handmade lacquerwork has also put it on the map (▷ 232). The attractive *zócalo* is at the heart of town, and on its east side is Uruapan's oldest building, the, arcaded Huatápera. This former hospital, built by town founder Fray Juan de San Miguel in the 16th century, is now the Museo Regional de Arte Popular (Tue–Sun 9.30–1.30, 3.30–6) and a good place to visit before you purchase lacquerware. To the left of the Huatápera is the Casa de la Cultura (Mon–Sun 9–8),

which houses temporary exhibitions, as well as a good display on the history of Uruapan. Behind here is the bustling Mercado de Antojitos, with numerous food stands selling local delicacies such as tamarind atole, a thick sweet warming drink, or *uchepos*, steamed pancakes served with pork and tomato. Four blocks west of the *zócalo* up Calle Independencia is the entrance to the Parque Nacional (daily 8–6), an attractive park with many paths, streams and waterfalls.

🚻 314 J9 ℹ Carranza 20 ☎ (452) 524 06 67 🕐 Daily 9–7 🚌 Buses from Pátzcuaro, Angahuan, Morelia

VALLE DE BRAVO

The resort of Valle de Bravo, on a branch road of Highway 134, is a charming old town on the edge of an attractive artificial lake. Set in a mountainous area with a temperate climate, it receives many weekenders from the capital who own second homes in the area. This weekend influx means that the town has some excellent restaurants and swanky boutiques—although many are closed during the week. The outdoor eateries on Callejón El Arco are testament to the town's

unpretentiousness, and the yellow and cream buildings, red-tiled roofs and cobbled streets make for a charming atmosphere. On the lake you can canoe, sail and fish.

🚻 315 K9 🚌 Buses from Toluca, Mexico City, Zitácuaro

VOLCÁN PARICUTÍN

Rarely do volcanologists get to watch the birth, growth and death of a volcano, but the Volcán Paricutín provided such an opportunity. It started erupting on February 20 1943, spewed lava for almost three years, then died down by 1952 into a quiet, gray mountain (460m/1,510ft), surrounded by a sea of cold lava. The church tower of San Juan Parangaricútiro, a buried Indian village thrusting up through the lava, is a truly fantastic sight. It can be reached on an organized tour from the little village of Angahuan, with horses and guide included.

🚻 314 J9 🚌 Buses from Uruapan .

Above *Gigantic Toltec* Atlantes *figures at Tula de Allende*
Opposite *Stained-glass ceiling at Jardín Botánico Cosmovitral, Toluca*

Above *Mural in the Palacio de Gobierno*

INFORMATION

www.turismozacatecas.gob.mx
314 J7 Avenida Hidalgo 403, 2nd floor (492) 922 67 51 Mon–Fri 8–8, Sat–Sun 10–6 Buses from Ciudad Juárez, Tijuana, Saltillo, and Mexico City via Aguascalientes, Leon and Querétaro Aeropuerto La Calera, 27km (17 miles) north

INTRODUCTION

Built on the fabulous wealth of its silver mines, Zacatecas is a delightful and uncommercialized colonial city. The cathedral, with its sublime facade, is one of the most extraordinary examples of Mexican baroque. Zacatecas sits in the middle of a rugged wilderness of *nopal* cacti and scrub 610km (380 miles) north of Mexico City. But the city is anything but frontierlike. Its colonial core is remarkably compact and its principal attractions are easy to see on foot. Avenida Hidalgo is the main street, running north–south, either side of which you'll find almost everything of interest. Cerro de la Bufa, overlooking the town, is helpfully linked to the middle of town by a Swiss-built cable car.

The name Zacatecas means "the place rich in long grass" in Nahuatl. The area was also rich in silver, and the fabulous deposits found by the Spanish quickly led to the city's official founding in 1546. The city prospered during the colonial era and by the beginning of the 17th century was producing a fifth of the world's silver supplies.

After Independence, with silver production on the wane, Zacatecas sought greater local autonomy, putting the state into conflict with the federal government. In 1835 a local militia was routed by General Santa Anna's forces in nearby Guadalupe. Santa Anna separated the city of Aguascalientes from Zacatecas, depriving the state of rich agricultural terrain and sowing seeds of bitterness that still exist today. In 1914, during the Revolution, Zacatecas was the stage for a key battle between the irregular forces of Pancho Villa and the troops of usurper president Victoriano Huerta, ending in an unlikely victory for Villa.

WHAT TO SEE

AROUND THE CATHEDRAL

The city's spectacular pink-tinted Catedral Basílica Menor (1730–52), with its detailed baroque facade, dominates the Plaza de Armas. This is flanked by the 18th-century Palacio de Gobierno, with a modern mural (1970) by Antonio Pintor Rodríguez showing the history of Zacatecas. Opposite, on Avenida Hidalgo, is the Casa de la Mala Noche (House of the Bad Night). According to legend, its owner, Manuel de Rétegui, was a near-bankrupt mine owner who spent his last *peso* to feed a beggar. He passed a sleepless night (hence the name), only to be roused from his gloom by his foreman, who had come to tell his boss of a miraculous discovery of a rich vein of silver, making them millionaires overnight. South of the cathedral is the handsome 19th-century arcaded Mercado González Ortega (▷ 233). Its south side opens onto the stepped Plazuela Goitia, overlooked by the Teatro Calderón, where young Zacatecanos rendezvous in the evenings.

MUSEUMS OF THE CORONEL BROTHERS

Pedro (1921–1985) and Rafael (born 1933) Coronel, two locally born brothers, both collectors and artists in their own right, each have an excellent museum housing their collections. The Museo Pedro Coronel (Fri–Wed 10–4.30), on Plaza Santo Domingo, one block north of the cathedral, has a remarkable collection of European and modern art, including works by Goya, Hogarth, Miró, Tàpies, and Picasso, as well as folk art from Mexico and around the world (take a guide to make the most of the collections). The Museo Rafael Coronel (Thu–Tue 10–4.30), in the ex-Convento de San Francisco, has a vast collection of masks and puppets, as well as an attractive garden.

CERRO DE LA BUFA

Meaning "pig bladder" in Spanish Aragonese, La Bufa is a rocky crag that dominates the city, giving breathtaking views for miles around. Here you will find three gigantic revolutionary statues, the most famous being a burly Pancho Villa astride his horse. The Museo Toma de Zacatecas (Museum of the Taking of Zacatecas; Tue–Sun 10–5) has relics of the battle that took place here in 1914. Next door is a pretty church, El Santuario de la Virgen del Patrocinio, dedicated to the city's patron. Directly behind is the station for the cable car or *teleférico* (daily 10–6; cancelled when windy).

MINA EL EDÉN

The El Edén mine makes for an interesting visit, whether you see it on a guided tour by day or as a chance to dance the night away in the mine's nightclub (▷ 233). To reach the mine, take Avenida Hidalgo south, turn right on Avenida Juárez, and continue along the left side of the tree-lined Calle Alameda until you reach the enormous yellow IMSS hospital. The mine entrance is just behind here. Whichever way you see it, you'll take a train 500m (1,640ft) into the heart of a mine where work first began in 1586, finally ending in 1960. The guided tour proceeds on foot for another 320m (1,050ft), passing hanging bridges, tortuously narrow tunnels and an altar to the Santo Niño de Atocha, emerging an hour later at the cable-car station for the trip up to La Bufa. Take warm clothing as it gets pretty chilly down there.

✉ Antonio Dovali, off Avenida Torreón 🕐 Daily 10–6

SHOPPING

Delightful Zacatecan handicrafts include silver jewelry, intricate leatherwork, and stone-carving. Wonderful examples can be found in shops inside the old Mercado Gonzalez Ortega on Hidalgo, next to the cathedral. There are also quite a few silver jewelry shops in the center of town. Huichol Indians sometimes sell their crafts around the Plaza Independencia as well.

TIP

» The city orchestra gives free concerts every Thursday at 6pm in the Plazuela Goitia. Farther down Avenida Hidalgo you'll find a weekend book market under the arcades.

Above *The twin towers of the pink stone baroque cathedral*

Below *The teleférico, traveling up the Cerro de la Bufa*

THE MISSIONS OF THE SIERRA GORDA

The drive to and over the Sierra Gorda is spectacular, crawling over big-country scenery to reach the five missions founded by Fray Junípero Serra in the 18th century. En route the huge Bernal monolithic outcrop provides a useful break in a long, dramatic and enjoyable drive known as the route of 700 curves.

THE DRIVE

Distance: 540km (335 miles)
Time: 2–3 days
Start/end at: Querétaro
Note: The road is in good condition and the journey is safe.

★ Leave Querétaro (▷ 216) on Highway 57, heading south. At Km 15 look for the sign and road feeding off on the left to Peña de Bernal. At Km 36 the monolithic outcrop of Bernal appears.

❶ Bernal is the third-largest outcrop of its type in the world after Sugar Loaf Mountain in Brazil and the Rock of Gibraltar in southern Europe. It's worth a stop to wander around the pleasant colonial heart of the town and to scramble on the lower slopes of the rock.

Back on the road, the curves begin gently at first, increasing as the road climbs through the first of many passes to reveal a spectacular view of the flats of San Pablo below. At Km 56 a fuel station marks the road off to the right to Jalpan. Climbing out of the valley, you can see the spectacular silhouette of Bernal in the distance. There's a viewpoint with a parking spot after Km 62 and again at Km 63.

Again the road sneaks through a pass, opening up to reveal the small village of Higuerillas below. Shortly after the roads from San Juan del Río (Highway 120) and Bernal merge there is a police checkpoint. There is nothing to worry about if you're polite and explain your plans *(Voy/Vamos a ver los misiones*—I/We're going to see the missions).

The road continues to rise and fall with the dramatic desert landscape, picking a route through the scrubby cactus and passing isolated buildings such as the Puerta del Cielo (Gateway to Heaven). As it climbs, it inches toward the bulbous massif of the Sierra Gorda. Soon after Cuesta Colorada, Bernal is visible again on the horizon. By Maguey Verde, trees have replaced the cactus because the higher altitude brings lower temperatures and with them, increased moisture.

The road clings to the mountainside as it drops through the maze of valleys, passing through small towns and villages, including Pinal de Amoles and Ahuacatlán, before finally arriving in Jalpan at around Km 175.

② This may be a good opportunity to stop for the night. The Jalpan mission was the first to be built by Fray Junípero Serra, and served as the model for the four other missions in the region. It dates from 1751 to 1758 and is considered to be one of the best examples of baroque architecture in the New World.

From Jalpan head northwest to Concá along Highway 69—the intersection marked by the Mexican flag. The route rides the contours of the broad valley, eventually crossing and climbing the valley of the Río Santa Maria. Gentle hills fringe this valley, hiding the harsh desert landscape to the west. Turn left at Km 35 next to Restaurant La Palapa. At the end of the cobbled drive, continue for one block and turn right, following the road until you arrive at the Misión de Concá.

③ Misión de Concá is simpler and less ornate than the mission at Jalpan; in fact it is the smallest church in the Sierra Gorda. There are images of maize and vegetables above the entrance.

Returning along the same route to Jalpan, turn left at the Mexican flag onto Highway 120; from here, it's 22km (13.5 miles) to Misión de Landa de Matamoros. It's a gentle climb to the pass, with a fairly quick drop immediately after to the town and a signposted turn to the left.

④ Misión de Landa de Matamoros was the last of the missions to be built and is the best preserved. It

has a small community museum with items that demonstrate the use of agriculture in the region. Carved saints decorate the elaborate facade.

Head out of the village the way you came. After 10.5km (6.5 miles) is La Lagunita. Here take the right turn to Misión de Tilaco.

⑤ Above the wide door of the Misión de Tilaco there are sculptures of St. Joseph and the Virgin, with angels above flying toward a garden.

The road heads west, climbing to reveal the plateau of Tilaco below, 16km (10 miles) from La Lagunita. Head back to Highway 120 and turn right. In 4km (2.5 miles) you'll reach the left turn to Misión de Tancoyol.

⑥ Although all five missions share the same style, Misión de Tancoyol, dedicated to Our Lady of the Light, is the simplest of the designs.

The return journey is less complex. Follow Highway 120 for 220km (136 miles), at which point it joins Highway 57. Continue on this road back to Querétaro.

TOURIST INFORMATION
✉ Plaza de Armas, Querétaro ☎ (442) 238 50 73 🕐 Mon–Fri 9–4

Above *Misión de Landa de Matamoros*
Opposite *The intricate facade of the Misión de Tilaco*

WHERE TO EAT
There are several good hotels with restaurants in Bernal and around the main plaza in Jalpan, and along Highway 120 on the way back to Querétaro.

WHERE TO STAY
HACIENDA MISIÓN CONCÁ
✉ Highway 69, 1km (half a mile) south of the turn-off for the mission
☎ (441) 296 02 55

HACIENDA MISIÓN JALPAN
✉ Downtown Jalpan ☎ (441) 296 02 55

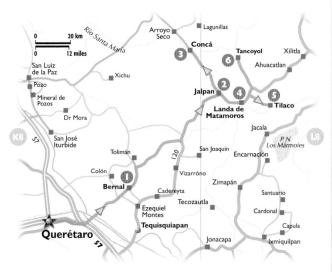

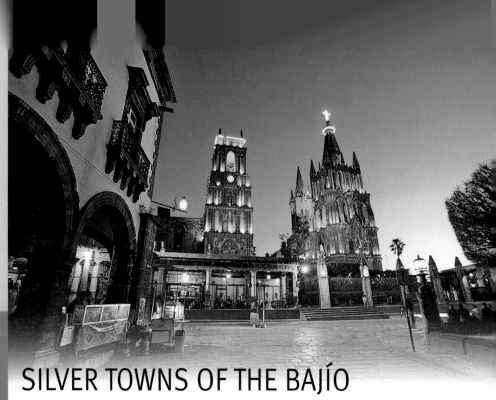

SILVER TOWNS OF THE BAJÍO

This easy drive passes through pleasant scenery, visiting some colonial jewels of the historic Bajío region.

THE DRIVE

Distance: Approximately 135km (84 miles)
Time: 1–2 days. An easy one-day trip, but make it two if you want more time to sightsee in San Miguel de Allende
Start/end at: Guanajuato

★ Guanajuato (▷ 210–213) is the best place to start and end a driving tour of the Bajío. Once you are familiar with the town's warren-like tunnels, it's an entertaining city to drive around, but parking is difficult. Head out of town through the Túnel Santa Fé under Cason del Quijo. At the first traffic circle (roundabout) take the turn almost straight ahead, marked La Valenciana. At the second traffic circle turn right. Climb out of Guanajuato, twisting past San Javier (to your right), to reach the Iglesia de la Valenciana.

❶ The Iglesia de La Valenciana, the splendid Churrigueresque church in Valenciana (▷ 213), was built for the workers of the nearby mine, once the richest in the world. A short distance down the hill the Hacienda del Cochera draws in passing visitors with the Museo de las Momias—a rather morbid display of mummies in positions of torture.

Continue climbing out of the valley of Guanajuato, the road twisting and turning to Santa Rosa.

❷ At Santa Rosa you can stop for a drink or breakfast and enjoy the splendid view across the forest.

The road continues to climb out of the valley, eventually reaching the open plains before hitting the outer suburbs of Dolores Hidalgo. At Km 39 turn left at the traffic circle, heading north into the middle of Dolores Hidalgo. After the bridge, take the fourth right turn, Calle

Ithacan, marked by a collection of blue signs saying, among other things, Centro Historical. Continue straight ahead for several blocks and on reaching the Plaza Principal pull up. There is a small parking charge.

❸ Dolores Hidalgo (▷ 207) is the home of the Mexican Independence movement, where the local priest Miguel Hidalgo rang the church bells issuing the famous call to arms, *El Grito* (The Cry), on September 16 1810. The revolt failed, Hidalgo was executed and Mexico waited a further 11 years to achieve independence from Spain.

Leave the plaza and return to the traffic circle—as you drive back up the road you'll pass many ceramics stores selling all manner of items from the appalling to the offensive. There are, however, some fine items among the junk, including Talavera tiles. Head straight on for about 3km (2 miles), turning left to San Miguel de Allende. Go straight across at the first intersection, then take the right fork at Km 10.7, marked San Miguel de Allende. The road drops into the town on Calle Hidalgo. Look for the road names—once you've reached Avenida Insurgentes you're a couple of blocks from the plaza so look for a parking spot.

❹ San Miguel de Allende (▷ 217) is a colonial town with cobbled streets and fine old mansion houses. It makes a convenient base for exploring the temples and churches of the region, and also has several good restaurants, so take your pick and stop for lunch before exploring the plaza. If you are staying overnight in San Miguel, park carefully and watch for time limits. Ask at your hotel.

Leave San Miguel de Allende where Calle Hidalgo meets the Plaza Allende and turn right, then take the second left down Avenida Zacatecas.

Take the right turn for Guanajuato from the plaza in San Miguel.

❺ Passing by the southern shoreline of Presa Ignacio Allende (dam), the road winds through cactus and grassy scrubland, with the lumpy massif of the hills around and Guanajuato appearing in the distant west.

At Km 37 turn right toward Guanajuato and León, and follow the road to Guanajuato. At the first traffic circle, marked Guanajuato Centro, go straight through. Peel off right at Km 72.6, with a sign for Guanajuato, and you will soon enter a short tunnel, then another at Km 74.2, followed by a stretch of speed humps. From here on *ayudantes* (helpers) appear at the side of the street offering parking and other services. A feeder lane comes in from the left; move to the left lane marked Guadalajara Centro. The road is cobbled from here onward as you pass over one traffic circle with a statue of miners and another (barely

noticeable) one. Move across to the middle lane and go straight ahead at the traffic circle before bearing right and heading into the tunnels of Guanajuato.

TOURIST INFORMATION

✉ Plaza de la Paz 14, Guanajuato
☎ (473) 732 19 82 🕓 Mon–Fri 9–7.30, Sat 10–5, Sun 10–2

WHERE TO EAT
CIAO BELLA
▷ 234.

MESÓN DE SAN JOSÉ
A secret spot hidden in a small courtyard of cobbled stone, with a good mix of *enchiladas* and *quesadillas*, blended with international dishes, and a children's menu. There's something to suit everyone's taste.
✉ Calle Mesones between Colegio and Presa, San Miguel de Allende 🕓 Daily 8am–10pm

Opposite *Night-time view of San Miguel de Allende's cathedral*
Left *Templo de San Cayetano towers behind La Valenciana mine*
Below *Dolores Hidalgo is renowned for its colorful pottery*

AROUND LAGO DE PÁTZCUARO

This drive takes you around Lake Pátzcuaro, through the Tarascan Indian villages on its shores, where the way of life has hardly changed.

THE DRIVE
Distance: 99km (61 miles)
Time: 8 hours
Start/end at: Pátzcuaro

★ Begin the drive at the northern edge of Pátzcuaro (▷ 216). Turn north on Highway 14 at the signs to Quiroga. After passing several small roadside handicraft stands and motels, the road climbs a small hill to a lookout point with a view of the lake. After 11km (7 miles) a sign appears on the east side of the road for the turn-off to the archaeological site of Tzintzuntzán.

❶ The cluster of restored structures at Tzintzuntzán, the first capital of the Purépecha Empire, includes an unusual round temple and five pyramid-shaped temples. About 40,000 Purépecha lived around the lake when the Spaniards arrived in the 16th century.

The road continues through the town.

❷ In the town of Tzintzuntzán, a daily market (at its busiest from Friday to Sunday) sprawls along the west side of the road in front of a 16th-century restored Franciscan monastery; pilgrims often shuffle on their knees to reach the church. Woodcarvers work in shops and stands on the east side of the road. Local crafts include making straw ornaments and producing green-and-blue ceramics.

From Tzintzuntzán the road continues for 7km (4 miles) past lake views, churches and rural homes to Quiroga (▷ 216).

❸ An important commercial and ceremonial base since pre-Hispanic times, Quiroga is known for its plaza lined with stands selling delicious local delicacies, including fragrant *carnitas* (roasted pork). Visitors stop here for *carnitas tacos*, bowls of *pozole* (hominy stew) and *menudo* (tripe soup).

Head west from Quiroga for 8.5km (5 miles), following signs south to Parque Chupícuaro.

❹ Wooded Parque Chupícuaro is on the edge of Lake Pátzcuaro. The park has lavatories and picnic tables, and is popular with families who picnic on food they've picked up in Quiroga.

Continue for 26km (16 miles) southwest of the park towards Erongarícuaro.

❺ This small lakeside town, formerly important for textiles, is known for its woodworkers. Families linger all day at Campestre Alemán, just south of town, where the restaurant fronts a lake stocked with trout, and offers boat rentals. Apple and pear trees provide shade.

About 2 miles (3km) south of Erongarícuaro is Tocuaro.

❻ This tiny town is home to several excellent mask-makers, many of whom will open their studios to visitors. Among the best artists is Gustavo Horta, whose gallery is called Puerta del Sol. It's on the north side of the main street near the entrance to town; no phone.

Continue southeast for 14km (8.5 miles) to the outskirts of Pátzcuaro to complete the drive. If you wish to extend the drive, turn south at the intersection with Highway 41, which becomes Highway 120 about 10km (6 miles) south of Pátzcuaro, to reach Santa Clara del Cobre.

⑦ The streets of Santa Clara del Cobre town are lined with shops. At the Museo del Cobre, workmen pound out patterns on flaming hot sheets of copper beside large fires.

Return to Pátzcuaro by driving north on Highway 120 for 24km (15 miles).

WHEN TO GO
If you intend visiting Pátzcuaro during the Day of the Dead celebrations (Nov 1–2), reserve accommodations well in advance.

TOURIST INFORMATION
✉ Calle Buenavista 7, Pátzcuaro ☎ (434) 342 12 14 🕐 Mon–Fri 9–3, 5–7, Sat 10–1

PLACES TO VISIT
MUSEO DEL COBRE
✉ Calle Morelos at Piño Suárez 🕐 Tue–Sun 10–3, 5–7 💵 $3

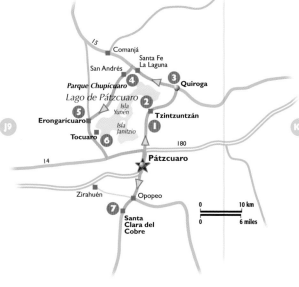

TZINTZUNTZÁN ARCHAEOLOGICAL SITE
🕐 Daily 9–6 💵 $4.50

WHERE TO EAT
CAMPESTRE ALEMÁN
Smoked trout, Hungarian goulash, and apple strudel are specialties.
✉ Carretera a Pátzcuaro, Km 14 ☎ (434) 344 00 06 🕐 Daily 1–7 ❓ No credit cards

LOS ESCUDOS
An excellent place to try *sopa tarasca* (soup made with toasted

tortillas, cream and cheese).
✉ Portal Hidalgo 73, Plaza Vasco de Quiroga, Pátzcuaro ☎ (434) 342 12 90 🕐 Daily 11–7

WHERE TO STAY
MANSIÓN DE LOS SUEÑOS
www.prismas.com.mx
As much a museum as hotel, this faithfully restored 17th-century home has 11 rooms decorated with handcrafted furnishings; art from the region fills the courtyards and

gardens. The restaurant serves excellent regional cuisine.
✉ Calle Ibarra 15, Pátzcuaro ☎ (434) 342 57 08 💵 $220

HOTEL MANSIÓN ITURBE
www.mansioniturbe.com
This colonial-era mansion has 12 rooms, all nonsmoking. Some face the plaza, others the courtyard. Viejo Gaucho restaurant serves *queso fundido* (melted cheese with *tortillas*), pizza and snacks and has live music Tuesday to Sunday nights.
✉ Portal Morelos 59, Plaza Vasco de Quiroga, Pátzcuaro ☎ (434) 342 03 68 💵 $100

HOTEL MISIÓN SAN MANUEL
Rooms at the front of this converted colonial-era mansion have tiny balconies and views of the plaza; those at the back are larger. The outdoor café serving coffee and home-made *pan dulce* (sweet bread).
✉ Portal Aldama 12, Plaza Vasco de Quiroga, Pátzcuaro ☎ (434) 342 10 50 💵 $50–$90

Opposite *Janitizio Island in the middle of Lake Pátzcuaro*
Left *Market stand in Quiroga*

COLIMA

DIF ARTESANÍA

Handsome wooden musical instruments, clay figurines, masks and ceramics are on sale at this great-value state-run crafts shop on Andador Constitución, leading north from Colima's main square.

✉ Calle Andador Constitución 12, Colima 🕐 Mon–Sat 10–2, 5–8, Sun 10–2

GUADALAJARA

ANTIGUA DE MEXICO

This is a wonderful antiques emporium with antique furniture, custom-made stonework and sublime articles for the home—an interior design fan's heaven. Unfortunately, quality doesn't come cheap. Shipping of your purchases is possible on request.

✉ Avenida Independencia 255, Tlaquepaque, Guadalajara ☎ (33) 363 534 02 🕐 Mon–Fri 10–2, 3–7, Sat 10–6

BALLET FOLCLÓRICO DE GUADALAJARA

This superb dance troupe performs every Sunday at 12.30pm in the Teatro Degollado. Their repertoire includes memorable renditions of some of the pre-Hispanic and regional dances.

✉ Teatro Degollado, Calle Degollado ☎ (33) 361 44 773 💲 $8–$30; reserve in advance

HUICHOL MUSEUM SHOP

Attached to the Huichol Museum, this is one of the best places to buy crafts made by the Huichol people of Jalisco and Nayarit. Exquisite bead bowls and yarn paintings are on offer, and staff will explain the symbolism of each piece. All works are left unfinished, as the Huichol believe only God can achieve perfection. Cash only.

✉ By the main entrance to Basilica of Zapopan, Guadalajara 🕐 Mon–Sat 9.30–1.15, 3–5.45

LIENZO CHARROS DE JALISCO

Authentic Mexican rodeo, including wild-mare riding and bull riding, takes place every Sunday at midday.

✉ Calle Dr. Michell 572, Guadalajara 💲 $5 entrance 🚌 Head south on Avenida Independencia, turning left at third traffic circle (roundabout)

LA MAESTRANZA

Bullfighting's the theme in this bar five minutes south of the Plaza de Armas. Arrive early for a seat—the place is heaving on weekends.

✉ Maestranza 179, Guadalajara ☎ (33) 361 358 78 🕐 Tue–Sun 1pm–3am

MERCADO LIBERTAD OR SAN JUAN DE DIOS

This vast covered market houses a panoply of local goods, ranging from Paracho guitars, cowboy hats, *huarache* sandals and good food on the first floor—try the *birria* (goat meat). The east end of the market is better for local crafts.

✉ South of Plaza Tapatía, Guadalajara 🕐 Daily 10–6

TONALÁ MARKET

At the Sunday and Thursday street markets you can find great bargains in pottery, glass and ceramics. The market is held on the central avenue, where buses from Guadalajara stop.

✉ Tonalá, 15km (9 miles) southwest of Guadalajara 🕐 Thu and Sun

ZOOLÓGICO GUADALAJARA

www.zooguadalajara.com.mx
Guadalajara's internationally acclaimed zoo has 2,000 animals. Exhibits include "Safari Masai Mara," where animals are free to roam.

✉ Paseo del Zoológico 600, Parque Natural Huentitán, Guadalajara ☎ (33) 367 444 88 🕐 Wed–Sun 10–5 (daily only during

Opposite *Blankets for sale at the Mercado Libertad in Guadalajara*

school holidays) 🚻 $4.50 🚌 Take Calzada Independencia Norte and turn right after ring road (Periférico Norte) at Paseo del Zoológico

GUADALUPE
SARAPES DE GUADALUPE
This gem of a workshop sells fabulous handmade *sarape* rugs and ponchos. Eusebio Salas Ramírez has been working here for more than 65 years, and is happy to show visitors the antique wooden looms they use.
✉ Avenida Colegio Militar 117, Guadalupe
🕐 Mon–Sat 8–6

GUANAJUATO
CASA DEL CONDE DE LA VALENCIANA
Right opposite the Templo de San Cayetano de Valenciana on the road to Dolores Hidalgo, this delightful antiques emporium consists of several large rooms of tasteful furniture. The locally made tin and copper lamps are particularly fine. Amex cards are not accepted.
✉ Plazuela de Valenciana, Guanajuato
☎ (473) 732 25 50 🕐 Mon–Sat 11–6
🚌 Take the road 4km (2.5 miles) out of Guanajuato toward Dolores Hidalgo

MERCADO HIDALGO
You can't miss the enormous iron-framed building housing this crafts market. Local specialties include basketware and embroidered dresses, flowers and *charamusca*—a confection of melted twisted brown or white sugar, usually with peanuts or coconut.
✉ Avenida Juárez, main entrance opposite Calle Mendizabal, Guanajuato 🕐 Daily 7am–9pm

LEÓN
ANTROPÍA
Live acts—from Pablo Milanés covers to Afro-Peruvian rhythms—can be seen and heard at trendy Antropía, north of central León in the Jardines del Moral district between López Mateos and Insurgentes. Cocktails and dips are served.

✉ Calle Niebla 202, León ☎ (477) 773 92 99 🕐 Daily 7pm–1am, Fri–Sat until 3am

EXPLORA SCIENCE MUSEUM
This is a great interactive science museum for kids with the added attraction of an IMAX screen. In the gardens there are two handsome old steam engines.
✉ Boulevard Francisco Villa 202, La Martinica, León ☎ (477) 711 67 11
🕐 Tue–Fri 9–6, Sat–Sun 10–7

MANZANILLO
GOLF LAS HADAS
Condé Nast voted this 18-hole Roy Dye-designed course one of the most scenic golf courses in the world—the 18th hole is truly spectacular. There's a laid-back clubhouse too.
✉ Avenida Los Riscos and Vista Hermosa, Peninsula de Santiago, Manzanillo ☎ (314) 331 01 01 🚻 $90 weekdays, $140 weekends, golf cart $20 extra

MORELIA
LA ANTIGUA VALLADOLID
This secondhand bookshop one block west of the Plaza de Armas has a good selection of pocket Spanish-English dictionaries, as well as books in English, French, and German. And the cappuccino in the café isn't bad either. Cash only.
✉ Calle Galeana 82, Morelia 🕐 Mon–Sat 10am–10.30pm

MERCADO DE DULCES
Morelia's block-long, arcaded Mercado de Dulces, alongside the Palácio Clavijero, overflows with stands selling local Michoacánense sweets—cloyingly sweet for some tastes, but worth sampling nevertheless. Try the guava paste rolls, sugar-cane drinks and tamarind balls dusted with chili powder.
✉ East side of Calle Valentín Gómez Farías, next to Palacio Clavijero, Morelia 🕐 Daily 10–6, but most stands tend to keep their own hours

LAS MERCEDES
Directly opposite the Mercado de Dulces, Las Mercedes is an epicurean interior design shop that

blends traditional crafts from the region—including fine Cocucha pots—with modern designs. Knowledgeable staff will help you pick your way through the kitchenware, Talavera ceramics and furniture (including pigskin chairs) on the large shop floor.
✉ Calle Madero 185, corner with Calle Valentín Gómez Farias, Morelia ☎ (443) 313 15 55 🕐 Mon–Sat 10–9, Sun 10–6

EL RINCÓN DE LOS SENTIDOS
This is a great place to catch soulful live *trova* music (Thu–Sat from 9pm) in a pretty courtyard decked out with cool modern sculptures, paintings and photographs.
✉ Calle Madero 485, Morelia ☎ (443) 317 59 74 🕐 Sun–Wed 10–12, Thu–Sat 10am–2am

PÁTZCUARO
CASA DE LOS ONCE PATIOS
Don't leave Pátzcuaro without wandering through the craft shops in this warren of courtyards. You'll find lacquerware, religious art, clay pottery and musical instruments of the highest quality—but not cheap.
✉ Between Calle Lerin and Calle Coss, Pátzcuaro 🕐 Daily 10–7, but most stores keep their own hours

LA CASA DEL FUEGO
This splendid colonial mansion across from the basilica has been converted into a fun bar with live music on Friday and Saturday nights (starts 8pm). Different rooms have different atmospheres, but all are decorated with modern art and painted in outlandish shades.
✉ Portal Pueblito No. 1, Pátzcuaro ☎ (434) 342 66 77 🕐 Wed–Thu 3–11, Fri–Sat 1–12.30

PUERTO VALLARTA
CLUB CHRISTINE
This is the resort's top nightspot playing the latest techno and house hits. The light show and decor are both spectacular.
✉ Krystal Vallarta Hotel, Avenida de las Garzas, Puerto Vallarta ☎ (332) 224 69 90 🕐 Tue–Sun from 10pm 🚻 Cover charge $20 ($45 for open bar)

ECORIDEMEX

Mountain biking in the mountainous jungle of the Sierra Madre around Puerto Vallarta is what this friendly tour company offers. There is a variety of different excursions, from relaxed to strenuous, all with an English-speaking guide. The office is two blocks behind the cathedral.

✉ Calle Miramar 382, Puerto Vallarta
☎ (332) 222 79 12 🕙 Mon–Sat 10–6

MUSEO DEL CUALE

Located at the far western end of Isla Río Cuale near Oscar's restaurant, this small archaeology museum focuses on the indigenous peoples of western Mexico and displays ancient figurines, pottery, jewelry, and more.

✉ Isla Río Cuale, Puerto Vallarta
🕙 Tue–Sat 10–3, 4–7 ✋ Free

ORIGENES

Less than one block north of the main square is this stylish interior-design boutique that stocks well-made furniture, basketware and ornaments, including original candles and lamps. Great for special gifts.

✉ Calle Zaragoza 160, Puerto Vallarta
☎ (322) 223 14 55 🕙 Mon–Sat 10–8

VALLARTA ADVENTURES

www.vallarta-adventures.com
Swimming with dolphins, whale-watching, snorkeling and sailing are organized by this, one of Puerto Vallarta's most established tour operators, with small groups and good safety. It's best to book online or by phone. The visit to the "authentic" Huichol village is not to be recommended.

✉ Paseo Las Palmas 39A, Nuevo Vallarta, Puerto Vallarta

VENUS MASSAGE

Pamper yourself with a massage (Swedish, Turkish or with aromatherapy oils), hot stone therapy and facials at this great health complex, next to Hotel Molino de Agua. Masseurs will also visit your hotel on request.

✉ Aquiles Serdán 220, Puerto Vallarta
☎ (332) 223 27 14 🕙 Daily 10–7

QUERÉTARO
DOÑA URRACA SPA

www.donaurraca.com.mx
This luxurious spa has views over the whole city. Choose from the Jacuzzi, the gym, massages, facials or a sauna; you'll come out feeling reinvigorated—even your wallet will have lost weight.

✉ Calle 5 de Mayo 117, Querétaro
☎ (442) 238 54 00 🕙 Daily 8–6

SAN BLAS
DIVING BEYOND ADVENTURES

www.divingbeyond.com
From December to May this eco-tour company leads adventure excursions in and around San Blas. Tours include scuba diving ($150 and up), whale-watching ($160), kayaking ($15–$55), fishing ($190) and jungle boat expeditions to La Tovara ($47).

✉ Juárez 187B, San Blas ☎ (323) 285 14 18

STONERS SURF CAMP

www.stonerssurfcamp.com
This is an efficiently run surfing school at the beginning of Playa El Borrego. Run by friendly former Mexican champion surfer José Manuel "Pompis" Cano, it rents out boards and bicycles and gives surfing classes. They can arrange canoe trips too.

✉ Playa El Borrego, San Blas ✋ $18 per hour for lessons

SAN MIGUEL DE ALLENDE
7TH HEAVEN

Attentive service and original jewelry, hats, clothes, and gifts await you in this fashionable boutique two blocks from the zócalo. Jewelry can be made to order. Prices are high but the quality of goods and a tranquil ambience make it worth the extra pesos. Traveler's checks are accepted, but not Amex cards.

✉ Calle Diez de Sollano 13, San Miguel de Allende ☎ (415) 154 46 77 🕙 Mon–Sat 10–8, Sun 11–3

CASA GROU

Three blocks south of the Escuela de Bellas Artes, before the Insituto Allende, you'll find this cool crafts

and antiques shop filled with local artesanía and fabrics, as well as rugs and paintings.

✉ Calle Zacateros 19, San Miguel de Allende ☎ (415) 152 16 23 🕙 Tue–Sat 10–3, 4–6

TEQUISQUIAPAN
TURISMO ALTERNATIVO

This local tour company opposite the bus station offers great half-day guided tours in English that take in local spas, haciendas, thermal pools, geysers, and an opal mine.

✉ Andador Comercial Vista Hermosa, local 1, Tequisquiapan ☎ (414) 273 27 42 🕙 Daily 10–6

URUAPAN
EL ARTE TARASCO

This is one of the best shops for exquisite handmade lacquerware, at the top of Calle Independencia opposite the entrance to the Parque Nacional. There's also a workshop where you can watch the painstaking process of layered painting taking place.

✉ Calle Culver City 32, Uruapan 🕙 Daily 9–2, 3–7

CASA DE LAS ARTESANÍAS DE MICHOACÁN

Crafts from around Michoacán state are sold here. Traditional lacquerware and pottery share space with superb examples of modern design, including silk scarves, as well as changunga, a potent fruit liqueur, and local sweets. In addition there is an exotic all-natural macadamia nut perfume.

✉ Calzada Fray Juan de San Miguel 129, Uruapan ☎ (452) 312 08 48 🕙 Mon–Fri 10–7, Sat–Sun 10–6

VALLE DE BRAVO
SALON SPA DE VALLE

Raymundo González is building himself a reputation as a great stylist, offering professional service at his trendy hair salon. Excellent facials and a relaxing massage are also available.

✉ Calle Nicolás Bravo 402, Valle de Bravo ☎ (726) 262 4919 🕙 Wed–Sat 10–3, 5–8, Sun 10–2

ZELÁMPAGO CLUB LOUNGE

Recline amid Moroccan splendor in this bar perched above Calle Pagaza. Soul and acid jazz are on the playlist, and a gas heater (and cocktails) will warm you on chilly evenings.

✉ Calle Joaquín Arcadio Pagaza 316, Valle de Bravo ☎ (726) 262 49 46 🕐 Fri–Sat 8pm–2am

ZACATECAS
MERCADO GONZÁLEZ ORTEGA

Built in the late 19th century, this richly ornamented arcade houses 10 classy boutiques—an excellent place to pick up Zacatecan silver, Huichol crafts, leather goods, antiques, and handmade sweets.

✉ Avenida Hidalgo, between the cathedral and Plazuela Goitia, Zacatecas 🕐 Mon–Fri 9–6, Sat 10–3 (shops have individual opening times)

LA MINA CLUB

A small train takes you the 450m (490 yards) or so to the entrance of this unusual nightclub buried in the depths of the "Del Grillo" hill (▷ 223). It is comfortably decked out around a circular dance floor, and has rocky walls, waiter service and international and Mexican hits on the playlist.

✉ Cerro Grillo, Zacatecas ☎ (492) 922 30 02 🕐 Thu–Sat 10pm–3am ✋ Cover charge $10

MUSEO RAFAEL CORONEL

Wander through the lovely gardens and ruins of the former Franciscan convent before stepping into this interesting museum. A variety of masks—4,500 of them from all over Mexico—will catch your eye with their vivid colors and exotic styles. Another wing of the museum is dedicated to puppets. The Ruth Rivera room features many of Diego Rivera's drawings. Ruth Rivera is the daughter of Diego Rivera and is married to Rafael Coronel.

✉ Calle Chevano (between Abasolo and Matamoros) ☎ (492) 922 81 16 🕐 Thu–Tue 10–5 ✋ $2

Right Leopards at Guadalajara's excellent modern zoo

FESTIVALS AND EVENTS

APRIL/MAY
FERIA DE SAN MARCOS

www.feriadesanmarcos.com
Originally an agricultural fair, this two-week event has become a vibrant cultural festival with dancing, bullfights, a rodeo, craft exhibitions, beauty pageants, *mariachi* bands, and live music.

✉ Aguascalientes 🕐 Last week April to first week May

OCTOBER
FESTIVAL CERVANTINO

The International Cervantino Festival draws around 150,000 visitors each year for a feast of recitals, concerts, plays, dance, and opera in a variety of locations around town to commemorate the writer Miguel de Cervantes, the author of *Don Quixote*.

✉ Guanajuato 🕐 Starts first week October

FIESTA DE LA VIRGEN DE ZAPOPÁN

This is when the revered Virgin returns from her annual pilgrimage of all the churches of Guadalajara. More than 150,000 people accompany her on the final leg of her journey back to the basilica in Guadalajara.

✉ Guadalajara 🕐 October 12

PRICES AND SYMBOLS

The restaurants are listed alphabetically within each town. The prices given are the average for a two-course lunch (L) and a three-course dinner (D) for one person, without drinks. The wine price is for the least expensive bottle. All the restaurants listed accept credit cards unless otherwise stated.

For a key to the symbols, ▷ 2.

BARRA DE NAVIDAD
SEA MASTER

Sea Master has a front entrance on the main drag and views across the bay to Melaque with waves lapping up on the beach just a few steps from your table. Open-sided, lit by bamboo lamp-shades and decked out with typical Mexican panache in bright yellows, pinks and blues, style is matched by a quality menu (mainly seafood) that includes a superb red snapper stuffed with shrimp, bacon and pecans. And for ultimate beach hedonism, order one of the pitchers of daiquiri. The service is great and the drinks are strong. Cash only is accepted for payment.

 Avenida Lopez de Legaspi 146, Barra de Navidad ☎ (315) 355 51 99 ⏰ Daily noon–11 🍽 L $12, D $18, Wine $14

COLIMA
LOS NARANJOS

Fresh and filling breakfasts ($6) are highly recommended in this restaurant halfway between Parque Nuñez and the Jardín Torres Quintero. Try the *nopales* with eggs à la Mexicana, or the fresh hotcakes dripping with maple syrup. For lunch and dinner there are tender steaks, spicy barbecued chicken drumsticks, and good *quesadillas*. The atmosphere family friendly.

✉ Calle Gabino Barreda 34, Colima ☎ (312) 312 00 29 ⏰ Daily 7.30am–11.30pm 🍽 L $11, D $15, Wine $11

GUADALAJARA
RESTAURANT SIN NOMBRE

You'll find this delightful restaurant housed in an 18th-century mansion a couple of blocks north of the Jardín Hidalgo in the southeastern suburb of Tlaquepaque. Candlelit tables are set in a wonderful garden under pergolas shaded with vines and palms. There are good Mexican options—melted cheese with mushrooms and a tasty guacamole—as well as more ambitious international dishes, including tender red snapper in butter and capers.

✉ Avenida Madero 80, Tlaquepaque, Guadalajara ☎ (33) 3635 4520 ⏰ Mon–Thu 11–10, Fri–Sat 11am–midnight 🍽 L $14, D $18, Wine $15

GUANAJUATO
CIAO BELLA

Just a few steps behind the Museo del Pueblo de Guanajuato, Luis Arturo Tinajero presides over this attractive Italian restaurant. There is a good wine list and the menu includes delicious walnut, pear and Parmesan salad, as well as the tasty *fusilli à la boscaiola* (fusilli in mushroom sauce). Tables are set in high-ceilinged rooms painted in oranges and yellows, with wine bottles suspended from the walls. Amex cards are not accepted.

✉ Calle Pocitos 25, Guanajuato ☎ (473) 732 67 64 ⏰ Mon–Sat 2–10, Sun–Mon 2–6 🍽 L $24, D $28, Wine $13

MANZANILLO
TOSCANA

French chef Michele Laugeri Giraud's creations have made Toscana one of the top landmarks in the Playa Azul zone of Manzanillo—without astronomic prices. The international menu changes weekly, but includes the likes of *gazpacho*, shrimp ravioli,

Opposite *In this region's restaurants you'll find plenty of local specialties*

and sea bass in a mango and ginger marinade. Tables are wafted by sea breezes coming in off the bay, and at weekends there's live music after 9pm. Amex cards are not accepted.
✉ Boulevard Miguel de la Madrid 3177, Manzanillo ☎ (314) 333 25 15 ⓘ Daily 7am–midnight 🖐 L $20, D $26, Wine $17

MORELIA

LAS MERCEDES

Three blocks west of the cathedral off Madero, Las Mercedes is an enchanting restaurant offering classy dining in an original setting. Tables are set in a colonial patio amid a forest of balls of lava called *heodas*, palms, orchids and enormous, locally made vases. Steak fillets, crêpes suzettes and tasty shrimps sizzling in garlic are just some of the menu's highlights. Service is impeccable. Amex cards are not accepted.
✉ León Guzmán 47 ☎ (443) 312 61 13 ⓘ Mon–Sat 1–midnight, Sun 1.30–7 🖐 L $25, D $30, Wine $11

PÁTZCUARO

LOS ESCUDOS

Housed under the arcades on the west side of the Plaza Quiroga, Los Escudos is a popular mid-range dining option with a family-friendly atmosphere. It is set on two levels under pink-painted beams, and serves a wide range of breakfasts ($10), including a good fruit platter. For later in the day, try the *sopa tarasca*, a tasty soup made from toasted *tortillas*, cream and cheese. In the summer there are tables outside. Cash only is accepted.
✉ Plaza Quiroga, Portal Hidalgo 73, Pátzcuaro ☎ (434) 342 12 90 ⓘ Daily 7am–10pm (breakfast until 1pm) 🖐 L $10, D $16, Wine $16

PUERTO VALLARTA

THE RIVER CAFÉ

www.rivercafe.com.mx

Tucked under the principal bridge over the Río Cuale three blocks from Puerto Vallarta's old heart, the River Café oozes trendy elegance. Diners can either eat inside at candlelit tables or on the terrace overlooking the river. While the crêpes, salads and meat options are reliably tasty, it's the seafood that really stands out—try the pan-seared yellowfin tuna accompanied by a delicate black truffle risotto.
✉ Isla Río Cuale local 4, Puerto Vallarta ☎ (322) 223 07 88 ⓘ Daily 9am–11pm 🖐 L $26, D $34, Wine $20

SAN MIGUEL DE ALLENDE

TIO LUCAS

Tio Lucas is situated within 50m (55 yards) of the Escuela de Bellas Artes in a pretty colonial house that opens onto an attractive whitewashed patio lit by pink paper lanterns. The pink theme is repeated in the painted tin folk art adorning the walls of the interior dining area. The filet mignon and T-bone steak in a mushroom sauce are good options from a menu that leans toward meat.
✉ Calle Mesones 103, San Miguel de Allende ☎ (415) 152 49 96 ⓘ Daily noon–11 🖐 L $17, D $20, Wine $14

TEQUILA

REAL MARINERO

Should you find yourself in Tequila in need of sustenance to soak up the local tipple, this is the place to head for. On the main square within stumbling distance of the Sauza and José Cuervo distilleries, the Real Marinero restaurant offers good seafood, including a first-class *ceviche*, at reasonable prices. There are also set meals at lunchtime.
✉ Paseo Benito Juárez 92, Tequila ☎ (374) 74 21 674 ⓘ Daily 9am–10.30pm (Wed, lunch only) 🖐 L $12, D $18

TOLUCA

BIARRITZ

This unpretentious café-restaurant within two minutes' walk of the cathedral supplies local delicacies at reasonable prices. Specialties include the *torta Toluqueña*, a roll containing cheese and Toluca's own chorizo sausage, as well as the extravagantly carnivorous *Molcajete*, a stone bowl filled with strips of local chorizo, barbecued ribs, chilies, and avocado, and accompanied by maize *tortillas*. Filling Mexican breakfasts ($7) make up the morning fare. Amex cards are not accepted
✉ Calle Nigromante 200, Toluca ☎ (722) 214 57 57 ⓘ Daily 8am–11pm 🖐 L $8, D $10, Wine $10

URUAPAN

VENTANAS AL PARAÍSO

The views are worth the elevator trip up to the top floor of Uruapan's highest building. The restaurant serves generous portions and the soups are good: *caldo tlalpeño* is a tasty vegetable and chicken soup, and *crema P'urhépecha* is an avocado bisque using local fruits.
✉ Calle Nicolás Bravo 100, Uruapan ☎ (452) 527 59 00 ⓘ Daily 3–11 🖐 D $22, Wine $10

VALLE DE BRAVO

DA CIRO

Five minutes' walk from Valle de Bravo's main square, Da Ciro serves delicious Italian cuisine in a colonial house. Starters include foie gras with a strawberry and arugula (rocket) salad, while dishes such as spaghetti with porcini and shiitake, and a prawn and saffron risotto top the mains. There is an excellent and extensive wine list. Unfortunately, like many of the town's restaurants, Da Ciro is open only on weekends.
✉ Calle del Vergel 201, Valle de Bravo ☎ (726) 26 201 22 ⓘ Fri–Sat 2–2, Sun 2–8 🖐 L $21, D $25, Wine $28

ZACATECAS

ACROPOLIS

Operating since 1943 next to the cathedral at a corner of the González Ortega market, this is Zacatecas' place to see and be seen. American diner-style tables next to windows are the place to watch the world go by, although they don't leave much legroom. Mexican breakfasts are served until 12.30 and there are good *chilaquiles* and *enchiladas*, as well as coffee, cake and ice cream. Amex cards are not accepted.
✉ Avenida Hidalgo, Zacatecas ☎ (492) 922 12 84 ⓘ Daily 8am–10pm 🖐 L $10, D $15, Wine $13

PRICES AND SYMBOLS

The prices are the average for a double room for one night including breakfast, unless otherwise stated. All the hotels listed accept credit cards unless otherwise stated. Note that rates can vary widely throughout the year.

For a key to the symbols, ▷ 2.

BARRA DE NAVIDAD
HOTEL LAS VILLITAS

In the heart of Barra de Navidad, this is a great boutique hotel with its own private entrance to the beach. The comfortable rooms have vaulted ceilings, spacious closets and thick mattresses on enormous beds. The terrace overlooking the beach, with a large Jacuzzi and attractive bamboo loungers, is a perfect place to watch the sunset. Reservations are essential in summer months.
✉ López de la Gaspez 127, Barra de Navidad ☎ (315) 355 53 54 🖐 $90–$120, excluding breakfast ⓘ 8, including 2 with sea views ⬙

GUADALAJARA
HOTEL FRANCÉS

One block south of the Plaza de Armas, this is Guadalajara's oldest hotel and a protected monument.

Rooms are grouped around a two-tiered covered courtyard with a marble fountain, a chandelier and a wonderful old elevator—all with gleaming brass fittings. Rooms are comfortable and elegantly furnished in sober oak with cream walls. Warning for those who go to bed early: on Friday nights from 9pm to 10pm there is *mariachi* music in the lobby. Parking is available.
✉ Maestranza 35, Guadalajara ☎ (33) 361 311 90 🖐 $65–$72, excluding breakfast ($8) ⓘ 60, including 10 suites

GUANAJUATO
CASA ESTRELLA DE LA VALENCIANA

www.mexicaninns.com
Sitting on the mountainside above La Valenciana church, this lovely hotel is constructed in contemporary Mexican style. Interiors are decorated with the pottery, tiles, and arts of the area. Guest rooms are named after local mines and all rooms have their own balcony or terrace, providing wonderful, panoramic views of the city and surrounding valley.
✉ Callejon Jalisco 10, Col. La Valenciana, Guanajuato ☎ (866) 983 88 44 🖐 $170–$190 ⓘ 8 ⬙ Outdoor

Above *Misión San Manuel in Pátzcuaro is full of historic interest*

HOSTAL CANTARRANAS

A superb budget option in the heart of Guanajuato, just half a block from the Teatro Juárez. Rooms are comfortable and clean; some have kitchenettes and others cater to groups as large as six. There is a roof terrace with superb views up to the Pípila. Credit cards are not accepted.
✉ Cantarranas 50, Guanajuato ☎ (473) 732 52 41 🖐 $35 in low season, $45 in high season, excluding breakfast ⓘ 12

HOSTERIA DEL FRAYLE

Housed in Guanajuato's original mint, founded in 1673, this is a marvelously convenient hotel just a block from the Jardín de la Unión. Well-appointed rooms are decorated with antiques and colonial religious art; some have balconies and handsome, high windows looking out onto the street below. Staff are professional and friendly. This is a perfect place to be for the Festival Cervantino (▷ 233), although it can be noisy. Amex cards not accepted.
✉ Sopeña 3, Guanajuato ☎ (473) 732 11 79 🖐 $70–$100, excluding breakfast ($5) ⓘ 37, including 5 suites

MORELIA

LA CASA DE LAS ROSAS

This tiny hotel is in Morelia's colonial heart, halfway between the Plaza de Armas and the Jardín de las Rosas. Its motto might well be "quality, not quantity"—there are only four rooms, each exquisitely furnished and endowed with huge beds overflowing with bulging down pillows. Staff are attentive to the last detail, and cater to your every whim. Valet parking is available.

✉ Guillermo Prieto 125, Morelia ☎ (443) 312 45 45 ✦ $235–$340, excluding breakfast ($10) ⓘ 4 ✦

PÁTZCUARO

MISIÓN SAN MANUEL

You'll find this atmospheric hotel in the heart of Pátzcuaro under the arches on the south side of Plaza Quiroga. Beamed balconies, antique gramophones, old typewriters and suits of armor all adorn the lobby and interior courtyard. The carpeted rooms, meanwhile, come with corner chimney pieces, have good reading lamps and are kept spotlessly clean by the pleasant staff. Parking is available.

✉ Portal Aldama 12, Pátzcuaro ☎ (434) 342 10 50 ✦ From $65 ⓘ 35

PUERTO VALLARTA

MAJAHUITAS RESORT

Unforgettable luxury is the order of the day at this divine hotel (accessible only by boat) in a protected cove on the spectacular Bay of Banderas between Quimixto and Yelapa, just 15 minutes south of Puerto Vallarta. Attractive individual and duplex *casitas* (cabin houses) dot the 7ha (17 acres) of private gardens and lush jungle, filled with an abundance of fruit trees and wildlife. The beach is gloriously pristine and the whole place runs on alternative energy sources. Snorkeling, kayaking, fishing and hiking are all available, as well as relaxing massages.

✉ Majahuitas, 21km (13 miles) southwest of Puerto Vallarta ☎ (322) 293 45 06 ✦ $375 Oct–Apr, $315 May to mid-Jun. Closed mid-Jun to Sep ⓘ 7 *casitas*

QUERÉTARO

LA CASA DE LA MARQUESA

www.lacasadelamarquesa.com

A beautiful mansion built in 1756 situated one block west of the Jardín Zenéa, this sumptuous hotel is utterly charming and an aesthete's heaven. Rooms are individually decorated—the Moorish room, for instance, comes with *mudéjar* chests and an Andalucian-style bedstead. Public areas are hung with velvet curtains and scattered with elegant chaise-longues and leather-backed armchairs. Don't forget to take a look inside the private chapel too—you can even ask for it to be set up as a private dining room if you want to celebrate or party.

✉ Madero 41, Querétaro ☎ (442) 212 00 92 ✦ $180–$350 ⓘ 25

MESON DE SANTA ROSA

This luxury hotel has been welcoming visitors for centuries: It used to be a caravan stop on the route to the north of the country and still has a drinking trough in the central courtyard. All rooms are tastefully decorated and have cable TV and a minibar; some have views over the central courtyard or the pool courtyard. Facilities include a sauna, Jacuzzi, boutiques, indoor and outdoor swimming pools, and a patio restaurant.

✉ Pasteur Sur 17, Plaza de la Independencia, Querétaro ☎ (442) 224 26 23 ✦ $200 ⓘ 21 rooms (15 suites and 6 guestrooms) ✦

SAN MIGUEL DE ALLENDE

CASA DE SIERRA NEVADA

www.casadesierranevada.com

Five magnificently restored colonial houses comprise this beautiful and luxurious hotel oozing with understated elegance. In each house, rooms are arranged around a tranquil, flower-filled patio; many have a private veranda, and all have massive oak beds, fresh flowers and intricately tiled bathrooms. This hotel is truly a treat.

✉ Hospicio 42 San Miguel de Allende ☎ (415) 152 70 40 ✦ From $312 ⓘ 31 ✦

HOTEL POSADA CARMINA

www.posadacarmina.com

Centrally located, this hotel is both beautiful and comfortable. In a colonial mansion, it is just a half-block south of the plaza. The two-story structure surrounds a courtyard with lovely orange trees growing around a stone fountain. Rooms are fairly large and well-furnished. Some will find the ringing bells of the nearby Parroquia to be a beautiful sound; others, searching for peace and quiet, may want to request a room at the back of the hotel, farther from the sound.

✉ Cuna de Allenda 7, San Miguel de Allende ☎ (415) 152 04 58 ⓘ 24 ✦ $120–$130

VALLE DE BRAVO

HOTEL BATUCADA

Three blocks north of the Plaza Independencia, this is a very appealing hotel ranged around an attractive courtyard with trickling fountain. The nine rooms are individually decorated, but all are furnished with beautiful antique Michoacanense chests and vases, and come with wood-burning fireplaces for cold nights. Bathrooms have antique bathtubs, spotlighting, and gorgeously fluffy towels. The corridors are painted in calming sky blue. Parking is available.

✉ Bocanegra 207, Valle de Bravo ☎ (726) 262 04 80 ✦ $180–$280 ⓘ 9

ZACATECAS

QUINTA REAL

www.quintareal.com

Standing in the shadow of Zacatecas' colonial aqueduct, the great novelty of this luxurious hotel is its incorporation into the beautiful old Plaza de Toros, which functioned as a bullring until 1976. The elegant dining room overlooks the arena, which is spectacularly lit at night and is regularly used as a backdrop for wedding photos. Rooms are stunning, with huge beds and sparkling bathrooms. There's a shop selling silver on site.

✉ Avenida Ignacio Rayon 434, Zacatecas ☎ (492) 922 91 04 ✦ $270 ⓘ 49

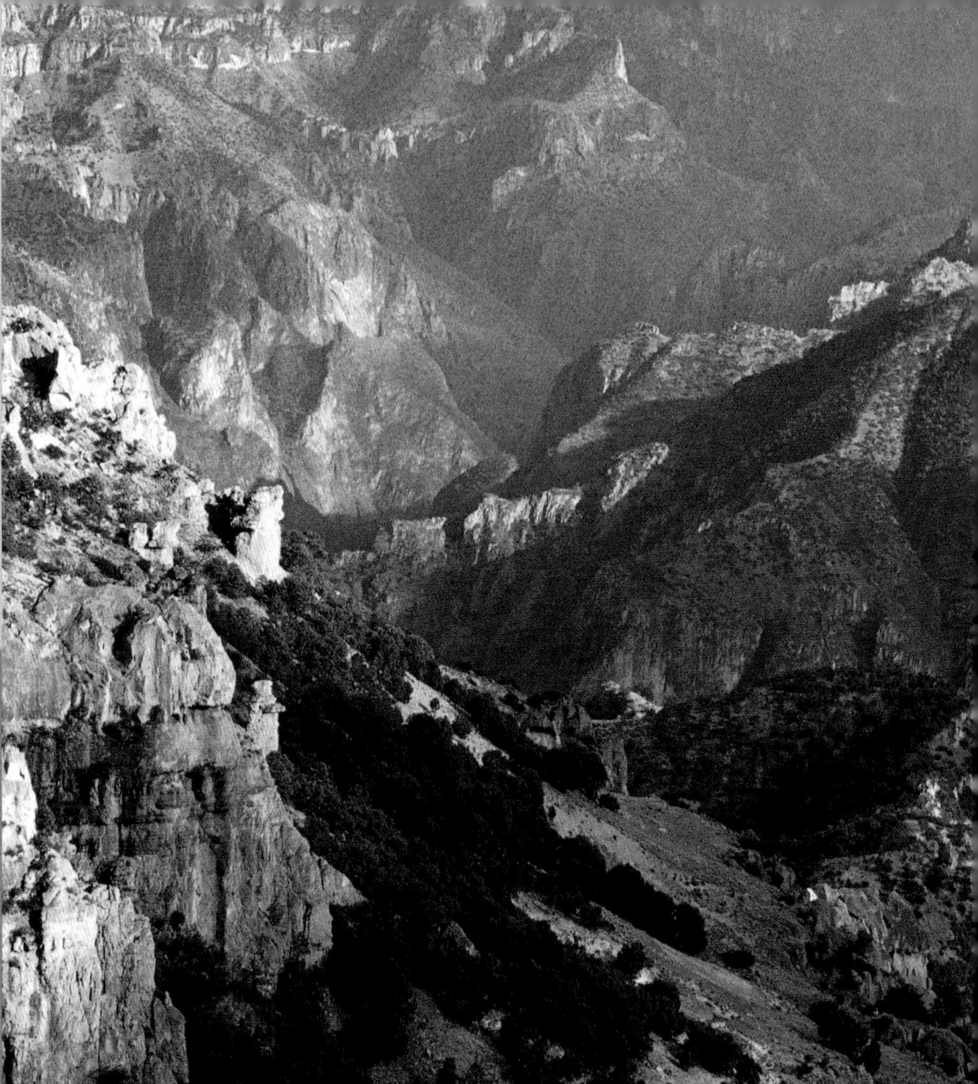

USA

na Mexicali

San Luis Río
Colorado

nada

San
tín

ario

Cataviña

Puerto
Peñasco

Nogales

Agua
Prieta

Ciudad
Juárez

Santa Ana

Nuevo
Casas
Grandes

Villa
Ahumada

Puerto
Libertad

Mazocahui

Gallego

Arados

Ojinaga

Hermosillo

Presa Plutarco
Elías Calles

Chihuahua

Guerrero
Negro

Bahía
Kino

Delicias

Santa
Elena

Piedras
Negras

Reserva
de la Biósfera
El Vizcaíno

Guaymas

Presa
Álvaro
Obregón

Ciudad
Obregón

Cuauhtémoc

Nuevo
Rosita

San
Ignacio

Santa
Rosalía

Barranca
del Cobre

Jiménez

Nuevo
Laredo

Nopoló

Chinobampo

Hidalgo
del Parral

Monclova

Ciudad
Constitución

Los Mochis

Tepehuanes

Gómez
Palacio

Saltillo

MONTERREY

Matamoros

Isla
Santa
Margarita

La Paz

Isla
Cerralvo

Culiacán

Torreón

Cuencamé

Linares

San
Fernando

La Cruz

Durango

Villa de
Guadalupe

Valle
del Salado

Ciudad
Victoria

Cabo San Lucas

Mazatlán

San José
del Cabo

Sierra
de
Durango

Fresnillo

Zacatecas

San Luis
Potosí

Ciudad
Mante

Tampico

Mexcaltitán

Aguascalientes

Ciudad
Valles

Islas Marías

NORTHERN MEXICO
AND BAJA CALIFORNIA

Northern Mexico, a region of arid desert, high plains, rugged mountains and spectacular canyons, stretches from the Gulf of Mexico in the east to the Gulf of California in the west. This is the Mexico of old black-and-white Hollywood Westerns. In fact, many of them were filmed in the desert surrounding the town of Durango. Farther west, across the Mar de Cortés, a narrow finger of land, the Baja California peninsula, stretches some 1,287 sun-bleached kilometers (800 miles) from the US–Mexico border to the famous rock arch at Land's End in Cabo San Lucas.

While the sun splashed beach resorts of Los Cabos and Northern Mexico's Mazatlán see the highest number of foreign visitors, the region has much more to offer the curious traveler. Near the Gulf of Mexico coast, the modern city of Monterrey sits high in the mountains and boasts some of the country's finest museums. In Northern Mexico's rugged interior lies the magnificent Barranca del Cobre (or Copper Canyon), a dramatic gash in the Earth's surface that's five times deeper and one-and-a-half times wider than Arizona's Grand Canyon. It is one of Mexico's most impressive sights.

Over in Baja California, intrepid travelers can ponder prehistoric cave paintings in the central badlands, get up-close-and-personal with Gray Whales in Laguna San Ignacio or surf the legendary waves of the peninsula's Pacific coast. For Mexican food lovers, the region is a spicy delight. This is the birthplace of *huevos rancheros* and the fish *taco*, and it is Northern Mexico's cuisine that most resembles what passes for Mexican food in the rest of the world. For those seeking a budget vacation, the region is quite affordable, with one exception. In the Los Cabos resort area you'll pay the highest prices for lodging, food and services in all Mexico. But when the sun shines practically year round, few are complaining.

REGIONS

NORTHERN MEXICO AND
BAJA CALIFORNIA

239

ALAMOS

www.alamosmexico.com

Inland from Navojoa on the northwest coast, the colonial town of Alamos is now a national monument. Although the area was explored by the Spanish in the 1530s, development did not begin for another 100 years, when the Jesuits built a mission where the Iglesia de la Purísma Concepción now stands on the main plaza. In 1683 silver mines were discovered near the village of Aduana, 3km (2 miles) west, and the population began to rise—the photogenic old mine site near the village of Minas Nuevas can be visited.

By the end of the 18th century, silver production reached its peak and Alamos was the world's greatest producer. However, by 1909 nearly all the mines had closed.

Most of the sights of interest are within easy walking distance of the Plaza de Armas. The Museo Costumbrista de Sonora (Wed–Sun 9–6) has a collection of items related to colonial life in Alamos and the history of mining in the area, with good explanations. At the end of January the Ortiz de Tirado Music festival takes place, an annual extravaganza in memory of Dr. Alfonso Ortiz Tirado (1893–1960), also known as "Mexico's Pavarotti."

➕ 311 F4 ℹ️ Calle Juárez 6 ☎ (647) 428 04 50 🕐 Mon–Fri 8–1, 2–5 🚌 Buses from Navojoa ✈ Airports at Los Mochis (south) and Ciudad Obregon (northwest)

BAHÍA DE LOS ANGELES

Since the 1940s the Bay of Angels has drawn a devout following of marine biologists and sportfishing enthusiasts, including the American novelist John Steinbeck. One of the major draws is the area's whale population, including sperm, orca, and humpback. In July and August you can hear the whales breathe as you stand on shore. Easier to spot, however, are the thousands of dolphins that gather in the bay from June to December, and the large colonies of seals. A boat and guide can be rented for around $120 a day.

The bay, sheltered by the forbidding slopes of Isla Ángel de la Guarda (Baja's largest island and now a nature reserve), is also a haven for boating, although the winds can be tricky for kayaks and small craft. Note that facilities in town are limited and the water supply is inadequate.

In the town (also called Bahía de los Angeles) there is a small but interesting museum, the Museo de Naturaleza y Cultura (Tue–Sat 9–noon, 3–5), with good information on mining techniques used in the region, as well as shells, fossils and a selection of arts and crafts produced by the Cochimi Indians.

➕ 310 C3

BAHÍA KINO

Bahía Kino is an attractive bay with azure waters, refreshing breezes and deserted beaches during the week. Pleasant public beaches provide a good balance between relaxation and adventure activities, with swimming, diving and sailing. The main attraction is sportfishing in the new Kino Nuevo area, a "winter gringoland" of condos, trailer parks, and a couple of expensive waterfront hotels.

On Avenida Mar de Cortés, the Museo de los Seris (Tue–Sun 9–1, 2–5) has exhibits about the Seri people, who used to live across El Canal del Infiernillo (Little Hell Strait) on the mountainous Isla Tiburón (Shark Island, (▷ 248). Now occupying a settlement at nearby Punta Chueca, the Seri go into Bahía Kino on weekends to sell their ironwood animal sculptures and traditional basketware. The old part of town—the fishing village of Bahía Kino—is more somnolent and down-at-heel.

➕ 310 D3 🚌 Buses from Hermosillo

BAHÍA MAGDALENA

"Mag Bay" is considered the finest natural harbor between San Francisco and Acapulco and provides the best boating on Baja's Pacific coast. The coastline is protected by two long, thin islands—Isla Magdalena and Isla Santa Margarita—and small craft can explore the mangrove-fringed inlets where bird and marine life flourishes. Naturalists flock to the bay to view the gray whales that come here in the winter season. One of the best places to view them is at Punta Entrada, at the southern tip of Isla Santa Margarita. Fishing is excellent in the area, and a clutch of restaurants serves excellent fish and seafood. On the narrow south end of Isla Magdalena is Puerto Magdalena, a sedate lobstering village.

From January to March gray whales can be sighted at Puerto Adolfo López Mateos farther north, where you can choose from a wide number of water-based activities such as kayaking, swimming, fishing, and diving.

➕ 310 D5–D6 (inset) 🚌 Road west from Ciudad Constitución (57km/35 miles) ends at San Carlos

Opposite *A juvenile gray whale breaches at Bahía Magdalena*

Below *The expanse of beach at Bahía Kino was named for explorer Eusebio Kino (1644–1711)*

INFORMATION

www.allaboutcabo.com

🔀 310 E7 (inset) 🚌 Bus from La Paz

TIPS

›› There are no beach bars or restaurants on Playa Santa Maria so you'll need to pack a lunch and drinks. The signed beach turn-off is on Mex.1, some 12.5km (8 miles) northeast of Cabo. Park in the guarded pay lot near the highway or farther down the dirt road at the beach.

›› Avoid Medano during American college "spring break" weeks in late March and April if you prefer a less raucous nightlife scene.

›› Driving on Mex. 1, watch for the "Chileno Bay Playa Publico" sign; a paved road leads to a large free parking lot.

Above *A cactus growing in a hotel's cactus garden at Cabo San Lucas*

CABO SAN LUCAS

Cabo San Lucas has grown from a sleepy fishing village immortalized as a "small boy's dreams of pirates" in John Steinbeck's 1940 novel *Log from the Sea of Cortez*, to a bustling, expensive international resort with a permanent population of 8,500. There are trailer parks, cafés and restaurants, condominiums, gift shops, nightclubs, and a marina to cater to the increasing flood of Americans who come for the world-famous sportfishing or to find a retirement paradise. Spanish explorer Francisco de Ulloa first rounded and named the cape in 1539 and the sheltered bay became a watering point for the treasure ships from the East; pirates rested here too. Now Cabo San Lucas is on the cruise ship itinerary. An interesting attraction is the Museo de Cabo (Tue–Sun 10–3, 6–8) on Plaza Amelia Wilkes.

BEACHES AND BAYS

Ringed by pounding surf, columns of fluted rock enclose Lover's Beach, a romantic, sandy cove with views out to the seal colonies on offshore islets (be careful if walking along the beach as huge waves sweep away several visitors each year). At the very tip of Cabo is the distinctive natural arch, El Arco; you can rent a boat to see it close up, but care is required because of the strong riptides. At the harbor entrance a pinnacle, Pelican Rock, is home to vast shoals of tropical fish; it's an ideal place for snorkeling and scuba diving, and glass-bottomed boats can be rented at the waterside.

Cabo's most popular spot for sunbathing and carousing is Medano Beach (Playa El Medano), which curves along the shore of Cabo San Lucas Bay north of town. The beachfront hotel zone begins just north of the main strand, where the surf is typically calm enough for swimming, the sand is soft, and the people-watching from the rowdy restaurants and bars is always entertaining.

Massive beachfront resorts have sprung up all along the Los Cabos Corridor coast, which separates Cabo San Lucas from San José del Cabo. Still, a few pockets of undeveloped bliss remain. To visit the Corridor beaches, a rental car is a must. Snorkelers flock to Playa Santa Maria, a pretty horseshoe-shaped bay with gorgeous sub-aquatic scenery.

Roughly 1.5 km (1 mile) northeast of Santa Maria is Chileno Bay, the most easily accessible beach on the Los Cabos Corridor. Backed by rocky bluffs and a lush palm grove, Chileno is a prime swimming, snorkeling and scuba destination. This is one of the few Corridor beaches with bathrooms, showers and a booth renting snorkel equipment.

BARRANCA DEL COBRE

www.coppercanyoninsider.com

Rugged, untamed and beautiful, the Barranca del Cobre is an unmissable experience on one of the world's greatest railway journeys. The Barranca del Cobre, or Copper Canyon, is a section of a series of canyons that forms part of the Sierra Madre, more commonly known as the Sierra Tarahumara. Five times deeper and one-and-a-half times wider than the Grand Canyon in the United States, it is one of Mexico's most amazing sights.

The Copper Canyon was first made accessible to visitors in 1961 with the opening of the Chihuahua al Pacífico Railway between Chihuahua in the north and Los Mochis on the coast. The journey is one of majestic beauty. The descent to the coast south of Creel passes through 86 tunnels and crosses 37 bridges, and is considered the most spectacular part of the trip. The best time to visit the canyons is from July to September; while there may be short bursts of rain in later summer, the weather is warm and the Sierra is at its most vibrant.

Creel, north of the Copper Canyon, is the commercial hub of the Tarahumara region, and a good starting point for reaching several of the canyons. It is named for Enrique Creel (1854–1931), governor of Chihuahua state in 1907, who initiated the building of the railway and planned to improve the lives of the Tarahumara people by establishing a colony here. His statue stands in the central square, just below the railway.

Batopilas, 120km (75 miles) south of Creel, is a former silver-mining town—quiet, palm-fringed and subtropical, hemmed in by the swirling jade-green river of the same name and the cactus-studded canyon walls. It is an excellent base for walking and is within easy reach of the Urique Canyon. Hotel Divisadero Barrancas, in El Divisadero, perches on the edge of the cliffs, with breathtaking views of the Urique Canyon.

Above *The red-brick Mission of Satevo in the former silver-mining town of Batopilas, surrounded by canyon walls*

➕ 311 F4 ℹ️ Amigos 3 tour office in Creel, Mateos 46, provides free maps and information 🚌 Buses from Chihuahua to Creel, then from Creel to Batopilas 🚆 Daily trains leave Chihuahua and Los Mochis between 6am and 7am, arriving around 8pm or 9pm. Delays are common. One-way ticket $130

CASAS GRANDES

Just a couple of hours' drive south of the US border is the most important archaeological site in northern Mexico—Casas Grandes, or Paquimé. A maze of multilevel adobe buildings, Casas Grandes was once a thriving community (probably a trading base) with more than 3,000 inhabitants. The city reached its peak between 1210 and 1261, before being destroyed by fire in 1340. Its commercial influence is said to have reached as far as Colorado in the north and into southern Mexico.

Today, significant archaeological reconstruction is under way and the site is well maintained, although few buildings are more than one floor high: The niches that held the beams of the upper floors are still visible in some structures. A water system, also visible, carried hot water from thermal springs to the north, and acted as drainage. You can see a ball court and various plazas among the buildings. The Museo de las Culturas del Norte includes a scale model of Paquimé and examples of

the distinctive local pottery which is made in the nearby village of Mata Ortiz, copying the original patterns, either black on black or beige with intricate red and gray designs.
➕ 311 F2 ☎ (636) 692 41 40 🕐 Tue–Sun 10–5 💲 $4.60 🚌 Buses from Chihuahua

CASCADA DE BASASEÁCHIC

In the state of Chihuahua, the spectacular Basaseáchic waterfall, at 311m (1,020ft), is the highest single-jump waterfall in North America and one of the country's natural wonders. Its sheer scale and power are overwhelming.

A paved road leads 1.5km (1 mile) to a vehicle parking area where you will find *taco* stands and a *mirador* (lookout point). From here, a path leads to the top of the falls and continues steeply downward to the turquoise pool at the bottom. If you wish to swim in the pool, the best time is in the morning when the sun still strikes the surface of the water. Two-thirds of the way to the bottom is the Mirador Ventana, offering the best viewpoint of the falls. From here a path leads to the top of the falls and continues steeply—hiking is difficult here, so take a tour from Creel. The best time to visit the falls is between July and September.
➕ 311 F4 🚌 Top of the falls is 3km (2 miles) from town (2km/1.2 miles by dirt road, 1km/half a mile by signed trail)

CHIHUAHUA

www.chihuahua.gob.mx

Chihuahua City, capital of the state of Chihuahua and hub of a silver-mining and cattle-rearing area, is 375km (233 miles) from the US border. A modern and rather run-down industrial sprawl, it lacks immediate appeal but it has strong historical connections, especially with the Mexican Revolution, and several engaging museums. Pancho Villa operated in the surrounding countryside, and once captured the city by disguising his men as peasants going to market. There are also associations with the last days of Independence hero Hidalgo.

One of the main attractions is the Quinta Luz (1914), Calle 10 No. 3014, where Pancho Villa lived with his official wife, Luz Corral, and which now houses the Museo Histórico de la Revolución Mexicana (Tue–Sat 9–1, 3–7, Sun 10–4). Exhibits include many old photographs, the car in which Villa was assassinated (looking like a Swiss cheese from all the bullet holes) and his death mask. The Museo Regional (Tue–Sun 9–1, 4–7), in the former mansion Quinta Gameros on Paseo Bolívar, has interesting exhibits and fine art nouveau rooms, including the dining room, the child's room which features Little Red Riding Hood scenes, the bathroom—with frogs playing among reeds—an exhibition of Paquimé ceramics (▷ 243), and temporary exhibitions.

The old tower of the Capilla Real, where Hidalgo awaited his execution in 1811, is in the Palacio Federal (Libertad y Guerrero). Worth closer inspection is the Catedral Metropolitana on Plaza Constitución, begun in 1717 and finished in 1789. The interior is mostly unadorned, with square columns, glass chandeliers and a carved altarpiece. Summer temperatures often reach 40°C (104°F), but be prepared for ice at night as early as November.

✚ 312 G3 ℹ️ Palacio Gobierno, Avenida Aldama ☎ (614) 410 10 77 🕐 Mon–Fri 8.30–6, Sat–Sun 10–3 🚌 Bus terminal is 8km (5 miles) southeast of town. Buses from Cuidad Juaréz, Creel

CUAUHTÉMOC

Cuauhtémoc is known for the 20 or so Mennonite villages (campos menonitas) which surround the town. Having fled from Europe in search of religious freedom in the early 20th century, almost 20,000 Mennonites from Belgium, Holland and Germany arrived in Mexico. The president during that time, Álvaro Obregón, established an agreement with the Mennonites that they could enjoy total liberty providing they worked the land. Many of the villages' inhabitants are blond, blue-eyed and speak old German; they can be seen in town (also in Chihuahua and Nuevo Casas Grandes) wearing their distinctive bib overalls and straw hats or long dresses and bonnets, and selling

their cheese and vegetables or buying supplies. There is a small but engaging Mennonite Museum (at Rubio Km 2.5, tel 625 582 1382) that re-creates the living conditions and lifestyle of the first immigrants, and you may be able to organize a visit to a cheese factory.

✚ 312 G3

DESIERTO VIZCAÍNO

The road from Guerrero Negro crosses the peninsula to San Francisquito overlooking the Gulf of California (77k/48 miles). These minor Bajan roads require high-clearance, preferably 4WD, vehicles carrying adequate equipment and supplies, water and fuel. A new gravel road from Bahía de Los Angeles (135km/ 84 miles) gives easier road access than from El Arco, 64km (40 miles) east of Guerrero Negro, and opens up untouched stretches of the Gulf coast. Southeast of El Arco is Misión de Santa Gertrudis (1752)—some stone ruins have been restored.

Some 2.5 million hectares (6.2 million acres) of the Desierto Vizcaíno are protected by the Reserva de la Biósfera El Vizcaíno, located south of the state border of Baja California Sur between the Gulf of California on the east and the Pacific Ocean on the west. Encompassed by the reserve are the desert, the Vizcaína Peninsula, Scammon's Lagoon (Laguna Ojo de Liebre; ▷ 248), Las Tres Vírgenes volcano, the Laguna de San Ignacio and several offshore islands.

The Vizcaíno Peninsula, which thrusts into the Pacific south of Guerrero Negro, is one of the remotest parts of Baja. Although part of the Vizcaíno Desert, the scenery of the peninsula is varied and interesting and there is an abundance of wildlife, including lynx and the endangered Cedros mule deer; isolated fishing camps dot the silent coast of beautiful coves and

Left *The ornate facade of the cathedral in Chihuahua*
Opposite *Grutas de García*

untrodden beaches which provides a remote watersport haven for divers, surfers and fishermen. Until recently only the most hardy ventured into the region; now an improved dry-weather road cuts west through the peninsula to Bahía Tortugas and the rugged headland of Punta Eugenia. It leaves Highway 1 70km (43 miles) beyond Guerrero Negro at the Vizcaíno Junction.

✚ 310 C4 🚌 You will need your own transport to explore the Vizcaíno desert

DURANGO

Victoria de Durango, capital of Durango state, was founded in 1563. Although the city has been modernized, it retains many graceful old buildings, including 18th-century Churrigueresque Casa del Conde de Suchil—now a bank—on Calle 5 de Febrero; the French-style Teatro Ricardo Castro, staging operatic, orchestral and dance productions; and the baroque cathedral (1695). A small Cinema Museum on Calle 16 de Septiembre (Tue–Sun 10–6), has a good collection of Mexican film posters, plus old cameras. To buy leather goods try Mercado Gómez Palacio, on Calle Pasteur between Avenida 20 de Noviembre and Calle 5 de Febrero. Parque Guadiana at the western edge of town, with its huge eucalyptus trees, is a pleasant place to relax. There are good views over the city from the hill called Cerro de Los Remedios, from which many flights of steps lead up to a chapel.

Halfway between Durango and Zacatecas to the southeast is Sombrerete, a pretty, colonial silver-mining town, which once rivalled Zacatecas at the height of its prosperity toward the end of the 17th century. Worth visiting is the partially restored Franciscan convent San Mateo (1567).

Some 7km (4 miles) north of the Durango road and 12km (7 miles) before Sombrerete is the Sierra de los Organos (Valley of the Giants), now a national park. It is named after the basaltic columns which are supposed to resemble organ pipes.

✚ 312 H6 ℹ️ Calle Florida 1106, 2nd Floor, Col. Barrio del Calvario ☎ (618) 811 11 07 🕐 Mon–Fri 8–8, Sat 10–2 🚌 Buses from Chihuahua, Mexico City

EL FUERTE

Founded in 1564, El Fuerte was of great strategic importance to the Spanish in their aspirations to lay claim to and settle Arizona and New Mexico, and was a key trading base for the abundant gold and silver which came from the nearby mines. Tranquil and low key, the town has interesting colonial architecture at its heart, an attractive plaza, cobblestone streets and several good restaurants. The Museo de El Fuerte (daily 9–9) is housed in a reconstruction of the fort (from which the town takes it name) which was built by the Spanish in the 17th century to fortify the city against attacks from local Indians. El Fuerte is the first stop after Los Mochis on the Chihuahua al Pacifico railway.

✚ 311 F5 🚂 First-class trains leave Los Mochis at 6am and arrive at train station, 10km (6 miles) from the town, around 7.25am; taxi to town $4.50 per person

ENSENADA

www.ensenada.tourism.com
Ensenada—Baja's leading seaport—on the northern shore of the Bahía de Todos Santos, is a popular place for weekenders from San Diego in the US. While most visitors head out to the attractions of nearby Estero beach, a couple of good museums in the town are worth seeking out. The Museo Histórico Regional (Tue–Sun 10–5), on Gastelum near Calle 1, has an ethnographic collection on peoples of Mesoamerica and temporary exhibits that focus on seminal historical events and themes. The Museo de Historia de Ensenada, Centro Social Cívico y Cultural Riviera, Boulevard Costero (daily 10–6) relates the history of Baja, detailing episodes which range from Amerindian history through an engaging series of ceramics, weapons, letters, and photographs, to the arrival of Catholic missionaries (information in Spanish and English).

While a tourist village atmosphere prevails at the heart of town, there is a lively and very American nightclub/bar zone at its northern edge. Small, rustic restaurants and a good fish market can be found on the harbor fringe. Beyond the waterfront the town has little of interest for visitors. The blue waters of the bay are home to dolphins and there are whale-watching trips (December–March), and bay and coastal excursions available from the Sportfishing Pier on Boulevard Costero. The Bodega de Santo Tomás, Avenida Miramar 666, between Calle 6 and Calle 7, is Mexico's premier winery, dating to 1888 (hourly tours Mon–Sat 11–4).

✚ 310 B1 ℹ️ Boulevard Costero 609 ☎ (646) 178 85 78 🕐 Daily 8–8 🚌 Buses from Tijuana, Mexicali, La Paz

GRUTAS DE GARCÍA

About 45km (28 miles) west of Monterrey, off the road to Saltillo, are the Grutas de García. They were formed more than 50 million years ago and are said to be Mexico's largest cave network. Guided tours, lasting around two hours, follow a 2.5km (1.5-mile) route through 16 caves dripping with stalagmites and stalactites. The caves are reached via a turn-of-the-20th-century cable car which leaves from the parking area, where there is a recreational complex and a swimming pool.

✚ 313 K5 ✉️ Salida a Garcí ☎ (818) 347 15 99 🕐 Daily 9–5 🚌 Buses from Monterrey 🚐 Tours from Monterrey

GUAYMAS

The port of Guaymas sits on a lovely bay backed by desert mountains and its main attraction is the excellent deep-sea fishing and gourmet seafood. Miramar Beach, on Bocachibampo Bay—its blue sea sprinkled with green islets—is the town's resort area. The 18th-century Iglesia de San Fernando is worth a visit; so too is the 17th-century Iglesia de San José de Guaymas, outside the town. The port area also has some buildings of note, including the Templo del Sagrado Corazón de Jesús, the Banco de Sonora, the Palacio Municipal (1899), the Ortiz Barracks and the Antigua Carcel Municipal (old Municipal Prison), constructed in 1900.

About 15km (9 miles) north of Guaymas is Bahía San Carlos. Above the bay a twin-peaked hill, the Tetas de Cabra, is a significant landmark. There is good fishing—marlin, tuna, snapper, wahoo—at San Carlos, with an international tournament held each July.

🚹 311 E4 🛈 Calle 19 and Avenida 6 ☎ (622) 226 03 13 🕔 Mon–Fri 9–3 🚌 Buses from Hermosillo

GUERRERO NEGRO

The shallow lagoons that surround Guerrero are some of the best places in Baja for whale-watching, especially during the mating season between January and March. Many local tour operators arrange trips on *pangas* (small fishing boats), with lunch on Isla Arena included. The town is the headquarters of Exportadora de Sal, the world's largest salt-producing firm, and salt is transported by barge to a deepwater port on Isla Cedros. From there, ore carriers take it to the US, Canada and Japan. Permits which enable you to tour the facility are available from Exportadora.

🚹 310 C4 🛈 Corner of Felix and Castinez ☎ (615) 157 17 77 🚌 Buses from Tijuana

HERMOSILLO

Capital of Sonora state, Hermosillo is a modern city, resort and heart of a rich orchard area. Reminders of an illustrious colonial past can be found around the central Plaza Zaragoza: The imposing neoclassical Catedral de la Asunción (1779) has a baroque dome and three naves; the Palacio de Gobierno, with intricately carved pillars and pediment, stands amid landscaped gardens; and the old traditional quarter lies a few blocks southeast of the plaza, where attractive houses and narrow streets wind around the base of Cerro de la Campana, which has fine views of the city. On the eastern slope of the hill is the Museo Regional de Sonora (Wed–Sat 10–5, Sun 9–4), with exhibits on Sonora's history and geology. Not far north of downtown (Calle Rosales and Transversal) is Ciudad Universitaria (University City), whose modern buildings of Mexican architecture blend effectively with Moorish and mission influences. The main building contains a large library, auditorium and interesting museum (daily 9–1, closed holidays). Many of the town's year-round fine arts and cultural events are open to visitors (details available at the tourist office).

About 2km (1.2 miles) south of Plaza Zaragoza, near the Periférico Sur, is the Centro Ecológico de Sonora (daily 8–5), a botanical garden and zoo with endemic species of plants and animals, including the rare Mexican gray wolf.

🚹 307 E3 🛈 Palacio de Gobierno, first floor ☎ (662) 217 00 60 🕔 Mon–Fri 8–5 🚌 Buses from Nogales, Agua Prieta, Tijuana, Mazatlán, Kino Nuevo

Opposite *Detail on an archway in Plaza de los Tres Pueblos in Hermosillo*
Below *Twin spires overlooking the town of Guaymas*

Above *Typical countryside around Hildago del Parral, famous for mining and for the assassination of Panch Villa*

HIDALGO DEL PARRAL

Hidalgo del Parral's history is split between its mining heritage (lead, copper and silver were produced here for more than 350 years) and Pancho Villa's assassination in 1923. Parral (as it's generally called) is a compact city with shaded plazas, bridges over the often dry Río del Parral, and several churches. In 1629 Juan Rangel de Viezma discovered La Negrita, the first mine in the area. Now known as La Prieta, it overlooks the city from the top of Cerro la Prieta. The mine owners were very generous benefactors to the city and left a legacy of many handsome buildings. Plaza Baca has a statue called *El Buscador de Ilusiones* (*The Dream Seeker*), a naked man panning for gold. The cathedral is on this square, and on the opposite side is the Templo San Juan de Dios, with an exuberant altarpiece painted gold. Across the road from the cathedral is the former Hotel Hidalgo (not in use), built in 1905 by mine owner Pedro Alvarado and given to Pancho Villa in the 1920s. Continuing on Calle Mercaderes, before the bridge is Casa Griensen, now the Colegio Angloamericano Isaac Newton. Griensen, a German, married Alvarado's sister. Behind this house is Casa Alvarado (privately owned), built at the beginning of the 20th century. Its limestone facade is carved with human faces and animals. Across the bridge at the end of Calle Mercaderes is the site of Villa's death, on the corner of Plaza Juárez. Also worth seeing is

the facade of the Teatro Hidalgo on Plazuela Indipendencia.

🚩 312 G4 ℹ️ No tourist office but you can get information from Museo Pancho Villa, Barrera 13 ☎ (627) 525 32 92 🚌 Buses from Durango, Zacatecas

ISLA TIBURÓN

Offshore from Bahía Kino (▷ 241), which draws the crowds for its lovely beaches, is the nature reserve of Isla Tiburón (Shark Island). Mexico's largest island is the ancestral home of the Seri, one of the indigenous cultures of North America. The Seri are no longer allowed to live on the island, which was protected as a reserve in 1963, but the Seri government organizes boat trips to Tiburón and the Seri people still fish the surrounding waters as part of their livelihood. A population of bighorn sheep and mule deer roam the mountain ranges, and there are birds such as peregrine falcons, frigates, and boobies. The waters around the island are excellent for scuba diving, with depths of 50m (165ft) or more common at the southern end.

🚩 310 D3 📄 Information on boat trips to the island from Seri government on main street in Kino Viejo ☎ (662) 242 05 57

LAGUNA OJO DE LIEBRE

Laguna Ojo de Liebre is also known as Scammon's Lagoon, after the whaling captain Charles Melville Scammon who came here in 1857. Its shores are part of the Parque Natural de la Ballena Gris, where California gray whales mate and give

birth between the end of December and February. Most leave by the beginning of April, but some stay as late as May or June.

They can be seen cavorting and sounding from the old salt wharf 10km (6 miles) northwest of Guerrero Negro on the Estero San José (estuary), or from a designated whale-watching area with an observation tower on the shore of Scammon's Lagoon, some 37km (23 miles) south of town.

🚩 310 C4 🚗 Unless you are going on an organized tour, you will need your own transportation. The access road for Laguna Ojo de Liebre branches off Highway 1, 8km (5 miles) east of the intersection. Whale signs lead the way to the park; the road is sandy in places, so drive with care

LA PAZ

La Paz, capital of Baja California Sur, is a relaxed modern city at the southern end of Bahía La Paz. First impressions certainly inspire you to move on fairly promptly, but though the ever-expanding outskirts are an ugly sprawl, the heart of the city still has touches of colonial grace, and the duty-free shopping can kill a few hours while waiting for the next ferry. The one real sight, other than the beaches, is the Museo Antropológico de Baja California Sur (daily 9–6), at Avenida Ignacio Altamirano and Calle 5 de Mayo (four blocks east of the plaza), with a small but admirable display of anthropology, history and prehistory, folklore and geology.

There are many beaches around La Paz, the most popular of which are on the Pichilingüe Peninsula. Heading northeast of town to the ferry terminal at Pichilingüe you'll pass Palmira, Coromuel, El Caimancito, and Tesoro, most of which have basic facilities and restaurants. There are buses to the ferry terminal from the bus station at Paseo Álvaro Obregón and Avenida Independencia.

🚩 310 E6 (inset) ℹ️ Carretera al Norte Km 5.5 ☎ (612) 124 01 00 🕐 Mon–Fri 8–3, Sat 9–1, 2–3; till 7pm high season 🚢 Ferries to Mazatlán and Topolobampo

LORETO

Tucked in between the slopes of the Sierra Giganta and the offshore Isla del Carmen, Loreto has gone through of a tourist revival, with the development of southern Baja and its attraction for fishing enthusiasts, who come here to enjoy some of the best fishing in Baja California. Loreto is also one of the most historic places in Baja, and was the first capital of the Californias. Spanish settlement of the peninsula began here with Father Juan María Salvatierra's founding of the Misión de Nuestra Señora de Loreto on October 25 1697. The mission church, on the *zócalo*, is the largest structure in town and perhaps the best restored of all the Baja California mission buildings. The museum (Tue–Sun 9–1, 2–6) beside the church is worth a visit for its displays on Bajan history.

Some 8km (5 miles) south of Loreto construction continues on the super-resort of Nopoló, which was tipped to rival the developments at Cancún, Ixtapa and Huatulco. An international airport, streets and electricity were all installed, then things slowed down as money was diverted elsewhere. In recent years, new investors have reignited the project and American expatriates are buying homes and condominiums. ✚ 310 D5 ▯ City Hall, Calle Madero ☎ (613) 135 04 11 ◷ Mon–Fri 9–5

LOS MOCHIS

Los Mochis, 25km (16 miles) from the coast in the state of Sinaloa, is the departure point for the Chihuahua al Pacífico Railway (see Barranca del Cobre, ▷ 243) which links the coast with the Sierra Tarahumara. Among the attractions here is the wonderful music, courtesy of the *mariachis*, who roam the lively nightspots and bars.

The city was founded in 1904 around a sugar mill built by the American Benjamin Johnson. The name is derived either from a local word meaning "hill like a turtle," or possibly from *mocho*, meaning one-armed, perhaps after a cowboy who was thus mutilated. Johnson's wife was responsible for building the Iglesia de Sagrado Corazón. A stairway leads up the hillside behind La Pérgola, a pleasant public park near the city reservoir, for an excellent view of Los Mochis. ✚ 311 F5 ▯ Buses from Mexico City, Guadalajara, Tres Estrellas de Oro, Ciudad Obregón, Tijuana, Mazatlán, Tres Estrellas de Oro, Tepic ✈ Airport Federal, 6.5km (4 miles) north

MAZATLÁN

www.gomazatlan.com
Mazatlán, the largest Mexican port on the Pacific Ocean, spreads along a peninsula at the foot of the Sierra Madre. With its stunning backdrop, golden beaches, excellent fishing and warm winters, its popularity has been increasing, gradually transforming the area from a laid-back visitors' haven to a smarter, more polished resort.

Approaching Mazatlán by sea from Baja shows the city at its most impressive—two pyramid-shaped hills, one with a lighthouse on top, the other the peninsula of Isla de la Piedra (Rock Island), guard the harbor entrance. The old part of town is around Plaza Machado, on Calle Carnaval—far and away the most interesting part of the city. Half a block from the plaza is the restored Teatro Ángela Peralta, the 17th-century opera house. The Acuario Mazatlán (Aquarium, daily 9.30–5.30), on Avenida de los Deportes III, just off the beach, includes sharks and blindfish. The Museo Arqueológico de Mazatlán (Mon–Sat 10–5, Sun 10–3), Calle Sixto Osuna 115, has exhibits on the state of Sinaloa. The Zona Dorada (Golden Zone) is a developed tourist area, with corresponding prices, including the beaches of Gaviotas, Los Sábalos, Escondida, Delfín, Cerritos, Cangrejo, and Brujas (north of Playa Brujas is a rocky area which is good for snorkeling. From Olas Altas the promenade curves northward around the bay, first as Paseo Claussen, then Avenida del Mar, which leads to Avenida Camarón Sábalo in the Zona Dorada. The sunsets are superb seen from this side of the peninsula; at that time of day high-divers can be seen and the fishing boats return to the north beach. Mazatlán is also renowned for its Carnaval (▷ 261). ✚ 312 G6 ▯ Carnaval 1317, near Plaza Muchado ☎ (669) 981 88 83 ◷ Mon–Fri 9–5 ▯ Buses from major cities west and north of the capital ✈ Aeropuerto General Rafael Buelna (MZT), 19km (12 miles) south

Below left Monumento a la vida, *Mazatlán*
Below *Loreto is undergoing an expansion of its tourist industry, building modern hotels*

INFORMATION

✚ 313 K5 🛈 Edificio Kalos, Zaragoza 1300 Sur ☎ (81) 8340 1080/8344 4343 ◷ Mon–Fri 8.30–6.30, Sat–Sun 9–5 (sometimes closed at lunchtime) 🚌 Several major bus routes converge at Monterrey, connecting it to the rest of Mexico and to Nuevo Laredo, Reynosa and Matamoros on the US border ✈ Aeropuerto Internacional General Mariano Escobedo (MTY), 24km (15 miles) east

MONTERREY

Monterrey has a thriving university, ebullient nightlife, diverse gastronomy, eclectic shopping and some of the finest museums in the country. Capital of Nuevo León state and the third-largest city in Mexico, Monterrey is dominated by Cerro de la Silla (Saddle Hill) from the east. Despite being one of Mexico's major industrial players, it is worth visiting for its fine museums.

The city's heart lies just north of the Río Santa Catarina. Plaza Zaragoza, Plaza 5 de Mayo, Explanada de los Héroes and Parque Hundido link with the Gran Plaza to the south to form the Macro Plaza, claimed to be the biggest civic square in the world. It runs north–south and is nine blocks long by two blocks wide; its focal point is the Faro del Comercio, a rust-red 70m (230ft) obelisk designed by Luis Barragán (1902–88). To the east of the Faro is the 18th-century cathedral, badly damaged in the war against the US between 1846 and 1847. The older area, east of the cathedral, is the Barrio Antiguo.

HISTORY AND ART

The Museo de Historia Mexicana (Tue–Fri 10–7, Sat–Sun 10–8) off the north end of the plaza is an excellent interactive museum, which reveals the history of Mexico from pre-Columbian times through to the modern era, highlighting the first great achievements in art, architecture and scientific knowledge of the Mesoamerican cultures.

The Museo de Arte Contemporaneo de Monterrey (MARCO), Calle Zua Zua (Tue–Sun 10–6, Wed until 8; closed Mon) is a superb modern art gallery. The permanent collection brings together the most influential Mexican artists including Frida Kahlo, Diego Rivera and Rufino Tamayo, alongside important contemporary Latin American and international artists.

NATURE

The serene Parque Ecológico Chipinque (daily 6am–8pm) lies on the southern outskirts of the city and offers easily accessible hiking and biking trails that wind through 1,620ha (4,000 acres) of mountainous pine forest. Bird-watching and rock climbing are other popular pursuits. The park is a 15-minute taxi ride from downtown.

Below *The orange tower of the Faro del Comercio (Lighthouse of Business), from which green lasers are beamed across the city at night*

MULEGÉ

Mulegé is a real oasis; a tranquil retreat outside of the spring break, and an increasingly popular hideaway for retirees from the US and Canada. There are lovely beaches, good diving, snorkeling and boating in the Bahía Concepción. The old Federal territorial prison (La Cananea), a short walk from the heart of town, has been converted into the Museo Mulegé (Mon–Fri 9–1). It became known as the "prison without doors" because the inmates were allowed out during the day to work in the town. Just upstream from the highway bridge on the south side of the river is the Misión Santa Rosalía de Mulegé (▷ 259), founded by the Jesuits in 1705. Above the mission there is a good lookout point over the town and its sea of palm trees. Facing the other way there is a fine view at sunset over the inland mesas. There is one bank in Mulegé, but it is wise to come with plenty of cash.

➕ 310 D4 🚌 Buses to the south do not leave at scheduled times; ask in town as everyone knows when they come through

PARQUE NACIONAL SIERRA DE SAN PEDRO MÁRTIR

The serrated peaks of the Cordillera's highest mountain range rise dramatically from the Sierra de San Pedro Mártir National Park. The highest peak in Baja, Picacho del Diablo (Devil's Summit) stands at 3,078m (10,098ft). A hiker's paradise, the park is crisscrossed by trails revealing an ethereal landscape of deep canyons where cascading waterfalls and petroglyphs provide wilderness adventure. The flora and fauna vary according to altitude and range from pine, yucca and sagebrush to sugar pine and the endemic San Mártir cypress, and provide a lush contrast to the barren beauty of so much of the Baja peninsula. Myriad trails afford wonderful views of the canyons and there are many hikes across open meadows to more challenging boulder-strewn rivers. From the observatory, which crowns the Cerro

de la Cúpula, 22km (14 miles) from the main park entrance, a trail leads to the Cañon del Diablo, the deepest canyon in the park.

➕ 310 B2 ✉ Main entrance at La Corona de Abajo 🚌 From Highway 1 follow signs for the Observatorio

REAL DE CATORCE

High in the Sierra Madre Oriental is Real de Catorce, one of Mexico's most interesting old silver-mining towns. Founded in 1772, it clusters around the sides of a valley with the river 1,000m (3,280ft) below. At its height in the late 19th century the town had a population of around 40,000, but because of falling silver prices after World War II hundreds of people left and many of the buildings became derelict. However, with increasing tourism and the reopening of a silver mine, the one-time ghost town is reviving.

The first church to be built was the Iglesia de Virgen del Guadalupe (1779), a little way out of town. Lovely ceiling paintings remain, as well as the black coffin used for the Mass of the *Cuerpo Presente*. Many of the images from this church were moved to the Iglesia de San Francisco (1817). Here the floor is made of wooden panels, which can be lifted to see the catacombs below. In a room to one side of the main altar are retablos, touchingly simple paintings on tin given as votive offerings to the saint for his intercession.

Guided tours are available from the Casa de la Moneda (the former mint which is now a museum), in front of the cathedral; they include the *palenque*—an eight-sided cock-fighting arena built in 1863, which seated 500 to 600 people (this is otherwise closed to the public).

➕ 313 K6 ℹ Calle Lanza, at Casa de la Moneda

SAN FELIPE

San Felipe is a tranquil fishing and shrimping port on the Gulf of California with a population of about 25,000. Long a destination for devoted sportfishermen and a

Above *Northern Mexico, with its deserts, canyons and mountains, has a diverse range of cacti*

weekend retreat for Americans, it has burgeoned into an easy-going beach resort with a clutch of budget trailer parks, and activities ranging from kayaking to golf. Alternatively, you can just stroll along the wide stretches of sand, contemplating the stunning sunsets.

San Felipe is protected from desert winds by the coastal mountains and is unbearably hot during the summer, but in winter the climate is perfect. There is a good view of the wide sandy beach from the Virgin of Guadalupe shrine near the lighthouse. *Día de la Marina* (Navy Day) is celebrated on June 1 with a carnival, street dancing and boat races.

➕ 310 C2 ℹ Avenida Mar de Cortés y Manzanillo, opposite Motel El Capitán ☎ (686) 577 11 55 🕐 Mon–Fri 8–8, Sat 9–1 🚌 Highway 5 heads south from Mexicali to San Felipe. After passing Río Hardy and Laguna Salada (Km 72)—a vast, dry, alkali flat unless turned into a muddy morass by rare falls of rain—the road continues to San Felipe. When floods close the road across the Laguna Salada use Highway 3 from Ensenada

SAN IGNACIO

The oasis of San Ignacio comes as a blessed relief after the arid landscape of the Desierto Vizcaíno (▷ 244). It's a very attractive stop on the way south, with its thatched roofs and pastel shades. Here the Jesuits built a mission in 1728 and planted the ancestors of the town's date palm groves. The beautifully preserved mission church, completed by the Dominicans in 1786 and one of the finest examples of colonial architecture in all Baja California, stands on the square.

In the barren hills to the north and south of the town are countless caves, many of which are decorated with ancient human and animal designs left by Baja's original inhabitants. These still defy reliable dating, or full understanding, and to reach most of them requires a trek by mule over tortuous trails. The easiest to visit are those near San Francisco de la Sierra, 45km (28 miles) north of San Ignacio: a guide is required by law. Tours can be arranged through most hotels and agencies in town, but they are expensive. The cave at the Cuesta del Palmarito, 5km (3 miles) east of Rancho Santa Marta (50km/31 miles northwest of San Ignacio), is filled with designs of humans with uplifted arms, in brown and black; a jeep and guide (if you can find one) are required. The same hotels and agencies will also arrange whale-watching tours to Laguna San Ignacio, one of the best whale-viewing sites in Baja.
✚ 310 D4

Above *Prehistoric drawings in the caves at Los Flechas, near San Ignacio, depicting figures pierced by a number of arrows*

SAN JOSÉ DEL CABO

Founded in 1730 by the Jesuits, San José del Cabo is now essentially a modern town divided into two districts: the Americanized resort sector, with swanky condos, golf courses, fine restaurants and Fonatur development on the beach, and the northern downtown zone, with government offices and businesses near Parque Mijares. The main attraction is the relaxed atmosphere and a more traditional and low-key Mexican way of life than in Cabo San Lucas (▷ 242).

The chief reference point is the main square, Plaza Mijares. From here narrow streets lined with restored adobe buildings meander into tranquil leafy enclaves. The attractive church on the square was built in 1940 on the final site of the mission of 1730; a tile mosaic over the entrance depicts the murder of Padre Tamaral by rebellious Indians in 1734. This area has become increasingly chichi, with small galleries and cosmopolitan coffee shops and boutiques. Most of the top hotels are west of San José along the beaches or nearby *estero* (estuary), although the Fonatur development blocks access to much of the beach near town. The best are Playa Nuevo Sol and Playa California, about 3km (2 miles) from downtown.
✚ 310 E7 (inset) 🛈 Palacio Municipal, on Plaza Mijares, has free maps and brochures 🚌 Buses from La Paz, Cabo San Lucas ✈ Los Cabos international airport, 13km (8 miles) north

SAN QUINTÍN

San Quintín's appeal lies in its proximity to the beach areas of Santa María to the south, where there are excellent conditions for inshore fishing. Several operators in town can organize fishing trips.

Brigades of dedicated clam diggers can be also seen along Playa Santa María. Good point breaks at Cabo San Quintín ensure a lively surf scene, despite the area's inaccessibility, and there is scuba diving; conditions for underwater photography are excellent.
✚ 310 B2 🚗 The coast of San Quintín is virtually impossible to explore without your own transport 🚌 Buses between Tijuana and Lázara Cárdenas

SANTA ROSALIA

Santa Rosalia, 38km (24 miles) north of Mulegé, was built by the French El Boleo Copper Company in the 1880s and laid out in neat rows of wood-framed houses, many with broad verandas, which today give the town its distinctively un-Mexican appearance. Most of the mining ceased in 1953, though the smelter, several smokestacks and much of the original mining operation can be seen north of town. There is a small museum off Calle Francisco with historic exhibits of mining and smelting. The cast-iron church of Santa Barbara, a block north of the main plaza, was built for the 1889 Paris' World Exposition from a design by Gustave Eiffel. It was then shipped to Baja. A car ferry service operates between Santa Rosalia and Guaymas from the small harbor.
✚ 310 D4

TIJUANA

The border town of Tijuana, the former playground for America's thirsty exiles from the prohibition years, is now driven by tourism, with the lure of inexpensive goods. More than 40 million people cross the border annually, fueling Tijuana's claim to be "the world's most-visited city": This is the frontline between the US and Mexico, where the two face up to each other in pleasure and politics. Often criticized as not being the "real Mexico," it is nevertheless a historic and impassioned place.

Tijuana came to prominence during the 1920s Prohibition in the US, when Hollywood stars and other Americans flocked to the sleazy bars and enterprising nightlife of Tijuana and Mexicali, both at that time little more than large villages. Today, tourism is the major industry. Although countless bars and nightclubs still vie for the visitor's dollar, it is duty-free bargains, greyhound racing and inexpensive English-speaking dentists that attract many visitors. It is your last, or first, opportunity to buy craftwork drawn in from all around Mexico, but remember that this border area is much more expensive than places farther south, and on weekends prices are hiked up even higher. The main drag, Avenida Revolución, runs directly south from the tourist kiosk on the edge of the red-light district and is awash with bars, restaurants and souvenir shops (usually open 10–9). It is generally regarded as one of the world's most popular streets for shopping.

TIJUANA SIGHTS

The Centro Cultural Tijuana, a spectacular building designed by Pedro Ramírez Vázquez, on Paseo de los Héroes at Mina, contains the excellent Museo de las Californias (Tue–Sun 10–5.30), which chronicles the history of the Baja peninsula. Visit the small Museo de Cera de Tijuana (Wax Museum; Mon–Fri 10–6, Sat–Sun 10–7) on Calle 1 y Madero to see historical figures and movie stars ranging from Pancho Villa to Marilyn Monroe and Michael Jackson. There are also handicraft shops, a restaurant, concert hall and the ultra-modern spherical IMAX Theater, where films are shown on a 180-degree screen.

The Jai Alai Palace (Palacio Frontón), downtown at Avenida Revolución and Calle 7, was built for jai alai, a fast paced and furious game in which ball speeds exceed 160kph (100mph). Today, the architecturally impressive venue hosts music concerts and boxing matches.

Tijuana has two bullrings: the Plaza de Toros Monumental at Playas de Tijuana is the only one in the world built on the sea shore. El Toreo bullring is 3km (2 miles) east of downtown on Bulevar Agua Caliente; *corridas* (bullfights) alternate between the two venues between May and September. The bulls are killed at the end of the fight so this is not for the squeamish or those concerned about animal rights.

INFORMATION

www.tijuanaonline.org

☩ 310 B1 ℹ Paseo de los Héroes 9365 (there is also an information booth at the US border crossing) ☎ (664) 607 39 07 🚌 Bus station 5km (3 miles) southeast of town

Below *The distinctive Tijuana Cultural Center is unmissable, both inside and out*

ON THE EDGE OF THE COPPER CANYON

This walk skirts the edge of the Urique Canyon, one of a series of dramatic gorges that make up the Barranca del Cobre, passing through pine forests and three lookout points.

THE WALK

Distance: 2.5km (1.5 miles)
Time: 3 hours
Start/end at: Hotel Divisadero Barrancas

HOW TO GET THERE

Visitors to El Divisadero usually arrive on Ferrocarril Chihuahua al Pacifico (tel (614) 439 72 10, www.chepe.com.mx), more commonly known as the Copper Canyon train, which runs for 653km (405 miles) between Los Mochis, on the Pacific Coast, to Chihuahua city. Alternatively, El Divisadero can also be reached by car via Highway 127 from Creel, which connects with Highway 16 from Chihuahua.

★ Urique is the deepest canyon in Mexico. El Divisadero sits some 2,392m (7,848ft) above sea level and provides extraordinary vistas into and across the canyon. The Tarahumara, who have remained one of Mexico's most traditional indigenous cultures, live in caves

and small settlements in and around the canyon. Tarahumara women sit alongside the train tracks, hotels and lookout points at El Divisadero, selling carved wooden dolls, hand-woven baskets, belts woven on back-strap looms and rustic pottery. Carry a bottle of water and snacks, as there are no restaurants along the route. A market next to the train station sells sodas, water and food, and vendors along the stairway to the station sell *tacos*, *burritos*, *quesadillas*, and other hot snacks.

❶ Begin your walk at the parking area at the Hotel Divisadero Barrancas, across a dirt road from El Divisadero train station. Head southeast on the dirt road, walking past a large dirt field where Tarahumara dancers often perform for tour groups. If you see people assembling there, wait for the show.

Continue on the dirt road until you see a sign and fence for Hotel

Barrancas on the west side of the road. Cross through the fence (there is an old, rickety gate, but this is not used) and turn south on the dirt trail alongside the edge of the canyon. Carry on for about 125m (135 yards) to cross a dirt airstrip that is occasionally used by private planes. Continue to the Mirador Elefante, a fenced-in lookout point at the edge of the canyon.

❷ From the viewpoint, look south to the rock formation that resembles an elephant and north to the Hotel Divisadero Barrancas—seemingly suspended over the canyon. Vendors selling local crafts gather here, but the selection is better farther on.

Stay to the right side of the fence as you continue to the next lookout, Divisadero Escalera.

❸ A narrow ladder is set in a crevice in the rocks below the lookout point. The Tarahumara use it to get to and from their homes in the canyon. The women climb up or down barefoot, carrying a large plastic bag stuffed with their wares on their heads. Tarahumara is a Spanish corruption of the indigenous word *Raramuri*, meaning "running people." They are extraordinarily fleet of foot, running long distances through the canyon chasing deer until the animals are exhausted and easy to capture. Unless you're exceptionally dexterous and strong, resist the urge to descend the perilous ladder. Again, women have their crafts on display for sale here.

From Divisadero Escalera walk southeast to reach the Piedra Volada (Balancing Rock), the most popular attraction in the area.

❹ A large stone hangs over the canyon, looking as if it's about to topple at any moment. Brave souls climb it and balance as the rock tips from side to side. The selection of crafts for sale at this point is of better quality than at the others. The beaded belts and wristbands are especially attractive. There are restrooms and trash cans here.

Either follow the driveway west to the main dirt road or backtrack along the trail you came along to the Hotel Divisadero Barrancas.

If you wish to continue, turn south at the road that runs along the edge of the canyon and follow it to the Hotel Posada Mirador for lunch, then return the same way to the Hotel Divisadero Barrancas.

WHERE TO EAT AND STAY
HOTEL POSADA MIRADOR
www.mexicoscoppercanyon.com
Perched on the rim of the canyon, this lodge has 51 rooms, most with fireplaces and canyon views. It's popular with group tours. Meals are served in a dining room with log ceilings; food is average.
✉ El Divisadero, Los Mochis ☎ (635) 578 30 20 ✋ From $280, including meals

HOTEL DIVISADERO BARRANCAS
www.hoteldivisadero.com
Right across the road from the train station, the hotel has 52 rooms;

most have fireplaces and some have canyon views.
✉ El Divisadero ☎ (614) 415 11 99
✋ $180–$220, including meals

HOTEL MANSIÓN TARAHUMARA
www.mansiontarahumara.com.mx
The turreted towers seem a bit out of place in the pine forest but the heated indoor pool, sauna and steam room feel good after a long hike.
✉ El Divisadero ☎ (614) 415 47 21
✋ From $165, including meals

WHEN TO GO
The best times to visit are September to November and March to June. It snows in El Divisadero from December to February.

Clockwise from below *Ponderosa pine in Copper Canyon; Tarahumara girls; view of Urique Canyon*

THROUGH THE HIGH MOUNTAINS OF BAJA

One of the most dramatic drives in Baja, this route takes in stunning views of the sea from high in the mountains. On the way you'll pass a small cluster of prehistoric petroglyphs (cave paintings) and an 18th-century mission church.

THE DRIVE
Distance: 74km (46 miles)
Time: 6 hours
Start/end at: Loreto

★ The dirt road into the Sierra de la Giganta is somewhat rough, but passable in a regular car, except during the rainy season (August to November). Ask in town about the road conditions, and don't attempt this drive after hard rains. There are plans to improve the road, since San Javier has become a popular side trip for passengers on cruise ships visiting Loreto. The road is part of the Camino Real (Royal Road), once used by the Spaniards in the 18th century as they established a chain of mission settlements throughout

the Californias. San Javier was chosen for some of the New World's first orchards and vineyards because of its exceptionally temperate climate and abundance of fresh water supplies.

From Loreto (▷ 249), turn south on Highway 1 to the west of town and continue for 2km (1 mile) to the turn-off on the west side of the road, marked San Javier. From here the road runs southwest, winding up Cerro la Gigántica (1,490m/4,888ft) through low hills. After 10km (6 miles) the road begins to climb steeply and signs to the petroglyphs start to appear. There is parking near the sign on the left-hand side of the road.

❶ Baja's petroglyphs are one of its great mysteries. No one knows who painted the large figures of humans and animals, although experts have determined that they date from 3000BC to AD1650. The most dramatic petroglyphs, with figures up to 4m (13ft) tall, are in remote caves high in the Sierra and are accessible only by hiking or riding a *burro* (donkey) for several days. The small cluster of paintings on the road to San Javier include faint red, white and black figures of deer and people.

From the petroglyphs, continue 10km (6 miles) on Highway 1 to Rancho las Parras, built in an oasis on both sides of the road.

Clockwise from left *Typical desert terrain near San Javier; statue of St. Francisco Javier in Misión San Javier; prehistoric petroglyphs*

② The private ranch has a small chapel on the east side of the road and tropical fruit orchards on the west, including 5,000 mango trees. Some of the olive, date and fig trees were planted by the Jesuits in the late 1700s. The ranch is not normally open to the public, but if the gates are open and there's someone around, ask to see Juan Angel (also known as Johnny Angel), the manager of the ranch. A garrulous gentleman in his 80s, he loves picking exotic fruits for guests to sample. If he takes you on a tour, offer 50 or so pesos for his time.

From the ranch the road climbs steeply, twisting along mountainsides with staggering views of canyons, orchards, small ranches and the sea for another 16km (10 miles) to San Javier.

③ The small settlement of San Javier sits in a deep valley surrounded by towering cliffs. Its 100 or so residents live in whitewashed homes lining the dirt street that ends at the mission church. The stone structure, built from slabs cut from a nearby *arroyo* (dry stream), was moved from its original location in 1720 to free up the fertile land for orchards. The Jesuits planted grapes, olives, figs and oranges in the valley, which supported a community of more than 500 residents in the mid-1800s.

From the outside the church is rather plain, although the entrance has a subtle Moorish look, with several domes and turrets. Inside, several oil paintings hanging over the main and side altars depict Jesus, Mary, Joseph, the trinity, and St. Javier. The church is an important pilgrimage site for people from all over central Baja, and on December 1, 2 and 3 the town is filled with thousands of pilgrims for the Feast of San Javier. Villagers, eager to sell home-made candies and local produce from stands along the street leading to the church.

To return to Loreto, retrace your drive down the mountain, then turn north (left) on Highway 1. Be sure to leave San Javier at least two hours before dusk as it is not advisable to drive the mountain road in the dark.

TOURIST INFORMATION
✉ Calle Madero at Salvatierra in the City Hall, Loreto ☎ (613) 135 04 11
🕐 Mon–Fri 9–5

WHEN TO GO
The best weather is during October and November, and April and May. Summers can be very hot and winters chilly and very windy.

WHERE TO EAT
LA PALAPA
A small restaurant next to the church serves bean and *machaca* (dried shredded beef) *burritos,* homemade cheese and *tortillas,* cold sodas and other simple fare. Take snacks and water for the drive.
✉ San Javier 🕐 Daily 10–7

CAFÉ OLÉ CALLE
Serves *tacos, burritos* and sandwiches for a picnic lunch.
✉ Madero 14, Loreto ☎ (613) 135 04 96
🕐 Daily 9–7

WHERE TO STAY
CASA DE ANA
www.hoteloasis.com
Simple rooms in adobe bungalows have hot showers and electricity for about two hours after dusk. Meals are available. Reserve at the Hotel Oasis, Calle de la Playa (tel (613) 135 01 12), in Loreto.
✉ On the main road at the entrance to San Javier 🖐 $45

THE SEA OF CORTÉS: LORETO TO MULEGÉ

This route goes from Loreto, site of the first mission in the Californias, to the oasis town of Mulegé. After passing through desert terrain with the Sierra de la Giganta looming to the west, the highway reaches the shores of the Sea of Cortés, where there are panoramic views of crystalline bays dotted with small islands.

THE DRIVE

Distance: 270km (167 miles)
Time: 8 hours
Start/end at: Loreto
Note: Watch for cattle wandering on the roadside and be prepared to drive slowly behind buses and trucks.

★ Turn north on Highway 1 at the west side of Loreto. The town and sea quickly disappear from view as you drive across the coastal plain past small ranches and palm groves. The road climbs steep hills and descends through *vados* (sudden dips in the road). After 23km (14 miles) you approach a military checkpoint where all vehicles must stop for inspection. Be aware that the officers may ask to look inside the vehicle's trunk (boot) in a routine check for weapons and drugs. After climbing steep hills and negotiating narrow curves for about 45km (28 miles), the Sea of Cortés appears to the east.

❶ The next 40km (25 miles) cover one of Baja's most spectacular drives along Bahía Concepción, a huge bay open to the north and sheltered by Punta Concepción. The entire bay is a national marine preserve that's home to frigates, blue-footed boobies, porpoises, whales, and many marine mammals, fish and birds. As you drive along the coastline you'll see volcanic islands, white-sand beaches and water in startling shades of blue and green.

Continue for a further 23m (14 miles), then turn east on a dirt road to Playa Buenaventura (there's a sign at the entrance).

❷ Guests swing in hammocks at Hotel San Buenaventura and lunch on ceviche and fried fish at the adjacent restaurant.

If you want to swim or go kayaking in the bay, stay on Highway 1 for another 20km (12.5 miles) until you reach a small sign on the right-hand side of the road to EcoMundo Baja Tropicales.

❸ This ecologically sensitive camp houses the largest kayaking outfitter on the bay.

The views of the bay continue as you drive north on Highway 1 toward Mulegé, passing Playa Concepción and Playa Santispac, both dotted with recreational vehicles and vacation homes. Continue for another 29km (18 miles) until you reach a large sign for the Hotel Serenidad on the right-hand side of the road. Turn right and follow the dirt road to the Hotel Serenidad on a cliff above the Sea of Cortés.

❹ The view of the sea disappears by the time you reach Hotel Serenidad and is replaced with lush palm groves and campgrounds.

Drive 10km (6 miles) along this busy stretch of Highway 1. A small bridge passes above the Río Santa Rosalia. Past the river is the turn-off east to the small town of Mulegé. At the intersection of the highway and the road into Mulegé called Calle Moctezuma (you won't see any street signs), turn right. Follow the road as it becomes a one-way street and bears right (southeast). Driving is difficult at this point, as the streets are narrow and unmarked. The main road becomes Calle Madero. There is parking next to Hotel Las Casitas, in Mulegé.

5 It's best to explore Mulegé (▷ 251) on foot. The main plaza is a block south of Las Casitas, and there are souvenir shops, *taco* stands and restaurants on side roads.

Back in your car, turn southwest on Calle Zaragoza and drive under the highway bridge along the riverbed and up a steep hill to the Misión Santa Rosalia de Mulegé—about 3km (2 miles) from the bridge.

6 The modest brick mission church of Santa Rosalia is usually locked, but the view from the churchyard over the river is worth a look. Established in 1705, the mission has been restored after hurricane damage and abandonment.

From the church, turn southeast on Calle Moctezuma and then south on Highway 1 to return to Loreto.

TOURIST INFORMATION
✉ Calle Madero at Salvatierra in the City Hall, Loreto ☎ (613) 135 04 11
🕐 Mon–Fri 9–5

WHERE TO EAT AND STAY
ECOMUNDO BAJA TROPICALES
The camp has simple *cabañas* with cots and hammocks. Communal showers have cold water only. The restaurant serves breakfast and lunch. Kayaks are available for rent.
✉ Highway 1 Loreto-Mulegé Km 111 at Playa Concepción ☎ (615) 153 04 09/153 03 20 ✋ $15–$25 per person

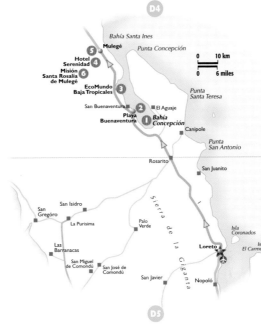

HOTEL LAS CASITAS
www.baja-web.com/mulege/casitas.htm
This former home is also Mulegé's informal visitor information office. The garden restaurant serves good Mexican food.
✉ Calle Madero 50, Mulegé ☎ (615) 153 00 19 🌐 $40 double ✋

HOTEL SAN BUENAVENTURA
www.hotelsanbuenaventura.com
Simple beachfront *cabañas* cost $25 per night. The restaurant is open for breakfast, lunch and dinner daily. Kayak rental is also available.
✉ Highway 1 Loreto-Mulegé Km 91, Playa Buenaventura ☎ (615) 155 56 16 ✋ $69–$99

HOTEL SERENIDAD
This is a great place for lunch, with Mexican specials and clean rest rooms. Guests dining here are allowed to use the cool, refreshing swimming pool. Rooms and cottages are both available for overnight stays.
✉ Mulegé, Highway 1 ☎ (615) 153 05 30 ✋ $65–$120

Opposite *A hazy sunset over the bay and mountains viewed from Loreto*
Below *The clear blue waters of Bahía Concepción are ideal for snorkeling*

CABO SAN LUCAS
BAJA CANTINA
Baja Cantina is one of the busiest spots, with a laid-back, holiday vibe. The dockside bar with a large-screen sports TV packs in the local gringo residents, who enjoy the all-day happy hour specials. There is a highly regarded restaurant where anglers can have their catch cooked.

✉ Marina, L-M Dock, Cabo San Lucas ☎ (642) 143 15 91 🕒 Daily 7am–1am

SOLMAR FLEET
www.solmar.com

Choose from a variety of fishing cruises, from short excursions in *pangas* (8.5m/28-foot boats) beginning at $75 to more luxurious sportfishing cruisers at $400–$700 for serious anglers interested in catching marlin, dorado, tuna and wahoo. Prices include rent of cruiser, on-board captain, live-bait tank, international premium tackle and fighting chairs. Live bait costs extra.

✉ Boulevard Marina, Cabo San Lucas ☎ (624) 143 06 46 🕒 Daily 8–5

EL SQUID ROE
www.elsquidroe.com

Hot and raw, the Squid Roe is where anything well and truly goes.

The dance floor, surrounded by a three-tier people-watcher's heaven, is the focal point. By 11pm gyrating hipsters are packed into every nook and cranny, with music ranging from hard core dance and garage to more light-hearted rock and pop. Dinner is served until 11.30.

✉ Boulevard Marina, Plaza Bonita, Cabo San Lucas ☎ (642) 143 12 69 🕒 Daily 12pm–3am

CHIHUAHUA
CASA DE LAS ARTESANÍAS DEL ESTADO DE CHIHUAHUA
There are many good *artesanía* shops in Chihuahua that sell everything from silver jewelry to weavings and musical instruments. The best collection of Tarahumara crafts, including ceramics, baskets and furniture can be found here. Prices are fair in Chihuahua, so bargaining is not necessary.

✉ Avenida Niños Heroes 1101, Chihuahua ☎ (614) 437 12 92 🕒 Mon–Fri 9–7, Sat 10–5

CREEL
EXPEDICIONES UMARIKE
www.umarike.com.mx

The professionally run Expediciones Umarike organizes adventurous

Above *Sportfishing attracts anglers from all over the world to Baja California*

pursuits in the Copper Canyon, including mountain biking and hiking to remote regions, rock-climbing, exploring colonial mining towns and thrilling rides across spectacular landscapes with 1,830m (6,000ft) descents. Guides speak both Spanish and English.

✉ Avenida Ferrocarril s/n, north of tracks west of Plaza, PO Box 61, Creel ☎ (635) 456 06 32 🔖 Trips range from 4 to 8 days and cost $560 and $1,150 respectively

ENSENADA
HUSSONG'S CANTINA
Hussong's Cantina is one of the liveliest spots in town. Earthy and raw, the vibe tips from light-hearted ebullience to frenzied revelry. Locals and visitors alike lap up the meandering *mariachi* soundtrack punctuated with *ranchera*.

✉ Avenida Ruíz 113, Ensenada ☎ (646) 178 32 10

LORETO
ARTURO'S SPORTFISHING FLEET
www.arturosport.com

Arturo's offers a multitude of marine activities, from snorkeling in the waters around Coronado to fishing and scuba diving in the Loreto Bay Marine Park. Trips explore the bay's five islands, where you dive among rainbow fish, Cortez angel fish and surgeon fish and a variety of other marine species. Dives are suitable for all levels of experience.

✉ Loreto ☎ (613) 135 07 66 ⊙ Trips leave daily at 9am ⬚ Day rates $130–$300

MAZATLÁN
THE FIESTA MEXICANA

One of the longest-standing dinner fiesta shows in the country, this regional extravaganza is great entertainment for all the family. Music, dancing, vibrant costumes, *mariachis*, fire throwing, magic shows, Mexican wedding and hat parties, and audience participation.

✉ Playa Mazatlán Hotel, Playa las Gaviotas, Mazatlán ☎ (669) 989 05 55 ⊙ Tue, Thu, Sat 7pm–10.30pm ⬚ Show ticket $35, includes an all-you-can-eat buffet

LA PAZ
KUMUTÚ

This excellent shop is a labor of love for owners Marta and Aldo, who sell and eulogize over their bright collection of regional products, from travel literature to wildlife guides, local food, wine and delicacies, ceramics, textiles, and maps. There is also a small café, which sells coffee, tea, cakes, and sandwiches.

✉ Calle Domínguez 1245, La Paz ☎ (612) 122 24 71 ⊙ Daily 10–7

EL TEATRO DE LA CIUDAD

El Teatro de la Ciudad is the cultural heart of La Paz and has a lively repertoire of performances ranging from classical music to theater, symphonies, ballet and experimental dance. The majority of performances are by local and Mexican artists, but there are occasional shows of international prestige.

✉ Avenida Navarro, La Paz ☎ (612) 125 04 86 ⬚ Depends on performance

ROSARITO
MERCADO DE LAS ARTESANÍAS

While Baja is certainly not renowned for being a shopping Shangri-la,

FEBRUARY/MARCH
LA PAZ CARNIVAL

This Pre-Lenten Mardi Gras (carnival) is becoming one of Mexico's finest. The *malecón* (waterfront) is converted into a swirling mass of dancing, games, restaurants and stands, and the street parade is highly entertaining.

✉ La Paz ⊙ Before Lent

MAZATLÁN CARNIVAL

Mazatlán is renowned for its carnival extravaganzas, with a spectacular array of parades, costumes, *mariachis*, live concerts, food and drink ,and general revelry. The hub of activity is Olas Altas *malecón* coastal boulevard, and festivities reach their climax on the eve of Ash Wednesday. Reserve rooms in advance.

JUNE
HECHO EN MEXICO JAZZ FESTIVAL

www.jazzinmexico.com

Jazz artists from all over Mexico perform at various Cabo bars and restaurants.

✉ Cabo San Lucas ⊙ Early June

Rosarito tends to provide a greater selection of goods than most towns, in terms of handicrafts. The artisans' market has a good selection of rather predictable souvenirs, ranging from hand-painted ceramics to tequila and sombreros.

✉ Boulevard Juárez 306, Rosarito ⊙ Daily 10–6

SERGIO'S SPORTFISHING CENTER

www.sergios-sportfishing.com

Sergio's offers daily group boat excursions to Todos Santos from 7am to 3pm for around $50 per person. Private boat charter services are also available, from *pangas* (small fishing boats) at $350 to a clipper sleeping up to 36 passengers

OCTOBER
BISBEE'S BLACK AND BLUE TOURNAMENT

www.bisbees.com

Every October, big game fishermen from around the world descend on Cabo San Lucas for a series of billfish tournaments. Bisbee's is one of the richest and tourney winners typically reel in blue marlin weighing more than 272kg (600lbs).

✉ Cabo San Lucas ⬚ Register online, entry fees are $600 and up

NOVEMBER
BAJA 1000 DESERT RACE

Competitors race over 1,600km (994 miles) along the length of the Baja Peninsula. The race begins in Ensenada and ends in La Paz, and any vehicle can be entered, ranging from a motorbike to a 2CV to a 10-ton truck—the only prerequisite being that you don't mind if it gets totally trashed. The road surfaces are hazardous to say the least and competitors see the event as a test of endurance.

✉ Ensenada ☎ (818) 225-8402 in US

for $4,000 (cheaper rates available Monday to Friday). Bonito, yellowfin tuna, albacore, barracuda, rockfish and bass are reliable catches.

✉ Malecon, Rosarito ☎ (646) 178 21 85

SAN JOSÉ DEL CABO
GORDO BANKS PANGAS

www.gordobanks.com

The Gordo Banks, close to the entrance to the Sea of Cortés, support a rich variety of marine life including yellowfin, marlin, dorado, and sailfish. Fishing excursions in *pangas* leave at 6.30am and include a bilingual guide and all fishing equipment ($210–$300, based on a six-hour trip and three anglers).

✉ Box 140, La Playa, San José del Cabo ☎ (624) 142 11 47

PRICES AND SYMBOLS

The restaurants are listed alphabetically within each town. The prices given are the average for a two-course lunch (L) and a three-course dinner (D) for one person, without drinks. The wine price is for the least expensive bottle. All the restaurants listed accept credit cards unless otherwise stated.

For a key to the symbols, ▷ 2.

CABO SAN LUCAS
MI CASA

Mi Casa is one of the most highly regarded Mexican restaurants in town. A restored colonial hacienda provides the setting with regional dishes served in a candlelit courtyard. The house special is *chiles en nogado*, a red pepper stuffed with creamy walnut sauce, but the seafood, fish and meat dishes are also recommended—try the *pescado sarandeado* (barbequed red snapper) or the chicken with *mole* sauce. While some dishes can be hard to fault, consistency is reputedly an issue.

✉ Plaza Mayor, Calle Cabo San Lucas, Cabo San Lucas ☎ (624) 143 19 33 ◉ Mon–Sat noon–3, 5.30–10.30, Sun 5.30–10.30 ✋ L $15, D $30, Wine $15

CHIHUAHUA
TONY'S

Steeped in the ranching traditions of Chihuahua, this highly regarded restaurant, which opened in the 1950s, is something of a local institution. The setting, a classical-style adobe building, decorated with photos of Chihuahua's local legends, is as engaging as the food is satisfying. Huge steaks and succulent *carne asado* (roasted or barbecued meat) are the house specials, served with rice, *tortillas* and guacamole. Vegetarians should think twice.

✉ Avenida Juárez 3901, Chihuahua ☎ (614) 460 29 88 ◉ Mon–Sat noon–9.30 ✋ L $$17, D $23, Wine $17

ENSENADA
EL CHARRO

It is hard to miss the aroma of spit-roasted chicken that exudes from El Charro, the locals' favorite. A simple but tasty Mexican repertoire ranges from fresh home-made *tortillas* with guacamole to fish and meat *tacos* and *burritos*, and even the Oaxacan dish of chicken smothered with deep-flavored *mole*. Serving the masses in a satisfyingly unpolished closet-sized setting since the 1950s,

El Charro is worth visiting as much for the gregarious ambience as for excellent cooking. Credit cards are not accepted.

✉ Avenida López Mateos 454, Ensenada ✉ (646) 178 21 14 ◉ Mon–Tue noon–9, Wed–Sun noon–11 ✋ L $9, D $14, Wine $12

LA EMBOTELLADORA VIEJA

This smart, Mediterranean-influenced restaurant has a gastronomic panache that makes it arguably the best restaurant in town. Located in the aging room of the Bodega de Santo Tomás, the Gothic interior with candelabras and exposed brickwork fuses decadence and sophistication with aplomb. The menu has excellent fish, seafood and meat dishes, served with an inspired selection of sauces and a monumental wine list.

✉ Avenida Miramar 666 and Calle 7, Ensenada ☎ (646) 174 08 70 ◉ Tue, Wed 11.30–10, Thu–Sat 11.30–11, Sun 11.30–6 ✋ L $15, D $25, Wine $20

LORETO
CAFÉ OLÉ

Right on the main square in the middle of town, this vibrant and inexpensive café is a great stop-off

for breakfasts, light lunches, snacks, decadent cakes and pastries, smoothies, milkshakes, and a medley of coffee varieties. The breakfast special is eggs with *nopal* (cactus), but *huevos rancheros*, fish *tacos* and seafood omelets feature on the broad menu and all are more than satisfying. Burgers and chicken dishes cater to the carnivorous. Credit cards are not accepted.
✉ Calle Madero 14, Loreto ☎ (613) 135 04 96 ⏰ Mon–Sat 7am–10pm
✋ L and D $12

CHILE WILLIE
On the waterfront at the northern end of the beach, this fine *palapa*-style restaurant has inventive fish and seafood dishes. The menu is a fusion of exotic Pan-Latin cuisine and American classics. Begin with an appetizer of choco clams—named for their color, not taste—followed by a fresh fillet of grilled fish doused in a heady liqueur sauce. Be sure to leave room for one of the delicious American-style diner desserts such as chocolate cake with huge peaks of ice cream swimming in chocolate sauce or a slab of key lime pie.
✉ Calle López Mateo, Loreto ☎ (613) 135 06 77 ⏰ Daily 11.30–11 ✋ L $14, D $20, Wine $15

LOS MOCHIS
EL FARALLÓN
El Farollón is the apogee of dining among the slim selection of quality restaurants in Los Mochis. Excellent seafood and fish are cooked to order—choose from the chef's special sauces or piquant marinades. The atmosphere is chic but relaxed, the dining room cool, and staff will elaborate on the menu's often bewildering descriptions.
✉ Calle Angel Flores, Los Mochis ☎ (668) 812 14 28 ⏰ Daily 8am–11pm
✋ L $13, D $18, Wine $14

LA PAZ
LA PAZTA
One block from the *malecón*, and next door to the Hotel Mediterrané,

this chichi Italian-Swiss restaurant is one of La Paz's hippest eateries. Exposed brick and contemporary art works provide the minimalist backdrop to a maximalist menu, with everything from pasta to fondue, wood-oven pizza, and Mediterranean meat and fish dishes. The wine list is monumental, the service discreet and the prices very reasonable by international standards. Breakfasts ($14) are also served.
✉ Calle Allende 36, La Paz ☎ (612) 125 11 95 ⏰ Wed–Mon 4–11 ✋ L $12, D $18, Wine $15

QUINTA SOL
This popular café caters to most dietary regimes with soya, gluten-free, vegan and vegetarian products. Salads, wholemeal sandwiches and *tacos* are all fresh and tasty, and fresh-fruit smoothies are reason alone for visiting. Credit cards are not accepted.
✉ Avenida Independencia and Calle Domínguez, La Paz ☎ (612) 122 16 92 ⏰ Mon–Sat 8–4.30 ✋ L $10

SAN JOSE DEL CABO
DAMIANA
Damiana occupies a beautifully restored late 18th-century hacienda in the heart of town, with a leafy courtyard patio. Inside, a bright Mexican theme prevails with burnished orange, terra-cotta tiles and local artworks. The menu includes lobster, jumbo shrimp, filet mignon and a few Mexican vegetarian choices.
✉ Plaza, San Jose del Cabo ☎ (624) 142 04 99 ⏰ Daily 10.30–10.30 ✋ L $17, D $35, Wine $20

MI COCINA
Mi Cocina is widely considered the gastronomic zenith of San Jose del Cabo. The setting is as sublime as the food, with a lush candlelit patio that is romantic, stylish and contemporary. The inspired and consistent menu injects traditional Mexican ingredients and recipes with European and Mediterranean influences. The house special is filet mignon with a rich piquant cream

sauce, but the fish and seafood dishes are also delectable with succulent lobster and stir-fried jumbo shrimps. For vegetarians, there is a selection of pasta dishes.
✉ Casa Natalia Hotel, Boulevard Mijares, San Jose del Cabo ☎ (624) 142 51 00 ⏰ Daily 6–10 ✋ D $35, Wine $22

TIJUANA
CIEN AÑOS
This classy restaurant is thought by many to be the finest in the city. Mexican *alta cocina* fuses spiced traditional regional recipes, including *mole* and *chiles en nogada*, with Maya-inspired twists. The more intrepid diner can try an appetizer of mescal worms, or sample one of the excellent tequilas on offer.
✉ Calle José María Velazco 1407, Tijuana ☎ (888) 534 60 88 ⏰ Mon–Thu 8am–11pm, Fri–Sat 8am–midnight, Sun 8am–10pm ✋ L $20, D $30, Wine $20

LA FONDA DE ROBERTO
Just out of town, La Fonda is as popular with San Diego residents north of the border as it is with the locals. It's a veritable kitsch fest: Fountains laden with plastic fruit, flags and dolls juxtaposed with human skulls provide a kaleidoscopic backdrop. The traditional Mexican dishes are well prepared and presented. Specials include *pechuga de angel* (a breast of chicken with squash flowers), *Oaxacan mole poblano* and *dedos de Montezuma* (cactus stuffed with strips of roast beef coated with a spicy sauce).
✉ La Sierra Motel, Cuauhtémoc Sur Oeste 2800, Tijuana ☎ (664) 686 46 87 ⏰ Noon–10pm ✋ L $12, D $18, Wine $18

TIJUANA TILLY'S
Tilly's is a monument to historic Tijuana, with atmospheric wall-to-wall black-and-white photos and a low-key, unpretentious vibe. Visitors come for the excellent steaks, seafood and Mexican dishes—all served with panache.
✉ La Leña, Avenida Revolución, Tijuana ☎ (664) 685 60 24 ⏰ Sun–Thu noon–midnight, Fri–Sat noon–3am ✋ L $12, D $16, Wine $14

PRICES AND SYMBOLS

The prices are the average for a double room for one night including breakfast, unless otherwise stated. All the hotels listed accept credit cards unless otherwise stated. Note that rates can vary widely throughout the year.

For a key to the symbols, ▷ 2.

CABO SAN LUCAS

DREAMS LOS CABOS

www.dreamsresorts.com

The main draw here is the 18-hole golf course designed by Robert Trent Jones, but for non-players there's still plenty to do. This all-inclusive resort has an outdoor pool, tennis courts, a gym, and spa. The studios have two double beds, a private bathroom with a shower, and a terrace with an ocean view. Suites have a separate bedroom with a king-sized bed, private bathroom with a tub, and a queen-sized sleeper sofa in the living room. The suites' private balconies also have views of the ocean. You can take your meals in one of the five restaurants, then relax in any of the six bars and lounges.

✉ Los Cabos Corridor, Km 18.5 Carretera Transpeninsular ☎ (624) 145 76 00 🖐 $450–$650 🛈 104 suites 🔵 🏖 🍸

FIESTA AMERICANA GRAND LOS CABOS

www.fiestamericana.com

This luxury beach resort has few rivals along the Los Cabos Corridor. The standard "deluxe" rooms feature contemporary décor, marble bathrooms and ocean view balconies, while suites boast a separate bedroom with a king-sized bed. Duffers will delight in the on-site Jack Nicklaus-designed 18-hole golf course. Sun worshippers can soak up the rays next to one of five swimming pools. Those seeking spa pampering will find the Fiesta's facility offers "vinotherapy," which uses unique wine-based skin treatments. At mealtimes, there are five restaurants to choose from.

✉ Los Cabos Corridor, Km 10.3 Carretera Transpeninsular in the Cabo del Sol development ☎ (624) 145 62 00 🖐 $200–$400 🛈 250 🔵 🏖 🍸

FINISTERRA

www.finisterra.com

Perched on promontory near "Land's End," this landmark hotel has fully appointed luxury suites and rooms with air-conditioning, television and views of the bay area. New extensions blend seamlessly with the original 1970s building, part of which was built into the rock face. Facilities include a mammoth swimming pool with a swim-up poolside bar and unsurpassed view, tennis courts and a good restaurant. And, should you get carried away by the romance of it all, there's even a wedding chapel.

✉ Domicilio Conocido, Cabo San Lucas ☎ (624) 143 33 33 🖐 $265–$450 🛈 287 🔵 🏖 Outdoor 🍸

SOLMAR SUITES

www.solmar.com

Set against a backdrop of granite cliffs, this secluded beachfront resort on the Pacific Ocean side of Land's End is a Cabo original. Built in the late 1970s and turned into an all-suite hotel in the 90s, Solmar is beloved by anglers for its sport fishing fleet. The resort also has three swimming pools, tennis courts, and a top-flight restaurant with palm-framed ocean views. All rooms have a private garden patio or sea view balcony. Some units include a kitchen.

✉ Avenida Solmar 1, Cabo San Lucas ☎ (624) 146 77 00 🖐 $150–$200 🛈 190 🔵 🏖 🍸

Above *Dreams Los Cabos at Cabo San Lucas is an all-inclusive resort*

CHIHUAHUA

HOTEL PALACIO DEL SOL

Handy for the main plaza, this modern hotel block provides good services and a range of facilities. Each room has a king- or queen-size bed, air-conditioning, and television. While the decoration may lack imagination, and be in need of upgrading here and there, the location and amenities—which include two restaurants, a very sociable bar, room service and laundry—and the warm welcome certainly compensate.

✉ Avenida Independencia 116, Chihuahua ☎ (614) 416 60 00 💷 $140 🏠 200 ⬛

POSADA TIERRA BLANCA

Clean and comfortable, the Tierra Blanca isn't going to win any awards for charm, but it's a good budget option near the main Plaza de Armas. Rooms are of the basic motel variety, and all have air-conditioning and cable TV. Traffic noise can be loud so light sleepers should request a room on the top floor of the quieter main building.

✉ Avenida Niños Heroes 102, Chihuahua ☎ (614) 415 00 00 💷 $75 🏠 94 ⬛ ⬛

COPPER CANYON

BEST WESTERN THE LODGE AT CREEL

www.bestwestern.com

A bit Americanized, yet comfortable, the Lodge at Creel's clean cabin-style rooms are heated by gas stoves and have a private porch. There's also a Honeymoon Suite with a Jacuzzi and kitchenette. The onsite Sierra Madre Restaurant serves Mexican and American standards in a ski lodge-like setting.

✉ Avenida Lopez Mateos 61, Creel ☎ (625) 456 00 71 💷 $100–$130 🏠 38 ⬛

HOTEL PARAISO DEL OSO

www.mexicohorse.com

In the middle of the Sierra and less then 2km (1 mile) from Cerocahui, this inviting family-run inn provides a wonderful sense of solitude. The comfortable hacienda-style rooms, with two double beds, are grouped around the central patio and powered by solar energy. A large communal dining room is where meals are served, and there's a sociable living room and a well-stocked library. Welcoming and informative host Doug Rhodes organizes horseback-riding, bird-watching and hiking trips. Reserve well ahead of time.

✉ Cerocahui, Copper Canyon ☎ (614) 421 33 72 💷 $185, including 3 meals per day 🏠 21

ENSENADA

CASA NATALIE HOTEL & SPA

Children are not allowed at this intimate boutique hotel aimed at couples looking for a luxurious romantic getaway. All eight beautifully furnished suites feature feather-soft king-size beds and private ocean view balconies. Guests can soak in the oceanfront Jacuzzi, lounge next to the infinity pool or enjoy massages at the onsite spa. Of course, all this pampering comes at an astronomical price, but top-flight service helps soften the blow. Weekend stays require a two-night minimum.

✉ 8km (4.8 miles) north of Ensenada on Highway 1, Ensenada ☎ (646) 174 73 73 💷 $200–$380 🏠 8 ⬛ ⬛

PUNTA MORRO HOTEL SUITES

www.punta-morro.com

A 20-minute stroll from the middle of Ensenada, this understated but excellent hotel draws a large following of both American and international guests with its superlative service, good facilities and comfortable minimalist accommodations. Each pleasantly designed room is fully equipped with air-conditioning, television, hair dryer and a kitchen with a small fridge, and all have wonderful sea views. There is an outdoor heated swimming pool, spa and Jacuzzi, plus a good restaurant and bar. Three-bedroom apartments are available for larger groups.

✉ 3km (2 miles) north of Ensenada on Highway 1, Ensenada ☎ (646) 178 35 07 💷 $155–$185 🏠 24 ⬛ ⬛ Outdoor

LA PAZ

CASA TUSCANY INN

Within easy walking distance of the *malecón* (waterfront), this charming little B&B is run by a hospitable couple of American expatriates. All four rooms have private baths, air conditioning, mini refrigerators and Wi-Fi access. The delicious breakfasts, included in the rate, are served in a peaceful courtyard. Credit cards are not accepted.

✉ Calle Nicolas Bravo 110, La Paz ☎ (612) 128 81 03 💷 $95–$135 🏠 4 ⬛

LORIMAR

Just two blocks from the *malecón*, this popular budget option may be lacking in creature comforts but it is very clean, has hot showers and provides an excellent base to meet fellow travelers. Run by a friendly and helpful Mexican-American couple, this is the best value for money in town by a long shot. There is a good-value restaurant and you can organize trips to Tecolote beach. Credit cards are not accepted.

✉ Bravo 110, La Paz ☎ (612) 125 38 22 💷 $38 🏠 20

MEDITERRÁNEO

www.hotelmed.com

This intimate hotel overlooking the *malecón* exudes relaxed Mediterranean panache. The whitewashed hotel, set around an idyllic palm-fringed courtyard, fuses Greek and Mexican style with aplomb. Each impeccable room is named after a Greek island and varies in size and design, with original art works. The outstanding La Pazta restaurant serves Greek and Italian dishes fit for the gods. There is also internet access, and bicycles and kayaks for rent.

✉ Allende 36, La Paz ☎ (612) 125 11 95 💷 $65–$95 🏠 9 ⬛

LORETO

DESERT INN AT LORETO

In a beautiful setting right on the seafront, the hacienda-style Desert Inn is a pleasantly designed complex of rooms and villas, each with cable television, air-conditioning and

safe-deposit boxes. Considered by many to be the best of the original "Presidente" *paradores*, facilities include a large swimming pool, tennis courts, a restaurant, and two cocktail bars. This is an ideal base for fishing enthusiasts, and there are boats for rent and organized tours.
✉ Sea of Cortés, 2km (1 mile) north of the *zócalo*, Loreto ☎ (800) 800 96 32 (toll free within Mexico) 📶 $79–$106 🛏 48 🅂 🏊 Outdoor

INN AT LORETO BAY
The Inn is set in its own secluded cove. All guestrooms have stunning views of the desert, the Giganta Mountains, the Loreto Golf Course or the Sea of Cortés, and all have air-conditioning and private bathroom, and the suites have a Jacuzzi on the balcony. The hotel complex has two bars and three restaurants: Salvatierra for fine Italian food, buffet-style Guaycura serving Mexican and international food, and the Snack-Shack set in the gardens.
✉ Boulevard Misión de Loreto, Loreto ☎ (613) 133 00 10 📶 $100–$250 🛏 156 🅂

MAZATLÁN
BEST WESTERN POSADA FREEMAN EXPRESS
www.bestwestern.com
The 12-story Posada Freeman was one of the city's first hotels. Located across the street from Playa Olas Altas and within walking distance of historic Old Mazatlán, this landmark is an excellent choice far away from the touristy hotel zone. Rooms are clean, comfortable and have either ocean or city views. The hotel's 12th floor "Sky Room" bar is a great place to watch the sun set.
✉ Olas Altas 79 Sur, Mazatlán ☎ (669) 985 60 60 📶 $100–$150 🛏 72 🅂 🏊 Outdoor rooftop

EL CID EL MORO BEACH HOTEL
This 28-story beachfront hotel tower near the northern end of the hotel zone is one of four El Cid properties in Mazatlán. Rooms at the El Moro feature contemporary décor and ocean views. A majority of the 310

units are one-bedroom suites with kitchens. The full range of amenities includes an onsite shopping mall and a water sports center, which offers tours to Deer Island in an amphibious vehicle.
✉ Avenida Camarón Sábalo S/N, Zona Dorada, Mazatlán ☎ (669) 913 33 33 📶 $125–$270 🛏 310 🅂 🏊

MONTERREY
SAFI CENTRO
www.safihotel.com
There's no lack of international hotel chains in Monterrey, and with global brands, you know what to expect. The locally owned Safi, located next to Alameda Park and only a short taxi ride from the city's major sights, offers stylish accommodations that run the gamut from basic rooms with king-size or double beds to a suite with private Jacuzzi. The small pool is in a pretty garden courtyard and the hotel restaurant is good.
✉ Avenida Pino Suarez 444 Sur, Monterrey ☎ (81) 8399 7000 📶 $90–$160 🛏 158 🅂 🏊 🍴

SAN JOSÉ DEL CABO
BEST WESTERN POSADA REAL
www.bestwestern.com
At the budget end of San Jose's beachfront hotel spectrum, this all-inclusive property offers clean comfortable rooms at a good price. All standard rooms have private balconies or patios and offer at least a partial ocean view. There are also eight suites. The pool is in a cactus filled garden.
✉ Malecón San Jose, Zona Hotelera, San Jose del Cabo ☎ (624) 142 01 55 📶 $135–$170 🛏 148 🅂 🏊 🍴

EL ENCANTO INN
www.elencantoinn.com
A change of pace from the massive beach resorts, this small colonial style hotel sits in the heart of downtown San José near art galleries and restaurants. The hotel consists of two buildings, directly across the street from each other. The "garden building" has large standard rooms, while the "pool building" features suites facing a

flower-filled courtyard with a pool. There's also an onsite spa.
✉ Calle Morelos 133, San José del Cabo ☎ (624) 142 03 88 📶 $95–$240 🛏 28 🅂 🏊

POSADA SEÑOR MAÑANA
www.srmanana.com
In a peaceful enclave a short walk from the main square, this neat *posada* is one of the best budget options in San José. Meandering walkways connect each of the simple, bright, rooms to the communal, well-stocked kitchen and leafy courtyard strewn with hammocks. It's worth looking at a selection of rooms—those on the lower level have been renovated. There is also a basketball court.
✉ Alvaro Obregon 1, San José del Cabo ☎ (624) 142 13 72 📶 $40–$60 🛏 11

PRESIDENTE INTERCONTINENTAL LOS CABOS
www.ichotelsgroup.com/intercontinental
Right on the beach, against the spectacular backdrop of the Sierra de San Lazaro Mountains, the Presidente Intercontinental is the mother of Mexican all-inclusive resorts. A variety of packages is available. There are six restaurants, seven bars, a cocktail lounge, travel agency, three pools, three tennis courts, car rental and a nearby golf course. Rooms are a good size, well equipped, and the large bathrooms are amply stocked with a range of complimentary goodies.
✉ Zona Hotelera, San José del Cabo ☎ (624) 142 92 29 📶 $250 🛏 390 (108 nonsmoking) 🅂 🏊 Outdoor (3) 🍴

TIJUANA
GRAND HOTEL TIJUANA
The soaring, monolithic Grand Hotel is lavish. Standard rooms, while lacking any Mexican identity, are plush and well equipped. Extensive facilities include an impressive business complex, golf course, Jacuzzi, gym and restaurant.
✉ Boulevard Agua Caliente 4500, Tijuana ☎ (664) 681 70 00/1-800 026 60 07 (toll-free in Mexico) 📶 $126–$180 🛏 422 🅂 🏊 Outdoor and indoor 🍴

PRACTICALITIES

Practicalities gives you all the important practical information you will need during your visit from money matters to emergency phone numbers.

WEATHER

CLIMATE

In Mexico, climate—as well as scenery, vegetation and even culture—is determined by altitude rather than latitude or longitude. Along the Pacific Coast, for example, things don't change that much from north to south, but head up into the mountains and the differences are immediately apparent. It is difficult, therefore, to make too many generalizations about climate.

The best time to go is the dry season, between October and April, although there are slight regional variations. The rainy season works its way up from the south, beginning in May and running through until August, September and even October. This is also hurricane season in the Caribbean and on

rare occasions the Yucatán and Gulf states get hit. Don't be put off by the term "rainy season." Most years, the rains only really affect visitors for an hour or two a day and, especially in the northern states of Baja, Sonora, Chihuahua and Coahuila, it can remain very hot and dry.

The highlands are mostly mild, but with sharp changes of temperature between day and night, sunshine and shade. There are only two areas where rain falls year-round: south of Tampico along the lower slopes of the Sierra Madre Oriental and across the Isthmus of Tehuantepec into Tabasco state; and along the Pacific coast of the state of Chiapas. In southern coastal areas it gets very hot and humid between June and September.

WHEN TO GO

Baja California is popular at different times of year for different reasons. During the winter, US and Canadian "snowbirds" head south to escape the cold and then head back when it warms up in the north. This doesn't put any real pressure upon available hotel rooms, but what does is the spring break influx of students, particularly in Baja California Norte and in the small oasis towns of Baja California Sur.

February to March are the best months for whale-watching in the Guerrero Negro area. Mid-April to mid-June is a good time to visit, too, because it is not too hot and the water is starting to warm up in the Sea of Cortés. October is also good

as it is still quiet and the sea is about as warm as it is going to get.

August is vacation time for Mexicans and this can make rooms scarce in the smaller resorts and in popular places close to Mexico City. *Semana Santa* (Easter week) witnesses an exodus from parts of the capital, putting pressure on transportation to, and hotel space within, many attractive regional towns and villages.

The Día de los Muertos (Day of the Dead) celebrations at the beginning of November and the Christmas holidays can also affect room availability.

For up-to-date weather information for your region in Mexico and for the latest hurricane reports, visit www.accuweather.com.

WHAT TO TAKE

» The key things to remember are travel and health insurance documents, money, credit cards and any medication you will need.
» Also vital are photocopies of essential documents, including passport, visa and travelers' check receipts if you lose the originals.
» Clothes that are quick and easy to wash and dry are a good idea. Loose-fitting clothes are more comfortable in hot climates and can be layered if it gets cooler.
» Sunscreen and a sun hat are essential (also Health, ▷ 272–273).
» Take all the camera film or memory cards and batteries you will require for the duration of your trip, ideally in a bag that is both

MEXICAN EMBASSIES AND CONSULATES ABROAD		
COUNTRY	**ADDRESS**	**CONTACT DETAILS**
Australia	14 Perth Avenue, Yarralumla, 2600 ACT, Canberra	Tel (02) 6273 3963 www.mexico.org.au
Canada	45 O'Connor Street, Suite 1500, K1P 1A4, Ottawa, Ontario	Tel 613 233 8988; www.sre.gob.mx/canada/
Ireland	19 Raglan Road, Ballsbridge, Dublin 4	Tel (353) 1667 3105; www.sre.gob.mx/irlanda
New Zealand	111–15 Customhouse Quay, 8th floor, Box 11–510, Wellington	Tel 472 0555
South Africa	2nd Floor, Alexandra House, Earlsfort Centre	Tel 01 661 5553
UK	16 St. George Street, Hanover Square, London, W1S 1LX	Tel 020 7499-8586; www.sre.gob.mx/reinounido/
USA	1911 Pennsylvania Avenue, NW, 20006 Washington DC	Tel (202) 728-1600; http://portal.sre.gob.mx/usa/

TIME ZONES

CITY	TIME DIFFERENCE
Amsterdam	+7
Berlin	+7
Brussels	+7
Chicago	0
Dublin	+6
Johannesburg*	+7
London	+6
Madrid	+7
Montréal	+1
New York	+1
Paris	+7
Perth, Australia*	+11
Rome	+7
San Francisco	-2
Sydney*	+13
Tokyo*	+12

Clocks in Mexico go forward one hour from the first Sunday in April to the last Sunday in October.
* One hour less during Summer Time

CUSTOMS

The list of permitted items is extensive and generally allows for things that could reasonably be considered for personal use. Large quantities of any item may attract suspicion. Those entering by trailer are subject to the same rules based on reasonable personal use. Adults entering Mexico are allowed to bring in up to:

» 20 packs of cigarettes
» 25 cigars
» 250g (8.8oz) of tobacco
» 200g (7oz) of medicines for personal use
» 3 liters (0.6 gallons) of wine, beer or spirits
» A reasonable amount of perfume for personal use

» Goods imported into Mexico with a value of more than $1,000 (with the exception of computer equipment, where the limit is $4,000) have to be handled by an officially appointed agent
» Gift items not exceeding a total of $300

water- and dust-proof. Choice may be limited in Mexico.
» In the highlands it can be cold at night, and most cheaper hotels do not have heating and provide only one blanket. A light sleeping bag that packs up tightly can be useful.
» Health precautions should be taken; important items include a first-aid kit, sunscreen and painkillers. Also handy are diarrhea treatments, such as Imodium and Pepto-Bismol. A mosquito repellent containing Di-ethyltoluamide (DEET) and anti-malarial tablets in key areas are also vital.

DOCUMENTS
TRAVEL INSURANCE

» Insurance is recommended. If you have financial constraints the most important aspect of any insurance policy is medical care and repatriation. Ideally, make sure you are covered for personal items too.
» Read the small print before leaving so you know what is covered and what is not, how to submit a claim and what to do in an emergency.
» Don't bring anything you can't afford to replace.
» Check whether your insurer has a 24-hour helpline, and note it.

PASSPORTS AND VISAS

» From January 1 2008, all visitors traveling from the US to Mexico, including US citizens, will have to show a valid passport.
» A passport is required for citizens from western European countries, Canada, Australia, New Zealand, Hungary, Iceland, Israel Japan, Singapore, South Korea, Argentina, Bermuda, Chile, Costa Rica, Uruguay, and Venezuela.
» Once proof of nationality has been verified, you will receive a Mexican Tourist Card (FM-T) at the point of entry or in advance at a consulate or embassy. The tourist card is issued for up to 180 days and should be returned to immigration when departing the country. Citizens of other countries need to obtain a visa before visiting, so check in advance.
» Tourist cards are not required for cities close to the US border, such as Tijuana and Mexicali.
» Renewal of entry cards or visas must be done at Servicios Migratorios (862 Ejercito Nacional, Mexico City, Mon–Fri 9–1). Only 60 days are given, and you can expect to wait up to 10 days for a replacement tourist card.
» There are immigration offices at international airports, and in cities such as Guadalajara, Oaxaca and Acapulco, which can renew tourist cards. To renew a tourist card by leaving the country, you must stay outside Mexico for at least 72 hours. Take travelers' checks or a credit card as proof of finance.
» Visitors not carrying tourist cards

need visas; multiple entry is not allowed and visas must be renewed before reentry (South Africans and those nationalities not listed here need a visa). Business visitors and technical personnel should apply for the requisite visa and permit.
» At border crossings with Belize and Guatemala, you may be refused entry into Mexico if you have less than $200 (or $350 for each month of intended stay, up to a maximum of 180 days). If you are carrying more than $10,000 in travelers' checks or cash, you must declare it.
» If a person under 18 is touring alone or with one parent, both parents' consent is required, certified by a notary or authorized by a consulate. A divorced parent must be able to show custody of a child. (These requirements are not always checked by immigration and do not apply to all nationalities.) Exact details are available from any Mexican consulate.
» Entry requirements can change at short notice: Check before travel.

LONGER STAYS

For a *Visitante Rentista* visa (non-immigrant pensioner) for stays over six months (up to two years) the following are required: passport, proof of income from abroad of $750 per month (or 400 days of the minimum wage), reduced by half if you own a house in Mexico, and your tourist card. For information call the Immigration Department of the Mexican consulate (▷ 268).

MONEY

THE PESO

The Mexican peso, usually represented by the dollar sign ($), has the potential of creating great confusion, especially in popular tourist places where prices are higher and often quoted in US$. The one- and two-peso coins and the 10- and 20-peso coins are similar in size; check the number on the coin. US$1 = approximately $10.20 Mexican pesos. Check currency conversion websites such as www.onada.com for the latest rates.

In this book, the dollar sign ($) indicates the US dollar.

BEFORE LEAVING HOME

» The three main ways of carrying money while visiting Mexico are with US dollars cash, US dollars travelers' checks (TCs), or plastic (credit cards). It is recommended that you take all three.

» Check with your credit or debit card company that your card can be used to withdraw cash from Automated Teller Machines (ATMs) in Mexico. It is also worth checking what fee will be charged for this and what number you should call if your card is stolen.

TRAVELERS' CHECKS

» Travelers' checks are a safer way of bringing in money as you can claim a refund if they are stolen—but commission can be high when you cash them.

» Checks from any well-known bank can be cashed in most towns if drawn in US dollars; travelers' checks from other currencies (including euros) are harder to cash, and certainly not worth trying to change outside the largest of cities.

» Denominations of US$50 and US$100 are preferable, though you will need a few of US$20. American Express and Visa US$ travelers' checks are the easiest to change.

ATMs

ATMs (cajero automático) are now found even in small towns in Mexico, allowing you to travel

PRICES OF EVERYDAY ITEMS (MEXICO CITY)	
Item	**Pesos**
Loaf of bread	13.50
Bottled mineral water (per liter)	8
Coffee and pastry at specialty coffee house e.g. Starbucks	70
Petrol (per liter)	7.92
Diesel (per liter)	6.50
Buses (local)	1–15
Buses (national)	50–1,000
Camera film (36 exposures)	43
20 cigarettes (on average)	25
33cl bottle of beer	10

without carrying large amounts of cash or travelers' checks. You will need a four-digit PIN. Amex (American Express), MasterCard and Visa are widely accepted in Mexico. Your card issuer may charge you for withdrawing cash; check current policy before traveling.

BANKS

» Larger branches of main banks in Mexico City are usually open from 8am to 7pm; most are open at least from 9am to 5pm.

» In smaller provincial towns some bank branches still close at 1.30pm. Larger branches also open between 9am and 12.30pm on Saturday mornings.

» Public holidays lead to a complete shutdown in virtually all services, including banks. It is worth keeping an eye on the calendar to avoid changing money on these days.

CASAS DE CAMBIO

» Casas de cambio are generally quicker than banks for carrying out exchange transactions, and generally stay open later; fees are not charged, but their rates may not be as good.

» You may be asked to show your passport, another form of ID or even proof of purchase (but remember to keep it separate from your travelers' checks).

TIPPING	
Restaurants	10–15 percent
Bell boys	equivalent of US$1
Lavatories	equivalent of US$0.20–0.25 depending on class of establishment
Fuel stations	3–5 percent of cost of fuel
Taxis	none, unless some kind of exceptional service is provided

CREDIT CARDS

» MasterCard, Visa and American Express are widely accepted in Mexico, whether you are paying for goods, withdrawing cash from ATMs or obtaining cash over the counter from banks.

» Credit cards are useful in hotels, restaurants, shops and when making a deposit to rent equipment.

» Credit card transactions are normally made at an officially recognized rate of exchange and are often subject to sales tax.

» In addition, many charge a fee of about 5 percent on credit card transactions; although it is forbidden by credit card company rules, there is not a lot you can do about this.

» Rates of exchange on ATM withdrawals are the best available for currency exchange, but your bank or credit card company imposes a handling charge.

» If you lose a card, contact the 24-hour helpline of the issuer in your home country immediately (find out the numbers to call before leaving home and keep them in a safe place).

» Most card issuers provide a telephone number where you can call collect from anywhere in the world in case of card loss or theft; request it before leaving home.

TAXES

» Airport departure tax is around $24 on international flights (dollars or pesos are accepted), but can be higher, depending on the airline you use and your destination; always check when purchasing your ticket if departure tax is included in the price.

» A sales tax of 15 percent is payable on domestic plane tickets bought in Mexico.

WIRING MONEY

If you need to make a transfer ask your bank if they can transfer direct to a Mexican bank without using an intermediary, which usually results in greater delays. Beware of short-changing at all times. Western Union (www.westernunion.com) has outlets throughout Mexico, but the service is more expensive than a traditional bank wire.

TIPS

» Dollars are easily changed in all cities and towns at banks and *casas de cambio*, and in the more popular places can sometimes be used if you are running short of pesos.

» Take a mix of large and small denominations—you don't want to get stuck trying to change a US$100 bill in a remote village.

» In the border states with the US, such as Baja California Norte, the most-used currency is the US dollar.

» Large branches of BITAL bank have been known to change travelers' checks in other currencies if you are stuck.

» Keep your spare money and travelers' checks in your hotel safe until you need them.

» Sell any currency left over at the end of your visit to avoid losing out on the exchange rate.

» If your budget is tight, it is essential to avoid situations where you are forced to change money regardless of the rate.

» Watch weekends and public holidays carefully and try not to run out of local currency.

» Take plenty of local currency, in small denominations, when making trips away from the major towns and resorts. It is also very useful for tipping.

Below *The 16th-century palace of Casa de Montejo in Merida now houses a branch of the National Bank of Mexico*

HEALTH

BEFORE YOU GO

» Ideally, see a doctor or travel clinic at least six weeks before departure for advice on risks, malaria and vaccinations; know your blood group, and if you suffer a long-term condition such as diabetes or epilepsy make sure someone knows, or have a Medic Alert bracelet/necklace.

» Get a dental checkup, especially if you are going to be away for more than a month.

» Take out adequate travel insurance (▷ 269).

» Check with your doctor whether you are up to date with BCG (against TB; recommended for stays of more than a month), tetanus, and polio.

» Make sure you have received vaccinations (and that they are still valid) for: hepatitis A, typhoid, and yellow fever. Mexico has no yellow fever and wants to keep it that way. If you arrive from Africa or South America the authorities may want to see your yellow fever certificate. You may also want to consider vaccination against rabies.

» Be aware of the risk of malaria in Mexico. Rural areas are at risk, including resorts in the rural areas of the following states: Campeche, Chiapas, Guerrero, Michoacán, Nayarit, Oaxaca, Quintana Roo, Sinaloa, and Tabasco. Before travel, check whether any anti-malarial medication should be used.

WHAT TO TAKE

It is a good idea to carry a first-aid kit with you, especially if you have children in tow. This could include the following:

» Antiseptic cream
» Insect repellent
» Antihistamine cream for insect bites or stings
» Band aids/plasters
» Water sterilization tablets or water purifier
» Bandages
» Calamine lotion
» Cotton wool
» Imodium (Lomotil) for emergency diarrhea treatment

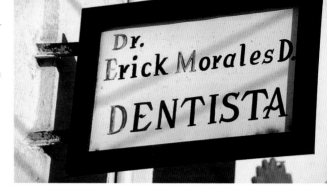

» Rehydration sachets
» Painkillers such as paracetamol or aspirin
» Wet wipes

GETTING TREATMENT

» The Social Security hospitals are restricted to members, but will take visitors in emergencies; they are more up-to-date than the *Centros de Salud* and *Hospitales Civiles* found in most towns, which are very cheap and open to everyone.

» Most medium- and larger-sized towns and cities have at least one hospital or clinic. In an emergency, an ambulance will take you to a nearby hospital for treatment. Your doctor may refer you to a local clinic or hospital, for example to get broken bones/sprains attended to.

FINDING A DOCTOR

» Your hotel can recommend local English-speaking doctors.

» Most of the higher-quality hotels that cater to foreign visitors have a doctor on call. Ask at reception.

» Most embassies have a list of recommended doctors.

FINDING A HOSPITAL

» Parts of rural Mexico are very poor and health services are often basic; communicable diseases are an ever-present threat. However, in large cities there is a thriving private sector and standards are high.

» In the event of an emergency requiring treatment, your embassy or consulate, or the larger hotels, should be able to recommend a local clinic or hospital.

» If you have the opportunity, ask your medical insurer whether they are satisfied that the establishment you have been referred to is of a suitable standard.

» A list of English-speaking private, public and specialist hospitals can be found on the website for the US embassy in Mexico, www.mexico. usembassy.gov.eng/eacs_medical_info.htm.

DENTAL TREATMENT

» There are many dentists all over Mexico. In the more touristy areas, it is possible to find dental surgeries offering the same services and technology that you might expect from your own country.

» Dental practices are easily found through the local directory and also simply by walking around a town or a city and enquiring at any places that look appropriate.

» Many dentists speak English and the cost is likely to be much cheaper than elsewhere in the world. However, be careful of those who are not adequately qualified.

» Despite the relatively low cost of dental work, it is still worth checking that your insurance plan covers you for it. Have a dental checkup before you go.

OPTICIANS

» Pack a spare pair of glasses or spare contact lenses and your prescription in case you break or lose them.

» Opticians can be found in the local directory under *Opticas*, or ask at the nearest pharmacy.

PHARMACIES

» Many of Mexico's pharmacies are open 24 hours a day. Some close at around 10pm, others stay open all night. In smaller towns, pharmacies take turns staying open on the "all night" shift—ask locally for details. They are recognizable by the green cross and *Farmacia* sign.

» You can buy most medicines over the counter in Mexico, but you should only buy medicines that you know are safe to self-prescribe.

» If you think you need something stronger see a doctor and get a prescription; don't just take the pharmacist's advice.

» Most medicine is inexpensive in Mexico, but keep receipts for claims on medical insurance.

» In Mexico City and some of the other major cities in Mexico, the larger supermarkets usually have a good pharmacy attached.

TAP WATER

» Use bottled or mineral water for drinking, except in hotels that normally provide *agua de garrión* (purified drinking water). Make sure ice is made from *agua purificada*. Remember that coffee water is not necessarily boiled.

» Bottled water is available everywhere, but make sure the cap is sealed as it is not unknown for bottles to be filled from the tap and passed off as bottled water.

» If bottled water is not available, it is essential that you purify drinking water with a preparation containing chlorine (for example Puritabs), widely available in pharmacies.

» There are a number of water filters available in personal and expedition size. They work either on mechanical or chemical principles, or may do both. Make sure you take the spare parts or spare chemicals with you.

HAZARDS

» Both dengue fever and cholera are on the rise in Mexico, so seek the relevant advice before visiting and be mindful about getting bitten or drinking non-purified water once in the country.

HEALTHY FLYING

» Visitors to Mexico from as far as Europe, Australia or New Zealand may be concerned about the effect of long-haul flights on their health. The most widely publicized concern is Deep Vein Thrombosis, or DVT. Misleadingly called "economy class syndrome," DVT is the forming of a blood clot in the body's deep veins, particularly in the legs. The clot can move around the bloodstream and could be fatal.

» Those most at risk include the elderly, pregnant women and those using the contraceptive pill, smokers and the overweight. If you are at increased risk of DVT see your doctor before departing. Flying increases the likelihood of DVT because passengers are often seated in a cramped position for long periods of time and may become dehydrated.

To minimize risk:
Drink water (not alcohol)
Don't stay immobile for hours at a time
Stretch and exercise your legs periodically
Do wear elastic flight socks, which support veins and reduce the chances of a clot forming

EXERCISES

1 Ankle Rotations	2 Calf Stretches	3 Knee Lifts
Lift feet off the floor. Draw a circle with the toes, moving one foot clockwise and the other counterclockwise	Start with heel on the floor and point foot upward as high as you can. Then lift heels high, keeping balls of feet on the floor	Lift leg with knee bent while contracting your thigh muscle. Then straighten leg, pressing foot flat to the floor

Other health hazards for flyers are airborne diseases and bugs spread by the plane's air-conditioning system. These are largely unavoidable, but if you have a serious medical condition seek advice from a doctor before flying.

USEFUL TELEPHONE NUMBERS

Emergencies (police, ambulance, fire): *emergencias*	060/080
To report a crime	061
Federal Highway Police: *Policia Federal de Caminos*	(55) 5684 2142
Anti-Rabies Center: *Centro Antirabbico*	(55) 5607 4093/4658
AIDS Information: SIDA	(55) 5644 7603
AIDS Support: *Telsida y Conasida*	(55) 5666 7432
Tourist Safety: *Infotur Seguridad Turistica*	(55) 5250-0123
	(01) 800 903 9200
Emergencies (English spoken)	(55) 52 50 04 93

» Although most insect bites are more of a nuisance that an actual hazard, proper insect repellent, as well as covering your skin with clothing will make your stay much more comfortable.

» There is a risk of malaria in the low-lying tropical zones—consult your own doctor on whether any anti-malarial medication will be necessary for your trip.

» Altitude sickness is a very real problem when visiting Mexico. The ideal prevention for this is to get acclimatized—do not try to reach the highest levels on the first few days of your visit. Mexico City lies at an altitude of 2,240m (7,349ft), so you will have this as well as pollution to contend with.

» The burning power of the tropical sun, especially at high altitude, is phenomenal. Always wear a wide-brimmed hat and use high-factor sunscreen.

» The high glare of the sun can also cause conjunctivitis, so a good-quality pair of sunglasses is essential—both at high altitude and at the beach.

BASICS

ELECTRICITY

» Mexico's electricity system is the same as in the US: 120 volts, 60Hz.

» Any electrical equipment you carry with you that operates at the higher 240 volts rate will need to be dual-voltage, such as hair dryers.

» A lot of electrical equipment (including video cameras, digital cameras, laptops) that operates on 12 volts via a product-specific adaptor will happily cope with dual voltage—check the adaptor and the device instructions to be sure.

» Most plugs in Mexico have two flat prongs. Some have a third, circular prong, and adaptors can be bought for these.

LAUNDRY

» Almost every town and city in Mexico has a number of *lavenderías*. These places normally wash and dry a load (about 3kg/7lb) of laundry for between $5 and $7.

» Self-service is generally not an option, although more coin-operated machines are beginning to appear.

» Dry-cleaning shops can be found in the larger towns and cities.

MEASUREMENTS

Mexico uses the metric system for all weights and measures.

CONVERSION CHART

From	To	Multiply by
Inches	Centimetres	2.54
Centimetres	Inches	0.3937
Feet	Metres	0.3048
Metres	Feet	3.2810
Yards	Metres	0.9144
Metres	Yards	1.0940
Miles	Kilometres	1.6090
Kilometres	Miles	0.6214
Acres	Hectares	0.4047
Hectares	Acres	2.4710
Gallons	Litres	4.5460
Litres	Gallons	0.2200
Ounces	Grams	28.35
Grams	Ounces	0.0353
Pounds	Grams	453.6
Grams	Pounds	0.0022
Pounds	Kilograms	0.4536
Kilograms	Pounds	2.205
Tons	Tonnes	1.0160
Tonnes	Tons	0.9842

PUBLIC RESTROOMS

» Almost without exception, used toilet paper should be placed in the receptacle provided, not flushed down the toilet. This applies even in quite expensive hotels. Failing to observe this custom blocks the drain or pan.

» Public restrooms (toilets) are a rare sight, and are often particularly unpleasant. Some now make a small charge for entry, and you'll find these are usually clean and tidy.

» If you cannot find a public restroom, use the facilities at a nearby restaurant or hotel, but make sure that you leave some money for the service provided.

» When you wash your hands, you will see a small, flat box, sometimes with a piece of cloth inside (and usually a couple of coins on it), placed beside one of the sinks. A small tip, depending on the class of establishment, is sufficient.

SMOKING

Smoking is not allowed on most forms of public transportation, including intercity buses, the metro and *colectivos*; there are usually nonsmoking areas in the better restaurants. The attitude toward smoking is more relaxed than in the US and some other countries.

VISITORS WITH DISABILITIES

» As in most Latin American countries, facilities for visitors with disabilities are severely lacking. Most airports, hotels and restaurants in major resorts have wheelchair ramps and adapted toilets (▷ 58).

» Sidewalks (pavements) are often in such a poor state of repair that walking is precarious.

» Some travel companies specialize in exciting, tailor-made holidays for individuals depending on their level of disability. For those with access to the internet, a Global Access-Disabled Travel Network Site, www.geocities.com/Paris/1502, provides travel information for adventurers with disabilities and has a number of reviews and tips from members of the public.

PLACES OF WORSHIP

Religion plays a vital part in the lives of many Mexicans. For this reason it is important to remain respectful of religious services at all times. Photography is allowed in most churches and cathedrals, but not when there is a service in progress.

Left *Ringing bells at Santiago de Jalpan*

Avoid wearing shorts or revealing clothing when visiting churches.

CHURCHES IN MEXICO CITY
Roman Catholic St. Patrick's, Bondojito 248, Tacubaya, tel (55) 55 15 19 93.

Evangelical Union Reforma 1870, Lomas de Chapultepec, tel (55) 55 20 04 36.

Baptist Capital City Baptist Church, Calle Sur 138 y Bondojito, tel (55) 55 16 18 62.

Lutheran Church of the Good Shepherd, Paseo de Palmas 1910, tel (55) 55 96 10 34.

Anglican Christ Church, Monte Escandinavos 405, Lomas de Chapultepec, tel (55) 52 02 09 49.

Jewish Beth Israel, Virreyes 1140, Lomas Virreyes, Nidche Israel (Orthodox), Acapulco 70.

LOCAL WAYS
» Casual clothing is adequate for most occasions, although men may need a jacket and tie in some restaurants.

» Topless bathing is increasingly acceptable in parts of Baja California, but take your cues from others.

» Most Latin Americans, if they can afford it, devote great care to their clothes and appearance; it is appreciated if visitors do likewise. How you dress is mostly how people will judge you.

» Remember that politeness—even a little ceremoniousness—is much appreciated. Men should always remove any headgear and say *con permiso* when entering offices. Shaking hands is much more common in Latin America than in Europe or North America.

» Always say *Buenos días* before midday, *Buenas tardes* in the afternoon or *Buenas noches* later in the evening, and wait for a reply before proceeding further.

» In shops and markets, saying *No, gracias* with a smile is always better than an arrogant dismissal.

» Try not to be impatient, and avoid criticizing situations in public; the officials may know more English than you think, and gestures and facial expressions are certainly open to interpretation.

» Punctuality is more of a concept than a reality in Latin American countries. The *mañana* culture reigns supreme and any arrangement to meet at, say 7pm, will normally rendezvous about 9pm. However, the one time you are late to catch a bus, boat or plane, it will leave on time; the rule is to arrive on time and be prepared to wait.

» If you have any complaints about faulty goods or services contact Profeco or Procuraduría Federal del Consumidor I, tel 01-800-468-8722; www.profeco.gob.mx, or visit the nearest city branch.

» ID is increasingly required when visiting offices or tourist sites within government buildings. It's handy to have some form of identification *(identificación* or *credencial;* a photocopied passport will usually do). Register your name and leave the ID with the security guard in exchange for a pass.

» There is a charge of $4 to $5 for the use of video cameras at historical sites. If you want to use professional camera equipment, including a tripod, the fee is $150 per day.

Below *Blue and white signs indicate parking zones for visitors with disabilities*

FINDING HELP

PERSONAL SECURITY

Mexico is generally a safe country to visit, although precautions over personal safety should be taken, especially in Mexico City and other large cities, especially when taking a taxi in the street.

» Make sure you have adequate insurance to cover any health emergencies, thefts or legal costs.
» Never carry valuables visibly or in easily picked pockets.
» Leave passports, tickets and important documents in a hotel safety deposit, not in your room.
» Never leave possessions visible inside the car and at night park in hotel parking areas.
» Avoid using the bus at night, particularly in Guerrero, Oaxaca, Veracruz and Chiapas.

EMERGENCY PHONE NUMBERS

General emergency number	060/080
(police, ambulance, fire)	

» Couples and women on their own should avoid lonely beaches.
» Be prepared for short-changing and overcharging.

LOSS OF PASSPORT

» If possible, scan the relevant pages of your passport and email them to yourself at an email account you can access anywhere (like www. hotmail.com).
» Always keep a separate note of your passport number and a photocopy of the page that carries your details, in case of loss or theft.

» If you do lose your passport or it is stolen, report it to the police and then contact your nearest embassy or consulate.

POLICE

The police service has an equivalent to the Angeles Verdes (Green Angels, ▷ 55), who help victims of crime to file a report. US citizens should present this report to the nearest embassy or consulate.

Otherwise, try to avoid the police if possible; they are rarely helpful and tend to make complicated situations even worse. Should you come into contact with them, try to stay as calm and polite as possible. Never offer a bribe unless you are fully conversant with the customs of Mexico.

EMBASSIES AND CONSULATES IN MEXICO CITY

COUNTRY	ADDRESS	CONTACT DETAILS
Australia	Ruben Dario 55, Colonia Polanco, 11580 Mexico DF	tel (55) 11 01 22 00
		www.mexico.embassy.gov.au
Canada	Calle Schiller 529, Colonia Polanco (Rincón del Bosque) 11580 Mexico DF	tel (55) 57 24 79 00
		www.canadainternational.gc.ca/mexico-mexique/index.aspx
Germany	Lord Byron 737, Colonia Polanco, 11560 Mexico DF	tel (55) 52 83 22 00
		www.mexiko.diplo.de/Vertretung/mexiko/es/Startseite.html
New Zealand	Jaime Balmes No. 8, 4th Floor, Colonia Los Morales, Polanco, 11510 Mexico DF	tel (55) 52 83 94 60
Spain	(Consulate General) Galileo 114, Colonia Polanco, 11560 Mexico DF	tel (55) 52 55 52 82
UK	Río Lerma 71, Colonia Cuauhtémoc, 06500 Mexico DF	tel (55) 52 42 85 17
		www.embajadabritanica.com.mx
US	Paseo de la Reforma 305, Colonia Cuauhtémoc, 06500 Mexico DF	tel (55) 50 80 20 00
		http://mexico.usembassy.gov/eng/main.html

COMMUNICATIONS

TELEPHONES

» Calls made to Mexican numbers are either local, regional or international.

» Most destinations have a 7-digit number (except Mexico DF, Guadalajara and Monterrey, which have 8-digit numbers).

» Most regions have a 3-digit code (except Mexico DF, Guadalajara and Monterrey, which have 2-digit codes). See the chart (right) listing the phone codes of the major regions in Mexico.

» The format of a number, depending on the type of call, should be as follows:
Local: use 7- or 8-digit numbers
Between regions: long-distance access (01), plus regional code (2- or 3-digit code), plus 7- or 8-digit number
International: international access, plus country code (52), plus regional code, plus 7- or 8-digit number.

» To call Mexico from the UK dial 00 52, followed by the regional code (2 or 3 digits, depending on the area) and then the 7- or 8-digit number.

» To call the UK from Mexico, dial 00 44, then drop the first zero from the relevant area code.

» To call Mexico from the US dial 011 52, followed by the regional code (2 or 3 digits) and then the relevant 7- or 8-digit number.

» To call the US from Mexico, dial 00 1, followed by the number.

CALL CHARGES

» There is a fixed charge for a local call, regardless of how long the call lasts. National and international calls vary in price according to time of day and distance.

» International calls are very expensive by US, European and Australian standards.

PAYPHONES

» Most public phones take phone cards only (Ladatel), costing 30, 50 or 100 pesos from shops and news kiosks everywhere. AT&T's US Direct service (www.att.com) is available. Dial 01-800-288-2872 for direct ATT access within Mexico. The access number for Canada Direct (www.canadadirect.com) is 01-800-123-0200.

» Commercially run *casetas*, or booths (for example Computel), where you pay after phoning, are up to twice as expensive as private phones, and charges vary from place to place. Computel have offices countrywide with long opening hours. It is better to call collect (reverse charge) from private phones, but better still to use the LADA system.

» Collect calls on LADA can be made from any blue public phone; ask for "*llamar por cobrar*".

» Silver LADA phones are for making local and direct long-distance calls, some take coins. Others take foreign credit cards (Visa, MasterCard, not Amex; not all phones that say they take cards accept them, others that say they don't, do).

» Pre-paid phone cards (such as Ladatel) are available, but are expensive for international calls.

» Of other pre-paid cards, the best value are those issued by Ekofon, available at various airport and other outlets.

» Ekofon provides a pre-chargeable account service, which may be opened from anywhere (including outside Mexico) by internet; go to www.ekofon.com or call (877) 522-8361 (US and Canada only).

» Accounts may be opened with as little as $5 and are rechargeable.

» Calls, which can be made from any telephone in the country, cost 3 pesos per minute to the US, 5 pesos per minute to Europe, 2.75 pesos per minute to Asia.

AREA CODES FOR MAJOR CITIES

Acapulco	744
Aguascalientes	449
Campeche	981
Cancún	998
Chihuahua	614
Cozumel	987
Cuernavaca	777
Durango	686
Guadalajara	33
Guanajuato	473
La Paz	612
Mérida	999
Mexico City	55
Monterrey	81
Morelia	443
Oaxaca	951
Puebla	222
Querétaro	442
San Cristóbal de las Casas	967
San José del Cabo	624
San Miguel de Allende	415
Taxco	762
Tijuana	664
Veracruz	229
Xalapa (Jalapa)	228
Zacatecas	492

INTERNATIONAL DIALING CODES

Australia	00 61
Belize	00 501
Canada	00 1
Costa Rica	00 506
Germany	00 49
Guatemala	00 502
Honduras	00 504
Ireland	00 353
Italy	00 39
New Zealand	00 64
Spain	00 34
UK	00 44
US	00 1

GUIDE TO TELEPHONE PRICES

TYPE OF CALL	(PER MINUTE)/LOWEST PRICE	HIGHEST PRICE
National calls	1.32 pesos	2.60 pesos
International (USA/Canada)	6.32 pesos	12.64 pesos
Other international calls	9.92 pesos	14.84 pesos
Mobile phones	2.50 pesos	

NB. Call charges vary and change, therefore it is important to check before making a call.

» The same account can be used for calls made from the US and Canada, at even cheaper rates.

CELL (MOBILE) PHONES

» If you want to be able to talk on the move, you can rent a cell phone while you are in Mexico, or if you have a triband GSM (Global System for Mobile) phone, you can take yours with you, but beware as the charges are high.

» Your telephone provider back home must enable international roaming on your account before you go, and have a reciprocal arrangement with Telmex in Mexico.

» If you are going to be in Mexico for a while, the best bet is to buy a Mexican mobile phone.

» Mexico's dominant telephone company, Telmex, has been rolling out its GSM network in Mexico. This means that users of GSM phones (Europe, Australia, et al) will soon be able to take them to Mexico and use them as if they were at home.

POST OFFICES

» You'll find a post office (Oficina de Correos) in almost every town and in every city in Mexico.

» In the major cities, opening hours are long, Monday to Friday 9 to 7, Saturday 9 to 1.

» In the more remote areas, post offices may only open in the morning.

SENDING A LETTER

» International services have improved and the bright red mailboxes found in many parts of the country are reliable for sending letters.

» Stamps can be bought from post offices or stamp machines, generally located outside post offices, at bus stations, airports and some commercial establishments (but not many).

» Airmail letters have to be weighed at the post office and stamps to the postage value bought.

» Rates are raised periodically in line with the devaluation of the peso against the dollar, but occasionally vary between towns.

» Parcel counters often close earlier than other sections of the post office in Mexico.

» Not all of these services are obtainable outside Mexico City; delivery times in or from the interior

may well be longer than those from Mexico City.

» Poste Restante (lista de correos in Mexico) functions quite reliably; mail is returned to the sender after 10 days if not collected (for an extension write to the Jefe de la Administración of the post office holding your mail; any other post office will help with this). Address the envelope with Favor de retener hasta llegada.

INTERNET ACCESS

» Internet access in Mexico is extensive and often easier and more reliable than the phone. Every major town now has at least one internet café, with more springing up daily.

» If money is tight and you have time, look around; prices vary from place to place, but are normally $2 an hour.

» Visit www.cybercafes.com for a selection of some of those in Mexico.

Above *Post box in Mexico City*
Below *Public telephone booth, Mexico City*

POSTAGE GUIDE PRICES	UNDER 20G	20–50G	500G–1KG
North America, Central America and the Caribbean	10.50 pesos	20.50 pesos	197 pesos
South America and Europe	13 pesos	20.50 pesos	275 pesos
Asia, Africa and Oceania	14.50 pesos	24.50 pesos	357.50 pesos

NB. Postal rates are subject to change.

OPENING TIMES AND TICKETS

It's very difficult to generalize about opening times for museums, tourist offices and shops in Mexico. Even when times are posted, they are not necessarily adhered to. The hours of business in Mexico City are extremely variable and in other parts of the country vary considerably according to climate and local custom. The siesta, though slowly disappearing in large cities, is still commonplace, particularly in hotter areas such as the Gulf coast and Yucatán, and many places will close for a few hours in early afternoon, usually from 1 till 3 or even 4.

BANKS

» Larger branches of main banks in Mexico City and those in the rest of the country are generally open Monday to Friday 9 to 5. Head offices and some larger branches are open 9 to 12.30 on Saturday mornings. In smaller provincial towns some branches close at 1.30.
» Public holidays lead to a complete shutdown in virtually all services, including banks. It is worth keeping an eye on the calendar to avoid the necessity to change money on days such as these.

SHOPS

» Shops in big towns and cities are normally open daily from 9 till between 8 and 10pm. Smaller towns will have more limited opening hours, and in hotter, non-tourist regions, will close between 1pm and 3 or 4pm for siesta. In smaller towns shops may close on Sundays, except tourist spots in high season.
» Christmas and Easter public holidays are observed; on other public holidays you'll find most things open in cities, bigger towns and resorts.

MUSEUMS, GALLERIES AND ARCHAEOLOGICAL SITES

» Museums and galleries tend to open from around 9 to 1 and from 3 to 6, but hours vary across the country and are seasonal; check

locally. Many close on Monday, but again this can vary.
» Many museums and archaeological sites offer free entry on Sundays.
» Archaeological sites are normally open all day, from 8 or 9 till 5.

RESTAURANTS, BARS AND CAFÉS

» Opening times vary wildly, depending on location and season. In Mexico City and large towns and tourist areas, places tend to open longer, often from 8 or 9 in the morning till 11 or 12 at night, though some open only from lunch (1pm).
» Cafés serving breakfast may open from around 6.30 or 7am.
» Bars will open from lunchtime onward, but again times vary around the country. Many are open till around 2 or 3 in the morning, or even later in tourist hotspots in high season.

POST OFFICES

In the major cities, opening hours are Monday to Friday 9 to 6 and Saturday 9 to 1. Smaller branches open shorter hours, often 9 to 3, and Saturdays from 9 to 1. In the more remote areas, post offices may only open in the morning on weekdays.

PHARMACIES

Many of Mexico's pharmacies are open 24 hours a day. Some close at around 10pm, others stay open all

night. In smaller towns, pharmacies take turns staying open on the "all night" shift—ask at your hotel for details.

CONCESSIONS

» Although an international student identity card (ISIC) offers student discounts, only national Mexican student cards permit free entry to archaeological sites, museums etc.
» SETEJ (Mexican Students' Union) issues student cards and offers ISIS insurance. To obtain a national student card you need two photos, passport, confirmation of student status and $13.30.
» For elderly visitors (age 60 plus, retirees or those on a long vacation) who can provide proof of address, a special card is available from the Instituto Nacional de la Senectud (INSEN), which gives free admission to museums, use of the metro, and 50 percent off bus and theater tickets.
» Children can often travel for reduced rates on buses, and free entry is usually given to them on sightseeing tours to museums etc. Also check out cheaper flights for children.

NATIONAL HOLIDAYS

If any of these holidays falls on a Thursday or a Tuesday, they are usually an excuse for a *puente*, a bridge or long weekend (which can have implications for travel, hotel accommodations and services). Sunday is a statutory holiday. Saturday is also observed as a holiday, except by the shops. There is no early-closing day in Mexico.

January 1	New Year
February 5	Constitution Day
March 21	Birthday of Benito Juárez
March/April	Maundy Thursday, Good Friday and Easter Saturday
May 1	Labor Day
May 5	Battle of Puebla
September 1	El Informe (Presidential Message)
September 16	Independence Day
October 12	Día de la Raza (Discovery of America)
November 20	Día de la Revolución (Revolution Day)
December 25	Christmas Day

TOURIST INFORMATION OFFICES IN MEXICO

Aguascalientes
Avenida Universidad No. 1001, Edifico
Torre Plaza Bosques 8 Piso, CP 20127
Aguascalientes, AGS
(tel (449) 912 35 11)

Baja California Norte
Boulevard Díaz Ordáz s/n, Edificio Plaza
Patria Nivel 3, CP 22400 Tijuana, BAJ
(tel (664) 634 63 30)

Baja California Sur
Carretera Al Norte Km. 5.5 Fracc. Fidepaz,
CP 23090 La Paz, BCS
(tel (612) 124 01 00)

Campeche
Avenida Ruiz Cortines s/n, Plaza Moch-
Couoh, Centro, CP 24000 Campeche, CAM
(tel (981) 811 92 00)

Chiapas
Boulevard Belisario Dominguez No. 950,
Planta Baja, CP 29060 Tuxtla Gutiérrez, CHI
(tel (961) 613 93 96)

Coahuila
Boulevard Luis Echeverría No. 1560, Edificio
Torre Saltillo Piso 11, CP 25286 Saltillo,
COA (tel (884) 415 17 14)

Colima
Portal Hidalgo No. 96 Centro, CP 2800
Colima, COL (tel (312) 312 28 57)

Distrito Federal (Mexico City)
Amberes No. 54, 2 Piso, CP 06600 Mexico
DF (tel (55) 55 25 93 80)

Durango
Calle Florida No. 1106, CP 34000 Durango,
DUR (tel (618) 811 11 07)

Guanajuato
Plaza de la Paz No. 14, CP 36000
Guanajuato, GNJ (tel (473) 732 19 82)

Guerrero
Avenida Costera Miguel Alemán 4455,
Centro Cultural y de Convenciones de
Acapulco, CP 39850 Acapulco, GUE
(tel (44) 484 24 23)

Hidalgo
Carretera Mexico-Pachuca km 93.5, Colonia
Venta Prieta, CP 42080 Pachuca, HID
(tel (771) 717 81 17)

Jalisco
Paseo de Gollado No. 105, CP 44100
Guadalajara, JAL
(tel (33) 3668 16 00)

Mexico (state)
Urawa No. 100, Edificio Centro de Servicios
Admvos. Puerta No. 110, CP 50150 Toluca,
MX (tel (722) 212 59 98)

Michoacán
Tata Vasco No. 80, Centro, CP 58000
Morelia, MIC
(tel (443) 317 80 52)

Morelos
Avenida Morelos Sur No. 187, Las Palmas,
CP 62050 Cuernavaca, MOR
(tel (777) 314 38 72)

Nayarit
Calzada del Ejército y Avenida México s/n,
Ex-Convento de la Cruz de Zacate, CP 63168
Tepic, NAY (tel (311) 214 80 71)

Nuevo Leon
Zaragoza No. 1300 Sur, Edificio Kalos Nivel
A-1 Desp. 137, CP 64000 Monterrey, NL
(tel (81) 8344 4343)

Oaxaca
Juarez No. 703, CP 68000 Oaxaca, OAX
(tel (951) 502 12 00)

Puebla
5 Oriente No. 3, Centro Histórico, CP 72000
Puebla, PUE (tel (222) 246 20 44)

Querétaro
Avenida Luis Pasteur No. 4, Norte, Centro
Histórico, CP 76000 Querétaro
(tel (442) 212 14 12)

Quintana Roo
Avenida Cobá, CP 77500 Cancún, QUI
(tel (998) 884 65 31)

San Luis Potosí
Hidalgo No. 5, CP 78000 San Luis Potosí,
SLP (tel (444) 812 27 70)

Sinaloa
1317 Carnaval, CP 82100 Mazatlán, SIN
(tel (669) 981 88 83)

Sonora
Palacio de Gobierno, Edif Estatal Norte 3er
Nivel, CP 83280 Hermosillo, SON
(tel (662) 217 00 60)

Tabasco
Avenida Los Ríos s/n, Calle 13 Tabasco
2000, CP 86035 Villahermosa, TAB
(tel (993) 316 51 34)

Tamaulipas
16 Rosales No. 272, CP 87000 Ciudad
Victoria, TAM (tel (834) 312 10 57)

Tlaxcala
Avenida Juárez esq, Lardizábal, CP 90000
Tlaxcala, TLA
(tel (246) 465 09 60)

Veracruz
Enríquez No. 214, Palacio Municipal, CP
91190 Xalapa, VER
(tel (228) 842 12 14)

Yucatán
Calle 59 No. 514 entre 62 y 64, Centro, CP
97000 Mérida, YUC
(tel (999) 924 93 89/930 37 66)

Zacatecas
Avenida Hidalgo No. 403 Segundo Piso, CP
98000 Zacatecas, ZAC
(tel (492) 922 67 51)

Canada
1610-999 West Hastings Street, Suite 1110, Vancouver, British Columbia V6C 2W2 (tel +1-604-669-2845)

France
4 rue Notre Dame des Victoires, Paris 75002 (tel +33-1-42 86 96 12)

Germany
Taunusanlage 21, Franfurt-am-Main D60325 (tel +49-69-71 03 38 95)

Italy
Via Barberini No. 3, 7° piso, Rome 00187 (tel +39-06-487-46 98)

Spain
Calle de Velázquez No 126, Madrid 28006 (tel +34-1-561-3520)

UK
Wakefield House, 41 Trinity Square, London EC3N 4DJ (tel +44-20-7488-9392)

US
225 N. Michigan Avenue, Suite 1850, Chicago IL 60601 (tel +1 312 228 0517); 1880 Century Park East, Suite 511, Los Angeles CA 90067 (tel +1 310 282 9112); 400 Madison Avenue, Suite 11C, NY 10017 (tel +1 212 308 2110); 975 Sunset Drive, Suite 305, South Miami, FL 33143 (tel +1 786 621 2909); 4507 San Jacinto, Suite 308, Houston TX 77004 (tel +1 713 772 2581)

GETTING INFO

For most visitors, the first port of call for information and maps is the Secretaría de Turismo (SECTUR), the Mexican Government Ministry of Tourism, which has offices throughout the country and abroad. As well as providing free information and various brochures and maps, these tourist offices—also known as turismos—will book your hotel. It's a good idea, however, to stock up on as many freebies as you can before leaving, as many offices in Mexico either run out or don't stock them. As well as SECTUR offices, there are offices run by state and municipal authorities.

» Standards of service vary greatly from place to place. Many people are extremely friendly and helpful, while others appear not to know much about the town in which they live.

» In Mexico City there are sporadically manned tourist booths dotted around which have handy maps and can provide information.

» Information is also available in the capital at Tourist Information Centers operated by the Mexico City Government at several places throughout the city. The website www.mexicocity.gob.mx gives comprehensive information on a wide range of topics, from business to pleasure, and even details of film locations.

» You can refer complaints to the Tourist Information Centers or to the Tourist Police, in blue uniforms, who are usually very friendly.

» The SECTUR main office in Mexico City can be called from anywhere in the country at local rates (tel 1-800/903-9200).

BOOKS, MAPS AND FILMS

BOOKS

There is a wide selection of travel literature on offer, including Carl Franz's The People's Guide to Mexico (John Muir Publications, Santa Fe, NM, 1998), which is practical and entertaining. Isabella Tree's Sliced Iguana (2001) describes her travels to various parts of Mexico, showing it as an exciting, diverse and delightful country.

From a national perspective works are also abundant as Mexico has produced widely respected writers, such as Carlos Fuentes. Of his many works, both Terra Nostra (1975) and The Old Gringo (1985) are well worth a read. Laura Esquivel's Like Water for Chocolate (1993), a novel about desire, love and rebellion, led to big-screen success.

There are dozens of works about Mexico from a foreign perspective. Among the most well known and most popular are Malcolm Lowry's Under the Volcano (1947), Graham Greene's The Power and The Glory (1940), and D. H. Lawrence's The Plumed Serpent (1926). Although these works are not contemporary, they provide a vivid and insightful view into Mexican life and culture that holds true today.

For an insight into different aspects of Mexican culture and the people's own perceived place in the world around them, try Octavio Paz's The Labyrinth of Solitude and Other Writings (1985). Coe, M. D., The Maya (Pelican Books, or large-format edition, Thames and Hudson) is essential reading for the Maya archaeological area. There are many good works on Mexican history, among which William Prescott's History of the Conquest of Mexico (1849) remains a popular choice.

A more up-to-date perspective can be found in Hugh Thomas' Conquest: Cortes, Montezuma, and the Fall of the Old Mexico (1995).

The informative annual Travelers Guide to Mexico (editor and publisher Chris Luhnow) can be found in more than 35,000 hotel rooms across Mexico.

MAPS AND LEAFLETS

Do not expect to find leaflets or books available at all the archaeological sites. Bloomgarden, Richard Panorama Guides and Easy Guides are all reliable, widely available and have plans and good illustrations.

Also available are Miniguides to archaeological and historical sites, published in various languages by INAH, $1.50 each.

The AAA (US) produces a Mexican map predominantly for the independent visitor. There is also a road atlas for the US, Canada and Mexico combined. To order a copy of the map or atlas, look up the website: www.theAA.com.

The Instituto Geográfico Militar sells topographical maps, scale

ESSENTIAL INFORMATION

PRACTICALITIES

1:100,000 or 1:50,000. The physical features shown on these are usually accurate; the trails and place names less so. National Parks offices also sell maps.

SPECIALIST MAP SHOPS
UK
National Map Centre, 22–24 Caxton Street, London SW1H 0QU, tel 020 7222 2466, www.mapsnmc.co.uk
Stanfords, 12–14 Long Acre, Covent Garden, London WC2E 9LP, tel 020 7836 1321, www.stanfords.co.uk

US
The Complete Traveler, 199 Madison Avenue, New York, NY 10022, tel 212/685-9007
Map Link inc, 30 S La Patera Lane, Unit 5, Santa Barbara, CA 93117, tel 805/692-6777, www.maplink.com

FILMS
On the international big screen Mexico has probably suffered more than most from stereotypical images painting the whole nation as a bunch of lazy, good-for-nothing scoundrels, crooks and corrupt officials, but things began to change with the international success of the 1992 movie *Como Agua Para Chocolate (Like Water for Chocolate)*.

Mexico's new film image was further enhanced by the 2002 hit *Frida*, which celebrated the life of the painter Frida Kahlo and her relationship with Diego Rivera, but it was the Oscar-nominated and Bafta-winning *Amores Perros (Love's a Bitch*, 2001), and *Y Tu Mamá También (And Your Mother Too*, 2001) that really put Mexican cinema on the map, as well as launching the glittering careers of Latin heart-throb Gael García Bernal and director Alejandro González Iñárritu (▷ 20).

The Mexican landscape has always featured on the international film scene and the Western genre relied heavily on the scenic locations around Durango, producing classics from the 1950s through the works of Sam Peckinpah up to the all-star *Mask of Zorro* (1998), starring Antonio Banderas.

Many other US productions have used Mexico's tropical locations for films, such as *Night of the Iguana*, *Romancing the Stone* and *Medicine Man*, and the 1997 blockbuster *Titanic*, which was shot at Rosarito, Baja California, close to Tijuana.

MEDIA
TELEVISION
» The national television network is largely controlled by Televisa, which owns and runs four of the six national channels, while the other two channels are owned and run by TV Azteca.
» Mexican television basically consists of adverts, soap operas *(telenovelas)*, sports (predominantly soccer/football), movies and comedy. As a general rule, the networks refrain from showing any material containing nudity, violence or offensive language.
» Once TV and Canal 22 are two channels that offer a much more cultural selection of viewing.
» It is only through satellite and cable television that visitors are likely to find channels that they recognize.
» The main providers, Multivisión and Cablevision, offer the now widely known Cartoon Network, MTV, ESPN and CNN. However, these are likely to be found only in mid- to upper-range hotels.

RADIO
» Mexico has approximately 1,000 short-wave and long-wave stations and so a short-wave (world band) radio offers a practical means to brush up on the language, sample aspects of popular culture and absorb some of the richly varied regional music.
» There are also radio stations available if you want to catch up on events at home or around the world. International broadcasters offer this service, often both in English and Spanish. Among the most popular is the BBC World Service: 648 kHz LW; check www.bbc.co.uk/worldservice/index.shtml for schedules and the relevant short-wave frequencies depending on your location.
» The Voice of America website, www.voa.gov, gives all schedules and frequencies for Mexico and the rest of Latin America.

NEWSPAPERS
» The influential national dailies are: *Excelsior, Novedades, El Día, Uno Más Uno, El Universal, El Heraldo, La Jornada* (www.jornada.unam.mx, more to the left), *La Prensa* (a popular tabloid, with the largest circulation) and *El Nacional*, which is effectively the mouthpiece of the government.
» There are influential weekly magazines such as *Proceso, Siempre, Epoca* and *Quehacer Político. Los Agachados* is a weekly political satirical magazine. *The News*, an English-language daily, is currently not available.
» The New York edition of the *Financial Times* and other mainstream British and European newspapers are available at Mexico City Airport and from the Casa del Libro, Calle Florencia 37 (Zona Rosa), Hamburgo 141 (Zona Rosa) and Calle Homero (Polanco), all in Mexico City. The *Miami Herald* is stocked by most newspaper stands.

USEFUL WEBSITES

www.visitmexico.com
Website of Mexico Tourist Board, a comprehensive multilingual site with information on the entire country.

www.sectur.gob.mx
Website of Tourism Secretariat, with less glossy links but equally comprehensive information.

www.mexperience.com
Well-constructed site updated daily, with current affairs, feature articles and advice on travel in Mexico. Look for the forum where comments from fellow visitors are exchanged.

www.mexconnect.com
A massive and comprehensive site devoted to Mexico. You will have to sign up as a member, but the level of information, news and articles on offer is vast and well worth a look.

Gorp.com/gorp/location/latamer/mexico.htm
An option for adventurers, with lots of detailed information, including good suggestions and tips on more adventurous travel.

www.wtgonline.com/data/mex/mex.asp
The online presence of The World Travel Guide Mexico, with an overview of Mexico for visitors, and a useful Essentials section with facts on visas, public holidays, money and health.

www.lanic.utexas.edu/la/mexico/
Mexico Reference Desk, a huge site containing a variety of information about Mexico, ranging from anthropology to sport and trade. Rather academic in tone, it is nevertheless an excellent source for background information.

www.mexonline.com
Another good source for information of all types on Mexico. It offers everything from places to stay, eat and visit, as well as more general information on Mexico's history, culture and everyday life.

MAJOR SIGHTS QUICK WEBSITE/PAGE FINDER		
SIGHT/TOWN	WEBSITE	PAGE
Acapulco	www.sectur.guerrero.gob.mx	143
Aguascalientes	www.aguascalientes.gob.mx	205
Barranca del Cobre	www.coppercanyoninsider.com	243
Campeche	www.campechetravel.com	106
Cancún	www.cancunmx.com	107
Chichén Itzá		108–111
Cozumel	www.islacozumel.com.mx	112–113
Cuernavaca	www.cuernavaca.gob.mx	179
Guadalajara	www.guadalajara.gob.mx	208
Guanajuato	www.guanajuato.gob.mx	210–213
Mérida		117
Monte Albán	www.oaxaca.gob.mx	146–147
Monterrey	www.allaboutmonterrey.com	250
Morelia		147
Museo Nacional de Antropológia	www.mexicocity.com.mx/musantro.html	72–75
Oaxaca	www.aoaxaca.com	148–151
Palenque	www.palenquemx.com	152–155
Puebla	www.poblanerias.com	182–183
San Cristóbal de las Casas	www.turismochiapas.gob.mx	157
San Miguel de Allende	www.turismosanmiguel.com.mx	217
El Tajín		185
Taxco	www.taxco.guerrero.gob.mx	186
Tijuana	www.tijuanaonline.org	253
Tulúm		192
Uxmal		122–123
Veracruz	www.veracruz-puerto.gob.mx/turismo	192
Xalapa (Jalapa)	www.xalapa.gob.mx/turismo	193
Zacatecas	www.turismozacatecas.gob.mx	222–223

www.cybercaptive.com
A site that holds a database of the location of many cyber cafés in Mexico.

www.eluniversal.com.mx
This online version of the popular *El Universal* newspaper has stories primarily in Spanish, but also offers translations into English on the major stories and articles. A useful tool to keep abreast of current events in Mexico.

www.jornada.unam.mx
The *La Jornada* newspaper is the most popular national daily in Mexico. This online site is only in Spanish, but is very useful for any who can read the language.

www.mexicocity.com.mx
An excellent site that caters specifically to Mexico City. With a large amount of information on restaurants, transportation, embassies and much more, it's a comprehensive resource if you are spending time in the capital.

www.planeta.com
Website run by Ron Mader. Forum for various environmental issues, but also features Mexican stories and travel articles.

SHOPPING

Mexico has taken to the shopping mall in a big way. These shiny, air-conditioned temples of retail therapy now grace every self-respecting large town and city. A highlight of any visit to Mexico, however, is to wander around the busy markets and *artesanía* (handicrafts) shops that appear with unerring regularity up and down the country, offering not only a mind-boggling variety of wonderful folk art, but also an exotic assault on the senses.

DEPARTMENT STORES
Mexico's big name is Sanborn's, with branches in all the major towns and cities. It sells a huge range of gifts, DVDs, video games and CDs, electrical goods, jewelry, cosmetics, books, chocolates and sweets. It also has good in-store cafés and restaurants (▷ 91).

MARKETS
Every Mexican town has a weekly market *(mercado)*, when people from the surrounding countryside come to buy and sell their wares. Mostly it's food and everyday household items, but many have a section devoted to *artesanía*, while larger towns may even have a separate crafts market.

Bargaining is usually the order of the day and there are often some good deals to be had, but it's a good idea to shop around first and check up on the value of certain items. When haggling, be courteous and good natured, and always bear in mind that, by First World standards, usually only a small amount of money is involved.

CRAFT SHOPS
It is usually cheaper to buy crafts away from the capital or major visitor areas, but not everyone has the time to visit the villages where the *artesanía* is still made.

Almost everything can be found in Mexico City, and most regional capitals have a Casa de las Artesanías with exhibitions, and sometimes sales, of local craftwork. You'll also come across FONART shops in the main towns and cities. These are run by a government agency and are designed to promote and preserve *artesanía* and artesans. Though relatively expensive, they always stock a wide range of excellent quality goods.

The main advantage of buying your souvenirs in more established shops—other than sheer convenience—is that shopkeepers will often ship items home for you, thus saving a huge amount of bureaucratic hassle.

OPENING HOURS
Opening hours are flexible and vary according to the region, city, town and type of shop. Small shops tend to close for a few hours around lunch, from around 1 or 2pm to 4 or 5pm. Climate is also a factor and in hotter areas, such as the Gulf coast and Yucatán, shops tend to close for longer in the heat of the day and stay open later in the evening. In larger towns and resorts, most shops open from 9am till around 8 or 9pm.

PAYMENT
Credit cards are acceptable in larger stores and boutiques in the main visitor hubs, though smaller shops and markets will only accept local currency. In more popular resorts such as Acapulco and Cancún it is just as easy to pay in US dollars and even dollar travelers' checks. Larger chains charge a sales tax of between 12 and 15 percent, depending on which state they are in.

WHAT TO BUY
Artesanía
Artesanía is an art form and a craft skill, lending functional, everyday items an inherent beauty and profound religious meaning. Each town has its own particular special crafts. Traditional indigenous communities the length and breadth of Mexico congregate in colonial towns such as Oaxaca, Pátzcuaro, San Cristóbal and Uruapan to ply their wares, and these visitor hotspots are good places to see the superb range of products on offer, from *huipiles* (traditional sleeveless blouses) to hammocks, from silverware to scary masks.

Ceramics
Ceramics are an excellent buy and can be seen at roadside stands, local markets or retailers in the main towns and resorts. One of the best examples is the Patambán pottery found in Michoacán and on sale in Uruapan. Also outstanding is the *bandera* pottery of Tonalá (Jalisco), decorated in the Mexican national colors. One of the most typical forms is the famous *árboles de vida* (trees of life) from Metepec (▷ 26). Guanajuato is famous for its Majolica pottery, and Puebla, one of the country's main bases for ceramics, for its decorative tiles.

Jewelry
For silver and gold work, known as *orfebrería*, look in Taxco and the markets in Mexico City. Jade jewelry is made in Michoacán, while semiprecious stones such as onyx, obsidian, amethyst and turquoise are found in Oaxaca, Puebla, Guerrero, Zacatecas and Querétaro. Beware of mistaking the cheapish pretty jewelry called *alpaca*, an alloy of copper, zinc and nickel, for the genuine stuff. By law, real silver, defined as 0.925 pure, must be stamped somewhere on the item with the number 925, unless the item is very small, in which case a certificate is provided instead.

Lacquerware
Olinalá is the focus of inspiration for *laca* (lacquerware) in Guerrero and its influence spreads to other towns such as Temalacacingo, 20km (12.5 miles) away, while the Sunday market in Chilapa is a good place to shop. Things to look for include large chests, boxes, furniture, toys, and gourds shaped into fruit and animal figures. Michoacán has the most elaborate lacquerwork, while Pátzcuaro and Uruapan are also good places.

Leatherwork
Leather goods can be bought in northern Mexico, particularly in the ranching towns of Durango and Zacatecas, and also in Central Mexico. Jackets, belts, boots and shoes are all good value, though make sure you road test the footwear as the quality is usually inferior to that found in Spain or Italy.

Masks
Masks are a vital component of Mexican festivals and make excellent souvenirs. They come in all shapes and forms, from animals such as eagles and monkeys, to papier-mâché skulls used for the *Día de los Muertos* (Day of the Dead) celebrations (▷ 26). Good places to seek out masks are the markets in Paracho, in Michoacán, and throughout Tlaxcala state, where you can find the wooden "old man" masks with white face, tiny moustache and crystal eyes peering out from behind huge eyelashes. At Papantla (Veracruz), black wooden masks stir up African spirits in magic rituals.

Textiles
Weaving and textile design go back a long way in Mexico. Many woven items are on sale in the markets, from *sarapes* (ponchos) and *morrales* (shoulder bags) to wall hangings, rugs and bedspreads, which are found around Oaxaca state. Synthetic materials are often used too, so make sure you know what you're getting before you buy.

Ponchos come in two distinctive types: the *sarape*, which is a long garment, and the *jorongo*, which is shorter. They are found all over Mexico but the former is worn especially in the Valle de Oaxaca, where it is made in Santa Ana del Valle, Teotitlán del Valle and San Luis Potosí.

Hammocks are another excellent buy and the best place to look is Mérida in the Yucatán peninsula. Different materials are used for making hammocks. Sisal is very strong, light and durable, but rather scratchy and uncomfortable, while cotton is soft, flexible and comfortable, though it doesn't last as long. The surest way to judge a good hammock is by weight: 1,500g (3.3 pounds) is a fine item, under 1kg (2.2 pounds) is junk. Also, the finer and thinner the strands of material, the more strands there will be, and the more comfortable the hammock. The best hammocks are the so-called 3-ply, but they are difficult to find. There are four sizes: single *(sencilla)*, double *(doble)*, matrimonial and family; buy at least a matrimonial for comfort.

Opposite *Sombreros are popular purchases*
Below *Brightly colored string hammocks*

Away from the hectic calendar of festivals that testify to Mexico's hedonistic tendencies, the cities and main resorts provide a year-round schedule of good times for local people and visitors alike. Mexico City, in particular, is a hotbed of cultural activity, with classical music concerts and performances of ballet and opera by touring companies, while university cities such as Xalapa are cultural centers in their own right, with art-house cinemas and lively student bars and clubs. Mexico City enjoys a vibrant nightlife, which starts late and usually continues till sunrise. Away from the capital, Guadalajara and the Caribbean and Pacific beach resorts such as Veracruz, Cancún and Acapulco are always buzzing after dark. The popularity of nightclubs and bars changes, and places come and go continually, so check out the latest scene before making plans. Tijuana's proximity to the US border has made it enormously popular with Americans who come to party.

CINEMA

Mexicans are avid cinema-goers and popular movies are inevitably sold out. Latest releases arrive very soon after showing in the US, often before their European debut, and are always shown in their original language, with Spanish subtitles—except in the case of foreign children's movies.

As in Europe and North America, the huge multiplex cinemas dominate. The largest chain is Cinemex, which you'll find in all the main towns and cities. You can buy tickets on the Cinemex website: www.cinemex.com.

Art-house cinemas, showing independent releases, are prevalent in the capital and large cities, as well as university towns such as Xalapa.

A night out at the cinema is relatively inexpensive, with prices ranging from $5–$7, and Wednesday nights are half-price in the capital. Complete listings are given in *Tiempo Libre* magazine (see Listings, ▷ 287).

CLASSICAL MUSIC, DANCE AND OPERA

The big cities, especially the capital, are the best places to hear good classical music concerts, or to see operatic and ballet performances by touring companies. One event particularly worth seeing in Mexico City is the Ballet Folcórico (▷ 92). Aimed at the tourist market, this distillation of various traditional folk dances may be more like a

Broadway or West End show than an authentic indigenous experience, but is a good night out nevertheless. Guadalajara also hosts its own impressive version, as well as a schedule of theater and dance. Away from the main cities, the best chance of seeing traditional forms of dance is at one of the myriad festivals that take place throughout the country.

LIVE MUSIC

It's difficult to avoid hearing live music, be it in on the street, at the beach, on the plaza or in a club. The main sources of this pervasive soundtrack are, of course, the *mariachi* bands (▷ 25), those groups of strolling Mexican minstrels who seem to magically appear, as if from nowhere, every time you sit down.

Plaza Garibaldi in Mexico City has always been a good place to hear *mariachi*, as well as other types of Mexican music such as *norteño* (a kind of Tex-Mex country) and *marimba*, but it gets very busy late at night and may prove a daunting experience for more sensitive visitors. Other types of Latin music, particularly Cuban, can also be heard in bars and clubs up and down the country.

The alternative rock scene is thriving, most notably *rock en Español* (▷ 21), which can be heard in the capital as well as the other larger cities. Details of gigs are given in *Tiempo Libre* (▷ 287).

THEATER

Mexican theater can be rather heavy going unless you're a fluent Spanish

speaker. Many of the country's finest theaters, however, double up as music or dance venues and it is worth checking these out, if only to see their grand interiors.

BARS AND NIGHTCLUBS
Places for drinking alcohol in Mexico run the whole gamut, from rough-and-ready *cantinas* to plush hotel cigar bars. Mexican *cantinas* are, of course, legendary. They are no place for shrinking violets, but an eye-opening introduction to the country's macho culture, where shots of tequila may be accompanied by shots of a different sort. These establishments are not really the place to go for a family night out. *Cantinas* are traditionally men-only affairs, though women may be tolerated if they are accompanied by a man.

Pulquerías are also working-class male preserves, where *pulque*, a thick, astringent fermented drink made from the maguey cactus, is drunk in copious quantities.

Further up the scale, much of Mexico's socializing goes on in restaurants, bars, cafés and lounges, as well as "pubs," a more recent feature on the drinking landscape.

Often based around some theme (such as Irish), pubs are aimed at visitors and young Mexicans.

Nightclubs come in all shapes and sizes and range from huge *über*-clubs with several dance floors to more intimate places where you might be able to hold a conversation.

Mexico City and the large resorts such as Acapulco, Cancún, Puerto Vallarta and Veracruz have the broadest range and you can choose one to suit your own musical preference, be it techno, house, hip-hop or Cuban groove. Many of the classiest places in the capital are in the more salubrious suburbs such as Zona Rosa, Condesa, Polanco and San Angel.

GAY AND LESBIAN
There are gay bars and clubs in the large cities such as the capital, Guadalajara, Monterrey and Veracruz, major resorts and in the towns along the US border. The lesbian scene is less developed but nevertheless exists and is growing.

In terms of attitudes toward gay and lesbian visitors, machismo and religion are deeply entrenched and prejudice is all-pervasive. This means that discretion is the order of the

day, particularly in rural areas, where even holding hands can offend.

OPENING HOURS
It's difficult to generalize about opening times in Mexico. Bars tend to stay open until around 1 or 2am, but opening times are flexible and vary considerably from place to place, depending on the night in question, or how busy the place is.

Clubs generally don't get going until the wee small hours and most young Mexicans don't leave until dawn. Many places charge a cover of $10–$20, though women are usually allowed in free.

Nightlife in more rural areas will obviously start earlier and finish earlier than in cities.

LISTINGS
Details of events in Mexico City can be found in *Tiempo Libre* (www.tiempolibre.com.mx) on sale at most newsstands every Thursday, costing $1.25. Elsewhere, the local newspapers, tourist offices and hotel concierges are excellent sources of information.

Above *Members of a* mariachi *band*
Opposite *Acapulco is famous for its nightlife*

SPORTS AND ACTIVITIES

In a way, Mexico has always been synonymous with sports, from that famous leap of Bob Beaman in the long jump at the Mexico City Olympics in 1968 to the movie reel of young Turks leaping from the cliffs at Acapulco into the crashing waves far below. Mexico's massive coastline of reefs and swells and expanse of mountain ranges cut by long rivers make it very well suited to outdoor adventure. The Caribbean offers superb diving off the Quintana Roo coastline, particularly off Isla Mujeres and Isla Cozumel. Even if you're not diving, the water is crystal clear, warm and impossibly blue, and the beaches refreshingly quiet. On the other side of the country is the wild Pacific with its giant rollers, a must for natural surfers and goofies alike who schlep down here in their droves to catch those waves in places like Puerto Escondido, Oaxaca state and the length of Baja California.

BASEBALL

Professional baseball *(beisbol)*, though not on a par with wrestling or soccer, commands quite a following. The season runs from April to August, with the top teams going forward to represent Mexico, along with the champions of Dominican Republic, Puerto Rico and Venezuela, in the Serie del Caribe, held in February.

BULLFIGHTING

Bullfighting is an integral part of Mexican life. Whatever your views, it is rooted in tradition and deeply symbolic. Mexico's *toreros* (matadors) have a reputation for

being particularly brave (or foolish) and are in demand in Spain. Unless you are vehemently opposed, it is worth attending a *corrida de toros* (bullfight) to experience this national obsession.

Mexico City's Plaza México is the largest bullring in the world, where *corridas* take place on Sundays at 4pm from October to April. Prices are low ($3–$5) if you are prepared to sit on the concrete sun *(sol)* terraces, but more expensive (up to $55) for a seat in the shade *(sombra)*. Posters—a fascinating art form in themselves—on display around the city advertise forthcoming events.

CANYONING

Canyoning, or canyoneering, is the practice of climbing up and down waterfalls, swimming across rivers and scrambling through caves and over massive rocks.

Two of the best locations for this infant sport are the Cañadas de Cotlamani, near Jalcomulco in Veracruz, and the Cumbres de Monterrey National Park.

CAVING

Caving, or speleology, in Mexico is more than just going down into deep dark holes. It is a sport more closely related to canyoning, as there are some excellent underground river scrambles. The best of these is probably the 8km-long (5-mile) Chontalcuatlán, a part of the Cacahuamilpa cave system near Taxco. Other possibilities are in Cuetzalan, near Puebla. Beside the Matacanes River circuit in Nuevo León, near Monterrey (see Canyoning) there are some large caves—the Grutas de La Tierrosa, La Cebolla and Pterodáctilo. The biggest cave systems are in Chiapas, especially around Tuxtla Gutiérrez.

CENOTE DIVING

There are more than 50 *cenotes* (natural sinkholes) on the Yucatán peninsula, accessible from Ruta 307 and often well marked. *Cenote*-diving has become very popular in recent years. However, it is a specialized sport and can be very dangerous: Unless you have a cave-diving qualification, you must be accompanied by a qualified dive master. A cave-diving course involves over 12 hours of lectures and a minimum of 14 cave dives using double tanks, costing around $600. Some of the best *cenotes* are "Carwash," on the Cobá road, good even for beginners, with excellent visibility; and "Dos Ojos," just off Ruta 307 south of Puerto Aventuras, the second-largest underground cave system in the world. It has a possible link to the Nohoch Nah Chich, the most famous *cenote* and part of a subterranean system recorded as the world's largest, with more than 50km (30 miles) of surveyed passageways connected to the sea.

CLIMBING

The main climbing region is in the highlands, with several peaks over 5,000m (16,400ft). The big glaciated volcanoes are within relatively easy reach of Mexico City. Although there are few technical routes, crampons, an ice axe and occasionally rope are required for safe ascents. The season is October to May. Now that Popocatépetl (5,452m/ 17,888ft) and Colima Volcano (3,842m/12,605ft) are sporadically erupting, the two

remaining challenges are Pico de Orizaba, Citlatépetl (5,760m/ 18,898ft), Mexico's highest volcano, and Iztaccíhuatl (5,286m/17,343ft), which offers the best technical climbing. Two good acclimatization climbs are Cofre de Perote (Nouhcampatépetl, 4,282m/14,049ft) and Nevado de Toluca (Xinantécatl, 4,583m/15,036ft).

DIVING

There's good diving off most of Mexico's coastline but two regions, Quintana Roo and Baja California, at opposite ends of the country, stand out. Cozumel, in Quintana Roo, has some of the best diving in the world and there are marine parks at Chankanaab and at Palancar Reef, with numerous caves and gullies and a horse-shoe-shaped diving arena. Southern Baja is warmer than the north but it is still advisable to wear a wetsuit, not least to protect from skin-irritating hydrozoa organisms. A diving organization, the Club de Exploraciones y Deportes Acuáticos de México (CEDAM), is based in Puerto Aventuras.

GOLF

Some of Mexico's best golf courses are attached to hotels. Check out information on www.worldgolf.com/ golfdestinations/mexico.

HIKING AND WALKING

Mexico's national parks were set up a long time ago primarily to

provide green recreation areas for city dwellers. In Chiapas, El Triunfo Biosphere Reserve protects Mexico's only cloud forest, on the mountains (up to 2,750m/9,020ft) above the Pacific coast. The main hiking route runs from Jaltenango (reached by bus from Tuxtla) to Mapastepec on the coastal highway. Groups need to book in advance through the state's Institute of Natural History, on Calzada de Hombres de la Revolución, by the botanical garden and Regional Museum (Apartido 391, Tuxtla 29000; tel (961) 612 36 63). Another fine area for hiking is Copper Canyon. Creel is the best base, but a good trek is from Batópilas to Urique—three days in the heart of the Barranca, through Tarahumara lands. The best hiking within reach of a major city is around Monterrey, particularly in the Cumbres de Monterrey National Park.

The Instituto Geográfico Militar sells topographical maps, scale 1:100,000 or 1:50,000. The physical features shown on these are usually accurate; the trails and place-names less so. National park offices also sell maps. Trekking should not be approached casually. Even if you only plan to be out a couple of hours you should have comfortable, safe footwear (which can cope with the wet) and a daypack.

Opposite *Scuba diving lesson, Cancún*
Below *Golf is a major attraction*

JAI ALAI

Also known as *frontón* or *pelota*, this fast-paced Basque game is played with a curved scoop attached to the player's hand, which is used to propel the ball against a large wall at high speed, rather like squash. This isn't so much a spectator sport, however, as a way to win, or lose, money on bets.

ROCK CLIMBING

This is an increasingly popular sport for Mexicans and there is very good climbing in most parts of the country. On the outskirts of the capital there are two convenient natural high-rises above the smog: the cliffs at Magdalena Contreras to the southwest and at Naucalpan to the northwest. Going north of the capital, 70km (43 miles) east of Querétaro is the Peña de Bernal, the world's largest monolith after Ayer's Rock in Australia. The north face route is 400m (1,312ft) in elevation. You have to go much farther north, to Monterrey, for the best rock in Mexico. Near the small town of Hidalgo is the Potrero Chico big wall, 650m (2,132ft) of limestone nirvana.

Contact the Club Alpino Mexicano, AC Coahuila 40, Espuina Córdoba, Colonia Roma, México DF; tel (55) 55 74 96 83, www.clubalpino mexicano.com.mx, for more details and advice.

RODEOS

Charrerías, as they are known in Mexico, take place mostly in northern towns and cities and are lively events, notable as much for their glitz and glitter as the horsemanship of the various competitors. In Baja *charrerías* are held most weekends from May to September.

SEA KAYAKING

This requires no special prior expertise and you can usually take off on your own in quiet waters for day trips. The warm waters of the Sea of Cortés off Baja California Sur are kayak heaven. Isla Espíritu Santo and Isla Partida are easily accessible

from La Paz, and whether in or out of your kayak you can experience a fine display of stingrays, sea lions, dolphins, porpoises, and occasionally gray whales and hammerheads. Farther up the coast, Loreto is another good base for renting gear and at Bahía Coyote, near Santispac, on the mainland side of the larger and more encompassing Bahía Concepción, there are many small islands you can explore in a day on calm waters. The Baja Sea Kayak Association is based in La Paz. The simplest kayaks are more like rafts and have no open compartments, so there's no need to worry about flooding. Agencies will assess your experience when renting out more advanced equipment or basic equipment for longer periods.

SOCCER

Bullfighting may be an obsession but soccer, or football *(fútbol)*, is by far the most popular spectator sport in Mexico. The biggest club teams are those from the capital, particularly América and Necaxa, who both play their home games at the Estadio Azteca (Aztec Stadium), and Guadalajara. Perhaps the biggest game in the soccer calendar is América (Mexico City) versus Chivas (Guadalajara), which fills the 114,000-seat Aztec Stadium. The university team, Pumas UNAM, who play their games at the Estadio Olimpico in Mexico City, are also a strong side, as are Cruz Azul, also based in the capital. Games are played on Sunday afternoons during the season, from August to May, and tickets are normally easy to come by at the ground; the exceptions are the big games and local derbies. Check the local newspapers for details.

Though Mexico has failed to emulate its South American counterparts in winning the World Cup, it has hosted the competition twice, in 1970 and 1986.

SPORT FISHING

Some of the best fishing is in the Sea of Cortés, particularly off La Paz, around Isla Espíritu Santo and

Isla Cerralvo, from Loreto, and off the Buena Vista resort (which has boats), near Los Barriles, 60km (37 miles) south of the Baja Sur capital. Here the high season for many species such as marlin, swordfish, sailfish, roosterfish, dorado, cabrilla and wahoo is May to September. For sierra, it is November to January, and yellowtail from March to May. There are international competitions in July and August and one in March dedicated to catching yellowtail. Tampico, in the Gulf of Mexico, is the focus for competition fishing for robalo (April), marlin (June) and sábalo (July and August).

SURFING

You can experience some of the world's most exhilarating surfing along Mexico's Pacific coast. Highlights are the huge Hawaiian-size surf that pounds the Baja shoreline and the renowned Mexican Pipeline at Puerto Escondido. There are many possibilities, from developed beaches to remote bays accessible only by 4WD vehicles. Many can be found at the estuaries of rivers where sandbars are deposited and points are formed. San Blas, in Nayarit state, is an excellent learning base. The waves are normally not too big and there are few rocks or dangerous currents. Surfing is best between July and October.

WHITEWATER RAFTING

The variety in Mexico's rafting rivers creates all types of opportunities. The attraction is not just the run but the trek or rappel to the start and the moments between rapids, drifting in deep canyons beneath hanging tropical forests, some of which contain lesser-known and quite inaccessible ruins. For sheer thrills, many of the best rivers are in the middle of the country.

The most popular is the Río Antigua/Pescados in Veracruz. The upper stretch, the Antigua, has some good learning rapids (Grade II running into Grade III) but, if you have more than one day, the

Pescados (the lower Antigua), closer to Jalcomulco, can give a bigger adrenalin rush, with some Grade IV whitewater. The biggest rushes in the country, however, are on the Barranca Grande and at Cañón Azul, where there is Grade V water.

Rafting in Chiapas covers the spectrum from sedate floats on rivers such as the Lacan-Há through the Lacandón jungle to Grade IV/V rapids on the Río Jataté, which gathers force where the Lacan Tum enters it and gradually diminishes in strength as it approaches the Río Usumacinta.

The season for whitewater rafting is generally July to September in the middle of the country, when rivers are fuller, but in Chiapas, January and February are better because the climate is cooler.

WILDLIFE-WATCHING

Mexico has an immense range of flora and fauna and presents spectacular wildlife-watching opportunities. The wetland lagoons and rain-forest sites provide some of the most vibrant birdlife. For the novice, the resplendent quetzal, with its flamboyant tail feathers, is an essential sighting. In Chiapas, El Triunfo Biosphere Reserve (▷ 158) protects many endemic species, including the rare azure-rumped

tanager. Other wildlife includes the harpy eagle, jaguar, tapir, and white-lipped peccary. It is also well worth visiting the Río Lagartos (▷ 118) and Río Celestún (▷ 105) reserves on the north and west coasts of Yucatán, well known for their flamingos. The Mapimí Biosphere Reserve, to the east of Ceballos, on the Gómez Palacio–Ciudad Jiménez highway, is home to giant turtles, now in enclosures at the Laboratory of the Desert.

In Baja California, the Sea of Cortés is one of the world's richest marine feeding grounds and in many places you can see hammerheads, whales and dolphins—if you go at the right time. The best time to watch for California gray whales is between December and February, but you can see them as late as May or June in some spots.

For information on national parks and biosphere reserves, contact the Instituto Nacional de Ecología I Periférico 5000, Colonia Insurgentes Cuicuilco, CP 04530, Delegación Coyoacán, México DF; www. ine.gob.mx. Other conservation organizations include Naturalia I Apdo Postal 21541, 04021 México DF, tel (55) 56 74 66 78, and Pronatura, Asociación Mexicano por la Conservación de la Naturaleza, Aspérgulas No. 22, Colonia San

Clemente, CP 01740, México DF, tel (55) 56 35 50 54, www.pronatura. org.mx. Both of these websites are in Spanish only.

WRESTLING

Wrestling—*lucha libre*—is a hugely popular spectator sport, second only to soccer. Imported originally from the US, it has evolved into a fast-flowing sport with its own complex rules and up to eight or even ten grapplers (*luchadores*) in the ring at the same time. The most important Mexican ingredient, however, is the use of masks to conceal the participants' identities. Fights can be seen in Mexico City at the Arena Coliseo, Calle Republica de Peru 73 (Metro Allende) and Arena México, Río de la Loza 94, Colonia Doctores (Metro Balderas) on Fridays.

ADVENTURE TOURISM

The adventure tourism organization in Mexico City, Asociación Mexicana de Turismo de Aventura y Ecoturismo (AMTAVE), Insurgentes Sur 1981-251, Colonia Guadalupe Inn, Mexico DF, can provide a list of reputable operators for all the activities listed here and their website, www. amtave.org, is also in English.

Above *Storks feature among the large number of bird species in Mexico*

HEALTH AND BEAUTY

Spas *(balnearios)* have a long tradition in the country and were used by the nobles of the great pre-Hispanic dynasties. The Mexican version is not the five-star beauty farm that American or British visitors will be accustomed to, but a far more rustic equivalent, often comprising a series of hot mineral baths of increasing temperatures and pretty basic changing facilities.

More exclusive options are available, however, to cater to wealthy vacationers from the capital as well as foreign visitors. Cuernavaca, in Morelos, is well known for its thermal springs, around which resort spas have developed, and there are also excellent spa resorts at Puerto Vallarta, San José del Cabo in Baja Sur, and at Punta Mita, Bahía de Banderas in Nyarit state. For more details, visit the global SpaFinder website: www.spafinder.com.

Beauty salons in Mexico are not hard to find, so any visitor needing an emergency manicure or pedicure will not have far to look.

FOR CHILDREN

Mexicans love children and touring with your family can bring you into closer contact with local people. Officials tend to be friendlier where children are concerned and teaching your child a little Spanish goes a long way. Moreover, even thieves and pickpockets seem to have some of the traditional respect for families and may leave you alone because of it.

One drawback for families touring in Mexico is that the anti-smoking movement has yet to reach the country, so restaurants and hotel lobbies can be smokier than you are used to.

FAMILY ATTRACTIONS

Swimming pools with slides, wave machines and cascades are all popular for family fun and can be found on both the Caribbean and Pacific coasts. Museums in Mexico, particularly in the capital, have also caught on to the vogue for interactivity, encouraging children to touch, push, prod and poke to get the most out of them. Zoos and aquariums are also easy to find in most cities and resorts for an introduction to Mexican wildlife.

TAKING CARE

» Excessive heat and sun can be damaging and uncomfortable, so ensure children drink enough water and are well protected from the sun with high-factor sunscreen, a T-shirt and a sun hat.
» To counter the risk of rabies, keep children away from animals. Ask your doctor about giving them a rabies vaccination before setting out on your trip.
» Take extra care with drinking water and food. Diarrhea can be dangerous for children, and it is a good idea to carry rehydration salts just in case.

TRAVEL TIPS

» For an overview of the practicalities of touring with children look at www.babygoes2.com.
» Overland travel in Latin America can involve a lot of time waiting for public transportation, so make sure you pack enough toys, books and things to amuse them.
» Food can be a problem if the children are not adaptable. It is easier to take snacks, drinks, bread and so forth with you on longer trips than to rely on rest stops where the chili-dominated food may not be to their liking.
» On long-distance buses children generally pay half or reduced fares. For shorter trips it is cheaper, if less comfortable, to seat small children on your knee. Often there are spare seats which children can occupy after tickets have been collected.

» In city and local excursion buses, small children do not generally pay a fare, but are not entitled to a seat when paying customers are standing. On sightseeing tours you should always bargain for a family rate—often children can go free. Note that children going free on long excursions are not always covered by the operator's travel insurance.
» When flying, check the child's baggage allowance, which is sometimes as low as 7kg (15lb).
» Many hotels offer family rates. If charges are per person, you can insist that two children will occupy one bed, counting as one tariff. If rates are per bed, the same applies. In either case you can almost always get a reduced rate at cheaper hotels.
» In the better hotels in more commercial resorts, it is quite common for children under 10 or 12 years to stay for no extra charge, as long as they are sharing your room.

Above *Children enjoy the waterslide in Cici Aqua Park, Acapulco*

FESTIVALS AND EVENTS

Fiestas are a fundamental part of life for most Mexicans, taking place the length and breadth of the country and with such frequency that it would be hard to miss one, even during the briefest of stays. They come in all shapes and sizes, from the fast and furious Veracruz Carnival (February/March) to the more sedate Blessing of Pets in Mexico City (mid-January). Some are highly Catholicized, while others incorporate Spanish colonial themes into what are predominantly ancient pagan rituals.

MAIN NATIONAL FESTIVALS

Carnival

One of the biggest and most riotous celebrations is Carnival, which takes place a week before Lent, in February or early March. It is a time for indulgence and excess before the hardships of Lent and is celebrated with parades, eating and dancing, most spectacularly in La Paz, Mazatlán and Veracruz. It builds up to a wild climax on the last day, Mardi Gras.

Easter

Another great time to be in Mexico is during Easter week. Thousands of people gather in towns all over the country for processions and Passion plays. In places like Mexico City's Ixtapalapa suburb, millions hit the streets to watch an annual crucifixion. Besides the main regional bases there are renowned parades in small towns, among them Valle de Allende near Hidalgo de Parral and Huaynamota, up in the mountains above Tepic.

Día de la Marina

June 1 is Navy Day, when coastal towns re-enact navy battles using fireworks for added effect.

Día de la Independencia

September 16, Independence Day, is marked by regional festivities and parades up and down the country, the most impressive being those in Mexico City.

Día de los Muertos

Between October 31 and November 2, across Mexico, rural cemeteries come alive as villagers set up all-night vigils to entertain returning souls. These celebrations, known as *Día de los Muertos* (Day of the Dead), are a fascinating spectacle. The ground blazes with candles and orange and red *cempasúchil* flowers, while the air is highly scented with copal (resin).

Two of the best places to witness it are the island of Janitzio and the village of Tzintzuntzán, both on Lake Pátzcuaro. In the cities, the *calavera*, or dancing skeleton, reigns over altars decorated with flowers, tissue paper cut into delicate shapes, food offerings and sugar skulls.

La Virgen de Guadalupe

Another important national celebration is held in honor of Our Lady of Guadalupe, on December 12. The pilgrimage of thousands to the Basílica de Guadalupe, in Mexico City, the most venerated shrine in Mexico (▷ 69), is the most impressive example, but there are big celebrations in Tuxtla Gutiérrez and San Cristóbal de las Casas.

Navidad

During the nine days before Christmas, groups of people go asking for shelter (*posada*), as did Joseph and Mary, and are invited into different homes. This culminates on the night of December 24 with *calendas*, a parade of floats representing scenes from the birth of Christ; every church prepares a float honoring their patron saint.

Above *A papier mâché figure on Día de los Muertos (Day of the Dead)*

Mexican cuisine today is a combination of indigenous and Spanish recipes, seasoned with French influence from the 19th century and topped with the 20th-century additions of Asian dishes and fast food from the US. The result is a very broad mix of styles and tastes to suit all budgets, from street-corner *tacos* to sophisticated dining—a far cry from the "Tex-Mex" served up elsewhere in the world.

TRADITIONAL MEXICAN FOOD

» *Tortillas* are the staple diet of all Mexicans, whether they are consumed at breakfast, eaten from a food stand by a roadside or enjoyed in a restaurant selling fine cuisine. The classic *tortilla* consists of unleavened corn dough which is pressed into a round, thin pancake then cooked on a hot griddle. They are best when handmade and served fresh, but as demand grows more and more are mass-produced.

» Mexicans eat *tortillas* in many forms as *antojitos*, or *botanas*, savory snacks that may be eaten by themselves or as a starter in restaurants and markets, or from street stands and pushcarts. Loosely translated as "appetizers," the most common of these include *tacos* (tortillas stuffed with any filling), *tostados* (tortillas topped with shredded meat, cheese, tomatoes and beans), *totopos* or *tostadaditas* (deep-fried and cut *tortillas*, more commonly known as *nachos*, dipped in a hot sauce), *quesadillas* (tortillas stuffed with cheese) and *enchiladas* (tortillas fried in cheese sauce and smothered in chili sauce).

» In addition to the corn *tortilla*, the chili pepper is another Mexican staple that is never far away from any kitchen. Mexico has more varieties of chili (over 200) than any other country, ranging from the relatively tame *jalapeño* to the red hot *habanero*, which will seriously blow the roof of your mouth off.

» Mexico has a wealth of tropical fruits, from the commonplace banana, mango, pineapple, guava and papaya to the bright pink, plastic-looking dragon fruits *(pitahaya roja)* that taste like sour kiwi fruits, and they all produce fantastic juices.

» The world can thank Mexico for chocolate, as the Mayan Indians first cultivated the cocoa plant in AD600. The Aztec emperor Moctezuma was said to have been the first person to add vanilla pods to chocolate in order to sweeten it. Boiling pots of the mixture are made and mixed with ground cinnamon, almonds and sugar.

» Adventurous palates may wish to taste some of the more unusual culinary offerings, such as *jumiles* (a type of beetle, eaten alive or fried, by themselves or in *tacos)* from Taxco, *chapulines* (small crickets fried with chili until they turn red and then served with lime) from Oaxaca, or *gusanos de maguey* (maguey worms, fried and seasoned with garlic and served with guacamole) from Tlaxcala. Other strange delicacies include *escamoles* (ant eggs) and for vegetarians there's *huitlacoche* (black corn fungus), which can be served in crêpes, omelets and *quesadillas*. Note: Recent tests have shown that *chapulines* can have a high lead content and may not be suitable for pregnant women or children.

MEALTIMES AND MENUS

» Breakfast *(desayuno)* is eaten early and often consists of coffee and *pan dulce* (sweet rolls and pastries), or eggs in many and varied forms. Lunch *(almuerzo/comida)* is the main meal of the day, eaten around 2pm, while supper *(cena)* is a light meal, often *antojitos*, eaten around 8pm.

» A meal in the classiest restaurants of Mexico City can cost anything from $15–$45 and more, while more modest establishments will charge from around $8–$14 for an à la carte dinner. The most economical eating by far is the set lunch *(comida corrida)*, which will generally cost around $4–$6 and is usually served between 1 and 5pm. In more expensive restaurants, the set lunch will be called *menu del día* or *menu turístico* and cost from around $7.

» Always check on local seasonal variations when ordering seafood. For example, lobster is best between April and October.

» Some restaurants give foreigners the menu without *comida corrida* (set meals), forcing them to order à la carte, often double the price. Try to avoid eating in restaurants that don't display a menu.

» McDonald's, Burger King, KFC, Pizza Hut and Domino's are everywhere, should you long for a hit of high cholesterol junk food.

» Vegetarians can eat well in Mexico and many national dishes are naturally meat-free. *Chiles rellenos, quesadillas* and *tacos* can all come with non-meat fillings. Eggs and cheese are widely available, as are salads, though be wary of restaurants washing vegetables in tap water. Vegetarian restaurants are becoming more widespread in the main resorts and large cities, while in more remote parts you may have to endure a rather bland diet of *tortillas* and cheese.

TIPPING AND PAYMENT

Tipping in restaurants should be around 10 to 15 percent of the bill. However, even if service is included waiters have been known to deduct a further tip from any change that is due to you; they will generally hand it back if challenged.

Unless otherwise stated, the restaurants listed for each region will accept credit cards.

SMOKING

In 2008 smoking was banned in all Mexico City restaurants and bars. You'll still find separated smoking and nonsmoking areas in the rest of the country.

MEXICAN TIPPLES

The native alcoholic drinks are tequila, made mostly in Jalisco, and *mezcal* from Oaxaca, both of which are distilled from agave plants. *Pulque* is a sweet fermented cactus drink and definitely an acquired taste. Also available is the Spanish aniseed spirit, *anís*, which is made locally. Imported whiskies and brandies are expensive, while rum is inexpensive and good.

Puro de caña (called *chingre* in Chinanteca and *posh* in Chamula) is distilled from sugar cane; stronger than *mezcal* but with less taste, it is found in Oaxaca and Chiapas.

Tequila is usually drunk in one hit with a lick of salt before (to encourage the thirst) and a suck on a lemon wedge after (to quash the bitter aftertaste). The poorer-quality tequilas are normally used to make cocktails such as margaritas, while the better tequilas, generally graded as *anejo* (aged) or gold, are smooth and should be sipped like a good brandy or malt whisky. The best brands are generally Herradura, Sauza and Cuervo.

Mezcal usually has a *gusano de maguey* (worm) in the bottle, considered to be a delicacy. The worm is, in fact, a butterfly larva which crawls into the heart of the agave plant and often ends up in the finished product. Although the larva used is traditionally coral pink in color, it does tend to fade after some time in the bottle.

WATER

Tap water should not be drunk, but there are always plenty of

non-alcoholic soft drinks *(refrescos)* and bottled mineral water available. Fresh fruit juices *(jugos)* are many and wonderful. The country's markets are often the best places to sample these juices, or the refreshingly delicious watered-down versions called *aguas frescas*, or *licuados* (milkshakes).

BEER

Mexican beer is excellent, particularly the blond varieties, which include Dos Equis-XX, Montejo, Bohemia, Corona, Sol, and Superior. Sometimes these beers are drunk with lime juice and a salt-rimmed glass. Negra Modelo, a dark variety, is one of the country's most distinctive beers.

WINE

Local wine is inexpensive and improving in quality, especially Domecq, Casa Madero and Santo Tomás. The white wines sold in *ostionerías* (oyster restaurants) are also usually good, especially Cetto Riesling Fumé. Some of the best wines produced in Mexico are those from Monte Xanic, near Ensenada, Baja California, though they are very expensive.

HOT DRINKS

Mexicans often round off a meal with chocolate, coffee (especially *café de olla*—with cinnamon) or *atole*, a sweet maize-based drink with milk.

Above *A cocktail served in a fresh coconut*
Opposite *A fast-food stand in Mexico City*

Each region of Mexico has its own special dishes, based on the best ingredients available locally. Some of the most unusual ones come from central Mexico and the southern states. If you don't speak Spanish *(castellano)* it can be daunting to work out exactly what's on offer. Following is a menu reader to help you familiarize yourself with some of the dishes and foods you are likely to come across. This is not a complete list by any means, but it includes many regional specials.

PESCADO (FISH)
atún tuna
cazón dogfish
dorado dolphin (fish)
huachinango red snapper
jurel yellowtail
mero grouper
pez espada swordfish
robalo bass
tuburón shark
trucha trout

FRUTAS (FRUITS)
aguacate avocado
coco coconut
duraznoz peaches
fresa strawberry
granada passion fruit
guayaba guava
higo fig
manzana apple
naranja orange
papaya pawpaw
piña pineapple
plátano banana
sandía watermelon

tamarindo tamarind
zarzamora blackberry

CARNE (MEAT)
albóndigas meatballs
chivo goat
chorizo/salchicha sausage
chuleta chop or cutlet
cordero lamb
costillas ribs
hamburguesa hamburger
hígado liver
jamón ham
lengua tongue
lomo tenderloin
pato duck
pavo turkey
perro caliente hot dog
pollo chicken
puerco pork
res beef
ternera veal
tocino bacon

MARISCOS (SEAFOOD)
almeja clam

calamares squid
camarones shrimps
cangrejo crab
langosta lobster
ostra oyster
pulpo octopus

LEGUMBRES (VEGETABLES)
aceitunas olives
cebolla onion
chícharos peas
frijoles beans
hongos/champiñones
  mushrooms
lechuga lettuce
nopales young leaves of the
  prickly pear cactus
palmito palm heart
rábano radish
zanahoria carrot

ENTREMÉS (SIDE DISHES)
arroz rice
huevo egg
mantequilla butter
mermelada jam

pan bread
papas fritas french fries
queso cheese

POSTRES (DESSERTS/PUDDINGS)
arroz con leche rice pudding
ate jelly made from quince
flan crème caramel
helado ice cream
membrillo jelly made from any fruit other than quince
torrejas bread soaked in honey and fried
turrón nougat

BEBIDAS (DRINKS)
agua mineral con gas/sin gas sparkling mineral water/still mineral water
café coffee
cerveza beer
leche milk
refrescos soft drinks
té tea
vino wine

COOKING METHODS
a la brasa flame-grilled
a la plancha grilled on a griddle
al horno baked/roasted
asado roast
borracho cooked with wine
frito fried
poché poached
relleno stuffed/filled

SOME REGIONAL SPECIALS
AQUASCALIENTES/DURANGO
menudo tripe
CHIAPAS
tamales chiapanecos maize pancake in banana leaves
CHIHUAHUA
machaca con huevo eggs with dried minced beef
COAHUILA/MONTERREY
frijoles charros beans with bacon and chili
GUANAJUATO
enchiladas mineras large tortillas filled with potato, chicken, lettuce and radishes
OAXACA
mole negro as mole (see right) but auce based on chili and chocolate

SAN LUIS POTOSÍ
enchiladas potosinas non-spicy coated red tortillas
TLAXCALA
sopa tlaxcalteca spicy soup with mushrooms and tortilla
VERACRUZ
huachinango a la veracruziana red snapper in sauce of tomatoes, olives and onion
YUCATÁN
sopa de lima chicken broth with giblets, fried tortillas, sweet chili and lime

OTHER DISHES
caldo de pollo chicken-based broth with vegetables and cilantro (coriander)
caldo tlalpeño highly spiced chicken soup, sometimes with rice, and avocado
ceviche raw fish in lime juice with tomatoes, onions, spices and chilis
chalupas fried tortillas, shaped like a boat, with sauce and salad
chicharrón pork crackling
chilaquiles rojos as above with red tomato sauce
chilaquiles verdes small fried tortillas with green tomato sauce
chiles en nogada stuffed peppers with white almond sauce and red pomegranate seeds, echoing the green, white and red of the Mexican flag
chilorio loin of pork in chili sauce
enchiladas verdes fried tortillas filled with chicken with green tomato sauce, sprinkled with onion and cream
enchiladas rojas as above with red mole
enfrijoladas fried tortillas with a bean-based sauce, with cheese, cream and onion
ensalada de nopales cactus-leaf salad
fajitas anything rolled up in a flour tortilla, but strictly should contain skirt steak
guacamole mashed avocado and green tomatoes, with onion, cilantro and sometimes with chili

huevos a la mexicana scrambled eggs with chili and tomatoes
huevos ahogados hard-boiled eggs in a tomato-based sauce
huevos motuleños fried eggs in a sauce of tomatoes, peas, cheese and fried banana
huevos rancheros fried eggs and diced chili in a tomato sauce on top of a tortilla
mixiotes chicken or rabbit wrapped in leaves of the maguey
mole a chili-based sauce, usually used to accompany cooked chicken or turkey
mole poblano mole sauce based on chili, almonds, raisins and chocolate
picadillo minced beef with tomatoes and other vegetables
pipián chicken or pork in a chili-based sauce with peanuts, almonds or pumpkinseeds
pozole a pot-au-feu with a base of maize and stock
quesadillas doubled-over tortillas, heated, slightly crisp, filled with one or more of beef, chicken, cheese, rajas (green peppers), spinach, flor de calabaza (pumpkin flower), chorizo (spicy sausage), nopal (cactus leaves) or huitlacoche (a fungus that grows on maize)
rope vieja beef pulled into fibrous strips with a tomato-based sauce and peas
salpicón cold cooked beef with salad
sopa Juliana soup made from lentils (lentejas) or broad beans (habas)
sopa de tortilla tomato-based soup with shredded tortillas
sopa azteca as above but with chili
tacos rolled up tortillas, usually filled with chicken or beef
tamales meat and chili sauce wrapped in corn dough and then in maize or banana leaves and steamed. Sweet tamales with pineapple, strawberries and nuts are also delicious, while chili and cheese tamales are suitable for vegetarians

While Mexico may not have the range of accommodations options of other popular destinations around the world, there are many international hotel chains in the major resorts and commercially oriented large cities. There are also several small, independent hotels in the lower and middle price brackets, which are good value by US and European standards. Away from the main visitor areas and cities, though, choice becomes more limited.

TAXES

Taxes vary from state to state. Most charge 15 percent, while others impose a 12 percent tax. There is also a hotel (or *hospedaje*) tax, ranging from between 1 percent and 4 percent, depending on the state, although it is generally levied only when a formal bill is issued.

Hotels

» Hotels in Mexico can be described as anything from *paradores* to *posadas* (inns), from *casas de huéspedes* (guesthouses) to plain *hoteles*. The name, however, gives little clue to the standards on offer. *Paradores*, for example, bear little relation to their classy Spanish counterparts, while a *casa de huéspedes* can be a rather grand and expensive affair. Prices at the most luxurious resort hotels are the same as you'd pay in Europe and America, but they also offer the same standards of comfort and service, with English spoken almost everywhere. Prices are also usually quoted in US dollars.

» Boutique hotels are spreading across Mexico to meet international demands for more intimate luxury accommodations. Hoteles Boutique de México (www.mexicoboutiquehotels.com) is a network of these small, independent hotels, all of fewer than 50 rooms and many of them refurbished 16th- and 17th-century haciendas.

» Though finding a room is rarely a problem, making reservations is a good idea in the peak season (November to April) and during busy times such as the Easter and Christmas holidays. There are often great seasonal variations in hotel prices in the main resorts and discounts can be negotiated in the low season (May to October), though this is more difficult in the most popular regions, such as the Yucatán and Baja California.

» All rooms should have an official price displayed in the reception area, though this is not always a reliable guide to quality. Prices are usually based on a room rate, so sharing works out cheaper. Single rooms can cost as much as 80 percent of the price of a double. A room with a double bed *(cama matrimonial)* is normally cheaper than a room with two single beds *(doble)*. Many hotels have large family rooms.

» Check-out time from hotels is generally 11am or noon, but most will be happy to store your luggage till the end of the day.

» Air-conditioning *(aire acondicionado)* adds significantly to the price of a room and often it is better to opt for a ceiling fan *(ventilador)*, unless it is unbearably hot and humid. Except in the top hotels, air-conditioning units can be noisy so a night's sleep is unlikely.

Above *Many historic buildings house hotels*

» In the highlands, where it can be cold at night, especially in winter, many hotels do not have heating. The cheaper ones often provide only one blanket so you may need a sleeping bag. This applies in popular visitor bases such as San Cristóbal de las Casas, Oaxaca and Pátzcuaro.

» Hotel rooms facing the street may be noisy, so make sure you always ask for the best and quietest available room. The very cheapest hotels are normally found in abundance near bus and railway stations and markets. These often do not have 24-hour water supplies, so ask when the water is available. Also, at this end of the market, reservations can prove meaningless. Ask the hotel if there is anything you can do to secure the room and, if arriving late, make sure they know what time you plan to arrive.

CASAS DE HUÉSPEDES AND POSADAS

Smaller than hotels, and often friendlier, these offer cheap and simple accommodations, though without the services and facilities of a hotel. Some *posadas* are more like small hotels, while others are, effectively, *casas de huéspedes*.

MOTELS

Motels, particularly in northern Mexico, are extremely popular and tend to provide accessible, economical accommodations close to the main roads. Farther south, the term "motel" picks up an altogether seedier interpretation and is used by those with a car who want to get

away for an hour or two with their lovers. You can recognize them by curtains over the garage and red and green lights above the door to show if the room is free or not. If you are driving, and wishing to avoid a night on the road, they can often be quite acceptable. They are usually clean, some have hot water, and in the Yucatán, they also have air-conditioning. They also tend to be less expensive than other, "more respectable," establishments.

YOUTH HOSTELS

Youth hostels *(albergues de junventud)* offer a viable alternative to budget hotels. Found mostly in tourist towns such as Oaxaca, San Cristóbal de las Casas, San Miguel de Allende and Mérida, they are usually good value, clean, safe places. While the hostels take non-members, YHA members pay a slightly reduced rate and, after about four nights, it normally works out to be cost effective to become a member. Services vary from place to place, but you often have to pay a key deposit.

For information contact Hostelling Mexico I Guatemala 4, Col Centro, Mexico City, tel (55) 55 18 17 26; www.hostellingmexico.com.

CAMPING

Organized campsites in Mexico are few and far between. Those that do exist are called trailer parks, and are more suited to RVs or campervans. Most of the trailer parks are in the well-traveled parts of the country, especially Baja and the Pacific

Coast. Playas Públicas, with a blue-and-white sign of a palm tree, are beaches where camping is allowed. They are usually inexpensive, often free, and some have shelters and basic amenities, but theft is common. Mosquito netting *(pabellón)* is available by the meter in textile shops and, sewn into a sheet sleeping bag, is adequate protection against insects. You can often camp in or near national parks, although you must speak first with the guards, and usually pay a small fee. In less official campsites, you can rent a hammock and a place to sling it for around the same price as pitching a tent.

CABAÑAS

Cabañas are rustic beach huts, usually with a palm-thatch roof and a bed, or place to sling a hammock, and little else. They cost from around $20 up to $30, though some Caribbean resorts feature luxury versions that can cost up to $125!

APARTMENTS

Self-catering can work out as an economical option, especially for groups of three or more, and there are many apartments for rent in the main resorts and larger towns and cities. Fully furnished and with all modern conveniences, these can cost from as little as $300–$350 per week for a two-bed apartment. Serviced apartments with full maid service are also available, though these are more expensive. A minimum stay of two or more nights is standard practice.

MAJOR HOTEL CHAINS		
NAME	**DESCRIPTION**	**CONTACT NUMBER**
Best Western	Largest hotel chain in the world with more than 120 mid- to upper-range hotels in towns and cities across Mexico	1-800 528 12 34 (toll-free); www.bestwestern.com
Camino Real	Classy Mexican chain with 18 hotels and more planned	1-800 901 23 00; www.caminoreal.com
Hyatt	Top-end international chain with five hotels and resorts in Mexico	www.hyatt.com
InterContinental	Giant international chain who own Holiday Inn and Crowne Plaza, among others. Mid- to upper-range hotels aimed at businesspeople and tourists in more than 50 towns and cities across the country	1-800 315 26 21 (toll-free) www.ichotelsgroup.com
Radisson Hotels	20 luxury hotels and resorts throughout Mexico	1-888 201 17 18; www.radisson.com

A little Spanish will make a difference to your visit. Once you have learned a few basic rules, it's an easy language to speak: It is phonetic and, unlike English, particular combinations of letters are always pronounced the same way. When a word ends in a vowel, n or s, the stress is usually on the penultimate syllable; otherwise, its on the last syllable. If a word has an accent, this is where the stress falls.

a	as in	pat	**ai, ay** as **i** in	side
e	as in	set	**au** as **ou** in out
i	as **e** in	be	**ei, ey** as **ey** in they
o	as in	hot	**oi, oy** as **oy** in boy
u	as in	flute		

Consonants as in English except:
c before **i** and **e** as **th**, *although some pronounce it as* **s**
ch as **ch** in church
d at the end of a word becomes **th**
g before **i** or **e** becomes **ch** as in loch
h is silent
j as **ch** in loch
ll as **lli** in million
ñ as **ny** in canyon
qu is hard like a k
r usually rolled
v is a b
z is a th, *but sometimes pronounced as* **s**

COLORS

black	negro
blue	azul
brown	café
cerise	cereza
gold	oro
green	verde
gray	gris
mauve	malva
orange	naranja
pink	rosa
purple	purpúreo
red	rojo
silver	plata
turquoise	turquesa
white	blanco
yellow	amarillo

CONVERSATION

I don't speak Spanish
No hablo español

Do you speak English?
¿Habla inglés?

I don't understand
No entiendo

Please repeat that
Por favor repita eso

Please speak more slowly
Por favor hable más despacio

What does this mean?
¿Qué significa esto?

Can you write that for me?
¿Me lo puede escribir?

My name is...
Me llamo...

What's your name?
¿Como se llama?

Hello, pleased to meet you
Hola, encantado/a

I'm from...
Soy de...

I live in...
Vivo en...

Where do you live?
¿Dónde vive usted?

Good morning/afternoon
Buenos días/buenas tardes

Good evening/night
Buenas noches

Goodbye
Adiós

This is my wife/husband/son/daughter/friend
Esta es mi mujer/marido/ hijo/hija/ amigo

See you later
Hasta luego

That's all right
Está bien

I don't know
No lo sé

You're welcome
De nada

How are you?
¿Cómo está?

What is the time?
¿Qué hora es?

USEFUL WORDS

yes	sí
no	no
please	por favor
thank you	gracias
there	allí
where	dónde
here	aquí
when	cuándo
who	quién
how	cómo
why	por qué
free	gratis
I'm sorry	Lo siento
excuse me	perdone
large	grande
small	pequeño
good	bueno
bad	malo

TIMES/DAYS/MONTHS/HOLIDAYS

morning	la mañana
afternoon	la tarde
evening	la tarde/ noche
day	el día
night	la noche
today	hoy
yesterday	ayer
tomorrow	mañana
now	ahora
later	más tarde
spring	primavera
summer	verano
autumn	otoño
winter	invierno

Monday .... lunes	
Tuesday .... martes	
Wednesday .... miércoles	
Thursday .... jueves	
Friday .... viernes	
Saturday .... sábado	
Sunday .... domingo	
month .... el mes	
year .... el año	
January .... enero	
February .... febrero	
March .... marzo	
April .... abril	
May .... mayo	
June .... junio	
July .... julio	
August .... agosto	
September .... septiembre	
October .... octubre	
November .... noviembre	
December .... diciembre	
Easter .... Pascua	
Christmas .... Navidad	
New Year .... El Año Nuevo	
All Saints' Day ...... Todos los Santos	
vacation .... las vacaciones	
pilgrimage .... una romería	

MONEY

Is there a bank/bureau de change nearby?
¿Hay un banco/una oficina de cambio cerca?

Can I cash this here?
¿Puedo cobrar esto aquí?

I'd like to change dollars/ sterling into pesos
Quisiera cambiar dólares libras para pesos

Can I use my credit card to withdraw cash?
¿Puedo usar la tarjeta de crédito para sacar dinero?

What is the exchange rate?
¿Cómo está el cambio?

GETTING AROUND
Where is the information desk?
¿Dónde está el mostrador de información?

Where is the timetable?
¿Dónde está el horario?

Does this train/bus go to...?
¿Va este tren/autobús a...?

Does this train/bus stop at...?
¿Para este tren/autobús en...?

Do I have to get off here?
¿Me tengo que bajar aquí?

Do you have a subway/bus map?
¿Tiene un mapa del metro/de los autobuses?

Can I have a single/return ticket to...
¿Me da un boleto sencillo/ de ida y vuelta para...?

Can I have a standard/first-class ticket to...
Quisiera un boleto de segunda/ primera clase para...

I'd like to rent a car
Quiero alquilar un coche

Where are we?
¿Dónde estamos?

I'm lost
Estoy perdido

Is this the way to...?
¿Es esto el camino para ir a...?

I am in a hurry
Tengo prisa

Where can I find a taxi?
¿Dónde puedo encontrar un taxi?

Please take me to...
Me lleva a..., por favor

Please slow down
Vaya más despacio por favor

Can you turn on the meter
Podría poner el metro

How much is the journey?
¿Cuánto cuesta el viaje?

Could you wait for me?
¿Me podría esperar aquí?

POST AND TELEPHONES
Where is the nearest post office?
¿Dónde está la oficina de correos más cercana?

What is the postage to...
¿Cuánto vale mandarlo a...?

I'd like to send this by air mail
Quiero mandar esto por correo aéreo

Hello, this is...
Bueno, habla...?

I'd like to speak to...
¿Podría hablar con...?

Who is speaking?
¿Con quién hablo?

What is the number for...
¿Cuál es el número de...?

Please put me through to...
Comuníqueme con..., por favor

Where can I buy a phone card?
¿Dónde puedo comprar una tarjeta de teléfono?

Extension..., please
La extensión..., por favor

SHOPPING
Could you help me please?
¿Me podría atender por favor?

How much is this?
¿Cuánto vale esto?

I'm looking for...
Estoy buscando...

When does the shop open/close?
¿A qué hora abre/cierra la tienda?

I'm just looking
Sólo estoy viendo

Do you have anything less expensive/smaller/larger
¿Tiene algo más barato/pequeño/ grande?

Do you have this in...?
¿Tienen esto en...?

This is the right size
Esta talla está bien

I'll take this
Me llevo esto

Do you have a bag for this?
¿Tiene una bolsa para esto?

Can you gift wrap this?
¿Me lo envuelve para regalo?

Do you accept credit cards?
¿Aceptan tarjetas de crédito?

I'd like ... grams
Me pone ... gramos, por favor

I'd like a kilo of ...
Me da un kilo de...

I'd like ... slices of that
Me pone ... pedazos de eso

This isn't what I want
Esto no es lo que quiero

Can I help myself?
¿Puedo servirme?

bakery
la panadería

bookshop
la librería

pharmacy
la farmacia

supermarket
el supermercado

market
el mercado

sale
las rebajas

NUMBERS

1	uno
2	dos
3	tres
4	cuatro
5	cinco
6	seis
7	siete
8	ocho
9	nueve
10	diez
11	once
12	doce
13	trece
14	catorce
15	quince
16	dieciséis
17	diecisiete
18	dieciocho
19	diecinueve
20	veinte
21	veintiuno
30	treinta
40	cuarenta
50	cincuenta
60	sesenta
70	setente
80	ochenta
90	noventa
100	cien
1,000	mil

HOTELS

Do you have a room?
¿Tiene una habitación?

I have a reservation for ... nights
Tengo una reservación para ... noches

How much per night?
¿Cuánto es por noche?

Double room
Habitación doble con cama de matrimonio

Single room
Habitación sencilla

Twin room
Habitación doble con dos camas

With bath/shower
Con baño/ducha

Swimming pool
La alberca

Air-conditioning
Aire acondicionado

Nonsmoking
Se prohibe fumar

Is breakfast included?
¿Está el desayuno incluido?

When is breakfast served?
¿A qué hora se sirve el desayuno?

May I see the room?
¿Puedo ver la habitación?

Is there an elevator?
¿Hay elevador?

I'll take this room
Me quedo con la esta habitación

The room is dirty
La habitación está sucia

The room is too hot/cold
Hace demasiado calor/frío en la habitación

Can I pay my bill?
La cuenta por favor

Could you order a taxi for me?
¿Me pide un taxi por favor?

RESTAURANTS
See also Menu Reader ▷ 296–297.

I'd like to reserve a table for... people at...
Quisiera reservar una mesa para ... personas para las...

A table for ..., please
Una mesa para ..., por favor

We have/haven't booked
Tenemos una/no tenemos reservación

What time does the restaurant open?
¿A qué hora se abre el restaurante?

We'd like to wait for a table
Queremos esperar a que haya una mesa

Could we sit here?
¿Nos podemos sentar aquí?

Is this table free?
¿Queda libre esta mesa?

Are there tables outside?
¿Hay mesas afuera?

Is there a car park?
¿Hay aparcamiento?

Where are the lavatories?
¿Dónde están los baños?

Can I have an ashtray?
¿Me da un cenicero?

I prefer nonsmoking
Prefiero no fumadores

Could you warm this up for me?
¿Me podria calentar esto?

Could we see the menu/wine list?
¿Podemos ver la carta/carta de vinos?

We would like something to drink
Quisiéramos algo a beber

What do you recommend?
¿Qué nos recomienda?

Can you recommend a local wine?
¿Puede usted recomendar un vino de la región?

Is there a dish of the day?
¿Hay un plato del día?

I am a vegetarian
Soy vegetariano

I am diabetic
Soy diabético(a)

I can't eat wheat/sugar/salt/ pork/beef/dairy/nuts
No puedo tomar trigo/azúcar/sal/ cerdo/carne (de res)/ productos lácteos/nueces

Could I have a bottle of still/ sparkling water?
¿Me podría traer una botella de agua mineral sin/con gas?

Could we have some more bread?
¿Nos podría traer más pan?

Could we have some salt and pepper?
¿Nos podría traer sal y pimienta?

How much is this dish?
¿Cuánto es este plato?

This is not what I ordered
Esto no es lo que había pedido

I ordered...
Habia pedido...

I'd like...
Quisiera...

May I change my order
¿Puedo cambiar la orden?

I'd prefer a salad
Prefiero una ensalada

How is it cooked?
¿Cómo está hecho?

Is it very spicy?
¿Esta muy picante?

The food is cold
La comida está fría

... is too rare/overcooked
... está demasiado crudo/ demasiado hecho

We would like a coffee
Quisieramos tomar café

May I have the bill, please?
¿Me trae la cuenta, por favor?

Is service included?
¿Está incluido el servicio?

What is this charge?
¿Qué es esta cantidad?

The bill is not right
La cuenta no está bien

We didn't have this
No tomamos esto

Do you accept this credit card (travelers' checks)?
¿Acepta usted esta tarjeta de crédito (cheques de viajero)?

I'd like to speak to the manager
Quisiera hablar con el jefe

The food was excellent
La comida fue excelente

We enjoyed it, thank you
Nos ha gustado, muchas gracias

breakfast
el desayuno

lunch
la comida

dinner
la cena

starters
los antojitos/botanas

main course
el plato principal

dessert
el postre

dish of the day
el plato del día

bread
el pan

sugar
el azúcar

wine list
la carta de vinos

knife
el cuchillo

fork
tenedo   r

spoon
la cuchara

waiter
el mesero

waitress
la mesara

TOURIST INFORMATION
Where is the tourist information office?
¿Dónde está la oficina de turismo?

Do you have a city map?
¿Tiene un mapa de la ciudad?

Can you give me some information about...?
¿Me podría dar información sobre...?

What sights/hotels/restaurants can you recommend?
¿Qué lugares de interés/ hoteles/ restaurantes nos recomienda?

Can you point them out on the map?
¿Me los podría señalar en el mapa?

What time does it open/close?
¿A qué hora se abre/cierra?

Are there guided tours?
¿Hay visitas con guía?

Is there an English-speaking guide?
¿Hay algún guía que hable inglés?

Can we make reservations here?
¿Podemos hacer las reservaciones aquí?

What is the admission price?
¿Cuánto es la entrada?

Is photography allowed?
¿Se permite tomar fotos?

Is there a discount for senior citizens/students?
¿Hay descuento para los mayores/ los estudiantes?

Do you have a brochure in English?
¿Tiene un folleto en inglés?

What time does the show start?
¿A qué hora empieza la función?

How much is a ticket?
¿Cuánto vale una entrada?

IN THE TOWN
church
la iglesia
castle
el castillo

museum
el museo

park
el parque

cathedral
la catedral

bridge
el puente

gallery
la galería de arte

river
el río

no entry
prohibido el paso

entrance
entrada

exit
salida

lavatories
los baños

men
caballeros

women
señoras

open
abierto

closed
cerrado

ILLNESS AND EMERGENCIES
I don't feel well
No me siento bien

Could you call a doctor?
¿Podría llamar a un médico?

I feel nauseous
Tengo ganas de vomitar

I have a headache
Tengo dolor de cabeza

I am allergic to...
Soy alérgico a...

I am on medication
Estoy tomando medicamentos

I am diabetic
Soy diabético

I have asthma
Soy asmático

hospital
el hospital

How long will I have to stay in bed/hospital?
¿Cuánto tiempo tendré que quedarme en la cama/ el hospital?

How many tablets a day should I take?
¿Cuántas pastillas debéna de tomar diario?

Can I have a painkiller?
¿Me da un analgésico?

I need to see a doctor/dentist
Necesito ver un médico/dentista

I have bad toothache
Tengo un dolor de muelas horrible

Help!
Socorro

Stop thief!
Al ladrón

Call the fire brigade/police/ ambulance
Llame a los bomberos/la policía/una ambulancia

I have lost my passport/wallet/ purse/handbag
He perdido me pasaporte/la cartera/ el monedero/ la bolsa

Is there a lost property office?
¿Hay una oficina de objetos perdidos?

I have had an accident
Tuve un accidente

I have been robbed
Me han robado

Where is the police station?
¿Dónde está la comisaría?

MEXICAN GLOSSARY

Ahuehuete: giant cypress, Mexico's national tree

Alameda: large plaza or city park

Animalitos: little clay animals, produced in Chiapas

Arbol de la vida: tree of life

Ayuntamiento: town hall or government office

Aztec: dominant empire in Central Mexico from the 14th century till Spanish Conquest

Avenida: avenue

Azulejo: decorative glazed tile

Bahía: bay

Baluarte: bastion, bulwark

Barranca: canyon

Barrio: suburb or area within a town or city

Cabo: cape, headland

Calle: street

Calzada: avenue

Campesino: peasant farmer

Cantina: bar, usually only frequented by men

Capilla: chapel

Casa: house

Cascada: waterfall

Cenote: freshwater sinkhole

Cerro: hill

Chac Mool: carved figure used for holding sacrificial offerings

Chaltun: underground water cistern for storing rainwater

Charrería: rodeo

Chinampas: floating gardens whose plants eventually root themselves to the lake bed

Churrigueresque: highly elaborate and decorative form of baroque architecture seen in many Mexican churches, named after 17th-century Spanish architect

Colectivo: small bus

Convento: convent or monastery

Criollo: Mexican-born Spaniard

Don/Doña: Sir/Madam

Ejido: communal farmland

EZLN: Ejército Zapatista de Liberación Nacional (Zapatista Army of Liberation), Chiapas guerilla group

Feria: fair/market

Fuente: fountain

Fuerte: fort

Finca: ranch or plantation

Fonart: government agency responsible for promoting crafts

Fonda: basic restaurant or boarding house

Gachupin: person of pure Spanish blood

Gringo: general term for a foreigner, especially North American, but not an insult

Gruta: grotto

Guayabera: style of man's shirt originally from Cuba

Hacendado: estate owner

Hacienda: large country house or estate

Henequen: hemp fibre used to make rope

Huipil: Maya women's embroidered blouse

Indigena: person of indigenous birth

IVA: 15 percent value-added tax

Lancha: small fishing boat

Luz y sonido: light and sound

Malecón: seafront promenade

Maquiladora: assembly plant using US imported material for re-export

Mariachis: famed wandering musicians notable for their sentimental ballads

Maya: still extant pre-Hispanic tribe who inhabit Southeast Mexico, Guatemala, Belize, Honduras and El Salvador

Mercado: market, usually selling local farm produce and crafts

Mestizo: person of mixed Spanish and Indian blood

Mezcal: alcoholic spirit made from the maguey (agave) family of plants. The worm found in some bottles is actually the larva of a moth that lives in the agave plant

Mirador: look-out point

Mixtec: ancient tribe from Oaxaca

Mudéjar: Spanish architectural style based on Moorish forms

Muelle: pier or jetty

NAFTA: North American Free Trade Agreement which includes Mexico, the US and Canada

Nahuatl: Aztec language

Norteño: northern, used to describe a style of food or music

Obsidian: a type of volcanic glass

Palacio: mansion

Palacio de Gobierno: state/federal authority headquarters

Palacio Municipal: municipal local government headquarters

Palapa: palm-thatched hut

Palenque: cockpit (for cock-fighting)

PAN: Partido de Acción Nacional (National Action Party), conservative party (currently in power)

Paseo: broad avenue or ritual evening stroll

Pemex: national oil company, Mexico's only provider of gas and oil products

Porfiriato: era of dictator Porfirio Díaz, also used for grandiose architecture of the time

Posada: inn

PRD: Partido Revolucionario Democrático (Party of the Democratic Revolution), left-wing opposition party

PRI: Partido Revolucionario Insitucional (Party of the Institutional Revolution), ruling party for 71 years until 2000

Pulque: alcoholic drink made from fermented maguey

Quetzal: rare Central American bird, prized by the Maya for its feathers

Retablo: decorative painted wooden altarpiece

Romería: procession

Sacbé (plural sacbeob): "white road"; a stone causeway linking Maya buildings and settlements

Sierra: mountain range

Stela: large freestanding carved stone monument

Talavera poblano: considered the crème de la crème of decorative *azulejos* (tiles)

Tenochtitlán: Aztec capital, site of present-day Mexico City

Teotihuacán: ancient city north of Mexico City

Tequila: alcoholic spirit made from the blue maguey plant only (see also Mezcal)

Toltec: tribe which ruled Central Mexico before the Aztecs

Tula: Toltec capital

Tzompantli: Aztec rack displaying skulls of sacrificial victims

Virreinal: period of Spanish viceroys

Wetback: illegal Mexican migrant in the US

Zapotec: tribe which ruled in Oaxaca until around the eighth century AD

Zócalo: main town plaza

BENITO JUAREZ.

KEY FIGURES IN MEXICAN HISTORY

Ignacio Allende: (1779–1811) Mexican soldier and Independence hero

Luís Barragán: (1902–1988) one of Mexico's most influential 20th-century architects

Miguel Cabrera: (1695–1768) Oaxacan artist

Plutarco Elías Calles: (1877–1945) president of Mexico (1924–28)

Cuauhtémoc Cárdenas: (born 1934) mayor of Mexico City and leader of the PRD

Lázaro Cárdenas: (1895–1970) president of Mexico (1934–40)

Venustiano Carranza: (1859–1920) president of Mexico (1917–20)

Bartolome de las Casas: (1474–1566) Spanish priest, known as a protector of Indians and a defender of their rights

Hernán Cortés: (1485–1547) Spanish conquistador and conqueror of Mexico

Cuauhtémoc: (1495–1525) the last Aztec emperor (1520–21)

Porfirio Díaz: (1830–1915) president of Mexico (1876–80, 1884–1911)

Vicente Fox: (born 1942) president of Mexico (2000–2006)

Carlos Fuentes: (born 1928) Mexican novelist, playwright and diplomat

Juan de Grijalva: (1489–1527) Spanish conquistador, explored the shores of Mexico

Vicente Guerrero: (1782–1831) president of Mexico (1829)

Miguel Hidalgo: (1753–1811) enlightened Catholic priest and leader of the Independence movement, famous for his *"grito"* (call to arms)

Victoriano Huerta: (1854–1916) president of Mexico (1913–14)

Agustín de Iturbide: (1783–1824) Mexican soldier and emperor (1821–23)

Benito Juárez: (1806–72) Zapotec lawyer who became president of Mexico (1861–63 and 1867–72)

Frida Kahlo: (1907–54) influential Mexican artist, married to Diego Rivera

Diego de Landa: (1524–79) Bishop of Yucatán, infamous for destroying all Maya documents, then writing an account of the Mayan civilization—Relaciones de las Cosas de Yucatán—around 1566

Ricardo Legorreta: (born 1931) one of Mexico's most renowned architects

Francisco Indalecio Madero: (1873–1913) president of Mexico (1911–13)

La Malinche: (c1505–c1528) daughter of a nobleman, consort and interpreter for Hernán Cortés. She played a significant role in the downfall of the Aztec empire

Maximilian of Habsburg: (1832–67) Emperor of Mexico (1864–67)

Moctezuma II: (Montezuma; 1466–1520) the penultimate Aztec emperor (1502–20)

José María Morelos: (1765–1815) Mexican patriot who took over leadership of the Independence movement after the death of Hidalgo in 1811

Álvaro Obregón: (1880–1928): president of Mexico (1920–24)

Juan O'Gorman: (1905–82) Mexican architect; studied painting under Diego Rivera

José Clemente Orozco: (1883–1949) one of the greatest mural painters of the 20th century

Octavio Paz: (1914–98) leading Mexican poet, particularly known for *The Labyrinth of Solitude* (1950)

José Guadalupe Posada: (1851–1913) considered Mexico's greatest lithographer, whose engravings and etchings satirized tyrannical politicians

Vasco de Quiroga: (1479–1565) Spanish priest who did much to help the Tarascans in Michoacán

Diego Rivera: (1886–1957) Mexican painter, famous for his murals depicting the life and history of the Mexican people

Antonio López de Santa Anna: (1797–1876) soldier and president of Mexico (periodically 1833–55)

David Alfaro Siqueiros: (1896–1974) one of Mexico's most original and eminent painters, renowned for his murals

Rufino Tamayo: (1899–1991) one of the great Mexican artists of the 20th century

Miguel Alemán Valdés: (1905–83) president of Mexico (1946–52)

Francisco "Pancho" Villa: (1877–1923) legendary Mexican bandit, real name Doroteo Arango

Emiliano Zapata: (1879–1919) peasant hero of Mexico and rebel leader during the Mexican Revolution

AZTEC AND MAYA DEITIES

Ah Mucen Cab: Maya god of bees

Ah Puch: Maya god of death

Centeotl: Aztec god of corn

Chac: Maya god of rain

Chalchiuhtlicue: Aztec goddess of running water; sister of Tláloc

Chaob: Maya god of the wind

Chicomecoatl: Aztec goddess of corn and fertility

Coatlicue: Aztec earth goddess—she of the serpent skirt

Coyolxauqhui: Aztec god of the moon

Ehécatl: Aztec god of the wind

Ekahau: Aztec god of travelers and merchants

Huitzilpochtli: Aztec god of war and the sun, supreme god

Itzamná: Maya god of creation

Ix Chel: Maya goddess of the moon

Ixtab: Maya goddess of suicide

Kukulkán: Maya name for Queztalcóatl

Mictlantecuhtli: Aztec god of death

Nacon: Maya god of war

Queztalcóatl: the plumed serpent, the most powerful and important of all Mexican gods

Tlacolotl: Maya god of evil

Tláloc: Toltec/Aztec god of rain

Tonatiuh: Aztec sun god

Xochipilli: Aztec god of flowers

Yum Cimil: Maya god of death

Yum Kaax or Yumil Kaxob: Maya god of maize

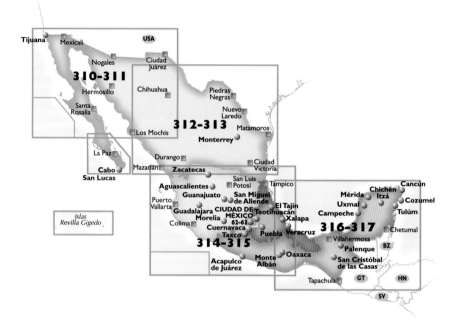

	0					100 km
310-317						
	0					60 miles

═══ Motorway (Expressway)	▨ Built-up area
▬▬ National road	■ City / Town
▬▬ Regional road	National park / Reserve
┄┄ Main road	● Featured place of interest
┄┄ Other road	✈ Airport
──── Railway	621 ▲ Height in metres
▨▨▨ International boundary	⌂— Ferry route
┅┅ Administrative region boundary	

MAPS

Map references for the sights refer to the atlas pages within this section or to the individual town plans within the regions. For example, Puebla has the reference ✚ 315 L9, indicating the page on which the map is found (315) and the grid square in which Peubla sits (L9).

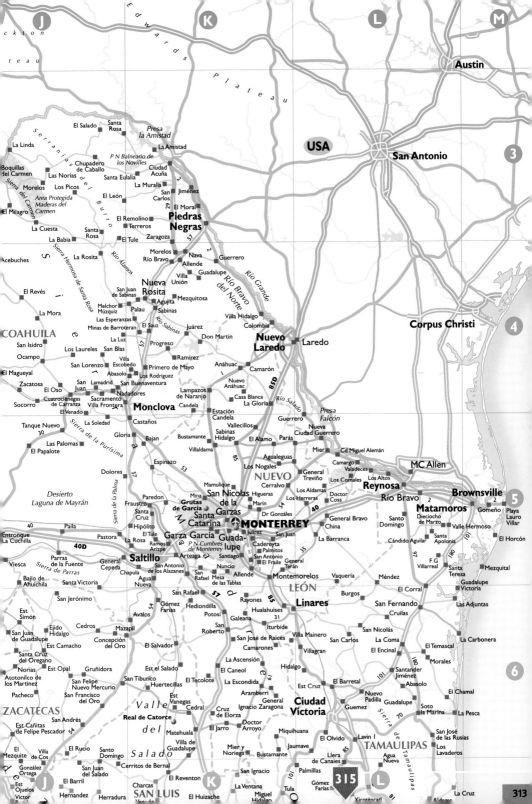

Name	Pg	Ref
Acala	316	P10
Acapulco de Juárez	315	K10
Acatlán	315	M9
Acatlán de Osorio	315	L9
Acatzingo	315	L9
Actopan	315	L8
Aduana	311	F4
Agua Blanca	317	R9
Agua Caliente de Garate	312	G7
Agua Dulce	316	P9
Agua Flores	310	B1
Agua Prieta	311	E2
Aguascalientes	314	J7
Agua Verde	314	G7
Aguila	317	Q10
Ajalpan	315	M9
Ajijic	314	H8
Akumal	317	S8
Alamo	315	M8
Aleman	316	P9
Alicante	312	H4
Altamira	315	L7
Altamirano	316	Q10
Alvarado	316	N9
Alvaro Obregón	312	G3
Alvaro Obregón	316	P9
Amatenango del Valle	316	Q10
Amatitán	314	H8
Amozoc	315	L9
Anáhuac	313	K4
Anáhuac	312	G3
Angangueo	315	K9
Angostura	312	F5
Antigua	316	M9
Antiguo Morelos	315	L7
Apaxco	315	L8
Aquila	314	H9
Arados	312	G3
Arandas	314	J8
Arizpe	311	E2
Armería	314	H9
Arrayan	314	G7
Arriaga	316	P11
Arroyo Seco	315	K8
Arroyo Zarco	315	K8
Arteaga	313	K5
Arteaga	314	J9
Ascensión	311	F2
Astapa	316	P10
Asunción Nochixtlán	315	M10
Asunción Tlacolulita	316	N11
Atenango del Río	315	L10
Atenquillo	314	H8
Atlacomulco	315	K9
Atlíxco	315	L9
Atolinga	314	H7
Atotonilco	315	K7
Atotonilco el Alto	314	J8
Atoyac de Alvarez	315	K10
Autlán de Navarro	314	H9
Ayutla	314	H8
Ayutla	316	M10
Ayutla de los Libres	315	L10
Baborigame	311	F5
Bacalar	317	S9
Bacoachi	311	E2
Bacobampo	311	E4
Bacubirito	311	F5
Bacum	311	E4
Bahía Asunción	310	C4
Bahía de los Ángeles	310	C3
Bahía Kino	310	D3
Bahia Santa Maria	310	C2
Bahía Tortugas	310	B4
Bajamar	310	B1
Bajío de Ahuichila	313	J5
Bajios de Agua Blanca	312	G5
Balancán	316	Q10
Balsas	315	K10
Banámichi	311	E2
Banderas	311	G2
Barra de Cazones	315	M8
Barra de Navidad	314	H9
Barra de Palmas	315	M8
Barra de Tonalá	316	N9
Barra Santa Elena	315	M11
Barreal	311	G2
Basaseachic	311	F4
Basihuare	311	F4
Bataques	310	C1
Batopilas	311	F4
Baturi	312	F5
Bavispe	311	F2
Beatriz Microondas	312	H4
Becanchen	317	R8
Benito Juárez	316	P10
Benjamin Hill	311	E2
Bermejillo	312	H5
Boca del Río	316	M9
Boca Paila	317	S8
Bochil	316	P10
Bocoyna	311	F4
Bonampak	317	Q10
Boquilla del Mezquite	317	H3
Boquillas del Carmen	313	J3
Buenaventura	317	S8
Burgos	313	L6
Cabo Pulmo	310	E6
Caborca	310	D2
Cabo San Lucas	310	E7
Cacahoatan	316	Q11
Cacahuamilpa	315	L9
Cacahuatepec	315	L10
Cacalotepec	315	M11
Cadeje	310	D4
Cadereyta	313	K5
Calderitas	317	S9
Calkiní	317	R8
Calotmul	317	S8
Calvillo	314	J7
Camalú	310	B2
Camarón	313	K4
Camarones	313	K6
Campeche	317	Q8
Cananea	311	E2
Cañas	314	J9
Canatlán	312	H6
Cancún	317	S7
Candelaria	317	R8
Candelaria Loxicha	315	M11
Canipole	310	D4
Canoas	315	L7
Cansahcab	317	R8
Cantamar	310	B1
Carapán	314	J9
Cárdenas	316	P10
Carichi	312	G4
Carmona	315	K9
Carrillo	312	H4
Casas Grandes	311	F2
Casa Vieja	311	D3
Castaños	313	K5
Cataviña	310	C2
Catazajá	316	Q10
Catemaco	316	N9
Ceballos	312	H5
Cedral	317	S8
Celaya	315	K8
Celestún	317	Q8
Cenotillo	317	R8
Cenzontle	312	H4
Cerralvo	313	K5
Cerritos	315	K7
Cerritos de Bernal	313	J7
Cerro Azul	315	M8
Cerro Gamo	310	D2
Cerro Prieto	312	G5
Chamela	314	G9
Chametla	314	G7
Champotón	317	Q9
Chandiablo	314	H9
Chankán Veracrut	317	S9
Chapala	314	J8
Chapalilla	314	H8
Chapulco	315	M9
Chapulhuacan	315	L8
Chapultepec	315	K10
Charco de la Peña	312	H3
Chekubul	317	Q9
Cheran	314	J9
Chetumal	317	S9
Chiapa do Corzo	316	P10
Chiautempan	315	L9
Chiautla	315	L9
Chicbul	317	Q9
Chichicapan	315	M10
Chicomuselo	316	Q11
Chihuahua	312	G3
Chihuahuita	311	E5
Chilapa	314	G7
Chilón	316	Q10
Chilpancingo de los Bravos	315	L10
Chinameca	316	N10
Chinampas	314	J7
Chinipas	311	F4
Chinobampo	311	F5
Chiquilá	317	S7
Cholula	315	L9
Chontalpa	316	P10
Chumpón	317	S8
Chunhuhub	317	S9
Chunyaxché	317	S8
Chupadero de Caballo	313	J3
Ciénega	312	H6
Ciénega de Escobar	312	G5
Cihuatlán	314	H9
Cintalapa de Figueroa	316	P10
Ciudad Acuña	313	K3
Ciudad Altamirano	315	K9
Ciudad Camargo	312	H4
Ciudad Constitución	310	D5
Ciudad del Carmen	316	Q9
Ciudad del Maíz	315	K9
Ciudad de México	315	L9
Ciudad de Río Grande	312	J6
Ciudad Guerrero	311	F3
Ciudad Guzman	314	H9
Ciudad Hidalgo	315	K9
Ciudad Ixtepec	316	N10
Ciudad Juárez	311	G2
Ciudad Lerdo	312	H5
Ciudad Obregón	311	E4
Ciudad Pemex	316	P10
Ciudad Serdán	315	M9
Ciudad Valles	315	L7
Ciudad Victoria	313	K4
Coahuayutla	314	J9
Coatepec	315	M9
Coatzacoalcos	316	N9
Cobachi	311	E3
Cocula	314	H8
Cojumatlán	314	J8
Colima	314	H9
Colombia	313	K4
Colomos	314	H8
Colotlan	314	H7
Comala	314	H9
Comalcalco	316	P9
Comanjá	314	J9
Comitán de Domínguez	316	Q11
Comonfort	315	K8
Compostela	314	H8
Concepción del Oro	313	J6
Concordia	312	G6
Conitaca	312	G6
Conkal	317	R8
Constancia	312	F6
Copala	312	G6
Copala	315	M9
Coroneo	315	K8
Cortázar	315	K8
Cotaxtla	315	M9
Cotija de la Paz	314	J9
Coxcatlán	315	M9
Coyoacan	315	L9
Coyotitán	312	G6
Coyuca de Benitez	315	K10
Coyuca de Catalán	315	K9
Cozumel	317	S8
Creel	311	F4
Cruces	311	F3
Cruz Grande	315	L10
Cuajiniculapa	315	L11
Cuarenta	314	J8
Cuauhtémoc	312	G3
Cuautepec	315	L8
Cuautitlán	315	L9
Cuautitlan	315	H9
Cuautla	314	H8
Cuautla de Mor	315	L9
Cucurpé	311	E2
Cuernavaca	315	L9
Culiacán	312	F6
Culiacancito	312	F6
Cumbres de Majalca	312	G3
Cusarare	311	F4
Custepec	316	P11
Cutzota	314	J9
Degollado	314	J8
Delicias	312	G4
Desemboque	310	D3
Díaz Ordaz	310	C4
Dieciocho de Marzo	313	L5
Dieciocho de Marzo	317	Q9
Dimas	312	G6
Dolores	313	J5
Dolores Hidalgo	315	K8
Donato Guerra	312	H6
Dos Casas	315	K9
Durango	312	H6
Dzibalché	317	R8
Dzibalchén	317	R9
Dzidzantún	317	R8
Dzilam de Bravo	317	R7
Dzitás	317	R8
Dzoyola	317	S8
Edzná	317	R9
Ejido Bonfil	310	B2
Ejido Eréndira	310	B2
Ejido Hidalgo	313	J6
Ejido Morelas y Pavon	310	C3
Ejido Uruapan	310	B1
Ejutla	315	M10
El Aguaje	310	D4
El Alamillo	311	F3
El Alamo	313	K5
El Alamo	310	B1
El Anuajito	311	E5
El Arco	310	C4
El Arenal	312	H6
El Atajo	314	H8
El Barretal	313	L6
El Burro	310	D3
El Caballo	312	J4
El Cajete	310	E6
El Camarón	316	M10
El Caneol	313	K6

Name	Pg	Ref
La Huacana	314	J9
La Huerra	314	H9
La Jarille	315	L7
La Junta	311	F3
La Laguna	312	H4
La Libertad	316	Q10
La Linda	313	J3
La Mancha	312	J6
La Máquina	312	G2
La Misa	311	E3
La Misión	310	B1
La Mora	313	J4
La Morita	312	H3
Lampazos de Naranjo	313	K4
La Muralla	313	K3
Landa de Matamoros	315	L8
La Nona	312	G6
La Nueva Victoria	316	N9
La Palma	314	G7
La Palma	317	Q10
La Paloma	311	D3
La Paz	310	E6
La Perla	313	H5
La Pesca	313	L6
La Piedad	314	J8
La Piedra	316	M9
La Pila	315	K7
La Pinta	311	F3
La Pocitos de Aguirre	311	E3
La Poza de Teresa	310	D5
La Poza Grande	310	D5
La Purisima	310	D5
La Recholera	312	H5
La Reforma	316	P10
La Revancha	317	Q10
La Rosa	313	K5
La Rosita	313	J4
La Rosita	312	J3
La Rumorosa	310	B1
Las Adjuntas	313	L6
Las Barrancas	310	D5
Las Brujas	315	L7
Las Cruces	310	E6
Las Cruces	316	P10
Las Cuevas	310	E6
La Selva	312	H3
Las Encantades	310	C2
Las Glorias	312	F5
Las Herreras	312	G5
Las Isabeles	310	B1
Las Lagunas	310	E6
Las Nieves	312	G5
Las Norias	313	J3
La Soledad	313	J5
Las Palomas	310	C4
Las Palomas	313	J5
Las Peñas	314	J10
Las Rosas	316	Q10
Las Vigas	315	M9
La Tinaja	315	M9
La Trinidad	310	E6
La Trinitaria	316	Q11
La Union	314	J10
La Venta	316	P10
La Ventana	310	C1
La Ventana	315	K7
La Ventosa	316	N10
La Viga	315	L10
La Zarca	312	H5
Lázaro Cárdenas	314	J10
Lázaro Cárdenas	317	S9
León	314	J8
Leona Vicario	317	S8
León Guzman	312	H5
Lerdo de Tejada	316	N9
Limón	315	L7
Limones	317	S9
Linares	313	K6
Llera de Canaies	313	L7
Loma	312	G3
Loma Bonita	316	N10
Loreto	310	D5
Los Arrieros	311	E3
Los Aztecas	315	L7
Los Barriles	310	E6
Los Chinos	311	E3
Los Gavilanes	310	C4
Los Herreras	313	L5
Los Hoyos	311	E2
Los Laureles	313	J4
Los Lavaderos	313	L6
Los Lirios	317	R9
Los Mártires	310	C4
Los Mochis	311	F5
Los Molinos	310	D2
Los Naranjos	316	M9
Los Nogales	313	K5
Los Picos	313	J3
Los Remedíos	312	G6
Los Rodriguez	313	K4
Lucio Vázquez	315	K7
Maclovio Herrera	312	H3
Madera	311	F3
Magdalena	314	H8
Magdalena de Kino	311	E2
Magdalena Tequisistlán	316	N11
Majahual	317	S9
Mal Paso	314	J7
Malarrimo	310	C4
Mama	317	R8
Manatlán	314	H9
Maneadero	310	B1
Maní	317	R8
Manuel	315	L7
Manzanilla	314	J8
Manzanillo	314	H9
Mapastepec	316	P11
Mapimí	312	H5
Maravatío	315	K9
Maravillas	312	H4
Marquelia	315	L10
Martinez de la Torre	315	M8
Mascota	314	H8
Matachic	311	F3
Matamoros	313	M5
Matanzas	314	J7
Mata Ortiz	311	F2
Matatlán	316	M10
Matehuala	313	K6
Matías Romero	316	N10
Matrimonio	312	J4
Maxcaltzin	315	L7
Maxcanú	317	R8
Maytorena	311	E4
Mazapil	313	J6
Mazatán	311	E3
Mazatán	316	Q11
Mazatlán	312	G6
Mazocahui	311	E3
Mecayucan	316	M9
Medias Aguas	316	N10
Méndez	313	L5
Meoqui	312	G4
Meresichic	311	E2
Mérida	317	R8
Mesa de Guadalupe	312	G5
Metepec	315	L8
Metepec	315	K9
Metztitlán	315	L8
Mexcaltitán	314	G7
Mexicali	310	B1
Mexico	310	D3
Mezcala	315	K10
Mezcalapa	316	P10
Mezquite	311	G2
Mezquitic	314	H7
Mezquitosa	313	K4
Mier	313	L5
Mier y Noriega	313	K6
Miguel Hidalgo	315	K7
Mil Cumbres	315	K9
Milpillas	311	F4
Milpillas	311	D2
Mina	313	K5
Minas de Barroteran	313	K4
Minas de Hércules	312	H4
Minatitlán	314	H9
Minatitlán	316	N10
Miquihuana	313	K6
Miraflores	310	E6
Misión de San Borja	310	C3
Misión de San Fernando	310	B2
Misión de San Telmo	310	B2
Mísol-Há	316	Q10
Mitla	316	M10
Mixquiahuala	315	L8
Mixtlán	314	H8
Mochicahui	311	F5
Mocorito	311	F5
Mocorúa	311	E4
Moctezuma	315	K7
Molango	315	L8
Momax	314	H7
Moncillo	312	H6
Monclova	313	K4
Monclova	317	Q9
Monte Escobedo	314	H7
Monte Mariana	312	J7
Montemorelos	313	K5
Montepío	316	N9
Monterde	311	F4
Monterrey	313	K5
Morales	313	L6
Morelia	315	K9
Morelos	311	E4
Morelos	313	K4
Morelos	312	G6
Morelos	314	J7
Motul	317	R8
Moyahua	314	J8
Mulegé	310	D4
Muna	317	R8
Naco	311	E2
Nacori Chico	311	F3
Nacozari de García	311	E2
Namiquipa	311	F3
Nanchital	316	N10
Naranjo	311	F5
Naranjos	315	M8
Nautla	315	M8
Nava	313	K4
Navojoa	311	E4
Nazas	312	H5
Neji	310	B1
Nexpa	314	J10
Nezahualcoy	315	L9
Nicolás Bravo	317	R9
Nogales	311	E2
Nombre de Dios	312	H6
Nonoava	312	G4
Nopoló	310	D5
Norias	313	J6
Norogachic	311	G4
Nueva Ciudad Guerrero	313	L5
Nueva Coahuila	313	Q10
Nueva Rosita	313	K4
Nuevo Campechito	316	P9
Nuevo Casas Grandes	311	F2
Nuevo Churumuco	314	J9
Nuevo Ixcatlán	316	N10
Nuevo Laredo	313	K4
Nuevo México	316	P10
Nuevo Morelos	315	L7
Nuevo Padilla	313	L6
Numaran	314	J8
Nuxco	315	K10
Oaxaca	315	M10
Ocampo	311	F4
Ocampo	314	J8
Ocosingo	316	Q10
Ocotlán	315	M10
Ocotlán	314	J8
Ohuisa	311	E3
Ojinaga	312	H3
Ojo Caliente	314	J7
Ojo de Carrizo	312	H3
Ojos Negros	310	B1
Opichén	317	R8
Opodepe	311	E3
Opopeo	314	J9
Oriental	315	M9
Orizaba	315	M9
Orozco	311	E4
Ortiz	311	E3
Otinapa	312	H6
Oxkutzcab	317	R8
Ozuluama	315	L8
Paamul	317	S8
Pacheco	313	J6
Pachuca de Soto	315	L8
Paila	313	J5
Palau	313	K4
Palizada	316	Q9
Palmar de Cuautla	314	G7
Palmarillo	316	N9
Palmas	317	S9
Palma Sola	315	M9
Palmillas	313	L7
Palmitos	313	K5
Palo Gordo	312	G6
Palomares	316	N10
Palomas	315	K7
Palo Verde	310	D5
Pánuco	315	L7
Papantla de Olarte	315	M8
Paracho de Verduzco	314	J9
Paracuaro	314	J9
Paraiso	316	P9
Parás	313	K5
Paredon	313	K5
Parras de la Fuente	313	J5
Paso de Ovejas	315	M9
Paso del Toro	316	M9
Paso Nacional	312	H5
Pastora	313	J5
Pathe	315	K8
Pátzcuaro	314	J9
Patzimaro	314	J8
Pedernales	312	G3
Pedro Montoya	315	K7
Pénjamo	314	J8
Pericos	314	G7
Perote	315	M9
Pesqueira	311	E3
Petatlán	315	K10
Peto	317	R8
Pichachic	311	F4
Pichilingüe	310	E6
Pichucalco	316	P10
Piedras Negras	313	K3
Pihuamo	314	H9
Pimientillo	314	G7
Pinos	314	J7
Pinotepa Nacional	315	L11
Piste	317	R8
Pixoyal	317	Q9
Placer de Guadalupe	312	G3

Place	Map	Ref
Soyaló	316	P10
Soyatita	311	F5
Suchil	312	H6
Tabasco	314	J7
Tacubaya	312	J5
Tahdzibichén	317	R8
Tajicaringa	312	H6
Talpa de Allende	314	H8
Tamazula	312	G6
Tamazula de Gordiano	314	H9
Tamazunchale	315	L8
Tampacan	315	L8
Tampico	315	L7
Tampico Alto	315	L7
Tamuin	315	L7
Tancitaro	314	J9
Tangancicuaro	314	J9
Tanque Nuevo	313	J5
Tanques	311	F4
Tapachula	316	Q11
Tapalpa	314	H8
Tapilula	316	P10
Tarandacuao	315	K8
Taretán	314	J9
Tasajeras	311	F4
Tastiota	311	D3
Taxco	315	K9
Tayahua	314	J7
Teabo	317	R8
Teacapan	314	G7
Teapa	316	P10
Tecalitián	314	H9
Tecamachalo	315	M9
Tecate	310	B1
Tecoh	317	R8
Tecolutla	315	M8
Tecomán	314	H9
Tecpan de Galeana	315	K10
Tecuala	314	G7
Tehuacán	315	M9
Tehuitzingo	315	L9
Tejolocachic	311	F3
Tejupilco de Hidalgo	315	K9
Tekantó	317	R8
Tekax de Álvaro Obregón	317	R8
Tekik	317	R8
Telchac Puerto	317	R7
Temascal	312	H6
Temascaltepec	315	K9
Temax	317	R8
Temezcal	315	M9
Temochic	311	F4
Temozón	317	S8
Tenabó	317	R8
Tenamaxtlán	314	H8
Tenancingo	315	K9
Tenejapa	316	P10
Tenixtepec	315	M8
Tenochtitlán	316	N10
Tenosique de Pino Suárez	317	Q10
Teopisca	316	P10
Teotitlán del Camino	315	M10
Tepalcatepec	314	J9
Tepantita	312	F5
Tepatitlán	314	J8
Tepechitlán	314	H7
Tepehuanes	312	G5
Tepeji del Río	315	L9
Tepeojuma	315	L9
Tepetitlán	316	Q10
Tepetongo	314	J7
Tepetzintla	315	L8
Tepic	314	H8
Tepich	317	S8
Teposcolula	315	M10
Tepuxtla	312	G6
Tequila	314	H8
Tequisquiapan	315	K8
Tequixquiac	315	L9
Tetamechi	311	F5
Teul González Ortega	314	H8
Texistepec	316	N10
Teziutlán	315	M9
Tiacolulan	315	M9
Ticul	317	R8
Tierra Blanca	315	M9
Tihosuco	317	S8
Tihuatlán	315	M8
Tijuana	310	B1
Tilzapotla	315	L9
Tinum	317	R8
Tinum	317	S8
Tixbacab	317	S8
Tixcancal	317	S8
Tixkokob	317	R8
Tixmucuy	317	R9
Tizimín	317	S8
Tlachichilco	315	L8
Tlacoapa	315	L10
Tlacotalpan	316	N9
Tlajomulco	314	H8
Tlalpujahua	315	K9
Tlaltenango	314	H7
Tlapacoyan	315	M10
Tlapacoyan	315	M8
Tlaquepaque	314	H8
Tlatlaya	315	K9
Tlaxcala	315	L9
Tlaxco	315	L9
Tlaxiaco	315	M10
Tocumbo	314	J9
Todos Santos	310	E6
Toluca	315	K9
Tomatán	310	C3
Tomatlán	314	G8
Tonalá	316	P11
Tonaya	314	H9
Tonila	314	H9
Topolobampo	311	E5
Torreón	312	H5
Torreón de Cañas	312	H5
Torres	311	E3
Tosanachic	311	F3
Totolapan	316	M10
Totontepec	316	N10
Totutla	315	M9
Tres Picos	316	P11
Tres Reyes	317	S8
Tula	315	K7
Tula de Allende	315	L8
Tulancingo	315	L8
Tulipan	316	Q10
Tulúm	317	S8
Tupilco	316	P9
Tuxcueca	314	J8
Tuxpan	314	H9
Tuxpan	315	K9
Tuxpan	314	G7
Tuxpan de Rodriguez Cano	315	M8
Tuxtla Gutiérrez	316	P10
Tzintzuntzán	314	J9
Tzucacab	317	R8
Uaymá	317	S8
Ucum	317	S9
Uman	317	R8
Unión de Tula	314	H8
Union Hidalgo	316	N10
Unión Juárez	316	Q11
Ures	311	E3
Uriangato	315	K8
Ursulo Galván	317	S9
Ursulo Galván	316	M9
Uruachic	311	F4
Uruapan del Progreso	314	J9
Uspero	314	J9
Va Comaltitlán	316	P11
Valerio	312	G4
Valladolid	317	S8
Valle de Allende	312	G4
Valle de Banderas	314	G8
Valle de Bravo	315	K9
Valle de Guadalupe	314	J8
Valle del Rosario	312	G4
Valle de Santiago	315	K8
Valle de Zaragoza	312	G4
Valle Hermoso	313	L5
Valle Hermoso	317	S9
Valle Las Palmas	310	B1
Valle Nacional	316	M10
Valparaiso	314	H7
Vaquería	313	L5
Vasconcelos	316	N10
Vega de Alatorre	315	M8
Venado	315	K7
Venustiano Carranza	310	B2
Venustiano Carranza	312	H6
Venustiano Carranza	316	P11
Venustiono Carranza	314	H9
Veracruz	310	C1
Veracruz	316	M9
Vicam	311	E4
Vicam Pueblo	311	E4
Vicente Guerrero	312	H6
Vicente Guerrero	311	E2
Vicente Guerrero	317	S8
Victor Rosales	314	J7
Viejo	310	B1
Viesca	313	J5
Vigia Chico	317	S8
Villa Ahumada	312	G2
Villa Ahumada y Anexas	312	G2
Villa Azueta	316	N10
Villa Coronado	312	H5
Villa de Guadalupe	313	K6
Villa de Orestes	312	G5
Villa de Pozos	315	K7
Villa de Ramoz	314	J7
Villa de Reyes	315	K7
Villa de Sarí	311	E3
Villa Flores	316	P11
Villa Frontera	313	J4
Villa García	314	J7
Villago Hidalgo	310	B2
Villa González Ortega	314	J7
Villagran	313	L6
Villagrán	315	K8
Villa Guerrero	314	H7
Villahermosa	316	P10
Villa Hidalgo	311	E2
Villa Hidalgo	313	K4
Villa Hidalgo	312	H5
Villa Hidalgo	314	J7
Villa Hidalgo	315	K7
Villa Insurgentes	310	D5
Villa Jesús Maria	310	C3
Villa Juanita	316	N10
Villa Juarez	311	E4
Villa Juárez	312	H5
Villa Juárez	315	K7
Villaldama	313	K5
Villa López	312	H4
Villa Mainero	313	K6
Villa Matamoros	312	G4
Villanueva	314	J7
Villa Ocampo	312	G5
Villa Pesquera	311	E3
Villa Unión	312	H6
Villa Unión	312	G7
Villa Unión	313	K4
Xagacia	316	M10
Xalapa (Jalapa)	315	M9
Xcabacab	317	Q9
X-Can	317	S8
Xcupil	317	R8
Xiatil	317	S8
Xichu	315	K8
Xicoténcatl	315	L7
Xicotepec de Juárez	315	L8
Xilitla	315	L8
Xmaben	317	R9
Xochiapa	316	N10
Xochicalco	315	L9
Xochihuehuetlán	315	L10
Xonacatlan	315	M9
Xpujil	317	R9
Yahualica	314	J8
Yajalón	316	Q10
Yalalag	316	M10
Yalina	316	M10
Yalsihon	317	S7
Yanga	315	M9
Yanhuitlán	315	M10
Yaqui	311	E4
Yautepec de Zaragoza	315	L9
Yávaros	311	E4
Yaxchilán	317	Q10
Yaxcopil	317	R8
Yécora	311	F3
Yecorato	311	F5
Yeloixtlahuacan	315	L10
Yerbanis	312	H6
Yermo	312	H5
Yucatán	317	S7
Yurécuaro	314	J8
Yuriria	315	K8
Zaachila	315	M10
Zacapu	314	J9
Zacatal	316	Q9
Zacatecas	314	J7
Zacatelco	315	L9
Zacatepec	315	M9
Zacatepec	315	L9
Zacatlán	315	L9
Zacatosa	313	J4
Zacoalco de Torres	314	H8
Zacualpan	315	K9
Zacualtipán	315	L8
Zamora	314	J8
Zape	312	G5
Zapopan	314	H8
Zapotic	314	H8
Zapotitic	314	H9
Zapotlán de Salinas	315	M9
Zapotlán Tables	315	L10
Zapotlanejo	314	J8
Zaragoza	311	G2
Zaragoza	311	F3
Zaragoza	313	K3
Zaragoza	315	M9
Zaragoza	315	K7
Zaragoza	316	P11
Zicuirán	314	J9
Zihuatanejo	314	J10
Zimatlan	315	M10
Zinacantán	316	P10
Zinacatepec	315	M9
Zináparo	314	J8
Zinapécuaro	315	K9
Ziraándaro	315	K9
Ziracuraretiro	314	J9
Zitlala	315	L10
Zumpango	315	L9

166 AA/P Wilson;
168 AA/C Sawyer;
171 AA/C Sawyer;
172 AA/C Sawyer;
174 AA/C Sawyer;
176 AA/R Strange;
177 AA/P Wilson;
178 AA/R Strange;
179 AA/R Strange;
180 AA/C Sawyer;
181 AA/R Strange;
182 AA/C Sawyer;
183l AA/C Sawyer;
183r AA/C Sawyer;
184 AA/C Sawyer;
185 AA/R Strange;
186 AA/R Strange;
187 AA/C Sawyer;
188 AA/R Strange;
189 AA/R Strange;
190 AA/C Sawyer;
191l AA/R Strange;
191r AA/C Sawyer;
192 AA/R Strange;
193 AA/P Wilson;
194 AA/R Strange;
195 AA/R Strange;
196 AA/C Sawyer;
198 AA/C Sawyer;
200 AA/C Sawyer;
202 AA/C Sawyer;
204 AA/C Sawyer;
205 AA/P Wilson;
206 AA/P Wilson;
207 AA/R Strange;
208 AA/C Sawyer;
209 AA/C Sawyer;
210 AA/P Wilson;
211l AA/C Sawyer;
211r AA/R Strange;
212 AA/R Strange;
213 AA/C Sawyer;
214 AA/C Sawyer;
215 AA/R Strange;
216 AA/P Wilson;
217t AA/C Sawyer;
217b AA/C Sawyer;
218 AA/R Strange;
219l AA/C Sawyer;
219r AA/C Sawyer;
220 AA/C Sawyer;
221 AA/R Strange;
222 AA/C Sawyer;
223t AA/C Sawyer;
223b AA/R Strange;
224 AA/C Sawyer;
225 AA/C Sawyer;

226 (www.visitmexico.com);
227l (www.visitmexico.com);
227r (www.visitmexico.com);
228 AA/C Sawyer;
229 AA/C Sawyer;
230 AA/R Strange;
233 (www.visitmexico.com);
234 AA/C Sawyer;
236 AA/C Sawyer;
238 © Macduff Everton/CORBIS;
240 Photolibrary Group;
241 AA/P Wilson;
242 AA/L Dunmire;
243 AA/F Dunlop;
244 AA/P Wilson;
245 AA/P Wilson;
246 AA/P Wilson;
247 AA/P Wilson;
248 AA/R Strange;
249l (www.visitmexico.com);
249r AA/L Dunmire;
250 (www.visitmexico.com);
251 (www.visitmexico.com);
252 AA/F Dunlop;
253 AA/P Wilson;
254 © Blaine Harrington III / Alamy;
255l AA/F Dunlop;
255r © Wolfgang Kaehler/Alamy;
256 © Bill Ross/Corbis;
257l © Macduff Everton/CORBIS;
257r © David Muench/CORBIS;
258 AA/L Dunmire;
259 AA/L Dunmire;
260 AA/C Sawyer;
262 (www.visitmexico.com);
264 AA/L Dunmire;
267 AA/R Strange;
268 AA/C Sawyer;
270 AA/R Strange;
271 AA/C Sawyer;
272 AA/R Strange;
274 AA/C Sawyer;
275 AA/C Sawyer;
276l AA/C Sawyer;
276r AA/C Sawyer;
278t AA/C Sawyer;
278b AA/C Sawyer;
282 AA/C Sawyer;
284 AA/P Wilson;
285 AA/R Strange;
286 AA/C Sawyer;
287 AA/C Sawyer;
288 AA/C Sawyer;
289 (www.visitmexico.com);
291 AA/C Sawyer;
292 AA/C Sawyer;
293 AA/R Strange;

294 AA/C Sawyer;
295 AA/P Wilson;
296 AA/C Sawyer;
298 AA/C Sawyer;
306 The AA;
309 AA/L Dunmire.

Every effort has been made to trace the copyright holders, and we apologise in advance for any accidental errors. We would be happy to apply any corrections in the following edition of this publication.

CREDITS

Managing editor
Marie-Claire Jefferies

Project editor
Lodestone Publishing Ltd

Design
Drew Jones, pentacorbig, Nick Otway

Picture research
Liz Stacey

Image retouching and repro
Michael Moody

Main contributors
Lisa Addison, Carolyn Bointon, Eli Ellison, Vanessa Hadley, Peter Hutchinson, Caroline Lascom, Maribeth Mellin, Alan Murphy, Rafe Stone, Nicholas Watson

Updater
Eli Ellison

Indexer
Marie Lorimer

Production
Karen Gibson

Published by AA Publishing, a trading name of AA Media Limited, whose registered office is Fanum House, Basing View, Basingstoke, RG21 4EA. Registered number 06112600.
A CIP catalogue record for this book is available from the British Library.

ISBN 978-0-7495-6232-8

KeyGuide is a registered trademark in Australia and is used under license.
Colour separation by Keenes, Andover, UK
Printed and bound by Leo Paper Products, China

We believe the contents of this book are correct at the time of printing. However, some details, particularly prices, opening times and telephone numbers do change. We do not accept responsibility for any consequences arising from the use of this book. This does not affect your statutory rights. We would be grateful if readers would advise us of any inaccuracies they may encounter, or any suggestions they might like to make to improve the book. There is a form provided at the back of the book for this purpose, or you can email us at Keyguides@theaa.com

A03807
Maps in this title produced from mapping © MAIRDUMONT / Falk Verlag 2009 and map data © Footprint Handbooks Limited 2004
Transport map © Communicarta Ltd, UK

Find out more about AA Publishing and the wide range of travel publications and services the AA provides by visiting our website at **www.theAA.com/bookshop**

Thank you for buying this KeyGuide. Your comments and opinions are very important to us, so please help us to improve our travel guides by taking a few minutes to complete this questionnaire.

You do not need a stamp (unless posted outside the UK). If you do not want to cut this page from your guide, then photocopy it or write your answers on a plain sheet of paper.

Send to: **KeyGuide Editor, AA World Travel Guides**
FREEPOST SCE 4598, Basingstoke RG21 4GY

Find out more about AA Publishing and the wide range of travel publications the AA provides by visiting our website at www.theAA.com/bookshop

ABOUT THIS GUIDE

Which KeyGuide did you buy? ....

Where did you buy it?...

When? ....month .... year

Why did you choose this AA KeyGuide?
☐ Price ☐ AA Publication
☐ Used this series before; title
☐ Cover ☐ Other (please state)

Please let us know how helpful the following features of the guide were to you by circling the appropriate category: very helpful (VH), helpful (H) or little help (LH)

Size	VH	H	LH
Layout	VH	H	LH
Photos	VH	H	LH
Excursions	VH	H	LH
Entertainment	VH	H	LH
Hotels	VH	H	LH
Maps	VH	H	LH
Practical info	VH	H	LH
Restaurants	VH	H	LH
Shopping	VH	H	LH
Walks	VH	H	LH
Sights	VH	H	LH
Transport info	VH	H	LH

What was your favourite sight, attraction or feature listed in the guide?

Page.................Please give your reason ....
....

Which features in the guide could be changed or improved? Or are there any other comments you would like to make?

....

ABOUT YOU

Name (Mr/Mrs/Ms)..

Address ....

....

....

....

Postcode... Daytime tel nos...

Email..
Please only give us your mobile phone number/email if you wish to hear from us about other products and services from the AA and partners by text or mms.

Which age group are you in?
Under 25 ☐   25–34 ☐   35–44 ☐   45–54 ☐   55+ ☐

How many trips do you make a year?
Less than1 ☐   1 ☐   2 ☐   3 or more ☐

ABOUT YOUR TRIP

Are you an AA member?   Yes ☐ No ☐

When did you book?.............. month................. year

When did you travel?.............. month................. year

Reason for your trip?   Business ☐   Leisure ☐

How many nights did you stay? ....

How did you travel?   Individual ☐   Couple ☐   Family ☐   Group ☐

Did you buy any other travel guides for your trip? ....

If yes, which ones?..

Thank you for taking the time to complete this questionnaire. Please send it to us as soon as possible, and remember, you do not need a stamp (unless posted outside the UK).
AA Travel Insurance call 0800 072 4168 or visit www.theaa.com

Titles in the KeyGuide series:
Australia, Barcelona, Britain, Brittany, Canada, China, Costa Rica, Croatia, Florence and Tuscany, France, Germany, Ireland, Italy, London, Mallorca, Mexico, New York, New Zealand, Normandy, Paris, Portugal, Prague, Provence and the Côte d'Azur, Rome, Scotland, South Africa, Spain, Thailand, Venice, Vietnam, Western European Cities.
Published in July 2009: Berlin

AA Travel Insurance call 0800 072 4168 or visit www.theaa.com